JEWS AND OTHER GERMANS

To Ron Walters
with many thanks
for being such an
outstanding teacher,

GEORGE L. MOSSE SERIES
IN MODERN EUROPEAN CULTURAL AND
INTELLECTUAL HISTORY

Advisory Board

Jews and Other Germans

Civil Society, Religious Diversity, and
Urban Politics in Breslau, 1860-1925

Till van Rahden

Translated by
MARCUS BRAINARD

THE UNIVERSITY OF WISCONSIN PRESS

This book was published with the assistance of a translation grant from the **Goethe-Institut** and support from the **George L. Mosse Program** at the University of Wisconsin–Madison.

The University of Wisconsin Press
1930 Monroe Street, 3rd Floor
Madison, Wisconsin 53711-2059

www.wisc.edu/wisconsinpress/

3 Henrietta Street
London WC2E 8LU, England

Originally published as *Juden und andere Breslauer*
© 2000 Vandenhoeck & Ruprecht, Göttingen

1   3   5   4   2

Printed in the United States of America

Library of Congress Cataloging-in-Publication Data
Rahden, Till van.
[Juden und andere Breslauer. English]
Jews and other Germans : civil society, religious diversity, and
urban politics in Breslau, 1860-1925 / Till van Rahden;
translated by Marcus Brainard.
p.   cm.—(George L. Mosse series in modern European
cultural and intellectual history)
Includes bibliographical references and index.
ISBN 0-299-22690-5 (cloth: alk. paper)
ISBN 0-299-22694-8 (pbk.: alk. paper)
1. Jews—Poland—Wroclaw—Social conditions.
2. Catholics—Poland—Wroclaw—Social conditions.
3. Protestants—Poland—Wroclaw—Social conditions.
4. Wroclaw (Poland)—Ethnic relations.
I. Title. II. Series.
DS134.66.W76R3413   2008
305.892´4043852—dc22   2007040520

CONTENTS

ACKNOWLEDGMENTS

Since its inception, modern civil society has had to negotiate a fundamental tension between the homogenizing force of the nation-state and the reality of pluralism, whether viewed as an end in itself or as the inevitable effect of individual freedom. I was first exposed to a historiography that explores this tension when I had the great fortune of spending a year as a graduate student at The Johns Hopkins University. There, Ronald Walters, Louis Galambos, and the late John Higham encouraged and supported my interest in the history of pluralism in America. Although this book is a history of Jews and other Germans in Breslau, the origins of this project reach back to my days in Baltimore, and I am delighted that its results are about to be published in the country where it all began.

It is a great honor to see this translation appear in the series that bears the name of George L. Mosse, one of the German-Jewish émigré scholars to whom I owe an enormous intellectual debt. Another is, of course, Peter Gay, and the title of this book deliberately echoes a collection of his equally brilliant and provocative essays. David Sorkin first suggested the possibility of a translation, and I thank him for his faith in the project. John Tortorice and Nadine Zimmerli of the Mosse Program in History accompanied this project over the years while overlooking my delays. I could not have wished for a better translator than Marcus Brainard, and I am grateful for his dedication, scholarly professionalism, and stylistic sensitivity. At the University of Wisconsin Press, Carla Aspelmeier, Adam Mehring, and Sheila Moermond supported this project. Their patience, generosity, and encouragement were remarkable.

This book grew out of my dissertation at the University of Bielefeld. As doctoral supervisor, Hans-Ulrich Wehler was unfailing in his support over the many years it took me to complete it. Heinz-Gerhard Haupt generously agreed to take on the role of second reader. As editors of the series in which the original German edition of this book appeared,

Helmut Berding and Hans-Peter Ullmann patiently urged me to clarify my argument and my prose.

I am extremely grateful to the following institutions for their financial support over the course of this project: the German National Academic Foundation; the German Historical Institute, Washington; the Polish Academy of Sciences; the Institute for European History, Mainz; the FAZIT-Foundation; the Vidal Sassoon International Center for the Study of Antisemitism; the Memorial Foundation for the Study of Jewish Culture; and the Leo Baeck Institute, New York.

In addition to the archives and research libraries mentioned in the bibliography, I would like to record my thanks to the wonderful staff of the University of Bielefeld's Library, the Klau Library (Cincinnati), the Robarts Library (Toronto), the Milton S. Eisenhower Library (Baltimore), and the Jewish National and University Library.

Earlier versions of some chapters of this book were given as papers at conferences and at seminars at universities in Germany, as well as Great Britain and Israel, Poland, Canada, and the United States. While I would like to thank the audiences on all those occasions for their comments, I would like to single out the following colleagues and friends with whom I had wonderful conversations about this project: Margaret L. Anderson, Werner T. Angress, Steven Aschheim, Olaf Blaschke, Jacob Borut, Michael Geyer, Svenja Goltermann, Monika and Woiciech Hann, Manfred Hettling, Christhard Hoffmann, Jerzy Kos, Walter Laqueur, Rainer Liedtke, Rebecca Manley, Kerstin Meiring, Thomas Mergel, Glenn Penny, Peter Pulzer, Andreas Reinke, Monika Richarz, Stefanie Schüler-Springorum, Helmut Walser-Smith, Martin Vogt, and Agnieszka Zabłocka-Kos. I owe a special thanks to Stefan-Ludwig Hoffmann, Marion Kaplan, Marline Otte, and Reinhard Rürup. Without their unfailing support and encouragement I would not have finished this book.

Nicole Velten's love and companionship mean everything to me. As I edited and slightly revised the translation, she buoyed my spirits when the work did not. Our son, David Caspar, doesn't have strong opinions on Jews and other Germans (yet), but helped me in countless other ways. The book is dedicated to my mother, Ingeborg van Rahden, and to the memory of my father, Günter Krämer-van Rahden.

JEWS AND OTHER GERMANS

Introduction

Jews lived in a world larger than themselves, and just as it is impossible to understand that larger world without its Jews, it is impossible to understand its Jews without their larger world.

Peter Gay, *Freud, Jews and Other Germans*

This is a book about relations between Jews and other Germans in Breslau from 1860 to 1925. Thus it belongs in the context of the contentious debate about the extent and limits of Jewish integration in modern German society. The study does not avoid the question of continuities between the relations of Jews and other Germans in imperial Germany and National Socialist anti-Semitism, but it addresses that question by going beyond it and analyzing the experience of German Jews before 1933 in view of the debate on multicultural society. By focusing on both the question of continuity and the relation between diversity and difference, this book seeks to meet the challenge of writing the history of German Jews simultaneously as a part of Jewish, German-Jewish, and German history.

This study argues, first, that neither a direct nor a "twisted road" led from the relations between Jews and other Breslauers before 1918 to the National Socialist policy of persecuting Jews.[1] From the mid-nineteenth century to roughly 1880, Jews were increasingly integrated in the Silesian capital. From the early 1870s to the end of imperial Germany, relations between Jews and other Breslauers were close and marked by mutual acceptance despite the existence of anti-Semitism. It was less the anti-Semitism of organized political parties than the "anti-Semitic mood of society," particularly among conservatives, that hindered a further increase in Jewish integration in the 1880s and 1890s.[2] Nevertheless, until 1914 the extent of Jewish integration remained high in

3

almost all spheres of social life in Breslau. Research into German anti-
Semitism in imperial Germany has often overstated its influence, since it
examined—understandably—primarily the successes of anti-Semitism
rather than its limits. The decisive turning point, this book argues, came
in the last years of the First World War and early in the Weimar Republic, when relations between Jews and other Breslauers deteriorated dramatically. Against the backdrop of experiences during the war and the
army's "Jew count" of 1916, the postwar crises and inflation, the high degree of Jewish integration eroded. While the socioeconomic situation of
Breslau Jews worsened after 1918, anti-Semitism increased and gained
in significance in many spheres of social life in the city. Yet the inher-
ently legitimate question of whether the experience of German Jews
prior to 1918 belongs to the prehistory of the Holocaust leads all too
easily to a one-dimensional understanding of the relations between Jews
and other Breslauers.

   This study therefore seeks, second, to relate the history of German Jews in imperial Germany to the contemporary discussion of the
challenge posed by a multicultural society. It claims to step out of the
long shadow of the paradigm of national homogeneity—which today is
largely a liberal Protestant paradigm—and seeks to write modern German history as a history of ethnic and religious diversity and difference.
For this reason the investigation dispenses with the premise that to this
day forms the starting point of many historical studies of nineteenth-
and twentieth-century German history, namely, that the telos of modern society is to become a homogeneous national state. By contrast, this
study is based on the assumption that ethnic and religious differences
cannot be overcome, that cultural plurality is not only desirable but also
unavoidable. In this sense, this book is intended as a contribution to a
German history under the sign of multiculturalism. Whereas German
Jews were regarded in the "nationalist narrative" as "rogues," the
American historian Samuel Moyn has argued that "they seem to have
a privileged role in the post-nationalist one where they are recuperated
as models of cultural hybridity, and as guides to a specifically modern
diasporic existence."[3]

   The concept of multiculturalism can be a source of misunderstanding, particularly because it is also claimed by those who have taken a
radically contrary stance toward liberal visions of society. In radical
multiculturalism, universalism and particularism are regarded as incompatible. This critique of modernity—which is not always fair and
sometimes rash—maintains, from the perspective of cultural relativism,

that the abstract promise of equality contained in the idea of a liberal society threatens to turn into, as Jörn Rüsen puts it, a "fury of the disappearance of difference."[4] That is why the sociologist Zygmunt Bauman has argued, on the example of the history of German Jews, that "the substance of modern politics, of modern intellect, of modern life, is the effort to exterminate ambivalence."[5] Not tolerance but "intolerance is, therefore, the natural inclination of modern practice." Against the backdrop of this critique, it is hardly surprising that the stance of German liberals on the question of Jewish equality was recently subjected once again to harsh critique. According to Michael Brenner, although Christian liberals rejected anti-Semitism, they "nevertheless denied Judaism . . . any right to exist." Still more devastating is Alan Levenson's appraisal. He reproaches the German liberalism of imperial Germany for a threefold failure: it neglected to develop "a sympathy for pluralism," to recognize "the personal as political," and to combat "outmoded stereotypes and low-level prejudices."[6]

The concept of multiculturalism employed by cultural relativists can be distinguished from the model of multicultural liberalism on which the present study relies. The latter vision of social order also breaks with the telos of national homogeneity and criticizes different varieties of the liberal tradition because they are regarded as having denied the right to ethnic or religious difference.[7] Unlike radical multiculturalism, however, multicultural liberalism does not reject the universalism of the traditional catalog of human and civil rights but instead expands it by adding an individualistically grounded right to be different. Following Jörn Rüsen, one can argue that particularity, difference, and plurality in modern society are based not only on "mutual acceptance of cultural difference" but also on the "assumption of equality sanctioned by human and civil rights."[8] The debate on the relationship between liberalism and multiculturalism has been conducted above all by North American and British intellectuals, such as the political scientist Will Kymlicka and the political philosophers Joseph Raz and Charles Taylor. According to Raz, "liberal Multiculturalism . . . recognizes the importance of unimpeded membership in a respected and flourishing cultural group for individual well-being." From this it follows for Raz that we "should think of our societies as consisting not of a majority and minorities, but of a plurality of cultural groups."[9]

To the extent that historical recollection and orientation are part of the self-description of modern society, a historiography under the sign of multiculturalism raises new questions, causes familiar objects to appear in a new light, and offers a chance to support the change in Germany's self-understanding from a homogenous, possibly even racially grounded, nation to a multicultural society. The road to the liberal civil state and the "challenge of multicultural democracy" presuppose a historical orientation in which diversity and difference, like class or gender, form central categories for historical reflection. A multicultural understanding of one's own history counts among the "rules of the game for the multiethnic republic." Yet so far neither historians nor the advocates of a multicultural society have taken up this challenge. The debate over the "homeland Babylon" is taking place in an ahistorical space.[10]

The history of German Jews between the mid-1860s and the 1920s forms an important part of a multicultural history in which questions of diversity and difference, of inclusion and exclusion become the focus of historical interest. Since no history of German Jews is conceivable without the "perspective of Auschwitz" (Thomas Nipperdey), since it is also always a (pre)history of exclusion, expulsion, and genocide, it is clear in this case of a "rupture in civilization" (Dan Diner) that the multicultural paradigm is not to be mistaken for the utopia of a new springtime of peoples and ethnic groups.[11] Despite the dreams of homogenizing nationalism, there can no more be a society without cultural conflict than a society without social tensions. The concept of multiculturalism includes conflict precisely because it characterizes a society in which a plurality of ethnic and religious groups continuously negotiate anew the terms of their coexistence and in which individuals must balance a multitude of particular and situational identities. The multicultural society does not put an end to conflict but encloses and defuses it—institutionally, through the constitutional state, which is based on human and civil rights; and ideally, through the mutual acceptance of difference.[12]

Anyone who wishes to write the history of relations between Jews and other Germans under the sign of multiculturalism would do well to rethink categories common to German-Jewish history, such as integration, subculture, and milieu, as well as assimilation and acculturation. Ultimately these concepts originate in the tradition of minorities studies that was committed to the paradigm of national homogeneity.[13] What defined the "minority" was neither number nor lesser legal status since that research tradition still regarded the Jews as a minority in the postemancipatory period. Instead, the decisive factor was the idea of a stable "majority" in which the minority was integrated and whose culture it adopted. According to this interpretation, the Jews advanced to the German bourgeoisie without their advancement having changed the character of the bourgeoisie. This idea explains why the historiography on the bourgeoisie has had so little to say about Jews; but it does not do justice to the cultural plurality of modern society. A German-Jewish history that inquires into diversity and difference in German society therefore presupposes a new understanding of integration, ethnicity, and assimilation.

Although Werner Mosse rightly has argued that integration is "seldom measurable," no study of the relations between Jews and other Germans can do without a definition of integration.[14] The question of Jewish integration cannot be answered without a sufficient theoretical framework. Here we shall combine Max Weber's and Niklas Luhmann's reflections on the functional differentiation of subspheres of societies in modernity with the concepts of exclusion and social closure.[15] In what follows, *integration* designates the result of a multitude of processes of inclusion in the central functional spheres of modern society (economy, politics, science, education, and law), as well as in everyday life. The generic concept of integration must be distinguished from the subsumable concept of inclusion: It is possible, for example, that a group could participate with equal rights in the economic sphere, thus experiencing inclusion, while being excluded from other spheres, such as from politics, so that one could not speak of integration. *Inclusion* designates here the generalized incorporation of the entire population in the individual functional spheres of modern society. As different ways of life are ever more rationalized in modern society, as the extent of functional differentiation widens, these subspheres of society regulate access increasingly in accordance with their "own internal logic" (Max Weber). Inherited privileges and other collective, ascribed conditions for access, such as status (*ständische Momente*), ethnicity, confession, and gender, are replaced by acquired prestige, that is, individual qualifications, such as wealth and ownership, income, and academic or professional credentials. Inclusion in the economic sphere, for instance, follows increasingly the price-oriented logic of the market. The concept of inclusion does not postulate equality of ownership, status, and power. The monopolization of ownership, status, and power, which is based on individual, acquired criteria, that is, *social closure*, can continue to exist.[16] In comparison with the usual concept of discrimination, the distinction between social closure and exclusion has the advantage of typologizing mechanisms of exclusion into individual criteria, on the one hand, and collective criteria, on the other. In contrast to the concept of social closure, exclusion designates every monopolization of ownership, status, and power in the social subsphere that is based not on individual but on collective, ascribed criteria, such as ethnicity, inherited status, confession, or gender.

Yet not all inclusion accords with that inner logic. The life world—including friendships and marriage circles, associational life, and residential patterns—is marked by diffuse forms of inclusion and exclusion. At the same time, in modern, functionally differentiated societies, ethnically or denominationally homogeneous circles of interaction can also be observed in daily life. But the existence of intra-Jewish sociability, Jewish associational life, or intra-Jewish marriage circles is not a clear index for the exclusion of the Jews in everyday life. That German Jews were not completely absorbed in the broader society can also indicate the efficacy of their ethnic identity. To do justice to the significance of that identity and the character of Jewish community ties between the mid-nineteenth and the early twentieth century, the concept of *situational ethnicity* is used in place of David Sorkin's model of subculture, which is suitable for the analysis of the partial integration of Jews prior to 1850 but not for the second half of the century. According to Sorkin, Jewish hopes of being integrated into German society were not fulfilled in the first half of the nineteenth century. Most states refused to confer political equality on the Jews, and many bourgeois associations continued to exclude them. For this reason, he argues, the Jews created a German-Jewish subculture, a kind of civil society parallel to the society of the "majority culture," a subculture comparable to the social democratic or Catholic cultural milieus in imperial Germany.[17] However, because German Jews, at least between 1860 and 1920, did not form a closed group with far-reaching demands for loyalty, unlike the Catholics, the character of their community ties cannot be described as either a subculture or a sociomoral milieu.

The coexistence of closedness and openness in the formation of modern German-Jewish groups and identities is best characterized as situational ethnicity.[18] An ethnic community distinguishes itself through the idea of a common origin and a common culture. Much like the modern nation, an ethnic group is an "imagined order" based on the "invention of a tradition."[19] Central to the imagined order of the ethnic community is the construction of boundaries. Ethnicity does not denote a fixed, unchangeable core of culture, tradition, and religion, but rather the marking of a cultural and social boundary that signals either membership or exclusion. Yet, unlike milieu barriers, ethnic boundaries need not be rigidly formed but are often fluid. Frequently, ethnicity structures the very social contact that transgresses group boundaries. Membership in an ethnic community thus does not exclude loyalty to other social formations and groups, such as class, sex, confession, professional group, and nation. It is precisely the concept of situational ethnicity, which seems to be particularly helpful in the analysis of German Jews, that emphasizes the high degree to which ethnicity can be bound to a concrete social situation.[20] Thus, while an individual's membership in an ethnic group can play an important role in specific situations, such as in family life or in participation in ethnic associations, in different contexts ethnicity becomes less significant, and other feelings of belonging predominate.[21]

Although German Jews in imperial Germany did not explicitly understand themselves as an ethnic group, many Jewish intellectuals who belonged to different Jewish factions used the concept of the tribe (*Stamm*) or the tribal consciousness (*Stammesbewußtsein*). With these terms they articulated the idea of a specifically Jewish loyalty based on the fiction of a common origin. They thereby articulated an idea of membership that resembles contemporary conceptions of ethnicity. "The Jewish tribe," the *Allgemeine Zeitung des Judentums* noted in 1870, is "chosen to provide in modern times the touchstone for the power of [both] the freedom of conscience and equality in the modern state."[22] The Jewish philosopher and ethnologist Moritz Lazarus also availed himself of these terms when he repudiated Heinrich Treitschke's attacks on the Jews in the Berlin debate on anti-Semitism of 1880. Rather than assimilating unconditionally, as Treitschke had demanded, Lazarus maintained that German Jews "had the duty" to preserve both "the intellectual peculiarity they possessed as a tribe and the inherited virtue and wisdom they possessed as a religion." Even a self-declared "German loyal to the Empire and of Jewish confession" exhorted German Jews in 1887 in the *Israelitische Wochenzeitschrift* to fight anti-Semitism based on each one's "reverence for his religion and his tribe." At the end of the Weimar Republic, the vaguely Zionist *Jüdisches Lexikon* reviewed this semantic tradition and noted that "in the last decades" the concept of "tribal community had become a much-used designation for the Jewish community or the Jewish people." Unlike the concept of a religious community, the encyclopedia concluded, the term "tribe" emphasized the "aspect of common descent and history."[23]

The concept of the tribe was attractive to German Jews because in general political speech it also stood for a form of particularity that, while not religiously founded, was nevertheless regarded as a legitimate expression of difference. Already in the gestation period of modern German nationalism, the concept found its way into political discourse. In 1815 the historian Friedrich Christoph Dahlmann wrote euphorically after Napoleon's defeat at Waterloo that now "the German tribes . . . [were] united, in the main, in their common claim to freedom." The nationalistic enthusiasm of the Napoleonic wars was echoed also in Jacob Grimm's preface to his *Deutsche Grammatik* from 1819, where he argued that "the German people" was striving "for its national reunification without the dissolution of the states and tribes that have emerged in history."[24] A good half century later, Theodor Mommsen stressed in his sharp critique of Treitschke that "the German nation [was] based . . . on the cohesion and, in a certain sense, the fusion of different German tribes," of which Jews were one "no less than the Saxons, Swabians, or Pommeranians." Rather than deny this "diversity," the public should "take delight in it."[25] The concept of the tribe made it possible to imagine the nation simultaneously as the unity of the German people and as a multiplicity of tribes. This idea of plurality stood in contrast to an older tradition that had thought of multiplicity above all as the coexistence of sovereign dynasties and the fragile unity of the German Empire. The liberal, antidynastic traditional line culminated in the preamble to the Weimar Constitution of 1919. Whereas the German princes had entered into "an eternal alliance" in the old imperial Constitution of 1871, the democratic constitution emphasized that "the German people, unanimous in its tribes," had given itself "this constitution."[26]

Finally, a history of the German Jews from the perspective of multiculturalism must redefine the concept of *assimilation*.[27] Older ideas about assimilation remained attached to the paradigm of minority studies, which implied the idea of an "asymmetrical relation between clearly defined entities."[28] Well into the 1970s, assimilation was regarded as a linear process of the "adaptation" of an ethnic community to the majority society, at whose quasi-self-evident endpoint of "complete fusion" the "minority" would have adopted all the behaviors and attitudes of the "majority."[29] True, the older models distinguished various levels of the assimilation process—the acculturation through which the "minority" in many respects conformed to the majority culture but without losing its awareness of its particular identity—from complete or radical assimilation. Yet there was no doubt about the fundamental direction of the assimilation process.[30]

Especially the American debate over ethnicity in the 1970s, which gave rise to fruitful collaboration between historians, sociologists, and anthropologists, decisively abandoned the classical assimilation model. Some rejected the concept of assimilation as useless, while others maintained it but stressed the persistence of ethnic identity, the reversibility of the assimilation process, and the active role of "minorities," which do not adapt themselves so much as actively appropriate elements of the "majority culture." The idea that one can distinguish between minority and majority culture thus proves to be elusive. In modern society, there is no universal majority culture dominating everything, but only a multiplicity of constantly changing particular identities that mutually influence one another. In addition to these particular visions, a public space of common culture is formed. The scope and content of this space are not the monopoly of a majority culture (say, of the Protestant bourgeoisie in Germany or the WASPs in the United States) but are subject to negotiations in which all cultural groups participate, even if they do not all have the same chances of finding an audience. Although the Jewish and Catholic middle classes in imperial Germany were smaller and less privileged than the Protestant middle class, they nevertheless did not simply assimilate to a "bourgeois firmament of values" but simultaneously helped to revaluate and negotiate the meaning of "bourgeois culture" and "civility" in political culture.[31] "The norm of the German spirit, which has been abstracted from somewhere and with which its sworn advocates are used to operating," the Zionist writer Gustav Krojanker wrote in 1922, "still must be confronted with a reality in which German culture proves to be the embodiment of quite different traditions."[32]

If the history of the German Jews were to become the focus of the historical interest in modern German history, that also would represent a break with the heretofore usual procedure of treating Jewish history as marginal.[33] By and large, that holds also for recent studies of German social history, whose achievement presumably consists in its having broken with the ideal of homogeneity proper to classical national history and having established conflict and difference as central categories of historical research.[34] However, it focuses primarily on socioeconomic dimensions of conflict and diversity, while religious and ethnic spheres remain underexposed. Christhard Hoffmann recently remarked that "even within the new Gesellschaftsgeschichte," German-Jewish history has remained "a peripheral subject for a few specialists."[35] More than forty years after the founding of the Leo Baeck Institute and more than thirty years after German historians such as Reinhard Rürup, Monika Richarz, and Arno Herzig began to explore the history of the German

Jews, Jews appear in the majority of historical studies only as victims or do not appear at all; at best they are extraterritorialized and treated in separate sections. Examples of the first variant of historiographic marginalization are provided by research in the fields of the social history of religion, liberalism, and the bourgeoisie, which thus far have largely ignored Jews.[36] In the second case, the German Jews are reduced to the passive role of victim because the interest lies exclusively in the history of anti-Semitism. Exemplary for this approach is the more than twenty-volume *Deutsche Geschichte der neuesten Zeit,* edited by Martin Broszat and others, the more than fifty-volume *Neue Historische Bibliothek,* edited by Hans-Ulrich Wehler, and the latter's *Deutsche Gesellschaftsgeschichte.*[37] The third variant, examples of which are the work of Thomas Nipperdey, Wolfgang Mommsen, and Wolfram Siemann, as well as the *Enzyklopädie deutscher Geschichte,* edited by Lothar Gall, can be characterized as historiographic marginalization only to a limited extent. These scholars are interested in not only anti-Semitism but also German-Jewish history, though not as part of general German history but as a special case to be treated separately.[38] Contrary to such marginalization, however, it is necessary to stress, following Peter Gay, that "it is impossible to understand" important aspects of modern German history "without its Jews."[39]

The period covered in this study extends from 1860 to 1925 and thus falls predominantly in the time of imperial Germany, which is generally not considered to be the epoch in which multiculturalism was born. Imperial Germany is associated first of all with the persistence of traditional elites and the failure of bourgeois liberalism, the ascent of a right-wing, völkish, radical nationalism, and the genesis of the ideology of a racist anti-Semitism whose political successes may have been limited but which increasingly poisoned everyday relations between Jews and other Germans. In the end, between the founding of the Prussian Empire in 1871 and the revolution of 1918, the course was thus set presumably for the rise of National Socialism. This interpretation, however, has been rightly subjected to critique over the past twenty years. Today the society of imperial Germany is regarded as more bourgeois and more modern than in the interpretations dating from the late 1960s and the 1970s.[40] Yet it remains uncontested that—if one disregards a few Jewish intellectuals such as Moritz Lazarus and Heinrich Graetz—the most resolute defenders of the liberal constitutional state and thus of Jewish equality still maintained the goal of a homogeneous nation-state. Instead of granting German Jews the right to be different, even the advocates of their legal equality, such as Theodor Mommsen, the later Gustav

Freytag, and Rudolf Virchow, demanded from the Jews in return for their emancipation their complete assimilation.[41] And it would surely be an unhistorical undertaking to look for pioneers of multiculturalism in the centers of power, be it at the Kaiser's court, in the government, in the upper echelons of bureaucracy, or even in the Reichstag.

Besides, to German Jews, the compromise character of the Prussian Constitution of 1850 proved to be a stumbling block on the path to full equality. The status of basic rights, like the constitution in general, had the character of a "dilatory compromise" in which liberal and constitutional elements were mixed with monarchic and feudal ones.[42] On the one hand, Article 4 seemingly guaranteed the equality of all "Prussians . . . before the law," particularly as it explained that "public offices . . . , in compliance with the conditions set by the laws, [are] equally open to everyone who is qualified." On the other hand, Article 14 limited equality before the law insofar as the "Christian religion" was to be "made the foundation of those state institutions connected with religious practice."[43] Moreover, the constitution left open the precise meaning of the principle of equality before the law. That made it possible to undermine the principle in that it did not require "the equality of the content of the law but only the equality of the application of the law."[44] As long as Prussia understood itself to be a "Christian state," the constitution already degraded the Jews to second-class citizens.[45]

Although multiculturalism cannot be found as an explicit vision among contemporaneous political ideologies, and the constitution granted only the two major Christian denominations the right to be different, several major German cities such as Breslau (and probably Berlin, Frankfurt, and Königsberg as well), nevertheless came to be spaces in which it was possible to experiment with models of the acceptance of difference.[46] The prerequisite for such experimentation was a high proportion of Jews in the population, a well-established Jewish bourgeoisie emerging during the 1840s or 1850s, self-confident organs of the Jewish community and individual representatives of Jewish interests, a stable left-wing liberal majority on the city council, and, finally, a non-Jewish population that at least in part was prepared to recognize specifically Jewish demands as the legitimate expression of Jewish particularity.[47] Reference to a right to difference would, of course, have been just as foreign to the Jews as to their fellow Protestant and Catholic citizens. But as long as matters lay in the hands of local institutions, be they municipal authorities or private institutions, Jews were able to participate with equal rights in municipal life without having to deny their Jewishness.

Jews figured as part of the diversity constituting the city's unity. To demonstrate that this was the case in Breslau is the task of this study.

Against the backdrop of both the debate about ethnic and religious diversity and difference and the discussion of the mechanisms of inclusion and exclusion, this book analyzes the relations between Jews and other Breslauers. The study situates the history of their relations in several general contexts of research: the history of the bourgeoisie, the history of education, gender history, and the history of the city as a space of political action. In particular, it analyzes the structure of and changes in the patterns of inclusion and exclusion in the following spheres: social structure; private and public socializing, especially associations and marriage circles; the school system; and city politics.

In doing so, this book can rely on a broadly developed historiography of the history of the German Jews.[48] While the interest in the 1960s and 1970s lay above all in the difficult emancipation process and the rise of German anti-Semitism, since the 1980s German research also has discovered the Jews as subjects of history. In contrast to the Zionist view of the history of German Jewry as the fall of doomed and over-assimilated Jews, recent studies have stressed that while the German Jews broke radically with tradition in the nineteenth century, at the same time they created a new and sustainable Jewish community. Modern diaspora Jewry, with German Jewry as a paradigmatic case, now figures again as a possibility of Jewish existence. In the course of reevaluating the history of the Jewish diaspora, such central concepts as assimilation and ethnicity have clearly gained in complexity. Thus a simple history of the success or demise of modern German Jewry can no longer be written today.[49] Whereas in the meantime numerous studies on the history of German anti-Semitism stand opposite a multitude of outstanding works on inter-Jewish history, thus far there have been hardly any studies of the history of relations between Jews and other Germans, although Jacob Katz, Paula Hyman, Marion Kaplan, and Alan Levenson have repeatedly pointed to the lacuna.[50] Despite the vast, virtually unsurveyable literature on German-Jewish history, an account of the extent and limits of Jewish integration in German society that meets the demands of modern social and cultural history has yet to be written.

In view of the extensive literature on German-Jewish history, this lacuna requires explanation. Though correct, the reference to the limited interest of general German historiography in the history of German Jews does not help us further here. The decisive reason is instead to be found in the fact that the history of relations between Jews and other Germans was hitherto investigated almost exclusively using two approaches, each of which has reduced the multiplicity of possibilities for contact and conflict to only one aspect: either anti-Semitism or a German-Jewish symbiosis.

Research on anti-Semitism is of limited use for an analysis of the dense web of relations between Jews and other Germans. It concentrates on anti-Semitism as a political ideology and movement, as well as on anti-Semitic associations.[51] For this approach, the central question—regardless of the answer in each case, regardless also of the method and the explanation of anti-Semitism—is what connecting lines extended between anti-Semitism in imperial Germany and the Shoah. Reinhard Rürup is doubtless correct in maintaining that, in light of the historical significance of the National Socialists' attempt to annihilate the European Jews, an "impartial view of German-Jewish history is no longer possible."[52] Yet the historiography of German anti-Semitism all too easily neglects dissenting voices and ambivalent positions, as well as spheres in which anti-Semitism had little or no influence but which also must be taken into consideration in an analysis of Jewish integration. A broadly conceived social and cultural history of the relations between Jews and other Germans cannot afford to inquire into the significance of anti-Semitism alone, since the history of relations between Jews and other Germans is not limited to the latter. Such a history instead attends to those aspects of relations in which political action, concrete living conditions, and cultural orientations are consolidated.

Also, historiography has frequently reduced the extent and limits of Jewish integration in Germany to the concept of German-Jewish "symbiosis." Already in imperial Germany, several assimilated German Jews—such as the leader of the Marburg school of neo-Kantianism, Hermann Cohen—had idealized Jewish-Gentile relations as a fruitful synthesis of two particularly distinguished cultures, "Germanness and Jewishness."[53] Of course, the excessively mythical concept of symbiosis is an easy target of polemics. And many have taken aim at it, especially Gershom Scholem: Does the "careless talk" of a German-Jewish symbiosis, he has asked, not fail to appreciate the constant refusal of non-Jews to accept Jews as Jews? Does the Shoah not appear to be less an "accident," and National Socialist anti-Semitism to be less a "resort to hatred," than a consequence of the exclusion of the German Jews by non-Jewish society? The limits of this debate for an investigation of the relations between Jews and other Germans are obvious. Methodologically, the discussion of symbiosis is usually restricted to the traditional

history of culture and ideas. At the same time, it makes little sense to
measure the ambivalence and contradictoriness of the relationship
between Jews and non-Jews against a nostalgically transfigured idea of a
cultural symbiosis.[54]

This history of relations between Jews and other Germans has a place:
Breslau. If justice is to be done to it, the Silesian capital must be studied
in its concrete aspects.[55] The city's topography—streets and buildings,
squares and railroad lines—is part of the history of Jews and other Breslauers. Beyond these fundamental considerations, there are practical
considerations that speak for the focus on local history. First, the micro-
perspective makes it possible to trace the multilayered and contradictory
mechanisms of inclusion and exclusion and to analyze the interaction
of several dimensions of relations between Jews and other Breslauers.
By claiming "to look closely" as well, this study also has the opportunity
to write a history of people with "names and a distinguishable history."[56] Moreover, similar to the penetrating local investigations of Richard Evans, David Blackbourn, and Martin Geyer, this study seeks to mediate between macro- and microhistory, between the history of society
and that of daily life.[57] Supraregional factors are taken into consideration, of course. The framework of the centralized state often restricted
the scope of action for local authorities, the municipal government, the
municipal school administration, and the branches of national associations and organizations. In the latter half of the nineteenth century, on
the other hand, cities were and remained largely independent in many
areas and defended their right to self-government. Due to population
growth, economic growth, and increasing self-confidence, cities remained an important "factor of political power in the state."[58] The
local approach reveals here more clearly than a consideration of the
centralized state that the debate about the scope of state and municipal
power was part of the conflicts between Breslau and Prussia. The validity of the results for Breslau will be checked by consulting those available for other cities. Because the present wave of local-historical research has also turned, after some delay, to the history of anti-Semitism
and of German Jews, it is easier to determine the validity of this study's
results.[59]

Because of Breslau's religious, political, and economic heterogeneity, the city is particularly well suited for a study of relations between
Jews and other Breslauers that inquires into the significance of cultural
diversity and difference, as well as that of the dynamics of inclusion and

exclusion. In the nineteenth century, Breslau was the second largest city in Prussia,[60] and since the late eighteenth century, it had been a center of German-Jewish life. Between 1800 and 1933, the Breslau Jewish community counted among the three largest in Germany. Between 1850 and 1914, the Jewish portion of Breslau's population vacillated between 4 and 8%.[61] The size of the community, the varied, extensive community life, the possibilities for studying at the university, and the major Jewish theological seminary made Breslau a magnet during the great Jewish migration of the nineteenth and early twentieth centuries.[62] Especially Jews from Silesia and Posen were drawn to Breslau.[63] Moreover, the city's religious climate was marked by the population's triconfessionality well into the twentieth century. Although the majority were Protestants (just under 60%), in addition to the large—by German standards— Jewish community many Catholics also lived in Breslau, making up a good third of the population. Contacts and conflicts thus arose in the metropolis on the Oder River both between Jews and Christians and between Catholics and Protestants.[64] The political climate of the city was dominated by the liberals, but since 1878–79 a strong conservative faction had also existed, as well as a branch of the Center Party that was important from the 1870s on, and quite early a successful social democracy.[65] Finally, Breslau counted among Germany's multifunctional cities, since it had industrial, service, and commercial enterprises, as well as national administrative institutions and a large university.[66] One is thus justified in understanding Breslau as a place in which central lines of development and fields of conflict converged in nineteenth- and twentieth-century German history. Nevertheless, Breslau is terra incognita for modern German and German-Jewish history. With the exception of investigations by Manfred Hettling, Andreas Reinke, and Leszek Ziątkowski, no studies of the history of Breslau in the nineteenth and twentieth centuries have reflected the current state of research and tapped into new source material.[67]

There is no cohesive source material on the history of Jews and other Breslauers. In integrating Jewish and German history, this study relies on diverse printed and archival sources. Many clues to the relationship between Jews and other Breslauers are found in the general press of the city, as well as in the local and supraregional German-Jewish press, and in the extensive holdings of the municipal authorities and the city council, as well as those of Prussian governmental authorities.[68] For the history of associational life, the school system, and city politics, the Breslau University Library's print and pamphlet collection also proved informative.[69] For microhistorical questions, the autobiographies, diaries, and correspondence of Breslau Jews and non-Jews were indispensable.[70] Since this study, unlike the majority of works on German-Jewish history, is also interested in lower-class Jews, serial sources such as tax rolls, marriage registers, and lists of high school graduates were crucial.[71] Numerous self-testimonies about the lives of bourgeois Jews are available; by contrast, hardly any family histories, letters, diaries, and autobiographies by lower-class Jews have survived.

This book comprises four fields of investigation: social structure, public and private sociability, the school system, and city politics. The first chapter, "The Social Structure of Jews, Protestants, and Catholics from the Mid-Nineteenth Century to the First World War," investigates the occupational profile and income structures of Breslau Jews and inquires into their significance for the relationship between Jews and other Breslauers. It becomes evident thereby that the social structure of the Jews was by no means primarily a bourgeois structure, though it was essentially more bourgeois than that of other Breslauers. Nevertheless, the social structure predestined Jews to be a core group of the city's bourgeoisie. A good quarter of the middle-class occupational and income groups in Breslau were Jewish. Yet the majority of Breslau Jews did not have an income that would have supported a bourgeois lifestyle; many Breslau Jews, especially single women, were poor.[72]

The second chapter, "Crossing Boundaries: Jews in Bourgeois and Jewish Associations," inquires into the significance of associational life for the relationship between Jews and other Breslauers. The extent of Jewish inclusion in the city's associational life was high. The great majority of associations were open to Jews: sports, cultural, and other social associations, the liberal representatives of Breslau's Masonic lodges, as well as professional organizations. Moreover, it is striking that several Breslau Jews played prominent roles simultaneously in associational life at large and in Jewish associations, a situation supporting the concept of situational ethnicity and indicating that Breslau Jews by no means had to deny their Jewishness in order to participate in the general associational life.

The third chapter, "Jewish-Christian Marriages, the 'New Woman,' and the Situational Ethnicity of Breslau Jews," explores the significance of gender relations for the history of Jews and other Breslauers. The quadrupling of the proportion of intermarriages reflects the fact that private contact between Jews and other Breslauers became more a matter of course. The analysis of marriage registers and available autobiographical testimonies suggests that the city's social life offered people manifold opportunities to get to know, to befriend, and possibly to marry one another across denominational boundaries. Lower-class Jews—and especially women—chose more often than bourgeois Jews to enter into a mixed marriage. Those who did so were usually more independent of their families, perhaps even more rebellious than those who entered into inter-Jewish marriages. The fact that these differences were particularly conspicuous in the case of women indicates that Jewish-Christian marriages were also an expression of a new and more likely egalitarian gender regime and an awakening of women's self-confidence.

The fourth chapter, "Unity, Diversity, and Difference: Jews, Protestants, and Catholics in Breslau Schools," investigates the experiences of Jewish schoolchildren. Between 1870 and 1918, all Jewish schoolboys and almost all schoolgirls in Breslau attended state or city schools, all of which were governed by a Christian school statute. The sociostatistical analysis and a sampling of the high school diplomas of Jewish schoolchildren do not reveal any structural discrimination. Exemplary for the school policies of the magistracy and the city council is the so-called Breslau school struggle, which escalated in the late 1860s and the early 1870s and was closely connected with what is known as the Kulturkampf, literally the "struggle of civilizations." After years of conflict between the city and the Prussian government, the municipal authorities opened the Johannes-Gymnasium. That was an important step on the path to the actual equality of the Jewish population, since several Jewish teachers taught at the school and Jewish religious instruction was obligatory.

Finally, the fifth chapter, "Liberalism, Anti-Semitism, and Jewish Equality," attempts, through the analysis of relations between Jews and other Breslauers, to elucidate the specific character of left-wing liberalism in Breslau and to investigate the extent of Jewish inclusion in local politics. Left-wing liberalism granted Jews the right to be different because local Jewish politicians helped to shape the local left-wing liberal movement. An essential element of the city's left-wing liberalism, indeed its driving force, was Jewish because Jews formed a core group. Jewish liberals decisively influenced central aspects of Breslau municipal politics. Together with non-Jewish liberals, they were able to repel political anti-Semitism, though it was temporarily successful in the early 1880s and 1890s.

The liberal nature of the municipal authorities' basic position was also expressed in concrete politics, which affected the special interests of Breslau Jews. Such was demonstrated by the city's stance on the controversial question of naturalization. From the perspective of the municipal authorities, the question of naturalization was a social question. They recommended that everyone who could burden the municipal and state welfare system be refused naturalization. As long as a Jewish immigrant could prove that he could support himself, the city recommended his naturalization. In nearly every case, the municipal authorities issued positive certificates to Jewish applicants. By contrast, the national authorities denied naturalization to almost every Jewish applicant. That is striking insofar as they even naturalized non-Jews against whose naturalization the city, arguing that these people probably would become welfare cases, had advised.

The conclusion first takes up the question of continuity and discontinuity and then traces how relations between Jews and other Breslauers deteriorated dramatically between 1916 and 1923 and anti-Semitism gained in significance in all the areas of our investigation. Against the backdrop of these dramatic changes, we then summarize the main theses of this study. It is precisely in view of the rapid increase in anti-Semitism between 1916 and 1925 that one gains an impressive picture of the high degree of Jewish integration in the prewar period.

1

The Social Structure of Jews, Protestants, and Catholics from the Mid-Nineteenth Century to the First World War

Diverse lines of differentiation ran through the Breslau population in the late nineteenth and early twentieth century. One of these boundaries, that between Jews and other Breslauers, is of particular interest in the present study. As with other boundaries, it is advisable not to consider the ethnic-denominational differences in an urban population in isolation, but rather to look for connections to other boundaries. This chapter explores the significance that socioeconomic inequality had for the relationship between Jews and other Breslauers. What follows is based on two guiding questions: How bourgeois were Breslau Jews, Protestants, and Catholics? And how Jewish, Protestant, or Catholic was the Breslau bourgeoisie? Thus the chapter analyzes and compares the income stratifications and occupational profiles of Jews, Protestants, and Catholics, which will also be differentiated by sex, age, and birthplace whenever possible. It investigates the social structure within the Jewish, Protestant, and Catholic populations and the proportion of the three denominations in the individual professional groups and income stratifications. This comparative investigation questions the prevailing view that the majority of German Jews belonged to the bourgeoisie from the mid-nineteenth century to the end of the Weimar Republic. Moreover, the comparative perspective makes it possible to determine the Jewish proportion of the Breslau bourgeoisie, the social strata that supported associational life (*Vereinswesen*), supplied almost all secondary-school students, and influenced local politics.

The first part attempts, following Max Weber, to grasp conceptually the strained relationship between class and status, which was constitutive of the "long nineteenth century." The bourgeoisie is understood thereby, following M. Rainer Lepsius, as a status group (*ständische Verge-sellschaftung*), which, while presupposing a bourgeois class situation, nevertheless cannot be reduced to the latter. Due to the rapid economic advancement of German Jews beginning in the mid-nineteenth century, their history is particularly suited for an analysis of the general strained relationship between class and status. In the second part, the upward social mobility of the Jews between the end of the eighteenth century and the founding of the German Empire will be sketched and the state of the relevant research discussed. Three deficits in the studies on the social structure of German Jews become evident thereby: First, they do not distinguish adequately between the petite bourgeoisie and the *Bür-gertum*, that is, the bourgeoisie proper. Second, they limit themselves almost exclusively to analyses of occupational structure while neglecting the more informative income stratification. Third, they almost completely ignore the proportion of single women in the overall Jewish population. The third part of this chapter analyzes the occupational profile of Breslau Jews in the German Empire, compares it with that of Catholics and Protestants, and inquires into the proportion of Jews in the individual occupations in the Silesian capital, especially in the bourgeois occupations. Yet since, particularly in the case of the Jews, the analysis of professions shifts one's attention to the actual heterogeneity of the class positions, the fourth part investigates Jewish income stratification in Breslau, compares it with Protestant and Catholic income stratifications, and thereby determines the proportion of Jews in the bourgeois income strata in the Oder metropolis. Through the analysis of the Jewish occupational profile and income stratification, it can be shown that the majority of Breslau Jews did not belong to the bourgeoisie. Since these results run counter not only to the prevailing consensus among scholars but also to the contemporary self-understanding, the fifth part attempts to grasp people's descriptions of themselves and others no longer as a substitute for sociohistorical stratification analysis but rather as reflections of the longings, hopes, and fears given expression in the widespread view that the majority of the Jews were bourgeois from the mid-nineteenth century on.

1. The Strained Relationship between Status and Class in Modernity: The Bourgeoisie as a Status Group

Three considerations make it attractive to write the history of social inequality in Breslau between 1870 and 1920 within the framework of a history of the relations between Jews and non-Jews. First, the analysis of the place of Jews within the social stratification of the German Empire makes it possible to investigate the strained relationship between class situations and status situations. The terminology used here derives from Max Weber. "Class situation" (*Klassenlage*) means the dimension of social inequality based on "the relative control over goods and skills" and on their "income-producing uses within a given economic order."[1] If class position constitutes the predominant moment of social inequality, then the "nature of an individual's opportunity in the market" decides the individual's fate. "Class situation," according to Weber, "is ultimately market situation."[2] Considerations of "'personal distinctions'" and the question of honor become completely unimportant relative to "'functional' interests." In Weber's ideal class society, the place of the individual within the social hierarchy is grounded in "mere economic acquisition and naked economic power."[3] By contrast, the status situation (*ständische Lage*) refers to forms of inequality "determined by a specific, positive or negative, social estimation of *honor*."[4] This status honor can derive from various sources. Feudal society, in which status honor is based on hereditary privilege, is thus only one special instance of the status situation. The social esteem of a status group can be based on the lifestyle, descent, personal selection (say, within a priestly estate), or on the esteem of a profession and is explicitly pitted against any "distribution of power which is regulated exclusively through the market" or "pretensions of purely economic acquisition as such."[5] In daily life, according to Weber, status honor is expressed "by the fact that above all else a specific *style of life* is expected from all those who wish to belong to the circle."[6]

Second, the investigation of the relationship between class and status situations makes it possible to question the idea that in the nineteenth century there was a linear development from an estate to a class society.[7] Weber himself has already indicated that status honor need not stand in contradiction to class position, but rather that frequently "class distinctions are linked in the most varied ways with status distinctions."[8] Above all, Weber rejects a teleological model of development in which the class society replaces the estate society. That does not mean that he ignores the connection between economic development and the prevailing form of social inequality. Rather, Weber stresses that "every technological repercussion and economic transformation" undermines stratification by status and gives rise to "naked class situations."[9] If the pace of technical and economic upheavals wanes, however, status honor can displace class position as a predominant criterion of social stratification. If one follows Weber, it is misleading to describe the nineteenth century as a "post-estate" epoch (Jürgen Kocka) in which class has replaced status and in which the bourgeoisie as a social class has superseded the estate social formation of the nobility as the social elite.[10] The status situation in Weber's sense is not a characteristic of "the old European society," the "residual forms" of which pass over into modernity.[11] Rather, the moment of social esteem, thus status honor, also often determines in the modern, functionally differentiated society the place of the individual within the social hierarchy. According to Weber, the capitalistic market economy does not undermine status in itself but rather the variations that are based on descent or personal selection. As a consequence, status groups dominate for which a specific class position is "by far the predominant factor. After all, the possibility of a style of life expected for members of a status group is usually conditioned economically."[12] The bourgeoisie in the nineteenth century provides rich illustrative material for this state of affairs. It was a social formation that presupposed bourgeois class positions as its condition of possibility but nevertheless had developed all the traits of a status group whose conceptions of social esteem and honor were grounded in a specific lifestyle. Whoever wanted to be a member of the bourgeoisie had to command a bourgeois income—that was the purely economic consideration—but beyond that (and this was decisive), he had to subject himself to the requirements of a bourgeois lifestyle in order to enjoy the status honor of the bourgeois. The status situation, the lifestyle and the social esteem, were always more important than the class situation. The particular challenge of an analysis of social stratification and mobility during the nineteenth century is to investigate the entanglement and the tension between class and status situations involved in the making of the bourgeoisie.

Third, no group in German society is more suitable than the Jews for an analysis of the strained relationship between class and status in the latter half of the nineteenth and the early twentieth century. Grounded in this strained relationship, the ambivalence of social position obtained for two reasons for Jews to a greater extent than for Protestants and Catholics. On the one hand, Jews enjoyed a more rapid upward mobility than other groups and therefore had to live more often with the stigma of the social climber, whose class situation (income and assets) and status situation (the social esteem based on lifestyle) diverged considerably. The bourgeois lifestyle of the climber was considered by other, tradition-conscious bourgeois to be somewhat too ambitious,

forced, and artificial. The "patrician arrogance of old-established bourgeois," according to Jacob Toury, "looked askance at all *homines novi.* . . .
The more economically threatened these patricians felt, the more exclusive they acted socially."[13] Typically enough, the positive assessment of
the social climber was expressed best in the English loanword *Selfmade-
man.*[14] Moreover, it was more difficult for Jewish climbers than for Protestant or Catholic parvenus to close the gap between the class situation
and status honor. They had to free themselves not only from the blemish
of the social climber but also from the stigma of the "Jewish." As early as
1817, Achim von Arnim complained in his lament about the "moneyed
nobility" that "the noble houses" of Berlin and Königsberg were "now
in the possession of merchants and Jews."[15] Anti-Jewish prejudice did
not have to be expressed in open enmity toward Jews. Yet even in its
weakest form, a specific reservation about Jewish social climbers remained. This did not prevent upward social mobility because the nature
of opportunity in the market, as Weber put it, knew no "personal distinctions." However, anti-Jewish sentiments did make it more difficult to
acquire bourgeois status honor in the eyes of other *Bürger.* The same assets and income could be regarded differently depending on social estimation as "prosperous" or "filthy rich"; one could speak of the "economic elite" or the "plutocrats."

Status honor, which is based on the claims of a bourgeois lifestyle,
comes to concrete sociohistorical expression in marriage and associational circles. The status situation of the bourgeoisie did presuppose a
bourgeois class situation, that is, the material means for a bourgeois style
of life. Conceptions of bourgeois honor, however, were based "above all
else" on the fact that a "specific style of life [was] expected from all those
who wish[ed] to belong to the circle." Such expectations went hand in
hand with "restrictions on social intercourse (that is, intercourse which
[was] not subservient to any other purposes)."[16] The making of the
bourgeoisie as a status group was therefore inextricably tied to habits
and manners, interior decorating, ways of eating, and forms of socializing, all of which were out of reach for anyone who did not command a
bourgeois income.

This chapter investigates the Jewish proportion of the bourgeois occupations and the bourgeois classes in Breslau, thus those income groups
that had at their disposal sufficient financial means to support a bourgeois lifestyle. An answer to the question of the role of Jews in the Breslau bourgeoisie as a status group is then sought in the following chapters,
which investigate the core areas of bourgeois lifestyle, associational life,

friendship and marriage circles, the secondary school system, and political life in the city.

2. The Social Advancement of Breslau Jews, 1780–1870

At the beginning one encounters an impressive story of climbing out of poverty and marginality. Yet in the course of the eighteenth century, the social situation of Jews in German-speaking Central Europe deteriorated. Many Jews were reduced to poverty, and many were forced to feed themselves by begging. Around 1750, almost three-fifths of all Jews belonged to the "penniless class" and lived on the edge of subsistence. "The poor are countless," a rabbi complained in the eighteenth century, "hundreds, thousands, hang around all over the place."[17] Even as late as 1829, the board of the Jewish *Gemeinde* estimated that of the nine hundred Jewish families living in Breslau, almost half, that is, four hundred, were unable to pay the community tax of at least six taler. In many cases, they were dependent on the *Gemeinde* for financial support.[18]

On balance, Jews succeeded in making a rapid social advance between the late eighteenth century and the founding of the German Empire. The nineteenth century was a time of increasingly rapid economic modernization in Central Europe. Modernization, Yuri Slezkine notes, is about "learning how to cultivate people and symbols, not fields and herds, . . . replacing inherited privilege with acquired prestige, and dismantling social estates for the benefit of individuals, nuclear families, and book-reading tribes."[19] The more feudal and guild barriers fell, the more the economy was liberalized, and the more trade and industry grew at the expense of agriculture, all the clearer was the road that beckoned to the hard worker, and the more chances emerged for the advancement of Jews from Central Europe. They built on centuries of experience in trade, on supraregional family networks, and well into the nineteenth century were also perhaps intellectually more alert and more venturesome and more flexible in reacting to economic changes than many of their Christian competitors. For German Jews, the thesis of general research into sociohistorical mobility does not hold true, namely, that the age of industrialization was not a golden age of greater upward mobility but rather a time of crisis for many, especially for traditional professional groups.[20] While the proportion of the total population that belonged to the lower classes continued to grow at least until midcentury, many Jews made the leap out of the lower classes and into the lower-middle class or even the upper-middle class.[21] From the perspective of many German-speaking Jews in Central Europe, the long nineteenth century was a golden age of economic advancement.

The best chances for advancement for Jews existed in urban centers, and Breslau was one of the most important in Prussia. The rapid upward social mobility of many Jews had occurred in barely two generations, as is shown by easily accessible sources (which are well known in the literature), namely, the income stratification and the occupational profile of Breslau Jews in the 1860s. Even as early as 1861, the *Allgemeine Zeitung des Judenthums* reported that in the Oder metropolis 30% of all voters in the first voting class were Jewish, although the Jewish proportion of the population was only 7%.[22] The Jews who succeeded in advancing economically did so especially because of their activity in trade. Rough conclusions may be drawn from the "Census and Population Description" in the *Preußische Statistik* from 1861–62, on which table 1 is based. Almost two-thirds (64.6%) of all economically active Breslau Jews made a living from trade. By contrast, only about 4% of Christians worked in this area, with the result that in the Oder metropolis almost every other person working in trade was Jewish. That was an unusually high proportion. In Berlin, Königsberg, and Cologne, the proportion was lower (33%, 24%, and 16%, respectively), though that was because in these cities Jews constituted a smaller proportion of the economically active population (table 2). Moreover, the occupational profile permits conclusions about the social stratification of the Jewish population in the early 1860s, even if such questions can be answered only imprecisely based on the *Preußische Statistik*. Because the Königliches Statistisches Bureau (Royal Statistics Bureau) categorized Jews and Christians differently and differentiated precisely only in the case of economically active Jews, these figures are available only for Jews working in trade. In the more precise classification, only the four subgroups of "bankers," "wholesalers and commission traders," "merchants with open shops," and finally "agents, suppliers, commission agents, and brokers" indicate a bourgeois class situation. This group encompassed 33% of all economically active Jews in Breslau. That, too, was unusually high. In Berlin, the corresponding proportion was only 29%, in Cologne 31%, and in Königsberg only 22%.[23]

At first glance, then, the history of Breslau Jews in the nineteenth century confirms the conventional view that the majority of German Jews belonged to the bourgeoisie in the late German Empire. There is hardly a study on the recent history of German Jews that does not cite Jacob Toury's estimate that as early as 1870 over 60% of German Jews lived in "safely bourgeois" conditions.[24] Monika Richarz says that prior to the First World War Jews had "belonged to the vast majority of the urban middle class." The reference here is not to the broad concept of the middle classes but rather, as one learns in the next sentence, to the bourgeoisie.[25] After 1870, "the large majority" of Jews, Shulamit Volkov argued in 1988, "belonged to the bourgeoisie." Somewhat more carefully in her recent survey, Volkov writes that the Jews made up "almost everywhere . . . a secure middle class."[26] According to Andrea Hopp's recent study on Jewish bourgeois families in Frankfurt am Main, "the majority of the Jewish population . . . in Frankfurt" around the turn of the century belonged "to the bourgeoisie."[27] In surveys of the German Empire, a similar judgment may be found, even in the works of respected experts such as Thomas Nipperdey and Volker Berghahn. According to Nipperdey, around the turn of the century 60% of German Jews belonged to the middle or upper bourgeoisie and another 25% to the petite bourgeoisie. While Berghahn is aware of the limits of available studies, he nevertheless speaks of the "rise" of German Jews "into the well-to-do bourgeoisie."[28]

The view that the majority of Jews were bourgeois is based on conceptual imprecision. Whereas the scholarship on the late nineteenth-century bourgeoisie usually distinguishes between the petite bourgeoisie, or *Kleinbürgertum,* and the bonne bourgeoisie, or *Bürgertum* proper, and is most interested in the latter, this distinction does not play an important role in German-Jewish history. However, if the history of relations between Jews and other Breslauers is to be written as part of the general history, it pays to distinguish between the *Bürgertum* and the *Kleinbürgertum,* which among Jews also included an army of clerks whose nickname was *Stehkragenproletarier,* proletarians in stand-up collars. Certainly, many petit-bourgeois Jews and non-Jews wanted to belong to the bourgeoisie; the distance to the bonne bourgeoisie was great, and it increased. The petits bourgeois, writes Nipperdey, "wanted to be bourgeois but they remained marginal."[29] The gulf between petit-bourgeois daily life and the lifestyle of the bourgeoisie was also visible to contemporaries. Eugen Altmann, a flax merchant in Breslau prior to the First World War, distinguished in retrospect in 1939 between the "man of the *Mittelstand*" and the "somewhat higher stratum of the *Bürgertum.*" The petit bourgeois was "the citizen holding one or even several newspapers," who loved the "afternoon cigar, the good nap" and whose cultural horizon consisted of "Ahlwardt," "Janusschauer," and "Zehngebote-Hoffmann." To the bourgeoisie, however, belonged only "people who traveled abroad, made contacts there, who were in correspondence with the representatives for whom they had voted, since their word already meant something, who were in charge or wanted to be!"[30]

One should not underestimate the will of many petits bourgeois to educate themselves and improve their social standing. Testimonies from members of this stratum, however, are rare and possibly not representative because it was precisely those whose desire to be bourgeois was particularly strong who wrote memoirs more often than other petits bourgeois. Adolf Riesenfeld (b. 1884) was one of the few Jews who wrote about his, as he himself said, "petit-bourgeois life."[31] After he had left the Elisabeth-Gymnasium in the spring of 1900 without a middle school certificate (das "Einjährige") on account of catastrophic grades, he first became an apprentice in his father's business and then in Sachs & Wohlauer, a Breslau manufactured-goods store. From 1903 to 1909, after he had taken over his father's business, he worked as a clerk and earned about nine hundred marks per year. Yet since he lived in his father's house and did not have to pay for any household expenses, his financial situation was better than it would otherwise have been given his low annual income. Nevertheless, it is astonishing how determinedly the young Riesenfeld oriented himself toward the bourgeois lifestyle even while still an office apprentice. When he traveled in the summer of 1901 to relatives in Berlin, he traveled fourth class, but once in the capital he went to the royal opera to hear Wagner's *Tristan and Isolde*.[32] Moreover, in the same year he purchased season tickets to the Breslau City Theater, sated his "hunger for reading . . . in the *Max'schen* lending library," "devoted himself more and more enthusiastically to the rhymes" of poems that "sometimes were pretty and quite thoughtful," had his father give him a bicycle so that he could become an "avid sports enthusiast," joined the Kaufmännisch-wissenschaftlicher Verein, a debate club for young Jewish merchants, in order to discuss the significance of "free love in our time."[33] After the end of his apprenticeship, dance lessons were added in the winter of 1903, even though Riesenfeld had to "buy all the clothes on credit"; what is more, he went not to the "more elegant" and mixed denominational Reif Dance School but to the "purely Jewish circle at the Baer Institute." Out of the dance school developed, in turn, a "tennis circle," to which Riesenfeld belonged from spring 1904 on; he had already sold his bicycle in 1903 to finance a summer vacation in the High Tatra Mountains (Slovakia).[34] "Out of the chaotic jumble of my thirst for knowledge," Riesenfeld judged in retrospect in 1917, "an incipient worldview crystallized." "A complete intellectual revolution" had made it possible for him "to lead an independently active and, above all, thinking life."[35]

Although the majority of studies on the social structure of German Jews is based on an analysis of professions,[36] there are nevertheless several, above all contemporary, analyses of Jewish income stratification.[37] The result of all the investigations is clear: in the German Empire, Jews were wealthier than other Germans, especially Catholics. The most comprehensive though also most dubious figures come from Werner Sombart, who sought in 1911 to underpin statistically his claim that there was a "monstrous superiority of the Jewish over the non-Jewish population in financial status." Sombart estimated that in 1905 Breslau Jews as a whole paid roughly four times as much in taxes as non-Jews.[38] According to Arthur Ruppin, Jews represented only a good 5% of Berlin's total population in 1898 but paid almost 30% of all taxes in Berlin.[39] In Frankfurt am Main, the average income of Jewish taxpayers was 427 marks, roughly three and one-half times higher than that of Protestant taxpayers.[40]

As a rule such studies compare the Jewish with the Christian population without differentiating the Jewish population by income. Generally, we hear nothing about income distribution, so these investigations do not permit any conclusions concerning how many Jews had an income that would have made a bourgeois lifestyle possible. One of the few surveys is for the income stratification of Frankfurt Jews in 1900 (see table 3).[41] If one takes 3,000 marks as the lowest annual income that would allow for a bourgeois lifestyle, then according to table 3 nearly 47% of all Frankfurt Jews did not belong to the middle classes. The actual proportion of lower-class Jews was even higher. Missing from the table are in fact all tax-exempt income earners with an annual income of less than 900 marks. As for how many Jewish income earners the Frankfurt table hides, we can only estimate. In Breslau, at least, nearly 35% of all Jewish income earners in 1906 paid taxes on an annual income of less than 900 marks; in Königsberg, more than a third of the Jewish population earned even less than 660 marks in 1905.[42] Even if we were to assume that in Frankfurt only 25% of all Jewish taxpayers earned less than 900 marks per year and for that reason are missing from the table, the proportion of Jewish heads of households who paid taxes on an annual income that definitely would not have permitted a class-appropriate bourgeois lifestyle would increase to 60%.

The thesis that the majority of German Jews belonged to the *Bürgertum* in the late German Empire lacks a distinction between bonne bourgeoisie and petite bourgeoisie and neglects the income levels of the Jewish population. The Oder metropolis is particularly well suited for the scrutiny of this view. Thus far, Breslau has not been known for having a particularly high proportion of impoverished lower-class Jews. On the contrary, Toury counts Breslau among the cities with a particularly high degree of socioeconomic embourgeoisement of the Jewish population.[43] The results from such a study of Breslau therefore will have a significance beyond the Silesian capital. Moreover, the state archives contain, completely preserved, Breslau's class lists and income tax rolls, which contain data on profession, denomination, age, income type, address, marriage status, and, at least for 1906, also birthplace. These Prussian tax rolls, which are regarded in the general literature on economic history as relatively reliable,[44] also afford insights into the extent of Jewish poverty because, unlike the tax rolls of the Jewish communities that Avraham Barkai used, they include tax-exempt Jews.[45] Finally, there are representative data sets for the entire Breslau population, so the significance of all the figures derived for the Jews can be weighted through a comparison with other Breslauers.[46]

Also Breslau is particularly suitable for an investigation of the occupational profile and income levels of single women, whether single, divorced, or widowed. Of all German metropolises around the turn of the century, Breslau, with 36%, had the largest proportion of women among all economically active individuals.[47] In what follows, it will be shown that the thesis that the majority of Jews belonged to the bourgeoisie does not do justice to the social structure of Breslau Jews since it neglects the proportion of Jews in the petite bourgeoisie and the lower classes. The occupational profile, but especially the income stratification, of the Jewish population in the German Empire was more heterogeneous than has previously been assumed.

3. The Occupational Profile of Jews and Other Breslauers

The Occupational Profile of Breslau Jews

At first glance the occupational profile of Breslau's total population and of the Jewish population hardly changed between 1876 and 1906 (tables 4 and 5). If one distinguishes on the basis of profession by the large groups of bourgeoisie proper, petite bourgeoisie, and lower classes, then a good 11% of all taxpayers belonged to the bourgeoisie in 1876 and a good 12% did in 1906; the proportion of the petite bourgeoisie also grew slightly for the same period from nearly 20% to a good 20%; finally, the size of the lower classes grew from 60% to 65%. Among the Jews, the proportions of professional groups remained roughly the same, even though more Jews than non-Jews made the leap from the petite bourgeoisie to the bourgeoisie; the proportion of the bourgeoisie grew from 40% in 1876 to 55% in 1906, whereas the proportion of the petite bourgeoisie sank from 30% to 25%, and the proportion of the lower classes remained virtually unchanged—16% in 1876 and 15% in 1906.

However, the fact that the proportions in the large groups hardly changed should by no means be mistaken for stasis. Between 1875 and 1905, Breslau's total population doubled, from 239,050 to 470,904 residents, and the Jewish population also grew by 30%, from 15,505 to 20,356.[48] Despite the population growth, the proportion of the *Bürgertum* between the early and the late German Empire did not decrease, but rather increased slightly, which suggests a certain social mobility. It was greater among the Jews than among the total population. The proportion of the bourgeoisie among Breslau Jews increased from 1876 to 1906 by roughly 13%, but among Protestants by only 0.5% and among Catholics by nearly 2% (tables 4 and 5). That the proportion of Breslau's bourgeoisie remained steadily high throughout the German Empire was due first and foremost to the social upward mobility of the Jews, who represented a good quarter of the Breslau bourgeoisie in 1906.

One should not overestimate the proportion of the bourgeoisie in the total population of Breslau. At the beginning and at the end of the German Empire, based on profession, nearly two-thirds of the Breslau population belonged to the lower classes, roughly one-fifth to the petite bourgeoisie, and only a good tenth to the *Bürgertum*. Even when one adds the petits bourgeois to the bourgeois professional groups, the middle classes have a proportion of only a good 30% in 1876 and 1906.[49] Granted, that exceeds the figures for the total German population, of which a maximum of 6% belonged to the professional groups of the bourgeoisie and a maximum of 9% to those of the petite bourgeoisie.[50] However, the fact that the proportion of bourgeois professional groups in a major city was greater than in the whole empire should not be overrated. Overall it is much more important to note that the majority of the Breslau population belonged to lower-class rather than bourgeois or petit-bourgeois professional groups.

The differences between the Jewish, the Protestant, and the Catholic occupational profiles were enormous and hardly decreased over the course of the German Empire (tables 4 and 5). If one looks only at the bourgeoisie, an impressive contrast arises between 1876 and 1906. Judging by profession, over 40% of Breslau Jews belonged to the *Bürgertum* in 1876, whereas only 10% of Protestants and only 5% of Catholics did. Thirty years later, the proportion of Jews in that group was almost 60%, while the proportion of Protestants was still a good 10%, and that of Catholics, just over 7%. Even if an analysis of occupations exaggerates the proportion of the bourgeoisie especially among the Jews, it should nevertheless already be clear that the proportion of the bourgeoisie among the Jews was greater than among other Breslauers.

The Jewish bourgeoisie lived off the trade of goods and money to a far greater degree than did Protestants and Catholics (tables 4 and 5). At the beginning of the German Empire, almost 90% of all Breslau Jews who belonged to the bourgeoisie were *Wirtschaftsbürger*, that is, merchants and bankers, industrialists, and other entrepreneurs whose claim to membership in the bourgeoisie rested on their property, wealth, and income. Merchants formed the lion's share (80%) of the Jewish *Wirtschaftsbürger*. By contrast, there were hardly any Jewish factory owners and manufacturers; their proportion among the Jewish *Wirtschaftsbürgertum* was only a good 2% and thus was barely higher than that of Jewish bankers, which was nearly 2%. The remaining proportion comprised managers, purveyors of luxury services, and independent gentlemen, the so-called *rentiers*. Still small in 1876 was the subgroup of the Jewish *Bildungsbürgertum*, that is, the educated elite of high-ranking civil servants and university professors, physicians, and lawyers for whom academic qualifications and professional credentials were the most important source of prestige and economic security. Within the Jewish professional structure, the number of Jews among higher-level civil servants remained virtually insignificant since it was a professional group that was and remained closed to Jews due to anti-Semitic discrimination.[51] The comparatively small group of Jewish *Bildungsbürger* includes almost exclusively physicians and other members of the free professions; almost 60% of Jewish members of the educated elite belonged to this group. Incidentally, there still were hardly any Jewish lawyers in 1876. Of the 226 Jewish *Bildungsbürger*, only 2 were lawyers and 1 a lawyer's widow. However, there were already signs that this would change. Although only 2 Jewish lawyers practiced in Breslau in 1876, there were already 34 Jewish legal interns.[52]

Unlike in its Protestant and Catholic counterparts, within the Jewish petite bourgeoisie the new lower-middle class, the *Neuer Mittelstand* of clerks and other white-collar workers, was already predominant at the beginning of the German Empire. Hence it is questionable whether the concept of *Neuer Mittelstand* is suitable to describe the changes within Jewish professional structure between the founding of the German Empire and the First World War. In 1876, Jews in particular worked as mid-level employees and employed management assistants who belonged to the new lower-middle classes; almost 70% of this professional group were white-collar workers; another 20% employed management assistants. By contrast, elementary school teachers, many of whom may have felt themselves to be *Bildungsbürger* despite their modest incomes, made up barely 7% of the Jewish new lower-middle classes. Much as in the new lower-middle classes, professional groups that were active in trade also predominated in the old lower-middle classes among Breslau Jews. Over 60% of all Jews in the so-called *Alter Mittelstand* earned their living as small traders and shopkeepers, tradesmen, and traveling salesmen. But at the beginning of the German Empire, there had also been many Jewish master craftsmen; after all, they represented 26% of all Jews in the old lower-middle classes. As the quantitative significance of the Jewish master craftsmen in the old lower-middle classes and of the white-collar workers in the new lower-middle classes shows, the professional structure already indicates a socioeconomically more heterogeneous Jewish population than is suggested by the view that the vast majority of Jews had belonged to the *Bürgertum*.

The analysis of the occupational profile in the Jewish lower classes also confirms the thesis of the socioeconomic heterogeneity of the Jewish population. The proportion of Jews whose profession indicates membership in the lower classes hardly changed between 1876 and 1906 and was a good 15% in each case. Within the Jewish lower classes, the distribution among smaller professional groups remained relatively stable. The slight shifts corresponded approximately to those in Breslau's total population. Between the founding of the German Empire and the First World War, the proportion of employed craftsmen among all lower-class Jews decreased from 40% to 30%, and the proportion of low-level employees increased from nearly 30% to almost 35%. In 1876, workers represented a good 10% of the Jewish lower classes; their proportion rose by 1906 to nearly 16% and thus corresponded almost exactly with the proportion of workers in Breslau's lower classes as a whole.

The proportion of the Jewish lower classes in the total Jewish population, however, was not only considerably smaller than the proportion of the lower classes in Breslau's total population; the Jewish lower classes also distinguished themselves structurally from the Catholic and Protestant lower classes. Within Breslau's lower classes, the proportion of low-level employees was a good 5% in 1876 and somewhat more than 9% in 1906, which was lower in each case than the proportion of this group in the Jewish lower classes. But one finds a professional group among non-Jews that was nowhere to be seen among the Jews, namely, low-ranking civil servants. In the sample years, the latter constituted a proportion of a good 3% and nearly 4% in the non-Jewish lower classes. Even a career as a low-ranking civil servant was closed to Jews. Breslau Jews who earned their living as domestic servants represented in 1876 16% and in 1906 17% of all Jewish members of the lower classes. In comparison with other Breslauers, however, this was a small proportion. Roughly 40% of all members of the Breslau lower classes worked as maids, housekeepers, washerwomen, or cooks. In view of the comparatively small group of Jewish domestics, it is hardly surprising that around 1890 in almost all Jewish households that employed domestic servants, it was Protestant or Catholic maids or nannies who worked there.[53]

Women made up the vast majority of the Jewish lower classes in Breslau; in 1906, their proportion was over 60% (table 6). That, too, distinguished the Jewish from the Protestant and Catholic lower classes, for among Protestants and Catholics women represented, with a good 52% and nearly 55% respectively, only slightly more than half of this professional group. This difference is all the more important because among Breslau's Jewish women the employment rate after the turn of the century was less than that among Protestant and Catholic women. Among all economically active Jews, only a good 30% were women, whereas the proportion of women among economically active Protestants and Catholics was a good 45% in each case. That it was above all women who belonged to the Jewish lower classes—an impression, incidentally, that the analysis of the income stratification will reinforce—may also be a reason that the significance of the Jewish lower classes has often been underestimated.

If one considers a characteristic other than profession in the narrower sense, namely, one's standing in his or her profession, it becomes clear that among Breslau Jews there was a higher proportion of self-employed people (*Selbständige*) and white-collar workers (*Angestellte*) than was the case among Catholics and Protestants, a contrast that even

intensified in the late German Empire (table 7). Among men, the difference between Jews and other Breslauers was particularly pronounced.
Whereas, according to the classification used in the Imperial Statistics of
1895, more than half of all economically active Jewish men in Breslau
were regarded as self-employed, among Protestants and Catholics only
about 20% in each case were self-employed. Among Jewish men, the
self-employment rate remained equally high until 1907 and had even increased by 1925 to a good 60%, while the rate among Protestants and
Catholics had decreased to 17% by 1907. Also, among economically active Jewish men, the proportion of white-collar workers was higher than
for Protestants and Catholics. Concerning white-collar workers, however, the contrast was even sharper in the case of economically active
women, particularly as fundamental changes in the female employment
structure are also reflected here. Already in 1895, 6% of economically
active Jewish women were white-collar workers, but only about 1% of
Protestant and Catholic women were; by 1907, the proportion of white-
collar workers among Jewish women had risen to 30% and by 1925
would even climb to 48%, while for Protestant and Catholic women in
1907 it was less than 10%. However, the category of "self-employed" in
the imperial statistics is misleading because it also includes high-ranking
civil servants and managers who did not work on their own authority.

If one draws not only on contemporary occupational statistics but
also on the tax rolls, it becomes clear that the proportion of the self-
employed among economically active Jews was higher than among other
Breslauers, but even among the Jews in the course of the German Empire the proportion of those who were truly self-employed sank. Since
the tax rolls provide precise data on the kind of income, they permit one
to draw distinctions according to the main source of income. Unlike in
the imperial statistics, what decides whether one was "self-employed" is
no longer one's standing in one's profession but rather whether one lived
primarily from revenues from dependent work, say, from wages and salary, as opposed to profits from independent business or returns on capital
investments (property or real estate) (table 8). Contemporaries probably
based their self-understanding more on what their income was than how
the imperial statistics categorized them. Here, too, the differences between Jewish and Christian men are particularly clear. At the beginning
of the German Empire, a good half of all of Breslau's economically active Jewish men were independent in the narrower sense, that is, they
lived primarily from an independently earned income, nearly 48% especially from business income and another 7% from interest and rental

revenues. By contrast, among Protestant and Catholic men, the corresponding proportion in 1876 was only 26% and 23%, respectively, of all those who were economically active. Although the proportion of Jewish men who lived above all from business income sank from 48% to 27% over the next thirty years, the contrast between Jews and other Breslauers had grown by 1906. Now a good 42% of all of Breslau's economically active Jewish men were independent in the narrower sense, whereas this held true of only 16% of Protestant and 15% of Catholic men. Unlike the occupational statistics, however, consideration of the chief source of income exposes the fact that the proportion of those who were independent in the narrower sense also sank among Jews. Presumably, the proportion of managers, at the expense of the self-employed entrepreneur, also increased among Breslau Jews in the German Empire. At least, that would explain the contradiction between the results derived from occupational statistics and those from the tax rolls and at the same time place in question the widespread thesis that the Jews had reacted inflexibly to the process of increasing economic concentration.[54]

Nevertheless, the high proportion of self-employed persons among Jews in comparison with Protestants and Catholics requires explanation. The condescending explanation offered in 1911 by the Zionist physician and demographer Felix Theilhaber, namely, that it is due to the Jewish "characteristic of individualism, the longing to become independent, to achieve a materially favorable situation," falls short of the mark.[55] Three other reasons are more plausible: The specific occupational profile of the Jews played an important role in this connection. They were particularly well represented in occupations in which the proportion of self-employed individuals was comparatively high, for instance, among *Wirtschaftsbürger*, especially in trade. Second, it was the result of the specific social standing of the Jews. As a rule, it was a matter not of personal experiences that an individual may already have had but of a fear of being stigmatized in the workplace. Economic independence protected Jews from the anti-Semitism of a non-Jewish superior or colleague, and, in fact, some Christian-owned businesses, such as Eichborn & Co., Bankers, in Breslau, refused to employ Jews.[56] The third reason for the high rate of self-employment is, finally, the great importance that was accorded to independence in the world of bourgeois values.[57] The path to the intellectual and emotional independence of the *Bürger* was long to be sure, but it also presupposed economic security. Many Jews wanted to be bourgeois. By being self-employed, they laid the groundwork for approaching that goal.

The Position of the Jews in Breslau's Professional Structure

Based on the occupational profile, the proportion of the bourgeoisie among Jews was higher than it was among Protestants and Catholics. In the Silesian capital, the proportion of Jews in the bourgeois professions was therefore higher than their proportion of the total population. Aside from a few studies on the small and surveyable group of the economic elite, scholarship on the bourgeoisie thus far has hardly touched the question of the Jewish proportion among bourgeois professions.[58] By contrast, the historiography on German Jews has limited itself to determining the Jewish proportion of individual subgroups, such as physicians or lawyers, without investigating the Jewish proportion among bourgeois professions as a whole. Yet even if the results gained in the foregoing for Breslau are applicable for only some German metropolises, such as Berlin, Frankfurt, Hamburg, and Königsberg, that fact has consequences for the historiography not only of the relations between Jews and other Germans but also of the bourgeoisie. A history of the urban bourgeoisie at the turn of the century without the Jews truncates its subject and may even miss it entirely. Within the Breslau bourgeoisie, Jews were a core group, not a small minority. Jews, as the following chapters will show, influenced the liberal and largest wing of the Breslau bourgeoisie that kept its distance from the Prussian and imperial state. Jews also contributed to the vitality of bourgeois associations, supplied a large portion of secondary-school students, and helped to shape Breslau local politics in essential respects, in fact, formed the very backbone of left-wing liberalism in Breslau, at least as long as the Prussian three-class suffrage system (*Dreiklassenwahlrecht*) was in effect.

The great significance of Jews to the bourgeois professions is evident particularly in the bourgeoisie proper (tables 9 and 10). Although Jews represented only 7% of all economically active individuals in 1876, their proportion of the high bourgeois professional groups was 28%. Conversely, Breslau Protestants and Catholics made up nearly 60% and nearly 35%, respectively, of all economically active individuals, but only 55% and 16% of the bourgeoisie in the Silesian capital. Jews were even more clearly overrepresented in the economic bourgeoisie, the largest group by far in the Breslau bourgeoisie. At the beginning of the German Empire, 30% of all *Wirtschaftsbürger*, and even 40% within the most important subgroup of self-employed merchants, were Jewish.[59] By contrast, the Protestant proportion of both professional groups at this time was only 60% and 50%, respectively, and the Catholic proportion, only

12% and 10%. At the end of the German Empire, the Jewish proportion of all the high bourgeois professional groups had decreased slightly, but the significance of the Jews to the economic bourgeoisie had nevertheless increased. In 1906, Jews represented only 6% of all economically active individuals but 27% of the high bourgeoisie. In view of the Protestant and Catholic proportions of all economically active individuals (58% and 34%, respectively), Protestants and Catholics remained underrepresented in the high bourgeoisie (their proportions being 53% and 20%, respectively). Within the economic bourgeoisie, the Jewish proportion was now 35%; in 1906, every other self-employed merchants was Jewish.

The Jewish proportion of Breslau's *Bildungsbürgertum* was less than that of the economic bourgeoisie, but it was still high and increased during the German Empire; in 1876, it was 12% and in 1906, nearly 16%. Given that many bourgeois careers in the civil service were largely closed to Jews during the German Empire, including university professorships and secondary-school teaching positions, the overrepresentation of Jews in the *Bildungsbürgertum* is remarkable.[60] The reason for this was the significant proportion of Jews in the subgroup of self-employed individuals, which was 29% in 1906 and thus barely less than the Jewish proportion of the economic bourgeoisie. The official, contemporary statistics on professions confirm the results derived from the tax rolls. Particularly striking was the Jewish proportion in the group of self-employed physicians and lawyers.[61] Of the good 450 Breslau physicians counted in the 1895 statistics on professions, almost half (44%) were Jewish. The proportion would later sink, but in 1907 Jews still represented 29% of the now 901 self-employed Breslau physicians. The number of Jews among Breslau lawyers was similarly high. Of the 485 self-employed lawyers who worked in "administration or administration of justice" in 1895, and the 835 who did so in 1906, 19% and 21% were Jewish in the respective years. The Jewish proportion of lawyers was probably about twice as high as stated in these figures since in the statistics on professions the category of the "self-employed" in "administration or administration of justice" also included high-ranking civil servants in the judiciary and administration, thus professions that were practically closed to Jews. This high proportion of Jews among Breslau's physicians and lawyers is not only a further indication of the great significance of Jews among bourgeois professional groups, but it is also remarkable because the vast majority of patients and clients of the Jewish doctors and lawyers were not Jews. Jewish physicians and lawyers were well respected

also among other Breslauers. People trusted their expertise and en-
trusted themselves to them even in situations in which their health or
legal integrity was at stake.

As for what contribution Breslau Jews made to the economic rise of
the Silesian capital in the nineteenth century, that must remain open
here, especially since such a question would have to be pursued within
the context of a study in economic history. Several consequences are
nevertheless obvious. Since, as was noted earlier, the self-employment
rate among Breslau Jews was higher than that among Protestants and
Catholics; many Protestants and Catholics worked in Jewish-owned
businesses and companies. That may have led to conflicts at times between Jewish employers and non-Jewish employees. In 1902, for instance,
a seamstress sued her Jewish employer: He was to reimburse the seamstress for the earnings she lost when the factory owner closed the workshop for the Jewish New Year holidays. In response, the entrepreneur
argued that if Christian employers were entitled not to compensate their
employees for earnings lost on high Christian holidays, it would be un-
fair to force him to do so for the high Jewish holidays. In this case, however, the *Gewerbegericht*, an arbitration court for trade and labor disputes,
decided in favor of the seamstress, and the Jewish employer had to compensate her for the lost earnings.[62]

Aside from such conflicts, daily working life in many Jewish-run businesses was marked by personal and natural interactions between Jews
and other Breslauers. Though only a small number of Jewish business
owners observed the Sabbath, even the "synagogal dayflies," as Ayre
Maimon has called them, took the high Jewish holidays seriously.[63] The
daily lives of many Christian employees were determined at least by residual rhythms of the Jewish calendar. But also the rest of the population could hardly fail to notice when many businesses and stores stayed
closed on high Jewish holidays. This helps to explain why the Breslau directory listed the Jewish alongside the Christian holidays on its cover.
The debate in Breslau on working on Sundays therefore was not merely
academic, nor was it merely a symbolic dispute, but affected the work
rhythms of many Jews, Protestants, and Catholics.

It is all the more remarkable that the municipal authorities and the
chamber of commerce opposed a prohibition of Sunday work and supported Jewish interests until the end of the German Empire. In a report
for the Prussian secretary of trade, for instance, the Breslau Chamber of
Commerce pleaded that "the so-called law-abiding businesspeople of
Jewish religion who close their businesses on the Sabbath out of religious

conviction . . . not be forced to sacrifice their conviction and work on the Sabbath because they cannot afford to keep their businesses closed for two successive days each week."[64] On the other hand, Jewish business owners and entrepreneurs took their Christian employees' rhythm of life into account. Like those Jewish families who celebrated Christmas for the sake of their Protestant or Catholic domestic servants, many Jewish business owners and entrepreneurs organized Christmas parties for their Christian employees.[65]

4. Income Stratification

The Income Stratification of Breslau Jews

A sociostructural analysis based on the occupations and not the incomes of income earners has only limited explanatory value.[66] Certainly, an occupations-based analysis of social inequality has the advantage that it takes account of the status dimension of the social stratification since it incorporates the social esteem of a profession in the analysis. At least one of the status considerations of social inequality remains visible. The cultural considerations that play a role in the emergence of the bourgeoisie involve more, however, than just the esteem of a profession: the world of bourgeois values, on the one hand, and a lifestyle appropriate to bourgeois deportment along with conspicuous consumption, on the other hand. Bourgeois daily life required adequate living conditions, a large, expensively furnished house, bourgeois clothing, at least one maid, a large banquet once or twice a year, fund-raising activities or even patronage, and sufficient means for bourgeois leisure activities and an education for one's children befitting one's station.[67] Bourgeois life cost money. "It is the most elemental economic fact," Max Weber notes, "that the way in which the disposition over material property is distributed among a plurality of people . . . in itself creates specific life chances."[68] Although the income range in the bourgeoisie was broad, long-term membership in it required a financial situation in keeping with the expectations that came with bourgeois status. Consequently, the available annual income of a household indicates whether a family commanded the financial means to live in accordance with bourgeois deportment.[69] On the other hand, the threats to the lives of members of the lower classes were greater, particularly as they grew older, for they were affected more severely by an illness or the death of the main breadwinner and poverty in old age.[70] Finally, through the Prussian

three-class suffrage system, adult men experienced the close connection
between income and political influence every two years in the local elections and every four years in the Landtag elections.[71]

Differences in income and the gulf between the bourgeoisie and the
petite bourgeoisie were visible to everyone, but especially to someone
who was familiar with the life of the bourgeois and the worker. Eugen
Altmann (b. 1876), for instance, son of a prosperous businessman, had
resolved to become a beer brewer after having attended a humanistic
Gymnasium. "Due to my red, chapped, and rough hands, my brewer's existence," Altmann recalled in 1939, "earned me, in my relation to the
class to which I had originally belonged, social boycott by all denominations." After Altmann had worked all over Germany as a beer brewer,
he fled the anti-Semitism of many brewers and switched in 1901 to his
father's flax business. "Now I had once again become 'capable of standing my ground,'" wrote Altmann; he continued: "Respectable bourgeois
society paid attention to me. The balloting for entry to the better club
was a formality. Invitation after invitation came from the best people, including Christian high society. Without being vain, let me say: 'Some
Christian fathers and even more mothers encouraged me [to pursue]
their daughter.' Even back then I assumed that this accommodation was
to be chalked up to an overestimation of my father's fortune."[72]

The lowest annual income a household had to have for a bourgeois
lifestyle was roughly 2,750 marks in 1876 and a full 3,000 marks in
1906.[73] While this is a pragmatic estimate, it is nevertheless a plausible
and conservative one.[74] That is confirmed, for instance, by the income
limits of the electoral classes in the Prussian Landtag elections and the
Breslau city council elections, on which the political power of the bourgeoisie was based. To be able to vote in the local elections of 1885 in the
second electoral class, one had to earn more than 2,700 marks per year;
to be able to vote in the first class, one had to earn at least 10,800 marks
per year. Ten years later, these income thresholds skyrocketed yet again.
In the first electoral class, now only adult men with an annual income of
over 54,000 marks were allowed to vote, and even for the second electoral class one needed an annual income of over 16,000 marks.[75] Moreover, the salaries of the *Gymnasium* teachers, ministers, and also many
lawyers, who frequently complained that their income was too small to
support a bourgeois household, were far above the limit of 2,700 and
3,000, respectively. In Breslau in 1906, a senior teacher at a *Gymnasium* earned about 4,500 marks a year, a gymnasial professor earned
a full 6,500 marks, and a *Gymnasium* director, roughly 9,000 marks. A

functionary at the Deutscher Anwaltsverein (German Bar Association) argued in 1914 that even an annual income of 5,000 marks would hardly enable a "station-befitting living"; in the opinion of a higher regional court council from Dresden, at least 12,000 marks per year were required for such a lifestyle.[76] In any case, the Breslau magistracy paid the salaried municipal councils, whom the magistracy surely expected to maintain a bourgeois lifestyle, an annual salary of a good 5,000 marks already in the mid-1860s and a good 8,500 marks in the mid-1880s.[77] Gustav Schmoller devised a similar classification of income groups. He distinguished between four large social groups: (1) the upper classes with an annual income of over 8,000 marks; (2) the upper-middle class with an annual income of between 2,700 and 8,000 marks; (3) the lower-middle class (which today we classify as the petite bourgeoisie) with an annual income of between 1,800 and 2,700 marks; and 4) the lower classes, which paid taxes on an annual income of less than 1,800 marks.[78] For the Statistical Bureau of the Hamburg Tax Deputation, only an annual income of 5,000 was regarded as a "good" income; it distinguished between "small" (600–1,000 marks), "moderate" (1,000–2,000 marks), "medium" (2,000–5,000 marks), "good," and "high" incomes, which were over 10,000 marks.[79] Finally, personal testimonies suggest that the limit of an annual income of 3,000 marks is more an underestimate than an overestimate. In 1908, Adolf Riesenfeld, then a twenty-four-year-old shipping agent, considered a "passable livelihood" to be an annual income of 5,000–7,000 marks.[80] Bertha Badt-Strauss, the daughter of the Jewish *Gymnasium* teacher Benno Badt, who earned almost 11,500 marks in 1906, stressed that her family was neither rich nor prosperous or wealthy, but lived in rather modest conditions—the furniture, for instance, "was simple and somewhat wobbly."[81] Of course, Badt's remarks illustrate that, depending on the class to which one belongs and which status one ascribes oneself, "poverty" or "modest conditions" can be experience differently: The "richest man may set himself goals," says Georg Simmel, "that . . . exceed his means, so that he sees himself psychologically as poor."[82]

Against the backdrop of these considerations, the Breslau population will be divided into four income groups in the following discussion. At the lower end are the "workers and casual laborers," who earned less than 1,100 and 1,200 marks per year in 1876 and 1906, respectively. The second group comprises the "petits bourgeois," who paid taxes on an annual income of between 1,100 and 2,750 marks in 1876 and between 1,200 and 3,000 marks in 1906. Next is the group of the "prosperous bourgeois," whose annual income was between 2,750 and 9,200 marks in 1876 and between 3,000 and 10,000 marks in 1906. Finally, at the top are the "rich or wealthy bourgeois," whose annual income was more than 9,200 and 10,000 marks in 1876 and 1906, respectively. This division seems plausible, but the same qualifications apply here, of course, as in the foregoing. As in all stratification analyses of the nineteenth and early twentieth centuries, one must draw attention to the potential "illusion of precision."[83] The present study claims only to present a more precise and, above all, more multidimensional analysis of the stratification of Jewish income than has been usual thus far.

A glance at the income levels of the most frequent bourgeois professions of Breslau Jews makes clear that the analysis of the occupational profile overestimates the proportion of the bourgeoisie in the Jewish population. Many income earners who pursued a bourgeois profession did not command an annual income that would have enabled a station-befitting lifestyle. The contrast between the bourgeois profession and the financial possibilities was particularly pronounced in the professions in which Jews were strongly represented, such as those of businesspeople and people with fixed incomes (tables 11 and 12). In this connection, the category of the *Kaufmann* possesses the greatest significance, as it included shopkeepers, people involved in commerce, and retailers, as well as merchants and wholesale dealers.[84] In the representative sample from 1906, 561 economically active individuals had bourgeois professions, thus nearly 57% of all Jewish income earners. Of these 561, no fewer than 342 had the job title of merchant, that is, *Kaufmann* or *Kauffrau*. However, in 1906 nearly half, and in 1876 more than half did not command a bourgeois income; nearly one-fifth even had an annual income below 1,200 marks. If one corrects the distortions within the professional group *Kaufmann*, the proportion of the bourgeoisie in the total Jewish population in Breslau in 1906 sinks from almost 60% to 40%. The case of the merchant is not atypical. Also in the large group of *rentiers*, there are many with low incomes. In comparison the less-common professions of physician and lawyer provide a reliable indication of a bourgeois income.[85] Whereas the bourgeois profession is suitable only to a limited extent for the delimitation of the bourgeoisie, almost no one among Breslau's Jewish income earners with petit-bourgeois occupations had an annual income that would have enabled a bourgeois lifestyle; in 1876, only 0.7% of accounting clerks (*Buchhalter*) and 4% of tradesmen (*Handelsmänner*) commanded such an income. By 1906, the income situation of this group had improved somewhat. But also after the turn of the century only 17% of all accountants and 5% of all tradesmen earned enough to run a bourgeois household.

Although the stratification of income in Breslau permits certain conclusions about the situation in other German cities, one must bear in mind that in Breslau the income level for wages and salaries was lower than in other German cities, even though the difference diminished somewhat during the German Empire. "Silesian wages," an employee of the Breslau Statistics Bureau noted in 1920 in retrospect, "have always been among the lowest in the entire empire." At the end of the nineteenth century, at any rate, the annual per capita income in Breslau of 400–500 marks was below that in Berlin (650–700 marks), Leipzig and Hamburg (both 700–750 marks), Dresden (800–850 marks), and Frankfurt am Main (1,000 marks). Also local wages were lower in the Oder metropolis than in other big cities. In the early 1880s, an adult male worker in Breslau earned 1.6 marks per day of work, but in Dresden and Leipzig he earned 2 marks, in Berlin and Frankfurt am Main 2.4 marks, and in Hamburg 2.5 marks. A journeyman carpenter in Altona in 1883–84 earned more than twice what he could earn in Breslau, and the income of a journeyman tailor in Munich in the same year was roughly two and one-half times as much as that of his Breslau counterpart.[86]

These differences diminished by 1914, however. Prior to the outbreak of the war, the local day wage in Breslau was 3.5 marks; in Berlin it was 4 marks; in Dresden, Leipzig, Frankfurt am Main, and Hamburg it was 3.8 marks. Despite the lower level of wages and income in Breslau, the quality of life in the Silesian capital need not have been lower, since in Breslau food was cheaper and rents were lower than in other big cities. In Berlin in 1880, an apartment cost on average a good 500 marks, but in Breslau only about 300 marks.[87]

Neither at the beginning nor at the end of the German Empire did the majority of Jewish income earners belong to the bourgeoisie, even if the proportion of bourgeois income earners was larger among Jews than among other Breslauers. The picture of the social stratification of Breslau Jews thus changes when one uses not profession but income as the most important indicator of the social situation and differentiates by age, sex, and birthplace. Since the studies on social structure based on profession overestimate the proportion of the bourgeoisie—and precisely because of the large proportion of merchants especially in the Jewish population—it is illuminating to contrast the results derived from professions with the analysis of the income stratification of Breslau Jews.

To determine as precisely as possible the proportion of the bourgeois classes among economically active Jews, I distinguish between three age groups: first, the "juniors": everyone under thirty years of age whose income, especially in the case of bourgeois professions such as student, was less than it was in later stages in life; second, the "established": the thirty- to sixty-year-olds who earned the highest income among their professional groups; third, the "seniors": those over sixty years of age who probably were no longer fully active and whose income had thus decreased. In what follows, I focus exclusively on the income levels of the "established," that is, on that age group with the smallest proportion of petit-bourgeois or lower-class Jews who earned little.[88]

The majority of "established" Jewish income earners in Breslau did not have an income in either 1876 or 1906 that permitted a bourgeois life-style (table 13). In 1876, almost two-thirds of all heads of Jewish households aged thirty to sixty years earned less than 2,750 marks. Of the Jewish women in this age group, thus the single, divorced, or widowed, almost 90% did not have a bourgeois income in 1876. After the turn of the century, the income situation of Breslau Jews had improved, but the majority of even the "established" income earners still had incomes that were too low for a bourgeois household. In 1906, 53% of all thirty- to sixty-year-old Jewish income earners earned less than 3,000 marks per year. Still, the income situation of male heads of households in particular did improve between 1876 and 1906. Almost 60% of all "established" Jewish men in 1906 earned more than 3,000 marks; 25% even commanded more than 10,000 marks. By contrast, the proportion of petit-bourgeois or lower-class households among "established" Jewish women in 1906 was over 85% and thus hardly differed from the proportion in 1876. Moreover, women's low level of income mattered far more after the turn of the century than it had in 1876 since their proportion of all thirty- to sixty-year-old Jewish heads of households had climbed from 19% at the beginning of the German Empire to 27%.[89] Even in the years prior to the First World War, the heyday of the Jewish bourgeoisie, the majority of economically active Jews thus did not have an income that would have permitted them to maintain a bourgeois household.

As for the Jewish immigrants from Eastern Europe, the proportion of those who did not command a bourgeois income was particularly high (table 14). Among Jewish men born in Breslau or elsewhere in Silesia, 43% and 48%, respectively, earned over 3,000 marks per year. Their average income was almost 8,000 and almost 7,000 marks, respectively. Breslau Jews born in Austro-Hungary, Poland, Russia, or another part of Eastern or Southeastern Europe earned less. Fully 80% of them paid taxes on less than 3,000 marks per year, and their average annual income was a good 2,700 marks, thus only a third of what Breslau-born Jewish men earned. The contrast among Jewish women was similar. Jewish women from Breslau and those from Silesia earned on average 1,560 and 2,345 marks per year, respectively. Still, one in eight had an annual income of over 3,000 marks. By contrast, Jewish women born in Eastern Europe paid taxes on an average annual income of nearly 500 marks, and of the seventeen women in the sample group, none earned more than 3,000 marks per year. However instructive this comparison may be, the reference to the Jewish immigration from Eastern Europe does not explain the high proportion of Breslau Jews with low incomes. Of all the Jewish men and women who earned less than 1,200 marks per year in 1906, only 11% and 7%, respectively, came from Eastern Europe, and of all the Jewish men and women whose annual income was less than 3,000 marks, only 10% and 6%, respectively, were from there.

Both at the beginning and at the end of the German Empire, Jewish poverty in Breslau had a female face; the analysis of Jewish poverty with the help of the Breslau tax rolls indicates time and again the importance of sex. Although age and place of birth did indeed play a role, what is most prominent is the income gap between Jewish men and women. Although in 1876 only 21% of all Jewish income earners were women, they represented 34% of all Jewish income earners who made less than 1,100 marks. The proportion of women among Jewish income earners who earned less than 1,200 marks in 1906 was 60%, although they represented only 30% of all Jewish income earners.

The proportion of low-income earners among Breslau Jews was particularly high for men and women who came from small households (tables 15 and 16). The larger the household, the higher was the proportion of income earners who had a bourgeois income, or who earned over 2,750 marks in 1876 and over 3,000 marks in 1906. Among the Jewish men who lived alone, only 12% earned a bourgeois income in 1876 and only 22% did so in 1906, whereas over 60% earned less than 1,100 marks per year in 1876 and fully 40% earned less than 1,200 marks per year in 1906. The Jewish men who headed a four-person household were, in contrast, more prosperous. Their average annual income of 5,609 marks in 1876 and 11,496 marks in 1906 was more than three times greater than that of the Jewish income earners who lived alone. Moreover, in 1876 over 40%, and in 1906 over 60%, commanded a bourgeois income. Among women, the contrast was less pronounced than among men, but it mattered because among the Jewish women whom the tax rolls listed as income earners the proportion of single-person households was greater than in the case of the men. That was particularly true of income earners who paid taxes on less than 1,100 marks in 1876 and less than 1,200 marks in 1906. In this income group, roughly 45% of all men lived alone in 1876 and 1906, while 70% of the women in 1876 and 90% in 1906 only had to take care of themselves. Of the Jewish women who lived alone, roughly 80% earned less than 1,100 marks in 1876 and less than 1,200 marks in 1906. Jewish women who headed a three-person household had a somewhat larger annual income. Among them, fully 60% paid taxes on less than 1,100 marks in 1876 and less than 1,200 marks in 1906, while a quarter earned between 1,100 and 2,750 marks in 1876, and nearly a third of the women heading a three-person household in 1906 even earned more than a bourgeois annual income of over 3,000 marks.

Such aggregate data, however, conceal individual tragedies, and those men and women who had to support a large family on a small income are also part of the history of Breslau Jews. For instance, in 1876 there lived in the household of the forty-two-year-old broker's widow, Jeanette Berg, four sons between fourteen and twenty-three years old and three daughters between sixteen and nineteen years old. Her husband, who, judging from the children's ages, must have died some ten years earlier, had left her no assets; she received neither an annuity nor a pension, living instead from her income as a worker, which earned her 450 marks per year. It is likely that her eldest children also earned something without its having been recorded in the tax rolls, and perhaps Jeanette received some assistance from relatives living outside Breslau or from Jewish welfare organizations. In any case, the family lived in bitter poverty. Jeanette's income was well below the subsistence level. In 1887, the Breslau Statistics Bureau estimated the subsistence level for an adult, that is, anyone over fourteen years of age, at 200 marks per year.[90] The total income of the Berg household would thus have had to be 1,600 marks per year to guarantee the family the minimum of support. It is unlikely that the tax rolls fail to say nothing about additional earnings of nearly 1,200 marks. The Bergs were poor indeed. Accordingly, they lived at Sonnenstrasse 14, in a row of houses in which almost only poor Jews lived.[91] In 1906, there were still many examples of Jewish families that were bitterly poor. Helene Hirschel (née Braun, b. 1866) came from Kempen, a city in the southwestern tip of the province of Posen. At the beginning of the 1880s, she emigrated to New York with her husband, the cigar maker Hermann Hirschel. Around the turn of the century, however, her husband died, and she returned to Kempen with her children. From there she moved to Breslau in October 1902. The widow first lived at Bohrauerstrasse 9, a large arterial street in the eastern part of Breslau's *Südstadt*. In 1906, however, she lived at Lewaldstrasse 15, a street in southwestern Breslau, near the large market halls and the freight depot Breslau-West. Helene Hirschel was now a cigar worker and had an annual income of 400 marks from which to feed herself and eight children, four of whom were under fourteen years old. At least her eldest daughter, Jessy Hirschel, who was born in 1883 in New York, contributed 400 marks, which she earned as an embroiderer, to the family's annual budget. Their relatives do not seem to have lived in Breslau, however, so the nine people in Helene's household lived more or less from a total of 800 marks.[92] Some impoverished Jews lived in the city's most destitute neighborhoods. In 1906, Moritz Krebs, born in the district of Kreuzburg, Upper Silesia, in 1860, his wife, and their two children had to subsist on his annual pension of 500 marks. While it was less than a half-hour walk from the fashionable lodgings of the well-heeled Jewish bourgeoisie around the Tauenzienplatz to the Krebs' tenement on Vincenzstrasse, they lived worlds apart. On Vincenzstrasse, near the Odertor railway station in northern Breslau, rents were low and apartments small. Most of the street's inhabitants were poor, as was the sanitation. It was so poor, in fact, that the inhabitants filed a desperate complaint to the municipal authorities during a cholera epidemic in the 1890s.[93]

These examples not only provide a glimpse of the poverty of Jews in the German Empire but also serve as reminders that an analysis of the income stratification of Breslau Jews must consider the size of the income earner's household. Someone who earned around 1,000 marks in 1876 and lived alone cannot be said to be poor in the narrower sense. However, someone who had to feed a family of six or seven from the same sum lived below the poverty line. Because the average income of four-person households was higher than that of single-person households, an analysis of the total Jewish population can hardly dispense with including the income earners' family members in the study. For the basic set, one is better advised to take not all Jewish income earners but rather the total Jewish population. Thus it is no longer a question of how many Jewish income earners had which income, but how many Breslau Jews, including their wives, children, and other family members, lived in the households that can be classed in one of the four income groups.

If one examines not only Jewish income earners but also the total Jewish population, it becomes clear that the majority of Breslau Jews did not live in households that had a bourgeois income. However, the proportion of petit-bourgeois and lower-class strata is now smaller, even when the households headed by women are included, as they should be in an analysis of the total population. Furthermore, a consideration of the income stratification of the total Jewish population also shows that the social situation of Jews improved in the German Empire. When one examines Jewish income earners, one finds that in 1876 almost every other Breslau Jew earned less than 1,100 marks, fully a quarter had a petit-bourgeois income of between 1,100 and 1,750 marks, and nearly a quarter more had a bourgeois annual income. Only a good 5% had an income of 9,200 marks, which made a wealthy bourgeois lifestyle possible. By contrast, consideration of the total Jewish population reveals that the income stratification of Breslau Jews was more bourgeois than the analysis of income earners has indicated (table 17). If one takes family members into account, then at the beginning of the German Empire 36% of all Breslau Jews belonged to a lower-class household that paid taxes on less than 1,100 marks, fully 30% of them lived in a petit-bourgeois household, and somewhat more than a third belonged to a bourgeois household, whose annual income was over 2,750 marks. Thus, based on income, a third of all Breslau Jews lived at the beginning of the German Empire in a household that can be characterized as working class, another third belonged to a petit-bourgeois household, and the remaining third to a bourgeois household.

In the subsequent thirty years, the income of Breslau Jews as a whole would improve markedly. The group of those belonging to a working-class household, which paid taxes on less than 1,200 marks per year, fell from 36% to 29%. Likewise, the proportion of those who lived in a petit-bourgeois household, with an annual income of 1,200–3,000 marks, sank from 31% in 1876 to 25% in 1906. Correspondingly, during the same period the proportion of those whose class situation can be called bourgeois grew. After the turn of the century, no longer a third, as in 1876, but almost half of all Jews belonged to a household that paid taxes on a bourgeois income of over 3,000 marks. Within the bourgeois classes, the proportion of those who lived in a wealthy bourgeois household with an annual income of over 9,200 marks (1876) and 10,000 marks (1906) had climbed from 8% in 1876 to 21% in 1906. When the household size is taken into account, the proportion of Jews with a sub-bourgeois income level diminishes in both sample years. Even more clearly than the analysis of income earners, the consideration of household size reveals that the income situation of Breslau Jews improved during the German Empire. Yet, even when the number of persons living in a household are included in the analysis of income stratification, our main thesis is still confirmed, namely, that at the beginning as well as at the end of the German Empire the majority of Breslau Jews did not belong to a household with a bourgeois income.

Although consideration of income stratification supports the thesis that the class situations within the Jewish population were quite heterogeneous, it permits only indirect and imprecise inferences about how unequal income distribution was within Breslau's Jewish population. To get an idea of the extent of the inequality of income distribution, a standard procedure is employed here: The group of the wealthiest and the poorest Jews is first determined and then this group's proportion of the total income of all Jewish households in Breslau is calculated (table 18). At the beginning of the German Empire, the uppermost 1% of Jewish income earners—seventy-five people in 1876—earned at least 32,400 marks per year; the top incomes were about 200,000 marks. This small economic elite earned 24% of the total income of all Jewish households in Breslau. Whoever paid taxes on at least 9,600 marks a year belonged to the uppermost 5% of Jewish income earners in 1876. This somewhat broader economic elite—it comprised 287 households—earned almost half the total income of all Jewish households in Breslau. By 1906, the extent of income concentration diminished, but it nevertheless remained large. After the turn of the century, the uppermost 1% of Jewish income earners paid taxes on 17%, and the uppermost 5% paid taxes on 43%, of the total income of all Jewish households in Breslau.

The picture of social homogeneity among the Jews that dominates the literature on German Jews is therefore misleading. This analysis of income distribution clarifies what the general calculation of Jewish income and the comparison of Jewish and Christian average income otherwise conceal: A significant part of the income of all Breslau Jews was earned by a small economic elite. In the mid-1870s, the incomes of Jewish Breslauers diverged even more widely than in the total Prussian population (24% as compared to 17–18% in the uppermost 1% of income earners; 46% as compared to 28% in the uppermost 5% of income earners), whose income distribution many contemporaries characterized as "plutocratic." After the turn of the century, the figures for the total Prussian population were slightly higher, at least for the 1% of the highest income earners, than those for Breslau's Jewish population

(Breslau Jews: 17%; Prussia as a whole: nearly 20%).[94] The analysis of
the income of heads of households elucidates the considerable socioeconomic differentiation among Breslau Jews both at the beginning and
at the end of the German Empire. While the average income of Jews
was higher than that of Christians, the extent of income concentration
among Breslau Jews was no less than in the total Prussian population.
The results for Breslau in 1876 and 1906 places in question Avraham
Barkai's thesis that among "German Jews . . . from the beginning of the
nineteenth century on, a process of a more egalitarian distribution of
income" had taken place. At least in Breslau, large differences in income
within the Jewish population had arisen already by the beginning of the
German Empire, thus prior to 1880, the point after which, according to
Barkai, the differences in income had grown more extreme.[95] What was
"monstrous," to use Sombart's aforementioned description, was not the
difference between Jewish and non-Jewish average income, but rather
the extent of inequality in the income distribution within Breslau's Jewish population.[96]

Only against the backdrop of the significant proportion of low-
income earners and of the large income gap among Breslau Jews does it
become comprehensible why, from the late nineteenth century on, there
was a bitter struggle within the Jewish community over the right to vote.
If the vast majority of Jews had belonged to the middle classes, the intensity of the dispute would have been incomprehensible. Traditionally,
the Jewish *Gemeinde*'s board of directors exempted low-income earners
from paying community taxes. Yet those men who were exempted not
only saved the taxes of at least 6 marks per year but also lost the right to
vote in the elections for the representative council. At the beginning of
the German Empire, the proportion of those who did not have a right to
vote was relatively small because the lowest income limit that obliged
one to pay Jewish community taxes and entitled one to vote was 600
marks. However, before the representative election of 1896, the election
committee raised the minimum annual income to 900 marks. In May
1906 in the representative council, a bitter dispute broke out over the
question of the right to vote. The board had moved—probably in part
in reaction to the hotly contested elections of the previous year—to increase the minimum income from 900 to 1,050 marks; in the debate,
some even called for a minimum of 1,200 marks. Representatives sympathetic to the opposition, such as the *Gymnasium* teacher Benno Badt and
the shipping agent David Schlesinger, criticized the board's motion in
vain as "depriving voters of their rights," which "today, when everyone

votes in the Reichstag elections," is out of step with the times. The board prevailed in the vote. Of the 5,000 Jewish taxpayers who had been entitled to vote in the 1905 elections, 437 (thus nearly 10%) suddenly lost their right to participate in choosing the *Gemeinde*'s representative council. Though they earned more than 900 marks, they earned less than 1,050. If the more far-reaching demand to raise the lower limit to 1,200 marks had been successful, 900 voters (almost one-fifth of those entitled to vote) would have lost their right to vote.[97]

The significance of the income gap was large also within Breslau's bourgeois classes. This social distance was experienced precisely by those who, like Max Born's father, married into a family whose income level and financial circumstances were well above their own. Gustav Born (1850–1900), born in Kempen, was the son of the physician Marcus Born, who had died in Görlitz in 1874. Although he had already worked for many years in the Anatomical Institute at the University of Breslau and had just completed his *Habilitation,* he had an annual income of only 1,200 marks in 1876. Gustav Born was, as his son, the physicist Max Born, recalled in the mid-1940s, "not a rich man but rather a young docent . . . with a small salary." His mother, Fanny Born, probably supported the twenty-five-year-old a little, although she still supported two daughters as well. After the death of her husband, she had purchased a house in Breslau with the inheritance and invested part of the savings, which yielded 3,400 marks per year in rental fees and interest. In the early 1880s, Gustav Born married Margarete Kauffmann, one of the daughters of the textile manufacturer Salomon Kauffmann, who in 1876, with an annual income of roughly 72,000 marks, belonged to the twenty richest Jewish families in Breslau. It was "not without resistance," Max Born recalled, that the Kauffmanns accepted Gustav Born, who in their eyes was impoverished.[98] After the official engagement, "an arrogance based on wealth" was given expression when Fanny Born was invited to the home of her future daughter-in-law's parents but was then treated there with condescension. Salomon Kauffmann did not appear at all, and Marie, his wife, also snubbed Gustav Born's mother by withdrawing after only a few minutes and leaving the visit to her children and the governess.[99] Both families kept their distance from each other, and the relationship between Gustav Born and his parents-in-law continued to be strained. There were repeated disputes because he did not want "his children to be instilled with the manner and outlook of a rich businessman's family." On the other hand, the Kauffmanns, Max Born reported further, expected his father "to lead a life at a social level that was far above his financial means and forced him to accept financial support" from his father-in-law.[100]

The petit bourgeois Adolf Riesenfeld, who in 1905 was a clerk with an annual income of about 900 marks, recalled in 1941 that it was "strange enough that within the relatively small Jewish community [in Breslau] . . . such a strong caste spirit developed . . . although social anti-Semitism strongly prevented contact between Christian and Jews really at all times and which should have caused the latter to develop the strongest connections among themselves." In any case, the liaison between Riesenfeld, then twenty-two years old, and the sixteen-year-old Charlotte Bodländer ended quickly after he had discovered that her family "did not count among the 'good' Jewish families"; the "different living standards of each family" created an insuperable distance between the two, he said.[101]

The income concentration among Breslau Jews did not escape Jewish commentators either and became an issue in conflicts between religious factions within Breslau's Jewish community. When after the turn of the century the conflict between the Liberaler Verein (Liberal Club) and the more orthodox Verein zur Förderung der Interessen des Judenthums (Society for the Promotion of the Interests of Judaism) came to a head, the *Jüdisches Volksblatt*, which sympathized with the orthodox minority, combined its critique of the prevailing reform-oriented "*Gemeinde* liberalism" with an attack on the Jewish economic elite in the Oder metropolis. "Just as in the ancient republics an oligarchy of old-established patrician families had gotten a foothold in the government," the weekly polemicized in view of the *Gemeinde* elections in December 1905; "likewise our community is dominated by a circle of rich people that does not let anyone take office who does not belong to the clique."[102] Just how much such election-campaign polemics clouded the vision of the *Jüdisches Volksblatt* becomes clear when one looks at the candidates from the list it supported. Among them were the businessmen Lippmann Bloch and Hermann Schottländer, as well as the counsellor of justice Max Schreiber, all of whom belonged to the economic elite. Bloch, who was born in 1849 in Tarnowitz, had an annual income in 1906 of nearly 65,000 marks; Schottländer, who was also born in 1849, though in Münsterberg, earned nearly 90,000 marks; and Schreiber, who was born in 1852 in Jauer, earned nearly 24,000 marks per year.[103] Not even two years later, the *Jüdisches Volksblatt* used the obituary for Theodor Oschinsky, a member of the representative council of the Jewish *Gemeinde*, to repeat its critique. The liberal majority, it said, had denied the Orthodox representative, to whom the *Jüdisches Volksblatt* had been sympathetic for years, a position that accorded with his authority. Oschinsky—who incidentally, with an annual income of nearly 63,000 marks, was one of the wealthiest Breslau businessmen—was "a victim" of the "oligarchic reign" and the "plutocratic line" that alienated the Breslau Jewish community "from Judaism."[104]

Although the majority of Breslau Jews did not have bourgeois income levels and despite the social inequality within the Jewish population, one should not lose sight of the fact that Jews were more prosperous on average than other Breslauers (table 19). As early as 1876, Jewish income earners paid taxes on an average of 2,875 marks, almost three times as much as Protestant and four and one-half times as much as Catholic income earners in Breslau. The greatest proportion of the general rise in income over the next thirty years was among Breslau Jews. The average income of Jewish earners increased by 1906 by over 80% to 5,200 marks, and now was three and one-half times as much as that of Protestant and five times as much as that of Catholic earners (1,458 and 1,024 marks, respectively), which had increased by nearly 50% and a good 60%, respectively.

Still more impressive is the comparison of the proportions of the income groups among Jews, Protestants, and Catholics (table 20). At the beginning of the German Empire, 24% of Jewish income earners in Breslau had a bourgeois income of over 2,750 marks; 5% even paid taxes on over 9,200 marks. Among Breslau Protestants, however, only 6%, and among the Catholics only 3% earned more than 2,700 marks. The proportion of income earners who paid taxes on over 9,200 marks was 2% among the Protestants; in the case of the Catholics, the proportion was so small that in the sample of 447 Catholic income earners no one earned that much. Thirty years later, the contrast was just as marked. A third of all Jewish income earners paid taxes in 1906 on more than 3,000 marks per year; by contrast, among Protestants not even one in ten did so; and among Catholics, only one in sixteen. If one focuses on the income group of the prosperous in the narrower sense, the Jewish income advantage becomes even clearer. Nearly 14% of all Jewish income earners earned more than 10,000 marks, 4% even more than 24,000 marks. Among the Protestants and the Catholics, by contrast, only 2% and 1%, respectively, of all income earners paid taxes on more than 10,000 marks per year.

Even when one takes family members into account, and thus considers the total Jewish, Protestant, and Catholic populations, the Jewish income advantage remains considerable (table 21). While in 1906 roughly 46% of all Breslau Jews lived in a household that had an annual income of over 3,000 marks, that held true for only 15% of all Protestants and 10% of all Catholics. When one focuses on the prosperous households, the contrast is again quite striking. While at the end of the German Empire 20% of Breslau Jews lived in a household with an annual income of more than 10,000 marks, only 2.6% of all Protestants and only 1.4% of all Catholics did so.

The Proportion of Jews in the Bourgeois Income Groups

What the analysis of professional structure has already shown, a consideration of income stratification confirms. Because of the significantly higher average incomes of Breslau Jews, they were overrepresented both at the beginning and at the end of the German Empire in the bourgeois income classes. A sizable segment of the bourgeois classes in the Silesian capital was Jewish. As regards profession and income, the Jews formed a core group of the Breslau bourgeoisie. If one compares the proportion of Breslau Jews in the bourgeois classes with their proportion in the bourgeois professions, it becomes clear that the significance of Jews to the Breslau bourgeoisie, particularly to the top of the bourgeoisie, must be judged greater than the analysis of occupational profile would have led one to suspect.

As early as the beginning of the German Empire, Jews were overrepresented—with their proportion of the population at a good 7%—in all income groups except among the low-income earners and the proletarians (table 22). Furthermore, 14% of the petit-bourgeois (annual income: 1,100–2,750 marks), 28% of the prosperous-bourgeois (annual income: 2,750–9,200 marks), and 32% of the wealthy-bourgeois (annual income: over 9,200 marks) income groups were Jewish. Protestants were represented in all the income groups roughly in accordance with their proportion of the population (58%), whereas Catholics were underrepresented in the higher income groups. Though Catholics made up 35% of the population, they represented only 27% of the petit-bourgeois, merely 20% of the prosperous-bourgeois, and only 5% of the wealthy-bourgeois income groups.[105]

By 1906 the Jewish proportion of the population had decreased to 4.3%, and its proportion in the petit-bourgeois and prosperous-bourgeois income groups sank, even though Breslau Jews continued to be overrepresented in both groups. After the turn of the century, 9% of all petit-bourgeois and 15% of all prosperous-bourgeois income earners were Jewish. The decline of the Jewish proportion of both income groups should not be given too much importance. More significant was the fact that the Jewish proportion of the wealthy or rich bourgeois (with an annual income of more than 9,200 or 10,000 marks, respectively) increased from 32% in 1876 to 40% in 1906. That increase is all the more important since the income limit for a bourgeois lifestyle during the same period rose considerably. That held true especially in the sphere of politics; in 1895, the lowest income for the second electoral class was already 16,000 marks.

In view of the great significance of local politics to the relationship between Jews and other Breslauers, it is worthwhile, finally, to analyze one last subgroup more precisely, namely, that of all men at least twenty-five years old and entitled to vote. Breslau Jews benefited in the city council elections from the threshold for the minimum income one had to earn to be permitted to vote, namely, 900 marks before 1896 and 600 marks from 1896 on. The proportion of Jewish men over the age of twenty-four who earned less than 900 or 600 marks, respectively, was smaller than among Breslau Protestants and Catholics. In the city council elections of 1876, Jews represented about 17% of those entitled to vote, although their proportion of the total population was only 7%. By 1906, that proportion would fall to 4.3%, but Jews still represented 8% of those entitled to vote.[106] How were these voters distributed among the three electoral classes? Unfortunately, no precise data on the income thresholds of the three electoral classes are available for 1876 and 1906, but only for 1868, 1885, and 1895, so we are forced to estimate for the missing years.[107] In the mid-1870s, those men who paid taxes each year on an income of 900–2,000 marks probably voted in the third electoral class; in the second class, those who earned 2,000–8,000 marks; and in the first, those whose annual income was over 8,000 marks. In 1905, the limits had shifted upward. To vote in the second class, a man now had to earn at least 8,000 marks; to vote in the first class, one had to earn over 20,000 marks per year. If one accepts this estimate, the following picture emerges (tables 23 and 24). At the beginning of the German Empire, the proportion of Jewish voters in the third electoral class was 12%; in the second, 23%; and in the first, roughly 35%. After the turn of the century, the Jewish proportion in the first two classes increased further. Among the voters in the third electoral class in 1906, 7% were Jewish; in each of the second and first classes, approximately 38%. To grasp just how impressive these figures are, one need only recall how much smaller the Jewish proportion of the population was in 1876 and 1906, namely, 6.7% and 4.3%.[108]

Because of their considerable income advantage over other Breslauers, Jews had the opportunity to participate actively in shaping local politics in the Silesian capital. On the other hand, this aspect of the three-class suffrage system was a thorn in the side of the anti-Semites. "More than 40% of the first electoral class," the editor of the *Schlesische Morgen-Zeitung* and conservative city councilor Kurt Nitschke complained in November 1910, "consists of . . . wealthy Jewish fellow citizens." That was why, he argued, the city council had a liberal-minded majority whose "leaders" were "Jewish lawyers."[109] What Nitschke failed to mention, however, was that a few days earlier the liberal list had received over 70% of the votes in the first electoral class.[110] Despite anti-Semitic hostilities, the Jewish city councilors managed to keep local politics in the Silesian capital on a left-wing liberal course until the end of the German Empire.

5. Embourgeoisement and the Jewish Bourgeoisie in Contemporary Perspective

The results presented here are at odds not only with the views prevailing in the literature but also with contemporary descriptions of German Jews from Jews themselves and other Germans. It may be fruitful, however, to grasp the contemporary descriptions of Jews not only as confirmation of the current research consensus but also as a linguistically constituted reality. While the contemporary view that most Jews were bourgeois as early as 1870 did not do justice to the socioeconomic situation of the majority of Jews, it was no less real on that account. When one no longer takes such descriptions as a substitute for a hitherto unavailable sociohistorical stratification analysis, one's eyes are opened to the yearnings, hopes, and anxieties that were inscribed in the common view that the majority of Jews had been bourgeois since the mid-nineteenth century. It is prosaic analysis of income stratification that allows us to reassess the cultural dimension of the constitution of the Jewish bourgeoisie in Germany.

There are three reasons why many Jewish observers during the German Empire thought that the majority of German Jews were already bourgeois in 1870. The first was their pride in what they had achieved. In the Jewish press in the German Empire, almost every obituary emphasized how the deceased had been able to rise out of the lower classes. Rarely is any mention made therein of shame felt over the poverty of the person's parents or grandparents. In the obituary by the Breslau local correspondent of the *Allgemeine Zeitung des Judenthums* for Leopold Freund, the publisher of the *Breslauer Morgen-Zeitung* who died in 1887, we read that he was "a *self made man*" "who had worked himself up from being a penniless compositor's apprentice to being the editor and owner of the most widely distributed Breslau newspaper." Freund, who was born in 1808 in Badewitz, in the district of Leobschütz, had himself stressed the poverty of his parents. "Poor and forsaken," in his youth he had "depended for years on [his] own abilities and on the support of [his] distant relatives in Leobschütz." He and his wife, Ida, née Oelsner, to whom he had been married since 1834, had still lived in depressing circumstances around 1840; he said: "Despite all my hard work and tremendous efforts, I could cover my expenses only with difficulty." However, in the mid-1840s Freund's "hard work" and "efforts" began to pay off, and he became a successful publisher. At the end of the 1860s, Freund was able to retire from actively running his firm; he had amassed such a great fortune that in 1876 alone he was earning 26,000 marks in interest on it.[111]

The theme of advancement is also to be heard in the *Jüdisches Volksblatt*'s obituary for Theodor Oschinsky, who died in 1907. Born in 1844 in the district of Pless, the merchant "had worked himself up from mean circumstances to a respected, solidly grounded position." Similar to Leopold Freund, Oschinsky also had successfully made the leap into the economic elite. Whereas in 1876 he paid taxes on an annual income of 4,800 marks, which was average at the time for businessmen, in the year before his death he earned nearly 63,000 marks per year.[112] Finally, although Emil Ludwig, the son of the ophthalmologist Hermann Ludwig Cohn, had converted to Protestantism, in 1908 he nevertheless described his great grandfather L. S. Cohn as the "son of a poor man" who, "as a businessman," managed "through cleverness to achieve prosperity, indeed wealth." "Painted by Resch the Elder in oil," Ludwig continued, "in a fur coat, clever, dignified, he looks quite the patrician, though with a Semitic aspect."[113]

Second, Jewish commentators viewed upward social mobility also against the backdrop of the quid pro quo established in the emancipation contract.[114] Legal equality was regarded thereby as payment in return for the Jews' "bourgeois improvement," which had already occurred or would occur in the future. This was a complex notion. The liberal pioneers of the emancipation expected the Jews to conform both culturally and religiously to the majority society. When Jewish observers emphasized in the late nineteenth century that the majority of German Jews belonged to the bourgeoisie, the boundaries between the economic and the generally cultural dimensions of "bourgeois improvement" dissolved. Because German Jews had become bourgeois, they had earned legal equality. Now other Germans were obliged to implement the equality of Jews also in the daily workings of politics. This complexity resonates in Toury's thesis of the "Jews' entrance into the German bourgeoisie."[115] Some contemporary commentaries, which at first read like an analysis of Jewish social structure, belong first and foremost in the context of the debate on the "bourgeois improvement" of the Jews. In 1890, the director of the Breslau Jewish orphanage, Michaelis Silberstein, linked his critique of anti-Semitism and his defense of Jewish legal equality with an analysis of the social structure of Breslau Jews. With the "Jew-baiting" around 1880, he said, a "regrettable movement has emerged that does our age no credit," a movement "by which Breslau has unfortunately not been spared." Despite the attacks, "influential people spoke up for the Jews in a fight that was forced on them" in order to prove that the Jews "always endeavored to keep step with their fellow citizens in spiritual development." Yet Silberstein based his thesis not on religious and cultural assimilation but on socioeconomic embourgeoisement. "If numbers are any proof," he continued, "then the following is incontrovertible proof that that was and is the case in Breslau, too. Among 17,445 Jewish residents, we now count: 3 government councilors, 11 professors, 128 physicians and public health counselors; furthermore, 53 jurists, including 3 counsellors of justice, 3 lower-court judges, 3 lower-court counselors, 1 provincial-court counselor, and 34 lawyers. We have 3 municipal counselors, 17 city councilors, and the chairman of that body . . . likewise a Jew. We have 3 government master builders, 2 master masons, and 1 master carpenter, 12 pharmacists, 8 accountants, etc."[116] It is only seemingly a question here of a detailed sociostructural analysis. With the meticulousness of an accountant, Silberstein attempts to prove that the Breslau Jews have completely fulfilled their side of the emancipation contract and thereby show that the anti-Semitic attack on the legal equality of the Jews was unfounded.

Third, from the 1890s on the Zionists formed another group that shared the view that the majority of the Jews belonged to the bourgeoisie. In their criticism of the "parvenu," however, the Zionists took the opposite tack. Now the talk was no longer of pride in what had been achieved or of the fulfillment of an emancipation contract. To them the social advancement of the German Jews in the nineteenth century was no success, but rather the root of all evil. From their perspective, the whole of West European Diaspora Jewry was degenerate. Instead of carrying out a subtle analysis of the Jewish social structure, they combined the critiques of civilization, the big city, and capitalism to depict the specter of the impending "downfall of the German Jews." In this view, Zionists regarded all German Jews as prosperous. They saw wealth and prosperity no longer as signs of success but as both an indication and a cause of moral depravity. For instance, Felix Theilhaber traced the "retrogression and decline" of the German Jews back to the "great spoiledness of Jewish women . . . , the material propensity, and the Jews' view of life that is bound up with it," in short, to the "effect of capitalism." The Jewish youth movement of the late Wilhelmine period adopted this diagnosis as well as the pessimistic critique of the bourgeois and his civilization. "The merchant who haggles and dickers," one could read in February 1918 in the *Blau-Weiß-Blätter*, "the physician helps merely in order to make money, the lawyer who perverts justice into injustice, seeks absolution for his sins, which he commits in broad daylight."[117] The youth movement author denied the bourgeois absolution while failing to notice that not all German Jews were businessmen, physicians, or lawyers. A consideration of lower-class Jews would have spoiled this simplistic argumentation. The view that all German Jews were bourgeois thus served as a counterimage to the farmer, who loved nature, was close to the earth, and lived, as Arthur Ruppin put it, off "the fruit from his clod of dirt," and whom the Zionists regarded as the embodiment of the healthy Jew of the future.[118]

Income-based sociostructural analysis does not render studies of the occupational profile of German Jews in the German Empire superfluous simply because the state of the sources does not permit precise investigations of income stratification in other cities. Like the investigation of professional structure, then, the analysis of income stratification has both its advantages and its disadvantages. There is no ideal method of sociostructural analysis. Both approaches are, above all, aids that enable us to investigate social inequality. Both are constructions. One must take care not to fall prey to the suggestive force of statistics.

Between the late eighteenth and the early twentieth century, many Breslau Jews succeeded in advancing economically. Although the nineteenth century was a period of high upward mobility for Breslau Jews, the view that the majority of Jews in the Silesian capital belonged to the bourgeoisie is misleading. If one distinguishes between the petite bourgeoisie and the bourgeoisie proper and considers the significant proportion of single women, it becomes clear that neither at the beginning nor at the end of the German Empire can the majority of Breslau Jews be assigned to the *Bürgertum,* the bourgeoisie in the narrower sense. Based on profession, about 40% of all Breslau Jews belonged to the bourgeoisie in 1876, and almost 60% did in 1906. However, since many who pursued bourgeois professions did not have a bourgeois income, the analysis of professions must be supplemented with an investigation of income levels. Even if one considers only the age group with the highest income, only a third of all thirty- to sixty-year-old Breslau Jews commanded a bourgeois income at the beginning of the German Empire, and less than half of them had such an income even at the end of the empire. Therefore, considerable evidence speaks for abandoning the view that the majority of Jews belonged to bourgeois professional groups and bourgeois income strata in the German Empire, or at least for qualifying that view considerably. There were petit-bourgeois and poor Jews not only in the country but also in major cities—among Jewish men but especially among Jewish women. Moreover, the view that the majority of Jews were bourgeois conceals the high degree of socioeconomic difference existing within the Jewish population itself.

The significance of the source material on which most of the studies on German-Jewish history are based, such as memoirs, diaries, and correspondence, is limited. Almost all the authors of such self-testimonies were from the bourgeoisie, mostly from the small stratum of the educated bourgeois; hence, these sources offer little information about the lives of most lower-class Jews. Also, the bourgeois authors of the autobiographies equated their specifically bourgeois experiences with those of all German Jews. Even as careful an observer as Norbert Elias said in retrospect in the early 1980s that "the Jews formed their own, firmly established stratum of the bourgeoisie" in the Silesian capital. With the exception of the "immigrants from the East who spoke Yiddish," he said, there were no poor Jews in Breslau.[119] To clear the blind spot of the self-testimonies, it is necessary to use many indirect testimonies, such as tax rolls and marriage registers.

If the proportion of the petits bourgeois and the lower classes among the total Jewish population was larger and the proportion of bourgeois classes was smaller than previously assumed, then that changes our picture of the relations between Jews, Protestants, and Catholics. That the analyses of professional structure and income stratification have preceded the investigation of sociability, the schools, and politics does not mean, however, that the present study proposes that the key to the relationship between Jews and other Breslauers is to be found in those analyses. The latter have served above all to describe the heterogeneous social structure of Breslau Jews, which will be kept in view in the following chapters, particularly in the history of Christian-Jewish mixed marriages. In that sense, there is not one history of the relations between Jews and other Breslauers, but many. The experiences of a bourgeois Jew differed from those of a petit-bourgeois Jew, and those differed in turn from the experiences of a lower-class Jew.

Even though the social structure of Breslau Jews in the German Empire was less bourgeois than one would have suspected based on the state of research, the proportion of the bourgeoisie among the Jewish population was larger than it was among Breslau Protestants and Catholics. Given their proportion of the total population, Breslau Jews were overrepresented in the city's petite bourgeoisie and *Bürgertum*. Within the professional groups of the bourgeoisie at the beginning and the end of the German Empire, more than a quarter of all Breslauers were Jewish; within the subgroup of the *Wirtschaftsbürgertum*, Jews even represented a third. Due to their income advantage, Jews continued to be markedly overrepresented also in the bourgeois income strata—the bourgeois classes. At the beginning of the German Empire, Jews made up nearly a third of Breslau's bourgeois classes, and at the end of the German Empire, still a quarter. As the following chapters will show, Jews influenced the largest faction of the Breslau bourgeoisie that was liberal and kept its distance from the Prussian and imperial state. Bourgeois Jews supported important parts of bourgeois associational life, supplied a good many of the city's secondary-school students, helped to shape local politics in essential respects as long as the three-class suffrage system was in effect, and formed the backbone of left-wing liberalism in Breslau. The three-class suffrage system endowed bourgeois Jews with the strength needed to keep local politics in the Silesian capital on a left-wing liberal course until the end of the German Empire. Within the Breslau bourgeoisie, Jews were a core group, not a small minority.

2

Crossing Boundaries

Jews in Bourgeois and Jewish Associations

The long nineteenth century was a blissful age for bourgeois associations. As voluntary associations, middle-class clubs and social organizations (*Vereinswesen*) provided an alternative to the society of old Europe
based on hereditary estates. It was no longer as a member of a hereditary social class or as someone associated with a group based on regnant
power structures but rather as a "free" individual that one belonged to
such clubs and organizations. The emergence of voluntary associations,
Thomas Nipperdey notes, was closely connected with the "individual-
ization and bourgeoisification of culture." Despite persistent exclusion,
clubs were therefore "fundamentally accessible to all."[1] In this sense, association life, according to Otto Dann, formed a structural characteristic that "arose with and was constitutive of bourgeois society."[2]

According to their self-understanding, many clubs saw themselves as
a society in miniature, as a space in which individuals could experiment
with different forms of sociability. Members could gain experience inside the club that would be of use to them outside it as well. The point
was to improve oneself morally in social life, to "cultivate" the self in the
emphatic sense. The clubs, particularly the political organizations, were
"great schools, free of charge, where all citizens [came] to learn the general theory of association," Alexis de Tocqueville had asserted in 1840.
The "art of association" became "the mother science; all stud[ied] it
and appl[ied] it." When "citizens are forced to be occupied with public
affairs," said Tocqueville, "they are necessarily drawn from the midst of
their individual interests and . . . torn away from the sight of themselves." Yet it was also a matter of acquiring concrete skills in the regular course of club life, such as rhetorical or negotiating techniques, or

the ability to lead a discussion. Many of the dignitaries in municipal administration probably developed their capacity to speak and act in clubs to which they already belonged before beginning their careers in local politics.[3] The *Breslauer Zeitung* went even farther in October 1879. The vigorousness of liberalism in the big cities, it said, was the "natural" consequence of "greater economic activity, . . . cooperation, and living together, the natural influence of the educated on the less educated, the number of educational institutions of every kind, the press, the social clubs" and the "common lectures in all cities."[4]

The heyday of associational life was not the early nineteenth century but the German Empire.[5] The Breslau directory lists a good 250 clubs in 1876, approximately 650 in 1902, and then nearly 800 in 1906. According to the directory's groupings, there were 174 organizations "for religion and charitable purposes," 117 for "school, education, and adult education," 94 for "business, trade, and land improvement," 67 for "politics and economics," 62 music and choral societies, 49 social clubs, 44 societies for science and art, and 40 military clubs.[6] Moreover, the criticism of club mania indicated the ubiquity of clubs. In the journal of the Verein für Geschichte und Altertum Schlesiens (Society for Silesian History and Antiquity), for example, the director of the Breslau City Library, Heinrich Wendt, warned of the "obvious excesses, lapses in taste, and ridiculousness" of associational life in Breslau. Unlike Tocqueville, Wendt believed that club mania encourages "craving for status," "solitariness," and an "addiction to gambling." Despite this criticism, Wendt judged the associations positively. The "modern club" is "a necessary concomitant of self-administration . . . ; indispensable for the amelioration of much of the damage that has arisen from our social circumstances; [the club] is often a training ground for our statesmen and social policymakers. And its effects on individuals are certainly not entirely negative."[7]

1. Early Bourgeois Anti-Semitism and the Jewish Subculture

Although in bourgeois associational life individuals came together in what was in principle an open form of association, Jews continued to be denied access to clubs well into the nineteenth century.[8] The masterminds of early liberalism justified the exclusion of Jews by pointing to their alleged "unsociability." Karl von Rotteck, for example, argued in 1847 that due to their "antisocial nature" Jews could not join the lodges;

as "standoffish elements," they threatened the intimacy of associational life.[9] Still in the 1840s many middle-class clubs in Frankfurt am Main, Darmstadt, and Gießen declared themselves against the admission of Jews.[10] In Breslau, for example, Henry Melford and Joël Bernard, two Jews, belonged to a local tobacco club of "students, young businessmen, and military officers." When it was accidentally discovered that Melford and Bernard were Jews, "they were denied entry despite their good manners, cultivation, and popularity."[11] In the early 1850s, while Gustav Freytag was at work on *Soll und Haben* (*Debit and Credit*), the Breslau merchants' guild was still refusing to admit Jews into its corporation. Only when the Jewish merchants boycotted the merchants' exchange and set up their own exchange were they able to gain admission to the merchants' guild.[12] The first joint ball of Jewish and Christian merchants in Breslau followed in 1870. Yet here too a certain distance was still noticeable. "Jewish and Christian merchants," the left-wing liberal *Breslauer Morgen-Zeitung* jested, "bargained, discounted, dined, supped, and drank hob or nob, they even spoused, but they never danced with one another. Isn't that very strange?"[13]

Because Jews continued to be denied access to the general associational life altogether or in part, they began in the first half of the nineteenth century to found their own clubs, which they modeled on the middle-class associations. From the 1820s on, German Jews created a "parallel associational life," which formed the most important component of a Jewish subculture.[14] "If German Jews could not enter bourgeois German society—if they could not achieve satisfactory, let alone total, social integration," reads David Sorkin's core thought, "they could create parallel institutions, gaining membership in the larger society in the sense that theirs closely resembled it."[15] Henry Melford and Joël Bernard, for example, reacted to their exclusion from the Breslau tobacco club by founding their own club. The Gesellschaft der Freunde, which was formed in January 1821, offered its members the chance to spend "evenings in noble sociability and in cozy circles" and to "keep their intellectual abilities sharp through beneficial engagement." The club set up an extensive library and subscribed to "the best and soundest newspapers," which were "to provide the material for the most fruitful conversation."[16] Soon many prominent Breslau Jews belonged to the club— for example, from 1835 on, the philologist Wilhelm Freund; from 1849, the book dealer and future city councilor Julius Hainauer; from 1852, the Reform rabbi Abraham Geiger; from 1854, the lawyer, future city councilor, and cofounder of the Deutsch-Israelitischer Gemeindebund

(Federation of Jewish Communities in Germany) David Honigmann; and from 1858 the botanist, future university professor, and honorary citizen of Breslau Ferdinand Julius Cohn.[17] Although the history of its founding suggests that the club had only Jewish members, its statutes from 1878 maintain that the Gesellschaft der Freunde was open to "every unmarried man of education and respectable reputation who possesse[d] the abilities and means to ensure his subsistence."

The Gesellschaft der Freunde was socially exclusive. The admission charge was 100 marks plus an obligatory donation to the widow and orphan fund. The annual dues increased from 24 marks in the 1860s to 36 marks in the 1870s and then to 56 from 1900 on.[18] The number of members increased from nearly 500 in 1871 to 666 in 1905, but then sank to 612 until 1920.[19] As early as the 1840s, the Gesellschaft der Freunde had become a respected club. The lyrics of the celebratory cantata for the twenty-fifth founder's day celebration in January 1846, for example, were written by Gustav Freytag, who at the time was also the house poet of the Zwingergesellschaft (which excluded Jews) and a guest of honor at their balls.[20] In the 1870s, the Breslau daily press reported extensively on the club's celebrations and on the talks it organized, which were attended by approximately 700 people.[21] The speakers whom the club was able to enlist included not only Jewish intellectuals, such as Berthold Auerbach, Karl Emil Franzos, Ludwig Geiger, and Moritz Lazarus, but also prominent non-Jews, such as Felix Dahn, Breslau's representative to the Reichstag Alexander Meyer, the pharmaceutics professor Theodor Poleck, and Albert Träger.[22]

The exclusivity of the Gesellschaft der Freunde was set in stone in the clubhouse it built in 1877–78 for almost 220,000 marks. Following the design of the Tempelhof architect Hubert Stier, a spacious neo-Renaissance building was erected on Neue Graupenstrasse in the rapidly growing *Südvorstadt*. The facade was a full 40 meters wide, and the building a full 20 meters deep. At the rear of the building was a garden in which the club held a summer festival each year. On the ground floor were the party rooms, the library and a reading room, three game rooms, a parlor and a dining hall, as well as a billiards room, which alone measured 6 by 8 meters. On the first floor, which the Gesellschaft der Freunde also rented out to other clubs, there was a banquet hall measuring roughly 360 square meters and a dining hall measuring 140 square meters.[23] The banquet hall was a popular venue. At the end of the German Empire and in the early Weimar Republic, readings were still given there by Kasimir Edschmid, Thomas Mann, and Armin T. Wegner.[24]

2. The Opening of Bourgeois Associations in 1848–1849

In the 1850s, 1860s, and 1870s, however, cities such as Berlin, Königsberg, Frankfurt, and Breslau opened almost all general clubs to Jews.[25] Often Jews even played an important role in the founding of these clubs, which frequently were close to the liberal parties. The majority of Breslau Jews were now active in both Jewish and general associations. In view of the far-reaching inclusion of Jews in bourgeois associational life after 1860, it is questionable whether Sorkin's concept of a German-Jewish subculture is useful for the latter half of the century. Certainly a Jewish associational life continued to exist. Yet now it was no longer a consequence of the partial or extensive exclusion of Jews from general associational life but part of new intra-Jewish forms of sociability. Because middle-class Jews also belonged to the general associational life from the 1860s on, they no longer had to simulate their participation in bourgeois society in the subculture of Jewish associational life. For German Jews, the Jewish clubs lost their compensatory function and became solely places in which they socialized as Jews, appropriated Jewish traditions, reinterpreted those traditions, and even invented new ones.[26]

One of the first and most respected clubs that opened itself to Jews and in which they then played an important role was the Schlesische Gesellschaft für Vaterländische Cultur (Silesian Society for Patriotic Culture). Founded in 1803 as a private club, it had about four hundred members in the 1840s and the 1880s, but then about one thousand members after the turn of the century. The club developed lively lecture and research activities and took the place of Silesia's missing academy. The club had set itself, the Schlesische Landeskunde judged in 1913, "the same goal as the academies, to teach, in rigorous, scholarly work, as many disciplines in the humanities and natural sciences, the sum of human knowledge," though without limiting itself "to promoting pure science and, following the model of the academies, to admitting only scholars to their circle."[27] Thus the club also appealed to the broad public. Its success was based on the fascination with natural history topics that had grown increasingly since 1848. Not programmatically but implicitly, it acted, as the Humboldt-Verein also would later, as a counterbalance to the power of state and religious interpretations in the explication of nature.[28]

From the 1850s on, Jews could assume leading roles in the Schlesische Gesellschaft für Vaterländische Cultur. From 1852 to 1857, the botanist

Ferdinand Julius Cohn headed the natural science division, which was regarded as the most important and the most respected in the society, and from 1856 to 1897 he oversaw the botany division.[29] In the 1870s and 1880s, two well-known Jews, Leopold Auerbach and Oscar Berger (1844–85), were secretaries of the medical division.[30] Moreover, Jewish scientists built up many of the new and innovative divisions. The health-care division, for instance, was shaped especially by Joseph Jacobi (1840–1907), physician and married to Selma, the sister of Gustav Born, who headed this division from 1879 to 1907.[31] At his side stood from 1892 to 1896 Hermann Ludwig Cohn (1838–1906), a well-known Breslau ophthalmologist nicknamed "Eye-Cohn" (*Augencohn*).[32] The founding of the philosophy-psychology division was initiated by Jacob Freudenthal, who headed it from 1903 until his death in June 1907. His successor was William Stern, who ran the division until 1914. From 1914 to 1930, it was headed by Richard Hönigswald, a Protestant of Jewish descent, the most important teacher of Norbert Elias, and, despite his apostasy, the spiritual leader behind the young Breslau Zionists in the early 1920s.[33] In 1903, the mathematical division was established, and its founder, Emil Toeplitz (1852–1917), was one of four Jewish senior teachers at the Johannes-Gymnasium, where he taught from 1879 and bore the title of professor from 1896 on.[34] However, the Schlesische Gesellschaft für Vaterländische Cultur could never entirely shed its fundamental Christian character. Typically enough, the club established a division for Protestant theology and one for Catholic theology in 1904, but never a division for Jewish theology, although there would have been sufficient local expertise in that area given the presence of Breslau's Jewish Theological Seminary.[35]

The most spectacular example of the opening of associational life in Breslau to Jews was the Kosmos Lodge (founded in 1849), in which Jews, Protestants, and Catholics sympathetic to the democratic movement gathered.[36] As early as July 1848, several reformers in the Friedrich zum goldenen Zepter (Friedrich with the Golden Scepter) Lodge had insisted that the exclusion of Jews and the state's overall control over the lodge be ended. Members were divided concerning the reformers' demands. The majority voted against the admission of Jews, and as a result the reformers left the Zepter Lodge and founded their own Reformverein Kosmos (Cosmos Reform Club) in 1849. Under the leadership of the merchant Carl Wilhelm Laßwitz (1809–1879), Protestant, Catholic, and Jewish Freemasons gathered there. Laßwitz, whom the police regarded as a "red republican," was the president of the Democratic Club in

Breslau during the revolution, belonged to the Prussian National Assembly in 1848, and in the 1860s became one of Breslau's leading left-wing liberals, whose position he represented in 1869 in the Prussian parliament's debate regarding the Johannes-Gymnasium.[37] Like the lodge Minerva zum vaterländischen Verein (Minerva Patriotic Club) in Cologne, the Kosmos Lodge was the first Prussian lodge open to Jews.[38] The other Breslau lodges opposed the liberal competition, prohibited social contact with Kosmos Lodge members, and denounced the latter to the Prussian government. Whereas the Cologne reform lodge ensured its survival by excluding its Jewish members so that it could gain admittance to a Prussian grand lodge, the Breslau Kosmos Lodge stood by its Jewish lodge brothers. Without the protection of a grand lodge, it was at the mercy of the police state that reigned during the restoration period. At the end of 1851, the Prussian secretary of the interior banned the Kosmos Lodge. The experiment of an interdenominational lodge in Prussia had failed after two years due to the resistance of the conservative lodges and the Prussian state.

Yet the defeat of the reformers could not change the basic trend. Even the Breslau Freemason lodges that had been particularly stubborn in upholding the exclusion of Jews began to open their doors to Jews in the 1850s. Officially, however, Prussian lodges could not permit the admission of Jews. As protector of the Prussian grand lodges, Wilhelm I had repeatedly threatened that he would strip the Freemasons of all state privileges if they admitted Jews. The Prussian lodges bowed to the royal pressure, though they did allow several Prussian Jews to apply for membership in a lodge outside Prussia, such as in Hamburg or Leipzig. With the approval of the Breslau lodges, several Breslau Jews applied successfully for membership in Leipzig Freemason lodges in the 1860s. Thus they could now all participate as visiting brothers in Breslau Masonic life.[39] However, this was possible only for a few prominent and prosperous Jews, such as the wealthy merchant Isaak Cohn or Hirsch Joachimsohn, a merchant and, since 1854, city councilor and in the 1860s a member of the representative council of the Jewish *Gemeinde*.[40] As character references, Joachimsohn provided the Leipzig lodge with the names of two leading members of the Breslau lodge Friedrich zum goldenen Zepter. Both emphatically supported his admission. Their own lodge would have admitted Joachimsohn long ago, they said, if the Prussian grand lodge association did not strictly forbid the admission of Jews. "Any lodge can consider itself fortunate to count this widely recognized man of honor among its members," read a letter of recommendation from a liberal Breslau counsellor of justice. Joachimsohn "would have been . . . admitted here long ago were it not that in *every* system privileged in Prussia it is *unfortunately* a rule not to admit any Jews." The Leipzig lodge brothers could gauge the great esteem for Joachimsohn not only from his function as city councilor but also from his membership in the representative council of the Jewish *Gemeinde*.[41]

The detour to a non-Prussian lodge was controversial among Jewish Freemasons. At least a Breslau lodge brother argued in November 1874 in the *Israelitische Wochenschrift* that "Freemasonry" is at best "superfluous" for Jews. Granted, Freemasonry does not saddle its members with "any duties whatsoever which could deter . . . even the most orthodox Jew . . . from the lowest Masonic degree [*Johannesgrad*]." Nevertheless, lodge membership is not advantageous to Jews. They are already "given the cultivation of heart and mind with universal standpoints, which do so much good in Freemasonry, . . . by their own religion . . . and an at least equally profound symbolism (our ritual laws)." Yet lodge membership is not just superficial but harmful. He sees, the Freemason argued, "a weakness of character in the well-known way in which Jews in Prussia have become or even will become Freemasons." Since Jews are not welcome in Prussian lodges, there is no excuse for Prussian Jews' having gone "abroad" to force themselves on "this society" "because the statutes guarantee the solidarity of Freemasons." But Prussian Freemasonry "insults my entire nation, my religion, or my relatives." It is therefore the "duty of every Jewish Freemason not to enter any Prussian Temple as long as the Prussian mother lodge has the practice of 'Christian virtues' as its aim."[42]

Breslau Jews actively contributed to the restraint of anti-Semitism in the city's associational life in the 1860s and 1870s by playing a leading role in the founding of new clubs, which would shape Breslau cultural life during the German Empire.[43] The gathering place of literary life in the city was the Breslauer Dichterschule (Breslau School of Poets). Every week the club held social evenings with readings and lectures at which the members presented their own work for discussion. Each summer, the club organized trips to the Silesian mountains. It also organized commemorations for such figures as Theodor Körner and Franz Grillparzer and celebrations in honor of living writers, such as on Gustav Freytag's seventieth birthday in July 1886, Felix Dahn's seventieth birthday, and Detlev von Liliencron's sixtieth birthday, both in 1904.[44] Contact among the members was presumably closer than in other clubs. "It is very pleasing" how the "contact among the members" has developed, it reads in the club's festschrift: "Despite the differences in denominations, professions, and later, too, political views, friendly relations were soon established which in part lasted for decades until the end of one's days."[45] From the mid-1860s on, the club published monthly reports, which later appeared under the title *Der Osten: Literarische Monatsblätter der Breslauer "Dichterschule"* (The East: Literary Monthly Reports of the Breslau "School of Poets"). The circle of writers covered a wide literary program.[46] Alongside representatives of Silesian regional literature, such as the rector and Silesian dialect poet Hermann Bauch, there were, for instance, enthusiastic followers of naturalism from the mid-1880s on. In the early 1890s, the *Monatsblätter* published early works by writers who later became well known, such as Otto Julius Bierbaum and Richard Dehmel, Arno Holz and Karl Kraus, and after the turn of the century also Carl Hauptmann and Max Brod, Emil Ludwig, Arthur Silbergleit, and Armin T. Wegner.[47]

Among the founding members of the Breslauer Dichterschule in 1859 were three Breslau Jews: the merchant Adolf Freyhan (1840–1909); the writer Oskar Justinus Cohn (1839–93), the younger brother of the botanist Ferdinand Julius Cohn; and Jakob Freund (1827–77).[48] While Freyhan and Justinus Cohn did not play a prominent role in Breslau's Jewish community, Freund was a teacher from 1856 on at the religious school of the synagogue and a well-known author of devotional literature. Freund, who was sympathetic to the Reform movement, had published *Biblische Gedichte* (Biblical Poems) in 1861, which was followed in 1867 by the widely read *Gebets- und Andachtsbuch für israelitische Mädchen und Frauen* (Prayer and Devotional Book for Jewish Girls and Women), and then in 1870 by his *Confirmationsreden* (Confirmation Talks). However, Freund clearly did not want to restrict himself to the genre of religious literature. For instance, in the play *Haman oder die Rechnung ohne Wirth* (Haman, or, the Unreckoned Price) he linked the Jewish tradition of the Purim play with the genre of the farce. Moreover, in 1857 he had already published *Gelegenheitsgedichte für Kinder* (Occasional Poems for Children), and in the 1870s was one of the most productive members of the Breslauer Dichterschule. Roughly a quarter of all the writings in the *Album Schlesischer Dichterfreunde* (Album of Silesian Poetry Enthusiasts) from 1874 were from his pen.[49] His only son, Julius Freund (1862–1914), influenced the style of modern revue theater after the turn of the century. He was the "house writer" of the Metropoltheater in Berlin, where he wrote successful revues between 1905 and 1914 and counted among the prominent nonlocal members of the Breslauer Dichterschule.[50] Already in the

1870s more Breslau Jews joined, among them two who from 1880 on would leave their mark on the club, Carl Biberfeld and Ludwig Sittenfeld, who edited the monthly reports from 1875 on.[51]

After the turn of the century, a younger generation of Breslau Jews was active in the Dichterschule, including Emil Ludwig (1881–1948); Bertha Badt (1885–1970), the daughter of Benno Badt; the future women's rights activist Clementine Cohn, who published under the pseudonym Clemens Berg; and Arthur Silbergleit (1881–1943), until he moved to Berlin in 1905 at Martin Buber's request to work for the Jewish journal *Ost und West*. Especially Silbergleit repeatedly took up Jewish themes in his writings for the Dichterschule, such as in his short story "Sabbat" from 1910.[52]

As in the Breslauer Dichterschule, Jews also played a leading role in the founding of the Humboldt-Verein für Volksbildung (Humboldt Society for Popular Education) in July 1869; a third of the twenty-four-member founding committee were Jewish.[53] The newly founded club expressly urged Jews to participate in the club.[54] Thus it was only logical, albeit remarkable, that the Breslau Humboldt-Verein, at the request of the Nikolaivorstadt's community association, planned the large centenary celebration of Alexander von Humboldt's birth on September 14 such that it would not conflict with Yom Kippur, which began in the evening.[55] In retrospect, the festschrift for the twenty-fifth anniversary of the club's founding said that "this accord" among Jews, Protestants, and Catholics was "only possible on the basis of *tolerance*, and it [was] precisely tolerance—which is the child of real education—that [was] the creed of the Humboldt-Verein, its answer to the question: What unites us in inner life?" A Kulturkampf, the text continues, will "never again find support in Germany," and "even the poisonous plant of anti-Semitism is isolating itself and consuming itself more and more; it is losing public credibility among decent people."[56]

Whereas elsewhere other Humboldt clubs remained "marginal phenomena," in Breslau its liberal bourgeoisie gathered in the Humboldt-Verein until 1914.[57] Even observant Protestant liberals who were initially skeptical about this association were active in it from the early 1870s on. With satisfaction, the *Schlesisches Protestantenblatt* noted in November 1872, "[I]n the club in question not just the atheistic position is represented but also the position that believes in and holds to God."[58] As early as 1876, just a few years after its founding, the club had 723 members. With the number of members rising to 895 in 1893, and then to 4,525 in 1906, the Humboldt-Verein grew to become one of the largest Breslau

clubs.[59] From its founding until the First World War, approximately a
third of the club's members were Jewish. Thus around 1906 some 1,500
Breslau Jews belonged to the Humboldt-Verein. So the club had more
Jewish members than all the Jewish clubs in the city with the exception
of the Israelitische Kranken- und Verpflegungs-Anstalt und Beerdigungsgesellschaft (Jewish Hospital and Burial Society), which had about
2,500 members around 1910. Even the Breslau chapter of the Centralverein deutscher Staatsbürger jüdischen Glaubens (Central Association of German Citizens of Jewish Faith), the second largest Jewish association in Breslau, had at this time only about half as many Jewish
members as the Humboldt-Verein.[60] Like the Israelitische Kranken-
und Verpflegungs-Anstalt und Beerdigungsgesellschaft, the Humboldt-
Verein also was able to attract members from the entire spectrum of the
Breslau Jewish community. In 1906 the club's membership included
Hugo Schachtel, the leader of the Breslau Zionists, as well as Markus
Brann, the successor of Heinrich Graetz at the Jewish-Theological
Seminary in Breslau, the liberal rabbi Jakob Guttmann, and his Ortho-
dox colleague Ferdinand Rosenthal.[61]

During the German Empire, the Humboldt-Verein developed a
comprehensive welfare and popular education agenda. At the turn of
the century, according the Heinrich Wendt, the club was the "uncontested leader" in the area of popular education in Breslau. "As part of
the great work of social reform," he said, the club played a leading role
in "the promulgation of the results of scientific research in wide, indeed
the widest circles."[62] "Through the work of the Humboldt-Verein," the
Schlesische Landeskunde judged in 1913, "a more general spectrum of educational interests [were] fostered with a greater variety and at a higher
intellectual level than in hardly any other German city."[63] The talks took
up the most varied topics. After the turn of the century, for instance, the
club was the first educational institution to offer classes in sexual enlightenment, though, of course, "separating men and women."[64] The name
of the club reflected its objective. It belonged to the popular education
movement, and so it also addressed the petit bourgeois and workers. Although the club, according to its founding statement, was founded in an
age of "enormous progress" and of "intellectual uplift among the civilized peoples of the present," the Humboldt-Verein was also, as was typical of middle-class liberals, patronizing toward the "backward classes."
It therefore wanted "to counteract the efforts of those dark powers who
[did] not want the light to shine, who aim[ed] to take [them] back into
the night of medieval ignorance, medieval superstition." Not without

an anti-Catholic barb, it continued: "Our aim is the light! . . . Our aim is humanity!"[65] In view of the Manichean conflict between the forces of light and those of darkness, the Humboldt-Verein had, according to the statute, "to work for popular education, . . . to spread the ideas of humanity and bring them to bear."[66]

Jews played an important role in this educational activity. Among the twenty-four-member committee, or the board of the directors of the club, there were four prominent Breslau Jews in 1876: Wilhelm Kalisch (ca. 1810–1902), managing clerk and later authorized signatory of the Heimann banking house and since 1855 member of the Gesellschaft der Freunde; Wilhelm Koebner, born in 1849, book dealer and later also publisher of Jewish religious literature; David Mugdan, born 1840, wealthy merchant, soon also city councilor, chairman of the Jewish community board, and trade judge; and finally Leopold Priebatsch (1834–1903), publisher and since 1862 member of the Gesellschaft der Freunde, in whose office, at Ring 58, there was a club library comprising fully five hundred volumes.[67] After the turn of the century, there were not four but six Breslau Jews on the club's board: the ophthalmologist and university professor Hermann Ludwig Cohn, the independently wealthy writer Adolf Freyhan, Adolf Heilberg (1858–1936), the merchant Louis Mugdan, the merchant Salo Sackur, and the merchant and writer Ludwig Sittenfeld.[68] Jews also played a leading role among the speakers at the club. Within the club's public, free, and well-attended series Sunday Talks, the well-known Breslau music and theater critic Max Kurnik early in 1870 delivered the lecture "Lessing, a Hero of Humanity"; Emil Ludwig's father, Hermann Ludwig Cohn, gave a lecture in November 1875, "Experiences regarding the Causes of Blindness"; in December of the same year, the botanist Ferdinand Julius Cohn, known as "Garden-Cohn," gave the talk "On the Discovery of the Microscopic World in 1675"; in January and February 1876, the historian Jakob Caro, one of Breslau's few Jewish university professors, presented "The Czarina Catherine II of Russia" and "On Petrarch as Politician"; and, finally, in March of the same year Wilhelm Freund, the long-time intellectual companion of Abraham Geiger, gave the lecture "The Question of Women's Emancipation."[69] Of the twenty speakers in winter 1892–93, six were Breslau Jews, including Adolf Heilberg, who doubtless touched on a sensitive contemporary topic when on December 4, 1892, he gave a lecture titled "The Idea of General Peace among Nations," which then appeared in the club's annual report.[70] And this tradition was continued after the turn of the century. In 1905–6, four of the seventeen speakers in the Sunday Talks series were Jewish: Hermann Hamburger, editor; Adolf Wohlauer, professor at the Johannes-Gymnasium; Isidor Ollendorff, legal counsel; and Adolf Heilberg, who this time dealt with a more innocuous topic: "What Should One Know about the Law when Traveling, at a Hotel, or on the Train?" In the series Neighborhood Talks for Everyone (*Vorstadtvorträge für jedermann*), two more Jewish members of the educated elite spoke: the lawyer Hermann Armer and the general practitioner Max Silber.[71] Finally, within the Akademie des Humboldt-Vereins (Academy of the Humboldt Society), in which Werner Sombart also gave a lecture titled "Socialism and Social Movement in the Modern Civilized Countries" during his time at the University of Breslau, several Breslau Jews offered classes, including the editor Hermann Hamburger ("Heinrich Heine and His Age"), the composer and pianist Felix Rosenthal ("Masters of Music"), and William Stern ("Philosophical Worldviews in the Nineteenth Century"), *Privatdozent* (private university lecturer), father of Günther Anders, founder of modern child psychology, and first university instructor of Edith Stein.[72]

In the early 1870s the clubs that continued to exclude Jews came under increasing public criticism. The Zeitgeist called for the total opening of general associational life. At that time, even the most important bastion of exclusive, Christian sociability in Breslau, the Zwingergesellschaft, was very nearly opened to Jews. Since from the early 1860s almost all Breslau clubs admitted Jews, criticism grew of the Zwingergesellschaft's anti-Semitic policy of exclusion. In March 1870, the liberal *Breslauer Zeitung* jested: "We live far off the beaten path / From all the bustle of the world / Yet whatever happens anywhere else / Comes one day to Breslau as well." "As Nero once Christians as quarry / To lions in their cage [*Zwinger*] gave, / So those shut themselves up still today / In Breslau's *Zwinger* fearfully: How does that fit, enlightened minds, / With the free school that you created, / Through which our mayor / Increases the fame of our citizenry?"[73] Early in 1876, the Breslau correspondent of the *Allgemeine Zeitung des Judenthums* reported on a "curiosity," namely, that "in the Silesian capital there is a so-called Verein christlicher Kaufleute [Christian Merchants' Club] that has in its statutes the hardly credible rule that Jews may be admitted neither as members nor as guests."[74]

Breslau's Zwingergesellschaft had almost bowed to public pressure and opened itself to Jews. The first step was taken by Leo Molinari. He was one of the wealthiest Catholic businessmen in the city and was the inspiration for Gustav Freytag's hero in *Soll und Haben* (*Debit and Credit*), the merchant Schröter.[75] As a prominent member of the club's board of directors, Molinari pleaded at a general meeting early in the 1870s that Jews be admitted, but his motion did not receive majority support.[76] At the end of that decade, however, the Zwingergesellschaft was the major exception to the rule. In Breslau, the ultramontane *Schlesische Volkszeitung* complained in July 1878 that there were "only very few associations left that follow the Zwingergesellschaft on the Jewish question, and that in fact means all the Catholic clubs and associations, the Provincial Club [Provinzial-Ressource], and the German Concert Society [Concertgesellschaft]."[77] Because the city's associational life as a whole was open to Breslau Jews, the Silesian anti-Semites praised the Zwingergesellschaft all the more emphatically. The organ of the Silesian conservatives, the *Schlesisches Morgenblatt*, celebrated the club in a multipart series of articles. "The Zwinger, our Zwinger, as we can rightly and proudly say," wrote the paper in October 1882, was one of the few Breslau clubs in which "a certain segment of the population has not succeeded in its fight for admittance." The "holy shrine" of the Zwingergesellschaft "is a place that has kept itself German in Breslau, which can hardly call itself German any longer."[78]

3. Anti-Semitism as Cultural Code: The Anti-Semitic Mood in the Conservative Bourgeoisie

Among the clubs that continued to exclude Jews, the Zwingergesellschaft was by far the most important because the Breslau and Silesian elite gathered there.[79] As early as the 1830s, the winter balls, or "*Thées dansants*, which often included a masked ball," "united" "the *crème* of Breslau society."[80] Many Christian members of the city's elite counted among the members of the Zwingergesellschaft in 1875, including, from the university, professors Lujo Brentano, Wilhelm Dilthey, Richard Förster, and Theodor Poleck. The city's political elite also met here; Lord Mayor Max von Forckenbeck was even an honorary member. Other members included Mayor Carl Bartsch, the municipal syndic and future mayor Gustav Dickhuth, the municipal council Julius Brückner, the chairman of the city council Georg Friedrich Lewald, and the city councilor and successor of Forckenbeck as lord mayor, Ferdinand Julius Friedensburg.

Nevertheless the Zwingergesellschaft was not typical for Breslau's urban bourgeoisie. Although the club was established as a merchants' club, the Kaufmännischer Verein (Merchants' Club) and Breslau

Chamber of Commerce (founded in June 1848) had taken over the role of representing the professions long ago.[81] In both bodies, Jewish businessmen made up 40–50% of the total membership and occupied many leadership positions. For instance, the chairman of the chamber of commerce from 1869 until his death was Isidor Friedenthal (1812–1886), the counsellor of commerce, city councilor, and long-time chairman of the Jewish *Gemeinde*.[82] The Zwingergesellschaft had long ceased to be a gathering place of Breslau's economic elite. At the beginning of the 1830s, the club was opened to higher-ranking officers, and since the 1840s the merchants had become a minority among the members.[83] In the Zwingergesellschaft, the proportion of high-ranking civil servants, officers, and noblemen was high and that of businessmen and entrepreneurs comparatively low.[84] Moreover, many members were not from Breslau but from the Silesian environs. Thus it was not the Breslau so much as the Silesian elite who gathered there. Those present from Breslau belonged to the faction of the urban bourgeoisie that was close to the state, the military, and the nobility. After Molinari's attempt to open the club to Jews had failed and anti-Semitism had grown more pronounced in public life after 1879–80, the Zwingergesellschaft symbolized the "anti-Semitic mood of society" (Friedrich Naumann) in the conservative Breslau bourgeoisie and the Silesian provincial nobility.[85] Among the bourgeois members, civil servants and members of the educated bourgeoisie empathetic with or otherwise close to state institutions were overrepresented, whereas businessmen and entrepreneurs were underrepresented. The exclusion of Jews served from about 1880 on as a symbol by which the conservative wing of the Breslau bourgeoisie set itself apart from the leftist liberal wing, a development that was noticeable also in Königsberg and in Berlin.[86] The anti-Semitism of the Zwingergesellschaft functioned as a "cultural code," served as "a sign of cultural identity," in order to distinguish a left-wing liberal from a conservative camp.[87] Because of the great symbolic significance of the Zwingergesellschaft, Breslau Jews appreciated the fact that Georg Bender, who as Breslau's lord mayor from 1892 to 1912 shaped local politics, did not join the club. Adolf Heilberg, a Jew, left-wing liberal, and city councilor from 1890 on, recalled in the early 1930s that Bender had refused to join because "as lord mayor [he could not] be a member of a club that exclude[d] from the very start a segment of the citizens that [was] as important to the life of the city as the Jewish population [was]."[88]

While in the 1860s more and more Breslau clubs opened their doors to Jews, in the late 1880s things began to change. In the early 1870s, it

seemed only a matter of time before all the clubs, save for Catholic or
Protestant religious associations, would admit Jews. However, in the
mid-1880s anti-Semitic members in several clubs that were open to
Breslau Jews tried to force Jewish members out of the clubs. Although
all the anti-Semitic attempts failed and almost all the clubs continued to
admit Jews, Breslau associational life had become polarized over the
"Jewish question" in the late 1880s and the early 1890s. Georg Bender's
refusal to join the Zwingergesellschaft reflects this state of affairs.

The first club in which the "Jewish question" sparked a bitter conflict was the Breslau chapter of the Deutscher und Österreichischer Alpenverein (German and Austrian Alpine Club). At the end of the 1880s,
approximately 20% of the members of the club (founded in the fall of
1877) were Jewish.[89] The Alpine Club considered itself an apolitical association open to followers of all political parties; in a song for the
founder's day celebration in January 1882, this was expressed as follows:

> Wherever you go these days,
> What do you hear? Politics!
> That would do us little good,
> That would bring us no happiness.
> We gather unconcerned
> About the quarrels of parties about
> Whether Windthorst or Benningsen
> Now is more important.
> Whether a protective tariff,
> Whether a defensive tariff
> Now is salutary for the people,
> You leave it to the others,
> For we, we hike
> In the Alps cheerful and free.
>
> . . . .
>
> Nationalists/Liberals,
> New and Progress Party,
> All peaceful
> And cozy
> Get on the board.[90]

In mid-December 1888, however, there was a row in the Breslau Alpine
Club. In the election of the club's board of directors, the law professor
Karl von Stengel (1840–1930), who was known throughout the city as an
anti-Semite, was not reelected to the board.[91] It was an open secret that
Stengel was voted out largely because of his anti-Semitic speech during

the Landtag elections in November 1888.[92] Stengel, who was originally
from Bavaria, had claimed, "[T]he hegemony of the Jews in many parts
of Breslau is as obvious as the nose on your face." In the Landtag elections, he said, it was therefore necessary "to take a good look at phys-
iognomies." "It is better," Stengel concluded his "brutal, anti-Semitic,
rabble-rousing speech," "to be a proud son of Germania than a slave of
Shem."[93] Yet because several non-Jewish members of the Alpine Club
were angry about Stengel's being voted out despite the anti-Semitic
speech, at the beginning of January a special general meeting was held.
Though Stengel was reelected there to the board by a narrow majority,
he would no longer be the deputy chairman. According to the *Breslauer
Zeitung,* "the vast majority of those who voted against Mr. von Stengel in
the general meeting before Christmas stayed away from yesterday's
meeting." It was "apparently not the intention of those who earlier
voted against Mr. Stengel to aggravate the differences that have arisen
in the club."[94]

Yet the differences between Stengel and the anti-Semitic members,
on the one hand, and the Jewish members, on the other, could no longer
be reconciled. Stengel turned down his election since he knew that it
was only the result of the large number of abstentions. "The professor,"
mocked the Breslau correspondent of the *Allgemeine Zeitung des Judenthums,* "has realized that anti-Semitism has a good deal of the world
against it after all and causes 'problems' for its advocates, himself, and
others."[95] Because of the disgrace, Stengel and several members who
sympathized with him left the club shortly thereafter—at least they no
longer belonged to the club in 1889.[96] Although the opponents of anti-
Semitism succeeded in teaching Stengel a lesson at the general meeting
in December 1888, many Jewish members left the club out of disappointment that the second general meeting had reelected Stengel to the
board after all. They no longer felt comfortable in a club in which a
heated debate on the "Jewish question" had erupted. The proportion of
Jewish members sank from roughly 20% in the 1880s to about 10% after
the turn of the century.[97] Hermann Ludwig Cohn, the merchant Siegfried Haber, the lawyer Adolf Heilberg, the factory owner Salomon
Kauffmann and his son Max Kauffmann, as well as the banker, city
councilor, and future city elder Fedor Pringsheim, counted among the
most prominent Jews who still belonged to the Alpine Club in 1888 but
had left it a year later.[98] It may have come easier to many Breslau Jews to
leave the club since the Riesengebirgsverein (Giant Mountains Club) offered an attractive alternative to it in the Oder metropolis, a club that,

only five years after its founding in 1881, had nearly 800 members, approximately 10% of whom were Jewish.[99] All in all, the Breslau Alpine Club had lost nearly 30% of its members within a few weeks; the number of members sank from 291 to 210.[100]

The increasing politicization of the "Jewish question" in Breslau associational life was also evident at the eighth German gymnastics festival, which took place in 1894 in Breslau. Since Jews played a prominent role in Breslau's gymnastics clubs, many Jews belonged to the committees that prepared for the festival. Carl Biberfeld was the celebrated author of the official festive performance of the gymnastics meeting, and among the select sights worth seeing that the festschrift recommended to the gymnasts from all over Germany was the New Synagogue.[101] Anti-Semites in Breslau and elsewhere tried to boycott parts of the gymnastics festival and to organize alternative events. But they were unsuccessful. The conservative *Reichsbote* noted in July 1894 that even among conservative Breslauers "the behavior of the anti-Semites, who avoided any and every form of positive cooperation and then tried to spoil the self-sacrificing work of others behind their backs, met with unanimous disapproval."[102]

Within the Breslau lodges, anti-Semitism also became a cultural code after 1890. Similar to the development of the Zwingergesellschaft and the confrontation over Jewish members in the Alpine Club, the "Jewish question" was a symbol that increased existing political tensions.[103] Among the three Prussian grand lodges, only the Royal York chose not to admit exclusively Christians to the lodge. Yet even the most liberal Prussian lodge, to which Breslau's Horus Lodge belonged as a branch lodge, rejected all membership applications from Jews from 1888 on. To protest against the renewed intensity of anti-Semitism among the Freemasons, a former grand master of the Royal York, the Berlin zoologist and National Liberal Hermann Settegast, founded liberal reform lodges, which were open to Jews. In Breslau, two of these so-called Settegast lodges were established: in 1893, the lodge Hermann zur Beständigkeit (Hermann for Perseverance) and in 1898, the lodge Settegast zur deutschen Treue (Settegast for German Loyalty). They were associated with the Frankfurt and the Hamburg Grand Lodge Alliance, respectively.

Roughly two-thirds of the members of the Hermann and the Settegast lodges were Jews, especially members of the bourgeois elite. Members of the Hermann lodge included the lawyer Hermann Armer (1863–1917)—at the same time also a member of the Israelitische Kranken- und Verpflegungs-Anstalt und Beerdigungsgesellschaft, the

Riesengebirgsverein, and the Humboldt-Verein[104]—the department store owner Georg Barasch; the chairman of the Breslauer Dichter-schule, Carl Biberfeld (also a member of the Israelitische Kranken- und Verpflegungs-Anstalt und Beerdigungsgesellschaft); the wealthy merchant Michael Fischhoff (1844–1907), who had applied three times between 1884 and 1895 in vain for Prussian citizenship;[105] the factory owner Simon Pfeffer (1862–1918), who, with an annual income of more than 770,000 marks, was one of the richest entrepreneurs in all of Breslau and an important patron of the new Jewish hospital construction;[106] and the pianist Hugo Markt (1862–1918), who wrote music criticism for both the left-wing liberal *Breslauer Zeitung* and the social-democratic *Volkswacht*, organized evening concerts at the Humboldt-Verein for years, and also was a member of the Israelitische Kranken- und Verpflegungs-Anstalt und Beerdigungsgesellschaft.[107]

Yet the "Settegast lodges" also had prominent non-Jewish members, mostly Breslau left-wing liberals. Among them, for instance, was the cofounder of the Hermann lodge, the rector of the municipal Höhere Töchterschule am Ritterplatz (School for Young Ladies on Ritterplatz), Martin Maass (1820–94). Born in Hamburg, Maass had already become a member of a liberal lodge in his hometown. After moving to Breslau in 1871, he could not decide whether to join one of the conservative lodges. In the 1880s, he was repeatedly a speaker at election rallies for the Progressive Party and, for instance, had delivered a much-discussed talk on January 10, 1881, "Progress and Reaction in Germany since 1815," in which he vigorously attacked anti-Semitism.[108] Furthermore, Maass had participated in debates on Jewish-Christian mixed marriages since the mid-1870s and had called for the "mixing of families . . . through reciprocal marriages."[109] Other prominent Jews were the legal council Oskar Poppe (1853–1905) and the manager of the *Breslauer Zeitung*, Lothar Linder (born 1854), who joined the lodge in 1899. Also connected to the *Breslauer Zeitung* was Alfred Oehlke, the long-time master of the second recently founded liberal lodge Settegast zur deutschen Treue and a prominent left-wing liberal politician. In 1900, the paper's editor in chief declared programmatically that Freemasonry was an "alliance among men," free from the "fetters of denominationalism."[110]

Against the backdrop of the growing anti-Semitic social mood among Breslau's conservative bourgeoisie, it is hardly surprising that the conservative lodges refused to interact socially with the liberal lodge brothers and tried to deny the respectability of the members of the newly founded lodges.[111] Until 1914, the conservative lodges demonstratively excluded their "lodge brothers" from both Settegast lodges. Only after the emperor ceased to recognize any parties in August 1914 did the two wings of Breslau's lodge system begin to interact. With the end of the war, the unity among the lodges quickly came to an end. As of November 1918 the conservative Freemasons began to avoid their liberal "brothers" all over again.

4. Social Life in the Club

Clubs offered the opportunity for varied contacts between Jews and other Breslauers.[112] Members met regularly for meetings, clubs organized excursions, and most associations held their founder's day celebration each year. The members of the Verein für Altertum and Geschichte Schlesiens (Society for Silesian Antiquity and History), for instance, could participate in an excursion to Grottkau and Koppitz. In Koppitz, they visited the manor house and park of Count Schaffgotsch; in Grottkau, the old parish church and the city hall. Now came the social part of the trip, namely, the "shared meal," with everyone in "a very cheerfully animated mood."[113] Moreover, members of the Humboldt-Verein not only disseminated the "ideas of humanity" but also organized founder's day celebrations, garden parties, and even summer excursions. In June 1882, the Humboldt admirers went to Zedlitz, which lay about fifteen kilometers north of Breslau. A song composed by Adolf Freyhan, a Jewish merchant from Breslau, offers the following description of the excursion:

> Through the fleeting waves of the Oder
> Steam-fired speeds the boat
> Rejoicing we see already the place
> Of our joyous celebration nearing . . .
>
> If the spirit's been refreshed
> By its delight in nature,
> So will usually the stomach
> Be served its meal.
>
> Girls, for your anxious waiting
> I see finally salvation blossom,
> Behold how full of grace
> A polonaise flows through the garden.
>
> Let us this day still cheerfully float
> In the nimble flight of dance,

For serious hard work and active striving,
The winter offers time enough.[114]

Even in the Alpine Club there were many forms of sociability between
Jews and other Breslauers, despite the conflicts in the late 1880s. Members went together on climbing tours in the Alps, and after talks the
Alpine Club members met "afterward in the Tucherbräu [pub]"; in
spring 1909, the club's board of directors expressly asked members also
to "participate in the drinking" afterward, since people got to know one
another "only by talking."[115] The high point of social life in the Alpine
Club, as in other clubs, was the yearly founder's day celebration. In January 1906, the club's board of directors had "invited [members] to a
'dance in Umhausen,' the popular summer resort in Ötztal." "At eight
o'clock the 'King of Hungary' hall filled with a colorfully dressed
crowd," read the report on the celebration; "about 150 ladies and gentlemen were present who soon took seats, to the sounds of merry tunes, at
the five tables awaiting them. . . . The meal was simple, though not exactly alpine [nor kosher, one might add]; Silesian Heaven [*Schlesisches
Himmelreich:* a stew of pork, dried fruit, and dumplings] and Austrian
apple strudel were served along with the international leg of veal to the
satisfaction of all the feasters. . . . After the meal, there was valiant dancing; the general dances were interrupted by two *Schuhplattler* [Bavarian
folk dances]. . . . In the next room, which had been transformed into a
cozy wine bar, guests sat during breaks and chatted among themselves
or listened to the songs and *Schnadahüpfel* [Austrian and Bavarian im-
promptu humorous-teasing songs] of a Tyrolean glee club. At twelve
o'clock the dancing and singing were interrupted for a moment so that
everyone could join in . . . a toast to the emperor with a threefold hur-
rah. After the first stanza of 'Heil Dir im Siegerkranz' [Hail to Thee in
the Victor's Laurels] had died away, the guests resumed dancing, singing, and yodeling."[116]

Social contact in the scholarly associations could also, under some
circumstances, presuppose a certain degree of intimacy. In any event it
was possible to speak openly in the forums about delicate topics. Hermann Ludwig Cohn gave a lecture, for instance, "On the Sexual Education of Schoolchildren" in October 1904 before the public health division of the Schlesische Gesellschaft für Vaterländische Cultur. In the
Fürstensaal in the city hall, where the city council otherwise debated, he
took up a topic on which he had delivered a controversial talk ten years
earlier at the Eighth International Healthcare Conference, titled "What

Can Schools Do to Prevent Children from Masturbating?"[117] Around the turn of the century, the question of masturbation came to occupy a "prominent place on the scale of middle-class anxieties."[118] Cohn knew full well that he had chosen a delicate topic for a scientific association. In his introductory remarks, he therefore said he hoped the audience would understand his efforts "to discuss this question, which [was] certainly not appetizing but not, as a result, any less important, from all sides." Yet he could not have asked for a better audience, he said, as this one, to which belonged "doctors and teachers and officials."[119] The audience had barely recovered from the fact that Cohn would be speaking not in general about the "sexual education of schoolchildren" but specifically about masturbation, when the ophthalmologist confronted them with the thesis "that there is no one at all who has never masturbated at some time."[120] While "the effects of masturbation in relation to tabes dorsalis and mental exhaustion have been exaggerated," there were nevertheless numerous eye diseases that led Cohn to the fact that patients "masturbate intensely."[121]

In view of the presumed health risks, Cohn made four demands. Teachers should prevent schoolchildren from masturbating in class or at recess. Moreover, teachers should inform their pupils of the "harmfulness" of masturbation, even though "the teachers would rather avoid the dirty topic altogether." Third, he pleaded for a principal-witness regulation, namely, that pupils who "report[ed] mutual masturbation" be assured that they would not be punished. Fourth, he demanded that the parents of schoolchildren be informed in writing and verbally about the topic and urged to explain the facts of life to their children early.[122]

Cohn's one-and-a-half-hour talk was followed by nearly four hours of discussion among Breslau's most eminent men of learning and prominent guardians of bourgeois respectability. The interest was so great that the city's arbiters of sexual propriety decided to continue their debate on November 14. It is hardly surprising that Cohn's theses were controversial. Many speakers argued that Cohn had exaggerated how widespread masturbation was; others asserted that schools should inform children of the facts of life only when they were over fourteen years old; some wanted to leave that to the parents entirely since they did not consider it an appropriate topic for school. Yet it is remarkable what a motley crew of learned men this was. Two protestant ministers spoke, including Presidial Senior Councilor (*Oberpräsidialrat*) Georg Michaelis (1857–1936), who would serve as imperial chancellor (*Reichskanzler*) in 1917; the pastor of the Breslau free church, Gustav Tschirn, and three distinguished teachers, including the *Realschule* principal and future rector of the Elisabeth-Gymnasium, Franz Wiedemann, and the municipal school inspector Hermann Hippauf.[123] The largest group was the physicians, which included several well-known Jews: Robert Asch (1859–1929), son of "old Asch" and a renowned obstetrician who would assist at the birth of Fritz Stern, his great-nephew, in 1926; the gynecologist and magistrate Ernst Fränkel (1844–1921); the aforementioned Joseph Jacobi; and two general practitioners, Martin Chotzen and Julius Samosch.[124] Of the non-Jewish physicians present, the university professors Buchwald and Tietze participated in the discussion, as did the director of the Breslau mental asylum, Clemens Neisser.[125] There was no trace of distance between the Jewish physicians and the other men of learning during these two-day, "unusually stimulating discussions" (Robert Asch). The open interaction seems to have been quite natural, at least natural enough for Michaelis to have defended the main speaker against the criticism that Cohn had exaggerated how widespread masturbation was: "I beg you," the future imperial chancellor said, "to think of your own youth and to examine yourself before God and your conscience. I am firmly convinced that if we now, here in this gathering, now at this hour, all agreed to write down silently and unobserved the word 'Yes' or 'No' on a slip of paper, . . . we would find that the statistics" would confirm Cohn's theses.[126]

5. Exceptionally Close: Friendships between Jews and Other Breslauers

How close the social interaction was among club members outside the club, and whether private friendships developed above and beyond mere membership in a club, is difficult to determine. Also, due to the nature of the sources, it is possible to investigate friendships only in the upper-middle and middle classes. In contrast, for lower-middle- and lower-class Breslauers there are sources concerning their marriage circles but not their friendship circles. Marion Kaplan in particular has argued that the number of contacts between Jews and other Germans declined as the interactions became more familiar. "Perhaps," in the sphere of private sociability, there was a "hardening of the lines between majority and minority." Since the cultivation of familial bonds required much energy, there often was little time left over for friendships. Precisely in the Jewish middle class, according to Kaplan, there was a desire to keep "to themselves," though the fear of rejection may also have played a role. "Of course, you had Christian acquaintances, such as colleagues of my father," a Jewish woman from Königsberg recalled, "but certainly not friends."[127]

Nevertheless there were friendships between Jews and other Breslauers, some close and others superficial. An early example is the friendship between an odd pair, Karl von Holtei (1798–1880) and Max Kurnik (1819–81). Holtei had made a name for himself in the 1820s and 1830s as a writer for the theater, but, disappointed with the 1848 Revolution, he became a conservative monarchist and from 1850 on defended the Silesian landed nobility and the provincial idyll. By contrast, Kurnik was one of the leading left-wing liberal journalists in Breslau from 1850 on; he founded the first telegraph office in Silesia, worked for many years as a theater critic for the *Schlesische Zeitung* and then the *Breslauer Zeitung*, and ultimately, from 1872 on, headed the progressive *Schlesische Presse*, which was published by Salo Schottländer's publishing house. The Protestant Holtei moved back to his hometown in the mid-1860s and spent his last years in the Catholic monastery of the Brothers of Charity, where his "good friends"—Kurnik and his wife—regularly visited him.[128] Even as early as the late 1850s, Theodor Mommsen and Jacob Bernays had a remarkable friendship. Mommsen esteemed Bernays's stupendous erudition. Several times a day, the Breslau university professor visited his colleague at the Jewish-Theological Seminary to ask him for advice and help. "I really don't have very stimulating contacts here," Mommsen wrote in 1856 about his situation in Breslau, "except for Bernays, who is always stimulating and repelling at the same time. . . . Nevertheless, we are very good friends, and I really have all possible respect for him, and by no means simply due to his erudition." Still, there remained a considerable distance between them. "That purely human ease on which everything is ultimately based," Mommsen added, "is not there and never will be."[129]

Many testimonies from the 1870s and early 1880s suggest that from the late 1860s on private contacts grew closer. Among the regular house-guests of the Gleiwitz-born merchant Wilhelm Silbergleit (1823–1881) and his wife, Seraphine, née Kern, in the 1870s was their neighbor, the historian and leading National Liberal Richard Roepell. "Those were wonderful debates at the Sunday luncheon with our cousin and more distantly related guests," recalled Anna Silbergleit thirty years later on the occasion of the seventieth birthday of her mother, Seraphine. Roepell was not at all the token Protestant in an otherwise exclusively Jewish circle: "The one who appeared most often and as a loyal family friend was Lunge, the district court judge and world traveler. For our parents, this friendship was one of the oldest household fixtures and began for him [Silbergleit] in his student years, when our parents, as a young married couple, moved into his [Roepell's] parents' house. That skinny little man, with his Biedermeier gallantry . . . was really a funny character who was known throughout the city. . . . As for the rest, he proved himself to be a loyal friend of the family at all times."[130] Marie von Forckenbeck, the wife of the lord mayor of Breslau, also maintained friendly relations with middle-class Jews until her death in 1876. She reported extensively to her husband, Max von Forckenbeck, who lived mostly in Berlin when the Reichstag was in session, about her social life in Breslau. In February 1874, she visited the wife of the Breslau garrison commander, General Tümpling; in March, she attended a large ball, which the city council chairman Georg Friedrich Lewald (1828–78) hosted, and received Leo Molinari and his wife. Finally, in February 1876, she and her daughters attended "a dance party at [Isidor] Friedenthal's," the long-time city councilor and chairman of the chamber of commerce.[131]

Close friendships developed in the 1870s particularly among left-wing liberal local politicians. That between Martin Kirschner (1842–1912) and Georg Pick (1847–93) can serve as an example here. In October 1873, the Breslau city council elected the Protestant Kirschner—previously he had been a county-court judge in Nakel, a city in the north of the province of Posen—to the post of salaried magistrate (*Stadtrat*). In May 1879, the city councilors appointed the future lord mayor of Berlin and militant left-wing liberal to the position of syndic of the City of Breslau.[132] Three years earlier, the Breslau Jew Georg Pick, son of the merchant Heinrich Pick, had become his colleague. On June 29, 1876, he became the first Jew that the city parliament had ever elected to the post of salaried magistrate of the Oder metropolis.[133] In the course of their work together in the Breslau magistracy, a close friendship developed between Pick and Kirschner, which was also facilitated by the fact that they lived barely a five-minute walk apart. In 1881, Pick lived at Schweidnitzer Stadtgraben 16b, about 100 meters east of the New Synagogue, and Kirschner lived at Tauenzienstrasse 1, roughly 50 meters southwest of his church. Their friendship continued even after Kirschner had requested his discharge in August 1879 in order to establish himself as a lawyer in Breslau.[134] In any event, when Georg Pick married the nine-years-younger Anna Sachs, daughter of the banker Siegmund Sachs and his wife, Ottilie, née Immerwahr, he chose Martin Kirschner as his "best man" at the civil wedding.[135]

Although an anti-Semitic mood had developed around 1890 in segments of the Breslau bourgeoisie, there continued to be close friendships between Jews and other Breslauers. Toward the end of the 1890s,
Max Born (b. 1882) met Ilse Späth, daughter of the principal pastor of
the Elisabeth Church, Hermann Späth. Every two weeks the two played
music together. "She was a pretty pastor's daughter," Born recalled almost fifty years later. "I wonder if she was even slightly in love with me
for a little while." Despite their friendship, however, a residual distance
remained between the two. A flirtation would have been possible, said
Born, but it would have "destroyed our musical comradeship." On the
other hand, a "serious involvement with a girl from a pious Protestant
family" would have been "against all my instincts and convictions." "I
was welcomed warmly in the pastor's house, but nevertheless found the
atmosphere strange."[136] By contrast, a close relationship between two
young men was less complicated. For instance, Hans Trentin (1866–
1926) and Alfred Kerr (1867–1947) had a close, lifelong friendship, which
even continued after Kerr had risen to be a feared Berlin theater critic.
Both had attended the Elisabeth-Gymnasium together and graduated
in 1887. Trentin, a captain's son born in the district of Pless in Upper Silesia, studied law and in 1907 became deputy mayor, an office he held
until his death. However, Trentin was more a bohemian than a mayor.
Since around 1900 he had lived "in sin" (*wilde Ehe*) with a woman from a
working-class family. Even though it was no secret in Breslau, he was able
to marry her only after the November revolution because he otherwise
would have risked his post as deputy mayor.[137] It is hard to say how representative these friendships were.[138] Yet the private relations between
Jews and other Breslauers are hardly surprising when one considers just
how many opportunities there were for them to meet one another in
daily life, say, at school or on the street. So perhaps it is not remarkable
that there were many friendships between Jews, on the one hand, and
Protestants and Catholics, on the other, but only that there were not
more of them and that in many of these friendships a residual distance
and detachment continued to be felt.

6. From Subculture to Situational Ethnicity

Particularly in the late German Empire, many Breslau Jews were active
in both general and Jewish associational life. They were not faced with
the choice of deciding to move in either general or inter-Jewish circles.
Their identity as Jews was neither all encompassing nor exclusive, but

rather situational and part of a plurality of identities. A comparison of membership lists from eight Jewish and fifteen general clubs in Breslau from the period after the turn of the century makes clear that more than half of all Jewish men (52%) who were members of at least one Jewish club were at the same time members of at least one general club; many even belonged to several general clubs (tables 25 and 26).[139] At the beginning of the German Empire, the proportion of Jewish men simultaneously active in Jewish and general associational life was still nearly 30%, as attested by a comparison of membership lists from three Jewish and eight general clubs. There may still have been remnants of a Jewish subculture around 1870, a space for social contacts for those Jews who did not otherwise participate in general associational life because they were denied access or preferred to keep to themselves. However, since this comparison of clubs at the beginning and the end of the German Empire considered only a small portion of all Jewish and general clubs, the proportion of Breslau Jews who were simultaneously active in Jewish and general association life was actually much larger. It is safe to assume that already around 1870 every other Breslau Jew who belonged to a Jewish club was also active in general associational life. After the turn of the century, this proportion probably rose to approximately 70%.

Unlike the notion of situational ethnicity, concepts that emphasize the closedness of inter-Jewish sociability do not do justice to the plurality of Jewish identity formation.[140] The notions of subculture and milieu do not help one to gain an adequate understanding of the patterns of sociability followed by many Breslau Jews. Precisely for middle-class Jews it was natural to belong simultaneously to Jewish and general clubs. In the 1870s, Hermann Auerbach (1831–1916), a wealthy, Breslau-born merchant with an annual income of over 40,000 marks, was a member of the Gesellschaft der Freunde, the Israelitische Kranken- und Verpflegungs-Anstalt und Beerdigungsgesellschaft, on the one hand, and the Frauen-Verein zur Speisung und Bekleidung der Armen (Women's Association for the Feeding and Clothing of the Poor) and the Humboldt-Verein, on the other. During the German Empire, Auerbach remained true to himself. On the one hand, he joined more Jewish clubs, such as the Gesellschaft der Brüder, the Centralverein deutscher Staatsbürger jüdischen Glaubens, and the Verein "Israelitisches Mädchenheim" ("Jewish Girls' Home" Association) in 1891, and supported with generous donations Jewish clubs such as the Israelitische Kranken- und Verpflegungs-Anstalt und Beerdigungsgesellschaft; on the other hand, he joined more general clubs, such as the Verein der vereinigten sechs Kleinkinder-Bewahr-Anstalten and the Riesengebirgsverein.[141] Even Auerbach's will preserved the complexity of his identity. While he designated the City of Breslau as his sole heir, he also required that a large portion of his legacy be used to establish the Hermann Auerbach'sche Stiftung für Waisenkinder (Hermann Auerbach Foundation for Orphans). As he wrote in his will, Auerbach wanted "to help, in keeping with the demands of true humanity and tolerance, to put an end to the (private and public) life-damaging persecution and discrimination, which unfortunately persist[ed] in a large segment of the people, of and against those fellow citizens who belong[ed] to a different religion." That is why he wanted to establish an institution for orphans that would be under the city's supervision and in which "no specific religious instruction" might be given, but "instead only the principles of general ethics, of humanity and tolerance, which [were] common to all religions present in Germany, [would] be taught."[142]

Such simultaneous participation in general and Jewish associational life can be illustrated by way of Louis Burgfeld (1828–1912), a *rentier* born in Rosenberg, Upper Silesia. Burgfeld lived at both the beginning and the end of the German Empire at Tauenzienplatz 8 and thus was a neighbor of Hermann Auerbach's, who lived in both 1880 and 1906 at Tauenzienplatz 4.[143] Like Auerbach, Burgfeld had belonged since 1855 to the Gesellschaft der Freunde and since 1867 to the Gesellschaft der Brüder; he was also a member of the Israelitische Kranken- und Verpflegungs-Anstalt und Beerdigungsgesellschaft and the Verein zur Verbreitung der Wissenschaft des Judenthums.[144] At the same time, Burgfeld was a member of the Frauen-Verein zur Speisung und Bekleidung der Armen, the Kaufmännischer Verein zu Breslau, the Humboldt-Verein, and, from 1873 on, the liberal Horus Lodge.[145] As he grew older, Burgfeld became even more active in Jewish and general associational life. From 1879 to 1882 and from 1893 to 1901, he was on the board of directors of the Industrieschule für Israelitsche Mädchen (Industry School for Jewish Girls) and the Israelitische Waisenanstalt (Jewish Orphanage), and belonged to the Verein "Israelitisches Mädchenheim" and the Verein für jüdische Geschichte und Literatur (Society for Jewish History and Literature). As a candidate of the Liberaler Verein der Synagogen-Gemeinde Breslau (Liberal Club of the Breslau Synagogue Community), he was on the board of governors of the Jewish *Gemeinde* from 1894 on and in 1898 took over the chairmanship of the *Armenkommission,* joined the Breslau chapter of the Centralverein deutscher Staatsbürger jüdischen Glaubens early on, and was one of the chief sponsors of the reconstruction of the

Jewish Hospital, whose eye clinic he cofinanced.[146] Moreover, Burgfeld not only remained a member of the aforementioned clubs but also joined the Riesengebirgsverein and the Bohn'scher Gesangsverein.[147]

Auerbach and Burgfeld are typical of many Breslau Jews who participated self-confidently in general associational life without denying their Jewish identity. Indeed, they counted among those who contributed to the revival of Jewish associational life in the 1890s. The *Allgemeine Zeitung des Judenthums* noted with satisfaction in March 1903 that, in recent years in Germany, "hundreds of [Jewish] clubs" had been formed. The motto "A bit more distance, a bit more Jewishness!" has "proven successful for us over the last decade not only in the religious sphere." Yet no new Jewish subculture had developed as a result, the paper said. Most Jews continued to be active in general associational life. "Anyone who is familiar with the charity and educational activities—which go beyond the middle classes—and their numerous clubs and associations," the paper continued, "knows that, thank God, there can be no talk whatsoever of a nascent, self-imposed isolation of the Jews."[148]

In summary, then, in the German Empire the degree of the inclusion of Breslau Jews in the city's associational life was high. From the 1850s on, the majority of Breslau clubs opened themselves to Jews. In many instances, they played an important role in the founding of new clubs, which broke with early middle-class anti-Semitism. From about 1870 on, the large majority of Breslau clubs were open to Jews: athletic, cultural, and other kinds of social clubs, the liberal Breslau Freemason lodges, as well as the professional and vocational associations. Clubs, such as the Zwinger-Gesellschaft, that continued to exclude Jews became increasingly the subject of public criticism. In the early 1870s, it seemed to be only a question of time before all Breslau clubs, except Catholic or Protestant religious clubs, would admit Jews.

In the course of the German Empire, a growing number of Breslau Jews played a prominent role in general associational life and in Jewish clubs. After the turn of the century, roughly two-thirds of all Jews who belonged to a Jewish club were also active in general associational life. That supports the thesis of situational ethnicity and shows that Breslau Jews by no means had to deny their Jewishness in order to participate in general associational life. Judging from the simultaneous involvement of Jews in Jewish and in general clubs, the inclusion of Jews in general associational life peaked around 1900 and not, as is frequently assumed, in the 1860s.[149]

Although more and more Breslau clubs opened themselves to Jews in the 1860s, the tide turned in the late 1880s. Now anti-Semitic members attempted to push Breslau Jews out of their clubs. Although all the anti-Semitic attempts failed and almost all clubs continued to admit Jews, Breslau associational life had become polarized in the late 1880s and early 1890s over the "Jewish question." Nevertheless, anti-Semitism did not become the social norm in Breslau associational life prior to 1914. Rather, it was a "cultural code" that signaled membership in the conservative milieu, which included parts of the Silesian nobility and the conservative wing of the Breslau bourgeoisie empathetic with or otherwise close to state institutions.

Since anti-Semitism in Breslau associational life was limited to narrowly circumscribed social groups, the widespread thesis that "on the eve of the First World War" "anti-Semitism flourished in the clubs" seems doubtful. In any case, one can hardly claim that the anti-Semitic mood of the conservative wing of the Breslau bourgeoisie was "an early preparatory phase . . . for the mass support" for National Socialist annihilation policies.[150] The claim that "the foul stench of anti-Semitism" penetrated "all spheres of social life" in the prewar years, or that "bourgeois society" was increasingly divided into "non-Jewish and Jewish associational life," finds no support in Breslau.[151] Although in associational life there was considerable contact between Jews and other Breslauers, which made possible a close coexistence, that contact can be characterized only with qualification as "unproblematic and normal," as Thomas Nipperdey has done.[152] The analysis of friendships clearly shows that even where there was more intimate contact between Jews and other Breslauers, some residual distance remained on both sides. That probably was most often the case in the upper-middle and middle classes, and less so in the lower-middle and lower classes. In any event, this supposition is suggested by the analysis of Christian-Jewish marriages in the next chapter.

3

Jewish-Christian Marriages, the "New Woman," and the Situational Ethnicity of Breslau Jews

In most models of ethnic relations, the so-called mixed marriage (*Mischehe*) marks the final step toward integration. Traditional, linear concepts of assimilation equate mixed marriages with total assimilation. The more external barriers are dismantled, the fewer the reservations about intermarriages become; the more open the private sphere is for friendships across religious and ethnic divides, the more likely intermarriages become.[1] However stimulating and fruitful these linear concepts of integration and assimilation may be, they nevertheless have only a limited usefulness in a historical analysis of marriages between Jews and other Breslauers. The traditional concepts ignore the gendered nature of intermarriages and cannot do justice to the plural identities of Breslauers who intermarried.

Jewish-Christian marriages are an indication that Jews and other Breslauers considered their relations perfectly natural. Whereas relations at club meetings may have been formally distant, those who married were prepared to share daily life. While in the presumably more widespread, short-term love affairs between Jews and non-Jews friendships were dissolved just as quickly as they were formed and those involved sought to keep their relationship secret, the partners in Jewish-Christian marriages chose to make their bond both permanent and public. The special character of marriage as the most intimate form of a "society of two" (*Gesellschaft zu zweien*) derives from its being a mixture of the private and the public. Whereas men and women could conceal a "flirtation" or dalliance, a marriage had consequences for their families, their friends, and their social life.

At no time in imperial Germany was it considered "normal" for Jews to marry other Breslauers. Such marriages differed remarkably from those within the Jewish community, being regarded by most contemporaries as a curiosity at best. Nor would the fourfold increase in the percentage of mixed marriages during the Wilhelmian era alter this perception. Although in the Weimar Republic the percentage of marriages between Jews and non-Jews remained high, the mixed marriage continued to be stigmatized as exceptional, unusual, and ultimately inappropriate. Because anti-Semites in imperial Germany and the Weimar Republic, and especially National Socialists, regarded marriages between Jews and other Germans as particularly reprehensible, such marriages came to be an important focus of enmity, especially because the daily lives of such couples exposed the senselessness of the anti-Semitic utopia of an "Aryan *Volksgemeinschaft*." However courageously many non-Jewish women and men may have tried to protect their spouses after January 1933, as of that date such marriages had no future in Germany.[2]

The historiography on German Jewry has usually discussed Christian-Jewish marriages in the context of the debate on the degree of Jewish assimilation. Like conversion to Christianity, mixed marriages have been regarded as an expression of "radical assimilation."[3] For example, in her pioneering study on Jewish women in imperial Germany, Marion Kaplan separates her discussion of Jewish marriage strategies from her cursory remarks on Christian-Jewish marriages. According to the dominant view, those who intermarried severed all ties with the Jewish community just as much as those who converted to Christianity. Although Jacob Toury concedes that the Jewish-Christian marriage was a sign of "complete social integration," he argues that it necessarily presupposed the "ultimate rejection of Judaism."[4] The sole point of contention between Zionist historians and their "liberal" critics was and is whether the rate of mixed marriages really jeopardized the future of German Jews. In any case, marriage between Jews and other Germans continues to have a bad reputation to this day.

In contrast to the traditional focus on assimilation, Kerstin Meiring has recently argued that intermarriages, too, attest to "the transformation of German Jews into an ethnic community with a new, . . . vital identity."[5] This perspective will be engaged in what follows in the present chapter. What holds for research into relations between Jews and other Germans in general applies equally to Christian-Jewish marriages

in particular: It is time for a reevaluation that avoids the dead ends of
the older discussions about the extent of assimilation or German-Jewish
symbiosis. Rather than being limited to a discussion of the nexus between assimilation and the rising number of marriages between Jews
and other Breslauers, the attempt is made here to link the history of
Jewish-Christian marriages with the history of gender relations (especially with the rise of the "New Woman"), the concomitant "debour-
geoisement" (*Entbürgerlichung*) of marriage patterns in Breslau's Jewish
middle class, and the history of the family.[6] Only at the end of this
chapter will previous debates about mixed marriages be addressed; at
that point, the argument will be made that, unlike in the case of conversion, marrying a Christian should not be equated with a rejection of
Jewishness.

The analysis of marriages between Jews and other Breslauers
will proceed in four steps. First, the task will be to demonstrate how the
historiographic debate on mixed marriages reproduces contemporaneous discourse and stereotypes. Second, a comparative social history of
both mixed and intra-Jewish marriages follows in which social origin,
age at marriage, the living circumstances of the marriage partners (particularly of women), and the role of the witnesses to a marriage are analyzed. Third, it will be argued that the increase in marriages between
Jews and other Breslauers after the turn of the twentieth century was
bound up with the rise of the New Woman. Fourth and finally, the discussion will return to the question raised at the outset of this chapter
and consider what Jewish-Christian marriages can tell us about relations between Jews and other Breslauers and about the changing nature
of the integration of Jews in German society.

1. The Negative Image of the "Mixed Marriage" in Contemporary Debates and Historical Scholarship

The mixed marriage contrasts starkly with nineteenth- and twentieth-
century ideals of purity and homogeneity. Any marriage between two
partners of different religious, ethnic, or racial groups ran counter to
the impulse to classify individuals unambiguously and to incarcerate
them within the "enclosure of a singular identity."[7] The mixed marriage became a symbol in which loathing and fascination went hand in
hand. The heated discussions about marriages between Catholics and
Protestants and between Jews and Christians in Germany, or between
whites and blacks in the United States, are rooted in such fantasies.[8]

Considered against the backdrop of both the ideal of purity and homogeneity and the desire to classify, the initially seemingly bizarre contemporary comments about marriages between Jews and other Germans begin to make sense, comments quite similar to those about mixed
marriages between Catholics and Protestants. For many Jewish and
non-Jewish contemporaries, the Jewish-Christian marriage symbolized
moral decay. When an impoverished aristocrat or a dashing but poor
lieutenant married a wealthy Jewish woman, they made the front page
of *Simplicissimus* in the form of a satirical cartoon.[9] The paper's treatment of the subject merely played on common stereotypes. Shortly after
the introduction of civil marriages between Jews and other Germans,
Emanuel Schreiber, a well-known Reform rabbi and former student of
Abraham Geiger, condemned such unions as typically being marriages
for money. Although he was not opposed to such marriages on principle, he claimed that it would be a long time before "mixed marriages
would also be happy ones." "As long as Christian barons, officers, and
artists hunt for wealthy Jewesses only in order to obtain the means with
which to hold their insistent creditors at bay or to enable them to continue to live prodigal lives more easily; as long as Jews are sought after
only for their money . . . , neither we nor any unprejudiced person—be
he Jew or Christian—can welcome the mixed marriage as a blessing."[10]

The Orthodox weekly *Der Israelit* likewise stressed the connection between mixed marriages and the dissolution of traditional gender roles.
The fact that young, unmarried women went "to the theater and to concerts, balls, and celebrations" and sought to gain access to the public
sphere reflected the "complete lack of religious education" among German Jews. To illustrate this "moral neglect," the paper's Breslau correspondent filed a sensational report in March 1892 that three young
women from that city's "most respected Jewish families" had been involved in sexual relations with Breslau officers. However, while the correspondent strongly condemned the women's behavior as immoral, he
simultaneously evoked the readers' sexual fantasies by describing the
events in detail. The "young girls . . . entered into thoroughly frivolous,
shocking relationships with several officers." Together, he reported, they
rented a villa in the neighboring town of Kleinburg so that they could
surrender themselves to their "nefarious doings"—assuming, that is,
that "their parents' homes hadn't served this purpose from time to time
already." In view of the dissolution of the gender order, the correspondent continued, "our gaze is involuntarily drawn back to the halcyon
days when morality and chastity formed the basis of true Jewish

womanhood," when young women avoided public spaces and "lived quiet, retiring, virginal lives in Jewish households under the watchful eye of their mothers and knew nothing of life beyond that which would prepare them for their future, circumscribed field of activity."[11] The more that Jewish leaders, such as the Orthodox Breslau rabbi Ferdinand Rosenthal, praised "familial love" as the "height of each and every national and religious community," the more threatening marriages between Jews and other Germans must seem to them.[12]

In scientific discussions, too, mixed marriages symbolized moral decay. The sexologist Max Marcuse argued that a great number of those who intermarried were "neurotics" and that intermarriages reflected the "psychological degeneracy" of those involved and "doubtless often" ended in "broken families." That the sociologist Werner Sombart also was convinced that children of intermarriages lacked "mental balance" is hardly surprising given his anti-Semitism. Yet even the rabbi and historian Arnold Tänzer and the Jewish doctor-cum-demographer Felix Theilhaber were convinced that the offspring of Jewish-Christian marriages often took up a life of crime.[13] Elsewhere, Theilhaber characterized mixed marriages as one of the "saddest and most mistaken institutions" of his time. Jews who entered into mixed marriages, he maintained, had "little interest in the family as such" but instead used their marriages "to pursue any number of other objectives." "They usually hail from the wealthiest circles," continued the leader of the racist branch of Zionism, "in which intentional or physically preexisting impotence or limited fertility is all too common."[14] The negative stance toward marriage between Jews and other Germans shared by Zionists and Reform Jews, liberal non-Jews and anti-Semites, reflected contemporary anxieties about the shifting gender order, middle-class prejudices about the sex lives of members of the lower classes, especially those of working women,[15] and the middle-class sense of crisis in the early twentieth century.

Further testimony to mixed marriages having functioned as a symbol in an atmosphere pervaded by intimations of crisis is to be found in their portrayal in memoirs written almost exclusively by middle-class Jews. According to Eugen Altmann, the high rate of intermarriage was no indication of a "good relationship," since such "marriages between Christians and Jews had a different basis than one that would have been expedient with regard to the objectives of mixing based on ethical motives." Mixed marriages "were entered into by [representatives of] unequal social categories, where the Jew provided the material advantage." Altmann was so confident of the accuracy of his assessment that he cited what he took to be precise percentages: "In 95 of every 100 cases," it was the "Jewish man who wed a Christian girl, usually his so-called mistress, who in most cases had not so much as set foot in his parents' home until the wedding day."[16] For the Breslau Zionist Willy Cohn, historian and in the 1920s one of the Jewish teachers at the Johannes-Gymnasium, mixed marriages symbolized the "ghastly" character of German left-wing liberalism. "The German Democrats," he recalled in the autobiography he wrote in 1940 and 1941, "were the party of the 'on the one hand,' 'on the other hand.'" Hence, it was "no accident that some Aryan democrats intermarried, for the essence of interracial marriage is also most often inconsistency."[17]

Without concerning itself with the reality of marriages between Jews and other Germans, part of the liberal public welcomed the growing number of Jewish-Christian marriages. In their view such marriages constituted an important step toward the total assimilation of the Jews. Instead of granting German Jews the right to be different, the liberals too shared the dream of a homogeneous nation. The Jews should abandon their resistance to "fusion by marriage," argued the left-wing liberal *Hamburger Fremdenblatt*, mouthpiece of the Progressive Party (*Fortschrittspartei*), in 1894: "The rigid rejection of such fusion" contradicts "the will, which definitely exists among German Jews, to be Germans" and prevents them from "becoming so in their blood as well."[18]

Historians have generally accepted these legends. For example, Monika Richarz has argued that there was a "high incidence of intermarriages between Jewish women and members of the aristocracy"; and Dirk Blasius has blamed the relatively high divorce rate in Jewish-Christian marriages on "a long tradition of instability in Christian-Jewish marriages."[19] Hannah Arendt and, more recently, Todd Endelman have claimed that the growing rate of intermarriage does not support conclusions about relations between Jews and non-Jews, since the majority of the partners in intermarriages whom the statistics classified as Christian were, in fact, converts with Jewish origins.[20] Contrary to Arendt and Endelman but likewise without documentation—for no historical studies were undertaken at the time on the identity of Jews who lived in mixed marriages—Alan Levenson has claimed that intermarriage led to "a severance of ties with the Jewish world."[21] The question therefore remains: What do the archival sources—which include municipal statistics, a quantitative analysis of records from the Breslau registrar's office, and a small number of extant autobiographical testimonies—tell us about the marriages between Jews and other Breslauers?

2. The Social History of Christian-Jewish Marriages

The increase in the number of Christian-Jewish marriages in Breslau mirrored patterns found in other large German cities. Between 1870 and the mid-1920s, the rate of intermarriage in Breslau soared, though it was consistently lower than in Hamburg and Berlin. While between 1876 and 1880 there were only 9 intermarriages for every 100 intra-Jewish marriages, between 1911 and 1915 the number grew to 35.[22] Between 1890 and the early 1920s, the rate of intermarriage quadrupled, rising from 11.2 to 39.2 and in the war years even to 52.8.[23] What is striking here is that in Breslau, unlike in Berlin and in Prussia as a whole, roughly the same number of Jewish women and men married a Christian partner. At any rate, the balanced gender ratio suggests that the increase in the rate of intermarriage cannot be reduced to a demographic surplus of men or women. Jews entered into marriage with other Breslauers because they wanted to marry a non-Jewish partner and not because they had not found a Jewish partner.[24] Between 1880 and 1899, 160 Jewish men and 145 Jewish women intermarried; between 1900 and 1914, 210 and 199 did so, respectively. It was only in the Weimar Republic that predominantly men married a non-Jewish partner: between 1919 and 1929, 426 men entered into a mixed marriage, while only 260 Jewish women did so.[25] The fact that the number of intermarriages increased considerably after the turn of the century indicates that the amicable and intimate relations between Jews and other Breslauers had become more a matter of course.

The history of Christian-Jewish marriages in Breslau contradicts both contemporary stereotypes and much recent historiography. Contrary to Arendt's and Endelman's speculations, such marriages generally involved spouses with exclusively Jewish or Christian backgrounds. Of the more than 350 Christian men and women who intermarried in Breslau between 1905 and 1920, only 20 were Jewish converts to Christianity. Nor were impoverished aristocrats typical candidates for Jewish-Christian marriages. Not one of the more than 600 Christian-Jewish marriages registered in Breslau between 1874 and 1920 involved an aristocrat marrying a Jewish woman. Nor were dashing officers very common; indeed, during the entire imperial era, there were only two recorded cases of such men entering into mixed marriages in Breslau, and only one of them—the Protestant first lieutenant Simundt—married into a respected upper-middle-class Jewish family. In the latter marriage, which took place in March 1882, the bride was Margarete Rosalie Sachs, the Breslau-born daughter of the banker Siegmund Sachs and his wife, Ottilie (née Immerwahr). Admittedly, Simundt himself was likely of Jewish origin, for he was born in Berlin in 1846, the son of the merchant Samuel Simon.[26] The second lieutenant was Otto Köppen, a Protestant who in June 1894 married Maria Elisabeth Eliason, a woman nearly his age. Yet this Christian-Jewish marriage did not accord with the contemporary stereotype either. The bride did not come from a wealthy Jewish family but was the daughter of the merchant Löbel Eliason and his wife, Hannchen (née Windmüller), both of whom had died prior to 1894. In 1876, at the age of sixty-three, her father had commanded a meager annual income of 1,500 marks. Since he had to feed himself, his wife, and their three daughters with this money and had no savings, the Eliason family's finances were modest even before the father's death.[27]

One of the most notable characteristics of Christian-Jewish marriages, but presumably of Protestant-Catholic mixed marriages as well, is that intermarriage was more common in the lower and lower-middle classes than in the middle class.[28] The social history of Jewish-Christian marriages in Breslau between 1874 and 1920 shows that lower- and lower-middle-class Jews—and this was true particularly of Jewish women—chose a Christian partner more frequently than did middle-class Jews. The social origins of Jewish women who married Christians were lower than the social background of those who entered into intra-Jewish marriages. This contrast was particularly pronounced at the beginning of the imperial era, but became noticeably less so after 1890, though it was still evident in 1920 (see table 27). Between 1874 and 1894, the two decades following the introduction of civil marriage, 73% of all Jewish women in intra-Jewish marriages had fathers with middle- or upper-middle-class professions, while 20% came from lower-middle-class families and only 7% from lower-class ones. For the same period, the social origins of the Jewish women who married Christians differed considerably. Of these women, not 73% but only 35% came from middle- or upper-middle-class households, 43% from a lower-middle-class ones, and no less than 17% from lower-class families.

By 1914, but especially during and in the years immediately following the First World War, the differences in social background between

Jewish women who intermarried and those who married Jewish men had begun to narrow. While the origins of women in intra-Jewish marriages remained virtually unchanged until 1920 and 75% of the women came from middle-class families, the percentage of Jewish women who married non-Jews and whose fathers had a middle-class profession rose from 35% at the beginning of the imperial era to over 45% between 1890 and 1910 and finally to 55% during and after the war.

As in the case of profession, the difference in income between those who intermarried and those who entered into intra-Jewish marriages was particularly marked among Jewish women (see table 28).[29] Of the Jewish women who married Christian men between 1874 and 1881 and for whom information on their father's income is available, 60% hailed from working-class families earning less than 1,100 marks annually. Only a quarter came from middle- or upper-middle-class households with a yearly income of more than 2,750 marks. By contrast, Jewish women who married Jewish men generally came from the higher-income brackets: only 13% of their fathers earned less that 1,100 marks annually, while 40% were well-to-do men who brought home between 2,750 and 9,200 marks a year; indeed, a further 20% were very wealthy men, whose yearly earnings exceeded 9,200 marks. At the very top of the economic scale, the contrast is particularly stark. Only one Jewish woman from a very wealthy family entered into a mixed marriage. In September 1876, Rosa Pringsheim—born about 1835 in the city of Oppeln and daughter of the wealthy banker Siegmund Pringsheim, whose income in 1876 was nearly 170,000 marks—married the municipal court judge (*Stadtgerichtsrat*) Bernhard Englaender, who was three years her senior. A convert to Protestantism, Englaender, like his bride, had been born into a Jewish family from Oppeln. Nevertheless, despite his apostasy—a move made most likely so as not to endanger his career in the judiciary—he sought his future wife within the Jewish community, just like those middle-class Jewish men who had remained true to their religion.[30] That practice seems to have been common. In any event, the brothers Albert and Gustav Neisser, two prominent Breslau converts, married women from the Jewish upper-middle class: Albert married Antonie Kauffmann, daughter of the textile manufacturer Julius Kauffmann, from Breslau; Gustav, Elsbeth Silberstein, daughter of the factory owner Philipp Silberstein, from Arnsdorf in the district of Hirschberg.[31]

Similarly, the annual income of Jewish men who married Christian women was considerably less than that of those who wed a Jewish spouse (table 29). In the case of men, it is more instructive to use their own income as a basis for comparison rather than their fathers'. Because of the grooms' more advanced age at marriage, it is difficult to classify their parental households unequivocally since their fathers were often already deceased and many parents did not live in Breslau. Of the Jewish men who married Christian women and could be unequivocally identified based on the tax rolls, only 18% had an annual income of more than 2,750 marks, while 60% fell into the decidedly lower-class bracket of those earning less than 1,100 marks per annum. By contrast, Jewish men in intra-Jewish marriages were clearly better off financially. Among this group, 28% commanded a middle-class income, while the percentage of those earning less than 1,100 marks was about 50%.

Just how unusual Jewish-Christian marriages were among the Jewish upper-middle class becomes clear in view of the only mixed marriage in which the Jewish groom could be classified as wealthy, thus as having an annual income of more than 9,200 marks. Theodor Stahl, born in Breslau around 1813, earned approximately 17,000 marks in 1881. Six years earlier, at the age of sixty-two, he had married Emilie Haertel, then twenty-seven, the Breslau-born daughter of a Protestant gardener. Beyond their considerable age difference, this case is remarkable in that the couple had already lived together prior to their marriage. This strongly suggests that the ceremony in May 1875 represented the legislation of a preexisting common-law marriage—a step that only the introduction of the civil marriage had made possible. Yet another noteworthy aspect of this case is that, whether voluntarily or under pressure from her husband, Emilie Haertel converted to Judaism after the wedding. This clearly contradicts the assumption that for Stahl the decision to enter into a mixed marriage would necessarily have meant the breaking of all his ties to his Jewishness.[32]

Typically men and women who entered into mixed marriages came from lower-class income situations. Thus, it is no coincidence that one can adduce Sara Neumann's family—which served in the foregoing as an example of Jewish poverty in Breslau—also in connection with Jewish-Christian marriages. One of Neumann's youngest children, her daughter Else Rosa, born in Ober-Glogau in the district of Neustadt in 1892, married the Protestant merchant Otto Rudolf Wagner, born in 1885 in Breslau and son of the Reichsbank clerk August Wagner. The Neumanns had meanwhile moved from Hildebrandtstrasse to the nearby cross street Anderssenstrasse, thus continuing to live in the poor Nikolaivorstadt. It was a fifteen-minute walk to the Wagners' house at Schiesswerderstrasse 15 in the western part of the Breslau suburb. Since they were neither neighbors nor coworkers, it is unclear where they met. Perhaps the merchant Otto Wagner knew Else's brother, the shop assistant Martin Neumann. In any case, both families approved of the marriage. One witness to the marriage was Martin Neumann and the other, Wagner's father, August.[33]

Although a higher degree of anti-Semitism among the middle class may partially account for the contrast, the most important reason for the differences in social background of Breslau Jews who entered into a mixed marriage and those who married a Jewish spouse is that middle-class families—whether Jewish, Protestant, or Catholic—followed more deliberate marriage strategies than did lower-class families. Those strategies aimed at maintaining and augmenting cultural, social, and economic capital; it was primarily middle-class men and women who had family fortunes to win or lose in marriage. In his novel, *Jenny Treibel* (1892), Theodor Fontane ridiculed middle-class marriage practices through the character of the *Gymnasium* teacher Schmidt: "They are continually liberalizing and sentimentalizing, but it is all a farce; when the time comes to show one's colors, gold is all that counts."[34] No doubt young middle- or upper-middle-class men and women were afforded some measure of choice. But their room to maneuver was limited by their parents, relatives, and friends, who controlled the young people's ability to initiate such marriages. Anna Auerbach—born about 1863 as one of five daughters of Wilhelm Silbergleit, the wealthy industrialist (income in 1881: 36,000 marks) and cofounder of the upper Silesian mining town of Bismarckhütte—recalled in 1905 that even as children it had been impossible for her sisters and her "to choose acquaintances independently, let alone friends." In her father's house, "a brusqueness dominated the daily routine that can only be described as extremely aristocratic," which only intensified "as [the] girls approached marriageable age."[35]

In this sense, middle-class marriages continued to be arranged, despite the ideal of marriage for love. Even as the open practice of marrying for money to accumulate capital fell increasingly into disrepute, the politics of marriage played an important role in the middle class's efforts to establish itself within society, for in middle-class marriages it was not only money that circulated but also the social standing of the families involved. In each case, Peter Gay notes, "courting rituals, parental roles, financial considerations formed distinct amalgams." Yet well into the early twentieth-century certain patterns prevailed. To a far greater extent than in lower-class families, the middle-class marriage was integrated into a system of "strategic marriage alliances" and was also meant to ensure and increase a family's economic capital and, above all, its social stand-ing.[36] Not intending to deny the significance of "economic motives in the search for a marriage partner," Anne-Charlott Trepp has recently argued that for the early nineteenth century the topos of the "arranged marriage" obscures the "real scope of action and choices available to women in looking for a husband." Trepp rightly warns against falling prey to the overly simplistic image of "polarized gender stereotypes." Nevertheless, her own analysis shows that even in the early nineteenth century the ability to choose could only be exercised on a playing field on which parents and relatives defined and enforced the rules.[37]

With Christian-Jewish marriages still a relatively recent phenome-non, members of the middle class were wary of taking the risky road of intermarriage. Anna Auerbach wrote of her and her four sisters' mar-riages in the 1870s and 1880s, "For each of us daughters, the prospect of marrying a converted Jew was unlikely, and a Christian of German blood thoroughly out of the question."[38] "Marrying out of faith was not done," Steffi Granby (née Klinenberger), daughter of a Breslau factory owner, recalled of her own generation.[39]

Proof that middle-class intra-Jewish marriages, unlike mixed mar-riages, did not formalize a romantic love relationship but amounted to strategic marriage alliances between two families is provided especially by the central role of the dowry. As long as middle-class marriages re-mained a way to secure and enhance social standing, Jewish, Protestant, and Catholic middle-class parents tried to supervise and restrict the love and sexual lives of their sons and especially their daughters to a much higher degree than did lower-class parents.[40] Because middle-class par-ents kept a tight, "loving-caring" rein on their children, it was very un-likely that someone from that class would find a partner without his or her parents' approval.[41] With good reason, Mary Jo Maynes has ques-tioned the view that, due to their poverty, the sexuality of members of the lower classes was "necessarily freer, more spontaneous, or somehow less [a] product of their society and culture" than middle-class sexual-ity.[42] Nevertheless, unlike the children of middle-class Jews, working-class Jewish men and women had more chances to establish intimate and possibly even sexual relations with other Breslauers—whether at work, dances, or fairs, or thanks to neighborly contact—something their par-ents hardly could have prevented, let alone supervised.[43] As a young man at the turn of the century, Adolf Riesenfeld, the son of a middle-class Jewish family, was at once fascinated and repelled by the gender relations among working-class men and women of his age. "On muggy evenings,

I would often stroll along the promenade [on the Liebichshöhe]," he recalled in October 1917. "On pleasant evenings, thousands of couples
would be wandering up and down it. Many men and girls also came
alone, searching for contact and often finding it. Most of them were
salesgirls and seamstresses, less often factory workers or housemaids.
There was also the occasional prostitute, mostly of the second-class variety. The better set avoided the streets at this time, where behavior was
not exactly always irreproachable."[44]

The importance of dowries further limited the possibilities for Jewish, Protestant, and Catholic middle-class women and men to choose a
partner on their own. The fact that working-class Jewish women were
much more likely to marry Christians than middle-class women provides further confirmation of this situation. As late as the early Weimar
Republic, dowries continued to play a critical role in intra-Jewish marriages. Jewish fathers with a moderate income could provide their
daughters with only a limited dowry. Due to their fathers' poverty, it was
difficult for these women to find a Jewish husband. And yet, unlike
middle-class Jewish women, working-class Jewish women were also freer
to choose their partners. Whereas middle-class fathers could use an often
considerable dowry to control whom their daughters would marry,
fathers of lower-class women lacked this means of exerting pressure.
The greater the dowry, the less room there was for individual agency.[45]

The Riesenfeld family of Breslau provides an interesting illustration
of the marriage strategies used by the city's Jewish middle class. The
father, who was born in 1853, was the owner of a successful shipping
company; around 1905, he earned roughly 20,000 marks a year. In
spring 1901, his eighteen-year-old daughter, Grete, met the man who
would become her first husband, the thirty-five-year-old Moritz Goldmann, at her uncle Samuel's house in Oppeln. In his memoirs, her
brother Adolf comments ironically that his future brother-in-law's visit
to their Oppeln relatives had "by chance" coincided with hers. Grete
must have made a good impression on Goldmann, her brother recalls,
"for since father's material assent"—that is, the dowry—"found favor
with . . . Goldmann, the bonds of Hymen were eagerly tied by the relatives. And as Grete's primary interest lay in soon becoming a bride, . . .
she put up no resistance. Indeed, she had all the less reason to do so as
Goldmann lived in Berlin and purportedly had an income of 10,000–
15,000 marks. So, for the most part, an agreement was already reached
before the marriage candidates had even met a second time."[46]

The marriage, which began in the autumn of 1901, had already fallen apart by January 1902. The Riesenfeld family was then left with a problem: a divorced nineteen-year-old daughter who was also expecting a child. It was, Adolf recalled, "the particular desire of our parents that Grete, after the failure of her first marriage, should find a new mate." This time the role of the marriage broker was played not by the uncle but by a "business and gambling associate" of his father's. This associate had a distant relative living in Vienna, a "university-trained pharmacist" who wanted to go into business for himself and hoped to obtain the necessary start-up capital "from other quarters." Grete's father offered the prospective son-in-law a dowry of 30,000 marks, in compensation for marrying a divorced woman with a child from her first marriage. This was, as Adolf Riesenfeld rightly observed, a "quite considerable sum for a young man with a monthly income of some 300 crowns [approximately 250 marks]." After the financial negotiations were completed at the end of 1904, Adolf Riesenfeld continued, "this gentleman then came to my parents' home and was invited to dinner." He made a "good impression on [their] parents and everyone else," including his sister Grete, so that nothing more stood in the way of her second marriage.[47]

Similar conditions governed Adolf Riesenfeld's own choice of a spouse. Although many of his friends went to the more fashionable Reifsche School of Dance, at which both Jewish and non-Jewish middle-class children took lessons together, Riesenfeld chose to attend the exclusively Jewish Baersche School of Dance. "From the 'dragons' perch,' the mothers looked on," recalled Willy Cohn, a contemporary of Riesenfeld's at the Baersche school, and stared with "gaping eyes" at the wooing efforts of the sons of the Jewish middle class. It was in this atmosphere that in 1904 the twenty-year-old salesclerk Riesenfeld met his future wife, the then sixteen-year-old "Mieze" Eckmann. "A lively girl," he remembered in his autobiography, "not at all pretty, but charming and quite reserved"—qualities he found "particularly attractive." After paying a "formal call on the Eckmann family," Riesenfeld inquired, to his satisfaction, about the financial situation of his prospective father-in-law, Leopold Eckmann, a junior partner "at the thriving S. Sternberg Fertilizer Company."[48] However, as long as Riesenfeld continued to earn his living as a traveling salesman, the two could not become officially engaged. Only in 1909, when he became a partner in his father's firm, was it possible to announce their engagement. The Eckmanns offered him a dowry of 15,000 marks, which, after their wedding in November of that year, was partly invested in his family's shipping company and partly used to furnish the young couple's apartment.[49]

Nevertheless, there was also a gender-specific difference between the two siblings' experiences. While for Grete Riesenfeld, or Goldmann, premarital sexual relations of any kind were out of the question, her brother, like other middle-class young men, was allowed to indulge in sexual encounters from puberty until marriage.[50] Between 1905 and 1909, during his extended engagement, Adolf had a string of love affairs with Jewish and non-Jewish working-class women. Despite his "true and deep attachment to Mieze," Riesenfeld recalled, for him it was perfectly natural that he should also seek "adventures elsewhere." Already at sixteen, during his apprenticeship at his father's company, he began a "dalliance" with a young woman, whose father worked at the firm. Forty years later, Adolf noted, "[It was] still a mystery to me to this day what I could have talked about with these girls and later on in the numerous other relationships I had with proletarian women." Such sexual excursions down the social ladder were far from uncommon. It seems likely, in fact, that, at the turn of the century, the ever-growing presence of commercial leisure and the remaking of the working class by increasing numbers of female casual laborers brought middle-class men into increasing contact with their social inferiors.[51] "Nearly all my friends," Riesenfeld notes, "had such relationships, and most of these girls belonging to another class were very adept at assuming the exterior social polish that enabled them to circulate with considerable confidence in a completely different milieu."[52]

Not all these women were Christian. Around 1905, Riesenfeld met Dora Weiss, a seventeen-year-old Jewish worker at an umbrella factory located next to his office. After the two had gone on numerous trips together to "the theater, Liebich's Music Hall, cafés, and [on] evening strolls," the young woman's parents invited him "to dinner on a Jewish holiday." However, since her family lived in "very modest circumstances," as Riesenfeld recalled, their "efforts to bring me into her family in no way accorded with my intentions. I therefore informed her straight out that there could be no talk of marriage, as I myself was already engaged." Thereafter, Dora's parents forbade her to see him and furthermore reproached the young man by letter. However, neither then in 1906 nor in hindsight did Adolf Riesenfeld appear to suffer any pangs of conscience: "It was already clear to me then," he wrote in 1942, "that Dora's mother had encouraged this harmless flirtation in the hopes that I would commit myself to her daughter in some more serious way." In any event, her parents would certainly have welcomed "an engagement with a young man from a well-off and respectable middle-class family."[53]

The more unlikely it was that an affair would lead to marriage—that is, if the woman was not Jewish and from a lower-class background—the less complicated it was for Riesenfeld. This casts doubt on Eugen Altmann's thesis that "95 of every 100" Jewish men who married a Christian woman were marrying their "mistress." Indeed, it was precisely outside the usual circles in which they moved that Riesenfeld and his friends sought their affairs. Only in this way could these relationships be kept secret from their parents and their social milieu in general, remain nonbinding, and be broken off without any risk to a man's reputation.[54] In fact, the precondition for Riesenfeld's intimate and sometimes sexual relationships with women from the lower class was that there be no question of marriage. And this applied especially to non-Jewish women. In autumn 1907, Riesenfeld began working as a traveling salesman for a company in Dresden. There he struck up a friendship with a female colleague, the "approximately eighteen-year-old" clerk Johanna Schindler. "Hanne," as Riesenfeld still referred to her in his memoirs, started out as "a good friend and unreserved admirer." Although she initially refused sexual relations, Riesenfeld managed to persuade her to become his "lover in the deeper sense of the word" by threatening to end the affair otherwise. In contrast to the relationship with Dora Weiss, this one appears to have received the approval of the young woman's parents. "Her mother," Riesenfeld recalled, "must have known what was happening and did not interfere with her daughter's wishes." The relationship with Johanna Schindler lasted until the end of March 1908, when Riesenfeld returned to Breslau to take up a position in his father's firm. Although at the time of departure his girlfriend believed herself—albeit mistakenly—to be pregnant, there was no question of their getting married. Still, had she been pregnant, Riesenfeld claims in his memoirs, he would have "helped her to the best of [his] abilities."[55]

At the same time, middle-class Jewish women tended to have a more sheltered adolescence than their lower-class counterparts; they hardly had a chance to meet a non-Jewish man, and they were practically barred from involvement in casual sexual relations both before and after marriage.[56] During a ski trip to the Silesian mountains in 1914, Lola Landau, the twenty-one-year-old daughter of a wealthy Jewish gynecologist from Berlin, met her first husband, Siegfried Marck. He was a fledgling *Privatdozent* in philosophy at the University of Breslau and the twenty-five-year-old son of an old, established Jewish banking family from Breslau. With both parents supervising their flirtation and encouraging their engagement, sense and sensibility rather than romance characterized their affair. "I would like to read Plato with you," was Siegfried Marck's way of proposing to her: "Do you like the idea?" While young Lola and both sets of parents liked the idea in 1914, the emotional basis of their union was soon spent and by 1919 their marriage had failed.[57]

In 1917, when riding a crowded streetcar in downtown Breslau, she encountered the man who would become her second husband, the non-Jewish writer Armin T. Wegner. "The car was packed," she recalled in her autobiography. "I was standing pinned" against the others "when I noticed a striking figure on the last platform" with a face "brilliant as if cut from precious stone and possessing such a perfectly symmetrical beauty that it appeared wrested from materiality like a work of art."[58] Meeting sporadically in literary circles and at political meetings of the peace movement, an equally secret and passionate romance soon developed between Landau and Wegner. Whereas Siegfried Marck, who in the meantime had become involved with a student of his, was willing to part on good terms, Lola Landau's father tried to block her from both divorcing Marck and marrying a non-Jew through emotional blackmail. "If you get divorced to marry that person," Theodor Landau remonstrated, "you might as well be dead. For me you won't exist anymore."[59] Even if Lola Landau's autobiography follows its own narrative logic, particularly as she wrote large parts of it while grieving in the wake of Armin Wegner's death in 1978, and even if their marriage was far from representative, the Breslau marriage records convey a similar picture.

3. Intermarriages and the "New Woman"

The sharp rise in the number of marriages between Jews and other Breslauers after the turn of the century coincided with the appearance of the New Woman.[60] Lola Landau's story is representative of many others. Jewish-Christian marriages were also the expression of both a new and more equitable order of the sexes and the increasing self-confidence of women. Those who entered into an intermarriage were not only more often from the lower classes; indeed, Jewish men—and especially Jewish women—were usually more independent from their families and perhaps even more rebellious than the partners in intra-Jewish marriages.[61] The greater independence of Jewish women who married non-Jewish men was expressed by several factors: their jobs, living conditions, and age at marriage, as well as the age difference between the bride and groom and the witnesses to their marriage. None of these factors says much on its own. Just because a woman was ten years younger than her husband need not mean that she was immature or naive.[62] Decisive here is that all indications point in the same direction. Jewish women who entered mixed marriages chose to do so on their own; intra-Jewish marriages, by contrast, continued to conform to the pattern of strategic marriage alliances.

Whereas women in intra-Jewish marriages rarely worked, many Jewish and Christian women who intermarried did have jobs, mostly as workers or petty clerks, at least at the time of their wedding (table 30). From 1874 to 1910, only 10% of women in intra-Jewish marriages had pursued a career prior to marriage; it was only during the First World War that the percentage rose to 30%, while in the postwar years it was 20%. Of Jewish women who had married a Christian between 1874 and 1910, at least 40% worked before marriage; during the war, that proportion rose to 45% and after the war, 50%. These women usually had lower- or lower-middle-class jobs. Of the five Jewish women who entered into a mixed marriage between 1874 and 1910 and pursued a "middle-class" career, three had artistic professions—namely, actress, artist, and singer.[63] In an age when particularly members of the middle class and the lower-middle class tended to look down on working women, many of these Jewish women worked a paying job because their parents were too poor to support them between leaving school and entering marriage.[64] These women had many opportunities to mingle with non-Jewish colleagues in the workplace. Their parents could hardly monitor these contacts, especially as their daughters were financially independent and the parents lacked a substantial dowry as a means of control. Working-class Jews fell prey far more easily "to the slogans of the antireligious," the *Jüdische Volkszeitung* complained in April 1917, particularly when they, due to their professions, lived "in social circles composed mainly of the uneducated and non-Jews."[65]

Mothers and fathers whose children married a non-Jew lacked still another means of control, since their children were less likely to be living with them. Many women who married a Christian either had their own apartment or even lived together with their partner before marrying (tables 31–34). This was remarkable at a time when premarital sex was taboo for women, virginity was a fetish, and when "living in sin," that is, in a *wilde Ehe*, was regarded as "a major cause of depravity . . . among the lower classes."[66]

In imperial Germany and into the postwar era, only about 5% of partners in intra-Jewish marriages had shared living quarters beforehand. By contrast, of the Jewish women who intermarried between 1874 and 1894, 37% had lived together with their future husbands before the wedding. Of the Jewish men who married a non-Jewish woman, roughly 50% had "lived in sin" before the civil ceremony. The contrast between intra-Jewish and mixed marriages grew less extreme after the turn of the century. Nevertheless, between 1905 and 1909 still a quarter of all Jewish women and a third of all Jewish men who intermarried had previously lived with their future spouse—a period during which roughly half of all Jewish women entering intra-Jewish marriages had never lived outside their parents' home. Of course, it is likely that a good many Christian-Jewish couples never legalized their relationship. At any rate, the sharp increase in the rate of intermarriages during the war years suggests that common-law marriages between Jews and other Breslauers were far from infrequent.

The respective ages of the spouses at marriage, and especially their age difference, also reflect the nexus between Jewish-Christian marriages and a new gender order (tables 35 and 36).[67] Between 1874 and 1884, the average age at marriage of Jewish women who married a Christian was twenty-nine years, and thus five years older and presumably more experienced and independent than their counterparts in intra-Jewish marriages, who were typically between twenty and twenty-four years of age at marriage.[68] Though the contrast was less marked after the turn of the century, the average age of women who intermarried was still two years more (twenty-eight between 1905 and 1909) than that of women in intra-Jewish marriages (twenty-six in 1905); only after the First World War did their ages coincide.

Yet particularly women who married outside their faith were much closer in age to their husbands than women in intra-Jewish marriages. Whereas only a few women who had intermarried were ten or more years younger than their husbands, in almost a third of all intra-Jewish marriages the husband was at least ten years older than his wife. In intra-Jewish marriages, the large age difference between the spouses reinforced the gender inequality enshrined in the legal order, especially as the husband in a respectable middle-class marriage was expected to be considerably older than his wife. Just how uncommon a marriage was in which the wife was older than the husband is shown by the scandal that the twenty-one-year-old Max Horkheimer caused. In 1916 he fell in love with his father's personal secretary, Rose Riekher, who not only was eight years older than he but also was not Jewish. His father was able to prevent this misalliance for quite some time; indeed, Horkheimer was able to marry Riekher only after he had obtained his *Habilitation*, that is, his postdoctoral lecture qualification.[69]

Throughout the imperial era and into the early Weimar Republic, men in intra-Jewish marriages in Breslau were on average seven years older than their wives.[70] The four-year age difference between Mieze Eckmann and Adolf Riesenfeld and the five-year difference between Lola Landau and Siegfried Marck were still below the average. Between 1874 and 1920, in 10% of all intra-Jewish marriages wives were older than their husbands; in roughly 60% of them, wives were at least six years younger; and in 25–30%, they were even more than ten years younger than their husbands. The seventeen-year age difference between Grete Riesenfeld and Moritz Goldmann appears to have been not at all out of the ordinary. In Jewish-Christian marriages, by contrast, the average age difference was less, and especially in early imperial Germany many Jewish women who married a Christian were older than their husbands. Between 1874 and 1910, the age difference in mixed marriages involving a Jewish woman was on average one to two years; only in the postwar period did it increase to almost four years. Nearly every other Jewish woman who married a non-Jew was older than her husband; only 28% of these women were six or more years younger; and only 13% were more than ten years younger. Between 1885 and 1918, the percentage of women in Jewish-Christian marriages who were older than their husbands dropped to 30%, yet at the same time the percentage of those who were six or more years younger sharply increased to a good 20%; roughly half of these women were the same age as or not much younger than their husbands. Whereas in intra-Jewish marriages, over half the women were younger than their husbands, from the beginning of the imperial era into the postwar years three-fourths of all Jewish women in mixed marriages were approximately the same age as their husbands.

Just as social origin, living circumstances, and age at marriage differed between intermarriages and marriages between Jews, so the witnesses to the respective ceremonies diverged (table 37).[71] What Hartmut Zwahr has shown regarding the choice of godparents in Christian families holds equally for the witnesses to marriages: their choice reflects "a substantial part of the social origins and milieu of the respective families."[72] While the influence of family members on the choice of a partner in intra-Jewish marriages is clear from the fact that they served as

witnesses to half of such marriages at the beginning and to two-thirds of
them at the end of the imperial era, the witnesses to Christian-Jewish
weddings tended to be neighbors, colleagues, or friends. If the fathers of
the bride and the groom were still alive, it was usually they who, in intra-
Jewish marriages, served as witnesses to their children's marriages at the
registry office. Father and son and father and daughter gathered before
the registrar, making it clear that the children were about to enter both
a marriage and a strategic alliance between two families.

There was seldom an analogous constellation at Christian-Jewish
weddings, but when it did occur, almost always the union involved a
Christian partner of Jewish origin. On October 14, 1889, the dentist
Hans Riegner and Elisabeth Franziska Cäcilie Bauer wed. He was Jewish and she Catholic, though of Jewish origin. The witnesses were the
bride's uncle, Moritz Bauer, who was Jewish, as well as both Otto Bauer,
the bride's father and co-owner of the prominent furniture factory
Bauer Brothers, and the groom's father, Paul Julius Riegner, a wealthy
Breslau hotel owner. In other respects, too, this marriage fit more the
pattern of intra-Jewish unions. Both hailed from Breslau's upper-middle
class, and the bride had just turned nineteen, was eleven years younger
than her husband, did not work, and still lived with her parents.[73]

Whereas the majority of intra-Jewish marriages continued to follow
the pattern of the arranged marriage, according to which the family or
a traditional matchmaker orchestrated the love relationship, those Jews
(particularly women) who chose a non-Jewish spouse seem to have done
so on their own and with relative freedom. They listened less to their
families than to their hearts. Even if Lola Landau made no explicit
mention of intermarriage in a programmatic article from 1929, she was
probably thinking of her own two marriages when she sharply contrasted the "economic institution of the middle-class marriage" to the
"companionate marriage." In the latter, "the economically and intellectually independent woman, with well-informed views and mature heart,
chose the man as a companion."[74]

After the turn of the century, Christian-Jewish and intra-Jewish
marriages became increasingly similar. In Breslau, the discrepancies in
age at marriage, social origin, and age difference between the partners
began to narrow. This was in part a reflection of the fact that, compared
to the beginning of the imperial era, mixed marriages had lost some
of their stigma of inappropriateness. Even among the middle class,
Christian-Jewish marriages had become a possibility. Simultaneously,
however, the middle-class strategy of forging marriage alliances between

families through their sons and especially their daughters was clearly eroding. The courting rituals and marriage practices of young men and—to an even greater extent—young women came to resemble more closely that of lower-middle-class and working-class Jews. While in other respects the lower-class population became more middle class during this period, the marriage pattern of Breslau's Jewish middle class underwent a "de-bourgeoisification" with the rise of the New Woman.

Around 1910 the first serious conflict over the issue of intermarriages took place within the Jewish *Gemeinde*. Although the opponents of such marriages ultimately won the day, other, more discriminating voices also entered into the debate—voices that maintained the distinction between mixed marriage and conversion.[75] At the general meeting of the Israelitische Kranken- und Verpflegungs-Anstalt und Beerdigungs-gesellschaft in June 1909, Zionist members of the society put forward the motion that doctors who had "left Judaism or the *Synagogengemeinde* or were in mixed marriages or whose children had left Judaism while still minors" should be excluded from employment at the Jewish hospital. The spokesman for members in favor of the motion was the lawyer Felix Hirschberg, who, as a candidate for the orthodox Verein zur För-derung der Interessen des Judentums (Society for the Advancement of the Interests of Judaism), had lost to the Liberaler Verein (Liberal Club) in Jewish *Gemeinde* elections the previous December.[76] "The problem lies just as much with mixed marriages as with leaving the congregation," Hirschberg argued, thereby defending a position that still prevails in the relevant historiography to this day. David Mudgan from the Religiös-Liberalen (Religious Liberals) represented the opposing viewpoint, ar-guing that the Jewish hospital—though it received neither state nor municipal funding—should also choose its doctors solely on the basis of their qualifications. The liberal Rabbi Jacob Guttmann tried to mediate. Anyone who had left the Jewish *Gemeinde*, he argued, had "forfeited the right to occupy a position financed by contributions from his former co-religionists." Nevertheless, although he strongly condemned conversion, his stand on mixed marriage was more moderate. "If someone marries a Christian out of love but still remains true to Judaism, he should not be seen as being either unworthy or unfit to be an employee of the Jewish hospital." Guttmann succeeded in winning over the society's board—on which liberals held the majority—to his position. Yet it was the mem-bers' assembly that had the last word. Here the Zionist and Orthodox camps joined forces and, continuing to set intermarriages on a par with conversion, outlawed the hiring of Jewish doctors married to non-Jews.

This policy still remained in force at the hospital during the Weimar Republic. In October 1927, a doctor applying for a position as head of ophthalmology was obliged to asseverate that he was "not engaged to marry a Christian lady nor was [he] intending to do so."[77]

Contrary to Dirk Blasius's claim, the rate of divorce in mixed marriages remained low, even if it was higher than in intra-Jewish marriages.[78] The intermarriage of the Breslau Jew Franz Ungerleider and the Protestant Gabriele Jakubczik, who married on April 3, 1920, and divorced on June 26 the same year, was anything but typical.[79] True, in intra-Jewish marriages divorce was much less likely than in mixed marriages: only 4% of all Breslau intra-Jewish couples married in 1905 obtained a divorce, compared to 11% of intermarriages between 1905 and 1909. Yet even among intra-Jewish couples wed in 1920, 18% successfully filed for divorce, mirroring the other side of the often over-hasty wartime weddings and the marriage epidemic of the postwar years that affected intra-Jewish marriage and intermarriage alike. The percentage of failed marriages increased to 30% among those that took place in the postwar years between Jews and other Breslauers, though this figure says less about the marriages than about the enormous pressure under which these unions were placed after 1933 in National Socialist Germany.[80] The fact that roughly 80% of Jewish-Christian marriages remained intact during this period, at least on paper, shows that they were substantially no less stable than other marriages.

4. Christian-Jewish Marriages and the Situational Ethnicity of Breslau Jews

It is misleading to equate marriages between Jews and other Breslauers with a blind desire for total assimilation. After the introduction of civil marriage in 1874, Jews and other Germans could marry out of faith without having to convert to their partner's religion. Jewish men and women who wanted to sever all ties with their Jewish background could, of course, still convert, but one can only speculate about how many Jews took this path to assimilation. Nevertheless, the Jewish spouses in contemporary intermarriage statistics consciously chose precisely not to convert and showed thereby that they did not take their marrying a non-Jew to be a rejection of their Jewish origins.[81] Whereas some Jewish partners in intermarriages converted after marrying, their number is likely to have been rather small, since it would have been easier for them to "assimilate" fully if they had converted before marriage.

Moreover, some Christian partners in these marriages converted to Judaism after the wedding, even though it is difficult to estimate this group's significance in quantitative terms. Many of the Protestants who converted to Judaism and about whom the Protestant church in Silesia kept meticulous records doubtless belonged to this group. In any event, in the whole of Silesia, forty-six Protestant men and women converted to Judaism in the years between 1880 and the turn of the century; eighty between 1900 and 1918; and fifty-two in the decade from 1918 to 1927.[82] In February 1922, a twenty-year-old Protestant industrial worker named Gertrud Luise Springer, daughter of Hermann Springer, a Breslau hatter, married the twenty-five-year-old Jewish coachman Benno Breslauer, son of a master tailor. Both children of this marriage—a son born in 1926 and a daughter born the following year—were Jewish from birth. Gertrud converted to Judaism after her marriage and remained true to her adopted religion until 1941, when she was obliged to quit the Breslau congregation in order to protect her husband and children.[83]

What is more, the religious upbringing of children born of Jewish-Christian marriages also suggests that one cannot equate such marriages with apostasy. Not all children born of mixed Christian and Jewish parentage were lost to Judaism. At least on paper, a considerable minority of them were raised Jewish.[84] If one looks at the religion of the offspring of all Jewish-Christian marriages recorded in Breslau, nearly 30% were nominally Jewish in 1890 and 1910, and as many as 35% were in 1900. In contravention of the Halakic tradition but in keeping with the patriarchal family structure, the father's religion appears to have been decisive. Until the turn of the century, intermarriages involving Jewish men did not pose any demographic "threat" to Breslau's Jewish community. On the contrary, in 1890 more than half of all children born of marriages between Jewish men and Christian women— whether Catholic or Protestant—were registered as Jewish. Nevertheless, the proportion of Jewish children in such marriages gradually declined: by 1900, it was only in marriages between Jewish men and Protestant women that the majority of such children were Jewish. After the turn of the century, the majority of children of mixed parentage were raised Christian even if the father was Jewish. If the mother was Catholic, only a quarter of the children were Jewish, but if she was Protestant, a third still were.

When Jewish women intermarried, the result—at least until around 1900—was a severe demographic "loss" from the perspective of the Jewish community. Only 4% of children born to a Jewish mother and a

Protestant father were Jewish in 1890; if the father was Catholic, then all the children were Christian. Yet already by 1900 the picture had changed. In that year, 20% of all such children were nominally Jewish; ten years later, this figure had risen to 24%. In contrast to the period around 1890, the independence and self-confidence that characterized Jewish women who intermarried began, at the close of the imperial era, to find expression in the religion of their children.

More important than these demographic number games so popular in those days is the fact that the question of whether marriages between Jews and other Breslauers were "Christian" or "Jewish" cannot do justice to the plurality of identities, and occasionally the degree of their hybridity, among the parents and their children. Many children of intermarriages derived their identity less from regarding themselves unambiguously as either "Christian" or "Jewish" than from crossing the boundary between these two designations. For example, when a Jewish-Christian couple's sixteen-year-old son, who had been baptized as Protestant, had to write a school essay on "what I know about my ancestors" in 1929, he noted proudly that he was a "hybrid [*Mischling*] of many nations and races."[85] In the daily life of these families, the Jewish and Christian traditions became intertwined. Even children who were nominally raised as Christians often took part in the family gatherings of their Jewish relatives.[86] Moreover, Jewish parents in mixed marriages often maintained Jewish traditions in the daily life of their families. For the three children of Lola Landau and Armin Wegner, at least, their Jewishness remained a possible identity. When his daughter Sybille was about to start school, Wegner wrote her while on an extended stay in Palestine, addressing her as "My child! My little Jewess!" He urged her to resolutely defend both her *Judentum* (Jewishness) and *Deutschtum* (Germanness) at school.[87]

For some Jews who chose a non-Jewish partner, their marriage was the final step toward their total assimilation; henceforth they no longer understood themselves to be Jews. For the majority, however, their marriage to a non-Jew did not contradict their identity as Jews; in such cases, the marriage constituted an instance of what was earlier termed "situational ethnicity." Even if Jews who intermarried did not always feel Jewish, in some situations—say, at family gatherings or religious celebrations—their Jewish identity was nevertheless given priority and remained part of their family life. Although this new form of Jewish identity disturbed both Jewish and non-Jewish observers, it was nevertheless one of many ways to live as a Jew and not deny one's Jewishness in early twentieth-century Breslau. Many Jews who married a non-Jew in imperial Germany had no intention of "breaking their ties to their Jewishness," but sought to preserve their Jewish identity in married life and to pass it on to their children. Jews who married other Germans were not harbingers of the allegedly imminent "downfall of German Jews," nor were they advocates of "radical assimilation." Rather, many of them practiced and possibly enjoyed Jewish identities that are best grasped as a form of situational ethnicity.

As long as research into Christian-Jewish marriages analyzes them exclusively in the context of radical assimilation, it cannot do justice to this aspect of the relationship between Jews and other Germans. Unlike conversion, intermarriage most often was not equated with a rejection of one's Jewishness. Jews who married Christian partners were experimenting with new forms of Jewish identity—gropingly and searchingly perhaps, but often successfully. Before the turn of the century, it was primarily lower-middle-class and working-class Jews who married other Breslauers. However, with the emergence of the New Woman around 1900, the numbers of Jewish middle-class sons and daughters choosing to marry Christians rose, though the Jewish-Christian marriage remained primarily a lower-class and lower-middle-class phenomenon. Among the middle class, the choice of a partner remained integrated in a system of strategic marriage alliances in which religious boundaries—whether Jewish, Protestant, or Catholic—were not crossed.

The fact that in imperial Germany and especially after the turn of the century the number of intermarriages rose sharply in Breslau shows just how matter of course intimate relations between Jews and non-Jews were. Sociability between Jews and other Breslauers did not end at the doorstep but continued in the private sphere. Neighborly or collegial contacts between Jews and other Breslauers could develop into friendships, love affairs, long-term relationships, or even marriages. The fact that the rate of intermarriage in Breslau quadrupled between the 1890s and the early 1920s indicates the limits of the thesis that from at least 1890 on anti-Semitism poisoned relations between Jews and other Germans. Social life in the city offered ample opportunities to meet, befriend, and perhaps even marry across religious and ethnic divides. That was particularly true of lower-class Jews and Christians; in view of this fact, it would be wise to take seriously here, too, "class" and "status" as categories of historical analysis.[88] The significance of economic inequality and class-based social distance was reflected in the contemporary debate on the phenomenon of mixed marriages between Jews and other Germans. In this context, members of the Jewish middle class discussed the love and sexual lives of lower-class Jews. That helps to explain why they employed stereotypes of the lower classes similar to those common among the German middle class in general.

4

Unity, Diversity, and Difference

Jews, Protestants, and Catholics in Breslau Schools

Whether and to what extent a minority was integrated into society as a whole, as well as which opportunities were afforded its members, was decided from the nineteenth century on chiefly in the school. This applied also to German Jews. At school at the very latest, a Jewish child came into contact with members of other religious or ethnic groups. Sometimes the child suffered discrimination; occasionally he or she formed friendships with other Germans. The school was a place of Jewish acculturation and a springboard for social advancement. From the mid-nineteenth century on, the large majority of German Jews attended public, usually Christian schools. In the end, schools in imperial Germany not only were objects of the sober administration of educational policies but also counted among the places in which politico-ideological conflicts were sparked. The left-wing liberal *Breslauer Zeitung,* for example, believed that schools were "sanctuaries of cultural progress dedicated to our nation's future."[1] Like the university and the arts club, the theater, and the concert hall, secondary schools, especially the humanistic *Gymnasien,* belonged to those institutions that reflected the middle-class ideal of *Bildung* (self-formation).[2] An analysis of relations between Jews and other Breslauers in the city's secondary schools thus promises not only to shed light on another key sphere of those relations but also to be fruitful in view of recent debates about the ambivalent nature of the concept of *Bildung* and the tension between universality and particularity inherent in it.[3]

We know little about the history of Jewish schoolchildren in German schools. Studies on Jewish schools have almost completely neglected the large majority of Jewish pupils who attended state, and thus usually

Christian, schools.[4] On the other hand, since the 1960s the flourishing field of educational history has limited itself to questions of political indoctrination, social control, and social mobility.[5] Only in roughly the last fifteen years have there been investigations of the relationships between religion, culture, and politics in the imperial German school system.[6] In contrast, for example, to North America, educational history in Germany has ignored the question of Jewish schoolchildren.[7] "The whole subject of Jewish schooling in this era awaits proper treatment," complained Geoffrey Field in 1980.[8] Little has changed in this regard over the past twenty-five years, even if the debate about multicultural child rearing will in all likelihood soon reach educational history.[9]

In the first part of this chapter, the Jewish "educational lead" and its causes are investigated. Whereas the analysis confirms the common view that Jews were overrepresented in secondary schools, it considerably relativizes the extent of that "educational advantage" by showing the close connection between the social structure of Breslau Jews and their success in school. The second part consists of an analysis of the history of the Johannes-Gymnasium, the school that embodied the Breslau magistracy's pluralistic school policies. Special attention is paid there to the school's prehistory, which was closely connected to the Kulturkampf. In the third part, the second conflict over school policy is investigated, namely, the conflict over the status of Jewish schoolchildren and teachers, which concerned not secondary but primary schools.

1. The Jewish "Educational Advantage": Jewish Students in Secondary Schools

Schools were an important aspect of relations between Jews and other Breslauers not only because of their political and cultural significance, but also and especially because nearly all Jewish schoolchildren in Breslau attended Christian schools in imperial Germany.[10] During the imperial era, there was no Jewish school system in Breslau that, as in the case of the Catholic milieu, united the group and closed it off from the outside world. Between 1825 and 1850, the Jewish school system lost its significance for the education of Jewish school-age children. In 1824, only 21 out of a total of 520 Jewish schoolchildren attended Christian schools; the large majority of them attended small, private Jewish schools; and the remaining 117 went to Breslau's Jewish Reform school, the Wilhelmsschule. By 1850 the situation had changed radically. Now 1,403 of the Jewish school-age children attended Christian schools and only a minority of 450 went to Jewish schools.[11] From 1874 on, all of Breslau's Jewish boys passed through public schools without exception. Only among Jewish schoolgirls was there a minority of 8–10% that attended a Jewish school during the imperial era, the Industrieschule für Israelitische Mädchen (Vocational School for Jewish Girls), which had been founded in 1802.[12]

Aside from religious instruction and the (seldom-observed) release of Jewish children on the Sabbath and on high Jewish holidays, Jewish schoolchildren experienced the same school day as their Protestant and Catholic counterparts. Instead of the Talmud and Torah, Jewish *Gymnasium* pupils read Tacitus and Cicero, Goethe and Schiller.[13] There was no "separation," Alfred Kempner (the future theater critic who wrote under the name of Alfred Kerr) recalled of his school days at Breslau's Elisabeth-Gymnasium.[14] Part of the Jewish school experience, therefore, was the educational pathos of the secondary schools, the nationalistic climate, the teachers' efforts to maintain discipline, and the fundamentally Christian character of the schools. Many Jewish schoolchildren took part as a matter of course in school celebrations. For example, Ludwig Geiger, the son of the Breslau Reform rabbi Abraham Geiger, recalled in 1910 that weekly devotional services, Reformation Day, and nationalistic celebrations were a constant feature of his time at the Maria Magdalena-Gymnasium in the 1860s. While today one might consider it institutional pressure to convert to Christianity, Geiger remarked that "listening to a prayer or a song, indeed even singing one, even if its . . . content was partially or wholly Christian, didn't hurt anyone." He continued: "On the contrary, it was precisely such gatherings that aroused and kept alive a sense of community. Everyone felt like a part of a whole."[15]

The majority of Breslau Jews sent their children not to an elementary school (*Volksschule*) but to one of the secondary schools. Informative in this connection is not the precise number so much as the ratio of distribution of school-age Jews, Protestants, and Catholics among the various school types. Only about 30% of all school-age Jewish boys went to a municipal elementary school; over two-thirds went to a *Gymnasium*, a *Realgymnasium*, or a *Realschule*, or their respective preparatory schools. Of the school-age Jewish girls, only 15% attended a municipal elementary school; another 15% the Industrieschule für Israelitische Mädchen; and nearly 70% a secondary or middle school. The contrast to the school-age Protestant and Catholic children is astonishing: nearly 85% of the latter went to an elementary school.[16]

It is likely that the middle and secondary schools served the Jews as substitutes for the denominationally bound elementary schools.[17] After having exceeded the age of compulsory education, Jews were more likely to leave school than Protestant and Catholic high-school pupils. As long as their children had to go to school, less wealthy Jewish parents presumably also accepted the high fees of the *Gymnasien* and their preparatory schools.[18] For children with less well-off Jewish parents, however, attending higher grades and earning the *Abitur*, the final exam given after nine years of *Gymnasium* training, were simply out of the question due to the high costs. Although it is true that many Protestant and Catholic *Gymnasium* pupils left school prior to acquiring the *Abitur*, Jews were overrepresented among the so-called early departees. The Jewish proportion among *Gymnasium* pupils likewise declined the closer the *Abitur* got. In the preparatory schools of Breslau's *Gymnasien*, fully half of the pupils were Jewish, while in the *Gymnasien* themselves fully a quarter of the school-age pupils were Jewish, among whom *Gymnasium* pupils who were no longer obliged to go to school amounted to just under a fifth.[19] In 1910 Jews still made up 25% of all preparatory pupils at the city's *Gymnasien*, but only 16% of *Gymnasium* pupils (table 38).

Because Jewish schoolchildren avoided elementary schools, they were overrepresented at secondary schools. At the beginning of the imperial era, Jews made up 7% of Breslau's population, but 21% of all secondary-school pupils and 28% of *Gymnasium* pupils. By the end of the era, the proportion of Jewish pupils dropped to 14% at secondary schools and 16% at the *Gymnasien*. Yet because in 1910 only 4% of Breslau residents were Jews, their proportion of secondary-school pupils clearly continued to exceed the proportion of the Jewish population. Even more than at boys' schools, however, Jews were overrepresented among the pupils at secondary girls' schools. In the early 1880s, Jews represented roughly 6% of the total population but 39% of all female pupils at both city girls' secondary schools. However, these figures are inflated inasmuch as many of the Protestant and Catholic girls who were secondary-school pupils attended private secondary girls' schools; Catholics, for example, attended the Ursulinenschule.[20] From the mid-1890s on, however, the statistics also accounted for the female pupils who attended private secondary girls' schools. In this period, Jews represented 5% of Breslau's population, but 25% of the female pupils at all secondary girls' schools. By 1910 the Jewish proportion of female secondary-school pupils fell to 19%, though it still was five times higher than the Jewish proportion of the population.[21] Thus at secondary schools there were four times as many Jewish schoolboys and five times as many Jewish schoolgirls than in the city's entire population. Although the Jewish educational advantage in Breslau was considerable and greater than in comparable cities, such as Frankfurt am Main, it remained only half as large as in the whole of Prussia.[22] This shows just how distorted the numbers are for Prussia as a whole, since they compare an essentially more urban Jewish population, which benefited from the superior educational opportunities in cities, with the more rural Protestant and Catholic population.

Denomination had hardly any influence on the choice of a type of secondary school. Between 1870 and 1910, Breslau's Jewish pupils favored the same type of school as their Protestant and Catholic schoolmates.[23] The greater proportion of Jews, Protestants, and Catholics among the secondary-school pupils attended the humanistic *Gymnasium;* the remainder was distributed between the *Realschule* (where no Latin was taught) and the *Realgymnasium.* Jews and Catholics, however, chose more frequently the *Gymnasium* and less often the *Realgymnasium* and the *Realschule* than did Protestants. The choices of Jewish and Catholic pupils diverged, however, after 1900. The proportion of Jewish pupils who chose the *Realgymnasium*—the "school with 'modern' features" (Thomas Nipperdey)—now increased and surpassed that of Protestants who did so, whereas that of the Catholics dropped. That the pattern of Jewish pupils' choices changed seems plausible against the backdrop of Prussian educational policy during the imperial era, particularly that of the so-called system of qualification.[24] Prior to 1900, an *Abitur* from a *Realgymnasium* limited one's options in choosing an area of study and a career, especially those that were closed to Jews, such as a career with the railroad, the postal service, and in construction and mining. However, since after 1900 such a diploma enabled one to pursue any career, it became more attractive to Jewish pupils.

Jewish *Gymnasium* pupils favored the schools of the city's elite. The smaller the percentage of pupils from the lower-middle class and the lower classes, the more exclusive was the school regarded. In the 1880s, middle-class pupils were overrepresented in four of Breslau's eleven secondary schools. At the Friedrich-, Elisabeth-, Maria Magdalena-, and Johannes-Gymnasien, nearly 90% of the pupils came from middle-class families; at the other secondary schools, however, only about 60%. If one considers the social background of the overall student body of the schools (rather than that of those who completed their *Abitur*), this impression is confirmed. At the four "elite schools" in 1884, the percentage of schoolchildren from lower-middle-class families was between 17% (Maria Magdalena-Gymnasium) and 49% (Johannes-Gymnasium), whereas at the other schools it averaged 58%.[25] At three of the four "elite schools," the percentage of Jewish pupils was unusually high in the 1880s, averaging 35%, 43%, and 44%, respectively. Only at the fourth, the Johannes-Gymnasium, which in contrast to the other three schools was located in a part of Breslau that had a small Jewish population, the percentage of Jewish pupils at the school was 19%, which was roughly equivalent to the percentage of Jewish pupils in all the city's secondary schools. Also noteworthy is their distribution at Breslau's two *Realgymnasien*. At the Realgymnasium am Zwinger, where only 29% of the pupils came from the lower-middle class, 19% of the pupils were Jewish in the 1880s; at the Realgymnasium zum Heiligen Geist, where 53% of the pupils came from lower-middle-class families, only 8% of the pupils were Jewish.[26]

Although the percentage of children from the lower-middle class among Breslau's *Gymnasium* pupils increased over the course of the imperial era, even after 1900 four of the by now twelve secondary schools were particularly exclusive. At these schools—the Johannes-, the Elisabeth-, the Maria Magdalena-, and the Wilhelm-Gymnasien— roughly 90% of all the pupils came from the middle class, whereas at the other *Gymnasien* only 50–80% of the pupils were from middle-class families.[27] Once again, Jewish pupils were overrepresented at the four exclusive schools. From 1900 to 1909, they accounted for approximately 30% of the pupils at the Johannes-, the Elisabeth-, the Maria Magdalena-, and the Wilhelm-Gymnasien, but only 16% of Breslau's secondary-school pupils altogether.[28] In Breslau, 84% of Jewish *Gymnasium* pupils earned their *Abitur* at the four elite schools, whereas only 57% of Protestant and only 16% of Catholic *Gymnasium* pupils did so.

Breslau's Jewish pupils not only were concentrated in the exclusive schools but also were presumably more successful than their Protestant and Catholic schoolmates. Jewish *Gymnasium* pupils received their *Abitur* earlier.[29] The average age of Jewish *Gymnasium* pupils in the 1880s was 18.8 years; after the turn of the century, 18.3 years. By contrast, Protestant *Gymnasium* pupils during the same period averaged 19.2 and 18.9 years of age, and the Catholics consistently averaged 19.8 years of age. Likewise, due to good grades, Jewish *Gymnasium* pupils were exempted from the oral exam more often than their Protestant and Catholic schoolmates. In the 1880s, one in eight pupils was exempted, and from

1900 to 1909 one in nine; but only one in eleven Protestant pupils and one in ten Catholic pupils were exempted.

A quantitative analysis of Breslau's secondary-school pupils indicates a high degree of Jewish inclusion in their schools throughout the imperial era. Presumably, success was determined by either good or bad grades, that is, by acquired as opposed to ascribed criteria. Breslau's *Gymnasien* and *Realgymnasien* were socially but not denominationally exclusive. Given the high percentage of Jews in secondary schools and the probable above-average success of Jewish pupils, there is no evidence of structural discrimination that would indicate exclusion. Nor would that change over the course of the imperial era. Their performance was no less above average in 1910 than it was in 1880. While anti-Semitism may have increasingly poisoned the atmosphere at Breslau's secondary schools, much as it had at the university, from the late 1880s on it had no effect on the educational opportunities of Jews up to graduation from the *Gymnasium*.

Secondary schools seemed in retrospect to many Breslau Jews to have been conservative, authoritarian, and stuffy, though seldom anti-Semitic. In 1916, Adolf Riesenfeld, who left the Elisabeth-Gymnasium in the spring term of 1900 without a middle school certificate (*das "Einjährige"*) after having had to repeat a year several times, recalled school as "a kind of prison that most [got] through without severe damage only because the young mind is elastic, and doesn't know any other state. Poor children. . . ."[30] Max Born, later a Nobel laureate for physics, recalled in the 1940s his time at the Wilhelm-Gymnasium, from which he graduated in 1901. "Our principal," Born writes, was conservative, "the typical Prussian civil servant, . . . perhaps a little narrow-minded and strict, though also just and friendly." At least "during his tenure," Born recalls further, "anti-Semitism was not tolerated."[31] A similar picture may be found in the memoirs written in the late 1930s by Ernst Marcus (1890–1982), who became a prominent Breslau lawyer in the 1920s. He attended the preparatory school of the Realgymnasium zum Heiligen Geist from 1895 to 1908 and then the *Realgymnasium* itself. "The scope of the teaching was quite narrow," Marcus noted. "The teachers were, with only a few exceptions, typical royalist Prussian civil servants." It was a miserable time for him since the "drill for the *Abitur,* which was to cap twelve years of school, . . . dominated the teaching." Particularly annoying, it seemed to Marcus in retrospect, was history class. Its "focus . . . was on 'Brandenburg-Prussian history.'" He learned about "non-German history" only "insofar as it touched on German history." However, he never experienced anti-Semitism at school. On the contrary, he—"the only Jewish pupil in my class"—"got on quite well and amicably" with his "classmates."[32]

Occasionally there were brawls between Jewish and Christian pupils. In spring 1886, according to the *Berliner Tageblatt*, a "number of Christian schoolmates" attacked the thirteen-year-old Alfred Schlesinger in Weissgerbergasse. The Christian pupils beat Schlesinger and called him "Jew boy." At that, Schlesinger flew into a rage, pulled an erasing knife, lashed out in all directions, and hurt one of the Christian pupils, the eleven-year-old Fritz Scheer. As a result, in autumn 1886 a trial was held at the district court in Breslau. In vain Schlesinger claimed he had acted in self-defense. The court fined him fifty marks; the district attorney had even called for a sentence of six months in prison.[33]

That Jews were overrepresented in secondary schools in imperial Germany is not a matter of dispute among scholars. The historian Viktor Kárády recently even went so far as to call Central European Jewry an "educational force in modernity."[34] What is disputed, however, is how the Jewish educational advantage can best be explained. Kárády provides a multilayered explanation, citing four reasons that so many Jews did so well in school. First, they were in a better position to benefit from the more varied and often superior educational opportunities in large cities because they were more urban than the non-Jewish population. Second, being members of the middle-class professional groups from which secondary-school pupils were drawn, they were overrepresented. Third, due to anti-Semitism, secondary schools were more important to Jews than to non-Jews since they had to legitimate their elevated socioeconomic status additionally by means of educational qualifications. Fourth, the Jews benefited from a tradition of "religiously grounded intellectualism."[35]

The significance of the fourth reason, the great importance of education in the Jewish tradition, is the most difficult to determine. Certainly, premodern Talmudic scholarship valued such things as acuity and wisdom, quick-wittedness and being widely read. It is questionable, however, whether in the late nineteenth century the self-understanding of Jewish *Gymnasium* pupils really constituted a "transformed and secularized" variant of the traditional educational ideal.[36] While evidence in support of this thesis can still be found regarding the early nineteenth century, the autobiographies of Jews who attended a secondary school in the imperial era in most cases remain silent about their motivation for doing so. The authors of the autobiographies came almost exclusively from middle-class families. The fact that they received a secondary education went without saying for them. They mentioned it without offering any justification. "Like the children of most wealthy families," Arye Maimon recalled in 1988, "I did not attend what today is called a grade school," that is, the first four years of elementary school, "but rather the preparatory school of a Breslau *Gymnasium*.[37] Moreover, the notion of a "religiously grounded intellectualism" among the Jews is closely associated, to this day, with the common thesis of a specifically "Jewish intellectuality." The idea of the "clever Jew" is ambivalent, however. The respectful admiration of "Jewish thinking" is countered by the fear of the clever, shrewd "Jew" who cheats his competitors in the competition for scarce goods, such as educational qualifications.[38]

It is hardly less difficult to judge Karády's third suggestion, that educational qualifications were particularly important to Jews as traditional outsiders. A good deal does support the argument that many Jews regarded going to school and in some cases the university as a chance to have their social advancement and their membership in the middle class certified. Yet the element of "social class legitimization" and "ennoblement" through secondary education, which Karády emphasizes, is not attested in the available memoirs. On the other hand, it is questionable whether these sources would make explicit the instrumental understanding of education on which Karády's thesis is based. Moreover, it remains an open question whether Protestant and Catholic schoolchildren were not just as convinced as the Jews about the import of educational qualifications with regard to social standing and status in imperial Germany.[39]

While the educational differences between urban and rural areas can partly explain the educational differences between Jews and non-Jews within Prussia as a whole, it does not explain the Jewish educational advantage in Breslau. Why was the percentage of Jews among pupils in Breslau's secondary schools four times that among the general population? It would seem promising to inquire into the connection between the social structure of the Jewish population, the social background of *Gymnasium* pupils, and the Jewish educational advantage. This question is interesting not only because of the socially exclusive character of the secondary schools but also because it permits one to gain indirect information about the significance of other factors. If the Jewish educational tradition and the ambition of outsiders were indeed of decisive significance, then the proportion of pupils from lower-middle-class and lower-class families among Jewish *Gymnasium* graduates would have to have been particularly large.

Breslau's *Gymnasien* and *Realgymnasien* were socially exclusive, indeed far more so than in many other Prussian cities. Secondary-school pupils came predominantly, the graduates almost entirely, from middle-class families. The social background of all secondary-school pupils can be determined only for the 1880s.[40] Judging by their fathers' professions, roughly 60% of the pupils at the five Breslau *Gymnasien* came from middle-class families; at the Maria Magdalena- and Elisabeth-Gymnasien, the percentage was even higher: 80 and 70%, respectively. On average, the proportion of *Realgymnasium* pupils from middle-class families was only slightly less; at the Realgymnasium am Zwinger, however, the proportion was 70%, which actually exceeded that at most *Gymnasien*. By contrast, during the same period in Minden, a small northwest German town of 20,000 inhabitants, for example, only 28% of *Gymnasium* pupils and 21% of all secondary-school pupils came from middle-class families.[41]

Even more exclusive than secondary-school pupils were the graduates from Breslau's *Gymnasien* and *Realgymnasien*. Judging by their fathers' professions, in the 1880s roughly 75% of those who completed their *Abitur* at these schools came from middle-class families, although the middle-class professional groups accounted for only 11% of the city's population. On the other hand, only 15% of the graduates came from the lower-middle class, which constituted roughly 20% of the total population; and barely 2% of all graduates came from the lower classes, the large majority of the population (table 39). By contrast, Cologne's secondary schools were comparatively open. There, in the first half of the 1880s, 35% of all *Gymnasium* graduates came from lower-middle-class families.[42]

At the end of the imperial era, Breslau's secondary schools were still socially exclusive. Now almost 80% of all *Gymnasium* and *Realgymnasium* graduates came from middle-class families, though only 12% of the total population pursued middle-class professions. Since the lower-middle class made up 20% of the population, they continued to be underrepresented among the graduates, constituting just under 19% of them (table 40).[43] And, as earlier, Breslau's secondary schools were still more exclusive than elsewhere. In Cologne, for example, during the same period 31% of all graduates came from lower-middle-class families.[44] Wolfgang Neugebauer's assertion of the "relative social openness of Prussian secondary schools" for children from the lower classes is hardly corroborated by Breslau's *Gymnasien* and *Realgymnasien*.[45] While it may be true true of small and medium-sized towns such as Minden or Duisburg, it does not hold for metropolises such as Berlin and Breslau in imperial Germany.[46]

Against the backdrop of the exclusivity of secondary schools and the social structure of the Jewish population, the Jewish educational advantage becomes relative. The close connection between class background and educational success can be clarified by means of a thought experiment. We start with a fictive magnitude, namely, the hypothetical percentage that each denomination would have had among Breslau's *Gymnasium* and *Realgymnasium* graduates if each were represented by its respective percentage of the social strata from which the graduates were drawn. The resultant percentage can then be contrasted with the real percentage (table 41). If educational success in secondary schools had been dependent on social background alone, graduates would have had to have been distributed in the 1880s as follows: 17% Jewish, 55% Protestant, and 18% Catholic. In fact, during this period 24% of Breslau's graduates were Jewish, 51% Protestant, and 24% Catholic. Thus, if one does not measure "overrepresentation" by the percentage of the denominations in the professional groups to which the graduates' fathers belonged, then the Jews were indeed slightly overrepresented, but hardly more than Breslau's Catholics; by contrast, the Protestants were underrepresented. This experiment yields a far more astonishing result when the focus is on the first decade of the twentieth century. Hypothetically, 20% of the graduates would have had to have been Jewish, 56% Protestant, and 23% Catholic; in fact, 20% were Jewish, only 48% Protestant, and 32% Catholic. If one considers the diverse social profiles of the three denominations in Breslau, after the turn of the century Jews were no longer overrepresented among *Gymnasium* and *Realgymnasium* graduates, Protestants were still underrepresented, and Catholics, who allegedly suffered from an educational deficit,[47] were even more starkly overrepresented than in the 1880s. At the beginning and especially at the end of the imperial era, the Jewish proportion of the graduates corresponded roughly to the proportion of Breslau Jews in the social sectors from which *Gymnasium* and *Realgymnasium* pupils came.

Moreover, there is no indication that lower-middle-class Jews sent their sons to secondary schools more frequently than did lower-middle-class Protestants or Catholics. Rather, children from lower-middle-class families were starkly underrepresented among Jewish graduates, whereas they were represented among Protestant graduates in keeping with their proportion of the population (tables 42 and 43). Measured by profession, in 1876 just under 30% of all Breslau Jews belonged to the lower-middle class. Of the Jewish graduates in the 1880s, however, only 7% came from lower-middle-class families. The proportion of children with lower-middle-class origins among the Protestant graduates corresponded, with 15%, almost exactly to the proportion of lower-middle-class Protestants in the total Protestant population, which was 18%. Finally, among the Catholic graduates, those from the lower-middle class—to judge from the occupational profile in 1906—were underrepresented. Only among Catholic graduates did sons from lower-middle-class families represent, with 37%, a larger percentage than would have corresponded to their percentage of the total Catholic population, namely, 19%.

If one considers the income rather than the professions of graduates' fathers, the thesis is confirmed that only a few Jews who came from the lower-middle class managed to graduate from a *Gymnasium* or a *Realgymnasium*. While some lower-middle-class Jews may have sent their children to middle or secondary schools, they took the children out of school once they had passed the age after which schooling was no longer compulsory because the burden of paying school fees was too great. There were hardly any children from low-income families among the Jewish *Abiturienten*. Unfortunately, an income analysis of the social background of the Jewish graduates is possible only for the period from 1875 to 1884, since such an analysis requires that the individual graduates be linked to their family's tax returns. It makes sense to do so only when, as in 1876, all Jewish wage earners were recorded. The analysis impressively confirms the close connection between social background and graduation from a *Gymnasium* (table 44). Among the 160 Jewish graduates whose parents' income could be unequivocally determined, only 2% came from a family whose annual income was under 1,100 marks, and 16% from a lower-middle-class family with an annual income between 1,100 and 2,750 marks. Measured by the income structure of the total Jewish population aged thirty to sixty years, then, lower-class families were grossly overrepresented among Jewish graduates and lower-middle-class families considerably so. By contrast, sons of middle-class families with an annual income of between 2,750 and 9,200 marks were slightly overrepresented among Jewish graduates, and those from upper middle-class families with an annual income of more than 9,200 marks were clearly overrepresented. Although only 8% of the total Jewish population aged thirty to sixty years belonged to the upper-middle class, 34% of all Jewish graduates in Breslau came from families with an annual income of more than 9,200 marks.

That it was just as unlikely for lower-middle-class Jews to complete their *Abitur* as it was for lower-middle-class Protestants and Catholics is shown by a consideration of the few Jewish graduates who grew up in poverty. One was Max Sohrauer, who graduated from the Realgymnasium am Zwinger in 1881 at the age of seventeen. He was the second oldest son of the merchant Wilhelm Sohrauer, who, due to the bankruptcy of his business in 1876, had an annual income of only 420 marks. It is probable that the father's income was greater before 1876, and it is possible that his income improved again after 1876.[48] Louis Neustadt (1857–1918), who later was editor of the *Jüdisches Volksblatt*, came from a family whose income did not support a middle-class lifestyle. He graduated in 1877 from the Elisabeth-Gymnasium. He was one of seven children of the rabbi Pinkus Neustadt (1823–1902), who directed the Jewish *Gemeinde*'s Hebrew School, for which he earned 1,200 marks per year. Given his income, Pinkus Neustadt and his wife must have made a great sacrifice to enable their eldest son to earn his *Abitur*. In any case, none of his younger brothers did so.[49] It is all the more important to stress just how unusual it was that Louis Neustadt attended and graduated from the *Gymnasium*, even if at first glance it seems to confirm the thesis that the educational advantage of Breslau's Jews was rooted in Jewish educational traditions.

The comparison of the social background of Jewish, Protestant, and Catholic graduates in imperial Germany relativizes the extent of the Jewish educational advantage. One's chances of successfully completing secondary-school studies were decided, above all, by the profession and income of one's parents. One's success in secondary schools was a function of how good one's grades were, not of collective criteria. Jewish *Gymnasium* pupils had just as good a chance of graduating with distinction as Catholic or Protestant pupils, assuming they managed to attend a secondary school in the first place. However, Jews were more likely to do so than their fellow Catholics and Protestants. The Jewish educational advantage was based primarily on the Jewish population's professional and income structures, which were rather exclusive in comparison with those of other Breslauers. On the other hand, factors such as the Jewish educational tradition or the pronounced ambition of outsiders had only negligible significance in the early, but especially the late imperial era. The question of how far these considerations would apply beyond Breslau must remain open until it has been determined whether these results apply to other metropolises as well.[50] It is likely that secularized Jewish educational traditions played a role during the rapid social advancement of German Jews between 1820 and 1870. But here, too, it would be necessary to consider whether the Jewish educational advantage in secondary schools and universities was not preceded by the socioeconomic advancement of Jews. Even if one grants a certain importance to a particular Jewish educational tradition, it remains questionable whether it was a direct line of tradition. The idea that the Jewish educational advantage was based on secularized Jewish educational traditions, an idea that had its origin in contemporary Jewish journalism, was itself an integral part of the "invention of a tradition," which is characteristic of modern German Jewry as a whole.[51]

2. Pluralism in Municipal School Politics and the Limits of Tolerance: The Johannes-Gymnasium, 1865–1933

In a history of relations between Jews and other Breslauers, the Johannes-Gymnasium, or Johanneum, holds a special place. The school, which opened in 1872, embodied the pluralist school policies of the liberal majority in the city council and magistracy. As in other metropolises, the City of Breslau wanted by no means to banish religion from the schools but rather to found a *Gymnasium* that embodied the idea of parity. Jewish, Catholic, and Protestant pupils and teachers were to enjoy the same rights, and the three denominations the same recognition.[52] As a consequence of this pluralism, the city entered into a struggle with the conservative Prussian state, which wanted to maintain the Protestant character of the school system, and with politically organized Catholics, who envisioned a segregated Catholic school system. The clashes began in 1863 and lasted until the early 1880s. The conflict's length and bitterness, and especially the liberal magistracy's endurance, sense of mission, and resoluteness, must be understood within the context of the Kulturkampf, literally a "struggle of civilizations" that marked the culmination of church-state conflicts in nineteenth-century Germany.[53] It is striking that Jewish liberals played an active role in the struggle. Together with liberal Protestants, Catholics, and dissenters, they succeeded in turning the Johannes-Gymnasium into a pluralist school and hoped that it would serve as a model for other schools.[54]

The Local Conflict and the Formation of the Catholic Milieu

In the 1860s all Breslauers were in agreement: The construction of new schools seemed imperative, since the population had grown faster than the number of secondary schools. The city council decided in 1863 to found a *Gymnasium*, a *Realgymnasium*, and three middle schools.[55] The debate about the denominational character of the schools was initiated by a Catholic citizens' movement that included both ultramontane and liberal Catholics. Its spokesman was Peter Joseph Elvenich (1796–1886), a professor of philosophy in the University of Breslau's Department of Theology, who had formerly been a leader of the Hermesian movement and would soon become a prominent Old Catholic. Equally interested in the conflict was Joseph Hubert Reinkens (1821–96), who became Germany's first Old Catholic bishop in 1873.[56] This broad Catholic coalition petitioned the magistracy on June 8, 1863, to open one of the schools as a first-class Catholic *Realschule*. Although one of Breslau's oldest *Gymnasien*, the Königliches Matthias-Gymnasium, was Catholic, all the secondary schools the city had opened since 1800 had a Protestant charter.[57] The city's leading Catholic newspaper, the *Breslauer Hausblätter*, had good reason to lament that the predominantly Protestant character of Breslau's secondary schools constituted "a glaring violation of the basic principles of parity the city [was] obliged to observe." "The discrimination against the denominational interests of Breslau's Catholic pupils in favor of those of the Protestants in secondary subjects" was held to be a "conspicuous fact for which the municipal authorities [were] responsible."[58]

In contrast to the Catholic citizens' movement led by Elvenich, the *Breslauer Hausblätter* raised the farther-reaching demand of building a separate Catholic school system. While that organ of ultramontanism complained about the "Protestantization" of *Gymnasien* and stressed that the Catholics of Breslau were entitled to their own secondary schools, *Hausblätter* articles also contained decidedly anti-Semitic and antiliberal digs. According to the paper, the clash over the Johannes-Gymnasium was symptomatic of the "Judaization" of Breslau politics. The municipal authorities wanted new "nondenominational" schools "in which Jews, Turks, and especially, of course, dissenters and atheists were allowed to instruct Christian adolescents." Eventually, the *Hausblätter* warned, "primarily Jewish and anti-Christian elements will usurp the teaching posts so as to corrupt the young with the magic potion of progress." In short, the city was planning to use the school's charter to "lock Christianity out of school."[59] "The Jewish press"—namely, the left-wing liberal *Breslauer Zeitung*—allegedly "worked on" the municipal authorities in advance to get them to ignore the interests of the Catholics.[60] David Honigmann, a Jewish liberal and one of the initiators of the pluralistic school policy, was the target of biting ridicule. The "Jewish doctor's" speech, said the *Hausblätter*, did not go down "like honey but rather was extremely tedious." Honigmann spoke out in favor of "nondenominational" schools "so that Israel and Judah, too, can instruct the Christian youth." The city council, continued the paper, had not brought an end to the debate but rather "observed Shabbat and voted, whereby Protestants, Jews, and dissenters" opposed the Catholics.[61]

Despite the resentment, the accusation of secularization was more justified than that of Protestantization. The magistracy, and especially the city council, did indeed want to secularize Breslau's secondary schools in 1865. All new schools were to be "nondenominational." Of course, "nondenominational" did not mean laicist or antireligious.[62] All pupils—thus not only Catholics and Protestants but Jews and dissenters as well—had to attend religious instruction. However, what raised the ire of ultramontane Catholics was the fact that all other subjects would no longer be informed by Christian doctrine. Secularized history or science instruction, the *Breslauer Hausblätter* argued in October 1865, was nothing but "a machine of destruction [pitted] against the church, faith, and the Christian ethos," and the "classroom" would become a "devil's workshop."[63] Six years later, with the bitter struggle over the Johannes-Gymnasium still going on, the *Hausblätter* further explained the Catholic position: Religion must, "as the factor that conditions educational activity in the school," form "the essence that pervades school instruction in its entirety." It would be impossible for "children to become steeped in the religious principles" if "clergymen were left with [only] a few class periods each week." The principal aim of education was "to strengthen the children's religious convictions," and this could be achieved only if children were "segregated along denominational lines, and if their teachers . . . observed the same religion as their pupils."[64] "Christian discipline," the paper elaborated, "seeks to enrich and bend the will, whereas nondenominational schools focus on developing cognitive capacities." The *Hausblätter* warned all the more urgently against "nondenominational schools," since, although they might "well be able to produce intelligent, calculating men, they [could] not produce men of character."[65] As early as the mid-1860s, Breslau Catholics opposed the interdenominational, pluralistic school system and criticized the allegedly secular *Gymnasien*. Their goal was instead to establish segregated, thoroughly Catholic schools as part of a Catholic milieu.[66]

As late as 1869—four years into the conflict, when the differences had long since become irreconcilable—a liberal Protestant commentator acknowledged that moderate Catholic demands were justified. The anonymous author, a self-professed "independent freethinker, . . . fully agreed with the 'separation of the school from the church,' or more precisely: the division of their respective administrative concerns." Most school subjects "have absolutely nothing to do with religion"; there are "no Catholic, Protestant, or Mosaic mathematics, chemistry, natural history, etc." Yet whereas radical secularizers are convinced that religious instruction alone is molded by denomination, argued the "independent freethinker," it is also true that within the field of history "one cannot cast off one's 'denomination.'" In contrast to "pure and free science," history lessons "should not be combined with the spirit of critique and doubt" but instead provide the pupils with "something positive, something concretely grounded." Such positive historical knowledge conveyed at school always has a denominational bias, he continued, because Catholicism and Protestantism, just like "spiritualism, materialism, and idealism," do designate not simply "an affiliation" but "a philosophy of life and a Weltanschauung."[67]

No less important than these general considerations, however, was the concrete situation in Breslau, for Protestants were "not the only ones" there. The Catholics in the Silesian capital had demanded that at least one of the new city schools be given a Catholic charter. "One can wish that this were not the case, that they would gladly send their children to . . . parity schools; but wishing doesn't change anything, because that's simply not the way things are." By rejecting the Catholics' demand, the city was provoking them to create "their own denominational school." Instead of supporting moderate Catholics, the city was playing into the hands of "radical agitators." An "institution produced by denominational agitation, and consecrated with anger and frustration, and influenced by those hellbent on segregation" would sharpen the sectarian conflict more than would a school "amicably proposed, built, maintained, and supervised by the community."[68]

In Breslau itself the Catholics could hardly hope to realize their goals, because a broad liberal coalition supported the municipal authorities' pluralistic school policy. In the city council meeting of October 26, 1865—which was attended by almost all councilors, the mayor,

and "an unusually large audience"—this liberal alliance demonstrated
its power for the first time.[69] In July 1865, the magistracy had proposed
that the "institutions of higher learning the city was planning to build"
not be given any "specific denominational character" and that, "of the
middle schools to be built first, two [were to be staffed] with Protestant,
one with Catholic teachers."[70] With only one dissenting vote, the city
council's school commission recommended accepting the magistracy's
proposal. On behalf of the commission, Moritz Elsner, a veteran liberal
journalist and one of the city's legendary Forty-Eighters, criticized the
Catholics' demand to maintain the Christian nature of secondary education. The natural sciences, history, and languages, he argued, should
be taught "objectively, without any denominational bias"; teaching general subjects with such a bias is "an abuse" of the school. He explicitly rejected the reproach of being anti-Catholic. Had the city's Protestants or
Jews put forward a similar request, he said, the school commission would
also have rejected it. Despite the neutral gesture, however, Elsner derided
ultramontane Catholicism by alluding to the small amount of taxes paid
by the Catholics: "In view of the Catholic petitioners, the Jewish inhabitants would be completely justified in demanding a Jewish *Realschule* and
a Jewish *Gymnasium*, and all the more so as they perhaps pay more taxes,
in proportion to their number, than the Protestants and Catholics."[71]

The Catholic spokesman in Breslau was no ultramontane radical
close to the *Breslauer Hausblätter*, but the provincial syndic general and
privy councilor Karl von Görtz, a good friend of Reinkens.[72] In a moderate tone, he declared that he was not "opposed to the principle of
nondenominational schools but to its immediate implementation." As
long as all the city's secondary schools were Protestant, it was perfectly
reasonable to demand another Catholic school. Görtz therefore introduced a motion that "if the principle of nondenominational schools
[were] ratified, a first-class Catholic *Realschule* should first be built to
accord with conditions of parity among denominations in Breslau"—
from which Görtz expressly excluded the Jews—and therefore "to lend
to the decrees . . . the consecration of justice."[73]

While Görtz was still trying to win support for the Catholic position,
a group of liberal councilors had taken a more radical position than the
magistracy and the school commission. The group demanded that none
of the new middle schools have a denominational character. The group's
speaker was Richard Roepell (1808–93), a historian who had been actively involved with the right wing of the liberal movement since 1848, a
Breslau city councilor since 1859, and a Protestant.[74] "The modern

era," argued Roepell, "calls for the nondenominational character of schools. . . . We should not force the middle schools . . . into the bounds of the past, namely, those of denomination, or provide the church with new means to interfere with municipal affairs." Like Elsner, Roepell could not go without taking a dig at the Catholics by reproaching them for their educational deficit. "It is proven that more Jewish pupils attend institutions of higher learning than do Catholic pupils." Therefore, "no tuition funds are available . . . for a new Catholic *Realschule*."[75]

The magistracy and city council wanted to secularize secondary schools also to enable the hiring of Jewish teachers, as especially David Honigmann (1821–85)—a Jewish city councilor who, unlike Elsner and Roepell, abstained from anti-Catholic digs—emphasized. "It would be advisable for the city administration to divest itself of its Protestant character," particularly as "building" parity schools would not involve the "banishing of religion" from them. The city's policy aims not only to grant equal rights and status to Judaism, Catholicism, and Protestantism, but also "to do away, at city meetings such as these, with all obstacles and considerations in the hiring of teachers that arise from taking account of their creed."[76] For some years, German Jews such as the Breslau philologist Wilhelm Freund had observed with increasing bitterness that it was impossible for Jewish teachers to secure positions at secondary schools.[77] To remind everyone present of this fact, Honigmann proposed that it be explicitly stated that it would be possible to hire Protestant, Catholic, *and* Jewish teachers at the schools.

In October 1865 the liberals carried the day. In each case, the farthest-reaching proposal received the wide majority of votes. The Breslau city council decided that the secondary and middle schools should have no denominational character and explicitly stated that Jewish teachers could be hired at all of them. The council recognized Catholic demands only insofar as they asked the magistracy to "uphold more than in the past the nondenominational character of the Realschule am Zwinger with regard to the hiring of teachers."[78] The new school policy thus resembled in essential respects those that the *Allgemeine Zeitung des Judenthums*, the voice of German Reform Jews, advocated. In April 1869, the newspaper argued that mixed schools "would not [cause] denomination-bound religious instruction [to] atrophy nor would [they] endanger religious life, but only prevent the abuse of [schools] for secular purposes."[79] Little surprise, then, that in August 1869 the leading Jewish weekly praised the Breslau school policy as an "example of steadfast independence well worth imitating."[80]

The Breslauer Schulstreit: A Conflict between the City and the State

Although the vast majority in the Breslau city council had supported a pluralistic school policy, the Catholics did not give up. In November 1865, the *Hausblätter* announced that Breslau Catholics, who had been reduced to "white slaves," would "try to ascertain whether the city [was] entitled to disregard their legitimate demands and [had] the authority to put state-recognized religious communities on the same level as tolerated sects."[81] Breslau Catholics were successful in their appeal to the provincial school board and the Kultusministerium (Ministry of Religious and Educational Affairs).[82] Henceforth, this was no longer a local conflict. Instead, the "Breslau school struggle" (*Breslauer Schulstreit*) attracted attention all over Germany.[83] An assorted crowd of liberals who held influential positions in the Breslau magistracy and city council now had to face both the ultramontane movement and the conservative Prussian state bureaucracy.

The provincial school board and the Kultusministerium rejected Breslau's liberal school policy and refused to allow the opening of the new parity secondary and middle schools. In particular, the Johannes-Gymnasium, the only *Gymnasium* among the new schools, had to have a "Christian character," the conservative secretary of religious and educational affairs, Heinrich von Mühler, announced in 1867.[84] Carl Gottfried Scheibert, who had been a member of the provincial school board in Breslau since 1855, considered the school to be "damaging to the German mind." According to Scheibert, the Christian faith should inform all aspects of education, and for that reason, Jews can never teach subjects that "touch on religious matters or can only be taught truthfully and fruitfully from a religious point of view." That holds as well, he noted, for "composition, mathematics, and grammar" teachers, because they are forced, "when giving encouragement, warnings, . . . , reprimands, etc., to draw on the motivating moral will dwelling" within themselves.[85]

The municipal authorities did not cave in, however, but instead petitioned the Prussian Landtag in January 1868 that the state accept the pluralist character of at least the Johannes-Gymnasium. Because the Landtag refused to consider the petition, the Breslau magistracy was willing to give way, especially as the need for new secondary schools had become even direr since 1863. Moreover, the new school buildings had been very costly. The bill for the Johannes-Gymnasium alone, which had been ready to open its doors in October 1866, came to sixty thousand taler.[86] Due to the ongoing conflict, the Johannes-Gymnasium, like the other new school buildings, had since stood empty, although, as the *Schlesische Zeitung* noted, "the need for new schools had grown with every term."[87] In June 1868, the magistracy proposed to the city council that it "open the Johannes-Gymnasium on October 1st as a denominational school."[88]

The city council's liberal majority, however, did not want to sacrifice their vision of a pluralistic school policy to what they regarded as the constraints of realpolitik. After Moritz Elsner and David Honigmann, in the council meeting of July 9, 1868, accused the magistracy of disregarding the resolutions passed at the city council meeting of October 1865, the chairman of the city council, Karl Gustav Stetter, a Protestant, proposed that the magistracy, together with the council, present the hitherto unsuccessful petition from January once again to the Landtag. The city councilors almost unanimously rejected the magistracy's motion and passed Stetter's instead.[89] Now the petition was again before the Landtag.

In late February 1869, the Prussian Landtag saw a contentious debate about the denominational character of Breslau secondary schools. Here ultramontane Catholics and liberals opposed each other just as irreconcilably as in the Silesian capital. What the liberals considered model school policy, Catholic members of the Landtag saw as a nightmare. Hermann von Mallinckrodt, for instance, urged the Landtag "to imagine what a nondenominational school in Breslau would look like in practice." Since half of Breslau's secondary-school pupils were Protestants and the other half was divided evenly between Catholics and Jews, "the proportion of teachers would have to be the same" and "the textbooks accordingly should not offend or oppose anyone." With that, the nightmarish picture of a misguided school policy was complete. In such schools, Mallinckrodt said, "a race will be educated that has come to doubt the highest goals and staggers through life without faith." Only denominational schools were able to educate pupils to be "faithful to God" and "loyal to their fellow men." Within a denominationally segregated school system, he continued, Jews should be granted equality. If Breslau Jews want "their own secondary school, then the city, in my opinion," has to build one. Yet Jews had no right to demand that "the Christian denominations . . . be so accommodating that they betray their principles." Mallinckrodt's idea of parity was not "that all the denominations be lumped together but that each be esteemed and respected in its distinctiveness."[90]

Two liberal Landtag members from Breslau defended the position of the municipal authorities. Both knew Breslau politics well. The Progressive member, the merchant Carl Wilhelm Laßwitz (1809–79), had been city councilor since 1860; the National Liberal member, the lawyer Wilhelm Lent (1824–86), since 1862. After a heated, five-hour debate, the liberals carried the day against Breslau's conservative and Catholic critics. The majority of Prussian members supported the liberal motion to forward the magistracy's petition to the government and to urge it to permit the city to establish a *Realschule* and a *Gymnasium* without "requiring that the schools be given a specific denominational character."[91]

After the debate in the Prussian Landtag, the municipal authorities hoped that a compromise could be reached that would be favorable to them, especially as the city in the meantime had sought to accommodate the Breslau Catholics by opening a Catholic *Realschule* in 1868, albeit only a second-class school rather than the first-class one the Catholics had demanded.[92] During the city council meeting of April 26, 1869, frictions surfaced within the liberal coalition. As in the meeting in October 1865, almost all city councilors showed up and "the gallery was quite full, even with women."[93] The minority envisioned a state completely neutral in religious matters. Its speaker was Wilhelm Bouneß, who had been city council chairman in 1864 and 1865 and represented Breslau in the Constituent Reichstag in 1867.[94] He reminded the city council that David Honigmann's motion, which the council had passed almost unanimously in 1865, "indisputably excluded any denominational character for the schools in question." Now it seemed that some "want[ed] to forge ahead with a different policy," which would entail giving the Johanneum a Christian character after all. Such a step would leave the city at the mercy of the conservative state bureaucracy. "What 'Christian' means with respect to these institutions," Bouneß warned, "can be learned from the notorious case of Jutrosinky, who was denied a position at a Christian school because he is Jewish."[95]

Unlike in 1865, the majority of liberal city councilors now wanted the schools to maintain a diffusely Christian character like that of the state. This, in essence, was the liberal-Protestant paradigm of cultural homogeneity, which, at least ideally, denied Jews a right to be different. Breslau's mayor, Arthur Hobrecht (1824–1912), had already suggested as early as June 1868 that the Johannes-Gymnasium be given a Protestant character in order to end the conflict. Now he reminded his audience that a complete separation of church and state was inconsistent with the Prussian constitution and warned against granting "non-Christian denominations rights that [did] not exist and whose denial [was] ameliorated by the fact that the great majority of Breslau inhabitants [were] Christians."[96] Remarkably, it was Richard Roepell, the same man who had introduced the most far-reaching motion in 1865, who now concisely presented the Christian-liberal view on the issue. Naturally, the Johannes-Gymnasium had to be a Christian school. "We call these schools Christian because the education they preserve and spread is Christian. No one hesitates to call Prussia a Christian state, or the Germans a Christian people. Were we not convinced that Jewish teachers familiarize themselves with Christian education, they would not find any position at our schools." Thus, yes, he implied, to the hiring of Jewish teachers at public, that is, "Christian," schools; no to the equal recognition of Judaism. The majority of councilors supported Roepell's view, though the margin of fifty-one to forty-four votes was unusually narrow. The city council decided to inform the provincial school board that the City of Breslau wanted the schools "to have a Christian but not narrowly denominational character" and demanded "that no members of any Christian or non-Christian religious community should be barred from teaching solely because of their religious beliefs."[97]

The mouthpiece of church-affiliated, liberal Protestants, the *Schlesisches Protestantenblatt*, articulated even more clearly the liberal-Protestant paradigm of cultural homogeneity. In June 1875, the weekly derided the demand of Jewish parents that their children be exempted from writing in school on the Sabbath as indicative of "the whole superficiality of Judaism." "Jewry, which claims to keep step with the times and to be able sincerely to reconcile itself with the ideals of modern culture," argued one of the *Schlesisches Protestantenblatt*'s four editors, the pastor Julius Decke, "is in fact shot through with religious superstition" and "religious narrow-mindedness." "A vigorous grasp of the genuinely human religious-moral ideal of life," Decke continued, "presupposes a complete reformation of the average Jewish character. Until that happens, the German people will consider Jews generally to be alien and disagreeable."[98]

The conflict over the Johannes-Gymnasium had long since stirred up the liberal and Catholic public in Breslau. On June 3, 1869, at a meeting of the Katholischer Volksverein (Catholic Citizens' Association), which had been founded two years earlier, 2,500 Breslau Catholics voted to petition the Prussian king to support the Catholic demand for a first-class *Realschule*. Peter Elvenich, the future Old Catholic, was still one of the group's spokesmen.[99] In 1869, the *Breslauer Hausblätter* reported with satisfaction that the leaders of the Catholic movement had "chosen Breslau as a testing ground for their powers" and that it was "incredible how zealous [they were] in this matter."[100] The Breslau liberals were outraged that the Catholics had taken their criticism of the municipal authorities to the king. Within two weeks, liberal city councilors collected more than 12,000 signatures for a statement of support for the magistracy in order to counter the "ultramontanes' passionate attacks on the mayor"—as the semiofficial *Chronik der Stadt Breslau* (Chronicle of the City of Breslau) put it twenty years later. On June 20, 1869, a deputation of Breslau citizens—among them, two prominent Jews, the dentist Moritz Fränkel and the printer Moritz Spiegel—formed a "solemn procession" to present the statement of support to Mayor Hobrecht. The deputation's speaker, Professor Christlieb Julius Braniss (1792–1873), and the mayor both used the occasion to reiterate the great symbolic significance of the conflict.[101]

The provincial school board and the Kultusministerium refused to allow the opening of the schools, even though the municipal authorities had complied with the Prussian state bureaucracy with their decision of April 1869. The city's willingness to give the schools a vaguely Christian character was not enough for the Prussian state bureaucracy. In August 1869, the provincial school board, which had coordinated its position with the Kultusministerium beforehand, answered that a school's religious character finds "its most meaningful expression" in the composition of the teaching staff. The state bureaucracy was outraged that the municipal authorities were claiming an area of authority for themselves that, according to the provincial school board, did not belong to them. "Only very special circumstances," the board argued, permitted the hiring of non-Christian teachers. Whatever those circumstances might be, each case had to be "evaluated and decided" by the state. In no uncertain terms, the provincial school board defended the traditional concept of Prussia as a Christian state: "To call an institution Christian . . . that is free to hire Protestants, Catholics, Jews, and dissenters as it likes," as Roepell and the magistracy had done, "is, to say the least, empty wordplay that does not do justice to the gravity . . . of the matter at hand."[102]

This curt rejection left little room for compromise. In September 1869, the municipal authorities announced that they believed they must "give up all hope of an unbiased assessment of [their] motives and intentions by the provincial school board." In response, the magistracy decided, with the city council's approval, to rent out the empty Johannes-Gymnasium. The city was playing for time, hoping that the conservative secretary of religious and educational affairs von Mühler would soon resign.[103] Yet Breslau schools continued to be jam-packed. Whereas the city could limit its financial losses by renting out the school building, such a measure could not put an end to the growing overcrowding of the city's secondary schools.

In summer 1870, a group of Breslau liberals once again tried to dilute the municipal authorities' pluralistic school policy. The mouthpiece this time was not a city councilman but the *Schlesische Zeitung*, which was close to the National Liberals. The external motive for this undertaking was the provincial school board's offer that the secretary of religious and educational affairs would allow the city to open the schools with the understanding that "the magistracy's choice of teachers [could] be confirmed only if it accord[ed] with the assumption, spelled out in the secretary's declaration, that the schools [were] to be Christian."[104] The *Schlesische Zeitung*, which hitherto had reported favorably on the municipal school policy, now entered the fray with a long editorial, which was reprinted in numerous other leading liberal German papers, perhaps because it represented National Liberal opinion on school policy more generally.[105] The secretary of religious and educational affairs had met the city halfway, it argued, and Breslau should accept his offer. Clearly "the inner nature of the new schools must be based on the generally Christian foundation of our nation's cultural life." The editorial only touched on the hiring of Jewish teachers, which the city councilors had demanded. It was desirable if the city could prevent the state from denying "the confirmation of teachers the municipal authorities had chosen by invoking the schools' denominational charter." To end the overcrowding of Breslau schools, the magistracy should accept a Protestant school charter for the Johanneum; in the long term, the spirit of "religious tolerance" would prevail. The city should not allow the "temporary reign of a rigid sectarianism . . . deprive us of the fruits of our labors."[106]

The Jewish press was alarmed by the *Schlesische Zeitung*'s editorial. In July 1870, the *Israelitische Wochenschrift*, whose left-wing liberal stance on school policy the *Breslauer Zeitung* had previously called "noteworthy," published a lengthy analysis of the "Breslau school struggle."[107] The blame for the current confusion, it said, lay with the city's magistracy and liberals like Roepell, who had told the Prussian state bureaucracy in 1869 that the new schools should have a generally "Christian character." Now the *Schlesische Zeitung* argued that "the inner nature of the new schools" was "based on the generally Christian foundation of [the] nation's cultural life." If that were correct, the *Israelitische Wochenschrift*

pointed out, the Prussian secretary of religious and educational affairs
would be justified in arguing that "schools grounded in such a spirit
could have no room for Jewish teachers." This was not, of course, what
the Breslau magistracy had intended, noted the paper; it had only
wanted to emphasize that the schools "had to be founded on a common
humane, moral basis, and it used 'generally Christian' to express that."
Thus the magistracy had "followed a widely held but . . . false usage according to which 'Christianity' is identical with 'humanity." In fact, "our
cultural life and our educational institutions based on it," the *Wochenschrift* argued instead, "have nothing to do with either Christianity or Judaism. The study of ancient and contemporary languages, . . . history
and geography, . . . mathematics and the natural sciences" is neither
Christian nor Jewish, but only study "that is grounded in specifically
Christian or Jewish ideas of faith, views, duties, etc."[108]

Unlike the *Schlesische Zeitung,* the magistracy did not want to rely on
the state bureaucracy's goodwill. When the Prussian secretary of religious and educational affairs stipulated on June 24, 1870, that the process of hiring teachers should be based on the premise "that the institutions [were] to be Christian," the magistracy answered on July 6, 1870,
that it amounted to an explicit "statutory prescription." Although the
city had been willing to accept the secretary's designation of the schools
as "generally Christian," it was unwilling to embed it in the school statute because it did not want to contradict the pluralistic character of its
school policy. As long as the state bureaucracy did not renounce the statutory prescription of the Christian character of Breslau's secondary
schools, the magistracy noted, the city felt obliged to continue to leave
the school buildings empty.[109]

"A Welcome Precedent"—*The Opening of the Johannes-Gymnasium*

Only after a political shift in the Prussian Kultusministerium, when the
National Liberal Adalbert Falk replaced the conservative von Mühler,
could the municipal authorities renew their hopes of realizing their pluralistic school policy. When von Mühler's dismissal became public in
late January 1872, the *Allgemeine Zeitung des Judenthums* speculated that his
successor would break with von Mühler's "clinging to formalities, . . . his
petty-minded sticking to the wording and the letter of the law." Legal
equality was the law; the new secretary of religious and educational affairs would now have to implement it administratively and "to cease
altogether to exclude qualified Jews from the staffs of public schools."[110]

No sooner had Falk taken office than the Breslau city council chairman, Georg Friedrich Lewald, received a letter from the Jewish salesman Adolph Wohlauer. He asked the city council "to take the appropriate steps regarding the opening of the nondenominational schools [there] . . . as soon as possible. Motives: the recent change of personnel and the current liberal climate in the Kultusministerium."[111] The magistracy sent its superintendent of schools, Heinrich Thiel, to Berlin to explain the city's position and to ask Falk for the permission the city had been denied by von Mühler for seven years. On April 1, 1872, Falk instructed the provincial school board that, when confirming the hiring the teachers for the Johanneum, it should "not consider abstract criteria," such as religious background, but decide only on the basis of the candidate's professional qualifications.[112] At the end of April, the city chose Professor C. F. W. Müller from the Joachimsthaler-Gymnasium in Berlin to be the Johanneum's principal.[113] In June, Müller and Thiel advised the magistracy in its choice of teachers. Now the municipal authorities were able to give "the principle a practical expression for which the municipal authorities had fought for so long." "The intention therefore was that among those chosen there should be at least one Catholic and one Jew."[114] In August 1872, readers of the *Allgemeine Zeitung des Judenthums* and the *Israelitische Wochenschrift* found the sensational news that "among the teachers chosen" for the Johanneum there was "indeed one of [their] coreligionists."[115]

The opening of the Johannes-Gymnasium on October 14, 1872, was thus both a triumph for Breslau's liberal municipal government and a major step toward tangible Jewish equality. Among the school's sixteen teachers, two were Jewish; they, too, were charged with teaching so-called *Gesinnungsfächer,* or ethical subjects such as history and German, and, at least initially, Jewish religious instruction was compulsory for Jewish pupils and part of their final exams—something formerly unheard of in Germany.[116] Thus the city accepted, at least symbolically, the right of Jews to be different. While, as the principal of the Realgymnasium am Zwinger had explained in 1865, the city's other secondary schools were dominated by the "spirit of Christian love" that respected "Judaism" solely as a "historical prerequisite for Christianity," Jewish religious instruction now had the same status as Catholic and Protestant instruction at the newly founded school.[117] In the Johanneum's "latest final exams, the subject of Jewish religion was part of the public examinations," the *Israelitische Wochenschrift* proudly reported in October 1874; the weekly lauded this "consideration of Judaism" and hoped it would be "a welcome precedent," one that other schools would follow.[118] In autumn 1897, the Johanneum celebrated the twenty-fifth anniversary of its opening; among the 16 professors and senior teachers, 4 were Jewish: Benno Badt, Ignaz Harczyk, Emil Toeplitz, and Adolf Wohlauer. At the city's other eleven *Gymnasien, Realgymnasien,* and *Realschulen,* 32 Catholics and 105 Protestants taught, but no Jews, apart from Gustav Krakauer, who taught at the Ober-Realschule, which had been founded in 1874.[119]

To do justice to the significance of October 14, 1872, the magistracy had decided to open the school "with all due ceremony." "Today," the *Israelitische Wochenschrift* wrote, is "significant" not only for Breslau "but for the entire German Fatherland."[120] Max von Forckenbeck, Breslau's newly elected mayor, emphasized in his address at the school's inauguration that "the opening of this *Gymnasium* signal[ed] that a right the city had long been denied [had] indeed been recognized, to establish institutions of higher learning that grant citizens who are given the same duties the same rights as well."[121] Forckenbeck expressed two hopes for the future: that the school will disprove the reproach that "nondenominationalism, that is, the principle that no denomination should receive preferential treatment," is "identical with a lack of religion," and that "this institution . . . will educate its pupils to become citizens who are true to their own convictions, independent, and impervious to religious persecution."[122]

The principal recalled, somewhat more diplomatically, the school's prehistory. The task of establishing the Johanneum as equal in quality to the traditional Breslau *Gymnasien* is "not only enhanced and ennobled . . . for us but also . . . facilitated by the fact that our *Gymnasium,* with the permission of the high municipal authorities in accordance with the city's wishes, is to be stamped with a special character." What distinguishes the school is "tolerance" and not, as the school's critics had claimed, "a lack of religion—how could the spirit of piety, whose cultivation I take to be the chief goal of our striving, grow in the soil of irreligiousness?"[123] "Our municipal authorities," reported the Breslau correspondent of the *Israelitische Wochenschrift,* "bravely" held fast "during von Mühler's sad system of stultification" to their demand that, in the hiring of teachers, the secretary of religious and educational affairs guarantee "complete equality regarding faith." "May" the Johanneum "blossom and flourish," the report said in conclusion, "and become a model for many schools to come."[124]

Although the municipal authorities and the school administrators repeatedly emphasized the principle of religious pluralism and tolerance, the "general Christian," specifically Protestant, character of the school was unmistakable. Even the school's opening ceremony was framed by two Protestant hymns, "Lord, Your Goodness Reaches So Far" ("Herr, deine Güte reicht so weit") and "Praise the Lord, My Soul" ("Lobe den Herrn, meine Seele").[125] When in the 1883–84 school year the usual celebration of Wilhelm I's birthday was cancelled because it fell during vacation, the school administrators decided to celebrate instead, "in view of the preponderance of Protestant pupils, the four-hundredth anniversary of Luther's birth."[126] Moreover, while the name of the school primarily expressed civic pride—Johannes der Täufer (John the Baptist) was the patron of the Oder metropolis—the appellation was also rooted in the Christian tradition. In any case, the courage to name the school after Humboldt or Lessing, as the Berlin magistracy had done in 1875 and 1882, and as the Frankfurt magistracy would do in 1887, was lacking among the Breslau liberals.[127]

Wherever liberal-Protestant tolerance dominated, anti-Catholicism was not far away. The city did appoint one Roman Catholic teacher, Robert Gregor Depène. But with the agreement of the magistracy, the city council, and the provincial school board, the Breslau school board and the superintendent of schools appointed an Old Catholic, a former priest named Jakob Buchmann, to the position of teacher of Catholic religious instruction.[128] The appointment was no accident. Born in 1807, Buchmann had been ordained in 1834 and from 1837 on had served as a priest in the small town of Kanth, some twenty kilometers southwest of Breslau. He became well known in 1850 with the publication of his book *Popularsymbolik*.[129] From the summer of 1864 on, Buchmann had been in close contact with Reinkens, to whom he had complained about "the disastrous administration" of the archbishop of Breslau, Heinrich von Forster.[130] In May 1871, Buchmann refused to sign a petition supporting the curatorial clergy of Munich.[131] In the following summer, he advanced to the rank of martyr of the Silesian Old Catholics. In June, Reinkens reported, "[Y]ou cannot imagine" how much Buchmann is suffering "from his chaplains." "They refuse to eat with him because he is considered a heretic; they turn their backs on him, because the apostle supposedly requires it."[132] In July, Reinkens reported in the liberal *Kölnische Zeitung* on the Buchmann affair; in October, he also wrote at length in the *Breslauer Zeitung* about Buchmann's dismissal; and in December, Buchmann himself published a series of articles in the *Rheinische Merkur* against the Jesuits, which Reinkens thought to be "excellent" and were published in 1872 as a pamphlet.[133]

In the city council meeting of November 15, 1872, the Catholics protested in vain against Buchmann's appointment as the Catholic religion teacher at the Johannes-Gymnasium. "It is a blatant affront," the *Schlesische Volkszeitung* commented, to appoint "a priest who has been excommunicated because of his Jansenism to teach Catholic pupils." One of the liberals' spokesmen, the Jewish city councilor Sigismund Asch, stressed that the city could not fire Buchmann now, since that would mean taking sides in an inter-Catholic conflict. The *Schlesische Volkszeitung* retorted sharply that Asch threw "Old Catholics, that is, non-Catholics," thus a sect, "together in the same pot" with the Catholic Church. Yet even if the magistracy was of Asch's opinion, the paper continued, it is unclear why the decision for an Old Catholic teacher of Catholic religion was made without consulting the parents of Catholic pupils. "We've not heard," the Catholic organ reported, "that the pupils were asked—as once were the Polish soldiers in Prussia—if they wanted to be Old or Roman Catholics."[134] Nevertheless, the city council almost unanimously rejected the resolution of its Catholic colleague Josef Rockel, which called for a Roman Catholic rather than an Old Catholic teacher of Catholic religion to be hired. Consequently, in winter semester 1872–73 and summer semester 1873, Buchmann was responsible for teaching Catholic religious instruction at the upper levels (*Prima, Sekunda,* and *Tertia*) of the Johanneum.[135] In September 1873, Buchmann gave up his position, officially "because of his health and his advanced age." His teaching duties were assumed by Benno Hirschwälder, also an Old Catholic and a regular teacher at the Johanneum who had already been assigned to teach Catholic religious instruction at the lower levels.[136]

When things had calmed down, the Johanneum's principal and the municipal school board found a pragmatic solution to the problem. Since Buchmann and Hirschwälder were "affiliated with the Old Catholics," the *Gymnasium*'s chronicle stated, the parents of seven of altogether thirty-four pupils had their children excused from Catholic religious instruction. Even though the parents wanted to have their children taught "privately by a priest," the magistracy ordered on April 4, 1873, that Catholic pupils who did not want to be taught by an Old Catholic teacher of Catholic religion were to report for Catholic religious instruction at the nearby Realschule zum Heiligen Geist.[137]

With that the conflict over the pluralistic character of the Johanneum seemed to have come to an end. The city had made concessions to the Catholics, and the Jewish public in and around Breslau had every reason to praise the Johanneum and the municipal school policy. Yet the

Prussian state strongly objected to Breslau's far-reaching policy of parity of Judaism with Protestantism and Catholicism. This time the dispute flared up over the importance of Jewish religious instruction. In January 1875, the magistracy had decreed that "the participation of Jewish pupils in the religious instruction taught at the school [was] obligatory." To have their children excused from religious instruction, Jewish parents could not, as was otherwise usual, turn to the school's principal, but instead had to approach the magistracy.[138] On February 14, 1876, the Kultusministerium ordered the municipal school board to end the obligatory character of Jewish religious instruction, thereby stripping it of its status as an examination subject.[139] The magistracy asked the board of the Breslau *Synagogengemeinde* for an assessment of "the value of the obligatory character of the Mosaic religious instruction" at secondary schools. In its response, the board of the *Synagogengemeinde* warned, "Now if such instruction . . . is officially given an elective character, that is, if in the eyes of the pupils and their parents it is given the stamp of irrelevance, unimportance, and indeed superfluousness, the result must necessarily be a nearly unanimous self-exemption from such instruction." Moreover, if the obligatory character of Jewish religious instruction were dispensed with, "the Christian pupils" would be given "the idea of an objective and therefore justifiable inequality of Judaism with the other denominations" and thereby "the sense of denominational differences" would be sharpened.[140]

Although the magistracy armed itself with the arguments of the Jewish community, the provincial school board rejected the magistracy's request to make Jewish religious instruction obligatory at all secondary schools and not just at the Johannes-Gymnasium.[141] At its meeting of April 23, 1877, the city council reacted. The Jewish city councilor, Julius Hainauer, spoke for the liberal majority. A bookseller, music vendor, and publisher born in Glogau in 1827, Hainauer was, as the director of the Gesellschaft der Freunde (Society of Friends), one of the most prominent figures in Jewish associational life, as well as in the cultural life of Breslau, such as in the Breslauer Orchester-Verein (Breslau Orchestra Society), which had made him an honorary member in 1871. As a friend of Abraham Geiger, whose *Israelitisches Gebetbuch* Hainauer had published in 1854, he was also close to the Reform movement. "Hainauer," his grandson Willy Cohn recalled, "was what one . . . calls a personality."[142] His voice thus carried weight when he emphasized in the city council meeting that the decree by the secretary of religious and educational affairs "revoked the principle of equality of all sufficiently

represented denominations expressed upon the school's founding."
The character of the Johanneum required, however, that, "as an interdenominational institution, no single denomination receive preference
within it." Now that Jewish religious instruction had lost its obligatory
character, the Johanneum had "become a Christian school." Yet that
was precisely what "the City of Breslau had once challenged." "Nearly
unanimously," the city councilors passed Hainauer's motion that "the
council [should] request of the magistracy that it, with respect to the Johanneum, apply once again to the Kultusministerium that it reinstate
the former relationship between Jewish religious instruction and that of
the Christian denominations, that is, to invest such instruction with an
obligatory character, and it also include Jewish religious instruction
among the subjects in the examination for the *Abitur.*"[143]

While the magistracy agreed with the city councilors in principle in
November 1877, it asked them nevertheless that it be permitted not to
petition the Kultusministerium. Informal talks had revealed that there
was "no chance" of a new request being approved. Nor did the intervention of the Verein jüdischer Religionslehrer Schlesiens und Posens
(Association of Jewish Religion Teachers in Silesia and Posen) persuade
the Kultusministerium otherwise. Consequently, Jewish religious instruction at the Johannes-Gymnasium remained elective and Judaism
de facto a second-class religion.[144] Nevertheless, Hainauer used the city
council meeting in November 1877 to underscore once again the cardi-
nal importance of the school. "Has the idea we associated with the
founding of the Johanneum really come to pass? Has the fine phrase,
which . . . the mayor spoke at the opening of the school, that in its rooms
all faiths should be equal, become reality? And may we take pride in still
seeing in the Johanneum an interdenominational *Gymnasium?*"[145]

Although the city was only partially able to achieve its goal of founding a model parity school, the liberal climate at the school was preserved. The school administration sought to initiate a disciplinary investigation, with the magistracy's approval, against one of the school's
teachers, the Protestant senior teacher Hermann Fechner, who had participated in 1880 in political agitation in support of the "Anti-Semitic
Petition" (*Antisemitenpetition*).[146] Although the provincial school board
reprimanded the school's principal for overstepping his competence
and not the anti-Semitic teacher, the city councilors intervened in the
conflict symbolically by giving Principal Müller, who had been offered a
position at an Altona *Gymnasium*, an unscheduled pay raise to keep him
in Breslau.[147] Although the principal had not been able to admonish the

teacher officially, Fechner seems to have withdrawn from political life increasingly after 1880. Admittedly, in January 1882, he was the vice secretary of the board of the New Election Committee (Neuer Wahlverein), a union of National Liberals and Conservatives.[148] But thereafter, as the *Jüdisches Volksblatt* noted at his death in August 1910, he no longer played any role in Breslau political life.[149]

The "Müller affair" attracted attention beyond the city, and for the second time the Prussian Landtag debated about the Johannes-Gymnasium in 1868. In the Landtag's notorious debate about the Anti-Semitic Petition in November 1880, the Center Party's representatives Peter Reichensperger and Julius Bachem used the Breslau conflict, as Bachem put it, to castigate the "Jewish-progressive terrorism in Breslau." The Breslau Liberal representative Alexander Meyer defended the municipal authorities in his response. The anti-Semitic agitation of a teacher at the Johanneum, he said, is particularly reprehensible as Breslau built the school "as a monument to the spirit of tolerance prevailing in it."[150]

Yet the Johannes-Gymnasium also played an important role in the political agitation by the Breslau anti-Semites in the late 1870s and early 1880s. In November 1880, a coalition of National Liberals, Center Party Catholics, and Conservatives succeeded in staging the city council elections as a conflict between Christians and Jews. Encouraged by their election victory, a coalition of Catholics and Conservatives organized a protest rally in January 1881 against the magistracy's school policy. The name of the event reflected their agenda: "Assembly of Christian Citizens" (Versammlung christlicher Bürger). To mark the end of the Kulturkampf, half the speakers were Catholic, half Protestant. The principal Catholic speaker was Joseph Wick (1820–1903), who had been leader of the Catholic movement in Breslau since 1848, editor of the *Breslauer Hausblätter* from 1863 to 1868, and canon in Breslau since 1871. The roughly four-thousand-person strong audience was enthusiastic when Wick called on them "to rise up against their common enemy," the Jews, and "to christen" the "hybrid" (*Zwitter*) that was the pluralist Johannes-Gymnasium. The "christening" of the school would have been an important victory in an anti-Semitic crusade, which, as the conservative *Schlesisches Morgenblatt* argued in November 1880 in a series on the "comprehensive solution to the Jewish question," should have culminated in "a thoroughgoing, internal and external change of Christianity."[151]

Despite these hostilities, the Johannes-Gymnasium would in the long run be a success and would gain a good reputation among the Breslau

Jews. Because of the Johanneum's "boundless tolerance," the manufacturer Julius Schaeffer and his wife, Charlotte, sent their son Hans to the
school around 1890. "A good spirit prevailed in that school," Willy Cohn
noted in his autobiography from 1940. "There were tensions, of course,
like everywhere in life," wrote Cohn, who attended the Johanneum
from 1898 to 1907 and himself taught there during the Weimar Republic. "In general, however, people got along well." Cohn's "best friend"
was a "Christian pupil, Kurt Gruhl," at the top of their class.[152] In more
sober terms, Norbert Elias—next to Ernst Cassirer, the second most important twentieth-century scholar in the humanities who attended the
Johanneum—recalled his schooldays (1905–15). It counted among the
"minority of city *Gymnasien* at which Jewish pupils hardly met with
the pressure of veiled or overt anti-Semitic hostility from teachers or
pupils."[153] Being hired at the Johanneum was not an award to Jewish
teachers for extensive assimilation. Hermann Warschauer (1840–80),
the first Jewish teacher at the Johanneum, openly professed his Judaism.
Before the city's *Wissenschaftlicher Verein* (Scholarly Society), of which he
had been a member since 1872, he gave a lecture titled "The High
Priesthood among the Israelites," in 1877.[154] Albert Wohlauer (1858–
1922) and Benno Badt (1844–1909), author of a much-read children's
Bible,[155] were both well known in the city for their involvement in the
Jewish community. Badt and Wohlauer, much as Willy Cohn would
later, played leading roles in the life of the Jewish community in Breslau.

Moreover, the Johanneum attracted a growing number of Jewish
pupils, though it was located in the Ohlauer Vorstadt, where a comparatively low number of Jews resided; from 1900 on, more than 30% of
the student body was Jewish. If the father's profession is taken as a sufficient criterion for determining the class from which the pupils came,
then the background of the graduates from the Johanneum was just as
socially exclusive as it was among Jewish secondary-school pupils as a
whole; between 1900 and 1909, almost 90% of the fathers in each of the
comparison groups belonged to the property-owning or the educated
middle class.[156]

However, the school did not become a kind of "golden ghetto"
for the sons of the Jewish middle class in Breslau. During the heated
debate about the denominational character of Breslau's elementary
school system, Lord Mayor Georg Bender defended, in 1910, the principle of nondenominational education with reference to the Johanneum, which had "become more popular among the Christian population." "It is highly esteemed by the population, has a good reputation,

and contributes substantially to the spread of amicability."[157] Non-Jews also regarded the Johannes-Gymnasium as an attractive school for their sons, even if the school had to compensate for the fact that it lacked an aura of tradition, whereas competitors, such as the Elisabeth-, the Maria Magdalena-, and the Friedrich-Gymnasien, could boast of having at least a one-hundred-year history.[158] In 1884, a good ten years after the Johanneum's founding, the percentage of its pupils with a lower-class background (39%) was 7% higher than the average at the city's five *Gymnasien* (32%). To that corresponded the comparatively high percentage (14%) of graduates from lower-middle-class families between 1874 and 1879.[159] However, while the percentage of graduates from lower-middle-class and working-class households rose between 1880 and 1910 from 17% to 21%, it was halved at the Johanneum from 14% to 7%.[160] As early as 1893, the Johannes-Gymnasium had the smallest proportion of *Freischüler*, that is, pupils on a scholarship, among all the city's *Gymnasien* and *Realgymnasien*. Only 10% of all Johanneum pupils were exempted from paying tuition because they came from low-income households.[161] The school clearly had succeeded in establishing itself as a respected elite school.[162]

The success of the Johannes-Gymnasium was also due to the fact that the city's political elite celebrated the school not only in soapbox speeches but also by sending their own sons there. Among the school's first graduates in spring term 1877 were Bruno Thiel, a Protestant and son of the superintendent of municipal schools, and in autumn 1877 Franz von Forckenbeck, a Catholic and son of the mayor. In spring term 1879, Eugen Dickhuth, a Protestant and son of Gustav Dickhuth, from 1865 to 1879 syndic and from 1879 to 1892 vice mayor of Breslau. In 1886, Dickhuth's second son, Max Paul, graduated from the Johanneum, and in 1887 Bruno Heyse, a Protestant and son of the district superintendent of schools, did so.[163] Prior to 1914, seven graduates from the Johannes-Gymnasium were sons of city councilors, more than at any other Breslau *Gymnasium;* six sons of city councilors graduated from the Maria Magdalena-Gymnasium, but none did from the Friedrich- and Elisabeth-Gymnasien. It was only with the Protestant clergy that the Johanneum was not popular. Of the seven sons of superintendents who graduated from a Breslau *Gymnasium*, none attended the model liberal school, six went to the traditional, conservative Elisabeth-Gymnasium and one went to the Maria Magdalena-Gymnasium.[164]

The conflict over the Johanneum exemplifies both the status of Jews in Breslau schools and the city's pluralistic school policy. Certainly, the

Gymnasium remained an exception even in Breslau, contrary to what the Jewish public had hoped, yet it acted as a symbol within the city and beyond. Until the end of the Weimar Republic, one of Breslau's most respected schools served as a reminder that it was possible to reconcile humanist ideals of education, Jewish equality, and a high degree of pluralism. The magistracy and the city councilors were prepared to accept the lengthy conflict with the Prussian state bureaucracy because of the complexity of the confrontation.

For the municipal authorities it was also a conflict about the extent of Breslau's powers concerning school affairs. Although the city did not deny that questions of the internal constitution of schools, such as those of curriculum, lay in the purview of the state, it sought to expand or at least to preserve the latitude it had already gained to decide organizational matters. In 1908, the mayor of Halle and former Breslau city councilor Richard Rive proudly emphasized to the Prussian conference of mayors that the municipal authorities had turned "the municipal educational system into the finest creation of civilization," even though in this sphere "it was the rights of self-governance that [had] experienced the least degree of implementation."[165]

There was also considerable friction among Breslau liberals, even if both sides supported the hiring of Jewish teachers. Two varieties of liberalism were at odds about how to address the tension between the universal and the particular. National Liberal city councilors opted for a Christian form of universalism. The legitimation of such universalism was held to come not from a universally human but from a Christian ethics. The state, the nation, the society, and thus also the school could not be "neutral" here, but ultimately had to be Christian.[166] In 1869, Abraham Geiger had perspicaciously accused one of the most prominent representatives of the Progressive Party, Rudolf Virchow, of lacking objectivity, saying that "when it came to Christianity, even he could not free himself from prejudice." Geiger's charge was based on the fact that, during a debate about Prussian school policy, Virchow had argued that "the whole of [their] modern education" rested "on a Christian foundation, not on a dogmatic foundation, but on a decisively Christian, moral one."[167] While these liberals certainly wanted to include Jewish teachers and pupils in public schools, for them inclusion meant not recognition but only toleration. For them Christianity was not only a code of morals to which they granted greater value for their own lives than to other moral codes, but a normative model that had validity for the entire society. Whereas these cultural Protestant liberals, like Heinrich von

Treitschke, for example, roundly rejected the reproach of "denomina-tional hypocrisy" as applying to them, they nevertheless became all the more angry at those who demanded "the literal parity in all things for everyone" and "no longer wanted to see" that the "Germans [were] in fact a Christian nation and the Jews [were] only a minority among [them]." "We have even seen," Treitschke continued, that "the removal of Christian pictures, indeed the introduction of the celebration of the Sabbath, was demanded in mixed schools."[168] The limits of these liberals' toleration derived from a Christian-tinged universalism and not, as the critique of liberalism asserts today, from the aporias rooted in general tensions between universalism and particularism.[169] Many Prot-estant liberals were able to invoke the universalist principle of liberalism only insofar as they stylized the particularism of their own cultural Prot-estantism as the only true universalism. They thus resolved the tension between particularism and universalism in favor of a cultural-Protestant particularism and at the expense of an abstract universalism.

Universalism with a Christian tenor competed with an abstract form of universalism shared by the Jewish press, Jewish city councilors, and other left-wing liberal Breslau city councilors, such as Wilhelm Bouneß and Moritz Elsner. It was based on the idea of universal morality, which was conceived of as neither specifically Christian nor Jewish but univer-sally "human." In their view, the state should be "neutral," schools should therefore be essentially free of religious content, and the role of religion in schools, as well as in public life in general, should be nar-rowly defined. The recognition of the other, of religious diversity and difference should occur only in religious instruction. While such ab-stract universalism also could lead to aporias, the abstract equality of individuals before the law went untouched. The status of Jewish pupils should not differ from that of Catholic or Protestant pupils, and neither should the status of Jewish teachers differ from that of Catholic or Prot-estant teachers.

The tension between particularism and universalism continued unabated, and denominational particularism could not be confined to religious instruction. As long as diversity and difference, and the plural-ity of perspectives, did not become the leitmotif of education, and as long as "denominational subjects" were supposed to communicate ob-jective knowledge and homogeneous historical narratives, the question of which particular culture would prevail over the others remained open at best. The spectrum of Catholics who criticized the magistracy was far too heterogeneous to warrant calling their demands antimodern and antiliberal. They were justified in criticizing the Protestant character of secondary schools and in becoming outraged over the appointment of an Old Catholic teacher of Catholic religion. However, whereas the city met the moderate Catholic demands at least partially, the Catholics made it easy for the municipal authorities to disregard their more far-reaching demands. Thomas Nipperdey's observation that Catholics proved unable "to make the right to be different . . . a universal" holds equally for Breslau.[170] In the end, even moderate Catholics were convinced that in a Christian state parity and pluralism was first and foremost a privilege of Protestants and Catholics. Beyond that, the ultramontane Catholics' assertion that the school's task was not to "develop cognitive abilities" but to sharpen "the religious consciousness of the children" awakened, to use Carl Schmitt's phrase, deep-seated "anti-Roman emotions" among Protestant liberals and confirmed their Manichean worldview.[171]

3. The Denominational Character of the Elementary School System and the Status of Jewish Schoolchildren and Teachers

At the center of the second controversy over policies concerning the status of Jewish pupils and teachers was the elementary school system. Likewise in this conflict, which began in 1904 and lasted until 1911, the left-wing liberal majority in the city council and in the magistracy ultimately prevailed. To be sure, this time the city pursued a more modest goal than it had in the struggle over the Johanneum. In comparison with the 1860s and 1870s, the Breslau liberals were in a weaker position. A liberal and pluralistic school policy was now contested also in the city council, and the left-wing liberal majority met with decisive resistance from city councilors affiliated with the Conservative and the Center Party. Since the number of opponents of a liberal school policy had increased in Breslau, the municipal authorities were no longer able to stand up so confidently to the state bureaucracy as in the 1860s and 1870s. The position of Jewish city councilors had also grown more difficult. Although the great majority of Breslau Jews held fast to the ideal of a nondenominational school system, since the turn of the century a vocal minority had called for a separate school system. Conservative and Catholic critics of the liberal school policy capitalized on this inter-Jewish controversy by accusing the Jewish city councilors of misrepresenting the interests of Breslau Jews.

Since there was no agreement in the Jewish community about which school best served the interests of Jewish pupils and parents, it also became more difficult for the municipal authorities to take the Jewish position into consideration. Presumably the local Jewish politicians, most of whom belonged to the liberal majority of the Jewish community, used their influence within the city council to prevent the establishment of a Jewish school system. This became evident during the negotiations between the city and the Jewish community concerning the takeover of the Industrieschule für Israelitische Mädchen as a municipal elementary school. Unlike in Hamburg, for example, where in 1871 nearly two-fifths and in 1903 over half of all Jewish schoolchildren attended Jewish schools, in Breslau in 1850 over 75% of all Jewish schoolchildren already went to non-Jewish schools. Since the early 1870s, the Industrieschule had been Breslau's last Jewish school.[172] The liberal Jews regarded it as a remnant of the early phase of emancipation, when public schools were still closed to the Jews.

Similar to Breslau's Wilhelmsschule, which was closed in 1848, the Industrieschule was a typical reform project aimed at "improving the social standing" of the Jews in the late eighteenth and early nineteenth century.[173] With the encouragement of the War and Domain Chamber (Kriegs- und Domänenkammer), a Jewish teacher by the name of Tobias Hiller founded the school in 1801. Although Hiller himself taught French at two Breslau *Gymnasien,* the school he founded imparted only basic knowledge in reading and writing, arithmetic, and Judaism. The emphasis of instruction was initially on handicrafts. Only after Carl Alexander became the school's principal in 1883 did the Industrieschule by and large adopt the curricula of the municipal elementary schools, though special emphasis continued to be placed on instruction in handicrafts. In the imperial era, the daughters of the Jewish middle class no longer seem to have attended the school. The Industrieschule was intended for "girls without means," according to the *Allgemeine Zeitung des Judenthums* in 1891, which also seems to be supported by the fact that many of the food stamps from the Israelitische Volksküche went to schoolgirls at that institution.[174] Beginning in the late 1890s, the school's financial basis began to crumble. Although the magistracy had supported it since 1858 — after 1900 with at least three thousand marks annually — and the Jewish community also subsidized it, the running costs were barely covered, and the teachers' salaries were a good third less than those at municipal elementary schools.[175] In the early 1890s the municipal school inspector had already proposed that the Industrieschule be transformed into a municipal elementary school, but that failed because of resistance from the Jewish community.[176]

After the turn of the century, the *Jüdisches Volksblatt* sought to push the transfer of authority over the Industrieschule to the city. The paper's editor, Louis Neustadt, the son of the Orthodox rabbi Pinkus Neustadt, noted that among Breslau's elementary schools there were no non-denominational schools but only Protestant and Catholic elementary schools, at which there were Jewish pupils but no Jewish teachers. Neustadt therefore demanded, in September 1904, that the city "integrate Jewish elementary schools into its denominational school system" and, as the first step, take over the Industrieschule. Later, another Jewish elementary school for girls and two for boys would be added.[177] Early in 1907, Neustadt organized a petition that asked the board of governors of the Jewish *Gemeinde* to initiate negotiations with the magistracy regarding the takeover of the school. The board first rejected the petition but then began to negotiate in September 1907 with the City of Breslau's school deputation.[178]

Since mid-April 1907 the school deputation counted among its members the counselor of justice Isidor Ollendorff, who was also a prominent member of the Jewish community administration.[179] Ollendorff, born in 1855, came from Neumarkt, a small town twenty miles west of Breslau, but had graduated from a Breslau *Gymnasium* and studied in Berlin and Breslau before establishing himself in 1883 in Breslau as a lawyer. From 1892 until his death, he was a member of the city council; he was a member of numerous associations in Breslau, the Schlesische Gesellschaft für Vaterländische Cultur, the Humboldtverein, and the Provinzialverein für Volksbildung (Provincial Society for Popular Education), and played an influential role from 1893 on also in the Jewish *Gemeinde*'s representative council. When after the turn of the century the differences between liberal and Orthodox Jews intensified there, he became one of the most important speakers for the liberal wing. Moreover, he was active in many other Jewish associations; in 1891 he was part of the founding committee of the Israelitisches Mädchenheim (Jewish Girls' Home); he was a member of the Lessing Lodge, and in June 1900 signed a leaflet in favor of Galician Jews. At any rate, the choice of Ollendorff for the school deputation in 1907 caused quite a stir. The conservative *Schlesische Morgen-Zeitung* regarded the choice as an "attack" of the Breslau city council "on the denominational school," whereas the *Jüdisches Volksblatt* hoped that Ollendorff would "also represent the rights of Jewish citizens wherever doing so [was] legitimate."[180]

A decisive point of contention would prove to be the question of whether, after the takeover of the Industrieschule, the city had the right to enroll Jewish schoolgirls from all over Breslau at the new Jewish elementary school even against the will of their parents or whether Jewish parents should have the right to decide between the Jewish school and the public elementary school. Hitherto the school had only four levels; with 150 schoolgirls, the class size was just under 40. If the Industrieschule were to become an elementary school, it would have to be expanded into an institution with seven levels. Since at the municipal elementary schools class sizes of about 50 girls were normal, the municipalized Industrieschule would have to increase the number of its pupils from 150 to 350 and thus would have to take in nearly all the Jewish girls at elementary schools. The school deputation therefore informed the board of governors of both the Jewish *Gemeinde* and the Industrieschule in November 1908 that the city could take over the school only if the municipal "school administration [was] authorized to send Jewish children from anywhere in the city to the Industrieschule, even against the will of their parents." Since the Jewish *Gemeinde*'s board of governors rejected that proposal, the magistracy decided in March 1909 against taking over the school.[181]

It is likely that the local Jewish politicians were not entirely blameless regarding the failure of the negotiations. At least that was a widespread impression within the Jewish community. At the Conference of Jewish Communities (Verbandstag der jüdischen Gemeinden) in Berlin in June 1909, the liberal rabbi Jakob Guttmann from Breslau attacked "the Jewish members of the magistracy, whose influence and actions [were] to be blamed for nothing coming of this affair."[182] On June 28, 1909, a fierce debate erupted at the representative council of the Jewish *Gemeinde*. The director of the university library, Leopold Cohn, claimed that the magistracy had made such exacting stipulations due to the "influence of two Jewish city councilors," Alfons Marck and Hugo Milch. At the city council meetings, he said, they had stressed that they did not want "any Jewish school" and demanded "in no uncertain terms" that the Industrieschule be closed down.[183] Due to the protests of the representative council of the Jewish community, the *Gemeinde*'s board of governors once again initiated negotiations. In the meantime, however, the majority of board members had also decided against a municipal Jewish school. In December 1909, the board informed the representative council of the Jewish *Gemeinde* that, on principle, the majority of board members rejected the proposal to transform the Industrieschule into a

Jewish elementary school because the "establishment of a Jewish elementary school [would] lead to disagreeable consequences regarding the denominalization of other schools, for instance, the preparatory schools for the *Gymnasien*."[184] The representative council of the Jewish community endorsed the board's position on January 26, 1910. The Industrieschule should thus continue as a small Jewish private school. The city's takeover of the school was undesirable, according to the council, because "a municipal Jewish school would thereby be created that it reject[ed] on principle."[185]

Thus the takeover of the Industrieschule ultimately failed not because of the magistracy but because of the liberal majority in the Jewish community, which decried the municipalized Industrieschule as a Jewish "ghetto school." At the end of the confrontation, the supporters of the Jewish school could be happy that the Industrieschule had survived, for at the Jewish *Gemeinde*'s representative council on January 29, 1910, a group of liberal representatives was formed that pleaded that the school be closed down completely. One of its speakers was the president of the representative council, Wilhelm Salomon Freund. The Industrieschule was founded at the beginning of the nineteenth century, he said, because the existing schools did not take Jewish schoolgirls. But today the elementary schools even provide Jewish religious instruction. Therefore, it is "not necessary to preserve the Industrieschule. . . . What was then a noble objective has been finished." Albert Wohlauer, professor at the Johannes-Gymnasium and since 1907 city councilor and member of the representative council of the *Gemeinde*, went even further. Regardless of whether the Industrieschule was a private or a municipal school, it had "denominational character," Wohlauer argued. "Yet that's just what we want to avoid. So far we've not had any denominational schools; we wish to protest vehemently against having any. We don't want to create a new ghetto." Orthodox representatives demanded that the Reform representatives respect the piety of the century-old school tradition. Wohlauer's motion to close down the Industrieschule subsequently received only two votes. By contrast, a large majority voted to end negotiations with the city about the Industrieschule once and for all.[186] Having a small, private Jewish school out of consideration for the Orthodox minority was also acceptable to most liberal Jews. The price for this decision, however, was that the Industrieschule had to continue to function as a one-room schoolhouse with uncertain funding. "For the time being, the time-honored Industrieschule is still alive," the *Allgemeine Zeitung des Judenthums* reported, "so long as it does not ultimately waste away."[187]

The liberal majority and the Orthodox minority agreed, however, that the city discriminated against Jews in the elementary school system. Whereas the Orthodox Jews felt that equality would be achieved sooner if the city would establish a Jewish school system, the liberals believed that it was possible to achieve Jewish equality in the public elementary school system. When the representative council of the *Gemeinde* met on January 26, 1910, Alfons Marck, who was not only a city councilor but also a member of the *Gemeinde*'s board of governors, defended himself against the accusations that Jakob Guttmann and Leopold Cohn had made against him. He rejected the Jewish elementary school, he said, also because "the magistracy was thinking of allowing Jewish religious instruction to be taught at four schools that have a large number of Jewish pupils. The teachers [of this subject] could be hired full time." This is, Marck concluded, "a much better program of emancipation" than the establishment of Jewish elementary schools.[188]

Unlike in the case of the Breslau school struggle in the 1860s and 1870s, the Breslau municipal authorities did not play a leading role in the overall conflict between liberal municipal administrations and the Prussian state about the denominational character of the elementary schools. Regarding the new contentious issue, Berlin municipal authorities had assumed Breslau's role. The Prussian secretary of religious and educational Affairs, Adalbert Falk, had permitted the Berlin magistracy in 1875 to hire Jewish teachers of Jewish religious instruction at Berlin elementary schools as full teachers. Since "full teachers" were allowed to teach all subjects and take on a so-called *Klassenordinariat*, that is, to serve as a class teacher, the Berlin magistracy had taken this to be recognition of the nondenominational character of elementary schools. Between 1879 and 1894, the school administration had hired a total of thirty-eight Jewish teachers at Berlin elementary schools.[189] The provincial school board, which had approved all these hirings, changed its position in 1895 and instructed the Berlin magistracy to give Jewish teachers responsibility for a classroom only when half the children in the class were Jewish. Yet, as the Prussian administration well knew, such was rare. The Jewish teachers whom the city had hired as full teachers were being demoted by the state, according to the Berlin magistracy, to "adjunct teachers with eligibility for a pension," thus second-class teachers.[190]

Since the positions had become entrenched after thirty years of conflict, Hugo Preuß used the Berlin city council meeting in December 1898 to clarify the position of the liberal majority. At issue, he said, was not a "specifically Jewish matter," since "great questions of principle

and law would be under discussion." Berlin advocated abstract universalism, Preuß argued in this remarkable soapbox speech, but Prussia,
Christianization. The "highest calling of the schools" was to serve "the
spirit of humane education," the "spirit of enlightenment and culture."
The "ministerial absolutism of the Kultusministerium" violated "a
higher authority," the "law of the German Empire, which [guaranteed]
the equality of religions." There could be no compromise, he said; "the
rift is insurmountable; between worldviews that are so heterogeneous,
there is no *modus vivendi*."[191]

Yet a compromise was reached after all. Although the secretary of
religious and educational affairs in principle maintained his position
that Jews could not teach any class in which almost all the pupils were
Christians, he nevertheless agreed to allow all previously hired Jewish
teachers to continue serving as class teachers. In October 1899, Preuß
once again criticized the compromise. The Berlin magistracy, he said,
did not vehemently oppose "bureaucratic anti-Semitism" but instead
had agreed to a comprise full of "elastic rules" and thereby gave "free
reign to arbitrariness." The majority of the city councilors supported
the magistracy, however, and Mayor Martin Kirschner rejected Preuß's
criticism. The compromise, the mayor said, was "at present the only
one that could be reached." Preuß's "harping on principles" risked
causing "self-administration within the school system [to be] completely
suppressed."[192]

It is against the backdrop of this compromise between the City of
Berlin and the Prussian state that the Breslau conflict over the hiring of
Jewish teachers at elementary schools must be understood. All parties
referred repeatedly to the Berlin struggle of the late 1890s. Since the
turn of the century, the Jewish community organs and the *Jüdisches Volksblatt*, the Breslau Jewish newspaper founded in 1896, followed with growing concern the situation of Jewish pupils at elementary schools. Although the number of teachers at the elementary schools had increased
between 1870 and 1903 from 353 to 1,183, after the turn of the century
there were 739 Protestant and 444 Catholic, but no Jewish teachers.[193]
For that reason, Jewish pupils at elementary schools received Jewish religious instruction not at their schools but in separate facilities maintained
by the Jewish *Gemeinde*. Given this situation, the fact that approximately
100 of the approximately 500 Jewish pupils at elementary schools attended Christian religious instruction is not surprising—no more so
than the Jewish community's annoyance at these developments.[194]

The Breslau magistracy seems to have avoided for a long time a conflict with the Prussian authorities about the hiring of Jewish teachers at municipal elementary schools. Instead, the city had attempted to reduce the exclusion of Jewish women teachers by hiring them in municipal libraries. This led to a scandal when city councilors negotiated the budget of the libraries on March 31, 1909. The conservative city councilor, Kurt Nitschke, complained that the wages of women librarians ate up too much money. Instead of hiring them permanently, he suggested that the city libraries be administered part-time by elementary school teachers, "who have the most interest in and understanding for the continued intellectual training of the youth," and who were Christian—which Nitschke did not mention, though everyone knew it. If the city already wanted to hire permanent female librarians, then he would ask that, "in these matters and particularly at public libraries, somewhat more parity achieved . . . of the five persons, four are of Jewish religion."

Since the city council had frequently discussed, from April 1907 on, how the city could put an end to the exclusion of Jewish teachers from the elementary schools, the liberals were outraged at Nitschke. Mayor Trentin reproached Nitschke for not voicing his real motives, that is, his intention was not to save money but to deny Jewish female teachers the opportunity to be hired even at public libraries. "The fact that these ladies are Jewish," the mayor noted to Nitschke, "is no accident. They are teachers who could not be placed in the positions for which they wished to be hired. Now if we offend against this parity . . . somewhat here, we nevertheless protect it in spirit by using the municipal administration to make up for the injustice" that Jews cannot be hired as regular teachers at municipal elementary schools. The liberal city councilor, Paul Hein, a Jew who had been active in the liberal parties since the early 1890s, mocked Nitschke for his sudden concern for parity. Surely it would please Nitschke if the "principle of parity were to be protected somewhat more also in other areas." As every city councilor knew the first salaried Jewish magistrate ever, Georg Pick, had resigned from office in 1888. Many Jews now hoped that he would not be the last Jew to hold such a position. Hein said that, when the time came to choose a paid Jewish city councilor, he hoped "one day to see our colleague, Dr. Nitschke, on our side as an ally."[195] The city council rejected Nitschke's motion almost unanimously. "Dr. Nitschke," the *Jüdisches Volksblatt* succinctly noted, "had to watch as his own friends abandoned him." In April 1909, the five female librarians—of which, incidentally, three were

Protestant and only two Jewish: Anna Freund (b. 1874) and Rosa Weiss-
mann (b. 1878)—accepted full positions, and in April 1910 the city hired
them permanently.[196]

This debate about hiring Jewish teachers at Breslau elementary
schools was initiated by Jewish city councilors. Carl Reich, Louis Hamburger, and especially Isidor Ollendorff opposed the magistracy at the
city council meeting of April 4, 1907. Whereas fifty Jews taught at Berlin
elementary schools, Ollendorff noted, there was not a single Jewish
teacher at Breslau elementary schools. Although his intention was not to
blame the magistracy for that, he nevertheless expected "Breslau to ex-
ercise justice and to support with all its energy the standpoint [they had]
elaborated." Reich went further and complained that the magistracy
lacked "a sense of justice and the courage to stand up for these things."
Instead of accepting the exclusion of Jewish teachers from the Prussian
elementary school system, he continued, the city should demand "parallel classes in religion for Protestant, Catholic, and Jewish pupils and
that Jewish teachers be hired and given the same rights as the teachers
from other denominations."[197] The municipal school inspector and the
lord mayor reacted to these reproaches of the city at first with incom-
prehension. Georg Bender was outraged, since he had acted a year
earlier as the spokesman of the left-wing liberal minority in the upper
chamber of the Prussian Landtag for interconfessional schools, that is,
Simultanschulen, and Jewish equality. "Incidentally, if you demand denominational schools," Bender had explained in 1906 to the supporters
of the Law for the Maintenance of Public Elementary Schools, "then it
is regrettable that the standing of the Jews and Jewish religious community is not equal to that of the other denominations. The Jews rank
among the best taxpayers in the country and are entitled to demand at
least the same consideration as the other minorities."[198] In the Breslau
city parliament, however, Bender appealed to the Jewish city councilors
to "be realistic." Although he considered their demands to be justified,
Reich and Ollendorff should "not think that it [would] be possible to
achieve them . . . under the current circumstances." The hiring of Jewish teachers at a Breslau elementary school would "not be approved."
Instead of dreaming of interconfessional schools, the Breslau Jews
should demand the establishment of Jewish schools. The state bureaucracy would approve that immediately.

The lord mayor's suggestion that a separate Jewish school system be
created embittered the Jewish city councilors. He is a city councilor, Ollendorff responded, not a representative of the Jewish *Gemeinde*, whose

responsibility it would be, if necessary, to propose that a Jewish elementary school system be established. Of course, the Breslau Jews would "never make such a proposal, since my fellow Jews are of the view that denominational barriers should not be raised still higher."[199] Despite the embitterment of the Jewish city councilors, they seem to have reached an agreement with the magistracy in the next days. In any event, at the next city council meeting, on April 18, 1907, the magistracy's sharpest critic, Isidor Ollendorff, of all people, was voted into the city's school deputation.[200]

With Ollendorff's election, the municipal authorities also began to champion the equality of Jewish teachers. The Prussian Law for the Maintenance of Public Elementary Schools of 1906 provided the Jewish community and the magistracy with the legal basis for hiring Jewish teachers at the city's elementary schools. According to an interpretation of the intentionally vague article 21, the local school administration was free to hire Jewish teachers even at Christian schools as long as at least twelve of the schoolchildren were Jewish.[201] Thus in Breslau it would have been possible to hire a Jewish teacher at seven elementary schools.[202] The magistracy decided, however, to hire Jewish teachers only at schools attended by well over twelve Jewish schoolchildren. In summer 1910, the city therefore advertised only four, instead of the possible seven, posts for Jewish teachers at four municipal Protestant elementary schools. The teachers would be charged with twelve hours of religious instruction and fulfill the remaining teaching load in any of the other subjects. In addition to Ollendorff, the school deputation also took on Ferdinand Rosenthal, the second head rabbi of the Jewish community, so that he could advise the commission concerning its choice of candidates.[203]

No sooner had the city advertised the positions than a storm of protest broke out in the conservative and ultramontane press. The attacks were so severe that the *Jüdisches Volksblatt* noted at the end of the summer, "Hopefully the Breslau municipal authorities will not allow itself to be influenced by the 'anti-Semitic capuchin's sermon' . . . and carry through what they have recognized to be just and right."[204] The *Deutsche Tageszeitung,* for example, earned the applause of the *Schlesische Volkszeitung* when it, as the organ of the Agrarian League, argued in mid-August 1910 that "German Christian parents" had "the incontestable right" to have "their children taught by Christian German teachers." Jews, it said, are unqualified "to bring up Christian children to be German Christian men and women." The Breslau magistracy's policy was reprehensible because, "when it comes to schools," "clear distinctions" have to be made.[205] Although none of the four Jewish teachers were to teach at a Catholic elementary school, the *Schlesische Volkszeitung* warned shortly thereafter "against the complete de-Christianization of the elementary schools." The magistracy's school policy was said to surpass "the worst times during the era of Falk and Bismarck's Kulturkampf." The liberals use "'justice and fairness toward Jewish citizens' as a pretext . . . to harm and restrict the rights of Christians." The four Jews among Breslau's roughly twelve hundred elementary school teachers "will become the battering ram that breaches the principle of Christian, denominational elementary schools in Breslau: *The Jew is the born enemy of Christian education.*" There is a threat of "school conditions" arising that resemble those "in today's France." The "Christian population of both denominations in Breslau" should follow the example set by Vienna's mayor Lueger and defend itself "in public rallies against this attack on our denominational elementary schools."[206]

Although the magistracy stuck by its decision to hire Jewish teachers, the anti-Semitic attacks seemed to be not entirely without effect, even if it was only that the magistracy wanted to avoid a conflict with the Prussian state bureaucracy. In September 1910, municipal school inspector Jakob Hacks (1863–1920) tried to calm things down at a meeting of the Verein katholischer Lehrer (Catholic Teachers' Association). As far as he was concerned, Jews should neither serve as class teachers nor teach any of the so-called ethical subjects, that is, German or history in particular.[207] On September 22, the magistracy's official submission was sent to the city councilors. The magistracy had obviously sought to avoid taking any fundamental position in the conflict over whether Jews could be full teachers, though without endorsing the anti-Semites' argument. The Jewish teachers were to teach not twelve hours of religious instruction each week, as the Elementary School Law prescribed, but nineteen hours, so that the teachers now had five to seven hours of their teaching load left over for other subjects. "This makes a referral to take on the responsibilities as a class teacher, even if it is legally permissible, virtually impossible here in Breslau. Likewise, no Jewish teacher will be able to teach German since each class requires 8–10 hours. But neither do we want to allow Jewish teachers to teach history since it is our view that instruction in history is best when it is linked to instruction in German and in religion."[208] Although the liberals in the magistracy "saw in the denial of the *Klassenordinariat* a slight against Jewish teachers," they were ready to make this compromise, the *Jüdisches Volksblatt* speculated, so that, "in this way, the school inspector can take the sting out of the opposition."[209]

Even though the magistracy had made concessions to the local opposition, Conservative and Center Party city councilors sharply attacked the magistracy on November 24, 1910. While they avoided open anti-Semitism, they nevertheless went to the limit of what could be said in a city council meeting without violating the rhetoric of "apolitical" local politics. Doubtless, a contributing factor to the strained atmosphere was the fact that the conservative-Catholic coalition, which had just barely missed having a majority among the city councilors in 1904, had lost eight seats only a few days earlier to the Social Democrats and liberals and now had barely a third of the city councilors.[210] The spokesman for the conservatives, Kurt Nitschke, accused the magistracy of having "adopted the *Synagogengemeinde*'s petition." Breslau Jews were by no means concerned with religious matters; otherwise they would not have petitioned that Jewish teachers be hired at municipal schools but "would have come with a petition to create a Jewish school. (Cheers from participants.)" The spokesman for the Catholics, Hans Herschel (1875–1928), also recommended the creation of a Jewish school; his sharp tone was surprising in that Jewish teachers were to teach only at Protestant schools. Although his was not a "racial standpoint," he rejected hiring Jews at an elementary school "as the first step toward an interconfessional school." Jewish teachers should not be permitted to teach "ethics" at either elementary or secondary schools, for "our schools do not exist only to relay knowledge but also to form character." Talking as if the magistracy had recommended the establishment of interconfessional schools or the banning of religious instruction from the schools, Herschel claimed that at issue "here was not at all the conflict between the Jewish and the Christian view but rather the struggle between the positive and the free, nondenominational, socialist view." And although even the *Jüdisches Volksblatt*, with its ties to the Orthodox minority, had called for the hiring of Jewish teachers at municipal elementary schools since 1904, Herschel alleged, "positive, Jewish circles" had "opposed the submission for completely different reasons. (Shouts: Oho!)"[211]

After the dispute was over, the *Schlesische Morgen-Zeitung*, whose publisher was Nitschke, attacked the liberal school policy once again. In the municipal administration, it said, a liberalism prevails that is led by "Jewish lawyers." The Jews "are calling for a breach of our denominational elementary school system, an infringement on the Christian character of our schools . . . for the sake of political principle." What was particularly difficult for the conservative paper to understand was that Breslau's Jews distinguished between the school and religious communities: Although the Jewish city councilors "maintain their claim to their religious privileges through their membership in the synagogue community, they demand that we Christians relinquish the same special privileges we have due to our denomination."[212]

Despite the protestations of the conservatives and Catholics, the magistracy and the liberal majority stood by the submission. The conflict between the magistracy and the Jewish city councilors, which had erupted in 1907, was thus ended. The representatives of the city asseverated to support in principle the farther-reaching demands of the Jewish city councilors. At the same time, the Jewish city councilors acknowledged that the magistracy was doing all it could within the limits set by the Prussian state bureaucracy. Municipal school inspector Hacks said that, although he was not of the view that Jews could not serve as class teachers, his hands were tied: "It is stipulated by the law." He said that he was glad the Jewish *Gemeinde* had made this petition and had not proposed to create a Jewish elementary school. It was not the magistracy's intention "that Jewish children, who later in life would have to associate economically with Christians, should be cut off from them already at school." Lord Mayor Bender concurred. Personally, he said, he preferred the interconfessional school over the denominational school; the best evidence for the superiority of the interconfessional school was the success of the Johannes-Gymnasium: "We cannot achieve what we want," he stated, "but can only act in accordance with the law."[213]

While Isidor Ollendorff, who had criticized the magistracy most openly in 1907, complained that the magistracy placed "certain constraints" on Jewish teachers, he acknowledged that the city was doing all it could that "stood a chance of being approved by the inspectorate." As the magistracy itself did not intend to discriminate against the Jewish teachers, Ollendorff hoped "that, since it already has a good deal of experience in these matters, the magistracy will promote Jewish teachers when they deserve it." Adolf Heilberg, the second Jewish city councilor to enter into the debate, said that he "was not in favor of dividing the population without reason." As a Jew he had to contradict Herschel's assertion that the denominationally segregated school is the prerequisite for "molding the character" of pupils. What is beneficial for the "molding of character," Heilberg emphasized, is not "segregation" but "mixing, differentiation, [and] creating a sense of community."[214]

In view of the anti-Semitism of the Catholic and the conservative city councilors, it is striking how self-confidently the Jewish city councilors presented themselves as liberals and Jews. In the debate there was not a trace of self-hatred, mimicry, or hide-and-seek. Ollendorff, for example, said that he was certain that the Jewish teachers did good work. "We Jews are well aware that we are in an exposed position, that we have to weather the sharpest criticism, that we have to do the best possible so as not to be forced onto the sidelines." Nor did Heilberg hide his Jewishness. "Now, I went to a school at which every day in class began with a [Christian] prayer, and it didn't hurt me a bit," Heilberg replied to Herschel, who had warned against hiring Jewish teachers because then the schools would have to dispense with school prayer. And Carl Reich, the third prominent Jew on the council to enter the debate, poked fun at Kurt Nitschke. Nitschke's suggestion that a Jewish school be created testifies to his "great love for . . . Jews," Reich said; but at the moment the Jews do not want one, and "when the Jews do want one, Dr. Nitschke will be the last person we'll ask for [support]."[215]

After the city council's school committee had looked into the matter over the turn of the year, on January 12, 1911, the city councilors debated one last time the hiring of Jewish teachers at elementary schools. Once again, many Jewish city councilors, including the counselors of justice Arnold Feige, Isidor Ollendorff, and Paul Hein, defended the liberal position. The school committee had recommended the acceptance of the magistracy's motion, and the majority of the city council did so. In vain, a Catholic city councilor had tried just before the vote to split the liberals by proposing that Jewish teachers indeed be hired but then charged solely with teaching religious instruction. The *Jüdisches Volksblatt* noted with satisfaction that "the last weak attempt to neutralize Jewish teachers as religion teachers" was unable to split the liberals and "was not endorsed even by the council's black-blue [i.e., conservative-Catholic] minority."[216]

Now the ball was in the Prussian state bureaucracy's court. Because of the great significance that the hiring of four Jewish teachers had from the government's perspective, the provincial school board left the decision to the secretary of religious and educational affairs. Berlin let Breslau wait nine months but consented in September, so that the city hired Breslau's first Jewish elementary school teachers (three men and one woman) to begin on October 1, 1911.[217] A year later, the *Jüdisches Volksblatt* reported that the number of Jewish schoolchildren in elementary

schools, which had been declining steadily since the 1890s, increased in
the foregoing year from 382 to 411. In the schools at which Jewish teachers taught, there were now 115 instead of 85 Jewish schoolchildren.[218]

A comparison of the conflict over the Johannes-Gymnasium with the
controversy over Jewish teachers makes clear how much the political atmosphere in Breslau had changed. That is reflected in the political composition of the city council. In the 1860s and 1870s, the liberals dominated the council and thus had hardly any need to make compromises in
the city. After the turn from 1879 to 1880, Liberal councilors still maintained their majority, but in campaigns in which anti-Semitism was often
pronounced, that majority dangerously melted away. In 1904, the Liberals held fifty-one seats on the council, the Free Union (Freie Vereinigung),
a coalition of conservatives and centrists, held forty-eight, and the Social
Democrats only two. After 1906, the Liberals once again had a small majority, with fifty-four city councilors, while the Right had forty-six, and
the Social Democrats two.[219] In the city council elections in 1908, the
Right also lost mandates to the Liberals; in November 1910, they even
lost a total of eight seats to the Social Democrats and the Liberals. "Anti-
Semitism no longer seemed to go down very well," the *Jüdisches Volksblatt*
commented on the Right's defeat.[220] Yet the Liberal city councilors were
unable to regain the unqualified supremacy they had enjoyed in the
1860s and 1870s, and their majority remained precarious.

Moreover, the symbolic value of hiring Jewish elementary school
teachers was less than that of opening an interconfessional *Gymnasium*.
In the conflict over the Johanneum, general questions of liberal school
policy converged with part of the emancipatory "Jewish question."
Civic pride was crystallized in the confrontation; Arthur Hobrecht, the
lord mayor at the time, gave it top priority.[221] In contrast, the question of
whether Jewish teachers should be hired at four elementary schools remained an isolated issue. Hence it was easier for the opponents of such
hirings to depict them as a special interest of the Jews and to nurse their
underlying anti-Semitism with Christian rhetoric.

Finally, the differences between the controversies also showed that
the increase in the state's influence limited more and more the city's
room to maneuver regarding school policy. Even before the Law for the
Maintenance of Public Elementary Schools of July 1906 had been en-
acted, Lord Mayor Bender and Heilberg, as spokesman of the liberals,
warned the Breslau city council in December 1905 that the new school
law would rob the local school administration of what independence it
still had.[222] The law of 1906 marked a caesura insofar as it succeeded in

standardizing elementary-school policy more than ever before. The elementary school, according to Wolfgang Neugebauer, "moved decidedly closer to the state school model." Likewise, the state's portion of the financing of municipal elementary schools had increased from barely 5% in 1886 to a good 11% in 1901.[223] The more the Prussian state intervened in school policy, the *Allgemeine Zeitung des Judenthums* had observed already in 1880, the slighter "the prospects of Jewish philologists finding a post" became. "For even if the citizenry is enlightened enough not to take exception to a candidate's Jewish faith, it nevertheless is all too happy to avoid any conflict with the state bureaucracy."[224] The conflict over the Jewish teachers at Breslau elementary schools between 1906 and 1911 confirmed the Jewish weekly's observation.

Striking, moreover, was the Center Party's resistance to the hiring of Jewish teachers, particularly the *Schlesische Volkszeitung*'s shrill polemics. In the 1860s, politically organized Catholics had criticized the Protestant character of Breslau's secondary schools and, within the limits of an entirely local affair, fought against Protestant anti-Catholicism. But now the Catholics defended the abstract position, namely, the concept of a "Christian state" and the principle of Catholic "parity," though no Catholic elementary school was affected and the Catholics had no complaints about the status of Catholics in the elementary schools. The Center Party was hardly concerned about the local situation. Instead, two conceptions of equality collided here: the Catholic principle of "parity" and the Jewish demand for abstract equality before the law.

For Center Party politicians, the idea of "parity" entailed two basic but divergent principles.[225] On the one hand, parity involved the idea of the equality of the two principal Christian denominations, an idea first established in 1648 with the Peace of Westphalia. In the foreground here stood the legal status of the Catholic Church. In Prussia, the convention of 1841 had once again confirmed the traditional legal principle of the parity of Protestantism and Catholicism. According to the leading Protestant theological lexicon, "parity" meant "the equal treatment of different church communities, in particular Protestant and Catholic churches, by the state." A prominent Catholic "legal lexicon" argued along similar lines in 1889: "The system of the parity state demands the right for each individual denomination to move freely in accordance with its own canonical constitution, which corresponds to its system of religion, regarding all things involved in the practice of the religion."[226] On the other hand, the battle cry of parity aimed at a quota system. At issue in this case were the rights of Catholic citizens, not of the Catholic

Church. All denominations, thus also the Jews, should be represented, in proportion to their numbers in the population, in leading positions in the government administration, the legal system, the military, school faculties, and the universities. In view of the Catholics' educational deficit, the demands for parity aimed in effect at establishing not just a temporary but also a permanent "affirmative action" program for Catholics.

The Catholic model of parity was at odds with the Jewish demand for abstract equality before the law. "We Jews have never called for parity," Fabius Schach emphasized in 1902 in the journal of the Centralverein Deutscher Staatsbürger jüdischen Glaubens (Central Association of German Citizens of the Jewish Faith). "What we are fighting for," he said, "is justice. We demand only that applicants who are well suited and morally impeccable not be turned down because they call God by a different name." Against the Catholic understanding of parity, Schach argued that "equality cannot and indeed should not be understood as meaning that the state is to assign each denomination, based on the last census, X number of officials but solely that state is to be not at all interested in a candidate's religion."[227]

From the Jewish perspective it was also problematic that Catholic politicians sometimes employed the narrow canonical sense of parity and other times the general sense. In the deliberations about the Law for the Maintenance of Public Elementary Schools in December 1905, for example, the Breslau lawyer Felix Porsch had rejected Jewish demands. For the Center Party, Porsch argued that Jews could not lay claim to the same status in Prussian elementary schools as Catholics and Protestants because, "according to the principles of [the] constitution, Christian pupils [had] to have a somewhat different status" than Jewish pupils.[228] For Jews, it was not only annoying that Porsch invoked the narrow canonical sense of parity. They also had serious doubts that the privileged status of Protestants and Catholics in the school system could be at all justified based on Article 14, to which Porsch appealed in his argument. In January 1906, the Berlin lawyer Felix Makower responded to Porsch. Makower, who headed the school commission of the Verband der Deutschen Juden (Association of German Jews), which had been founded in 1904, demonstrated in light of the history of Article 14 that it referred only to national holidays and pastoral care in the military but not to the schools.[229]

All in all, the inclusion of Jews in the Breslau elementary school system remained limited because the municipal authorities were less successful in this case than they had been in the conflict over the

Johannes-Gymnasium. The city did regard the hiring of Jewish teachers as a first step, which they hoped to be able to build on as soon as the Prussian state would tolerate the complete inclusion of Jews in the teaching faculties. Yet that was still a long way off. Up to the end of the German Empire, Jews in Breslau's elementary schools remained second-class teachers because they, unlike teachers at the Johanneum, could not teach ethical subjects or take on a full position as class teacher. The significance of this discrimination went well beyond the personal fate of individual Jewish teachers. It was a symbolic act of exclusion. Before the eyes of their colleagues, the parents, the schoolchildren, and the public in general, the Prussian school administration slighted the Jewish elementary teachers solely because of their Jewishness. While the municipal authorities stuck to the fundamentally liberal line regarding school policy, they were much more hesitant in their handling of the conflict over the denominational character of elementary schools than they were regarding the founding of the Johannes-Gymnasium. In both conflicts, the Jewish community and the city cooperated to secure as much equality for Jewish schoolchildren and teachers as seemed possible in view of the Prussian government's anti-Semitic stance.

The great majority of Breslau Jews obviously approved of the fact that Jewish schoolchildren almost exclusively attended public schools. The public school system offered Jewish schoolchildren from bourgeois families the educational opportunities for which their parents hoped. Individuals within the Jewish community who called for the establishment of new Jewish schools were largely ignored. A minority of radical Reform Jews even wanted to shut down the Industrieschule. In the domain of schools, as we saw earlier regarding associational life and Jewish-Christian marriages, the openness of Jewish forms of sociability and community-building were also visible. Jewish schoolchildren attended Breslau's public schools, not Jewish schools. Anything else would have been incompatible with their situational ethnicity.

5

Liberalism, Anti-Semitism, and Jewish Equality

Local politics had a considerable influence on relations between Jews and other Breslauers. At the same time, the history of Breslau politics remains incomprehensible if one fails to consider the important role that Jews played in left-wing liberalism in Breslau and the extent to which anti-Semitism contributed to the changes in the political atmosphere there in the late 1870s. The present chapter focuses on the city's government, as well as its political parties—organizations whose aim it was to influence city hall. Following Karl Rohe, I understand politics here to be the "sphere in which what are ultimately *pivotal decisions* are made that bear on general coexistence in society."[1] This narrow concept of politics comes at a price, however, a fact that feminist historiography in particular has demonstrated in recent years with very good arguments. Yet many of the dimensions encompassed by gender history's broad concept of the political, such as the private and the prepolitical spheres, have already been discussed in the preceding chapters.[2]

Thus far only first steps have been taken toward providing an account of the significance of local politics for Jewish integration that would meet the requirements of a sophisticated political history. By contrast, numerous studies have analyzed the Prussian government's continuous, occasionally heightened discrimination against Jews in the judiciary, at universities, and in the army.[3] Yet they have ignored local politics even while providing isolated evidence that municipal authorities affected the social standing of Jews.[4] Interest in local politics has increased sharply over roughly the past thirty years. In view of the strength of the liberal parties in most German metropolises, local politics is regarded as an ideal test case to determine how capable of reform German society was before 1914 and how bourgeois was the political culture in the German Empire. In reference to municipal public works and municipal socialism, historians of urbanization have argued that in the late nineteenth century "city governments flourished tremendously" and that, due to their increasing self-confidence, cities became an important "part of political power in the state."[5] Yet although Jewish politicians made an important contribution to the late flowering of left-wing liberalism, and local politics in large German cities often dealt with questions of Jewish integration, the historiography of urbanization and urban liberalism has barely investigated this area. Over the past twenty-five years, the historiography of German-Jewish relations and research into anti-Semitism have discovered the local sphere, even though there is still hardly any new literature on the history of Berlin Jews, the largest Jewish community in Germany by far. Most of the studies on the history of Jews in German metropolises have ignored their reciprocal relations with local politics, while research into anti-Semitism has focused primarily on organized anti-Semitism, which—if one disregards cities such as Dresden—had very little success on the local, municipal level.[6]

Following these strands of research, which thus far have hardly been related to one another, the present chapter investigates the reciprocal relations between local politics, anti-Semitism, and the history of Breslau Jews. The chapter comprises three parts, each of which discusses a different aspect of the political dimension of relations between Jews and other Breslauers. The first part analyzes the rise and fall of anti-Semitism in Breslau and identifies the reasons for the failure of the anti-Semites. The second investigates the stance of the municipal authorities on the question of the immigration, naturalization, and deportation of foreign, mostly Eastern European, Jews. Finally, the third part focuses on the symbolic dimension of local politics and analyzes the award of the title of honorary citizen of Breslau, the highest honor in the realm of urban middle-class values, to two Breslau Jews.

Particular attention is paid in all three parts to the conflict between the City of Breslau and the Prussian state. By way of these examples from Breslau political life, each of which was particularly significant for the relations between Jews and other Breslauers, this chapter takes up Dieter Langewiesche's call for the investigation of the "reciprocal relation between the central state and municipal authorities over an extended period of time."[7] The conflicts between the City of Breslau and the state analyzed in the previous chapter with regard to the schools, rather than being isolated incidents, instead formed part of a larger field of conflict between local authorities and the state, a field in which, for example, the question of the naturalization of Jewish immigrants and the award of honorary citizenship were of great importance.

Moreover all three parts are variations on the thesis that left-wing liberalism in Breslau was not a continuation of a premodern, traditional, patrician form of early liberalism, but was instead closely connected with a new type of left-wing liberal politics. It was not a collectively but rather an individually oriented liberalism that did not aim to establish a community conforming to Christian tenets. Although Breslau's left-wing liberals did not speak out programmatically in favor of cultural pluralism, in their concrete politics they did recognize the right to be different and thus helped to create a denominationally pluralistic society.[8] Breslau's left-wing liberals were not pioneers of multiculturalism, but at least regarding school policy, the question of Jewish immigration, and that of the award of honorary citizenship, the municipal authorities were willing to allow Jews to participate equally as Jews and to consider the Jewish population part of a multiplicity within the unity of the city, a multiplicity to which even Eastern European Jews belonged— as the positive judgment of Jewish immigrants makes clear.

There are two reasons for this stance, which was unusual among German liberals in the late nineteenth century. First, Breslau's left-wing liberals were prepared to acknowledge a right to be different because they were not at the forefront of the social liberalism championed by Friedrich Naumann. The municipal authorities dealt sensitively with issues of cultural diversity and equal opportunity because they ignored issues of equal economic opportunity. There is little indication that Breslau distinguished itself through its social and welfare policies. On the contrary, the rift between left-wing liberals and Social Democrats ran deeper in Breslau than in other metropolises. And that is why in the Social Democrats' weekly *Kommunale Praxis*, which positively acknowledged the efforts of many liberal municipal administrations, Breslau served repeatedly as the appalling example of a magistracy in which cold-hearted Manchester liberalism prevailed. "The working conditions in Breslau," the *Kommunale Praxis* judged in 1905, were "known to be the worst of any municipality."[9]

Second, Breslau liberals granted Jews a right to be different also because Jewish local politicians exerted a decisive influence on the city's left-wing liberal movement. The literature on German liberalism has repeatedly emphasized its close ties to Protestantism.[10] However, as in other large Prussian cities, Breslau liberalism was influenced equally by

Protestants and Jews. An essential dimension of—indeed, the driving force behind—urban left-wing liberalism was Jewish because Jews formed a core group within it and influenced politics.[11] For that reason, Jewish voters found Prussia's three-class suffrage system quite congenial. Although Jews made up barely 7% of the population, in the 1860 city council elections almost a third of first-class voters (31.2%) came from the Jewish middle class, and the Jewish portion among first-class voters had even risen to nearly 37% by 1874. The importance of Jewish voters was also evident in the Prussian Landtag elections. In 1888 Jews made up a good quarter (26%) of the voters in the first class and nearly a fifth (19%) in the second, even though the Jewish portion of the population had decreased in the meantime to a fully 5%.[12] Just how much the political influence of Breslau Jews depended on the three-class suffrage system is shown by a consideration of Vienna, where "the middle class," as the *Neue Preußische Zeitung* noted with envy in 1896, was able "to really express its dislike of the dominance of the Jews in local elections."[13] Unlike in the Oder metropolis, Jews played almost no role in Viennese local politics since the Viennese curial system did not hierarchize voters by income but primarily strengthened the position of homeowners, teachers, and civil servants, among which Jews were barely represented. Around 1880, the Jewish portion of city councilors (6%) was even less than the Jewish portion of the Viennese population (10%). Whereas Viennese Jews were helpless in the face of the anti-Semitic challenge posed by Karl Lueger's Christian Socialist Party, Breslau Jews were able to use their political influence to restrain anti-Semitism and to gain acceptance for their own views.[14]

Without the support of Breslau's Jewish middle class, the liberals would have lost their majority on the city council long before 1918 and would not have had a chance in the Prussian Landtag elections. Much as in Berlin, where according to the last lord mayor of the German Empire roughly a quarter of all city councilors were Jewish, up to 30% of the left-wing liberal city councilors in Breslau and 40% of the left-wing liberal delegates to the Landtag were Jewish.[15] "The 'liberal' group" in the city council, the longtime leader of left-wing liberalism, Adolf Heilberg (1858–1936), recalled in 1934 about the period from 1890 to 1918, "included Jewish businessmen, doctors, and lawyers, but also a lot of people, large and small, who thought freely, were of the opinion that Jews after all are also decent, respectable people, and were disgusted by the social arrogance of reserve officers, high public officials, 'schoolmasters,' and so forth, and maintained their 'civic pride' in the face of these exclusive circles."[16]

Jewish liberals influenced key elements of Breslau politics: school policy and the circumscription of anti-Semitism, the municipal authorities' stance on Jewish immigrants from Eastern Europe, and the award of honorary citizenship. This new understanding of the history of urban liberalism is not readily applicable to each and every context. Nevertheless, in cities such as Berlin, Frankfurt, and Königsberg it is likely that one could show many parallels to Breslau.[17]

1. The Rise and Fall of Organized Political Anti-Semitism

Although contemporaries referred to the first wave of modern anti-Semitism as the "Berlin movement," anti-Semitism also marked Breslau politics between 1879–1882 and the early 1890s. Already in 1872, thus before the *Gründerkrach* (the depression of 1873), the Silesian capital's Catholic press had adopted an anti-Semitic stance, though it did not affect the general political atmosphere in the city.[18] That was because no other Breslau newspaper followed suit, the majority of Breslau Catholics did not belong to the Catholic milieu, and the liberal parties had monopolized political life in the city. "At least nine-tenths of our fellow Catholic citizens," the *Breslauer Zeitung* noted in 1872, had no connection with ultramontanism and had to endure, like the lord mayor of Breslau, Max von Forckenbeck, being mocked by the ultramontane press as "'Also'—or merely 'Baptized'—Catholics."[19]

Although the Kulturkampf inflamed passions also in Breslau—as especially the history of the founding of the Johannes-Gymnasium shows—there was still room enough for ironic, detached observations. Forckenbeck's victory in the Breslau city council elections in July 1872 was also remarkable in that his candidacy for the office of lord mayor in Berlin had failed precisely because many liberal city councilors in Berlin believed that a Catholic was unsuited to head a predominately Protestant municipality.[20] Under the title "How the Breslauers Greeted Their New Mayor, Max von Forckenbeck," a poem written on the occasion of his taking office recounted his election:

> Catholic was he, what a squall;
> There weren't no dilly-dallyin.'
> Nor did the tower of our city hall
> The least bit shake or go a shudd'rin'![21]

In the Reichstag elections of 1877, the Center Party received merely 12% of the votes since it was able to win over barely a third of the Catholic voters.[22] By contrast, the left-wing liberal party not only garnered more votes by far than the other middle-class parties but also won the runoff against the Social Democrats with nearly 60% of the votes.[23]

However, in 1878 the political atmosphere in Breslau suddenly changed. Part of the Protestant bourgeoisie turned away from the liberal parties and from now on supported Breslau's conservative movement. The *Schlesische Zeitung*, the oldest and most respected daily, which hitherto had been sympathetic to the right wing of the liberals, now backed the Conservative Party and adopted part of the Conservatives' catalog of anti-Semitic demands.[24] The anti-Semitism of the Catholic press now grew more important. In 1878 and 1879 articles and commentaries appeared almost daily with the most absurd anti-Jewish delusions.[25] The growing significance of anti-Semitism was also reflected in Breslau voting patterns. After an unusually hotly contested election for the Prussian Landtag, the left-wing liberals lost all three Breslau mandates, including one to a candidate whom the National Liberals and the Conservative Party had fielded together. During the electoral college (*Wahlmännerversammlung*) in early October 1879, there was a row. When the conservative delegates urged the undecided National Liberals to vote against the left-wing liberals, whom they denounced as representatives of an allegedly Jewish liberalism, many Jewish delegates left the polling station in protest. Encouraged by the success in the Landtag elections, the Breslau conservatives decided in early 1880 to found their own newspaper, the *Schlesisches Morgenblatt*, which alongside the Catholic papers soon became the most important mouthpiece of an aggressive anti-Semitism.[26]

The anti-Semitic movement devoted itself henceforth to local politics. In November 1880, a coalition of National Liberals, Center-Party Catholics, and Conservatives managed to stage the city council elections as a conflict between Christians and Jews. With the support of the Catholic newspapers, the *Schlesische Zeitung* and the *Schlesisches Morgenblatt*, the coalition founded the so-called Freie Vereinigung (Free Union) in order to organize antiliberal electoral alliances in the individual wards. The Freie Vereinigung did not try to hide its anti-Semitic character. Rather, it placed an election announcement in all the city's nonliberal daily newspapers in which it promoted its candidates with the argument that they would "defend the true interests of the entire citizenry in the sense of the Christian, German middle class."[27] On the morning of the elections, the *Schlesisches Morgenblatt* reminded voters about the Freie Vereinigung's objective: the "fight against the dominion of progress and of Semitism at city hall."[28] That evening Breslau's left-wing liberalism suffered its worst defeat in local elections during the imperial era. Although they won all the seats in the first class thanks to the three-class suffrage system, the left-wing liberals lost two-thirds of all mandates up for election in the second and third classes to the Freie Vereinigung.[29] With resignation, the *Israelitische Wochenschrift* assessed the political situation in early December 1880: The Silesian capital, it said, "has the by no means enviable distinction of being the place where the mob rages most gleefully and riots most fiercely against the Jews."[30]

Yet unlike in Berlin, for instance, Breslau's first wave of anti-Semitism had dried up by 1882. Already by the end of January 1881 the *Israelitische Wochenschrift* revised its pessimistic assessment from the foregoing December and reported that the anti-Semites were unable to turn their election victory into concrete political successes. "The day-to-day issues, insofar as they are this body's responsibility," the journal noted, "are certain to be treated in a liberal fashion."[31] In the Landtag elections of 1882 and 1885, left-wing liberals won all three of Breslau's seats, also thanks to the support of Breslau's Center Party, which had parted with its conservative allies out of disappointment and whose anti-Semitism had disappeared almost completely by the end of 1881.[32] In the local elections during the 1880s, the left-wing liberals succeeded, moreover, in regaining at least a few of the seats they had lost in 1878 and 1880. Until the end of the German Empire, they would successfully defend their majority on the city council. The renewed self-confidence of local liberalism found expression in 1887 in the city councilors' choice of Wilhelm Salomon Freund as the council chairman. At the same time, Freund, who occupied this respected and influential position until 1915 and who in 1901 became the second Jew to be named an honorary citizen of Breslau, embodied all that the city's anti-Semites disdained: He belonged to the leadership of Breslau's left-wing liberals, whom he had represented in the Prussian Landtag from 1876 to 1879 and in the Reichstag from 1879 to 1881, presided over the representative council of the Jewish *Gemeinde* for many years, was on the board of directors of numerous Jewish and bourgeois associations, and counted among the richest and most successful of Breslau's lawyers.[33]

In addition to political anti-Semitism in the broad sense, which was to be found especially in the coalition of Center Party Catholics, Conservatives, and right-wing National Liberals, in the early 1890s there was an independently organized anti-Semitic movement in Breslau. As in many other cities, in Breslau internal differences weakened the political influence of organized anti-Semites, although initially they prevailed in several instances.[34]

At the end of 1891, the Breslau chapter of the Deutsch-Socialer Verein (German Social Club) was formed, which in 1893 joined the scattered remnants of Breslau section of the Deutscher Reform-Verein (German Reform Association), which had been founded in spring 1881.[35] Yet hardly had the Breslau Deutsch-Socialer Verein celebrated its inauguration in November 1892 when an organizational rift occurred.[36] At the end of February 1893, the Breslau anti-Semites, who had broken off from the Deutsch-Socialer Verein due to the rift, established the Deutsch-Nationaler Verein (German National Association). The founding declaration attacked "business and hooligan anti-Semitism"; in the newly established party the focus would be not on concrete political work but rather on "scientific anti-Semitism."[37] In early March 1893, the *Jüdische Presse* scoffed that the "'pure' shameless anti-Semites" in Breslau had "split into three groups. At the top parades the Deutsch-socialer Verein . . . A second association calls itself the Deutsch-socialer Provinzialverband [German-Social Provincial Association], which allegedly has a different program." Although the clubs claim to have 1,800 members, "their organ, the pitiful *Ostwacht* [Eastern Watch], appears completely behind closed doors." Finally, one could mention the Deutsch-Nationaler Verein, whose members were previously "kicked out" by the other two groups.[38] Toward the end of March, the *Deutsche Ostwacht* itself noted that among Breslau's anti-Semites certain "elements" were trying to introduce "a short-sighted, personal club mania into the German-social movement." In early April 1893, an internal flyer of the Deutsch-Socialer Verein circulated, calling on its members "to remain true to the old club."[39] Moreover, in October, an overt struggle over the leadership of the Deutsch-socialer Provinzialverband erupted. To quell the conflict, the umbrella association of Silesian anti-Semites was forced to "mediate in the decision of party leadership."[40] Prior to that, the Breslau anti-Semites had conducted what proved to be an equally unsuccessful and expensive election campaign, one that far exceeded the means of the Deutsch-Socialer Verein. Consequently, the treasurer had to disclose the party's debt at the general meeting at the end of October.[41]

The "club mania," the precarious financial situation, and the left-wing liberal triumph in the Breslau Landtag elections on October 31,

1893, began to put a damper on the members' enthusiasm. In March 1893, Hermann Ahlwardt had filled one of the city's largest auditoriums with his speech "Why Must Anti-Semitism Prevail?" When in the following December Otto Böckel, who was equally prominent, spoke in a smaller auditorium, the gathering, as even the *Deutsche Ostwacht* had to admit, was "unfortunately not as well attended as one would have expected."[42] Moreover, if listeners stayed away, the financial risk of inviting one of the masterminds of German anti-Semitism to the Silesian capital increased. Böckel long remained the last high-caliber ideologue of anti-Semitism to make his way to Breslau.

In February 1894, Hugo Kretschmer gave an indication of just how low spirits were among Breslau's anti-Semites and provided an astute analysis of the organizational weaknesses of the Deutsch-Socialer Verein. The mentor of Breslau anti-Semitism tried to have a serious talk with party members, admonishing them to avoid past errors. Instead of "quiet, decisive work," the club had "sunk a lot of money . . . into useless gimmickry, on pictures, paraphernalia for pranks, rubber stamps, and the like, things that couldn't move any sensible man to join our movement but, on the contrary, are revolting him." Moreover, due to their undisciplined manner, such as "making fun of the Jews, even if done in an 'animated' state," many anti-Semites deserved to be called "hooligan anti-Semites." The low regard for the movement in Breslau, he said, is therefore hardly surprising. "One should live moderately," read his somewhat feeble remedy, "and be aware of the seriousness of our cause and demand the same of all party members." Come what may, one must avoid self-destruction: "No one should be envious of another's success, nor should one club fight against another."[43]

The anti-Semitic propaganda, however, particularly in the early 1890s, was not only an attack against the alleged "Jewish hegemony" but also an appeal of anti-Semites that they renew themselves morally. It was not only Jews who acted ethically reprehensibly but also "Germans," especially "German women and girls." "Our Bourgeoisie," Kretschmer's lead article from March 1894, is instructive here. Written for the paper's final issue, it was intended to explain the weaknesses of anti-Semitism in Breslau and at the same time formed the political legacy of the prophet of organized anti-Semitism in the Oder metropolis. The principal evil, he said, is not "Semitism"; the "contemporary bourgeoisie is degenerate." In large segments of the same, "the purely superficial quality of stylishness [*Schneidigkeit*]"—that is the central term, which, interestingly enough, has a negative connotation here—suppressed the ideal of "manly seriousness." The "emptiness of modern 'stylishness,'" "dandy-ism of every sort," is particularly evident in relations between the sexes. Young bourgeois men, he said, are destroying the patriarchal order of the family by marrying so as to climb the social ladder. "Well-to-do women," Kretschmer noted in his awkward prose, "make demands on life to which they are not entitled, by virtue of neither their wealth nor their husbands' income. For nowadays 'educated' girls often enough consider it their [right] to understand absolutely nothing about house-keeping and also to play the 'young lady' in their marriages!"[44]

In this remarkable document of soul-searching among Breslau's anti-Semites, there is no sign of the common stereotype of a Jewish threat to Christian virtuousness, be it by the Jewish man who seduces the lascivious Christian woman, be it by the beautiful and no less sinful and sexually uninhibited *belle juive*. For Kretschmer, the enemy of hier-archical relations between the sexes was not an external but an internal enemy. The "Germans," that is, the non-Jews, themselves had strayed from the path of virtue. More urgent than the "fight against Semitism" was the "serious effort to ban all rotten elements from society."[45] Kretschmer thereby made use of a motif that had already been current in the early 1880s. "And now, gentlemen, for a serious remark," Max Liebermann von Sonnenberg had declared in 1882 in Breslau; "allow yourselves to be told that we all are thoroughly jewified. We must drive the Jew out of very own hearts and gain another view of life. We must learn to feel once again like Christian Germans."[46]

Due to the organizational weaknesses of the anti-Semitic parties, the ambitious attempt to maintain their own press organ, the *Deutsche Ost-wacht*, also failed. There was no lack of good will, and the anti-Semites were well aware of the importance of a Silesian party paper. In the struggle against the "disgraceful hegemony of the Jews," the press was regarded as the "best means and the greatest aid." The *Deutsche Ostwacht* therefore appealed to the "dear Catholics, dear Protestants," in short, the "dear Germans," to support "above all the spiritual cement of [their] immediate home, the provincial anti-Semitic press."[47] Hugo Kretsch-mer had founded the weekly *Deutsche Ostwacht* in October 1892, but it soon became clear that the newspaper could not support itself. As early as September 1893, a rumor was circulating that it would soon be shut down. Thus in fall 1893 and spring 1894 the Deutsch-socialer Provinzial Verband für Schlesien (German-Social Provincial Association for Silesia) frantically, but unsuccessfully, attempted to found a *Deutsche Ostwacht Genossenschaft* (*Deutsche Ostwacht* Society) to enable the continued publication of the paper.[48] Yet by the end of January, Kretschmer had to acknowledge with resignation that "the self-sacrifice of the members of the German-Social Party lack[ed] the scope that would have been necessary . . . to enable the publication of the weekly."[49] When the paper was closed on March 31, 1894, one of the main supports of organized anti-Semitism in Silesia collapsed. Its lack of financial success was even more surprising since in other regions local party papers provided the chief source of income for important party functionaries. The Dresden anti-Semite Oswald Zimmermann, for instance, earned six thousand marks per year as editor of the *Deutsche Wacht.*[50]

Another reason for the weakness of anti-Semitism in Breslau lay in the inner logic of a specifically "apolitical" language of local politics that limited the scope of what could be said. It was in the topos of apolitical local politics that the "generally common way of talking about the limits and competencies of political action" emerged that defined the "accepted frame of action" of Breslau politics in the German Empire.[51] Neither the independently organized anti-Semites nor those in the conservative camp or in the Center Party were able to dress their criticisms of liberal local politics in the right rhetoric. As a result, they were unable to convince a broader public of their ideas on issues of local politics beyond their close circle of followers. Whoever sharply criticized the policies of the magistracy and the city council was quickly suspected of politicizing municipal affairs in an inadmissible way. Breslau civic pride surpassed party differences. Whoever violated its rhetoric was quickly regarded as a denigrator of the city.

The depths of local politics were hardly worthy of notice for organized anti-Semites since they were too busy building their anti-Semitic castles in the clouds. Whenever the *Deutsche Ostwacht* did address the situation in Breslau, however, it used language that must have wounded even the most rudimentary local civic pride. In March 1893 it published a lengthy analysis of "Breslau life." According to the article, Breslau "civil servants and officers" are "truly provincial." City life is shaped by "that not so much Talmudic as tawdry 'society' . . . which is so well represented here." Despite "all their refinement by the *Uebercultur*," their hallmark is their "not only rough-hearted but positively uncouth morals." The city council, which usually represented the self-confidence of the middle class, was said to be completely under the control of the Jews, hence the deportment of the city councilors: "They are 'fine' in dress and airs despite their slimy behavior, unwashed hands, and constantly dirty fingernails." Frighteningly "provincial" is no less the cultural level of the Christian residents, whose "spiritual pleasures" are "completely lacking in sophistication" due to their "vulgar taste." Not even Breslau's nightlife shows a trace of the "refinement and elegance other cities can boast of in this regard."[52]

This excited tone—which, while likely effective among party members in assuring one another of their stance, hardly helped the anti-Semites to win over new followers—also characterized Catholic anti-Semitism, in which the experience of the Kulturkampf also was always reflected. In the *Breslauer Sonntagsblatt,* a supplement of the *Schlesische Volkszeitung,* a rhymed warning to Breslau was published immediately before the assembly of delegates to the Prussian Landtag, a warning that likely did not impress many Breslauers outside the ultramontane milieu:

> "O Breslau, o dear Breslau,
> You old diocesan town,
> Who has within so many Jews
> and enemies of Christians.
>
> How did it come to pass,
> What have you done then,
> That you have allowed
> The Jews to take control?
> . . . .
> They already sit in the council
> Almost always at the top
> And have the say and vote
> The Christian—can obey.
> . . . .
> O do not be Christian
> Just in name alone,
> O make your words and deeds
> Accord with that name you bear.
>
> Do not deny the sign
> That's breaking through the clouds,
> For in the cross alone is there life,
> In the cross salvation and light!"[53]

Also a seven-part series "On the Jewish Question," published at the turn of the year in 1879–80 in the Catholic *Deutscher Volksfreund,* culminated in an analysis of Breslau local politics, in which anti-Semitism and offensive criticism of the city council, as well as of the city administration, achieved a symbiosis. "The children of Israel . . . are increasingly making their way into higher social circles," and that is why "the Jew has the say in the magistracy and the city council, and pushes many things through that are of doubtful benefit to the commonweal, such as the sewer system . . . and the like."[54]

The "paranoid style of politics" (Richard Hofstadter) practiced by the anti-Semites was at odds, moreover, with the unwritten laws of local Breslau politics, which followed other rules than did politics in Prussia or in the empire. Quite diverse newspapers, such as the conservative *Breslauer Communal-Zeitung* and the left-wing liberal *Schlesische Presse*, were in agreement about the "apolitical" character of local politics. In October 1880, at the height of the first wave of anti-Semitism in Breslau, the *Breslauer Communal-Zeitung* proclaimed, "[T]he parquet of the city council auditorium is neutral ground on which solely municipal interests, which promote the commonweal, may be championed, but not political or private interests."[55] Two years earlier, the *Schlesische Presse* had argued that "community affairs" should be discussed in the spirit of "intelligent and prudent objectivity," but in any case should be kept clear "of influences of one-sided or even denominational party tactics."[56] Doubtless the topos of "apolitical" local politics was a proven means of equating one's own political interests with the common good and of ensuring that the politics of local dignitaries be carried over into the age of the political mass market. The idea that the city council was a "neutral ground" nevertheless contributed to the mitigation of local political conflicts.[57]

The specifically apolitical character of local political action holds the key to understanding why the anti-Semites' room for maneuvering in the Breslau city council remained tightly circumscribed. As long as the liberal councilors maintained their majority in the city council, every overtly anti-Semitic motion in the city council was regarded as an offense against "intelligent and prudent objectivity." A subtle mechanism separated what could from what could not be said, the sober, objective language of local politics from the demagogic "bickering among parties." As early as spring 1880, city councilors sympathetic to the anti-Semites experienced firsthand the limits of what could be said in the council. In order to avoid being charged with unduly politicizing the city council, the first advance of local anti-Semitism occurred in connection with two seemingly minor issues: the election of a new board of directors of a municipal hospital and the award of a contract for lumber for the municipal lumberyard. In both instances, the anti-Semites failed due to the resolute resistance of liberal city councilors, among whom Jews played a prominent role.

On March 23, 1880, the city council had to decide on new members of the board of directors of the Aller-Heiligen-Krankenhaus (All Saints' Hospital). As was usual in such cases, the city council's election and constitution committee drew up a list of candidates in advance. Normally, the city councilors followed the committee's recommendations, particularly concerning minor decisions on personnel, without debate. The list included the names of five renowned doctors, among whom were four Breslau Jews. Prior to the meeting, anti-Semitic city councilors had, as Councilor Simon would scoff in the ensuing debate, distributed to a "chosen few" slips of paper with the demand to remove three of the four Jewish doctors from the proposed list and choose three Christian doctors in their place. Contrary to the principle of professional qualification, the anti-Semites insisted on proportional representation. To ensure that their advance went as smoothly as possible, without having to reveal the anti-Semitic motive, Councilor Seidel had moved that the list be decided upon by secret ballot. To thwart the plan of the anti-Semitic city councilors, Councilor Julius Friedländer, retired municipal judge and leader of Breslau's left-wing liberals, moved that the matter be dealt with in a secret session.[58] Since Friedländer's counterstrategy met with broad support, the anti-Semites were forced to disclose their motives. Although Councilor Hermann Seidel acknowledged the candidates' high professional qualifications, as spokesman for the anti-Semites he criticized the committee's list: "Among the gentlemen the election and constitution committee has recommended to us, there are five doctors, and of these five, only *one* is a Christian." It was now clear that the critics' motive had nothing to do with concerns about possible professional shortcomings of the candidates, but rather was anti-Jewish ressentiment. The anti-Semites had violated the unwritten laws of "apolitical" local politics.[59]

Immediately "heated protest" arose in the city council. The liberals withdrew their proposal of a secret session. It is, Councilor Milch declared, "in the interest and [necessary for the preservation of] the honor of the city and this body that the gentlemen at least have the courage to say in open session that we are divided into Christian and Jewish city councilors." Milch explicitly referred to the code of honor in effect in local politics. "Each of us," he appealed to his colleagues, "represents the entire citizenry. In the interest of my coreligionists and the City of Breslau, I would like it made known in the press how matters are discussed in this hall." Cornered, Seidel attempted to save the situation by referring to the heated general debate on the "Jewish question." In Breslau, too, he said, the political atmosphere has "now grown so extreme that one does and indeed must take cognizance of such distinctions."[60]

The closing speech in this highly emotional debate came from Moritz Elsner (1809–94), a city councilor since 1863, one of the most respected members of the body, and, at a good seventy years of age, the doyen of liberalism in Breslau. In the Revolution of 1848–49, Elsner had been the "most important representative" of radical democracy in Silesia, then counted among the prominent victims of reactionary politics, and finally, after 1862, began a second, successful career as editor of the influential *Breslauer Morgen-Zeitung.* "What impact would it have on the whole monarchy," Elsner asked his colleagues, not without bitterness, while also appealing to their civic pride, "if the Breslau city council now suddenly wanted to reflect on Jew-baiting in its vote. . . . For God's sake, don't let the spirit that now prevails in many circles gain ground here." Elsner's voice carried weight. "Almost unanimously," as the minutes soberly noted, the city councilors rejected the motion for a secret ballot and confirmed the election and constitution committee's recommendations.[61]

Three weeks later, in the city council meeting of April 15, 1880, came the sequel. The stumbling block this time was the magistracy's bidding policy. While the organized anti-Semites preferred to demand an open economic boycott of Jewish businesses, anti-Semitic city councilors tried to force the magistracy to consider not only economic criteria in awarding contracts but also the applicants' personal qualifications. The political mood for this attempt was favorable. Economic liberalism, in the spirit of which municipal contracts were usually awarded, had lost favor in the course of the stock market crash and the depression of 1873–79. Often the critique of "economic rationalism" (*Schlesisches Morgenblatt*) and anti-Semitism went hand in hand. "Thanks to the predominantly Jewish element," the Catholic *Deutscher Volksfreund* argued in January 1880, the "principle 'cheap and bad'" dominated economic life in the city. For that reason, "in the case of all bids . . . Christian applicants must be given preference over Semitic ones."[62]

In this atmosphere the magistracy recommended that the municipal building authorities purchase the necessary lumber from the lumber trader Isidor Witkowski.[63] His bid was 600 marks less than his nearest competitor, the old, established Breslau firm Lauterbach Lumber. Witkowski had come to Breslau around 1875 and was a member of the Jewish community, which is not surprising since his first name gave him away as a Jew. His lumberyard earned him 4,200 marks in 1877; that was no small sum, especially as he owned neither a house nor property, but neither was it considerable. The anti-Semitic spokesman for the magistracy's critics was Councilor Geier, who contrasted the upstanding, reliable businessman with the industrious and suspect newcomer. Geier argued that while Lauterbach was more expensive, he was also "more efficient" than Witkowski: "Lauterbach's firm is a business that owns large forests, one that therefore always has the kind of wood we need in stock and, due to his far-reaching business, offers the guarantee that delivery will occur brilliantly." By contrast, he continued, while Witkowski is "an industrious man, he has a very new business, which, in my opinion, would give cause for complaint." Obviously the anti-Semitic city councilors wanted to set an example in Witkowski's case. The liberals' response therefore had to be one of principle. Their main spokesman, the Protestant city councilor Anton Storch, thus replied to Geier that it was "imperative" that the City of Breslau "maintain the bidding process" hitherto in effect "as long it has not been notoriously shown that the lowest bidder is unreliable." Witkowski, he noted, had made the lower bid and was known to be reliable. All other criteria, such as personal dislike or fondness for someone, were thus out of place. "If we make a principle of what Mr. Geier is saying," he said in his sharp concluding remarks, "that would mean nothing but that the contract will be awarded only to the one who, forgive the somewhat vulgar expression, has the most 'spunk,' and nothing more."[64] Unlike in the debate on the election of the new board of directors of the hospital, the magistracy's opponents had concealed the anti-Semitic logic of their argument. Yet once again the anti-Semites were unsuccessful; the large majority of city councilors upheld the magistracy's motion. The contract went to Witkowski.

More important than the liberals' tactical victory here, however, was that the language of anti-Semitism not only did not find fertile ground in the Breslau city council but became virtually taboo. Whereas the Reichstag and the Prussian Landtag repeatedly debated the "Jewish question" until the end of the German Empire and the city councils in Potsdam and Dresden passed laws against kosher butchering, the Breslau city council held no further "debates on the Jews" after the meeting of March 15, 1880, until 1918. Doubtless, anti-Semitism had played a role in the run up to several city council elections, for instance in 1906 and 1912. A number of successful candidates styled themselves as opponents of the alleged "hegemony of the Jews" in Breslau. In the city council elections in November 1912, for example, the *Schlesische Morgen-Zeitung* fought against the "Jewish bloc," thus the left-wing liberals and the Social

Democrats, and recommended that its readers support the "coalition of all German-Christian elements."[65] However, as soon as the anti-Semites entered the council chamber in the Breslau city hall, they had to dispense with anti-Jewish rhetoric. The aura and self-understanding of the city council limited their opportunities to speak and act as anti-Semites in local politics. At the same time Heinrich von Treitschke freed the anti-Semitic movement from a "restraining sense of shame" at the national level, the Breslau liberals succeeded in making anti-Semitism taboo in the city council.[66] When in April 1905 the anti-Semitic city councilor Stein characterized the political stance of the progressive city councilor Heilberg as a "truly Jewish move," the lord mayor and the chairman of the city council forced the anti-Semite to apologize in the next meeting.[67] The language of anti-Semitism was the language of the gutter and the masses but not of local politics.[68]

The summer of anti-Semitism was as brief as it was hot. Similar to the "Berlin movement," Breslau anti-Semitism was not an independent movement but rather a part, albeit a central one, of the general shift in party-political power relations in the city.[69] Although the liberals had practically monopolized Breslau politics prior to 1878, the right wing of National Liberalism, the Center Party, and the Conservatives nevertheless succeeded in mobilizing a broad following. The left-wing liberals maintained their dominance in local politics, however, because the Breslau Jews, thanks to the Prussian three-class suffrage system, played a more significant role in the city council elections than their proportion of the population would have led one to expect, and because the inner logic of the "apolitical" language of local politics limited the anti-Semites' room for maneuvering.

2. Local Boundaries: The Naturalization and the Expulsion of Foreign Jews

In modern nation-states the question of nationality is of central significance. The universalistic claim of human rights crashes against it and is reduced to the particular rights of the citizen of individual states. Whereas in the course of the nineteenth century the rights of its citizens tended to grow within the German nation-state, the state became increasingly closed to the outside. Prior to the founding of the empire, most German states had not distinguished between citizens of other German states and those who today are called foreigners.[70] With the founding of the North German Confederation in 1866 and the German

Empire in 1871, however, the signs pointed toward the uniform citizenship of all Germans, a trend that was completed in the citizenship law of
July 22, 1913.[71]

The fact that in modern societies the "boundary between citizens
and aliens" has become "more important than ever" was experienced
by the immigrants who in their migration crossed one of the new boundaries.[72] The national boundary did not simply divide two territories but
possessed a far-reaching political and legal significance. Whoever left his
or her native land was now a foreigner. Immigrants crossed the boundary but did not leave it behind them. From now on, the local boundary
determined their lives. The boundary was, as Etienne Balibar puts it,
"not only an obstacle that was very difficult to overcome" but remained
"a place that one encountered continually."[73] The police authority kept
the foreigners under surveillance; they had no right to vote and could
not move freely; they were denied the right of assembly; and they continued to be in danger of expulsion even after having lived in the country for years. There was only one way out of this state of a partial lack of
rights and limited opportunities: naturalization, the acquisition of citizenship in the nation in which one now lived.[74]

The national politics of naturalization can be systematized in view
of the opposite poles of the principle of territoriality (*ius soli*) and the
principle of descent (*ius sanguinis*).[75] According to the principle of territoriality, West European nation-states naturalized all children who were
born within a nation's boundaries and often also all immigrants who
could demonstrate that they had lived in the country for a long period of
time. What was decisive here was that after a certain period immigrants
were entitled to naturalization or at least to far-reaching protection
from expulsion. By contrast, in Germany it was the principle of descent
that prevailed—at least in the realm of codified law. From the mid-
nineteenth century on, a right to citizenship was granted on principle
only to the offspring of provincial citizens (*Landesangehörige*). With the
emergence of a völkish nationalism, the principle of descent was based
no longer on the formal criterion of provincial citizenship but rather on
the fiction of an ethnically constituted *Volkskörper*, or national body. Even
after having lived for years in Germany, immigrants were entitled neither to naturalization nor to protection from expulsion. Whom the state
naturalized and whom not was, during the German Empire, a matter
left up to the state bureaucracy's "discretionary judgment, unfettered by
legal constraints."[76] The *Jüdisches Volksblatt* rightly complained in March
1910 about the "foreigner's lack of rights in Prussia" and considered a

"lawful resolution of [the] alien law" to be "absolutely essential." In September 1909, the newspaper had already, in the run-up to debates on the reform of the nationality law, pointed to the arbitrary naturalization practice. All parties "that have subscribed to the principle of equality regardless of denomination" should "also speak out on the question of the naturalization of Jewish foreigners, as well as the administrative authorities' discretionary right of expulsion and if possible establish through corresponding bills a *right to naturalization,* even if under the most difficult preconditions and requirements, but nevertheless a right."[77]

In the following, we shall investigate by way of the example of foreign Jews in Breslau the concrete naturalization and expulsion practices—which have been neglected by researchers so far—of the Prussian government authorities from 1865 to 1918 and compare them with the stance of the municipal authorities.[78] The experience of foreign Jews will not be isolated thereby but rather viewed as part of the state's and the city's general immigration policies. The first question is whether the immigration of East European Jews led to "real" problems, which could help explain the anti-Jewish stance of the Prussian government authorities. Next it is necessary to investigate the attempts of anti-Semites to halt the immigration of East European Jews and determine whether they influenced Prussian government policies and, if so, in what way. Then there is the question of whether conflicts arose between the Prussian state and local authorities regarding the naturalization of Jewish immigrants. It may be possible to infer from the city's stance what the stance of the silent majority of Breslau's population was toward East European Jews. Finally, we shall sketch the concrete expulsion practices of the municipal and the Prussian authorities.

Despite its intensive economic relations with East European countries, Breslau was not a center for the immigration of East European Jews. In 1880, before the great westward migration of East European Jews, only a good 5% of all Breslau Jews had been born in czarist Russia (2.7%) or in Austria-Hungary (2.6%).[79] But even after the first three great migratory waves of East European Jews in 1882–86, 1891–92, and 1905–8, comparatively few East European Jews lived in Breslau, such that in 1901 only 7.2% of all Breslau Jews did not have German citizenship. In all the Jewish communities in Germany with more than ten thousand members, this was the smallest proportion of foreign Jews: In Berlin, the proportion was nearly 19%, in Frankfurt am Main and in Cologne 13.5%, in Munich 35%, and in Hamburg 16%. Particularly stark is the contrast between the Breslau figures and the proportion of foreign Jews in the Jewish population in centers to which East European Jews immigrated, such as Leipzig and Dresden, where the proportion of foreigners in 1910 was 65% and 52%, respectively.[80]

But the statistical snapshot hardly does justice to the highly mobile society in the German Empire. By contrast, the figures on immigration and emigration show Breslau to be a way station. Many East European Jews settled there for a short time before they, in most cases, moved westward. The Jewish immigrants from Eastern Europe formed part of the "vagabondage of the working population," of which Gustav Schmoller spoke in 1889 with an undertone of cultural despair.[81] From 1882 to 1914, 4,239 Russian and 6,816 Austro-Hungarian Jews immigrated to Breslau. Almost the same number, namely, 4,218 Russian and 5,783 Austro-Hungarian Jews, notified the police that they were moving from Breslau. Many immigrants stayed only a few days, such as the Hungarian-born Jewish-American artist Julius Neuberger, who arrived from Budapest on May 18, 1903, and continued on to Berlin already on June 1. Others spent several months in the Silesian capital, such as the Bulgarian-Jewish tailor Elia Nissin, who moved from Berlin to Breslau at the end of November 1902 and then moved on to Vienna at the end of March 1903. And still others remained in Breslau for years, such as the Rumanian-Jewish architect Izil Behrmann, who moved from Munich to Breslau on August 20, 1902, and lived there for nearly five years before moving to Berlin in January 1907.[82]

Although a considerable number of East European Jews migrated to Breslau, they formed only a fraction of all the migratory movements; this must be stressed in opposition to the "fable of the mass immigration of the Jews," which is still prevalent in the literature today.[83] Aside from exceptional years, such as 1906, in the entire prewar period East European Jews represented only 0.5% of all the immigrants to Breslau, and the Polish and Russian Jews, whom the anti-Semites especially hated, represented only 0.1–0.2%. Even in the entire Jewish immigration, the proportion of *Ostjuden* until the beginning of the twentieth century was only 10–15% and reached roughly 20% only in the decade preceding the First World War. Contrary to the widespread reference-book assertion that Jews were more mobile than the rest of the population, Breslau Jews were less mobile than the rest of the city's population. The average Jewish migration movement, the sum of annual immigrants and emigrants, between 1880 and 1914 was barely a quarter of the Silesian capital's Jewish residents, whereas the entire migration movements made up nearly a third of Breslau's entire population (table 45). However, among the Jewish immigrants from Eastern Europe the proportion of Russian to Austrian Jews reversed. Until about 1905 Austrian Jews outnumbered Russian Jews, and in the decade before the war the proportion was even. In the period immediately following the war, however, the majority of *Ostjuden* came not from the succession states of the Habsburg Empire but rather from Russia and Poland (tables 46 and 47).

As a junction in the Silesian railroad network, moreover, Breslau was an important transit station in the great migration of East European Jews, who fled persecution and economic hardship from Eastern and Southeastern Europe to North America and Western Europe.[84] Since 1863, the Upper Silesian Railroad, the most important of the lines leading from Breslau to the East and an inexpensive means of transportation, linked, with its Warsaw–Vienna line, the Silesian capital with Kraków and the Austrian Northern Railroad.[85] On that line, to the east of Kattowitz, was the small town of Myslowitz. One of the most important German border stations was located there from 1893 on; at that station, while on their way to the emigration harbors in Bremen and Hamburg, Jewish immigrants had to undergo an often capriciously unpleasant hygienic inspection.[86] In early 1882 the number of transit immigrants fleeing persecution and economic hardship increased dramatically. Three times a week, between two hundred and three hundred Jewish refugees passed through the Breslau train station. By mid-May, an ad hoc committee from the Jewish community had already collected fifty thousand marks with which to provide the Russian Jews with food and clothes during their brief stay in the city. Moreover, despite the success of the anti-Semitic movement in the Silesian capital, an interdenominational committee was formed, with the encouragement of Mayor Ferdinand Friedensburg; one member was Felix Porsch, who already at that time led Breslau's Center Party.[87] The reactions in Breslau to later waves of refugees were similar.[88] The Jewish community organized humanitarian assistance, and the municipal authorities followed suit with a certain delay, though their support sometimes seemed halfhearted. With the encouragement of Mayor Bender and several Jewish city councilors, an interdenominational committee was formed once again in 1905 for the collection of money for "unfortunate victims of the political turmoil in Russia."[89]

Despite Breslau's importance as a transit station for Jewish migrants, these migration movements, which were not recorded in the statistics, did not cause any real problems. They occurred over a period of thirty years, the Jewish refugees as a rule left Breslau after a few hours, and the

hygienic inspections at the border were so thorough that the Jews passing through posed no danger, even during the cholera epidemics of
1892 and 1905.[90] Although the East European Jews constituted only a
fraction of all the migration movements in Breslau and there are no indications that they caused any real social or economic tensions, they
took on special significance in the imagination of anti-Semites. Long
before the topos of the *Ostjude* had been established in modern anti-
Semitism, a plethora of stereotypes condensed into the idea of the East
European Jew. From the perspective of the Christian bourgeoisie, the
"Polish Jew" symbolized immoral business practices, threatened the
ethos and the emotional balance of the up-and-coming middle classes,
and jeopardized all attempts to achieve the internal unity of the young
nation. Moreover, the stigmatization of the "Polish Jew" jeopardized
the symbolic inclusion of the German Jews because for anti-Semites of
the most varied shades and colors the line between German Jews and
"Polish Jews" was in flux.[91]

It was Gustav Freytag in particular who popularized the topos of
the "Polish Jew," in which was condensed a mixture of nationalism,
the canon of bourgeois virtues, and anti-Semitism. However, Freytag's
"Polish Jew" did not inhabit a counterworld to the canon of middle-
class values but represented the enemy within.[92] Born in Kreuzberg in
Upper Silesia, the "'poet' of the times and German *Bürgertum*" lived in
Breslau, with interruptions, from 1835 to 1847.[93] In 1849, six years before *Soll und Haben (Debit and Credit)*, Freytag published a brief retrospec-
tive sketch in *Grenzboten*, "The Jews in Breslau," in which he attempted
to show that "the Jewish element [was] a sickness for life in the eastern
parts of Prussia." The majority of Breslau Jews, he said, were "Polish,
horse-trading Jews." They twisted the middle-class values of work and
frugality beyond recognition. "Black and busy, like an ant," said Freytag,
"the Polish Jew of the old school" pursues his business, whereby "nothing in the world will surpass him in his frugalness." He is incapable of
true feelings, the prerequisite of all middle-class virtue. The world of
bourgeois values therefore remains closed to him: "The foreign Jew has
left his heart in his homeland with his family; he thinks of nothing, he
dreams of nothing, he wants nothing but to speculate."[94] While Freytag
reached only a small number of readers with this essay in *Grenzboten*,
with *Soll und Haben* he published the most successful German novel in
the second half of the nineteenth century. By 1890, 36 editions had
been published, by 1922 the 114th, and the largest lending library in Berlin had 2,300 copies on hand, a number to which no other novel came

even close. Even Franz Mehring, the Marxist literary critic, who considered Freytag's "literary gifts mediocre," acknowledged in 1910 that *Soll und Haben* was a "novel that faithfully reflects the bourgeoisie of those days." Freytag knew, he said, how "to stir the moral sauce in which the German bourgeoisie always wants to have its profit served."[95]

The success of *Soll und Haben* frightened the Jewish press, and it did not tire of pointing out the anti-Semitic character of the bestseller. The *Israelitische Wochenschrift* characterized the work as early as 1870 "as a novel that was both epoch-making and brimming with spitefulness toward the Jews." In 1886 the *Allgemeine Zeitung des Judenthums,* though more moderate in tone, basically reached the same conclusion: "When a distinguished writer," the editor noted, "who represents . . . good or bad types from other classes, but selects from one class of people only morally depraved figures as types and representatives and thereby brands the entire class: then he is following a spiteful bias."[96] In the protagonist, Veitel Itzig, Freytag not only condensed a catalog of anti-Jewish ressentiment but also assigned Breslau a central place in the anti-Semitic landscape. Few readers, particularly not Breslauers, could have failed to notice that the Silesian capital was the scene for the corrupt and deceitful misdeeds of the "Polish Jew."

The success of *Soll und Haben* was also based on the fact that Freytag took up ideas that were common in the conservative Breslau bourgeoisie. As the freemasons debated once again in the early 1870s whether they should admit Jews to their lodges, a Breslau freemason warned that Jews should be admitted only with "great caution." In the Oder metropolis, "that peculiarly Polish-Jewish element" prevails "to which a German does not so easily get accustomed. Given the unusual effort that this element exerts to advance itself, persons [are likely to] turn to the lodges . . . who do not belong there." In West Germany, "and even in Berlin," the concerned Freemason continued, "Jews could be admitted without any harm"; but in Breslau he "still has misgivings."[97]

Into the late 1870s the negative image of the "Polish Jew" had no demonstrable influence on the naturalization policy regarding Jewish immigrants from Eastern Europe. From 1865 to 1875, the district governor (*Regierungspräsident*), with the approval of the magistracy, had awarded Prussian citizenship to nearly every Jewish applicant. In this period, sixty-two Jews applied for naturalization, of whom only four came from Eastern Europe. The district governor naturalized fifty-six applicants; one applicant had withdrawn his application, in two cases the magistracy had advised against naturalization due to the applicants' extreme poverty, and the remaining three applicants had criminal records.[98] The successful applicants came from all social classes; only twenty-one of them earned less than three hundred talers per year. In addition to wealthy businessmen such as David Thumin from Lemberg, poor Jews also applied, such as the cigar maker Naftali Meier Immerglück, who made barely four hundred marks per year, or the peddler Samuel Zarek from Petrikau, a small town that lay a good two hundred kilometers south of Minsk.[99] Nor did a longer stay in Prussia seem to be required; in most cases the length of the applicant's stay was not even recorded. In the four cases in which the magistracy had noted it, it was between two and five years, and thus lay far below the prescribed period common at that time.[100] In the 1860s and 1870s, there does not seem to have been any conflict in Breslau—nor incidentally in Königsberg—over the question of naturalizing East European Jews. The municipal authorities and the Prussian state followed a naturalization policy that accorded more with the principle of territoriality than of descent.[101]

Although the anti-Semites were probably not aware of the inclusive naturalization practices, and many anti-Semites put even Jews who had lived in German lands for many generations on a level with recent Jewish immigrants from Eastern Europe, a determined campaign against East European Jews began in the late 1870s. Its goal was first of all to stop Jewish immigration and then to expel Jews who had already immigrated. In November 1879, Heinrich von Treitschke made himself the spokesman of intellectual anti-Semitism, which would soon reach a broad spectrum of the population, for Treitschke played the role of "a well-meaning, honest man" (Wolfgang Mommsen) and distanced himself from the "filth and coarseness" of the anti-Semitic movement. "Across our eastern borders," Treitschke wrote in the *Preußische Jahrbücher,* "come year after year droves of ambitious, pants-selling youth from the inexhaustible Polish cradle, whose children and children's children will one day rule Germany's stock exchanges and newspapers."[102]

Treitschke's polemic "Our Prospects," a key text in the history of political ideas in the German Empire, ignited the so-called *Berliner Antisemitismusstreit,* or Berlin debate on anti-Semitism, which despite its name resonated far beyond the German capital. In Breslau the city's entire press discussed Treitschke's article; even the Catholic papers agreed with the arch-Protestant.[103] Two fierce opponents of Treitschke were Breslau Jews: the historian Heinrich Graetz, who taught in the Jewish Theological Seminary, and the important Reform rabbi Manuel Joël. Treitschke's attacks on East European Jews gave rise ultimately to the atmosphere for

the anti-Semitic petition (*Antisemitenpetition*) of 1880–81, the principal demand of which was that Jewish immigration be stopped. The petition
drive was particularly successful in Silesia. Almost a third of all signatures, namely, fifty thousand, came from Silesia, five thousand of them
from Breslau alone.[104]

Doubtless the petitioners sought to expand their ideological hegemony through the mobilizing effect of the signature drive. Yet they ultimately aimed to establish an anti-Semitic naturalization practice. The
conservative *Schlesisches Morgenblatt*, which promoted the petition for
months, noted soberly, "[T]he petitioners expect the fulfillment of their
wishes through administrative channels." The leadership of the Prussian bureaucracy approved of the petition movement, especially as the
secretary of the interior, Robert von Puttkamer, regarded the Jewish immigrants as "a true plague." He reacted to the increase in Jewish immigration from Eastern Europe that began in 1881 with strict border inspections. The anti-Semitic administrative practice culminated in 1885–
86 in the expulsion of roughly ten thousand Polish and Russian Jews by
the Prussian authorities.[105] On a single day, October 8, 1885, the Breslau
district governor, for example, deported over one hundred Jewish immigrants from the Silesian capital.[106] In reaction to the liberal press's criticism that the mass expulsion was an arbitrary measure on the part of
the state, the *Schlesisches Morgenblatt* pointed out that in Breslau "cleanli-
ness and peace and quiet" had been improved by the expulsions. A lead
article in the *Schlesische Zeitung* shows the extent to which the delusion
about the mass immigration of Jews had spread also in bourgeois circles
and how far advanced was the symbiosis between anti-Semitism and
nationalism. The critics of the Prussian government lack "patriotism,"
the paper declared; they have instigated a "war" against the government "because, true to its duty to the nation, it is establishing rules
meant to protect the German nature and German culture within its
own borders against the outbreak of Polandism and Semitism."[107]

The anti-Semites' demand to restrict Jewish immigration also influenced the Prussian authorities' naturalization policies. Although the
sources for the late 1870s and the 1880s have been preserved only in-
completely, individual naturalization proceedings, in addition to the
wave of expulsions in 1886–86, provide evidence of a clear turn of the
tide. The Jewish religion instructor Adolf Wolf Poznanski, for example,
applied in summer 1887 for German citizenship. According to the record of the police interview on June 29, 1887, Poznanski was thirty-
three years old, came from the vicinity of Warsaw, had studied at the

rabbinical seminary in Berlin from 1872 to 1877, spent two years studying in England and France, resumed his training at the Breslau Jewish Theological Seminar in 1879, and completed his studies in 1881. He then attended the Catholic Matthias-Gymnasium in Breslau and graduated in 1884. After studying philosophy and history for three years in Halle, he received his doctorate in 1887. Also, in 1884 he had begun teaching Jewish religion in secondary schools and in the meantime taught at four schools in Breslau. The magistracy approved his naturalization and certified that he would have a secure annual income of nearly two thousand marks. Even the police inspector in charge seems to have been taken with him and reported to the chief of police following the interview that Poznanski, who had no criminal record and was unsuspicious politically, had "a very good command of German, . . . [had] already lived in Prussia for fifteen years . . . , and [was] an honest man, who [had] won respect in his circles."[108]

Although Poznanski was an almost perfect candidate for naturalization, he was denied citizenship. The Breslau chief of police summarized in his concluding report on July 23, 1887, first the positive result of the interview and the positive judgment of the magistracy and the responsible police inspector, but then concluded by saying that he did not consider Poznanski's naturalization "to be in the state's best interest and request[ed] the rejection of his application." The district governor followed this recommendation on August 12, and an appeal to the Silesian provincial authorities was also unsuccessful. On December 7, 1887, the provincial governor (*Oberpräsident*) informed Poznanski that he also denied his acceptance into the Prussian association of subjects (*Untertanenverband*), but wanted "hereby to grant him permission, revocable at any time, to reside in this city." Clearly the Jewish religion instructor was no better off now than before; after all, he had already had the precarious status of a foreign Jew in Prussia before he had applied for citizenship. The local boundary continued to determine his life.[109]

Even the language of racist anti-Semitism can be found sporadically in the official statements of the Prussian authorities. In March 1894, the Breslau district governor reported to the provincial governor on an application for citizenship by the brothers Hermann and Richard Jäger. Both were Catholic, had lived their entire lives in Breslau, worked as shop assistants, and lived with their mother, who had separated from their father, the Hungarian-Jewish choir singer Ignatz Jäger, already in 1883. Because of their father's Hungarian citizenship, Hermann and Richard Jäger were also Hungarians and therefore had applied for German citizenship.

As shop assistants, moreover, they had sufficient income, particularly as their mother had assets of about 100,000 marks. Nevertheless, the district governor spoke out against their naturalization "in view of their descent."[110] And yet racist anti-Semitism as a criterion for exclusion does not seem to have been the rule, as the naturalization of the Austrian Jew and law student Martin Leuchtag shows. The report of the chief of police from April 1908 on Leuchtag (born in Breslau in 1888) noted that his father, Richard, the owner of a women's coat factory, had a fortune of 700,000 marks. The chief of police stressed that the applicant was not only a "moral, honest, and hardworking man," but also that he belonged "to the German tribe." Martin Leuchtag had himself justified his application by saying that he felt "completely German, specifically Prussian" and it was his "most fervent desire to serve the king of Prussia, [his] true sovereign." His wish was fulfilled. Leuchtag was naturalized and served, after receiving his doctorate and completing his probationary training, as staff sergeant until he fell in battle in June 1916.[111]

The district governor's office could not, however, decide on the naturalization of foreign Jews completely by itself because in the naturalization proceedings the magistracy also had to be heard. According to the contemporary view, the report of the "local authorities," thus here the magistracy's, was to be considered "decisive as long as, under the prevailing circumstances, it [had] not been clearly demonstrated that it [was] based on erroneous assumptions."[112] As long as the left-wing liberals could defend their majority in local Breslau politics, there were constant conflicts between the city and the state over the question of naturalization. In their assessment of candidates for naturalization, the Breslau municipal authorities, like those in Königsberg, followed solely the logic of social closure, understood here as the monopolization of property, status, and power based on individual, acquired criteria.[113] For the municipal authorities, naturalization policy was a social issue. In principle, they supported immigration, since it promoted the economic development of the Oder metropolis, but recommended that all those applicants for naturalization be rejected who might burden the municipal and state welfare system. The Prussian government, which had the last word in naturalization proceedings, followed the principle of exclusion, understood here as the monopolization of property, status, and power based not on individual but on collective, ascribed criteria—thus, for example, on ethnicity, status, denomination, or gender. Between 1908 and 1914, the Breslau magistracy recommended the naturalization of fifty-eight Jewish applicants. By contrast, the district governor denied almost all of them citizenship and naturalized only eight. That was conspicuous since he even naturalized non-Jews whose naturalization the city had discouraged because of the probability of their becoming welfare cases.[114] The state's exclusion of Jewish applicants was thus a classic case of anti-Semitic exclusion.

Though there is no indication that the city questioned the anti-Semitic interpretation of the principle of *ius sanguinis*, the municipal reports are characterized, in contrast to the Prussian administration's, by an inclusive outlook. The magistracy's recommendations consistently contain impartial or positive judgments on the Jewish applicants; they stressed the latter's virtuous character and were unusually detailed. It may be that the municipal authorities made an effort to provide some Jewish applicants with a particularly positive certificate of good conduct. The city was represented before the district governor's office by the magistrate responsible for municipal Poor Relief Administration. The magistrate would base his judgment on municipal records of relief for the poor and an informal assessment by one of the city's three hundred district prefects (*Stadtbezirksvorsteher*)—an honorary official elected by the city council. Because the district prefects were respected citizens with an intimate knowledge of their municipal district's social fabric, an analysis of their reports provides a good basis from which to infer the attitude of the Breslau vox populi toward Jewish immigrants from Eastern Europe.[115]

In a typical report, District Prefect Hugo Hartmann recommended in November 1910 that the Turkish Jew Hirsch Chaimoff be naturalized. Chaimoff was born in Minsk in 1860, had married there, and moved to Breslau about 1885. Sometime around 1888 he had lived for a while in Copenhagen, and then, in the following year, he had settled permanently in the Silesian capital. Chaimoff worked as a factory manager in the Sultan cigarette factory; he "[has] held the same job already for twenty years, has an annual income of about 4,000–5,000 marks and has . . . already saved a tidy sum," Hartmann explained in his long report. "Moreover," he concluded, "Mr. Hirsch Chaimoff's entire family made a very good impression on me."[116] On December 3, 1909, District Prefect Emil Sattler judged of the family of Chaim Frenkel, a cigarette manufacturer born in Minsk, that they were not only able to feed themselves but were also "very decent people who enjoy[ed] a good reputation and [were] elegantly furnished."[117] Finally, the case of Russian-born commercial clerk David Flor is interesting. In 1908, at the age of nineteen, he applied for German citizenship. The district prefect raised objections. Flor, he said, "frequents a hostess bar" and has given "the police and city officials trouble" with his application. The magistracy vehemently contradicted the report of the self-appointed guardian of public morals and endorsed Flor's naturalization: "The applicant cannot be faulted for having 'caused the police and the city officials trouble' through his application for naturalization."[118]

It is also noteworthy that the municipal authorities by no means understood naturalization to be a prize for assimilation. In September 1913, the Hungarian Moritz Weiss applied for German citizenship. He worked as a religion teacher and as a rabbi in one of Breslau's small synagogues. On September 10, 1913, District Prefect Jesenich expressed his support for Weiss's naturalization. According to Jesenich, Weiss earned 4,000–5,000 marks annually. "My inquiries," he added, "yielded only impeccable appraisals from his landlady, Mrs. Schwarz, Freiburgerstrasse 40, as well as from Mr. Kober, Wallstrasse 10, a student of the applicant's." Weiss's professional position alone already guaranteed moral maturity: "The applicant's high intellectual caliber rules out any misgivings (religious activity)."[119] Even though the Prussian authorities refused to naturalize Chaimoff, Frenkel, Flor, and Weiss, as well as nearly every other Jewish applicant, the attitude of the magistracy and the district prefects indicates that, at least for a significant portion of Breslau's population, even East European Jews were regarded by no means as a threat but rather as members of Breslau society.[120]

Neither the municipal authorities nor the district governor treated female applicants differently than their male counterparts, provided they were single women. The nationality of female minors and married women was automatically considered to be that of the father or the husband, respectively. In the case of applications by single women, the district prefects and the magistracy recommended naturalization, but in almost every case the district governor rejected them. In their reports on female applicants, however, district prefects emphasized other characteristics than in the case of male applicants, particularly their "decency" and their virtuous sexual morals. Minna Seelig, who had immigrated to Breslau from the United States, was one of the Jewish women who applied for German citizenship in vain. In his report from February 1910, the district prefect had recommended her naturalization, since she was "a decent person" and "well-off." The Russian Jew Bertha Baumann, née Rosenbaum, from Slaworzeno was more fortunate in April 1914. After the responsible district prefect had praised her as "a most decent woman," the district governor granted her German citizenship at the end of May 1914.[121]

The municipal authorities' emphatically inclusive attitude toward the majority of Jews who applied for Prussian citizenship certainly does not mean, however, that the magistracy was guided by humanitarian considerations. With regard to poor immigrants, whether Jewish or not, the City of Breslau resolutely followed its policy of social closure. The municipal authorities feared that Breslau might become a magnet for the migrant poor. In a city council meeting in December 1905, Magistrate Georg Martius, head of the Breslau Poor Relief Administration, warned the council not to improve the facilities of the municipal shelter for the homeless. Almost all the homeless in Breslau, he said, "are work-shy persons who have several previous convictions for begging and vagabonding and have no place whatsoever in Breslau." The municipal homeless policy, Martius continued, does not solve any social problems but serves "in its present form only to burden us with foreign tramps and make it easier for them to stay here!"[122] The district prefects and the Poor Relief Administration meticulously examined the economic situation of each applicant in order to keep poor immigrants away from the city. In some cases, the municipal authorities not only rejected a naturalization due to poverty but even sought to have the applicant expelled. For instance, the district prefect and the magistracy's Poor Relief Administration advised against naturalizing the sixty-two-year-old Austrian ropemaker Anton Ischpan. The responsible magistracy official, Tilgner, noted on August 18, 1908, that Ischpan had "already received assistance from public poor-relief funds earlier"; moreover, "according to our inquiries," there is "a danger that later he will once again fall back on public poor relief."[123] Also in the case of the forty-year-old carpenter Wenzel Kowarnik the city warned against naturalization. As far as the district prefect was concerned, Kowarnik "only wants to be naturalized so he can receive welfare." The magistracy's negative judgment on August 11, 1910, was every bit as clear: "A son of the applicant has received public poor relief at the All Souls Hospital, and there is a danger that Kowarnik himself or his family will again become a burden on the public welfare system."[124]

The naturalization of women was likewise treated by the city primarily as an economic issue, even if here an applicant's deviant sexual ethics occasionally mattered. When the Russian cigarette maker Helene Jankowski applied for naturalization in July 1908, the district prefect at first raised no objections. After a review of the case by the Poor Relief Administration, however, the magistracy advised against her naturalization and wrote the Breslau chief of police on July 20, "[The applicant has] been on welfare for years. In view of her three children, we suspect that she will continue to fall back on poor relief." The Poor Relief Administration even informed Lord Mayor Bender of the case, and the responsible magistrate noted, "Helene Jankowski, who has been given continuous support, and her three children are Russian subjects." With the approval of the lord mayor, the magistrate recommended that "the expulsion of Jankowski and her children be initiated at once." What spoke against the cigarette maker and single mother was not merely her poverty but rather, from the magistracy's perspective, her dubious sexual morals. On July 22, 1908, a magistracy assessor summarized the basic stance of the magistracy: Expulsions of foreigners have "occasionally been initiated by us even when no more welfare was drawn but there was a danger that there would be a need for poor relief later. A very strict procedure was considered necessary particularly when the case concerned persons who were sexually not beyond reproach (for instance, those who have contracted sexually transmitted diseases, etc.). Since Jankowski had four [*sic*] children out of wedlock, she can hardly be considered, in connection with the welfare worker's report, to be sexually beyond reproach."[125]

That does not mean, however, that the magistracy treated the naturalization of female applicants in principle also as a moral issue. Helene Jankowski's violation of middle-class sexual ethics was a criterion for the municipal authorities only as long as she threatened to burden the municipal welfare system. When the unmarried father of the children promised to pay monthly alimony of fifty marks to Jankowski, the magistracy withdrew its petition for expulsion immediately in September 1908.[126] But if a female applicant could not show that she had sufficient income, the magistracy's economic logic came into play. When in 1911 Martha Fischer, the widow of a locksmith, applied for citizenship, the magistracy strongly advised against her naturalization. According to the district prefect, the applicant was almost completely without means and "a mendacious person." He therefore "vigorously" advised that she be "expelled."[127]

The principle of social closure affected low-income Jewish applicants, such as the thirty-nine-year-old Russian widow Rose Cukiermann, just as it did the non-Jewish poor. Rosa Cukiermann had lived with her parents until 1890 in the Kowno district, then followed her parents, Leib and Theophilia Walk, to Tilsit in East Prussia, from whence the Walk family moved in 1899 to Thorn in West Prussia, and finally settled in 1902 in Breslau. In 1909, Rosa left Breslau and moved to Radom, a city one hundred kilometers south of Warsaw, because she had married the electrical engineer Israel Mose Cukiermann, who lived there. After her husband's death in December 1917, she returned to Breslau with her two daughters, Edwarda and Anna, who had been born in Radom, to live with her parents. Although the responsible district prefect recommended her naturalization in December 1917, the magistracy warned against it after having reviewed her financial circumstances, for she was "completely impoverished." In his statement, the chief of police combined the economic with an anti-Semitic logic. The "impoverished Polish Jew" Rosa Cukiermann was not "a desirable addition to the population." Despite this negative stance, the naturalization proceedings nevertheless took a happy turn for Rosa, for her parents had been naturalized in the course of their twenty-seven years in Prussia. "While the applicant cannot be characterized as a desirable addition to the population," the chief of police noted on February 27, 1918, "because she had Prussian citizenship before her marriage, she nevertheless has a right to have her citizenship restored based on article 10 of the Nationality Act of July 22, 1913."[128]

The outbreak of the First World War led to a liberal turn in the Prussian government's naturalization policy. The army needed soldiers for the war. Suddenly even Jews of Polish and Russian descent could become Prussian citizens without having earned a legal right to naturalization. Already in October 1914 the district governor urged the magistracy to process the applications of war volunteers immediately. The Prussian Ministry of the Interior, he said, had ordered "that the naturalization paperwork for military conscripts and war volunteers be dealt with immediately."[129] Foreign Jewish men could now become Prussian citizens within a short time if they were prepared to risk their lives in the war. Of the fifteen Jewish men naturalized between August 1914 and November 1918, thirteen had volunteered to serve in the military.[130] The Chaimoffs, who had applied unsuccessfully for Prussian citizenship before 1914, now also took advantage of this opportunity. Already in September 1914, the two youngest sons—Joseph (twenty-three years old) and Leo (seventeen years old)—had joined the army and shortly thereafter applied for naturalization. The district prefect was again full of praise; the sons, like all the Chaimoffs, were "very decent people . . . all happy to be Prussians (or Germans), and . . . in Breslau already for decades." A few weeks later, both sons were German citizens. The district governor naturalized them on October 9 and 26, 1914, respectively. A year later, Joseph Chaimoff was dead; he fell on September 25, 1915.

Leo survived him another year and a half, but then was killed on March 10, 1917.[131] Their father, along with his wife and their twenty-two- and twenty-nine-year-old daughters, were granted Prussian citizenship in May 1916. The father had already filed his application in early 1915; perhaps his second-oldest son's death in action helped to bring the Prussian authorities round. Although their younger brothers had already died by this point, in fall 1917 the eldest sons—Jakob (thirty-three years old) and David (twenty-nine years old)—volunteered for the army and applied for citizenship. To shed the stigma of being a foreigner, they too were prepared to risk their lives. David and Jakob Chaimoff both were lucky. The district governor naturalized them on April 16, 1918, and, unlike their younger brothers, they each survived the war in one piece.[132]

The restrictive policy of the Prussian authorities regarding Jewish immigrants from Eastern Europe met with the resistance of the municipal authorities but also that of the Breslau Chamber of Commerce. The rigid surveillance of foreigners living in Breslau endangered important trade relations with East European partners.[133] When the Prussian authorities reacted to the wave of Jewish refugees in the early 1890s with strict border inspections, the chamber of commerce took up a sensational case as an occasion to force a fundamental clarification. In February 1895, a foot gendarme in Gleiwitz had picked up two Jewish businessmen from Czenstochau who wanted to travel to Breslau on business and, despite sufficient identification papers and the intervention of their Silesian business partners, sent them back to the border. The chairmen of the Breslau Chamber of Commerce, Salomon Kauffmann and Siegfried Haber, therefore turned directly to the Silesian provincial governor's office on March 8, 1895. Since they "could add other, similar incidents" to this case, they requested that the border inspections be eased due to the "importance of a border traffic for Silesian trade." "Due to its geographic location, our province depends on the Russian and Austrian hinterland," Kauffmann and Haber appealed to the provincial governor's economic expertise; it is precisely "the individual's movement back and forth" that is "the essential mediator of trade." Because of the uncertain legal status of the Russian Jews, to which the chamber of commerce alluded with the formulation "complicated legal conditions," it was urgently necessary, they said, to make border traffic easier instead of restricting it further. Otherwise, "the Province of Silesia" would be in danger of having "its market restricted." However, the provincial governor feared a potential Jewish immigration more than economic losses in Silesia's trade with Eastern Europe. The Oppeln district governor argued in his statement from April 3, 1895, which the provincial governor adopted on April 29, with regard to Jewish travelers, "the strict application of passport regulations is necessary." Economic considerations must come after the "interest in avoiding a new Russian influx and the interest in turning back impoverished emigrants."[134]

In view of the economic significance of foreign trade relations, the chamber of commerce accused state authorities repeatedly of damaging the Silesian economy through their anti-Jewish policies. In May 1911, for example, the chamber of commerce asked the district governor "most obediently for a . . . moderation of the treatment of the Russian-Jewish flax merchants in the interest of the businesses involved." Unlike in 1895, the district governor's office proved conciliatory this time. On June 22, 1911, it informed the Breslau chief of police that the chamber of commerce had argued convincingly that the "expulsion of the Russian-Jewish flax merchants living [there] would destroy Breslau's important flax trade." Therefore, the Russian-Jewish flax merchants living in Breslau were to be permitted to stay until further notice. However, in order to avoid any misunderstanding of the Prussian government's anti-Semitic base line, the district governor added that any "Russian-Jewish flax merchants" new to Breslau were to be denied permission to remain in the city.[135] The next conflict occurred in January 1914. At the end of 1913, the Breslau chief of police had denied the Jewish tobacco buyer Hirsch Palakiewicz from Russia a residence permit and reacted to the chamber of commerce's reproaches with the advice that the Breslau cigarette manufacturers should send their own buyers to the areas in Bulgaria where tobacco was grown.

To help improve the chief of police's economic expertise, the chamber of commerce prepared an extensive report on the Breslau cigarette factories' buying policies. There are no "Germans who are suited for this difficult job and have sufficient experience." "The precise knowledge of the circumstances and especially the trust of the individual tobacco growers, which is necessary for the purchase, is possessed only by . . . Russians who have already been in this business for a long time. . . . The German cigarette industry is thus totally dependent on Russian buyers for the purchase of uncured Turkish tobacco."[136]

The representatives of the Prussian state did not refuse in principle, then, to consider immigration problems also from an economic perspective, but only when Jewish immigrants were concerned. In the case of Catholic farmworkers from Galicia and Poland, the district governor most definitely allowed himself to be guided by economic considerations. In a confidential letter from April 1900, the district governor criticized the police authorities for their "unnecessary strictness" toward "migrant foreign seasonal workers." To guarantee that "the need for workers [was] met," he said he expected "an accommodation going as far as possible." Whereas only five years earlier the provincial governor had required the strict application of passport regulations regarding Jewish business travelers, now the district governor said that "identification not issued by the police could also be regarded as sufficient" identification papers.[137]

At least the legal situation of Austro-Hungarian Jews improved in January 1912 after the City of Breslau and the chamber of commerce had found an unexpected ally in the Austrian government in their fight against the rigid immigration policies of the Prussian authorities. In a secret letter, the Silesian provincial governor informed the Breslau chief of police on January 22, 1912, that the Austrian government had repeatedly protested against the arbitrary and harsh treatment of Austrian Jewish businessmen in Prussia, since it ran "counter to the spirit of contractual trade agreements." Therefore the Prussian secretary of the interior had allowed the provincial governor "to grant foreign Jews permission to stay without a specified time limit in those districts, subdistricts, and municipalities in the administrative districts of Breslau and Liegnitz that are not nationally endangered." However, the "milder policy" is not to be employed toward all foreign Jews, but only toward those who "are not of Polish descent; come from Austria and possibly even Hungary; . . . appear to be completely secure financially; belong to socially and culturally higher social circles."[138] Even if anti-Semitism continued to play a role in the provincial governor's position, the lines between anti-Jewish impulses, nationalism, class snobbery, and economic opportunity had blurred beyond recognition.

The partial lack of rights of foreign Jews living in Breslau also manifested itself in the Prussian authorities' practice of expulsion. Although the legal status of all foreigners living in Prussia was precarious, the representatives of the state treated foreign Jews more arbitrarily than other foreigners. In principle, the district governor and the chief of police could expel all foreigners who were unemployed or destitute, or politically out of favor, thus mostly social-democrats, as well as foreigners who had been convicted of homelessness or begging, prostitution or pimping, or other offenses or violations. The government authorities made their decision about expulsion at their discretion, without regard for the individual's family situation, without citing any reasons, and completely beyond the reach of the courts, which could have guaranteed a minimum of the rule of law. Unlike in many West European countries, foreigners did not acquire any protection from expulsion even after they had lived in Prussia for decades. They neither had a right to be heard nor could they fight an expulsion process in court, but at most only file an appeal with the provincial governor.[139] One had to be as fixated on the authoritarian state as Heinrich von Treitschke to defend Prussia's practice of expulsion, which looks arbitrary when compared to other countries, as "true humanity." "With the simple explanation: we find you disagreeable," Treitschke had argued, a state must "be able to expel foreigners who become a nuisance to it, even if it has made an agreement that ensures that the subject of the other state can stay."[140]

The proportion of Jews among the foreigners expelled from Breslau was not conspicuously large since the majority of the expulsion proceedings affected people who had come to the Silesian capital above all because of their poverty. Few Jews were among the migrant poor. In a random sample of forty-one expulsion proceedings in Breslau toward the end of the German Empire, there were only five foreign Jews.[141] The majority of those expelled were poor, unemployed workers, including many prematurely dismissed seasonal workers who had come from Silesian estates to Breslau to keep themselves above water there through begging and petty crimes. From a sample of twenty-five foreigners expelled from Breslau between 1903 and 1918, eight each were expelled for theft and begging, five for fraud, four for homelessness, two each for prostitution and vagabondage, and one for illness.[142] The age of those expelled also indicates that the group in question included hardly any Jews. Whereas most East European Jews had already lived in Breslau for a long time and had started a family, the expulsion proceedings affected mainly young people. In a third sample of fifty-two expulsion proceedings in Breslau, thirty-eight of those expelled were under thirty years of age (and eleven of these were even under twenty), and only ten were over forty.[143] The expulsion proceedings against the worker Jurko Hennisch and the maid Maria Cernuch can serve as examples here. The Breslau chief of police expelled Hennisch, a Catholic originally from Galicia, in 1910 as a "troublesome foreigner" after he had drawn a "crowd" at the train station on January 5, 1910, through his "helpless drunkenness." The twenty-six-year-old Cernuch, also a Catholic but from Sternberg in Moravia, had first worked as a cook, seamstress, and maid, but then earned her living as a prostitute. As a consequence, she was sentenced in February 1917 to four weeks in prison for "prostitution," in January 1918 to nine months for abortion, and, after serving her sentence, was expelled from Breslau.[144]

Jews among the migrant poor were expelled by the chief of police just as ruthlessly. In July 1910, for instance, a policeman arrested Salomon Herstein, a sixteen-year-old Jew from Kraków, in the train station. For attempted theft, the Breslau district court condemned him on August 25, 1910, to a draconian sentence of six months in prison since he had already been convicted of the same offense in 1907 in Berlin. After Herstein had served his sentence, the Breslau chief of police expelled him in January 1911 "from Prussia as a troublesome and homeless, penniless, unemployed, and uncredentialed foreigner." The twenty-five-year-old Josephine Herzfeld, a Jew from Vienna, was no more fortunate in 1911. After the deaths of her parents, she had tried to live from prostitution and was under the supervision of the local vice squad in Braunschweig. On July 25, 1911, she arrived in Breslau, where a police officer arrested her on the evening of July 27. In the interrogation on July 29, she stated that she intended "to engage in prostitution until she had earned enough to return home," and thus requested that she also be "placed under the supervision" of the vice squad in Breslau. Already on August 4, 1911, however, the chief of police ordered her expulsion, and on August 10 Josephine Herzfeld departed for Vienna.[145] The expulsion practice thus was hardly immigrant-friendly, but rather followed in the aforementioned cases the rules of social closure. Without any protestation from the municipal authorities, the police department sought to keep the foreign poor out of the Silesian capital. The brutal treatment of impoverished Jewish immigrants manifested not primarily anti-Semitism but rather "the general German suspiciousness toward all lower-class Eastern Europeans."[146]

Apart from that the Prussian state pursued a specifically anti-Semitic policy of expulsion, for they even expelled Russian Jews who were not guilty of the slightest offense and were neither unemployed nor impoverished nor politically suspect. In 1905, one of these expulsion proceedings struck the then twenty-year-old Isaak Jackersohn, a Jewish flax merchant from Vitebsk, Russia.[147] In the framework of a private feud, Jackersohn was the victim of a deliberate indiscretion at the Breslau police department in September 1904. The chief of police wrote in January 1905 to the district governor that, while the proceedings against Jackersohn for adultery had been abandoned, he asked the latter to consider "whether under the circumstances expulsion from Prussian territory seem[ed] called for." Thus, although a court had cleared Jackersohn of all charges, he had lived in Breslau without interruption since September 1901, and meanwhile was even engaged to a young Breslau woman, and although Jackersohn ran a flourishing flax business in Breslau, the district governor demanded on February 9, 1905, that he leave Prussia within four weeks. In vain Jackersohn tried to have the expulsion order repealed. On February 15, the mother of his fiancée approached the Breslau chief of police, von Bienko, whom she gave the "most solemn oath" that "Jackersohn [was] an upright, orderly, honest, and modest man who had erred due to the enticement of foolish people." The wedding of her daughter and Jackersohn, she said, was set for April 15. As a Breslau citizen who had always supported herself and her child "in an honest way," she would be no means "entrust her daughter to this man as his wife if [she] had not carefully investigated the matter and had not reached the true conviction that he [was] innocent, and had merely been the instrument of evil people." While the chief of police did take the time to speak with the mother personally, he nevertheless upheld the order. He would neither support an appeal to the district governor to rescind the expulsion nor approve a future naturalization application by Jackersohn. Jackersohn nonetheless managed, with the help of the Russian consulate, to postpone the date of his expulsion for six months, which enabled him to wrap up his business affairs.[148] After the flax merchant had moved to Trautenau in Austrian Silesia and continued to conduct his business from there, in fall 1905 he requested permission through a Berlin lawyer "to stay at least temporarily in those places to which he imported flax from Russia." Otherwise, according to the lawyer in his appeal to the Silesian provincial governor, "the expellee" is faced with "the end of [his] business and the destruction of his existence." Just as the chief of police paid no attention to Jackersohn's private circumstances, likewise the provincial governor took no interest in the petitioner's economic future. On January 26, 1906, he informed Jackersohn that in the future even a brief stay in Prussia would be denied.[149]

Just how difficult it was to be naturalized and how easily one could be expelled was common knowledge among Breslau Jews. Once again, the expulsion proceedings against Isaak Jackersohn are instructive. In view of the Prussian authorities' readiness to expel Russian Jews for slight misdemeanors, the businessman Ludwig Freudenthal took advantage of Jackersohn's precarious legal status to avenge his wife's affair. On September 14, 1904, Freudenthal wrote to the Breslau chief of police, von Bienko; he claimed Jackersohn had "managed, with sly cunning and threats, to bring my wife, with whom I was happily married for eleven years, to commit adultery." To pay for the adultery, Freudenthal requested that "the foreigner Isaak Jackersohn be expelled from German soil . . . due to this crime." In the hearing on September 20, 1904, Jackersohn said that he "did not associate with the woman in a criminal manner"; rather, Ludwig Freudenthal had "started the whole thing in order to have a reason for divorce." Since, on November 12, 1904, the district attorney's office abandoned proceedings against Jackersohn that had been initiated on account of adultery, the matter seemed at first to have run aground.

However, Freudenthal contacted the chief of police a second time on December 13. Unfortunately, he wrote, he would divorce his wife at the end of December but would have to drop charges against Jackersohn lest he end up sending her to prison as well. "Yet I am of the view," he continued, "that the crime of adultery is still the same thing even without Jackersohn's conviction [and thus feel justified] in requesting his expulsion." "Sir, please do not misunderstand me," Freudenthal went on, obviously well informed about the routine expulsions of Russian Jews, "when I take this opportunity to point out that roughly fourteen days ago a young man, likewise a Russian, named Grünblatt, was ordered to be expelled immediately without his even having done anything wrong." Furthermore, Freudenthal threatened that he would write directly to the Prussian secretary of the interior if von Bienko did not do something. After the expulsion proceedings had already run their course, Freudenthal protested a third time to the chief of police. He said, "[I find it] exasperating . . . that thus far all my humble requests have not been considered . . . while daily I hear of new expulsions of Russians in Breslau. . . . for instance, the other day a local bookkeeper of Russian descent, named Lewin, was sent an expulsion order." When the district governor granted Jackersohn the unusually long grace period of six months in view of his business affairs before he had to leave Prussia, Freudenthal intervened a fourth and final time by giving the chief of police a report on Jackersohn that he had had a Breslau private eye, Kreditschutz C. F. Schneider, prepare. In their view, the flax agent could most certainly be expelled immediately since "Isaak Jackersohn had no need of staying in Breslau for a longer period of time. . . . He could just as easily live in Kattowitz or in Myslowitz or in Czenstochau, in Kraków, etc." He may act "like a gentleman here," but he "associates mostly with Poles and Russians, has extravagant tastes, spends a lot of time in cafés, is said to gamble and to spend a lot of money on himself."[150]

The precarious legal status of foreign Jews living in Prussia seems to have encouraged widespread denunciations. In January 1902, for instance, the Breslau chief of police received a postcard from a German living in Paris who chose to remain anonymous. The author warned the police authorities about a "high-caliber vagrant and con man" who used many pseudonyms. The "alleged Lewkowitz . . . Jarmelowski or Karmelowski" had left Paris for Strassburg with his wife and four children a few days earlier and planned to travel to Breslau from there. It was likely that he would have seemingly genuine identification papers since "it [was] often a general custom among Jewish cattle- and calf-dealers in the countryside to employ the first Jewish vagrants as . . . kosher butchers and teachers."[151] Another informer thought it unnecessary to remain anonymous. Erich Baum, who resided at Carlstrasse 43, contacted the police department in February 1902 to warn it about Adolf Lustig, a Jewish egg dealer from Galicia. Lustig employed his unemployed cousin Josef, "who [was] an Austrian subject," and had him hawk eggs in Breslau. At least the Breslau police did not leave the tips unchecked. The police investigation revealed that Adolf Lustig did not hawk his eggs at all but only offered his customers home delivery. Moreover, Josef Lustig was found to have helped out in the shop only for a few weeks and in the meantime had again found work as a lumber salesman. In view of the situation, a policeman noted, "the report was probably filed by Baum only out of professional jealousy."[152]

Foreign Jews who intended to move to Breslau consulted the police department to get some degree of certainty about their legal status before they moved to the Silesian capital. The Viennese Jewish clerk Josef Mandl, for instance, had worked in Breslau in the late 1890s for a lengthy period, had become engaged there, and now wanted to settle in the Oder metropolis. In October 1898, he inquired with the chief of police "if, under the aforementioned circumstances and on the assumption of a genuinely respectable way of life, [he] would be granted permission to take up permanent residence." "On principle and out of concern due to earlier expulsions of foreigners," both he himself, Mandl continued, and "the family of [his] future wife" agreed that he could get married only after a positive reply from the police department.[153] Whereas the chief of police answered Mandl, saying that he could presumably settle in Breslau, the Polish Jew Josef Glückslein had no such luck three years later. He was, he wrote to the police authorities on July 25, 1901, an employee of a metal factory in Oświęcim and had received a job offer from the Breslau firm Archimedes Steel and Iron Corporation. But

Glückslein's prospect of an attractive new job was promptly shattered when the chief of police wrote in reply on July 27 "that permanent residence [could] not be granted to him."[154]

As long as they were not dealing with poor immigrants, the municipal authorities and the Breslau Chamber of Commerce seem to have followed in their immigration policies the inclusive maxim of the Marburg professor of constitutional law Sylvester Jordan. He had outlined a remarkable utopia of a liberal immigration policy already in 1847 in Rotteck and Welcker's *Staats-Lexikon*. "A government that is strong through the love of a free and thus also liberal people, because in their spirit and heart is rooted its political system," Jordan, a constitutional monarchist, had argued, "need not fear foreigners since they cannot pose it any danger; rather, that government will desire their frequent visits to and long stays in the state because the state can only profit intellectually and materially from the expansion of such commerce."[155] Yet since the Prussian government ultimately had its hand on the rudder regarding questions of naturalization and migration, neither the city nor the chamber of commerce could prevail with their liberal policies. The anti-Semites thus were able to put part of their ideology into anti-Semitic practice. The local boundary continued to determine the lives of foreign Jews in Breslau. This border was particularly high for Jews, and the danger of expulsion was particularly acute for them. The Prussian state treated foreign Jews as second-class foreigners, just as German Jews were regarded as second-class citizens.[156] In Breslau as well, as Etienne Balibar remarks, the "polysemy of the border" was evident since "in practice" it did "not have the same meaning for everyone."[157]

The anti-Semitic demand to limit Jewish immigration was motivated, moreover, solely by ideology and did not reflect, for instance, the "real" problems triggered by immigration. There was no mass Jewish immigration. The municipal authorities argued from a socioeconomic standpoint and therefore supported the naturalization of foreign Jews. By contrast, anti-Semitic motives marked the Prussian government's policies on Jewish immigrants. There was constant conflict with the municipal authorities over the question of the naturalization of Jewish immigrants, moreover, presumably since the anti-Semitic turn of the Prussian state in the early 1880s, but in the 1890s at the latest. For the municipal authorities, the question of naturalization was a social and economic issue. They recommended that naturalization be denied to everyone who might burden the municipal and state welfare system. As long as a Jewish immigrant did not fall under the poverty clause, the city recommended his naturalization. Almost always the municipal authorities reported positively on Jewish applicants. By contrast, the state authorities denied naturalization to almost all Jewish applicants. That was conspicuous since they naturalized even such non-Jews against whose naturalization the city advised because they probably would become welfare cases. After 1880, the Prussian state took the principle of exclusion as its point of orientation, whereas the city, thus the district prefects and the magistracy, maintained the principle of social closure and therefore approved the naturalization of almost every Jewish applicant.

The "nationalistic re-formation of the Nationality Act" occurred not only "under the sign of an offensive world politics" but also under that of a völkish anti-Semitism.[158] Whereas several million East European Jews in the stream of the "great migration" (Simon Dubnow) flowed into the United States, France, and the United Kingdom, the anti-Semites created a public atmosphere that enabled the Prussian government, without much protest from Jews or liberals, to reduce the Jewish immigration into Germany to a trickle and to stop the naturalization of Jews almost completely.[159] The Prussian authorities' exclusionist naturalization and expulsion policies indicate, moreover, the limits of the rule of law in the German Empire and deserve in this regard the same attention as the anticlerical legislation during the Kulturkampf and the Socialist Law. Under these policies, the state's representatives treated foreign Jews more arbitrarily than other foreigners, although their legal status also was precarious.

As early as 1909, Edgar Loening, professor of constitutional and canon law at the University of Halle, judged the responsible state authorities harshly—though justifiably so against the backdrop of expulsion practice in Breslau—in the *Handwörterbuch der Staatswissenschaften*. Due to "indeterminate and malleable" laws, foreigners living in Germany were "at the mercy of state governments." Loening was likely thinking of cases such as Jackersohn's expulsion when he added that it was "not impossible for the expulsion law to be used in the service of private objectives, to gain personal revenge, or to rid local traders and merchants of successful competitors."[160] The Breslau *Jüdisches Volksblatt* also complained bitterly in 1911 about the "manipulation of the alien law, especially when it [came] to foreigners of Jewish faith." "In the land of poets and thinkers, the foreigner still has no rights; at any moment, the authorities can expel him from the country without giving any reasons, nor does the law tolerate him in this respect, for he cannot appeal his case to any judge."[161]

In the face of this negative situation for Jewish migrants, it is easy to lose sight of the inclusionist stance of the municipal authorities and the chamber of commerce. Given the well-known anti-Semitic bias of the Prussian government, it is worth noting, however, how tenaciously the magistrate and the city's economic elite fought with the state over the question of the immigration of foreign, thus especially East European Jews. In the city of Breslau prior to the First World War even the so-called Polish Jews, we may conclude, were regarded not as threatening foreigners but as potentially equal members of the Breslau population, as part of a multiplicity in the unity of the city.[162]

3. Honored Jews: Ferdinand Julius Cohn, Breslau's First Jewish Honorary Citizen

In symbolic politics in the narrower sense there are forms of political action that are not aimed at a concrete political goal but whose purpose lies precisely in symbolic action. This includes honors and celebrations.[163] The highest and most coveted honor within Breslau's symbolic order and the heart of municipal civic pride was the title of honorary citizen. Beyond cultural particularity—for instance, that of denomination—it was based on an ethic of individual achievement and symbolized great service to the city of Breslau. In conferring the title of honorary citizen, however, the city not only rendered the service of the honoree visible but at the same time also gave expression to the municipal authorities' self-understanding, a municipal civic pride. Together with the city council, the magistracy could confer this distinction, according to section 6 of the Prussian Municipal Government Act (Städteordnung) of 1853, "to men who had German citizenship and civil rights, and who have rendered a great service to the city."[164]

The title of honorary citizen was hard to come by, and it had to be for it to retain its solemn aura. Honors comparable to the title of honorary citizen, Arthur Schopenhauer had warned in 1851, lose their value "through unjust or indiscriminate or excessive distribution." One should thus "be as careful with their conferment . . . as a merchant is when signing bills."[165] Breslau's municipal authorities followed Schopenhauer's advice. Between 1870 and 1914, the magistracy and the city council awarded only nineteen men the title of honorary citizen. It could happen that the city did not name any honorary citizens for several years, such as between 1886 and 1889 or between 1904 and 1906. The title of honorary citizen was a "rare distinction," the *Schlesische Zeitung* soberly observed.[166] Also in terms of social status, the circle of honorary citizens was tightly circumscribed. In this regard, the conferment of the distinction followed the logic of social closure. Only members of the bourgeois elite and the aristocracy were eligible. Anyone who belonged to the lower classes or the petite bourgeoisie had no hope of receiving the distinction.[167] To be an honorary citizen of Breslau was something special, and it is hardly surprising that the city spent a good deal of money on the conferment of the title. At the turn of the century, drawing up a certificate of honorary citizenship cost nearly 1,500 marks.[168]

A marked difference separated the municipal title of honorary citizen, which breathed the spirit of the bourgeois ethic of achievement, from the national system of titles and decorations. Hence it is surprising that, unlike the conferment of decorations and aristocratic titles, the title of honorary citizen has gone unnoticed in the debate on the supposed feudalization of the German middle class.[169] The three Hanseatic cities of Hamburg, Bremen, and Lübeck, for instance, intentionally dispensed with a system of titles and orders but still conferred the title of honorary citizen. Hamburg even went so far as to forbid senators and judges from accepting any national honors.[170] Honorary citizenship conferred by a Prussian city was expressly not regarded as an aristocratic title, since the conferment of the latter remained a privilege of the Crown until 1918.[171] As a consequence, the state took the monarch as its own point of orientation when setting the schedule for conferring decorations. Honors were conferred on the occasion of the coronation festival or when the king officially toured a province.[172] By contrast, the conferment of the title of honorary citizenship took its cue from the honoree's own biography. Concrete occasions included the end of the honoree's term of office, the fiftieth anniversary of having received his doctorate, or an even-numbered birthday. In conferring decorations, the monarch celebrated the appearance of absolute power, whereas in conferring honorary citizenship the cities focused on the individual and his accomplishments. The state system of titles and orders was also structured hierarchically. Most titles and decorations were divided into first-, second-, third-, and fourth-class honors. By contrast, there was only one class of honorary citizen and thus the community of honorary citizens was egalitarian.

Unlike honorary citizenship, state decorations and honors rapidly lost standing in the course of the German Empire because their number constantly increased and gained a reputation of being for sale. While the Prussian state conferred a good 4,000 decorations in 1867, it conferred almost 36,000 in 1913. The loss of standing was particularly evident in the case of the lower-level decorations; a fourth-class decoration must have seemed to be almost an insult to distinguished citizens.[173] Candidates for state decorations increasingly preferred "to dine à la carte from the menu of decorations."[174]

Some even snubbed the monarch and turned down the decoration offered to them. For instance, Oskar Huldschinsky (1846–1930), a Jewish heavy industrialist from Upper Silesia, declined the Order of the Crown because he received it not as "one of Germany's greatest industrialists" but because "he now sail[ed] with the emperor."[175] A left-wing city council chairman from the small Silesian town of Sagan also turned down a fourth-class Order of the Crown in 1896. The Prussian Ministry of the Interior did manage to convince him to accept it by threatening to charge him with lese majesty, but the chairman made a laughingstock of himself in the liberal and social-democratic press in Silesia.[176] Thus while in the German Empire the monarchic-hierarchic honors were increasingly devalued, the award of honorary citizenship, which was based on individual achievements, remained hard symbolic capital.

In 1897 Breslau was one of the first larger cities in Germany to confer honorary citizenship on a Jew. Prior to Breslau, probably only Erfurt and Schwerin could boast of a Jewish honorary citizen; the former had conferred honorary citizenship in 1860 on the mathematician Ephraim Salomon Unger (1789–1870) and the latter in 1876 on the lawyer and long-time city councilor Lewis Jacob Marcus (1809–81).[177] Even cities such as Königsberg and Mannheim, where, as in Breslau, anti-Semitism was hardly successful prior to 1918, did not choose a Jew as an honorary citizen until 1907 and then only one each. And not until 1914 did the magistracy and the city council of Berlin, the most important center of German-Jewish life, name, with Oskar Cassel, the first Jewish honorary citizen of the German capital.[178] Among the nineteen honorary citizens of Breslau around the turn of the century, two were Jews: the botanist Ferdinand Julius Cohn (since 1897) and the counselor of justice Wilhelm Salomon Freund (since 1901).[179] For the analysis of the relations between Jews and other Breslauers, it is therefore worth investigating whom the city actually honored, with what arguments it justified honoring two Jews, and how the Breslau public responded to honoring them.

Because the title of honorary citizen was rare, it is necessary to ask not only whom the City of Breslau made honorary citizens but who was missing from the list. Among the nineteen honorary citizens of Breslau in the German Empire, there were no district governors of the administrative district of Breslau, no chiefs of police (with the exception of Baron August von Ende), no Catholic archbishops, and no presidents of the Protestant consistory, finally no commandants of Breslau and almost no commanders of the Silesian army corps.[180] Not even Bismarck, on whom in 1895 on the occasion of his eightieth birthday a virtual shower of honorary citizen titles poured from Trier, Bayreuth, Altona, and hundreds of other German cities, was made an honorary citizen of Breslau.[181] Nor did the Breslau municipal authorities make the city's lord mayors and the chairmen of the city council honorary citizens automatically at the end of the terms of office. Ferdinand Friedensberg, who had been lord mayor from 1878 until 1891, and a total of four city council chairmen between 1866 and 1886—Karl Gustav Stetter, Wilhelm Lent, Georg Lewald, and Friedrich Beyersdorf—were denied this honor.

That there were two Jews among Breslau's nineteen honorary citizens is all the more surprising as the city honored in twelve cases individuals who held positions that were closed to Jews: three provincial governors and two high-ranking military officers, three lord mayors, and four mayors. In the case of the provincial governors and high-ranking military officers, the honors served primarily as an instrument, albeit one used infrequently, of municipal "foreign policy." That was a common practice. The *Handwörterbuch der Preußischen Verwaltung* expressly states in 1911: "[T]he occasion for this honor is not limited to immediate service to the conferring city; the conferment can also be for outstanding achievements as a statesman and general, or as a scholar, artist, industrialist, etc."[182] As an instrument of municipal foreign policy, the award of honorary citizenship symbolized that the city belonged to a larger political unity, be it the Prussian state or the German nation. That held true particularly in the case of three Silesian provincial governors. Yet even such awards were not automatic. Of the nine provincial governors who held office between 1870 and 1914, six came away empty-handed. The magistracy honored only those provincial governors who had headed the Silesian provincial government for a longer period of time, namely, Otto Theodor von Seydewitz, Hermann von Hatzfeldt, and Robert von Zedlitzsch und Trützschler. Furthermore, the honor followed as a rule only after their term of office had ended. With the conferment of honorary citizenship, the city thanked the recipient for his generous cooperation and cultivated its relations with the Prussian state. By honoring the predecessor, the magistracy and the city council signaled the new provincial governor that the City of Breslau was prepared to work together with him amicably.

A conciliatory gesture toward the Prussian state was also reflected in the honoring of Field Marshal Helmuth von Moltke in 1890, who had already been made an honorary citizen of Berlin in 1871, as well as of Hamburg and Cologne in 1879. Moltke was also highly esteemed in bourgeois circles beyond Breslau; and the city honored his strategic talent, for Moltke embodied like no other the modernity of the Prussian military. Wilhelm von Tümpling, the commanding general of the Sixth Army Corps stationed in Silesia, was honored already in 1880, probably to improve relations with the military stationed in Breslau. Unlike Moltke, Tümpling did not particularly distinguish himself either in 1866 or in 1870–71, but did set himself apart by having headed up the Sixth Army Corps seventeen years longer than any of his predecessors or successors.[183]

The largest group among Breslau's honorary citizens, however, were not representatives of the Prussian state but a total of seven former lord mayors and mayors of the city. The conferment of honor on them, which took place immediately after their terms of office, indicated once again the high esteem that the heads of the municipal government enjoyed, as well as the close connection between the citizenry and the political leadership they elected. Wholly in keeping with the Municipal Government Act, the distinction was an instance of solemn and freely given thanks to those "who [had] rendered a great service to the city." Since the honor went to a person as representative of an office and not to the person himself, it functioned simultaneously as a hint to his successor in the position. The new lord mayor or mayor might likewise receive that rare distinction one day should he support the magistracy's interests.

With the unanimous decision in both cases and in both committees to confer honorary citizenship on two Jews, the municipal authorities honored a successful and self-confident embourgeoisement of the Jews in the nineteenth century, which ended not with the denial but with the affirmation of Jewish identity. Breslau's first Jewish honorary citizen, the famous professor of botany Ferdinand Julius Cohn (1828–98), on whom the municipal authorities conferred honorary citizenship in November 1897 on the occasion of the fiftieth anniversary of his having received his doctorate, embodied the success story of Jewish assimilation. Already in view of the surname Cohn—according to Dietz Bering, "the surname with the most powerful anti-Semitic charge"—it could not escape even the most superficial of observers that the honoree was Jewish.[184] Moreover, Ferdinand Julius Cohn had never attempted to hide his Jewishness. His grandfather had still experienced the precarious legal situation and material plight peculiar to premodern Jewry. According to Ferdinand Cohn's biographer in the *Schlesische Lebensbilder*, the grandfather, Jacob Cohn, who had first worked as a proofreader at a Hebrew printing shop in Dyhernfurth, lived in the early nineteenth century as "one of those wretched Jews who populated the Breslau ghetto, on Carlsstrasse." His son Isaak, who was born in 1806 in Dyhernfurth, managed to rise to the bourgeoisie. With borrowed money, around 1828 he opened a small rapeseed-oil business, which was used for lighting. Remarkably, the shop was no longer located in the Jewish quarter but on Ohlauerstrasse in the eastern part of downtown Breslau. "My father thereby distanced himself," Ferdinand Julius Cohn recalled in his memoirs, "from the narrow confines of the Jewish quarter and thus made the first step to amalgamate himself and his family with the general life of the city." His business was successful, and Isaak Cohn enjoyed from roughly the 1840s on the emblems of bourgeois respectability. He was a Prussian privy counselor of commerce, Austro-Hungarian consul, a freemason in the Apollo Lodge in Leipzig from 1858 on, chairman of the factory section of the City of Breslau's trade commission for many years, and founded as the president of the merchants' association the Breslau commercial school.[185]

With pride Ferdinand Julius Cohn looked back in the autobiography he penned in 1898 on the success story of his father, whom he celebrated as a typical representative of Breslau's first generation of wealthy Jewish businessmen. "Poor lads [*Bocher*] from Upper Silesia and Posen, having immigrated to Breslau, [and] much sharper, more alert, and more frugal than their Christian competitors . . . gradually became wealthy and respected businessmen through their hard work, frugality, and reliability." This fascinating testimony of Cohn's is like a mirror image of Freytag's *Soll und Haben* (*Debit and Credit*), with which Ferdinand Cohn was quite familiar. In contrast to Gustav Freytag, who villainized the ascent of these *homines novi*, Cohn legitimated the career of the Jewish bourgeoisie with the self-confident reference to the rational aspects of the world of bourgeois values, to "hard work, frugality, and reliability," to "great energy and great ambition."[186]

Ferdinand Cohn's tough, virtually unbreakable will to climb the social ladder and to win laurels in the world of learning was honored by the city. The oil dealer's son succeeded in entering the educated elite, though he long had suffered discrimination and exclusion. As a precocious and extremely gifted "child prodigy" and as a Jew he was subjected to the ridicule and "rough treatment" of his schoolmates during his entire time at Breslau's Maria-Magdalenen-Gymnasium.[187] The end of his school days would change nothing. "The law and my faith prevent me from devoting myself to jurisprudence or serving the state as a teacher or civil servant," the sixteen-year-old Ferdinand Julius Cohn wrote in 1844 in his curriculum vitae prior to his final exams for his *Abitur*, summing up the discrimination that awaited him as a Jew. Yet he added self-confidently that he hoped for "the beautiful dawn of general freedom and equality," which would enable him "from above at a university to have a useful influence on the minds of youth."[188] This prophecy about his own influence would be fulfilled, but the path there was long and arduous. At the University of Breslau, where Cohn studied between 1844 and 1846, he could not receive a doctorate because he was a Jew. The faculty was unsuccessful in its appeal to the ministry to allow the talented scientist to receive his doctorate in Breslau despite his being a Jew. As a result, Cohn was forced to transfer to Berlin and earned his doctorate there.[189] By 1850 he was already a *Privatdozent*, was soon one of the leading German botanists, and "founded," according to the *Encyclopaedia Britannica*, "bacteriology as a science." With limited funding and against the will of the University of Breslau, in 1866 he founded an institute of plant physiology, where numerous groundbreaking studies in bacteriology were written. For many years he also led the botanic section of the Schlesische Gesellschaft für Vaterländische Kultur (Silesian Society for Patriotic Culture), advised the city on the landscaping of the botanical gardens and of the Südpark, and worked for the municipal parks commission. Nevertheless the typical fate of a Jewish *Privatdozent* befell him. The Prussian secretary of education von Mühler informed him at the end of the 1860s that as long as he was the secretary Cohn would not become "a professor in Prussia." His wife, Pauline Cohn, née Reichenbach, recalled that "the long years of waiting for a fixed position and fruitful teaching conditions were for him, who was so enthusiastic about his profession, difficult to bear."

The discrimination here was against both the Jew and the political nonconformist. Ferdinand Cohn was one of the few members of Breslau's bourgeoisie who did not take part in the 1850s in the exclusion of his teacher, the important botanist Christian Nees von Esenbeck (1776–1858). During the Revolution of 1848, Nees von Esenbeck had actively supported the radical democratic movement and in the backlash thereafter made contact with the early workers' movement. As a consequence, the seventy-five-year-old Nees von Esenbeck was removed from this professorship in Breslau and dismissed without a pension in January 1851.

Although now almost all the Breslau professors avoided Nees von Esen-beck, Cohn visibly maintained his friendship with him, supported the now completely destitute man, and, on the occasion of his funeral in March 1858 anonymously mocked in a newspaper the cowardice of the Breslau professorate:

> Cautiously, wisely, for the knowledge giant,
> That loyal man, last respects you would not grant,
> Because he spoke and lived without trepidation,
> You showed him no respect at his last station.
> That's nothing new, it's no masterpiece,
> You'll always lag far, far behind Mr. Nees.[190]

Ferdinand Cohn's more than twenty, economically precarious years as a *Privatdozent* were ended only by the national-liberal secretary of education Adalbert Falk, who in 1872 made the forty-four-year-old a full professor.[191]

In conferring honorary citizenship on him, the municipal authorities honored simultaneously Ferdinand Cohn's scientific achievements and his solidarity with the City of Breslau. He was read the magistracy's justification from October 26, 1897, to the city council, "a loyal son of our city and at the same time exceptional as a researcher and teacher, as well as a citizen and human being."[192] Cohn's double role as citizen and as brilliant natural scientist also formed the core of the justification on the extravagantly decorated certificate of honorary citizenship. The text, which the municipal councilor Karl Jaenicke drafted and Lord Mayor Bender painstakingly revised, honors Cohn as "the meritorious teacher at our university . . . whose name is spoken with honor insofar as science has a home in the world; . . . the exceptional writer, who is understandable even for laymen . . . ; the all-venerable fellow citizen of his hometown, to which he has been loyal despite tempting offers from afar, who has increased its renown, and who places his rich knowledge at its service whenever it is needed."[193] According to Bender's instructions, the artistic design of the certificate of honorary citizenship was to highlight both aspects. "For the presentation, the following plan should be followed," wrote the lord mayor to the commissioned artist: "(1) The City of Breslau's coat of arms is to be placed prominently—next to it, the east gable of the city hall might be depicted. . . . (2) Beyond the artistically decorative writing, the honoree's relation to the university and to botany, but especially his study of plants and enjoyment of flowers should be portrayed."[194]

The high point was doubtless the solemn presentation of the certificate of honorary citizenship during the celebration, to which Cohn, on the occasion of the fiftieth anniversary of his doctorate on November 13, 1897, had invited the guests. Fascinatingly, the simultaneity of civic pride, scientific reputation, and self-confident Jewishness is also reflected here. The location of the celebration was the impressive apartment of Ferdinand Cohn and his wife in an exclusive residential building at Tauenzienstrasse 3a. The building, with a neoclassical facade stood in the heart of the Schweidnitzervorstadt, where many upper-middle-class families had settled since the 1870s. It bordered on the extravagantly decorated Tauenzienplatz, from which the Schweidnitzer Strasse, with its numerous elegant shops and bank buildings, extended to the north and the Kaiser-Wilhelm-Strasse led to the residential suburbs of Krietern and Kleinburg to the south.[195] From the loggia of the Cohns' apartment, one had a view of the mansion of the banking family Eichborn with its private park. The New Synagogue was barely fifty meters away. Diagonally opposite on Agnesstrasse stood the clubhouse of the Lessing Lodge, which belonged to the B'nai B'rith organization, and a few hundred meters away was the elegant clubhouse of the Gesellschaft der Freunde, one of the city's exclusive Jewish social clubs.[196] With nearly 26,000 marks, the Cohns also commanded a high annual income for a university professor's family. Ferdinand Cohn had a fortune of 380,000 marks, which he presumably inherited from his father upon his death in 1883. The majority of heads of the other households also commanded annual incomes that made possible a bourgeois lifestyle. The Cohns shared the third floor with Ferdinand Cohn's seventy-six-year-old mother-in-law, Natalie Reichenbach, who each year received roughly 12,000 marks in pension annuity from her fortune of 300,000 marks. On the ground floor lived the fifty-year-old Jewish businessman David Lipmann, who had a fortune of 1.3 million marks and who earned a net annual income of 52,000 marks. On the second floor lived the thirty-eight-year-old Jewish dentist Wilhelm Sachs, who, with a fortune of 440,000 marks and a net annual income of almost 54,000 marks, certainly was among Breslau's wealthiest dentists.[197] On the fourth floor lived the thirty-two-year-old Protestant factory owner Arthur Deter, who made 22,500 marks after taxes from his assets and business. In the apartments of their employers or under the roof lived a large domestic staff—two servants, three maids, two nannies, a coachman, and the building superintendent.[198]

The guest list from the celebration on November 13, 1897, also suggests just how closely integrated the first Jewish honorary citizen of

Breslau was in the social life of the city. Among those present counted the leading representatives of the university, the Jewish *Gemeinde*, and the municipal authorities. "Early in the morning," Pauline Cohn recalled, "letters and dispatches had already arrived from all over, from near and afar; gradually our apartment was transformed into a palm and flower garden of the most magnificent kind."[199] In the course of the day, representatives of all the city's dignitaries had come. The rector of the university and the dean of the philosophical faculty led off the appreciations and honors, praising Cohn's scientific contributions and presenting him a *tabula gratulatoria*. Then followed representatives of the board and the representative council of Breslau's Jewish *Gemeinde*. They honored, above all, the self-confident Jew. Despite all the troubles caused him by the Prussian university system, Cohn had held fast to his Jewishness. Breslau's first honorary citizen was a member of many Jewish organizations, such as the Brüdergesellschaft (Society of Brothers), was a popular speaker at the *Gesellschaft der Freunde*, belonged to the scientific committee of the Viennese Gesellschaft für Sammlung und Conservierung von Kunstgegenständen und historischen Denkmälern des Judentums (Society for the Collection and Conservation of Jewish Art Objects and Historical Monuments), and had as a young scientist refuted the anti-Semitic phantasm of the desecration of the host by demonstrating that the red spots on the wafers that had served the anti-Semites as proof of the desecration of the host were the result of fungal growth in damp churches.[200]

The climax of the celebration was the painstakingly staged entrance of the magistracy and the city council chairman, which preceded the conferment of honorary citizenship. Lord Mayor Bender had asked five representatives from each of the two municipal bodies to come to the Fürstensaal of the city hall and don their official dress in order then to ride together in the magistracy's carriage to the Cohns' apartment roughly eight hundred meters away.[201] The staging of municipal civic pride had the desired success. According to Pauline Cohn, "the gathering was moved deeply when the noble figure of Lord Mayor Bender appeared with the city council chairman Freund . . . , accompanied by magistracy delegates and city councilors, in solemn official dress and presented . . . the certificate of honorary citizenship."[202]

Cohn knew full well the significance of this honor. Although he had previously accepted "with a grin" a third-class Order of the Red Eagle from the king of Prussia, now he thanked the city, as his wife recalled, in "a tremulous voice," for the award of honorary citizenship. It was, Cohn said in his acceptance speech, "such a magnificent honor that even a man who could boast of having made a contribution a thousand times greater would not be able to achieve anything greater" than this. He expressly took up the award's meritorious character. The award of honorary citizenship did not merely honor him as a person—"a born-and-bred Breslauer who grew up in the Breslau air, was trained in Breslau schools"—but primarily "a tribute" to the university to which he had "belonged for more than half a century." Through Cohn's stylization of the university as the "most brilliant jewel" in Breslau's "civic crown," the royal underpinnings of the university faded in importance. Like the Municipal Government Act of 1808 and free "self-administration," the University of Breslau was "a daughter of the great age of Stein and Hardenberg, . . . of Goethe, Fichte, and the Humboldt brothers."[203]

After the end of the marathon of honors, speeches, and words of thanks, the colorful mixture of city, academic, and Jewish dignitaries remained together. The social part of the celebration followed. The guests had breakfast in the impressive dining room and gathered once again on the next evening for the grand university banquet. And again there were speeches from colleagues and the lord mayor of Breslau. Yet the high point of the banquet on November 14, according to Pauline Cohn, was "a humorous song by [their] friend Felix Dahn, who had so often tuned his lyre for [them] on festive and solemn occasions before," in which the society lion and author of the anti-Semitic bestseller *Ein Kampf um Rom* (1876; *A Struggle for Rome*) honored the freshly minted first Jewish honorary citizen of Breslau.[204]

The significance of the conferment of honorary citizenship on Ferdinand Julius Cohn was reflected in the numerous reports on the celebration in the general Breslau and the German-Jewish press, in which the city's tribute eclipsed the numerous other tributes paid the honoree on that day. The social event of conferring honorary citizenship, an event buoyed by municipal civic pride, transcended party differences. In Breslau, all newspapers reported on the event—even papers such as the *Schlesische Zeitung* and the *Schlesisches Morgenblatt*, which often endorsed governmental anti-Semitism—honored Cohn's contributions and emphasized the great significance of the award of honorary citizenship. That was all the more true of the national Jewish press and the journal of the *Verein zur Abwehr des Antisemitismus* (Association for the Defense against Anti-Semitism), in whose reports the honor from the municipal authorities stood in the foreground.[205]

The singular status of the award of honorary citizenship at a time that was rich in honors is also reflected in the memories of the event and the place of Ferdinand Julius Cohn in Breslau's collective memory. For Cohn and his wife, Pauline, the certificate of honorary citizenship was the most "precious treasure" among all the honors, and Cohn's widow devoted an entire chapter of the "pages of remembrance" (*Blätter der Erinnerung*, the subtitle of the memoir of Cohn that she edited) to the precise depiction of the celebration and the conferment of the honor.[206] At Cohn's funeral on June 28, 1898, the lord mayor staged the city's final tribute to the honorary citizen. He personally penned a long obituary, which was published in all six Breslau daily newspapers and which honored Cohn as a "great scholar," a "loyal, helpful citizen," and a "member and advisor of the municipal administration." The certificate of honorary citizenship, "which we were privileged to present to him, thus expressed only what had long been alive in the hearts of his fellow citizens." Moreover, the lord mayor ordered a "beautiful wreath," on whose ribbon, according to Bender's instructions, were printed the city's coat of arms and the inscription "Our Son and Honorary Citizen." At the funeral service at Tauenzienstrasse 3a and at the burial in the Jewish cemetery, all the magistracy appeared in official dress.[207] Finally, in celebration of the tenth anniversary of Ferdinand Cohn's death, the magistracy decided in June 1908 to erect a monument to the honorary citizen at the entrance of Breslau's Südpark, in whose landscaping Cohn had taken part as an advisor. At the unveiling of the monument, which was made by Ferdinand Cohn's niece, the Vienna-based sculptor Ilse Conrat, there gathered once again a circle similar to that at the celebration in November 1897: Lord Mayor Bender, the chairman of the city council Wilhelm Salomon Freund, other members of the magistracy, representatives of the university, and many of Cohn's relatives.[208]

Although honorary citizenship, unlike the many councilor titles, was officially not a title that could be used with one's name, the first Jewish honorary citizen of Breslau was increasingly referred to no longer as "Cohn the botanist" but as Cohn the "botanist and honorary citizen." Breslau's *Jüdisches Volksblatt*, for instance, spoke repeatedly of Cohn as the "honorary citizen of Breslau." The deceased Cohn was not only "a pride of the Jewish community," noted the Mainz journal *Der Israelit: Central-Organ für das orthodoxe Judenthum*, but also "the greatest son of the city . . . and its honorary citizen." Both the archivist of the Jewish community in Breslau, Rabbi Aron Heppner, who drew up a list of all "Jewish personalities in and from Breslau who were true to their faith till beyond the grave," and the entry on Ferdinand Julius Cohn in the *Jüdisches Lexikon* from 1927 referred to only one among Cohn's many honors, the certificate of honorary citizenship. The best-known travel guide to Breslau during the Weimar Republic, *Komm ich zeige Dir Breslau,* placed the "honorary citizen" Ferdinand Julius Cohn alongside Ferdinand Lassalle and the ophthalmologist Hermann Ludwig Cohn, as one of three Breslau Jews on a brief list of "famous personalities" from Breslau.[209]

Breslau was one of the first German cities in the broader sense and probably the first German metropolis to confer honorary citizenship on a Jew. The municipal authorities thereby simultaneously honored the successful and self-confident Jewish embourgeoisement of the nineteenth century. Certainly, the award of honorary citizenship was also a reward for acculturation, but in neither case was it an assimilation that ended in a disavowal of Jewish identity and conversion to Christianity. With Ferdinand Julius Cohn and Wilhelm Salomon Freund, the city honored Jews who were self-confident and who maintained their Jewishness and, as a result, had to endure discrimination. Both Cohn and Freund were also social climbers, and the city honored that quality in each as exemplary and central to their success stories. Instead of villainizing them as parvenus and unwelcomed intruders, the municipal authorities emphasized in conferring honorary citizenship on them the rational, meritocratic aspects of the bourgeois canon of values. In relation to that, the emotional dimensions of the world of bourgeois values that were inscribed in middle-class anti-Semitism and which marked the social climber as a half-educated parvenu and nouveau riche faded in importance. Municipal civic pride, which found expression in the award of honorary citizenship, was therefore grounded in an ethic of individual achievement. The honor formed a successful foil to the hierarchic-feudal title, order, and ennoblement system with which the Prussian state rewarded a servile submissiveness to the monarchy. The high esteem of the award of honorary citizenship stood in sharp contrast to the rapid loss of esteem of state decorations. There was little evidence of aristocratization or feudalization of the Breslau bourgeoisie. The conferment of honorary citizenship was based on an individualistically oriented liberalism, which was pluralistic, at least regarding denomination. The inner logic of honorary citizenship, too, brought into view a political blueprint of a pluralist *Bürgerlichkeit,* a liberal, bourgeois civility, which Breslau Jews helped to shape, which was open to them, and in which they participated literally as men of civic honor.

Conclusion

The extraordinary pastness of our story results from its having taken place before a certain turning point, on the far side of a rift that has cut deeply through our lives and our consciousness. . . . it took place back then, long ago, in the old days of the world before the Great War, with whose beginning so many things began whose beginnings, it seems, have not yet ceased.

Thomas Mann, *The Magic Mountain*

Over the course of the First World War and in the years thereafter, relations between Jews and other Breslauers deteriorated dramatically. The high degree of Jewish integration visible in the prewar period eroded between 1916 and 1925. Among Breslau Jews, their sense of both security in and belonging to the middle class yielded to the fear of anti-Semitism, which since the early 1920s permeated many areas in which it had played a negligible role prior to 1914. For Breslau Jews, the Weimar Republic proved to be more a curse than a blessing. Although the Weimar Constitution assured the equal rights of German Jews in society and did away with the last legal loopholes to which anti-Semites had repeatedly appealed, the fact that now, unlike in the prewar period, Jews found themselves confronted almost daily with anti-Semitic agitation, violence, and discrimination indicates the gap that existed between constitutional ideal and constitutional reality in the years following the Great War. To be sure, Jews still felt at home in Breslau even after 1918, but that home had become uncomfortable, if not downright dangerous.[1] For Jews, more than for other Breslauers, danger became the sign of the new times.

The deterioration of relations between Jews and other Breslauers between 1916 and 1925 had a number of causes. Following the German

231

Army's "Jew count" of 1916, anti-Semitic ideology became more radical and dynamic while also joining forces with völkish nationalism,
which seized large segments of the conservative middle class and for
which "the Jew" became the "ultimate enemy."[2] Parallel to that, a general brutalization of politics and society occurred between 1916 and
1923. In part, this was an expression of wartime experiences and the
decivilization that accompanied them. But the brutalization increasingly followed its own laws. As elsewhere, in Breslau it was especially
young people, who had been spared any experience of the front, who
took part in the violent riots.[3]

Reasons specific to Breslau can also be given as to why relations
between Jews and other Breslauers rapidly deteriorated. It was significant that, within a brief period of time, the Jewish bourgeoisie lost
much of the political and economic power that had enabled it to participate in the shaping of Breslau politics in the prewar period. The rise of
anti-Semitism in the postwar period should not be interpreted as a reaction to the Jews' privileged status. Rather, it was precisely the Breslau
Jews' loss of power from 1918 on that formed an important precondition
for the spread of anti-Semitism.[4] Since Germany's eastern border had
shifted west, many shared the provincial governor's view that Breslau
had become the "only and final bastion of Germandom in the East."
Breslau indeed had been a frontier city since 1918. That was visible, for
example, from the large number of refugees from the former province
of Posen and the now Polish parts of Upper Silesia. The fact that the
confrontation over the German-Polish border in Upper Silesia went on
for years increased the political volatility of the situation. It was particularly momentous that the Oder metropolis became an operational base
for Freikorps and paramilitary organizations that often shared the radical anti-Semitism of the völkish right wing and were hardly averse to
using violence.[5]

The rise of anti-Semitism coincided with the Breslau Jews' loss of
economic significance. Since the strong economic standing of the Breslau Jews began to erode after 1916, their influence decreased at precisely
the moment they needed it more than ever to fight anti-Semitism. The
Jews' standing in the city's economy worsened as a result of inflation
and hyperinflation. It is likely that the far-reaching economic changes
were much harder on the Jews than on other Breslauers since inflation
wiped out the assets of many *rentiers*. While in the prewar period 18% of
all Breslau Jews lived primarily off the returns on their capital assets,

only 14% could do so in 1925. The *rentiers*' world, which had symbolized the economic security of the prewar period, had shrunk; the age of the independent gentleman had come to an end.[6] Likewise, the growing number of Jewish immigrants from Poland and Russia—who fled the turmoil caused by the war and civil war as well as poverty and anti-Semitic riots—increased Jewish poverty in Breslau. Between 1919 and 1923, 4,273 mostly poor Eastern European Jews came to the Oder metropolis, but only 3,088 of them later left Breslau. The surplus of 1,185 Polish- and Russian-Jewish immigrants in the postwar period therefore was greater than in the entire period from 1882 to 1913. Although many Russian and Austrian Jews had left the city during the war, the proportion of foreigners among the Breslau Jews rose from 7% to 9% between 1910 and 1925.[7] Just how severely the economic situation of the Breslau Jews deteriorated after 1914 cannot be determined, since no tax rolls were retained after 1906. It is striking, however, that complaints about "Jewish want" and poverty became increasingly frequent in the Jewish press from 1920 on. "The incessant increase in the cost of all necessities of life," the *Jüdische Volkszeitung* complained in June 1922, "has allowed want and distress to enter even into areas that previously were able to get by comfortably. Inflation and its consequences are making themselves felt most severely among the *Mittelstand*," that is, the petite bourgeoisie.[8]

In Breslau associational life, anti-Semitism took on a new quality with the politicization of daily life. Already at the turn from 1918 to 1919, anti-Semites stylized a trifling incident into a scandal, which they then used as a pretense for excluding all Jews from the Boy Scouts: A Jewish Boy Scout had told a Christian member that he could understand why revolutionary soldiers had torn off officers' epaulets. What the Jewish scout could not know was that he had spoken with the son of one of these officers.[9] One of the associations that excluded Jews after 1918 was the Breslau branch of the Alpenverein, of all things. Unlike in 1888–89, when the Jewish members succeeded in keeping anti-Semitism out of the association, the anti-Semites prevailed in November 1924 at the Alpenverein's second "Jewish debate": the Breslau chapter excluded all Jewish members. The mountains were to be "free of Jews."[10] Anti-Semitism also gained ground in the Breslau medical profession. In imperial Germany, Jews had often been presidents of professional associations. In 1923, however, anti-Semitic doctors began their efforts to take over the leadership of such associations. When they did not succeed, they founded an opposing organization, the Verein christlicher Ärzte

(Christian Doctors' Association). This anti-Semitic professional association demanded the boycott of all Jewish doctors and sought to undermine their reputation.[11]

Likewise in the schools, relations between Jews and other Breslauers
deteriorated. After 1918 Jewish teachers encountered anti-Semitic ani-
mosity more and more frequently. In 1921, when the municipal school
board planned to give the Jewish senior teacher Willy Cohn a position at
a girl's *Gymnasium*, the Victoriaschule, the parents' council—a product
of the revolution—sought to block the appointment by slandering
Cohn before the school inspector. In response, the school board offered
the Jewish teacher a position at the Elisabeth-Gymnasium, at which traditionally only Protestants had taught and which was regarded as one
of the most conservative secondary schools in Breslau. Once again, the
parents' council demanded that Cohn be moved immediately to another post. Yet this time the school board did not give in, particularly as
the principal of the Johannes-Gymnasium, Alexis Gabriel (1875–1939),
had given Cohn an excellent reference for his probationary period at
the liberal Modell-Gymnasium.[12] Many non-Jewish students attempted
to surpass the anti-Semitism of the parents' councils. They "embel-
lished" the school building with swastikas, handed out thousands of anti-
Semitic leaflets, and sought to undermine the Jewish teachers' authority
by bringing their hatred of the Jews with them into the classroom. In
March 1921, anti-Semitic incidents had become so frequent that the
municipal school inspector publicly demanded that the school administration take resolute action against the students' anti-Semitism.[13] Arye
Maimon also recalled of his school days at the Realgymnasium am
Zwinger that after the revolution "anti-Semitism began to take hold
in the school." In the student council elections, a Jewish list of candidates competed against a Christian list. In spring 1921, the differences
grew so intense that the school administration cancelled the usual graduation party to prevent anti-Semitic students from attacking Jewish
graduates.[14]

The dramatic increase in anti-Semitism's influence was most clearly
visible in the sphere of politics. The high degree of inclusion of Breslau
Jews in local politics before 1918 was based, among other things, on the
Prussian three-class suffrage system. When this disappeared with the
November Revolution, bourgeois Jews lost their political influence,
which they had used prior to 1918 to strengthen left-wing liberalism and
restrain anti-Semitism. Due to the general disenchantment with bourgeois politics and because Jews, as a result of the repeal of the three-class

suffrage system, now represented only 5% instead of 30% of the voters in local elections, left-wing liberalism declined in Breslau.[15] That political movement, which had been able to win the majority of mandates between 1860 and 1918 without interruption and had still had eighty-three city councilors at the end of the German Empire, soon was only a splinter party. Although *Der Volksstaat,* the weekly newspaper of the Silesian Deutsche Demokratische Partei (German Democratic Party), recognized early on the importance of anti-Semitism in its opponent's ideological arsenal and fought against it, left-wing liberalism secured only five seats in the 1924 local elections and thus held only one seat more than the radically anti-Semitic Deutschvölkische Freiheitspartei (German Völkish Freedom Party).[16] It is telling that, in the Reichstag elections of July 1932, Breslau of all places, a stronghold of left-wing liberalism in imperial Germany, would be the city in which the National Socialists had their greatest success, winning 43% of the votes, while the Deutsche Staatspartei (German State Party) was completely crushed, winning only 1% of the votes.[17] Bourgeois Jews who did not want to work together with what was now the strongest political force in the city, the Social Democrats, lost their political home in the early twenties.

The municipal authorities' stance, for example, on the question of naturalizing Jews from Eastern Europe clearly changed. Before the war, the city had maintained a liberal position and the state an anti-Semitic one, but afterward they exchanged roles. While the Prussian minister of the interior noted in spring 1919 that in the naturalization process "even the appearance of unfavorable treatment for reasons of confession" was to be avoided in the future, the local authorities now adopted an anti-Semitic stance.[18] Compared with the prewar period, the nationalization of thought had taken a quantum leap. Among the enemies of the fatherland, Jews from Eastern Europe assumed a prominent position. The *Ostjude,* or "Eastern Jew"—a semantic cipher that had not existed in this form prior to 1914—became a "focal point of crisis symbolism."[19] As elsewhere, so too in the Breslau press there appeared after 1918 a flood of articles about the alleged danger posed by the "Eastern Jews."[20] Even those who criticized the exclusion of Eastern Jews often took an ambivalent position. In the *Jüdische Volkszeitung,* Fritz Becker, Zionist and director of the Jüdische Arbeiterfürsorgestelle (Jewish Workers' Welfare Office) in Breslau, stated in 1922 in an article titled "Zur Ostjudenfrage"—a term that would not have been used in the Jewish press prior to 1914: "[T]his immigration has to be rejected as a matter of principle." The immigrants who had still worked as laborers and craftsmen in Poland, he said, became "traders and peddlers" in Breslau.[21] The ideological dynamic of the discourse about the Eastern Jew was also evident in the stance of the municipal authorities. While prior to 1914 district prefects referred only to an applicant's economic means and general lifestyle, now it was a matter of whether he had already conformed to the national, putatively homogeneous community. Selma Farnik, for example, was considered by the district prefect to be a "desirable addition to the population" because of her "German nature."[22] Likewise, the merchant Georg Persicaner's application was received positively because he "demonstrated the will and ability to conform to the German character and the German cultural community."[23] The more such decisions were oriented by fanciful notions of national purity, the sooner anti-Semitism slipped into the reports of the municipal authorities. In 1923, for example, the district prefect warned urgently against naturalizing the confectioner Abraham Pikarsky; he was said to be a "Polish Jew" and spoke "Yiddish jargon" at home. Since "his deep Eastern roots . . . [could] be discerned in him even from a great distance," the prefect therefore asked "urgently" that his application be rejected. The "foreigners office" at the police station supported the district prefect: the application definitely had to be rejected because Pikarsky, "as a typical Eastern Jew," did not have "a particularly high level of civilization."[24]

This new quality of political anti-Semitism was also reflected in the growing readiness to engage in individual, but especially collective acts of violence against Jews. As elsewhere, the radicalization of anti-Semitism and the increasing acceptance of violence as a legitimate weapon for use in political confrontation hardened into the "terroristic quality" of enmity toward the Jews.[25] With the applause of the *Schlesische Zeitung*, which in the meantime had aligned itself with the Deutschnationale Volkspartei (German National People's Party), and the support of local German-nationalist politicians, the Freikorps and the Third Marine Brigade controlled the Oder metropolis during the Kapp putsch in March 1920. Among the six killed in the counterrevolution, the best known was Bernhard Schottländer, who was particularly despised by the rebels. "In the end," the *Jüdische Volkszeitung* noted, he was "martyred because of his religion."[26]

Born in 1895, Schottländer came from one of Breslau's richest Jewish families but since the revolution had worked as a journalist for the *Schlesische Arbeiter-Zeitung*, the newspaper of the Unabhängige Sozialdemokratische Partei Deutschlands (USPD; Independent Social Democrats of Germany). Early in 1920 he had become a key figure among the city's radical leftists and played a leading role in the Breslau chapter of the USPD and two Jewish socialist organizations, the Bund and the Poale Zion. Although he was "anything but a good speaker," the Breslau lawyer Max Moses Polke recalled in 1939, "his followers, workers and intellectuals alike, looked up to him like a savior."[27] After the rebels had taken control of Breslau on March 14, 1920, they kidnapped and tortured Schottländer and then brutally murdered him in much the same way as Rosa Luxemburg and Gustav Landauer had been murdered the year before. His mutilated corpse was found on June 23 near a steamboat stop in Oswitz, roughly five kilometers northwest of Breslau.[28]

Yet the anti-Semitic violence was aimed not only at prominent Jews; on the contrary, in postwar Breslau at least two pogromlike riots occurred. Nearly six months after the Kapp putsch, and immediately following a demonstration for a German Upper Silesia, anti-Semites demolished a department store that belonged to a Breslau Jew and attempted to storm a hotel in which primarily Jewish guests from Eastern Europe were staying. The young men had already smashed all the hotel windows and rounded up all the Jewish guests in the lobby by the time the police arrived and drove away the rioters.[29]

Yet the anti-Semitic riots of August 1920 paled in comparison with the events of July 20, 1923, "Black Friday." The last time there had been such a manifestation of collective violence against Jews in Breslau was in June 1844.[30] Following a mass meeting to protest unemployment and hyperinflation, a violent pogrom broke out, which probably had been planned in advance and in which some five hundred people, mostly young men, participated. The violence lasted from the early afternoon until late in the night, and resulted in several deaths and numerous injuries. By the time the police regained control of the city in the early morning hours of July 21, the rioters had looted well over one hundred businesses, almost all of which belonged to Jews. "Whenever the crowd came upon a Christian store, for example," the left-wing liberal weekly *Die Freie Meinung* noted, "the cry rang out: 'That's not a Jew!' And the mob, having been stirred up with anti-Semitic hatred, moved on. To the nearest Jew."[31]

What is striking here is not only the new quality of anti-Semitic violence in the postwar period but also the indifference with which a segment of the Breslau bourgeoisie reacted to it, either quietly accepting or openly approving of the violent acts against the Jews. Willy Cohn, who at the time was a teacher at the Elisabeth-Gymnasium, was appalled at how his colleagues reacted to the discovery of Schottländer's body. "In the last days, the body of Bernhard Schottländer, the shamefully murdered newspaper editor, was found," Cohn noted on June 27, 1920. "In our teachers' room, I have yet to hear a single word in condemnation of the murder!"[32] After the riots that followed the nationalist demonstration for a German Upper Silesia at the end of August 1920, the *Schlesische Zeitung* denied that the violent rioters were in any way anti-Semitic. Rather, the newspaper said, the riots were a direct and inevitable reaction to the allies' policies, especially those of the French, toward Germany.[33] "The fact that that rabble-rousing organ seeks to find blame only in others and not in itself," the *Jüdische Volkszeitung* remarked acerbically, "suggests that it will continue to work at spreading hatred among our people. It will simply have the manuscript of the article ready for the day after the first Jewish pogrom to justify what happened."[34] Likewise after "Black Friday," the anti-Semitic character of which was more obvious than it had been in August 1920, the *Schlesische Zeitung* rejected any attempt to link rampant anti-Semitism to the riots. What was decisive, the conservative daily claimed, was the Bolshevik threat, not anti-Semitism. "Certain bourgeois publications, whose publishers vacillate between the Iron Cross and the star of the Soviets and the Star of David," have fallen prey to the "lie that anti-Semites had instigated the destruction." The looting was limited to Jewish businesses because the clothing industry is run almost exclusively by Jews."[35] In reality, the paper maintained, it was the communists who were responsible for the riots: "The attempt to make it look as if the masses of callow young men and their female companions were stirred up by anti-Semites is just plain stupid."[36]

Liberal journalists who had counted on the middle class to denounce the outrage were appalled by its silence. Alfred Oehlke, the publisher of the *Breslauer Zeitung,* condemned the indifferent reaction of the bourgeoisie no less than the riots themselves. Whereas he praised the resolute reaction on the part of both the police and the organized labor movement, he censured Breslau's middle classes. Instead of intervening, he said, many bourgeois men and women chose to stand by and watch, and as a consequence they were no less guilty than the rioters for what happened. "Anyone who did not make common cause with the hooligans," Oehlke said indignantly, "behaved as if the matter did not concern them in the least." In that dark hour when "civic freedom, independence, and responsibility" were needed, the bourgeoisie showed its "servile spirit" instead of fulfilling its "self-evident duty . . . [to] take immediate action when law and order is disturbed in the streets."[37]

Against the backdrop of the rapid increase in anti-Semitism and the dramatic deterioration of relations between Jews and other Breslauers between 1916 and 1925, one gets an impressive picture of the years preceding the First World War. From 1860 to 1914, a high degree of Jewish integration in urban society can be observed. From approximately 1850 on, many areas opened to Jews that had previously been closed to them despite the increasing bourgeoisification of society. In the early 1870s, there were even signs that Jews might be given access to spheres in which traditional anti-Semitism had persisted. Granted, the anti-Semitic sentiments of the conservative wing of the Breslau bourgeoisie did prevent the further increase in Jewish integration in the 1880s and 1890s. But anti-Semitism was by no means the social norm in Breslau; at most, it was a cultural code. It signaled one's membership in a conservative milieu, which included supporters of traditional and the new populist conservatism.

Until 1914 relations between Jews and other Breslauers remained close and the degree of Jewish integration high. Given that anti-Semitism in associational life in Breslau remained confined to closely circumscribed social groups, the common thesis that anti-Semitism pervaded associational life already in Wilhelminian Germany is dubious. The history of Christian-Jewish marriages also shows that social life in Breslau offered manifold opportunities—especially to lower-class Jews and non-Jews—to meet, befriend, and possibly even marry one another across confessional and ethnic lines. Likewise in the Breslau school system, signs of inclusion predominated, as especially the history of the Johannes-Gymnasium makes clear. The fact that during the imperial era there was no Jewish school system in the Oder metropolis is by no means evidence of the blind desire of Breslau Jews to assimilate and to deny their Jewish identity. With respect to the school, too, the openness of Jewish forms of sociability and community building was visible. Jewish schoolchildren attended Breslau's public schools and not Jewish schools because doing otherwise would have been incompatible with their situational ethnicity. Breslau's secondary schools offered Jewish schoolchildren from bourgeois families educational opportunities that their parents desired for them. Individual conflicts in which anti-Semitism played a role should not be allowed—precisely in view of the developments after 1918—to obscure the high degree of Jewish inclusion in the school system. At least with respect to the schools, the city of Breslau showed itself to be prepared to some extent to permit Jews to participate on an equal basis as Jews.

In Breslau's politics the left-wing liberal majority succeeded in containing the influence of anti-Semitism. Yet it was not just a matter of resisting anti-Semitism. Because Jews formed a core group of the city's bourgeoisie and the rhetoric of "apolitical" local politics limited the room for anti-Semites to maneuver, the standing of left-wing liberals in local politics was strengthened. Due to the prominent role that middle-class Jews played in left-wing liberalism, it dealt sensitively with questions that had a bearing on the status of the Jews and their right to be different. With respect not only to the school system but also to other areas, Breslau left-wing liberals championed a pluralistic understanding of urban sociability and civil society in which Jews—and in fact not only prominent members of the bourgeoisie, such as Ferdinand Julius Cohn, but also Jewish immigrants from Eastern Europe—were regarded as part of a plurality in the unity of the city.

Certainly Breslau Jews also suffered discrimination and exclusion, as the experiences of Jewish teachers and the second-class status of Jewish religious instruction show. But the Breslau anti-Semites remained a minority: in politics, in associational life, and in the school. However, the limits of Jewish integration in Breslau were not the effect of the activities of the city's anti-Semitic movement. During the entire period, the left-wing liberal majority's room to maneuver was restricted by the anti-Semitic policies of the Prussian state, which sought to restrict the integration of Jews. That was particularly evident in Breslau regarding the schools and immigration policies. Whenever Breslau Jews left the city, they encountered numerous barriers—for instance, in the university, the military, the legal system, and government bureaucracy in general. The history of Jewish integration in Germany was part and parcel of the negotiating process, first of all, over the areas in which the state had jurisdiction and those in which the city had jurisdiction. The further the Prussian state extended its power at the expense of the cities, the fewer possibilities they had of countering the state's anti-Semitic policies.

In the confrontations over the extent and limits of their integration, Breslau Jews, especially the Jewish middle class, played an active role. Bourgeois Jews defined the character of many of the associations that were part of the milieu of left-wing liberalism in the city and the left-wing liberal majority on the city council. Although they always had to seek out allies among the Protestants, the Catholics, and the dissenters, they nevertheless took a confident stand in questions bearing on the concerns of Breslau Jews. The specific sense of *Bürgerlichkeit*, of bourgeois civility, that found expression in many associations, in the school system, and in local politics will remain incomprehensible as long as one fails to consider the decisive role that Breslau Jews played therein. In the Oder metropolis, the definition of bourgeois culture and that of bourgeois civility were not a monopoly of Protestant majority culture but the subject of negotiations in which the Jewish middle class participated confidently and successfully.

Breslau Jews found it easy to participate in these negotiations because in imperial Germany they did not form a closed group with far-reaching demands of loyalty. They did not see themselves confronted with the choice of regarding themselves either as part of bourgeois society at large or as part of a Jewish subculture. Their identity as Jews was neither all-encompassing nor exclusive, but rather situational and part of a plurality of identities. The coexistence of closedness and openness that characterized the forms of community building and identity formation proper to the Breslau Jews can best be described as situational ethnicity. They regarded themselves as border crossers in a culturally pluralistic world. Many Jews believed that plurality and unity, universality and difference are compatible; they believed, to cite Hermann Auerbach once again, in a "universal ethics of humanity and toleration," which was "common to the religions present in Germany."

Nevertheless, the majority of Breslau's Christian left-wing liberals were unable to support this model of explicit "cultural pluralism."[38] Although many of them staunchly defended the legal equality of Jews and fought anti-Semitism, they still were unwilling to grant Jews a right to be different that would have been based on the principle of cultural pluralism. Other Breslauers, insofar as they affirmed the equality of Jews, did grant the Jews the right to be different in many areas: since Jews were equal members of bourgeois society, their particular identity as Jews had to be accepted. Nevertheless, the understanding of universalism shared by most non-Jewish liberals was essentially Christian, mostly taking the form of cultural Protestantism. Auerbach's basic thesis that liberal universalism is rooted in a Judeo-Christian tradition remained foreign to them. And yet one should not lose sight of the fact that, in their everyday coexistence, other Breslauers were willing to grant Jews the right to be different and to experiment with diverse forms of pluralism. It would be ahistorical to reproach the Christian liberals with anti-Semitism simply because they rejected "cultural pluralism" as an abstract vision of society. The idea that humanity, civilization, and liberalism have their roots in Christianity was a phenomenon common throughout Europe. A culturally pluralistic self-understanding of the

"Judeo-Christian tradition" that is not confined to speeches during the week of Jewish-Christian brotherhood can be found among Western democracies to this day only in the United States and Canada—and even there only since the 1960s.[39]

Even if relations between Jews and other Breslauers prior to the First World War cannot be described as a harmonious symbiosis, they were close and marked by a large degree of mutual recognition. A direct or twisted line of continuity that leads from imperial Germany to National Socialism and the Holocaust cannot be drawn in view of the history of Jews and other Breslauers before 1914. Only as a consequence of the First World War, Germany's defeat, and the postwar crisis did relations between Jews and other Breslauers deteriorate dramatically. The experiences of Jews in imperial Germany are, above all, part of a history of the difficult and continual conflict characterizing the history of many European states as well as that of the United States: the conflict between the idea of a homogeneous nation-state and the concept of a multicultural society.

ABBREVIATIONS

AMW   Akta miasta Wrocławia
APW   Archiwum Państwowe we Wrocławiu
BUW   Biblioteka Uniwersytecka we Wrocławiu
CAHJP   Central Archives for the History of the Jewish People
GŚŁ   Gabinet Śląska-Łużycki
LBI   Leo Baeck Institute
OPB   Oberpräsidium Breslau
PPB   Polizei-Präsidium Breslau
UBW   Universtätsbibliothek Wrocław
USC   Urząd stanu cywilnego (Standesamt Breslau)

TABLES

For additional commentary on the data in the following tables (half of which appear in chapter 1), see the main text.

Table 1. Professional structure of employed Jewish and non-Jewish population in Breslau, 1861–62

	Jews		Non-Jews		
	No.	%	No.	%	% of Jews in employed population
A. Agriculture	11	0.3	261	0.4	4.0
B. Industry	361	10.1	38,032	59.5	0.9
C. Commerce	2,311	64.6	2,518	3.9	47.8
D. Transportation	49	1.4	3,467	5.4	1.4
E. Personal services	134	3.7	12,119	19.0	1.1
F. Education, teaching, arts, civil service	202	5.7	2,418	3.8	7.7
G. Unemployed, others	506	14.2	5,127	8.0	9.0
Total	3,574		63,942		

Source: Preußische Statistik, vols. 5–6 (Berlin: Landesamt, 1864), 148–49 and 152–53.

Note: Soldiers are not counted among the non-Jews; for Jews, categories 7–11 are summarized under F.

Table 2. The Jewish proportion of economic sectors in Breslau, Berlin, Cologne, and Königsberg, 1861–62

	% of gainfully employed Jews				Factor of under- or overrepresentation			
	Breslau	Berlin	Cologne	Königsberg	Breslau	Berlin	Cologne	Königsberg
A. Agriculture	1.90	2.60	0.00		0.36	0.81	0.00	
B. Industry	0.90	0.70	0.30		0.17	0.22	0.17	
C. Commerce	47.80	33.20	15.50	24.40	9.02	10.38	8.61	10.76
D. Transportation	1.40	0.30	0.10		0.26	0.09	0.06	
E. Personal services	1.10	1.00	4.40		0.21	0.31	2.44	
F. Education, teaching, arts, civil service	7.70	5.30	1.40		1.45	1.66	0.78	
G. Unemployed, others	9.00	6.90	0.70		1.70	2.16	0.39	

Source: *Preußische Statistik*, vols. 5–6 (Berlin: Landesamt, 1864), 148–49 and 152–53.

Note: In 1861–62, 5.30% of all gainfully employed individuals in Breslau were Jewish, 3.20% in Berlin, 1.80% in Cologne, and 2.30% in Königsberg.

Table 3. Estimated income structure of Jews in Frankurt am Main and Frankfurt, 1900

	The income structure of Jews in Frankfurt am Main				The estimated income structure of Jews in Frankfurt			
	Under 900 marks	900– 3,000 marks	3,000– 9,500 marks	Over 9,500 marks	Under 900 marks	900– 3,000 marks	3,000– 9,500 marks	Over 9,500 marks
% of heads of households	N/A	46.9%	31.5%	21.7%	25.0%	35.1%	23.6%	16.3%

Source: *Zeitschrift für Demographie und Statistik der Juden* 1, no. 4 (1905): 12–13.

Table 4. The professional structure of Breslau Jews, Protestants, and Catholics in 1876 (men and women)

	Jews		Protestants		Catholics	
	No.	%	No.	%	No.	%
Bourgeoisie	**2,485**	**43.3**	**76**	**10.5**	**23**	**5.3**
Wirtschaftsbürger (Economic elite)	2,203	38.4	67	9.2	14	3.2
Businessmen	1,836	32.0	35	4.8	7	1.6
Manufacturers/entrepreneurs	46	0.8	6	0.8	2	0.5
Bankers	42	0.7	—	—	—	—
High services	164	2.9	3	0.4	4	0.9
Managers	39	0.7	1	0.1	—	—
Rentiers,						
Counselors of Commerce	59	1.0	—	—	—	—
Bildungsbürger (Educated elite)	226	3.9	20	2.8	6	1.4
Professors, *Gymnasium* teachers	25	0.4	6	0.8	1	0.2
Liberal professions	128	2.2	5	0.7	—	—
Writers, artists	16	0.3	2	0.3	1	0.2
Students	46	0.8	2	0.6	3	0.7
High-ranking civil servants	56	1.0	9	1.2	3	0.7
Petite bourgeoisie	**1,678**	**29.2**	**129**	**17.8**	**84**	**19.3**
Old middle class	684	11.9	77	10.6	54	12.4
Master craftsmen	178	3.1	41	5.7	25	5.7
Traders, small shopkeepers	422	7.4	5	0.7	9	2.1
Landlords	20	0.3	11	1.5	5	1.1
Other independent occupations	41	0.7	13	1.8	9	2.1
New middle class	994	17.3	52	7.2	30	6.9
Teachers	70	1.2	10	1.4	6	1.4
Mid-level civil servants						
and employees	720	12.6	38	5.2	21	4.8
Employed businesspeople	193	3.4	2	0.3	1	0.2
Lower classes	**938**	**16.3**	**441**	**60.8**	**298**	**68.3**
Low-level civil servants						
and employees	275	4.8	25	3.4	20	4.6
Workers	101	2.9	91	12.6	64	14.7
Employed craftsmen	406	7.1	128	17.7	96	22.0
Domestic servants,						
employed service personnel	152	2.6	179	24.7	117	26.8
Invalids, welfare recipients	4	0.1	5	0.7	1	0.2
Others	**638**	**11.1**	**79**	**10.9**	**31**	**7.1**
Total	5,739		725		436	

Source: My own calculations based on APW, AMW, K 150, vols. 1–18 and 20–36, as well as APW, AMW, K 151, vol. 19, and the Prussian tax rolls, APW, AMW, K 146, vols. 18 and 20. For 1876, I have included all the Jewish income earners. On the criteria for the random sample survey in the case of Protestants and Catholics, see Manfred Hettling, *Politische Bürgerlichkeit: Der Bürger zwischen Individualität und Vergesellschaftung in Deutschland und der Schweiz von 1860 bis 1918* (Göttingen: Vandenhoeck & Ruprecht, 1999), appendix.

Table 5. Professional structure of Breslau Jews, Protestants, and Catholics in 1906 (men and women)

	Jews		Protestants		Catholics	
	No.	%	No.	%	No.	%
Bourgeoisie	**557**	**56.9**	**125**	**11.0**	**48**	**7.2**
Wirtschaftsbürger (Economic elite)	451	46.1	69	6.1	31	4.7
Businessmen	349	35.6	28	2.5	12	1.8
Manufacturers/entrepreneurs	17	1.7	9	0.8	3	0.5
Bankers	2	0.2	—	—	1	0.2
High services	9	0.9	2	0.2	5	0.8
Managers	6	0.6	4	0.4	0	0.0
Rentiers,						
Counselors of Commerce	67	6.8	23	2.0	10	1.5
Landowners	1	0.1	3	0.3	0	0.0
Bildungsbürger (Educated elite)	92	9.4	42	3.7	13	2.0
Rabbis, priests	2	0.2	2	0.2	1	0.2
Professors, *Gymnasium* teachers	5	0.5	15	1.3	3	0.5
Liberal professions	46	4.7	9	0.8	4	0.6
Engineers	5	0.5	4	0.4	0	0.0
Writers, artists	7	0.7	6	0.5	2	0.3
Students	27	2.8	6	0.5	3	0.5
High-ranking civil servants	14	1.4	14	1.2	4	0.6
Administration officials	14	1.4	3	0.3	0	0.0
Justice officials	0	0	4	0.4	1	0.2
Local officials	0	0	1	0.1	0	0.0
Other civil servants	0	0	3	0.3	2	0.3
Officers	0	0	3	0.3	1	0.2
Petite bourgeoisie	**234**	**23.9**	**237**	**20.9**	**123**	**18.6**
Old middle class	98	10.0	65	5.7	30	4.5
Master craftsmen	16	1.6	43	3.8	14	2.1
Traders and						
small shopkeepers	62	6.3	4	0.4	3	0.5
Landlords	2	0.2	9	0.8	6	0.9
Other independent						
occupations	15	1.5	1	0.1	3	0.5
Farmers, small farmers	0	0	3	0.3	1	0.2
Homeowners	3	0.3	5	0.4	3	0.5
New middle class	136	13.9	172	15.1	93	14.0
Teachers	15	1.5	25	2.2	6	0.9

Continued on next page

Table 5—*continued*

	Jews		Protestants		Catholics	
	No.	%	No.	%	No.	%
Mid-level civil servants	4	0.4	53	4.7	27	4.1
Mid-level employees	112	11.4	51	4.5	40	6.0
Employed businessmen	4	0.4	23	2.0	12	1.8
Technicians	1	0.1	17	1.5	5	0.8
Foremen	0	0	3	0.3	3	0.5
Lower classes	**153**	**15.6**	**745**	**65.5**	**485**	**73.2**
Low civil servants						
and employees	52	5.3	98	8.6	58	8.7
Workers	24	2.4	160	14.1	85	12.8
Employed craftsmen	47	4.8	185	16.3	127	19.2
Domestic servants,						
employed service personnel	27	2.8	299	26.3	212	32.0
Handicapped, dependent on charity	3	0.3	3	0.3	3	0.5
Others	**35**	**3.6**	**29**	**2.6**	**7**	**1.1**
Total	979		1,136		663	

Source: My own calculations based on APW, AMW, K 156. For Jewish heads of households, I have included every tenth income earner. On the sample of Protestants and Catholics, see Manfred Hettling, *Politische Bürgerlichkeit: Der Bürger zwischen Individualität und Vergesellschaftung in Deutschland und der Schweiz von 1860 bis 1918* (Göttingen: Vandenhoeck & Ruprecht, 1999), 359–63.

Table 6. Proportion of men and women in the bourgeoisie, the petite bourgeoisie, and the lower classes for Jews, Protestants, and Catholics in Breslau, 1906

	Jews		Protestants		Catholics	
	Men	Women	Men	Women	Men	Women
Bourgeoisie	**77.4%**	**22.6%**	**64.0%**	**36.0%**	**68.7%**	**31.3%**
Wirschaftsbürger						
(Economic elite)	73.6%	26.4%	55.1%	44.9%	58.1%	41.9%
Bildungsbürger						
(Educated elite)	94.6%	5.4%	78.6%	21.4%	84.6%	15.4%
High-ranking civil servants	85.7%	14.3%	64.3%	35.7%	100.0%	0.0%
Petite bourgeoisie	**75.2%**	**24.8%**	**74.7%**	**25.3%**	**80.5%**	**19.5%**
Old middle class	77.6%	22.4%	86.2%	13.8%	90.0%	10.0%
New middle class	73.5%	26.5%	70.3%	29.7%	77.4%	22.6%
Lower classes	**37.9%**	**62.1%**	**47.8%**	**52.2%**	**45.2%**	**54.8%**
Low-level civil servants						
and employees	42.3%	57.7%	58.2%	41.8%	67.2%	32.8%
Workers	16.7%	83.3%	50.7%	49.3%	41.2%	58.8%
Employed craftsmen	55.3%	44.7%	76.2%	23.8%	76.4%	23.6%
Invalids, welfare recipients	11.1%	88.9%	25.1%	74.9%	22.2%	77.8%
Others	**11.4%**	**88.6%**	**3.4%**	**96.6%**	**28.6%**	**71.4%**

Source: Breslau tax rolls for 1906, APW, AMW, K 156.

Note: In 1906, 310 (31.7%) of all Jewish, 522 (46.0%) of all Protestant, and 310 (46.8%) of all Catholic taxpayers (including all those who were exempted from paying taxes) were women.

Table 7. Rate of self-employment among Jews, Protestants, and Catholics in Breslau, 1895 and 1907

	Jews		Protestants		Catholics	
	Men	Women	Men	Women	Men	Women
1895						
Self-employed	51.3%	39.6%	19.5%	37.5%	19.1%	35.4%
Employee	21.8%	5.5%	11.0%	1.2%	8.0%	0.8%
Worker	26.9%	54.9%	69.5%	61.3%	72.9%	63.8%
1907						
Self-employed	51.2%	35.9%	16.6%	31.1%	17.0%	30.3%
Employee	27.3%	29.6%	13.9%	8.3%	11.1%	6.5%
Worker	21.5%	34.5%	69.5%	60.6%	71.9%	63.1%
1925						
Self-employed	60.4%	30.7%				
Employee	33.8%	47.7%				
Worker	5.2%	8.5%				
Helpers	0.6%	13.2%				

Source: "Die Ergebnisse der Berufs- und Gewerbezählung vom 14. Juni 1895," *Breslauer Statistik*, vol. 18 (Breslau: Morgenstern, 1900), 92; "Die Ergebnisse der Berufs- und Gewerbezählung vom 12. Juni 1907," *Breslauer Statistik*, vol. 28, pt. 3 (Breslau: Morgenstern, 1909), 112; Heinrich Silbergleit, *Die Bevölkerungs- und Berufsverhältnisse der Juden im deutschen Reich* (Berlin: Akademie-Verlag, 1930), 201.

Note: Helpers = family members who help in the household.

Table 8. Status distribution of Breslau Jews, Protestants, and Catholics, 1876 and 1906

	Jews				Protestants				Catholics			
	Men		Women		Men		Women		Men		Women	
	No.	%	No.	%	No.	%	No.	%	No.	%	No.	%
1876												
Other	567	12.6	397	32.4	32	7.4	145	50.3	14	5.2	103	62.4
Salary	1,471	32.6	399	32.6	285	66.1	119	41.3	192	71.6	51	30.9
Industry and trade revenue	2,158	47.8	161	13.1	95	22.0	10	3.5	54	20.1	7	4.2
Interest and rental revenue	318	7.0	268	21.9	19	4.4	14	4.9	8	3.0	4	2.4
1906												
Other	16	2.4	15	4.8	3	0.5	6	1.1	4	1.1	1	0.3
Salary	371	55.4	215	69.4	522	83.3	474	89.9	302	83.9	302	95.0
Industry and trade revenue	198	29.6	11	3.5	73	11.6	9	1.7	35	9.7	2	0.6
Interest and rental revenue	85	12.7	69	22.3	29	4.6	38	7.2	19	5.3	13	4.1

Source: My calculations based on APW, AMW, K 150, vols. 1–18 and 20–36, as well APW, AMW, K 151, vol. 19, and the Prussian/national tax rolls, APW, AMW, K 146, vols. 18 and 20, as well as APW, AMW, K 156. On the specification of the categories, see Hettling, *Politische Bürgerlichkeit,* 49–50.

Note: In 1876, the group "Other" includes only those persons who have no income of their own. The decline in the size of the group is due to the fact that the 1906 tax rolls list the precise income of the tax-exempt low-income earners, while in 1876 an income is often not listed.

Table 9. Proportion of Jews, Protestants, and Catholics in professional groups in Breslau, 1876

	Jews		Protestants		Catholics	
	Z	%	Z	%	Z	%
Bourgeoisie	**3.113**	**28.2**	**6.084**	**55.1**	**1.847**	**16.7**
Wirtschaftsbürger (Economic elite)	2.761	30.0	5.331	57.9	1.115	12.1
Businessmen	2.301	40.8	2.782	49.3	0.558	9.9
Manufacturers/entrepreneurs	0.058	8.3	0.464	66.7	0.174	25.0
Bildungsbürger (Educated elite)	0.280	11.7	1.623	67.9	0.488	20.4
High-ranking civil servants	0.072	7.1	0.695	68.7	0.244	24.1
Petite bourgeoisie	**2.099**	**11.0**	**10.315**	**53.9**	**6.726**	**35.1**
Old middle class	0.856	7.6	6.143	54.3	4.321	38.2
Master craftsmen	0.223	4.0	3.303	59.9	1.986	36.0
Traders, store owners	0.532	31.9	0.406	24.3	0.732	43.8
New middle class	1.244	15.9	4.172	53.3	2.405	30.8
Teachers	0.086	6.2	0.811	58.6	0.488	35.2
Mid-level civil servants						
and employees	0.906	16.2	3.013	53.9	1.673	29.9
Lower Classes	**1.172**	**1.9**	**35.234**	**58.5**	**23.803**	**39.5**
Low-level civil servants						
and employees	0.345	8.8	1.970	50.3	1.603	40.9
Workers	0.209	1.7	7.302	57.8	5.123	40.5
Employed craftsmen	0.510	2.8	10.257	55.6	7.667	41.6
Domestic servants,						
employed service personnel	0.187	0.8	14.314	60.0	9.340	39.2
Others	**0.798**	**8.3**	**6.317**	**65.9**	**2.474**	**25.8**
Total	7.18		57.95		34.85	

Source: See table 8.

Note: The proportion of Jews, Protestants, and Catholics in the professional groups can be calculated only on the basis of data for the total population and the Jewish population. If the calculation were based only on the data for the total population, justice would not be done to the inter-Jewish distribution, since the data for the total population contains too few Jewish households. I therefore take the inter-Jewish distribution from the data for the Jewish population. To render both datasets compatible, the line percentages could not be calculated using absolute numbers but only by means of a standardized value Z. I calculate Z by multiplying the percentages from table 4 by the percentages of Jews, Protestants, and Catholics, respectively, in the data for the total population (AG). For the Jews (N = 90), AG was 0.072 (7.2%), for the Protestants 0.58 (58.0%), and for the Catholics 0.348 (34.8%). The sum of the Z-columns then yields the proportion of Jews, Protestants, and Catholics, respectively, among all the heads of households. The remaining 2.4% made up the group "Others." To avoid making the table unnecessarily complicated, I did not include the "others" in the calculations due to the group's small size. Since the line percentages are approximate values, this seemed legitimate to me.

Table 10. Proportion of Jews, Protestants, and Catholics in professional groups in Breslau, 1906

	Jews		Protestants		Catholics	
	Z	%	Z	%	Z	%
Bourgeoisie	**3.2433**	**26.9**	**6.38**	**52.9**	**2.4408**	**20.2**
Wirtschaftsbürger	2.6277	33.9	3.538	45.6	1.5933	20.5
Businessmen	2.0292	49.6	1.45	35.5	0.6102	14.9
Manufacturers/entrepreneurs	0.0969	13.3	0.464	63.5	0.1695	23.2
Rentiers, Counselors of						
Commerce	0.3876	18.9	1.16	56.4	0.5085	24.7
Bildungsbürger	0.5358	15.9	2.146	63.9	0.678	20.2
Liberal professions	0.2679	28.6	0.464	49.6	0.2034	21.7
High-ranking civil servants	0.0798	8.1	0.696	71.1	0.2034	20.8
Petite bourgeoisie	**1.3623**	**6.9**	**12.122**	**61.3**	**6.3054**	**31.9**
Old middle class	0.57	10.6	3.306	61.2	1.5255	28.2
Master craftsmen	0.0912	3.0	2.204	73.3	0.7119	23.7
Traders, store owners	0.3591	47.2	0.232	30.5	0.1695	22.3
New middle class	0.7923	5.5	8.758	61.3	4.746	33.2
Teachers	0.0825	5.0	1.276	76.7	0.3051	18.3
Mid-level civil servants	0.0228	0.6	2.726	65.8	1.3899	33.6
Mid-level employees	0.6498	12.3	2.61	49.3	2.034	38.4
Lower classes	**0.8892**	**1.4**	**37.99**	**59.6**	**24.815**	**39.0**
Low-level civil servants						
and employees	0.3021	3.7	4.988	60.5	2.949	35.8
Workers	0.1368	1.1	8.178	64.6	4.339	34.3
Employed craftsmen	0.274	1.7	9.454	58.2	6.509	40.1
Domestic servants,						
employed service personnel	0.1596	0.6	15.254	58.1	10.848	41.3
Others	**0.2052**	**9.8**	**1.508**	**72.3**	**0.3729**	**17.9**
Total	5.703		58.000		33.934	

Source: My calculations based on APW, AMW, K 156.

Note: For an explanation of the table, see the clarifications of table 9. In this case, Z is based on table 5. For 1906, AG is 0.057 (5.7%) for Jews, 0.58 (58%) for Protestants, and 0.339 (33.9%) for Catholics.

Table 11. The connection between profession and income among Breslau's Jewish income earners in 1876

Marks	Businessman No.	%	Physician No.	%	*Rentier* No.	%	Accountant No.	%	Trader No.	%
Under 1,100	304	17.2	13	13.1	38	21.0	44	31.4	177	72.8
1,100–2,749	614	34.7	29	29.3	55	30.4	95	67.9	56	23.1
2,750–9,200	653	36.9	44	44.4	64	35.4	1	0.7	10	4.1
Over 2,000	198	11.2	13	13.1	24	13.2	—	—	—	—
Total	1,769		99		181		140		243	

Source: My calculations based on APW, AMW, K 150, vols. 1–18 and 20–36, as well as APW, AMW, K 151, vol. 19, and the Prussian tax rolls, APW, AMW, K 146, vols. 18 (1876) and 20 (1877–78), and 21 (1878–79).

Note: The group of rentiers also included all independently wealthy individuals and the group of physicians included administrators and dentists. Doubtless, age played an important role. Young physicians or businessmen earned less than their established colleagues. Yet that hardly diminishes the table's meaningfulness. Of the 304 "businessmen" with an income of less than 1,100 marks, only 75 were under thirty years of age. The group of Jewish lawyers was still too small in 1876 to permit meaningful observations to be made.

Table 12. The connection between profession and income among Breslau's Jewish income earners in 1906

Marks	Businessman No.	%	Physician No.	%	Lawyer No.	%	*Rentier* No.	%	Accountant No.	%	Trader No.	%
Under 1,200	61	17.8	5	16.1	1	10.0	36	48.6	10	43.5	15	68.2
1,200–2,999	88	25.7	7	22.6	1	10.0	7	9.5	9	39.1	6	27.3
3,000–9,999	107	31.3	11	35.5	2	20.0	21	28.4	3	13.0	1	4.5
Over 10,000	86	25.1	8	25.8	6	60.0	10	13.5	1	4.3	—	—
Total	342		31		10		74		23		22	

Source: APW, AMW, K 156.

Table 13. Income stratification of "established" Jewish income earners in Breslau by sex, 1876 and 1906

	1876						1906					
	Men		Women		Together		Men		Women		Together	
	No.	%	No.	%	No.	%	No.	%	No.	%	No.	%
Lower stratum	539	22.9	407	73.6	946	32.6	49	12.2	106	73.1	155	28.4
Lower-middle stratum	836	35.6	85	15.4	921	31.7	115	28.7	18	12.4	133	24.4
Upper-middle stratum	752	32.0	51	9.2	803	27.7	136	33.9	13	9.0	149	27.3
Upper stratum	224	9.5	10	1.8	234	8.1	101	25.2	8	5.5	109	20.0
Total	2,351		553		2,904		401		145		546	

Source: My calculations based on APW, AMW, K 150, vols. 1–18 and 20–36, as well as APW, AMW, K 151, vol. 19, and the Prussian tax rolls, APW, AMW, K 146, vols. 18 (1876) and 20 (1877–78), and 21 (1878–79), as well as APW, AMW, K 156.

Notes: The lower stratum in 1876 was less than 1,100 marks and in 1906 was below 1,200 marks annually; the lower-middle stratum in 1876 was 1,100–2,749 marks and in 1906 was 1,200–2,999 marks; the upper-middle stratum in 1876 was 2,750–9,200 marks and in 1906 was 3,000–10,000 marks; the upper stratum in 1876 was over 9,200 marks and in 1906 was over 10,000 marks annually.

The numbers for 1876 and 1906 took account of the increase in the cost of living between the two sample years. The four-year mean of the cost of living index, as calculated by Ashok Desai, increased during the period under investigation here by 9.4% from 106 (1875–1878) to 116 (1905–1908); Desai, *Real Wages in Germany, 1871–1913* (Oxford: Clarendon Press, 1968), 117.

Table 14. Annual income of Breslau Jews by sex and birthplace, 1906

Marks	Unknown	Breslau	Silesia	EP/WP/Po	Posen	Ger.	WE	Russia	AH	Overseas
Men										
Under 1,200	5	40	60	5	39	5	3	2	17	—
	29.4%	29.0%	22.9%	16.1%	26.4%	21.7%	75.0%	50.0%	42.5%	—
1,200– 2,999	6	39	77	12	42	8	—	1	16	2
	35.3%	28.3%	29.4%	38.7%	28.4%	34.8%	—	25.0%	40.0%	66.7%
3,000– 9,999	5	32	77	7	34	6	—	1	6	—
	29.4%	23.2%	29.4%	22.6%	23.0%	26.1%	—	25.0%	15.0%	—
Over 10,000	1	27	48	7	33	4	1	—	1	1
	5.9%	19.6%	18.3%	22.6%	22.3%	17.4%	25.0%	—	2.5%	33.3%
Average income	2,966	7,916	6,886	8,930	7,012	4,712	5,903	2,778	2,721	5,436
Total	17	138	262	31	148	23	4	4	40	3
Women										
Under 1,200	4	53	101	4	44	10	—	6	10	2
	66.7%	76.8%	75.4%	66.7%	71.0%	71.4%	—	100.0%	90.9%	100.0%
1,200– 2,999	1	7	16	2	7	3	—	—	1	—
	16.7%	10.1%	11.9%	33.3%	11.3%	21.4%	—	—	9.1%	—
3,000– 9,999	1	7	11	—	6	1	—	—	—	—
	16.7%	10.1%	8.2%	—	9.7%	7.1%	—	—	—	—
Over 10,000	—	2	6	—	5	—	—	—	—	—
	—	2.9%	4.5%	—	8.1%	—	—	—	—	—
Average income	1,079	1,560	2,345	825	1,658	1,278	—	431	500	350
Total	6	69	134	6	62	14	0	6	11	2

Source: APW, AMW, K 156.

Note: Silesia = all places in Silesia excluding Breslau; "EP/WP/Po" = East and West Prussia, Pomerania; "Ger." = all other German regions; "WE" = Western and Southern Europe; "AH" = Austro-Hungary, Balkans; "Overseas" = United States and overseas. The sample included a total of 670 Jewish men and 310 Jewish women.

Table 15. Annual income of Breslau Jews by sex and number of family members, 1876

Marks	1	2	3	4	5-6	7-8	9 or more
Men							
Under 1,100	1,272	191	100	105	138	53	13
	60.9%	31.2%	22.5%	3.2%	22.0%	25.6%	16.3%
1,100– 2,749	562	204	186	154	210	64	23
	26.9%	33.3%	41.8%	34.1%	33.5%	30.9%	28.8%
2,750– 9,200	203	177	120	141	211	70	32
	9.7%	28.9%	27.0%	31.2%	33.7%	33.8%	40.0%
Over 9,200	53	41	39	52	67	20	12
	2.5%	6.7%	8.8%	11.5%	10.7%	9.7%	15.0%
Average income	1,721	3,762	4,050	5,609	4,853	5,361	5,479
Total	2,090	613	445	452	626	207	80
Women							
Under 1,100	752	103	53	39	15	7	—
	84.1%	71.0%	64.6%	68.4%	41.7%	70.0%	—
1,100– 2,749	75	26	22	10	11	1	1
	8.4%	17.9%	26.8%	17.5%	30.6%	10.0%	100.0%
2,750– 9,200	52	12	6	7	8	2	—
	5.8%	8.3%	7.3%	12.3%	22.2%	20.0%	—
Over 9,200	15	4	1	1	2	—	—
	1.7%	2.8%	1.2%	1.8%	5.6%	—	—
Average income	1,255	1,749	1,360	1,438	2,378	1,107	
Total	894	145	82	57	36	10	1

Source: See table 4.

Table 16. Annual income of Breslau Jews by sex and size of household, 1906

Marks	1	2	3	4	5–6	7–8	9 or more
Men							
Under 1,200	121	18	16	9	7	4	1
	40.5%	17.3%	14.8%	11.7%	10.8%	28.6%	
1,200– 2,799	112	21	29	19	15	6	1
	37.5%	20.2%	26.9%	24.7%	23.1%	42.9%	
3,000– 9,999	45	40	40	18	23	1	1
	15.1%	38.5%	37.0%	23.4%	35.4%	7.1%	
Over 10,000	21	25	23	31	20	3	—
	7.0%	24.0%	21.3%	40.3%	30.8%	21.4%	—
Average income	3,219	10,022	7,971	11,495	9,518	11,082	1,730
Total	299	104	108	77	65	14	3
Women							
Under 1,200	211	15	8	—	—	—	—
	77.9%	62.5%	61.5%	—	—	—	—
1,200– 2,999	33	3	1	—	—	—	—
	12.2%	12.5%	7.7%	—	—	—	—
3,000– 9,999	19	4	2	1	—	—	—
	7.0%	16.7%	15.4%		—	—	—
Over 10,000	8	2	2	1	—	—	—
	3.0%	8.3%	15.4%		—	—	—
Average income	1,403	5,523	4,082	7,792	—	—	
Total	271	24	13	2	—	—	—

Source: APW, AMW, K 156.

Table 17. The income structure of the total Jewish population in Breslau, 1876 and 1906

Marks	Men		Women		Total		Household (Ø)
	No.	%	No.	%	No.	%	
				1876			
Under							
1,100	3,635	29.9	1,407	72.8	5,042	35.8	1.8 persons
1,100–							
2,749	3,980	32.8	307	15.9	4,287	30.5	2.8 persons
2,750–							
9,200	3,449	28.4	179	9.3	3,628	25.8	3.5 persons
Over							
9,200	1,079	8.9	41	2.1	1,120	7.9	3.6 persons
Total	12,143		1,934		14,077		2.5 persons
				1906			
Under							
1,200	317	19.6	265	72.4	582	29.3	1.4 persons
1,200–							
2,999	452	28.0	42	11.5	494	24.9	2.1 persons
3,000–							
9,999	454	28.1	37	10.1	491	24.8	2.6 persons
Over							
10,000	394	24.4	22	6.0	416	21.0	3.1 persons
Total	1,617		366		1,983		2.1 persons

Source: See table 4 and APW, AMW, K 156.

Note: All family members are also included in the figures.

Table 18. Social inequality within Breslau's Jewish population, 1876 and 1906

	Highest 1% of Jewish income earners			Highest 5% of Jewish income earners			Total income all Jewish households
	Income level	Total	Proportion	Income level	Total	Proportion	
1876	32,400	3,940,000	23.9%	9,600	7,608,000	46.1%	16,518,557 marks
1906	52,500	858,520	16.7%	21,500	2,199,881	42.9%	5,126,655 marks

	Lowest 25% of Jewish income earners			Lowest 50% of Jewish income earners			Total income all Jewish households
	Income level	Total	Proportion	Income level	Total	Proportion	
1876	420	139,896	0.8%	1,200	1,253,949	7.6%	16,518,557 marks
1906	600	67,772	1.3%	1,530	317,378	6.2%	5,126,655 marks

Source: See table 4 and APW, AMW, K 156.

Note: The figures for 1876 include all Jewish households; those for 1906 include only every tenth household.

Table 19. Average income of all Breslau income earners by denomination and its increase, 1876 and 1906

	Average income in marks		
	1876	1906	Growth
Protestant	976	1,458	49.4%
Catholic	633	1,024	61.8%
Jewish	2,875	5,200	80.9%

Source: See table 4 and APW, AMW, K 156.

Table 20. The income structure of all income earners in Breslau by denomination, 1876 and 1906

Marks	Jews		Protestants		Catholics	
	No.	%	No.	%	No.	%
1876						
Under 1,100	2,841	49.50	593	80.10	385	86.10
1,100– 2,749	1,549	27.00	105	14.20	50	11.20
2,750– 9,200	1,042	18.20	32	4.30	12	2.70
Over 9,200	307	5.30	10	1.40	—	—
Total	5,739		740		447	
1906						
Under 1,200	407	42.00	854	74.00	531	78.30
1,200– 2,999	238	24.50	192	16.60	104	15.30
3,000– 9,999	190	19.60	88	7.60	39	5.70
10,000– 23,999	135	13.90	20	1.70	4	0.60
Over 24,000	42	4.30	6	0.50	1	0.15
Total	970		1,154		678	

Source: See table 4 and APW, AMW, K 156.

Note: Family members are not included in the calculations.

Table 21. Income structure of the total population of Breslau by denomination, 1906

Marks	Jews			Protestants			Catholics		
	No.	%	Household	No.	%	Household	No.	%	Household
Under									
1,200	582	29.3	1.4 persons	1,453	65.1	1.7 persons	994	71.1	1.9 persons
1,200–									
2,999	494	24.9	2.1 persons	450	20.2	2.3 persons	268	19.2	2.6 persons
3,000–									
9,999	491	24.8	2.6 persons	270	12.1	3.1 persons	117	8.4	3.0 persons
Over									
10,000	416	21.0	3.1 persons	59	2.6	3.0 persons	19	1.4	4.7 persons
Total	1,983		2.1 persons	2,232		1.9 persons	1,398		2.1 persons

Source: See table 4 and APW, AMW, K 156.

Note: Household = average size of household.

Table 22. The proportion of Jews, Protestants, and Catholics in income groups in Breslau, 1876 and 1906

	Jews		Protestants		Catholics	
Marks	Z	%	Z	%	Z	%
1876						
Under 1,100	3.564	4.5	46.458	58.1	29.963	37.5
1,100– 2,749	1.944	13.8	8.236	58.5	3.898	27.7
2,750– 9,200	1.310	27.6	2.494	52.6	0.940	19.8
Over 9,200	0.382	32.0	0.812	68.0	—	—
Total	7.2		58.0		34.8	
1906						
Under 1,200	2.394	3.3	42.920	59.7	26.544	36.9
1,200– 2,999	1.397	8.6	9.628	59.4	5.187	32.0
3,000– 9,999	1.117	14.9	4.431	59.2	1.932	25.8
10,000– 23,999	0.792	39.9	0.992	49.9	0.203	10.2
Over 24,000	0.245	41.8	0.29	49.5	0.051	8.7
Total	5.7		58.0		33.9	

Source: See table 4 and APW, AMW, K 156.

Note: The proportion of Jews, Protestants, and Catholics in the professional groups can be calculated only on the basis of data for the total population and the Jewish population. If the calculation were based only on the data for the total population, justice would not be done to the inter-Jewish distribution, since the data for the total population contains too few Jewish households. I therefore take the inter-Jewish distribution from the data for the Jewish population. To render both datasets compatible, the line percentages could not be calculated using absolute numbers but only by means of a standardized value Z. I calculate Z by multiplying the percentages from table 4 by the percentages of Jews, Protestants, and Catholics, respectively, in the data for the total population. For the Jews (N = 90), the percentage of the total population was 0.072 (7.2%), for the Protestants 0.58 (58.0%), and for the Catholics 0.348 (34.8%). The sum of the Z-columns then yields the proportion of Jews, Protestants, and Catholics, respectively, among all the heads of households. The remaining 2.4% made up the group "Others." To avoid making the table unnecessarily complicated, I did not include the "others" in the calculations due to the group's small size. Since the line percentages are approximate values, this seemed legitimate to me.

Table 23. Income stratification of all men eligible to vote in Breslau by denomination, 1876 and 1906

Marks	Jews		Protestants		Catholics	
	No.	%	No.	%	No.	%
1876						
900–						
1,999	1,034	37.2	88	56.4	50	64.1
2,000–						
7,000	1,365	49.2	56	35.9	27	34.6
Over						
7,000	378	13.6	12	7.7	1	1.3
Total	2,777		156		78	
1906						
660–						
7,999	362	70.7	397	94.7	226	97.4
8,000–						
20,000	100	19.5	15	3.6	5	2.2
Over						
20,000	51	9.9	7	1.7	1	0.4
Total	513		419		232	

Source: See table 4 and APW, AMW, K 156.

Note: Those who were eligible to vote were over twenty-four years old and had an income of at least 900 marks prior to 1896 and 600 marks from 1896 on. The income groups are oriented not by the four social classes but rather by the three elector classes. Needless to say, the figures here are estimated. The income limits for the electoral classes were known only for 1868, 1885, and 1895. See Hettling, *Politische Bürgerlichkeit*, 409 and 411.

Table 24. The proportion of Jews, Protestants, and Catholics among men eligible to vote in Breslau by income, 1876 and 1906

	Jews		Protestants		Catholics	
Marks	Z	%	Z	%	Z	%
1876						
900– 1,999	6.547	11.9	30.86	56.1	17.628	32.0
2,000– 7,000	8.659	22.9	19.609	51.9	9.515	25.2
Over 7,000	2.394	34.8	4.127	60.0	0.358	5.2
1906						
660– 7,999	6.236	6.7	55.589	59.5	31.555	33.8
8,000– 20,000	1.720	37.8	2.113	46.5	0.715	15.7
Over 20,000	0.873	39.8	0.998	45.4	0.325	14.8

Source: See table 4 and APW, AMW, K 156.

Note: On the calculations here, see the clarifications for tables 22 and 23.

Table 25. Proportion of Jewish members in select general associations in Breslau, ca. 1880

Name	Source	Proportion of Jewish members
Breslauer Bürgerschützen-Corps	Mitglieder-Verzeichnis des Breslauer Bürgerschützen-Corps am 1. Januar 1888 (Breslau: n.p., 1888). (BUW, GŚŁ Yh 523)	2 of 60
Constitutionelle Bürgerressource	Statut und Mitglieder-Verzeichniß der constitutio-nellen Bürger-Ressource (in Springer's Etablissement) pro 1869/70 (Breslau: n.p., 1870).	several, about 5–10%
German and Austrian Alpine Club (Deutscher u. Österreichischer Alpenverein)	Verzeichnis der Mitglieder der Section Breslau des Deutschen und Österreichischen Alpenvereins, April 1888 (Breslau: Breslauer Genossenschafts-Buchhandlung, 1888). (BUW, GŚŁ Yz 300, 303)	many, about 20%
Women's Association for the Feeding and Clothing of the Poor (Frauen-Verein zur Speisung und Bekleidung der Armen)	62. Jahresbericht des Frauen-Vereins zur Speisung und Bekleidung der Armen (Suppen-Anstalten) in Breslau 1893/1894 (Breslau: n.p., 1894). (APW, AMW, III, 7434)	many, about 20–30%
Society "Eintracht" (Gesellschaft "Eintracht")	Gesellschaft "Eintracht": Mitgliederverzeichnis, 1880 (Breslau: n.p., 1880). (BUW, GŚŁ Yz 66)	almost all Jewish
Humboldt Society for Popular Education in Breslau (Humboldt-Verein für Volksbildung in Breslau)	7. Jahresbericht des Humboldt-Vereins für Volksbildung in Breslau für das Vereinsjahr 1875–1876 (Breslau: n.p., 1876). (BUW, GŚŁ Yv 608)	many, about 35%
Merchants' Club of Breslau (Kaufmännischer Verein zu Breslau)	Bericht des kaufmännischen Vereins zu Breslau für das Jahr 1882: Nebst Statut und Mitgliederverzeichnis (Breslau: n.p., 1883). (BUW, GŚŁ, Yn 234, 235)	many, about 50%
Giant Mountains Club (Riesengebirgsverein)	Mitglieder-Verzeichnis der Section Breslau des Riesengebirgs-Vereins am Ende des Jahres 1883 (Breslau: n.p., 1883). (BUW, GŚŁ Yz 336)	several, about 5–10%
Society for Silesian History and Antiquity (Verein für Geschichte und Altertum Schlesiens)	Mitglieder-Verzeichnis für 1901, Zeitschrift des Vereins für Geschichte und Altertum Schlesiens 35 (1901): 390–414.	several, about 5%

Table 26. Proportion of Jewish members in select general associations in Breslau, ca. 1905

Name	Source	Proportion of Jewish members
Radfahrer-Verein "Wratislavia"	Breslauer Radfahrer-Verein "Wratislavia": Mitgliederverzeichnis Mai 1902 (Breslau: n.p., 1902). (BUW, GŚL Yz 334)	None, although open according to its statutes
Evangelischer Local-Verein zur Fürsorge für entlassene Strafgefangene	14. Jahresbericht des evangelischen Local-Vereins zur Fürsorge für entlassene Strafgefangene zu Breslau pro 1895 (Breslau: n.p., 1895).	Jewish members despite its name, about 5%
Bohn'scher Gesangsverein	Emil Bohn, Bohn'scher Gesangsverein: Hundert historische Concerte (Breslau: Hainauer, 1905), 143–44.	many, about 15–20%
Breslauer Kindergartenverein	"Breslauer Kindergarten-Verein: Rechenschaftsbericht für die Geschäftsjahre 1915/16 und 1916/17." (AMW III 7363)	many, about 20–30%
German Colonial Society, Section Silesia (Deutsche Kolonial-Gesellschaft, Abt. Schlesien)	Mitgliederlisten der Abtheilung Breslau der Deutschen Kolonial-Gesellschaft, 1896 (Breslau: n.p., 1896). (BUW, GŚL Ym 33)	several, about 10%
German and Austrian Alpine Club (Deutscher u. Österreichischer Alpenverein)	9. Bericht der Sektion Breslau des Deutschen und Österreichischen Alpenvereins, 29: Vereinsjahr 1906 (Breslau: Stenzel, 1907).	several, about 5–10%
Women's Association for the Feeding and Clothing of the Poor (Frauen-Verein zur Speisung und Bekleidung der Armen)	70. Jahresbericht des Frauen-Vereins zur Speisung und Bekleidung der Armen (Suppen-Anstalten) in Breslau 1902 (Breslau: n.p., 1902). (APW, AMW, III, 7435)	many, about 20–30%
Johannisloge "Hermann zur Beständigkeit" im Orient Breslau	Mitglieder-Verzeichnis der . . . St. Johannisloge "Hermann zur Beständigkeit" im Orient Breslau, 1907 (Breslau: n.p., 1907).	many, about 70–80%
Humboldt Society for Popular Education in Breslau (Humboldt-Verein für Volksbildung in Breslau)	37. Jahresbericht des Humboldt-Vereins für Volksbildung für das Vereinsjahr 1905–06 (Breslau: Breslauer Genossenschafts-Buchdruckerei, 1906).	many, about 30%
Giant Mountains Club (Riesengebirgsverein)	Mitglieder-Verzeichnis der Section Breslau des Riesengebirgs-Vereins am Ende des Jahres 1908 (Breslau: n.p., 1908). (BUW, GŚL Yz 336)	several, about 5–10%
Schlesischer Verein für Luftschiffahrt	"Schlesischer Verein für Luftschiffahrt: Mitgliederliste" (n.d. [ca. 1908]). (BUW, GŚL Yz 315k)	several, about 10%

Continued on next page

Table 26—*continued*

Name	Source	Proportion of Jewish members
Johannis-Loge "Settegast zur deutschen Treue"	Mitgliederverzeichnis 1905: Johannis-Loge "Settegast zur deutschen Treue"; Or. Breslau, gestiftet am 16. Februar 1901 (Breslau: n.p., 1905).	many, about 70–80%
Verein für die Besserung der Strafge-fangenen in der Provinz Schlesien	15. Bericht des Vereins für die Besserung der Straf-gefangenen in der Provinz Schlesien (Breslau: n.p., 1896). (APW, AMW, III, 7577)	many, about 20%
Society for Silesian History and An-tiquity (Verein für Geschichte und Altertum Schlesiens)	Membership directory for 1901, in Zeitschrift des Vereins für Geschichte und Altertum Schlesiens 35 (1901): 390–414.	several, about 5–10%
United Crèches (Vereinigte Kleinkinderbewahr-Anstalten)	Die sechs Vereinigten Kleinkinderbewahr-Anstalten zu Breslau im Jahre 1906/1907 (Breslau: n.p., 1907). (BUW, GŚL 26955 II)	many, about 20%
Verein für Velociped-Wettfahrten	Mitglieder-Verzeichniss des Vereins für Velociped-Wettfahren in Breslau, 1894 (Breslau: n.p., 1894). (BUW, GŚL 29261 III)	several, about 5–10%

Table 27. The social origins of Jewish women in intra-Jewish and Jewish-Christian marriages in Breslau, 1874–94 and 1905–20

	1874–94				1905–20			
	Intra-Jewish marriages		Jewish-Christian marriages		Intra-Jewish marriages		Jewish-Christian marriages	
	No.	%	No.	%	No.	%	No.	%
Upper-middle class	322	72.7	36	35.6	171	75	79	53.7
Upper-middle-class merchants	246		28		146		59	
Middle and lower-middle class	88	19.9	43	42.6	45	19.8	47	32.0
Lower class	29	6.5	17	16.8	6	2.6	15	10.2
Others	4	0.9	5	5.0	6	2.6	6	4.1
Total	443	100	101	100	228	100	147	100

Source: Marriage records of Breslau registrar's offices I and II, 1874–94, (APW, USC Wrocław) and marriage records of Breslau registrar's of-fices I–IV, 1905–20, now at USC, Wrocław.

Table 28. Annual income in marks of Jewish parents in Jewish-Christian marriages and intra-Jewish marriages in Breslau, 1874–81 or 1875 and 1881

| | Jewish-Christian marriages | | | | Intra-Jewish marriages | | | |
| | Husband's parents | | Wife's parents | | Husband's parents | | Wife's parents | |
Marks	No.	%	No.	%	No.	%	No.	%
Under 1,100	2	33.3	12	60.0	9	37.5	10	12.7
1,100–2,749	1	16.7	3	15.0	9	37.5	20	25.3
2,750–9,200	3	50.0	4	20.0	5	20.8	34	43.0
Over 9,200	—	—	1	5.0	1	4.2	15	19.0
Unknown	30		28		127		72	
Total	36		48		151		151	

Source: See table 4 and AMW, K 150: Class tax rolls, City of Breslau 1876 (35 vols.).

Note: Percentages refer only to those cases for which information on income was available.

Table 29. Annual income in marks of Jewish grooms in Jewish-Christian marriages and intra-Jewish marriages in Breslau, 1874–81 or 1875 and 1881

| | Jewish-Christian marriages | | Intra-Jewish marriages | |
Marks	No.	%	No.	%
Under 1,100	13	59.1	61	53.0
1,100–2,749	5	22.7	22	19.1
2,750–9,200	3	13.6	26	22.6
Over 9,200	1	4.6	6	5.2
Unknown	14		36	
Total	36		151	

Source: See table 4 and AMW, K 150: Class tax rolls, City of Breslau 1876 (35 vols.).

Note: Percentages refer only to those cases for which information on income is available.

Table 30. Percentage of women "out to work" before marriage

	Intra-Jewish marriages				Jewish-Christian marriages							
					Jewish women				Non-Jewish women			
	Out to work		Without profession		Out to work		Without profession		Out to work		Without profession	
Year of marriage	No.	%	No.	%	No.	%	No.	%	No.	%	No.	%
1874–84	17	8.9	197	92.1	22	43.1	39	56.9	20	44.4	25	55.6
1885–94	23	10.0	206	90.0	19	47.5	21	52.5	31	64.6	17	35.4
1905–9	9	11.0	73	89.0	20	40.0	30	60.0	—	—	—	—
1914–18	14	28.6	35	71.4	23	45.1	28	54.9	—	—	—	—
1919–20	15	20.8	57	79.2	15	50.0	50	50.0	—	—	—	—

Source: See table 27.

Table 31. Living status of Jewish women before marriage, 1874–84 and 1885–94

| | 1874–84 | | | | 1885–94 | | | |
| | Jewish-Christian marriages | | Intra-Jewish marriages | | Jewish-Christian marriages | | Intra-Jewish marriages | |
	No.	%	No.	%	No.	%	No.	%
With parents	15	25	149	70	7	33	143	62
By themselves	24	39	53	25	6	29	86	38
With future spouse	22	36	12	6	8	38	—	—

Source: See table 27.

Table 32. Living status of Jewish women before marriage, 1905–9 and 1919–20

	1905–9				1919–20			
	Jewish-Christian marriages		Intra-Jewish marriages		Jewish-Christian marriages		Intra-Jewish marriages	
	No.	%	No.	%	No.	%	No.	%
With parents	11	22	42	51	11	37	31	39
By themselves	27	54	37	45	15	50	67	57
With future spouse	12	24	3	4	4	13	3	4

Source: See table 27.

Table 33. Living status of Jewish men before marriage, 1874–84 and 1885–94

	1874–84				1885–94			
	Jewish-Christian marriages		Intra-Jewish marriages		Jewish-Christian marriages		Intra-Jewish marriages	
	No.	%	No.	%	No.	%	No.	%
With parents	—	—	24	11	1	3	29	13
By themselves	19	42	178	83	19	50	200	87
With future spouse	26	58	12	6	18	47	—	—

Source: See table 27.

Table 34. Living status of Jewish men before marriage, 1905–9 and 1919–20

	1905–9				1919–20			
	Jewish-Christian marriages		Intra-Jewish marriages		Jewish-Christian marriages		Intra-Jewish marriages	
	No.	%	No.	%	No.	%	No.	%
With parents	2	3	9	11	4	9	10	13
By themselves	51	66	70	85	32	68	67	83
With future spouse	24	31	3	4	11	23	3	4

Source: See table 27.

Table 35. Average ages of husbands and wives and age differences between husbands and wives

| | Jewish-Christian marriages | | | | | | Intra-Jewish marriages | | |
| | Jewish men | | | Jewish women | | | | | |
	H	W	Difference	H	W	Difference	H	W	Difference
1874–84	34.3	26.6	7.7	30.2	28.6	1.6	32.8	25.3	7.5
1885–94	35.3	29.8	5.5	27.6	26.4	1.2	32.8	25.6	7.2
1905–9	33.7	27.2	6.5	30.2	28.1	2.1	32.8	26.0	6.8
1914–18	34.9	28.3	6.4	31.2	28.5	2.7	36.5	29.1	7.4
1919–20	37.2	30.1	7.1	31.7	28.0	3.7	35.4	27.9	7.5

Source: See table 27.

Table 36. Age differences between husbands and wives in percentages (percentage of marriages, in which the husband is X years older)

| | Jewish-Christian marriages, husband Jewish | | | | Jewish-Christian marriages, wife Jewish | | | | Intra-Jewish marriages | | | |
	<0 yrs.	0–5 yrs.	6–10 yrs.	>10 yrs.	<0 yrs.	0–5 yrs.	6–10 yrs.	>10 yrs.	<0 yrs.	0–5 yrs.	6–10 yrs.	>10 yrs.
1874–84	15.6	33.3	22.2	28.9	45.6	29.5	14.8	13.1	11.2	30.8	27.6	30.4
1885–94	16.7	29.2	37.5	16.7	30.0	50.0	12.5	7.5	10.0	30.6	33.6	25.8
1905–9	14.3	40.2	19.5	26.0	26.0	48.0	16.0	10.0	11.2	31.8	30.8	26.2
1914–18	12.3	36.0	30.7	21.0	33.3	39.2	11.8	15.7	10.2	38.8	24.5	26.5
1919–20	11.6	55.1	18.8	14.5	15.2	63.0	10.9	10.9	9.7	27.8	33.3	29.2

Source: See table 27.

Note: Years < 0 when the wife was older.

Table 37. Witnesses to Jewish-Christian and to intra-Jewish weddings, 1874–84, 1905–9, 1914–18, and 1919–20

| | 1874–84 | | | | 1905–9 | | | | 1919–20 | | | |
| | Mixed marriages | | Intra-Jewish marriages | | Mixed marriages | | Intra-Jewish marriages | | Mixed marriages | | Intra-Jewish marriages | |
	No.	%	No.	%	No.	%	No.	%	No.	%	No.	%
I. Parents	54	25.0	217	50.0	52	23.0	84	51.0	41	28.0	78	55.0
II. Relatives	—	—	—	—	19	8.0	22	13.0	14	9.0	19	13.0
III. Neighbors	23	11.0	33	8.0	18	8.0	5	3.0	10	7.0	8	6.0
IV. Colleagues	17	8.0	1	0.2	42	19.0	24	15.0	27	18.0	24	17.0
V. Friends, etc.	120	56.0	177	41.0	95	42.0	29	18.0	56	38.0	13	9.0
Total	214		418		226		164		148		142	

Source: See table 27.

Table 38. The composition of pupils at preparatory schools of Breslau Gymnasien by denomination

| | Jewish | | Protestant | | Catholic | | Other | |
	No.	%	No.	%	No.	%	No.	%
1893–94	198	49	184	45	23	6	1	NA
1904–5	133	24	373	67	53	9	0	0
1909–10	141	22	408	63	96	15	1	NA

Source: Verwaltungsbericht des Magistrats der Königlichen Haupt- und Residenzstadt Breslau, 1892–1895 (Breslau: Grass, Barth & Co., 1895), 190; ibid., *1904–1907* (Breslau: Grass, Barth & Co., 1907), 235; ibid., *1907–1910* (Breslau: Grass, Barth & Co., 1910), 230.

Table 39. The class origin of Gymnasium graduates in 1880–89 in comparison with the class origin of the total population of Breslau in 1876

	% of total population	% of graduates	Class origin index
Upper-middle class	**11.5%**	**74.0%**	**6.50**
Economic middle class	7.9%	43.0%	5.50
Educated middle class	2.7%	12.0%	4.30
Senior civil servants/ officials	0.9%	19.0%	21.00
Old/new middle class	**19.5%**	**15.0%**	**0.80**
Lower classes	**60.0%**	**2.0%**	**0.03**
Unclassifiable	**9.1%**	**8.7%**	—

Source: See table 4 and the *Jahresschulberichte aller höheren Schulen Breslaus, 1880–1889*, Pädagogisches Zentrum, Berlin. The table is based on Peter Lundgreen, Margret Kraul, and Karl Ditt, *Bildungschancen und soziale Mobilität in der städtischen Gesellschaft des 19. Jahrhunderts* (Göttingen: Vandenhoeck & Ruprecht, 1988), 273.

Table 40. The class origin of Gymnasium graduates in 1900–1909 in comparison with the class origin of the total population of Breslau in 1906

	% of total population	% of graduates	Class origin index
Upper-middle class	**12.4%**	**76.6%**	**6.20**
Economic middle class	7.7%	42.2%	5.50
Educated middle class	3.7%	14.5%	3.90
Senior civil servants/ officials	1.0%	19.9%	19.9
Old/new middle class	**20.3%**	**18.8%**	**0.90**
Lower classes	**65.3%**	**2.2%**	**0.03**
Unclassifiable	**2.0%**	**2.4%**	—

Source: See table 5 and the *Jahresschulberichte aller höheren Schulen Breslaus, 1900–1909*, Pädagogisches Zentrum, Berlin. The table is based on Peter Lundgreen, Margret Kraul, and Karl Ditt, *Bildungschancen und soziale Mobilität in der städtischen Gesellschaft des 19. Jahrhunderts* (Göttingen: Vandenhoeck & Ruprecht, 1988), 273.

Table 41. Denomination, social stratification of total population, and social background of Breslau's Gymnasium graduates, 1880–89 and 1900–1909

	1880–89				1900–1909			
	PCC	PCG	HPC	RPC	PCC	PCG	HPC	RPC
Jewish								
Upper-middle class	**28.0%**							
Economic middle class	30.0%	43.0%	12.9%		35.0%	42.0%	14.7%	
Educated middle class	12.0%	12.0%	1.4%		16.0%	15.0%	2.4%	
Senior civil servants/officials	7.0%	19.0%	1.3%		8.0%	20.0%	1.6%	
Old/new middle class	**11.0%**	**15.0%**	**1.6%**		**7.0%**	**19.0%**	**1.3%**	
Lower classes	**2.0%**	**2.0%**	—		**1.0%**	**2.0%**	—	
Total			17.3%	24.0%			20.0%	20.0%
Protestant								
Upper-middle class	**55.0%**							
Economic middle class	58.0%	43.0%	25.0%		46.0%	42.0%	19.3%	
Educated middle class	68.0%	12.0%	8.0%		64.0%	15.0%	9.6%	
Senior civil servants/officials	69.0%	19.0%	13.0%		71.0%	20.0%	14.2%	
Old/new middle class	**54.0%**	**15.0%**	**8.0%**		**61.0%**	**19.0%**	**11.6%**	
Lower classes	**59.0%**	**2.0%**	**1.0%**		**60.0%**	**2.0%**	**1.2%**	
Total			55.0%	51.0%			56.0%	48.0%
Catholic								
Upper-middle class	**17.0%**							
Economic middle class	12.0%	43.0%	5.0%		21.0%	42.0%	8.8%	
Educated middle class	20.0%	12.0%	2.4%		20.0%	15.0%	3.0%	

Continued on next page

Table 41 — *continued*

	1880–89				1900–1909			
	PCC	PCG	HPC	RPC	PCC	PCG	HPC	RPC
Catholic								
Senior civil servants/officials	24.0%	19.0%	4.6%		20.0%	20.0%	4.0%	
Old/new middle class	35.0%	15.0%	5.3%		32.0%	19.0%	6.1%	
Lower classes	40.0%	2.0%	0.8%		40.0%	2.0%	0.8%	
Total			18.0%	24.0%			23.0%	32.0%

Source: See tables 4 and 5, as well as the *Jahresschulberichte aller höheren Schulen Breslaus, 1880–89* and *1900–1909* (Bibliothek für Bildungs-geschichtliche Forschung des Deutschen Instituts für Internationale Pädagogische Forschung in Berlin).

Note: PCC = percentage of denominations by social class (over professional groups), see tables 9 and 10; PCG = percentage of social class among all graduates; HPC = hypothetical percentage of denominations among all graduates (PCC x PCG); RPC = real percentage of denominations among all graduates.

Table 42. Social background of Jewish, Protestant, and Catholic Gymnasium graduates in 1880–89 in comparison with the professional background of the total population in 1876

	Jews			Protestants			Catholics		
	SPC	SBG	COI	SPC	SBG	COI	SPC	SBG	COI
Upper-middle class	43.0%	87.0%	2.00	10.0%	83.0%	8.30	5.0%	44.0%	8.80
Economic middle class	38.0%	74.0%	1.90	9.0%	39.0%	4.30	3.0%	21.0%	7.00
Educated middle class	4.0%	11.0%	2.80	3.0%	14.0%	4.60	1.0%	9.0%	9.00
Senior civil servants/officials	1.0%	2.0%	2.00	1.0%	30.0%	30.00	1.0%	15.0%	15.00
Old/new middle class	29.0%	7.0%	0.20	18.0%	15.0%	0.80	19.0%	25.0%	1.30
Lower classes	16.0%	2.0%	0.10	61.0%	1.0%	0.02	68.0%	3.0%	0.04

Source: See tables 4 and 5, as well as the *Jahresschulberichte aller höheren Schulen Breslaus, 1880–89* and *1900–1909* (Bibliothek für Bildungs-geschichtliche Forschung des Deutschen Instituts für Internationale Pädagogische Forschung in Berlin).

Note: SPC = social background of total population by denomination (based on table 4); SBG = social background of graduates; COI = class origin index (SBG/SPC).

Table 43. Social background of Jewish, Protestant, and Catholic Gymnasium graduates in 1900–1909 in comparison with the professional background of the total population in 1906

	Jews			Protestants			Catholics		
	SPC	SBG	COI	SPC	SBG	COI	SPC	SBG	COI
Upper-middle									
class	57.0%	95.0%	1.70	11.0%	82.0%	7.50	7.0%	57.0%	8.10
Economic									
middle class	46.0%	80.0%	1.70	6.0%	37.0%	6.20	5.0%	25.0%	5.00
Educated									
middle class	9.0%	8.0%	0.90	4.0%	18.0%	4.50	2.0%	14.0%	7.00
Senior civil									
servants/officials	1.4%	7.0%	5.00	1.2%	27.0%	22.5	0.6%	19.0%	31.70
Old/new									
middle class	24.0%	2.0%	0.10	21.0%	14.0%	0.70	19.0%	37.0%	1.90
Lower classes	16.0%	1.0%	0.06	66.0%	1.4%	0.02	73.0%	4.5%	0.06

Source: See tables 4 and 5, as well as the *Jahresschulberichte aller höheren Schulen Breslaus, 1880–89* and *1900–1909* (Bibliothek für Bildungsgeschichtliche Forschung des Deutschen Instituts für Internationale Pädagogische Forschung in Berlin).

Note: SPC = social background of total population by denomination (based on table 5); SBG = social background of graduates; COI = class origin index (SBG/SPC).

Table 44. Social background of Breslau's Jewish Gymnasium graduates (by father's income) 1875–84 in comparison with the income structure of the total Jewish population

		SBJG		
Marks	ISJP	No.	%	COI
Under 1,100	32.6	3	1.9	0.06
1,100–2,749	31.6	25	15.6	0.50
2,000–2,759		18	11.2	
2,750–9,200	27.7	77	48.1	1.70
Over 9,200	8.1	55	34.3	4.20
Total		160		

Source: Jahresberichte der Breslauer Gymnasien (Bibliothek für Bildungsgeschichtliche Forschung des Deutschen Instituts für Internationale Pädagogische Forschung in Berlin) and tax records for 1876 (AMW, K 150, vols. 1–18 and 20–36, as well as APW, AMW, K 151, vol. 19, and the Prussian tax rolls, APW, AMW, K 146, vols. 18 and 20).

Note: The percentages refer only to cases in which the father's income was known. Of the 226 Jews who graduated from a Breslau Gymnasium or Realgymnasium between 1875 and 1884, the families of 160 could be classified.

ISJP = income structure of total Jewish population (only those 30–60 years of age); SBJG = social background of Jewish graduates; COI = class origin index (SBJG / ISJP).

Table 45. Proportion of Jewish population in general migration movements in Breslau, 1882–1923

	Jewish population			Total Breslau population		
	Resident population	Migration volume	Mobility code no.	Resident population	Migration volume	Mobility code no.
1882–84	17,445	4,253	243	272,912	80,169	294
1890–94	17,754	4,085	232	335,186	97,838	292
1900–1904	19,743	4,672	237	422,709	122,006	289
1910–13	20,212	4,421	219	512,105	140,811	275
1919–23	23,240	6,174	266	557,139	142,181	255

Source: "Die Zu- und Abgezogenen nach Religion," *Breslauer Statistik* vol. 8, pt. 2 (Breslau: Morgenstern, 1883)–vol. 36 (Breslau: Morgenstern, 1919); *Statistisches Jahrbuch der Stadt Breslau für 1922* (Breslau: Morgenstern, 1922): 28–29; *Statistisches Jahrbuch der Stadt Breslau für 1924* (Breslau: Morgenstern, 1924): 12. The figures here are based on the author's own calculations of the mobility code numbers of the Jewish and the entire population of Breslau. A general overview may be found in Monika Richarz, "Die Entwicklung der jüdischen Bevölkerung," in *Deutsch-jüdische Geschichte in der Neuzeit*, by Steven M. Lowenstein, Paul Mendes-Flohr, Peter Pulzer, and Monika Richarz, ed. Michael A. Meyer, vol. 3, *Umstrittene Integration, 1871–1918* (Munich: C. H. Beck, 1997), 13–38, here 28.

Note: The mobility code number measures the average annual migration volume in thousands of the mean annual population; the migration volume is the sum of immigrants and emigrants; see Dieter Langewiesche, "Wanderungsbewegungen in der Hochindustrialisierungs-periode: Regionale, interstädtische und innerstädtische Mobilität in Deutschland, 1880–1914," *Vierteljahrschrift für Sozial- und Wirtschafts-geschichte* 64 (1977): 1–40, here 2–3n7.

Table 46. Jewish immigration to and emigration from Breslau and their balance, 1882–1923

	Jewish immigration		Jewish emigration		Balance	
	General	Russian/ Austrian	General	Russian/ Austrian	General	Russian/ Austrian
1882–84	6,379	841	6,380	783	-1	58
1885–89	10,368	1,000	10,387	1,080	-19	-80
1890–94	10,490	1,129	9,936	958	554	171
1895–99	11,027	1,355	9,876	1,115	1,151	240
1900–1904	12,307	1,831	11,053	1,545	1,254	286
1905–9	11,589	2,628	11,694	2,485	-105	143
1910–13	9,032	1,819	8,650	1,524	574	295
1914–18	14,367	1,340	16,312	1,471	-1,945	-131
1919–23	18,255	4,273	12,617	3,088	5,638	1,185

Source: See table 45. Prior to 1882, Prussian immigration statistics did not differentiate by denomination. Only after the anti-Semitic turn in national immigration policy in 1880–81 did the authorities separate out Jewish immigrants for expulsion. See Dieter Gosewinkel, "'Unerwünschte Elemente': Einwanderung und Einbürgerung von Juden in Deutschland, 1848–1933," *Tel Aviver Jahrbuch für deutsche Geschichte* 27 (1998): 71–106, here 78 and 82.

Table. 47. General immigration to and emigration from Breslau and their balance, 1882–1923

	Immigration	Emigration	Balance	Balance of Jewish Immigration	Balance of "Eastern Jewish" Immigration
1882–84	130,367	110,141	20,221	-1	58
1885–89	238,142	205,488	32,354	-19	-80
1890–94	260,632	228,558	30,094	554	171
1895–99	296,574	261,787	34,787	1,151	240
1900–1904	322,796	287,235	35,561	1,254	286
1905–9	347,973	312,744	35,229	-105	143
1910–13	297,374	265,870	31,504	574	295
1914–18	420,466	452,898	-32,432	-1,645	-131
1919–23	381,186	329,717	51,469	5,638	1,185

Source: See table 45.

Table 48. Political composition of the councils in Germany's six largest cities on the eve of the war

	Liberals	Social Democrats (SPD)	Center	Conservatives
Berlin (1914)	98	44	—	—
Breslau (1910)	57	12	—	33
Cologne (1911)	19	—	32	—
Dresden (1913)	38	16	—	31
Frankfurt (1912)	44	23	1	3
Munich (1911)	30	14	14	2

Source: James J. Sheehan, "Liberalism and the City in Nineteenth Century Germany," *Past and Present* 51 (1971): 116–37, here 132.

NOTES

Introduction

1. Karl A. Schleunes, *The Twisted Road to Auschwitz: Nazi Policy toward German Jews, 1933–1939* (Urbana: University of Illinois Press, 1970).

2. Friedrich Naumann first coined the phrase "anti-Semitic mood of society" (*antisemitische Gesellschaftsstimmung*) in his "Die Leidensgeschichte des deutschen Liberalismus" (1908), in: *Werke*, ed. Theodor Schieder, vol. 4 (Cologne: Westdeutscher Verlag, 1964), 292; cited in Thomas Nipperdey and Reinhard Rürup, "Antisemitismus: Entstehung, Funktion und Geschichte eines Begriffs," in *Emanzipation und Antisemitismus: Studien zur "Judenfrage" in der bürgerlichen Gesellschaft*, by Reinhard Rürup (Frankfurt a. M.: Fischer, 1987), 120–44, here 140.

3. Samuel Moyn, "German Jewry and the Question of Identity: Historiography and Theory," *Year Book of the Leo Baeck Institute* 41 (1996): 291–308, here 308. Moyn's essay is the first in the *Year Book* to give expression to postmodern and postcolonial reflections from "cultural studies." In general, see Jonathan Boyarin and Daniel Boyarin, eds., *Jews and Other Differences: The New Jewish Cultural Studies* (Minneapolis: University of Minnesota Press, 1997). Michael Weingrad is quite skeptical about how the pioneers of French postmodernism have addressed Jewish history and Jewish identities in their reflections. See his "Jews (in Theory): Representations of Judaism, Anti-Semitism, and the Holocaust in Postmodern French Writing," *Judaism* 177 (1996): 79–98.

4. Jörn Rüsen, "Identität und Konflikt im Prozeß der Modernisierung: Überlegungen zur kulturhistorischen Dimension von Fremdenfeindschaft heute," in *Universalgeschichte und Nationalgeschichte: Festschrift für Ernst Schulin zum 65. Geburtstag*, ed. Gangolf Hübinger, Jürgen Osterhammel, and Erich Pelzer (Freiburg: Rombach, 1994), 333–43, here 340.

5. Zygmunt Bauman, *Modernity and Ambivalence* (Cambridge: Polity Press, 1991), 7–8. On Bauman, see Shulamit Volkov, "Minderheiten und der Nationalstaat: Eine postmoderne Perspektive," in *Geschichte und Emanzipation: Festschrift für Reinhard Rürup*, ed. Michael Grüttner, Rüdiger Hachtmann, and Heinz-Gerhard

Haupt (Frankfurt a. M.: Campus, 1999), 58–74. In general, see Susan Mendus, *Toleration and the Limits of Liberalism* (London: Palgrave Macmillan, 1989).

6. Michael Brenner, "'Gott schütze uns vor unseren Freunden': Zur Ambivalenz des 'Philosemitismus' im Kaiserreich," *Jahrbuch für Antisemitismusforschung* 2 (1993): 174–99, here 175; Alan Levenson, "Philosemitic Discourse in Imperial Germany," *Jewish Social Studies* 2, no. 3 (1996): 25–53, here 45; see also Gary A. Abraham, *Max Weber and the Jewish Question: A Study of the Social Outlook of His Sociology* (Urbana: University of Illinois Press, 1992), esp. 71–126. Instructive analyses of the liberal stance toward Jewish emancipation are offered by Dagmar Herzog, *Intimacy and Exclusion: Religious Politics in Pre-Revolutionary Baden* (Princeton, N.J.: Princeton University Press, 1996), and Stefan-Ludwig Hoffmann, *Die Politik der Geselligkeit: Freimaurerlogen in der deutschen Bürgergesellschaft, 1840–1918* (Göttingen: Vandenhoeck & Ruprecht, 2000). Brenner's, Herzog's, and Levenson's critique is nothing new; the Israeli historian Uriel Tal had developed it quite convincingly already in 1969; see his *Christians and Jews in Germany: Religion, Politics, and Ideology in the Second Reich, 1970–1914*, trans. Noah Jonathan Jacobs (1969; Ithaca, N.Y.: Cornell University Press, 1975). German historians have virtually ignored this book; see, e.g., the "hatchet job" that Bernhard Unckel does on it in just a few lines in *Historische Zeitschrift* 237 (1983): 738.

7. Even American liberalism, which responded much more sensitively to cultural diversity than did the abstract-universalist tradition of French liberalism, maintained the ideal of homogeneity under the motto *E pluribus unum*. See John Higham, "Ethnic Pluralism in Modern American Thought," in his *Send These to Me: Immigrants in Urban America*, 2nd ed. (Baltimore: Johns Hopkins University Press, 1984), 198–232.

8. Rüsen, "Identität und Konflikt," 342.

9. Joseph Raz, "Multiculturalism: A Liberal Perspective," in his *Ethics in the Public Domain: Essays in the Morality of Law and Politics* (Oxford: Clarendon Press, 1994), 155–76, here 174. See also the two special issues of *Deutsche Zeitschrift für Philosophie* 43, no. 5 (1995) and 46, no. 3 (1996), edited by Axel Honneth and devoted to "multiculturalism." For a line of argumentation similar to Raz's, see, e.g., Will Kymlicka, *Multicultural Citizenship: A Liberal Theory of Minority Rights*, 2nd ed. (Oxford: Oxford University Press, 1996). Kymlicka's theses have initiated a fruitful discussion; see David D. Laitin, "Liberal Theory and the Nation," *Political Theory* 26 (1998): 221–37, as well as José Brunner and Yoav Peled, "Das Elend des liberalen Multikulturalismus: Kymlicka und seine Kritiker," *Deutsche Zeitschrift für Philosophie* 46 (1998): 369–91; see also Charles Taylor, *Multiculturalism and the Politics of Recognition*, ed. Amy Gutmann (Princeton, N.J.: Princeton University Press, 1992), and Michael Walzer, "Multiculturalism and Individualism," *Dissent* 41 (1994): 185–91.

10. See Daniel Cohn-Bendit and Thomas Schmid, *Heimat Babylon: Das Wagnis der multikulturellen Demokratie* (Hamburg: Hoffmann & Campe, 1993), and Claus Leggewie, *Multi Kulti: Spielregeln für die Vielvölkerrepublik* (Berlin:

Rotbuchverlag, 1993). Pleas for multiculturalism as the central concept of European history may be found, e.g., in Michael Geyer, "Multiculturalism and the Politics of General Education," *Critical Inquiry* 19 (1993): 499–533; Michael Geyer and Konrad Jarausch, "The Future of the German Past: Transatlantic Reflections for the 1990s," *Central European History* 22 (1989): 229–59, here 259; John R. Gillis, "The Future of European History," *Perspectives: American Historical Association Newsletter* 34, no. 4 (1996): 4–6, esp. 4 and 5; Atina Grossmann, "Remarks on Current Trends and Directions in German Women's History," *Women in German Yearbook* 12 (1996): 11–25, esp. 12 and 19–20; Malachi Haim Hacohen, "Dilemmas of Cosmopolitanism: Karl Popper, Jewish Identity, and 'Central European Culture,'" *Journal of Modern History* 71 (1999): 105–49, esp. 107–8. Among German historians of the nineteenth and twentieth centuries, only the circle around Klaus Bade has thus far taken up the concept of multiculturalism, though it has confined itself mostly to the classical themes of migration and minority studies; see Klaus J. Bade, Leonie Herwartz-Emden, and Hans-Joachim Wenzel, eds., *Institut für Migrationsforschung und Interkulturelle Studien (IMIS): Bericht, 1991–1997* (Osnabrück: Universitätsverlag Rasch, 1998).

11. Thomas Nipperdey, *Deutsche Geschichte, 1866–1918*, vol. 2, *Machtstaat vor der Demokratie* (Munich: C. H. Beck, 1992), 290; Dan Diner, "'Rupture in Civilization': On the Genesis and Meaning of a Concept in Understanding," in *On Germans and Jews under the Nazi Regime: Essays by Three Generations of Historians*, ed. Moshe Zimmermann (Jerusalem: Magnes Press, 2006), 33–48.

12. Concerning the problems of constitutional law inherent in multicultural liberalism, see esp. Kymlicka, *Multicultural Citizenship.*

13. The main arguments of the history of minorities may be found in Trude Maurer, *Die Entwicklung der jüdischen Minderheit, 1780–1933: Neuere Forschungen und offene Fragen* (Tübingen: Niemeyer, 1992), 11. Here I follow Etienne Balibar's skeptical assessment of the concept of minorities in "Ambiguous Universality," *Differences* 7, no. 1 (1995): 48–74, here 53–54; according to Balibar, the distinction between "majority" and "minority" is dissolving increasingly "because a growing number of individuals and groups are not easily inscribed in one single ethnic (or cultural, linguistic, even religious) identity . . . among these 'others,' and among the 'nationals' as well . . . , *more individuals are not classifiable:* marrying partners from different 'cultures' and 'races,' living across the fictitious boundaries of communities, experiencing a divided or multiple 'self,' practicing different languages and memberships according to the private and public circumstances."

14. Werner Mosse, *German-Jewish Economic Élite, 1820–1935: A Socio-Cultural Profile* (Oxford: Oxford University Press, 1989), 337–38; a lack of preliminary conceptual reflections is lamented also by François Guesnet in his *Lodzer Juden im 19. Jahrhundert: Ihr Ort in einer multikulturellen Stadtgesellschaft* (Leipzig: Simon-Dubnow-Institut für jüdische Geschichte und Kultur, 1997), 9.

15. A sketch of Weber's theory of differentiation and modernization may be found in Max Weber, "Zwischenbetrachtung: Theorien der Stufen und

Richtungen religiöser Weltablehnung," in his *Gesammelte Aufsätze zur Religions-soziologie*, 8th ed., vol. 1 (Tübingen: Mohr Siebeck, 1986), esp. 536–73; see also the important "Vorbemerkung" and "Über einige Kategorien der verstehenden Soziologie," in his *Gesammelte Aufsätze zur Wissenschaftslehre*, 7th ed. (Tübingen: Mohr Siebeck, 1988), 1–16 and 427–74, esp. 441–73, respectively. See also M. Rainer Lepsius, *Interessen, Ideen und Institutionen* (Opladen: Westdeutscher Verlag, 1990), 53–62. On the transition from collective to individual presuppositions of access, see esp. Frank Parkin, *Marxism and Class Theory: A Bourgeois Critique* (London: Tavistock, 1979), 60–71, as well as Rudolf Stichweh, "Inklusion in Funk-tionssysteme der modernen Gesellschaft," in *Differenz und Verselbständigung: Zur Entwicklung gesellschaftlicher Teilsysteme*, ed. Renate Mayntz et al. (Frankfurt a. M.: Campus, 1988), 261–93. On the connection of political and social equality under the law with the guiding idea of the "civil society," see Utz Haltern, "Die Gesellschaft der Bürger," *Geschichte und Gesellschaft* 19 (1993): 100–134, here 125–27; see Geoff Eley's influential critique of "teleological" equations, e.g., of lib-eralism and democracy, or of bourgeois and liberal, in his "German History and the Contradictions of Modernity: The Bourgeoisie, the State, and the Mastery of Reform," in *Society, Culture, and the State in Germany, 1870–1930*, ed. Geoff Eley (Ann Arbor: University of Michigan Press, 1996), 67–103, here 86–90, as well as his "Nations, Publics, and Political Cultures: Placing Habermas in the Nineteenth Century," in *Habermas and the Public Sphere*, ed. Craig Calhoun (Cambridge, Mass.: MIT Press, 1992), 289–339, here 307–17.

16. Weber's concept of social closure was expressed first in his *Economy and Society: An Outline of Interpretive Sociology*, ed. Guenther Roth and Claus Wittich (Berkeley: University of California Press, 1978), 1:43–46 and 341–43. Especially Frank Parkin has made this concept fruitful for the investigation of social in-equality and ethnic stratification. In the present study, the concept of exclusion has been sharpened into ethnic exclusion; see Parkin's *Marxism and Class Theory*, as well as his "Strategies of Social Closure in Class Formation," in *The Social Analysis of Class Structure*, ed. Frank Parkin (London: Tavistock, 1974), 1–18. On Parkin's interpretation of Weber, see Raymond Murphy, *Social Closure: The The-ory of Monopolization and Exclusion* (Oxford: Clarendon Press, 1988). The system-theoretical discussion of inclusion/exclusion is also important; see Niklas Luh-mann, *Die Gesellschaft der Gesellschaft* (Frankfurt a. M.: Suhrkamp, 1997), 594–865, esp. 618–34. The distinction between forms of exclusion based on individual criteria and those based on collective criteria is foreign to the system-theoretical discussion, however. Presumably it fears introducing traces of the normative into its theory. Yet that is unnecessary since, while the distinction between exclu-sion and social closure can be normatively charged, above all it limits the scope of the concept of exclusion, which is far too broad in system theory. At any rate, Luhmann himself distinguishes only between the exclusion that can be traced back to social stratification and "class rule" and a second variant based on "function-specific forms of deviation intensification" since in the functionally

differentiated society the "exclusion effect" is "intensified" by "multiple dependencies on functional systems" (Luhmann, *Die Gesellschaft der Gesellschaft*, 631).

17. David Sorkin, *The Transformation of German Jewry, 1780–1840* (New York: Oxford University Press, 1987), esp. 5–7 and 112–13. Sorkin's thesis was already developed by Henry Wassermann, "Jews, Bürgertum and Bürgerliche Gesellschaft in a Liberal Era in Germany, 1840–1880" (PhD diss., Hebrew University, 1984) (according to the English abstract), and Jacob Katz, *Out of the Ghetto: The Social Background of Jewish Emancipation, 1770–1870* (Cambridge, Mass.: Harvard University Press, 1973; repr., Syracuse, N.Y.: Syracuse University Press, 1998), 54. Sorkin's concept is developed further by Rainer Liedtke, *Jewish Welfare in Hamburg and Manchester, c. 1850–1914* (Oxford: Oxford University Press, 1998), and Andreas Reinke, *Judentum und Wohlfahrtspflege in Deutschland: Das jüdische Krankenhaus in Breslau, 1744–1944* (Hanover: Hahnsche Buchhandlung, 1999). An important critique of Sorkin may be found in Jacob Borut, "'Verjudung des Judentums': Was There a Zionist Subculture in Weimar Germany?" in *In Search of Jewish Community: Jewish Identities in Germany and Austria, 1918–1933*, ed. Michael Brenner and Derek J. Penslar (Bloomington: University of Indiana Press, 1998), 92–114, esp. 93–96.

18. What is new here is the concept's precise formulation as situational ethnicity, not the application of the concept of ethnicity to German Jews in general. See Shulamit Volkov, "Die Erfindung einer Tradition: Zur Entstehung des modernen Judentums in Deutschland," *Historische Zeitschrift* 253 (1991): 603–28; Marion A. Kaplan, *The Making of the Jewish Middle Class: Women, Family, and Identity in Imperial Germany* (New York: Oxford University Press, 1991), esp. vi and 64; as well as Steven M. Lowenstein, "Jewish Residential Concentration in Post-Emancipation Germany," in his *The Mechanics of Change: Essays in the Social History of German Jewry* (Atlanta: Scholars Press, 1992), 153–82, esp. 174–75.

19. Thus I follow those who emphasize the constructed nature of ethnicity. The classic argument in this regard is developed by Fredrick Barth in his introduction to *Ethnic Groups and Boundaries: The Social Organization of Cultural Difference*, ed. Barth (Bergen: Universitets Forlaget, 1969; repr., Long Grove, Ill.: Waveland Press, 1998), 9–38; important are Werner Sollors, *Beyond Ethnicity: Consent and Descent in American Culture* (New York: Oxford University Press, 1986); Sollors, ed., *The Invention of Ethnicity* (New York: Oxford University Press, 1989), ix–x; and Sollors, "Konstruktionsversuche nationaler und ethnischer Identität in der amerikanischen Literatur," in *Nationale und kulturelle Identität: Studien zur Entwicklung des kollektiven Bewußtseins in der Neuzeit*, ed. Bernhard Giesen (Frankfurt a. M.: Suhrkamp, 1991), 537–69; Marion Berghahn, *German-Jewish Refugees in England: The Ambiguities of Assimilation* (London: Macmillan, 1984), 9–20. For introductions to ethnicity studies, see Thomas Hylland Eriksen, *Ethnicity and Nationalism: Anthropological Perspectives*, 2nd ed. (Ann Arbor: University of Michigan Press, 2002), and Marcus Banks, *Ethnicity: Anthropological Constructions* (London: Routledge, 1996).

20. See Jonathan Y. Okamura, "Situational Ethnicity," *Ethnic and Racial Studies* 4 (1981): 452–65; Barth already argued along similar lines in his introduction, 16. Stimulating are also John Higham's concept of pluralistic integration and Peter Medding's reflections on segmented identity; see Higham, *Send These to Me*, 233–48, and Peter Y. Medding, "Jewish Identity in Conversionary and Mixed Marriages," *American Jewish Yearbook* 92 (1992): 3–76, here 16–19. An important empirical application of the concept of segmented identity is provided by Kerstin Meiring in *Die christlich-jüdische Mischehe in Deutschland, 1840–1933* (Hamburg: Dölling & Galitz, 1998).

21. Here the perception of oneself and that of others become so intermingled that they are virtually inseparable. This must be taken into consideration regarding the question of who is "Jewish." Jens Malte Fischer's definition is apt: "A Jew is whoever considers himself to be one, identifies with Jewry, or is considered to be one for so long that he considers himself to be a Jew." Jens Malte Fischer, "Gustav Mahler und das 'Judentum in der Musik,'" *Merkur* 51 (1997): 665–80, here 673. To be sure, this definition presupposes detailed biographical investigations. For the sake of economy, within the scope of this study we shall regard someone as "Jewish" if his or her name appears on Jewish community lists, if he or she is a member of a Jewish organization, or if his or her confession was listed as "Jewish" on the Breslau tax, marriage, or high school graduate registers. Stefanie Schüler-Springorum, *Die jüdische Minderheit in Königsberg/Preußen, 1871–1945* (Göttingen: Vandenhoeck & Ruprecht, 1996), 17–18, operates similarly. In general, see Leon Botstein, *Judentum und Modernität: Essays zur Rolle der Juden in der deutschen und österreichischen Kultur, 1848 bis 1938* (Vienna: Böhlau Verlag, 1991), 15–17.

22. "Die Reichen," *Allgemeine Zeitung des Judenthums* 34 (1870): 569–72, here 570 and 572.

23. Moritz Lazarus, *Was heißt national? Ein Vortrag von Prof. Dr. M. Lazarus*, with a foreword by Isid. Levy (Berlin: Philo Verlag, 1925), 46; "Noch eine Stimme über Lazarus' Broschüre," *Israelitische Wochenschrift* 18 (1887): 99; Max Joseph, "Stammesgemeinschaft," in *Jüdisches Lexikon*, vol. 4, pt. 2 (Berlin: Jüdischer Verlag, 1930), 628–29. In general, see George L. Mosse, *German Jews beyond Judaism* (Bloomington: University of Indiana Press; Cincinnati: Hebrew Union College Press, 1985), 107–8; Steven E. Aschheim, *Brothers and Strangers: The East European Jew in German and German-Jewish Consciousness, 1800–1923* (Madison: University of Wisconsin Press, 1982), 97; Hacohen, "Dilemmas of Cosmopolitanism," 117 and 119.

24. Friedrich Christoph Dahlmann, cited in Christof Dipper, "Der Freiheitsbegriff im 19. Jahrhundert," in *Geschichtliche Grundbegriffe: Historisches Lexikon zur politisch-sozialen Sprache in Deutschland*, ed. Otto Brunner, Werner Conze, and Reinhart Koselleck, vol. 2 (Stuttgart: Klett-Cotta, 1975), 506; Jacob Grimm, *Deutsche Grammatik*, vol. 1 (Göttingen: Dieterich, 1819), xiv; further examples of the use of this concept from the period of early nationalism may be found in

Dieter Grimm, "Verfassung," in *Geschichtliche Grundbegriffe*, vol. 6 (Stuttgart: Klett-Cotta, 1990), 878; and Reinhart Koselleck, "Volk, Nation, Nationalismus, Masse," in *Geschichtliche Grundbegriffe*, vol. 8 (Stuttgart: Klett-Cotta, 1997), 386. In general, see the article "Stamm" in the *Deutsches Wörterbuch von Jacob Grimm und Wilhelm Grimm*, vol. 10, division 2, pt. 1 (Leipzig: S. Hirzel, 1919), 634–44, esp. sec. 2, 3d, cols. 642–43, as well as the compound nouns from "Stammesart" to "Stammesgenossenschaft," 655–56. See also my "'Germans of the Jewish *Stamm*': Visions of Community between Nationalism and Particularism, 1850 to 1933," in *German History from the Margins, 1800 to the Present*, ed. Neil Gregor, Mark Roseman, and Nils Roemer (Bloomington: Indiana University Press, 2006), 27–48.

25. Theodor Mommsen, "Auch ein Wort über unser Judenthum," in *Der Berliner Antisemitismusstreit*, ed. Walter Boehlich (Frankfurt a. M.: Insel, 1965), 212.

26. Gerhard Anschütz, *Die Verfassung des Deutschen Reichs vom 11. August 1919*, 14th ed. (Berlin: Hermann Gentner Verlag, 1932), xii; see also 2. Drawing a contrast with the individual states, which seem to Anschütz to be "chance formations of dynastic statecraft," he defines "tribes" in this most important of contemporary commentaries on the Weimar Constitution as "these great natural divisions of the German people" (32). See also Wilhelm Heile, *Stammesfreiheit im Einheitsstaat* (Berlin: Fortschritt, 1919), and Willibalt Apelt, *Geschichte der Weimarer Verfassung* (Munich: Biederstein, 1946), 127–31. Due to the democratic and antidynastic orientation of the preamble, it was the target of conservative criticism; see, e.g., Fritz Hartung, "Stammesbewußtsein," in *Politisches Handwörterbuch*, ed. Paul Herre, vol. 2 (Leipzig: Koehler, 1923), 723, and Axel Freiherr von Freytag-Loringhoven, *Die Weimarer Verfassung in Lehre und Wirklichkeit* (Munich: Lehmann, 1924), 50–55.

27. Particularly stimulating in this connection are Russell A. Kazal, "Revisiting Assimilation: The Rise, Fall, and Reappraisal of a Concept in American Ethnic History," *American Historical Review* 100 (1995): 437–71, and Elliot R. Barkan, "Race, Religion, and Nationality in American Society: A Model of Ethnicity from Contact to Assimilation," *Journal of American Ethnic History* 14 (1995): 38–75. For the context of the American discussion, see Philip Gleason, *Speaking of Diversity: Language and Ethnicity in Twentieth-Century America* (Baltimore: Johns Hopkins University Press, 1992). Concerning specifically (German-) Jewish history, see esp. Steven E. Aschheim, "German History and German Jewry: Boundaries, Junctions, and Interdependence," *Year Book of the Leo Baeck Institute* 43 (1998): 315–22; Berghahn, *German-Jewish Refugees in England*, 9–20; Marion A. Kaplan, "Freizeit—Arbeit: Geschlechterräume im deutsch-jüdischen Bürgertum, 1870–1914," in *Bürgerinnen und Bürger: Geschlechterverhältnisse im 19. Jahrhundert*, ed. Ute Frevert (Göttingen: Vandenhoeck & Ruprecht, 1988), 157–74; Jonathan Frankel, "Assimilation and the Jews in Nineteenth-Century Europe," in *Assimilation and Community: The Jews in Nineteenth-Century Europe*, ed. Jonathan Frankel and Steven J. Zipperstein (Cambridge: Cambridge University Press,

1992), 1–37; David Sorkin, "Emancipation and Assimilation: Two Concepts and Their Application to German-Jewish History," *Year Book of the Leo Baeck Institute* 35 (1990): 17–34; Till van Rahden, "Treason, Fate, or Blessing? Concepts of Assimilation in the Historiography of German-Speaking Jewry since the 1950s," in *Preserving the Legacy of German Jewry: A History of the Leo Baeck Institute, 1955–2005,* ed. Christhard Hoffmann (Tübingen: J. C. B. Mohr, 2005), 349–73; Shulamit Volkov, "Jüdische Assimilation und Eigenart im Kaiserreich," in her *Jüdisches Leben und Antisemitismus im 19. und 20. Jahrhundert* (Munich: C. H. Beck, 1990), 131–45, as well as her "Minderheiten und der Nationalstaat," 72.

28. Elisabeth Bronfen and Benjamin Marius, "Hybride Kulturen: Einleitung zur anglo-amerikanischen Multikulturalismusdebatte," in *Hybride Kulturen: Beiträge zur anglo-amerikanischen Multikulturalismusdebatte,* ed. Elisabeth Bronfen, Therese Steffen, and Benjamin Marius (Tübingen: Stauffenburg, 1997), 1–29, here 19; the authors reject the concept of assimilation because it tends "to overlook the complex processes of interaction and reciprocity within cultural evolution, reducing them to an asymmetric, teleological process between two ahistorical entities" (19).

29. Wilhelm E. Mühlmann, "Assimilation," in *Wörterbuch der Soziologie,* ed. Wilhelm Bernsdorf, vol. 1 (Frankfurt a. M.: Fischer, 1972), 57–58; Volkov was critical of this position already in "Jüdische Assimilation und Eigenart im Kaiserreich," 132–33.

30. The most influential study in this connection is Milton Myron Gordon's *Assimilation in American Life: The Role of Race, Religion, and National Origins* (New York: Oxford University Press, 1964). Concerning its reception in German-Jewish history, see Maurer, *Die Entwicklung der jüdischen Minderheit,* 171–75.

31. Manfred Hettling and Stefan-Ludwig Hoffmann, "Der bürgerliche Wertehimmel: Zum Problem individueller Lebensführung im 19. Jahrhundert," *Geschichte und Gesellschaft* 23 (1997): 333–59. Even if outlines of a "bourgeois firmament of values" existed before Jews represented an important part of the German middle class, one should not underestimate the significance of the processes of revaluation and negotiation. That holds especially when one grasps identities as both particular and situational, on the one hand, and open and changeable, on the other; see, e.g., Stuart Hall, "Cultural Identity and the Diaspora," in *Identity, Community and Cultural Difference,* ed. Jonathan Rutherford (London: Lawrence & Wishart, 1990), 222–37, here 222; regarding German-Jewish history specifically, see Marline S. Otte, *Jewish Identities in German Popular Entertainment, 1890–1933* (Cambridge: Cambridge University Press, 2006).

32. Gustav Krojanker, ed., *Juden in der deutschen Literatur: Essays über zeitgenössische Schriftsteller* (Berlin: Welt-Verlag, 1922), 10, cited in Gerd Mattenklott, "Juden in der deutschsprachigen Zeitschriftenliteratur im ersten Drittel des 20. Jahrhunderts," in *Juden als Träger bürgerlicher Kultur in Deutschland,* ed. Julius H. Schoeps (Stuttgart: Burg-Verlag, 1989), 149–66, here 151.

33. Here I engage the thinking of Shulamit Volkov, Steven Aschheim, and others: Volkov, "Reflections on German-Jewish History: A Dead End or a New Beginning," *Year Book of the Leo Baeck Institute* 41 (1996): 309–20, here 315–20; Aschheim, "German History and German Jewry"; John A. S. Grenville, "Die Geschichtsschreibung der Bundesrepublik über die deutschen Juden," in *Studien zur jüdischen Geschichte und Soziologie. Festschrift Julius Carlebach* (Heidelberg: Carl Winter Universitätsverlag, 1992), 195–205; Moshe Zimmermann, "Jewish History and Historiography: A Challenge to Contemporary German Historiography," *Year Book of the Leo Baeck Institute* 35 (1990): 35–54; Shulamit S. Magnus, *Jewish Emancipation in a German City: Cologne, 1798–1871* (Stanford: Stanford University Press, 1997), 7–9, esp. 7: "Events in Jewish and non-Jewish history appear . . . like trains on parallel tracks, casting shadows on each other in passing but having no fundamental relationship." The question of the integration of Jewish history into general history is also being debated for other national histories: Robert Uri Kaufmann, "Wie man zum 'Fremden' erklärt wird: Fremd- und Selbstbildnis der Juden in der neueren Schweizer Historiographie," *Traverse* 3 (1996): 120–28; Aram Mattioli, "Juden und Judenfeindschaft in der schweizerischen Historiographie—Eine Replik auf Robert Uri Kaufmann," *Traverse* 4 (1997): 155–63; Sylvie Anne Goldberg, "On the Margins of French Historiography," *Shofar: An Interdisciplinary Journal of Jewish Studies* 14 (1996): 47–62. Pioneering in this connection are David Feldman, *Englishmen and Jews: Social Relations and Political Culture, 1840–1914* (New Haven, Conn.: Yale University Press, 1994), 7–15, and David A. Hollinger, *Science, Jews, and Secular Culture: Studies in Mid-Twentieth-Century American Intellectual History* (Princeton, N.J.: Princeton University Press, 1996), 10–14. David Katz understands his synthesis in *The Jews in the History of England, 1485–1850* (Oxford: Clarendon Press, 1994) as an attempt to follow "the Jewish thread through English life between the Tudors and the beginning of mass immigration in the nineteenth century" (ix).

34. This escapes the otherwise interesting polemics of Michael Geyer and Konrad Jarausch, who claim that "German 'Gesellschaftsgeschichte' has become every bit as univocal and as national" as older interpretations of German history; Geyer and Jarausch, "Future of the German Past," 236. An early critique, which claims that German historiography has been fixated to this day on the nation-state, may be found in James J. Sheehan, "What Is German History? Reflections on the Role of the 'Nation' in German History and Historiography," *Journal of Modern History* 53 (1981): 1–23, here 4 and 22; by contrast, Sheehan maintains that German history is also the history of experiences that "do not fit within the boundaries of the nation, the history of cultural richness and regional diversity, of economic activities and social institutions without national configuration, of relationships which stretch across legally-defined frontiers" (22). See also Margaret Lavinia Anderson, *Windthorst: A Political Biography* (Oxford: Clarendon Press, 1981), 5–7. The fact that the long shadow of the ideal of

homogeneity is a European-wide problem and not just specific to German historiography is shown by Gérard Noiriel, *The French Melting Pot: Immigration, Citizenship, and National Identity*, trans. Geoffroy de Laforcade (Minneapolis: University of Minnesota Press, 1996), 1–44, and Feldman, *Englishmen and Jews*, 10–14.

35. Chisthard Hoffmann, "The German-Jewish Encounter and German Historical Culture," trans. Louise Willmot, *Year Book of the Leo Baeck Institute* 41 (1996): 277–90, here 285. I do not share Hoffmann's optimism that things have changed in the meantime but instead find Shulamit Volkov's assessment of the situation on target: "the overall picture remains quite bleak" ("Reflections on German-Jewish History," 318).

36. To give but two examples: Wolfgang Schieder, "Sozialgeschichte der Religion im 19. Jahrhundert," in *Religion und Gesellschaft im 19. Jahrhundert*, ed. Wolfgang Schieder (Stuttgart: Klett-Cotta, 1993), 11–28, here 14–15; and Dieter Langewiesche, "Liberalismus und Region," in *Liberalismus und Region: Zur Geschichte des deutschen Liberalismus im 19. Jahrhundert*, ed. Dieter Langewiesche and Lothar Gall (Munich: Oldenbourg, 1995), 1–18, here 12–14. Thus far, in neither the Bielefeld nor the Frankfurt "Bürgertumsprojekt" has there been anything more than passing interest in the Jewish middle class; typical of the Bielefeld project is the monograph series edited by Wolfgang Mager and others titled Bürgertum: Beiträge zur europäischen Gesellschaftsgeschichte; typical of the Frankfurt project is Jürgen Hein and Andreas Schultz, eds., *Bürgerkultur im 19. Jahrhundert: Bildung, Kunst und Lebenswelt* (Munich: C. H. Beck, 1996). Surveys of more recent research may be found in Friedrich Lenger, "Bürgertum, Stadt und Gemeinde zwischen Frühneuzeit und Moderne," *Neue Politische Literatur* 40 (1995): 14–29, and Jonathan Sperber, "*Bürger, Bürgertum, Bürgerliche Gesellschaft: Studies of the German (Upper) Middle Class and Its Sociocultural World*," *Journal of Modern History* 69 (1997): 271–97. The fact that the marginalization of Jewish history is not exclusively a German problem becomes evident from a survey of recent Anglo-American essay collections in which Jews find practically no mention: Eley, *Society, Culture, and the State in Germany;* Roger Chickering, *Imperial Germany: A Historiographical Companion* (Westport, Conn.: Greenwood Press, 1996); and David Blackbourn, "The German Bourgeoisie," in *The German Bourgeoisie: Essays on the Social History of the German Middle Class from the Late Eighteenth to the Early Twentieth Century*, ed. David Blackbourn and Richard J. Evans (London: Routledge, 1991), 1–45, who mentions Jews only in the context of the growing anti-Semitism of the Weimar Republic (see 27 and 29).

37. In each of the three examples, there is a volume—by Hermann Graml, *Reichskristallnach: Antisemitismus und Judenverfolgung im Dritten Reich* (Munich: Deutscher Taschenbuch Verlag, 1988), and by Helmut Berding, *Moderner Antisemitismus in Deutschland* (Frankfurt a. M.: Suhrkamp, 1988)—or corresponding sections about German anti-Semitism, yet one searches in vain for references to the history of the German Jews. Wehler's blind spot may derive from his ascribing "membership in ethnic associations" to "anthropological constants," thus

to "nature," with the result that ethnicity as a category drops out of the history of "socictics" altogether. See Hans-Ulrich Wehler, *Deutsche Gesellschaftsgeschichte*, vol. 3, *1849–1914: Von der "Deutschen Doppelrevolution" bis zum Beginn des Ersten Weltkrieges* (Munich: C. H. Beck, 1995), 700.

38. Thomas Nipperdey, *Deutsche Geschichte, 1800–1866* (1983; 5th ed., Munich: C. H. Beck, 1991), *Deutsche Geschichte, 1866–1918*, vol. 1, *Arbeitswelt und Bürgergeist* (Munich: C. H. Beck, 1990), and vol. 2, *Machtstaat vor der Demokratie* (Munich: C. H. Beck, 1992); Wolfram Siemann, *Vom Staatenbund zum National-staat: Deutschland, 1806–1871* (Munich: C. H. Beck, 1994). In Nipperdey there are at least a few remarks on the position of Jews among the educated classes (*Deutsche Geschichte, 1866–1918*, 1:388). The "re-ghettoization" of Jewish history is reflected also institutionally. In the meantime, there are five independent research institutes for Jewish history in Germany (in Duisburg, Hamburg, Leipzig, Potsdam, and Trier), but only at the Ludwig-Maximilians-Universität in Munich is there a professorship for Jewish history in the department of history.

39. Peter Gay, *Freud, Jews and Other Germans: Masters and Victims in Modernist Culture* (New York: Oxford University Press, 1978), 11. Regarding the relationship between German-Jewish and general German history, Steven Aschheim has argued that the important aspects of general German history can be grasped only "dynamically as negotiated constructions in which . . . the role of the Jews . . . is conceived . . . as well-nigh *co-constitutive*" ("German History and German Jewry," 316–17).

40. To give but a few examples: Hans-Ulrich Wehler, *Das deutsche Kaiserreich, 1871–1918* (Göttingen: Vandenhoeck & Ruprecht, 1973), and *Gesellschaftsge-schichte*, vol. 3, esp. 1250–95; Geoff Eley and David Blackbourn, *The Pecularities of German History: Bourgeois Society and Politics in 19th-Century Germany* (Oxford: Oxford University Press, 1984); Nipperdey, *Deutsche Geschichte, 1800–1866*, and *Deutsche Geschichte, 1866–1918*, vols. 1 and 2; Wolfgang J. Mommsen, *Bürgerstolz und Weltmachtstreben: Deutschland unter Wilhelm II, 1890–1918* (Berlin: Propyläen, 1995), and *Das Ringen um den nationalen Staat: Die Gründung und der innere Ausbau des Deutschen Reiches unter Otto von Bismarck, 1850–1890* (Berlin: Propyläen, 1993); James Retallack, *Germany in the Age of Kaiser Wilhelm II* (London: Macmillan, 1996). However, in the debate on the "special path" (*Sonderweg*) of German history, neither the history of the German Jews nor (and that is even more remarkable) anti-Semitism has played a role for either the opponents or the advocates of the thesis.

41. Concerning the contemporary critique of the liberal ideal of homogeneity by Jewish intellectuals, see, e.g., Tal, *Christians and Jews in Germany*, 107–9. In this connection, Ulrich Bielefeld has spoken aptly of national "fantasies of purity"; see his "Bürger—Nation—Staat: Probleme einer Dreierbeziehung," in *Staats-Bürger: Deutschland und Frankreich im historischen Vergleich*, ed. Rogers Brubaker (Hamburg: Junius, 1994), 7–18, here 18. See also Christian Geulen, *Wahl-verwandte: Rassendiskurs und Nationalismus im späten 19. Jahrhundert* (Hamburg:

Hamburger Edition, 2004). A special path of German history is not to be found there: "Advocates of minority rights make stringent demands upon those they defend," Jacques Kornberg has stressed. "The relationship between the persecuted and their defenders is often a minefield of conflicting agendas." See Jacques Kornberg, "Vienna, the 1890s: Jews in the Eyes of Their Defenders (The Verein zur Abwehr des Antisemitismus)," *Central European History* 28 (1995): 153–74.

42. Hans Boldt, "Die preußische Verfassung vom 31. Januar 1850: Probleme ihrer Interpretation," in *Preußen im Rückblick*, ed. Hans-Jürgen Puhle and Hans-Ulrich Wehler, Geschichte und Gesellschaft Sonderheft 6 (Göttingen: Vandenhoeck & Ruprecht, 1980), 224–46, here 229. The provisions of the Prussian constitution continued to be decisive even after 1870–71 since neither the constitution of the North German Alliance nor the imperial constitution contained a catalog of human rights; see Ernst Rudolf Huber, ed., *Dokumente zur Deutschen Verfassungsgeschichte*, vol. 2, *Deutsche Verfassungsdokumente, 1851–1900*, 3rd ed. (Stuttgart: Kohlhammer, 1986), 272–86 and 384–401. In the negotiations over the constitution of the North German Alliance, Bismarck had already rejected the Progress Party's demand to protect basic rights under federal law since that demand was incompatible with the federal character of the alliance; see Ernst Rudolf Huber, ed., *Deutsche Verfassungsgeschichte seit 1789*, 3rd ed., vol. 3, *Bismarck und das Reich* (Stuttgart: Kohlhammer, 1988), 655–56; for general background, see Dieter Grimm, *Deutsche Verfassungsgeschichte, 1776–1866* (Frankfurt a. M.: Suhrkamp, 1988), 216–17, and Wehler, *Deutsche Gesellschaftsgeschichte*, 3:201–2 and 302–4, as well as 1343–44 and 1360–61.

43. Ernst Rudolf Huber, ed., *Dokumente zur Deutschen Verfassungsgeschichte*, 3rd ed., vol. 1, *Deutsche Verfassungsdokumente, 1803–1850* (Stuttgart: Kohlhammer, 1978), 501–2; on Article 14, see also Huber, *Deutsche Verfassungsgeschichte seit 1789*, 3:115–16.

44. Huber, *Deutsche Verfassungsgeschichte seit 1789*, 3:102–3, quotation from 102. "The clause," commented the constitutional law scholar Gerhard Anschütz in 1912 on Article 14, clause 1, "is a maxim not for him who makes the law but for him who applies it; equality before the law is in truth equality before the judge and the administration; art. 4, clause 1 prohibits the judge, but not the lawmaker, from making distinctions"; Anschütz, *Die Verfassung des Deutschen Reichs*, 109, cited in Huber, *Deutsche Verfassungsgeschichte seit 1789*, 3:102.

45. On the significance of the idea of the "Christian state" for the status of the Jews, see Peter Pulzer, *Jews and the German State: The Political History of a Minority, 1848–1933* (Oxford: Blackwell, 1992). It was especially in the concept of "parity" that competing visions of the relationship between equality and difference were expressed; see esp. chapter 4, section 3 of this volume.

46. Peter Fritzsche, *Reading Berlin 1900*, 2nd ed. (Cambridge, Mass.: Harvard University Press, 1998), esp. 132–33; Schüler-Springorum, *Die jüdische Minderheit;*

and Jan Palmowski, *Urban Liberalism in Imperial Germany: Frankfurt am Main, 1866–1914* (Oxford: Oxford University Press, 1999).

47. Here I have gained important ideas from David Feldman, "Jews and the State in Britain," in *Two Nations: British and German Jews in Comparative Perspective,* ed. Michael Brenner, Rainer Liedtke, and David Rechter (Tübingen: Mohr Siebeck, 1999), 141–61.

48. A number of surveys provide helpful introductions to the discussion: Michael Brenner, Stefi Jersch-Wenzel, and Michael A. Myer, *Deutsch-jüdische Geschichte in der Neuzeit,* ed. Michael A. Meyer, vol. 2, *Emanzipation und Akkulturation, 1780–1871* (Munich: C. H. Beck, 1996); Steven M. Lowenstein, Paul Mendes-Flohr, Peter Pulzer, and Monika Richarz, *Deutsch-jüdische Geschichte in der Neuzeit,* ed. Michael A. Meyer, vol. 3, *Umstrittene Integration, 1871–1918* (Munich: C. H. Beck, 1997); Shulamit Volkov, *Die Juden in Deutschland, 1780–1914* (Munich: Oldenbourg, 1994). Among the more recent monographs, see esp. Kaplan, *Making of the Jewish Middle Class;* Steven M. Lowenstein, *The Berlin Jewish Community: Enlightenment, Family and Crisis, 1770–1830* (Oxford: Oxford University Press, 1994); and Sorkin, *Transformation of German Jewry.* New publications are documented annually in the bibliography of the *Year Book of the Leo Baeck Institute;* for the literature from the 1980s, see Maurer, *Die Entwicklung der jüdischen Minderheit.*

49. In general, see Todd M. Endelman, "The Legitimization of the Diaspora Experience in Recent Jewish Historiography," *Modern Judaism* 11 (1991): 195–209; Paula E. Hyman, "The Ideological Transformation of Modern Jewish Historiography," in *The State of Jewish Studies,* ed. Shaye J. D. Cohen and Edward L. Greenstein (Detroit: Wayne State University Press, 1990), 143–57; and Frankel, "Assimilation and the Jews."

50. Jacob Katz, "Methodischer Exkurs," in *Vom Vorurteil bis zur Vernichtung: Der Antisemitismus, 1700–1933* (Munich: C. H. Beck, 1989), 251–52 (Katz wrote this chapter on methodology specifically for the German edition and it is not included in the original English edition published as *From Prejudice to Destruction: Anti-Semitism, 1700–1933* [Cambridge, Mass.: Harvard University Press, 1980]); Paula Hyman, "Review of Pierre Birnbaum, *The Jews of the Republic: A Political History of State Jews in France from Gambetta to Vichy,*" *Journal of Modern History* 70 (1998): 198–99; Kaplan, *Making of the Jewish Middle Class,* ix, 13, and esp. 240; Levenson, "Philosemitic Discourse in Imperial Germany," 49; Maurer, *Die Entwicklung der jüdischen Minderheit,* 179; Volkov, *Die Juden in Deutschland,* 120–21; Magnus, *Jewish Emancipation in a German City,* 8–9; Tal, *Christians and Jews in Germany,* 15. See also James J. Sheehan, "Different, Ignoble and Alien," *Times Literary Supplement,* July 31, 1992, 8: To understand the history of relations between Jews and other Germans, "we must venture into that difficult terrain where political action, social life and cultural values intersect. Here, in the everyday world, we will find the origins of the questions they posed to each other." Interesting

approaches to a history of relations between Jews and other Germans are of-
fered by Ulrich Baumann, *Zerstörte Nachbarschaften: Christen und Juden in badischen
Landgemeinden, 1862–1940* (Hamburg: Dölling & Galitz, 2000); Helmut Walser
Smith, "Religion and Conflict: Protestants, Catholics, and Anti-Semitism in
the State of Baden in the Era of Wilhelm II," *Central European History* 27 (1994):
282–314, and "Alltag und politischer Antisemitismus in Baden 1890–1900,"
Zeitschrift für die Geschichte des Oberrheins 141 (1993): 280–303; Fritz Stern, *Gold and
Iron: Bismarck, Bleichröder and the Building of the German Empire* (New York: Knopf,
1977); and W. Mosse, *German-Jewish Economic Élite* (though both treat only the
interactions among elites); as well as Jacob Toury, *Soziale und politische Geschichte
der Juden in Deutschland, 1847–1871: Zwischen Revolution, Reaktion und Emanzipation*
(Düsseldorf: Droste, 1977), 119–38; and Werner Jochmann, "Akademische
Führungsschichten und Judenfeindschaft in Deutschland, 1866–1918," in his
Gesellschaftskrise und Judenfeindschaft in Deutschland, 1870–1945 (Hamburg: Christians, 1988), 13–29 (the latter two studies, however, focus primarily on exclusion
and leave the local context almost completely unilluminated).

    51. See esp. Volkov, *Jüdisches Leben und Antisemitismus,* 13–75; Berding, *Mo-
derner Antisemitismus in Deutschland;* Rürup, *Emanzipation und Antisemitismus;* J. Katz,
From Prejudice to Destruction; Norbert Kampe, *Studenten und "Judenfrage" im Kaiser-
reich: Die Entstehung einer akademischen Trägerschicht des Antisemitismus* (Göttingen:
Vandenhoeck & Ruprecht, 1988); Richard S. Levy, *The Downfall of the Anti-
Semitic Political Parties in Imperial Germany* (New Haven, Conn.: Yale University
Press, 1975); Peter Pulzer, *The Rise of Political Anti-Semitism in Germany and Austria*
(1964; 2nd rev. ed., Cambridge, Mass.: Harvard University Press, 1988). Among
the numerous more recent publications, see esp. Paul Lawrence Rose, *German
Question/Jewish Question* (Princeton, N.J.: Princeton University Press, 1992);
James F. Harris, *The People Speak! Anti-Semitism and Emancipation in Nineteenth-
Century Bavaria* (Ann Arbor: University of Michigan Press, 1994); Anthony
Kauders, *German Politics and the Jews: Düsseldorf and Nuremberg, 1910–1933* (Oxford:
Oxford University Press, 1996); Olaf R. Blaschke, *Katholizismus und Antisemitismus im Deutschen Kaiserreich* (Göttingen: Vandenhoeck & Ruprecht, 1997; 2nd ed.,
1998); Wolfgang Altgeld, *Katholizismus, Protestantismus, Judentum: Über religiös
begründete Gegensätze und nationalreligiöse Ideen in der Geschichte des deutschen Nationalismus* (Mainz: Matthias-Grünewald-Verlag, 1992). Generally, see my review essay,
"Ideologie und Gewalt: Neuerscheinungen über den Antisemitismus in der
deutschen Geschichte des 19. und frühen 20. Jahrhunderts," *Neue Politische Literatur* 41 (1996): 11–29. Older surveys of the literature are provided in Dirk Blasius,
"'Judenfrage' und Gesellschaftsgeschichte," *Neue Politische Literatur* 23 (1978): 17–
33; Reinhard Rürup, "Zur Entwicklung der modernen Antisemitismusforschung," in his *Emanzipation und Antisemitismus,* 145–58; Ismar Schorsch, "German Antisemitism in the Light of Post-War Historiography," *Year Book of the Leo
Baeck Institute* 19 (1974): 257–71; Shulamit Volkov, "Antisemitismus als Problem
jüdisch-nationalen Denkens und jüdischer Geschichtsschreibung," in her

Jüdisches Leben und Antisemitismus, 88–110; Steven E. Aschheim, "Between Rationality and Irrationalism: George L. Mosse, the Holocaust, and European Cultural History," *Simon Wiesenthal Center Annual* 5 (1988): 187–202; and Anthony La Vopa, "Jews and Germans: Old Quarrels, New Departures," *Journal of the History of Ideas* 54 (1993): 675–95.

52. Reinhard Rürup, "Jüdische Geschichte in Deutschland," in *Zerbrochene Geschichte: Leben und Selbstverständnis der Juden in Deutschland*, ed. Dirk Blasius and Dan Diner (Frankfurt a. M.: Fischer, 1991), 79–102, here 79.

53. Hermann Cohen, *Deutschtum und Judentum, mit grundlegenden Betrachtungen über Staat und Internationalismus*, 3rd ed. (Gießen: A. Töpelmann, 1916); on Cohen and his role as the pioneer of neo-Kantianism, see Ulrich Sieg, *Aufstieg und Niedergang des Marburger Neukantianismus: Die Geschichte einer philosophischen Schulgemeinschaft* (Würzburg: Königshausen & Neumann, 1994), 395–97.

54. Gershom Scholem, *Judaica*, vol. 2 (Frankfurt a. M.: Suhrkamp, 1970), 11–46; Wolfgang Benz, "The Legend of a German-Jewish Symbiosis," *Year Book of the Leo Baeck Institute* 37 (1992): 95–102; Maurer, *Die Entwicklung der jüdischen Minderheit*, 3–4, 40, 163–64, and 167–71. Scholem's influence is evident also in the contributions to *Year Book of the Leo Baeck Institute* 41 (1996) by Evyatar Friesel ("The German-Jewish Encounter as a Historical Problem: A Reconsideration," 263–76), C. Hoffmann ("German-Jewish Encounter," 277–90), and Moyn ("German Jewry," 291–308). It is hardly helpful to speak, like Peter Gay, of a "love affair" instead of symbiosis; Gay, *Freud, Jews and Other Germans*, x and 114.

55. Thus the present study does not undertake an analysis of other spheres of the relationship between Jews and other Breslauers in which local factors played a negligible role, such as the university or theological controversies. A planned chapter on residential patterns had to be abandoned because a computer error almost completely destroyed the databases I had compiled. Unfortunately, there were too few sources for an analysis of daily contacts in the economic sector.

56. Wolfgang Hardtwig, "Alltagsgeschichte heute: Eine kritische Bilanz," in *Sozialgeschichte, Alltagsgeschichte, Mikro-Historie*, ed. Winfried Schulze (Göttingen: Vandenhoeck & Ruprecht, 1994), 19–32, here 21; the phrase "to look closely" comes from the Italian microhistorian Giovanni Levi, cited in Hans Medick, "Mikro-Historie," in *Sozialgeschichte, Alltagsgeschichte, Mikro-Historie*, 40–53, here 40. In general, see Giovanni Levi, "On Microhistory," in *New Perspectives on Historical Writing*, ed. Peter Burke (Cambridge: Polity Press, 1992), 93–113.

57. The fact that the microhistorical approach by no means neglects macrohistorical questions was stressed in the editorial of *Historische Anthropologie* 1 (1993): 1–4, esp. 2. See David Blackbourn, *Marpingen: Apparitions of the Virgin Mary in a Nineteenth-Century German Village*, 2nd ed. (New York: Vintage, 1995); Martin H. Geyer, *Verkehrte Welt: Revolution, Inflation und Moderne; München, 1914–1924* (Göttingen: Vandenhoeck & Ruprecht, 1998); Richard J. Evans, *Death in Hamburg: Society and Politics in the Cholera Years, 1830–1910* (Oxford: Clarendon

Press, 1987). On the relationship between micro- and macrohistory, see Richard J. Evans, *Rituals of Retribution: Capital Punishment in Germany, 1600–1987*, 2nd ed. (London: Penguin, 1997), ix. For Jewish history, pioneering studies in this connection include Gershon David Hundert, *The Jews in a Polish Private Town: The Case of Opatów in the Eighteenth Century* (Baltimore: Johns Hopkins University Press, 1992); Steven J. Zipperstein, *The Jews of Odessa: A Cultural History, 1794–1881* (Stanford, Calif.: Stanford University Press, 1985); Bill Williams, *The Making of Manchester Jewry, 1740–1875* (Manchester: Manchester University Press, 1976).

58. On this see Dieter Langewiesche, "'Staat' und 'Kommune': Zum Wandel der Staatsaufgaben in Deutschland im 19. Jahrhundert," *Historische Zeitschrift* 248 (1989): 621–35; see also Horst Matzerath, *Urbanisierung in Preußen, 1815–1914* (Stuttgart: Kohlhammer, 1985), 347–72, quotation from 371; Nipperdey, *Deutsche Geschichte, 1866–1918*, 2:154–63. By contrast, Wolfgang Mommsen emphasizes the limits of municipal self-governance that the "old authoritarian state" set for Prussia's communities; see his *Das Ringen um den nationalen Staat*, 394–405, here 400; for a similar account, see Wolfgang Hardtwig, "Großstadt und Bürgerlichkeit in der politischen Ordnung des Kaiserreichs," in *Stadt und Bürgertum im 19. Jahrhundert*, ed. Lothar Gall (Munich: C. H. Beck, 1990), 19–64, here 57–58. On the conflict between municipal and state power, see Hermann Beckstein, *Städtische Interessenpolitik: Organisation und Politik der Städtetage in Bayern, Preußen und dem Deutschen Reich, 1896–1923* (Düsseldorf: Droste Verlag, 1991); concerning Jewish history in particular, see Magnus, *Jewish Emancipation in a German City*, 5–6.

59. On the history of municipal and regional anti-Semitism in Germany, see, e.g., Inge Schlotzhauer, *Ideologie und Organisation des politischen Antisemitismus in Frankfurt am Main, 1880–1914* (Frankfurt a. M.: W. Kramer, 1989); David Peal, "Anti-Semitism and Rural Transformation in Kurhessen: The Rise and Fall of the Böckel Movement" (PhD diss., Columbia University, 1985); Albert Lichtblau, *Antisemitismus und soziale Spannung in Berlin und Wien, 1867–1914* (Berlin: Metropol, 1994); Kauders, *German Politics and the Jews;* Christhard Hoffmann, "Politische Kultur und Gewalt gegen Minderheiten: Die antisemitischen Ausschreitungen in Pommern und Westpreußen, 1881," *Jahrbuch für Antisemitismusforschung* 3 (1994): 93–120; James Retallack, "Conservatives and Antisemites in Baden and Saxony," *German History* 17 (1999): 507–26; Daniela Kasischke-Wurm, *Antisemitismus im Spiegel der Hamburger Presse während des Kaiserreichs, 1884–1914* (Hamburg: LIT, 1997). None of these studies can match John W. Boyer's monumental, two-volume history of anti-Semitism in Vienna: *Political Radicalism in Late Imperial Vienna: Origins of the Christian Social Movement, 1848–1897* (Chicago: University of Chicago Press, 1981) and *Culture and Political Crisis in Vienna: Christian Socialism in Power, 1897–1918* (Chicago: University of Chicago Press, 1995); comparable studies on the history of anti-Semitism in German metropolises are a desideratum. Publications on the history of large Jewish communities include Schüler-Springorum, *Die jüdische Minderheit;* Magnus, *Jewish Emancipation*

in a German City; Reinhard Rürup, ed., *Jüdische Geschichte in Berlin: Essays und Studien* (Berlin: Edition Hentrich, 1995); Andrea Hopp, *Jüdisches Bürgertum in Frankfurt am Main im 19. Jahrhundert* (Stuttgart: Franz Steiner, 1997). On the deficits of many local studies, see Monika Richarz, "Luftaufnahme—oder die Schwierigkeiten der Heimatforscher mit der jüdischen Geschichte," *Babylon* 8 (1991): 27–33.

60. Between 1861 and 1910 alone, the population quadrupled from roughly 120,000 to 500,000 residents. See Gerd Hohorst, Jürgen Kocka, and Gerhard A. Ritter, *Sozialgeschichtliches Arbeitsbuch: Materialien zur Statistik des Kaiserreichs, 1870–1914* (Munich: C. H. Beck, 1980), 45; and *Breslauer Statistik*, vol. 33, pt. 1 (Breslau: Morgenstern, 1914), 65 and 89–90.

61. Concerning Breslau in general, see Leszek Ziątkowski, "Rozwój liczebny Ludności żydówskiej we Wrocławiu w latach, 1742–1914," *Sobótka* 46 (1991): 169–89, as well as *Breslauer Statistik,* vol. 33, pt. 1, 89–90.

62. Taking as its example the largest Jewish association in Breslau, the "Chewra Kadischa," an exemplary study of community life in the city is Reinke's *Judentum und Wohlfahrtspflege in Deutschland.* On Jewish students in Breslau, see the overviews in Kampe, *Studenten und "Judenfrage" im Kaiserreich,* 83 and 85. On Jewish student organizations in Breslau, see Lisa F. Swartout, "Dueling Identities: Protestant, Catholic, and Jewish Students at German Universities, 1890–1914" (PhD diss., University of California at Berkeley, 2002), and her "Mut, Mensur und Männlichkeit: Die Viadrina, eine jüdische schlagende Verbindung," in *In Breslau zuhause? Juden in einer mitteleuropäischen Metropole der Neuzeit,* ed. Manfred Hettling, Andreas Reinke, and Norbert Conrads (Hamburg: Dölling und Galitz, 2003), 148–66.

63. Thus, in 1880 30% of all Breslau Jews came from Silesia (20% of whom came from Upper Silesia) and just under 20% from the province of Posen; the lion's share, over 40%, were from Breslau itself and only about 5% came from Russia or Austro-Hungary. See *Breslauer Statistik,* vol. 7 (Breslau: Morgenstern, 1881), 124; and Bernhard Breslauer, *Die Abwanderung der Juden aus der Provinz Posen* (Berlin: Berthold Levy, 1909).

64. The Breslau Jews found themselves in what was for the German region a unique situation. Only Frankfurt was roughly comparable. The Catholic portion of the population in Frankfurt, however, was considerably less than 30%. See *Breslauer Statistik,* vol. 9 (Breslau: Morgenstern, 1885), 139, and Heinrich Silbergleit, *Die Bevölkerungs- und Berufsverhältnisse der Juden im deutschen Reich* (Berlin: Akademie-Verlag, 1930), 56–67.

65. Manfred Hettling, "Von der Hochburg zur Wagenburg: Liberalismus in Breslau von den 1860er Jahren bis 1918," in *Liberalismus und Region,* ed. Langewiesche and Gall, 253–76; Thomas Kühne, *Handbuch der Wahlen zum Preußischen Abgeordnetenhaus, 1867–1918* (Düsseldorf: Droste Verlag, 1994); Adam Galos and Kazimierza Popiołka, eds., *Studia e materiały z dziejów slaska,* vol. 7 (Breslau: Zaklad Narodowy im. Ossolinskich, 1966); Theodor Müller, *Die Geschichte der*

Breslauer Sozialdemokratie, vol. 2 (Breslau: Sozialdemokratischer Verein, 1925), 400–403.

66. Hans-Dieter Laux, "Dimensionen und Determinanten der Bevölkerungsentwicklung preußischer Städte in der Periode der Hochindustrialisierung," in *Die Städte Mitteleuropas im 20. Jahrhundert,* ed. Wilhelm Rausch (Linz: Österreichischer Arbeitskreis für Stadtgeschichtsforschung, 1984), 87–112, esp. 90–91; see also Albert Holz, "Commerzielles Verhalten von Breslau," *Jahresbericht der Schlesischen Gesellschaft für vaterländische Cultur* [Historisch-staatswissenschaftliche Abtheilung] 69 (1891): 3–23; data for 1882 and 1895 are from *Breslauer Statistik,* vol. 18 (Breslau: Morgenstern, 1900), 168.

67. Manfred Hettling, *Politische Bürgerlichkeit: Der Bürger zwischen Individualität und Vergesellschaftung in Deutschland und der Schweiz von 1860 bis 1918* (Göttingen: Vandenhoeck & Ruprecht, 1999); Reinke, *Judentum und Wohlfahrtspflege in Deutschland;* Leszek Ziątkowski, *Dzieje Żydów we Wrocławiu* (Wrocław: Wydawnictwo Dolnośląskie, 2000). An overview of the literature on Silesian-Jewish history may be found in Margret Heitmann and Andreas Reinke, eds., *Bibliographie zur Geschichte der Juden in Schlesien* (Munich: Saur, 1995), and Marcin Wodziński, ed., *Bibliographie zur Geschichte der Juden in Schlesien II: Bibliography on the History of Silesian Jewry II* (Munich: Saur, 2004). Characteristic is, e.g., the small number of studies treating Breslau in the standard urban history bibliographies: see Wilfried Ehbrecht et al., "Neue Veröffentlichungen zur vergleichenden historischen Städteforschung," *Blätter zur deutschen Landesgeschichte* 128 (1992): 387–852 (for Breslau, 2 titles; Berlin, 112; Hamburg, 71; Cologne, 58; Frankfurt a. M., 53; and Munich, 42). For comprehensive histories of Breslau, see Norman Davies and Roger Moorhouse, *Microcosm: A Portrait of a Central European City* (London: Jonathan Cape, 2002), and the recent multivolume history of Breslau: Cezary Buśko, *Historia Wrocławia,* vol. 1, *Od pradziejów do konca czasów habsburskich* (Wrocław: Wydawn. Dolnośląskie, 2001); Teresa Kulak, *Historia Wrocławia,* vol. 2, *Od twierdzy fryderycjańskiej do twierdzy hitlerowskiej* (Wrocław: Wydawn. Dolnośląskie, 2001); Włodzimierz Suleja, *Historia Wrocławia,* vol. 3, *W Polsce Ludowej: PRL i III rzeczypospolitej* (Wrocław: Wydawn. Dolnośląskie, 2001); a good reference guide is Jan Harasimowicz, ed., *Encyklopedia Wrocławia* (Wrocław: Wydawn. Dolnośląskie, 2000); on Jewish life in Nazi Breslau, see Abraham Ascher, *A Community Under Siege: The Jews of Breslau under Nazism* (Stanford, Calif.: Stanford University Press, 2007).

68. See *Staatsarchiv Breslau—Wegweiser durch die Bestände bis zum Jahr 1945* (Munich: Oldenbourg, 1996).

69. See Heinrich Wendt, *Katalog der Druckschriften über die Stadt Breslau* (Breslau: Morgenstern, 1903), and *Katalog der Druckschriften über die Stadt Breslau: Nachtrag* (Breslau: Morgenstern, 1915). The copy in the Gabinetu Śląsko-Łużyckiego (Silesian-Lusatian cabinet, GŚŁ) of the Wrocław University Library contains handwritten additions for the period after 1915.

70. Miriam Gebhardt has rightly cautioned against the use of self-testimonies without considering the history of their origins; see her *Das jüdische Familiengedächtnis: Erinnerung im deutsch-jüdischen Bürgertum, 1890–1932* (Stuttgart: Franz Steiner, 1999). To address this legitimate objection, I have, as a rule, stated when the memoirs were written. For an exemplary guide to one of the collections used in this study, see Harry Liebersohn and Dorothee Schneider, *My Life in Germany before and after January 30, 1933: A Guide to a Manuscript Collection at Houghton Library, Houghton University* (Philadelphia: American Philosophical Society, 2001).

71. Just how difficult it is to write a history of relations between lower-class Jews and non-Jews is emphasized also by Guesnet in his *Lodzer Juden im 19. Jahrhundert*, 21.

72. The Jewish middle class lived above all in the city's exclusive and expensive residential areas and contributed significantly to the move of the city's middle class out of the inner city into the residential suburbs after the turn of the century. Since many poor Jews lived in the residential areas with a lower Jewish population, the residential concentration of lower-class Jews was probably less than that of the Jewish middle class.

Chapter 1. The Social Structure of Jews, Protestants, and Catholics from the Mid-Nineteenth Century to the First World War

1. Max Weber, *Economy and Society: An Outline of Interpretive Sociology*, ed. Guenther Roth and Claus Wittich (Berkeley: University of California Press, 1978), 1:302; the distinction between status situation (*ständische Lage*) and class situation (*Klassenlage*) concerns, of course, ideal types. Common to both status and class is their reflection of the "distribution of power, economic or otherwise, within its respective community" (Weber, *Economy and Society*, 2:926).

2. Weber, *Economy and Society*, 2:928.

3. Ibid., 2:936.

4. Ibid., 2:932. See also Georg Simmel's and Arthur Schopenhauer's reflections on "honor"; Simmel, *Soziologie: Untersuchungen über die Formen der Vergesellschaftung* (Frankfurt a. M.: Suhrkamp, 1992), 599–603; and Schopenhauer, "Aphorismen zur Lebensweisheit," in *Sämtliche Werke in fünf Bänden*, ed. Hans Henning, 2nd ed., vol. 4, *Parerga und Paralipomena: Erster Theil* (Leipzig: Insel, 1923), 371–580, here 426–59.

5. Weber, *Economy and Society*, 2:928. Since Weber understands professional prestige to be a form of estate honor, he does not distinguish, contrary to Heinz Reif, between "property, acquisition, and professional classes" but only between "property and acquisition classes"; Heinz Reif, "Von der Ständezur Klassengesellschaft," in *Scheidewege der deutschen Geschichte*, ed. Hans-Ulrich Wehler (Munich: C. H. Beck, 1995), 79–90, here 84.

6. Weber, *Economy and Society*, 2:932. "Linked with this expectation," Weber notes, "are restrictions on social intercourse (that is, intercourse which is not subservient to economic or any other purpose. These restrictions may confine normal marriages to within the status circle. . . . Whenever this is not mere individual and socially irrelevant imitation of another style of life, but consensual action of this closing character, the status development is under way" (ibid.).

7. See, e.g., Lothar Gall, *Von der ständischen zur bürgerlichen Gesellschaft* (Munich: Oldenbourg, 1993); Reif, "Von der Stände- zur Klassengesellschaft." The description of bourgeois society as a class society may also be found in Thomas Nipperdey, *Deutsche Geschichte, 1866–1918*, vol. 1, *Arbeitswelt und Bürgergeist* (Munich: C. H. Beck, 1990), 255; see also his "Verein als soziale Struktur in Deutschland im späten 18. und frühen 19. Jh.," in *Gesellschaft, Kultur, Theorie: Gesammelte Aufsätze zur neueren Geschichte* (Göttingen: Vandenhoeck & Ruprecht, 1976), 174–205, here 183.

8. Weber, *Economy and Society*, 2:932.

9. Ibid., 2:938. The fact that Weber expressly rejects a teleological model in *Economy and Society* does not mean that he does not defend elsewhere, particularly in his more popular scientific and political writings, the idea that there had been a development from a status to a class society. On such occasions, Weber usually refers to a narrow understanding of status, in the sense of an estate based on hereditary privilege.

10. Jürgen Kocka, "Das europäische Muster und der deutsche Fall," in *Bürgertum im 19. Jahrhundert*, ed. Jürgen Kocka, vol. 1 (Göttingen: Vandenhoeck & Ruprecht, 1995), 9–75, here 14 and 18. According to Kocka, the bourgeoisie formed a "social class" in Weber's sense (12 and 59n13). Kocka's sharp opposition between property and acquisition classes, on the one hand, and social classes, on the other, has no basis in Weber, however. For Weber, the concept of social class is merely a specification of the concept of class position; it denotes "the totality of those class positions between which individual and generational mobility is easy and typical" (Weber, *Economy and Society*, 1:302); thus in Weber's concept of "social class" the primacy of the purely economic is preserved, even if, according to Weber, the "status group comes closest to the social class and is most unlike the commercial class" (1:307). Though Kocka justifiably writes that the "common denominator and the delimiting particularity" of the bourgeoisie was not the "same class position" but rather the bourgeois "culture and lifestyle," the bourgeoisie was not, if one follows Weber, a social class, but rather a status group; see Kocka, "Das europäische Muster," 11, 17, and 62. In recent research on the bourgeoisie, the approach of interpreting the bourgeoisie as a status group is most often connected with the work of M. Rainer Lepsius; however, unlike in Weber, in Lepsius there is occasionally a lack of conceptual clarity; see the critique in Hettling, *Politische Bürgerlichkeit: Der Bürger zwischen Individualität und Vergesellschaftung in Deutschland und der Schweiz von 1860 bis 1918* (Göttingen: Vandenhoeck & Ruprecht, 1999), 18–22. An interesting plea for

grasping the bourgeoisie as a class may be found in Thomas Mergel, *Zwischen Klasse und Konfession: Katholisches Bürgertum im Rheinland im 19. Jahrhundert* (Göttingen: Vandenhoeck & Ruprecht, 1994), 6–14; following Pierre Bourdieu, Mergel's concept of class encompasses the moment of status insofar as he extends "the concept of the market beyond the sphere of economic commerce" (9); in his critique of those who have referred to the status dimension of embourgeoisement, however, Mergel levels the distinctions between status situation and (hereditary) estate (8).

11. One finds this idea, for example, in Gerhard A. Ritter and Klaus Tenfelde, *Arbeiter im Deutschen Kaiserreich* (Bonn: Dietz, 1992), 126. Something similar is also found in Nipperdey, who says that "the estate idea, for which descent and education, professional tradition, lifestyle, and self-understanding—not the class position—were what counted," was the expression of "pre-bourgeois German traditions." Yet if one follows Max Weber, it is precisely education, lifestyle, and self-understanding that make up the core of a bourgeois lifestyle based on status; see Nipperdey, *Deutsche Geschichte, 1866–1918*, 1:377.

12. Weber, *Economy and Society*, 2:935.

13. Jacob Toury, *Soziale und politische Geschichte der Juden in Deutschland, 1847–1871: Zwischen Revolution, Reaktion und Emanzipation* (Düsseldorf: Droste, 1977), 129.

14. See Weber, *Economy and Society*, 2:934; Nipperdey, *Deutsche Geschichte, 1866–1918*, 1:388–89; in the latter one finds Nipperdey's striking formulation about the German Jews as "model students of the bourgeois way of life and education" (406); see also Georg Simmel's observation that, well into the nineteenth century, "the lowly people" suspiciously watched "the emergence of great wealth"; "the most wicked horror stories" were told about the Rothschilds "and in fact not in the sense of moral ambiguity, but rather in a superstitious way, as if a demonic power were at play"; Georg Simmel, *Die Philosophie des Geldes*, ed. David Frisby and Klaus Christian Köhnke (Frankfurt a. M.: Suhrkamp, 1989), 318. On the "self-made man," see below concerning Leopold Freund, as well as Stefan-Ludwig Hoffmann, *Die Politik der Geselligkeit: Freimaurerlogen in der deutschen Bürgergesellschaft, 1840–1918* (Göttingen: Vandenhoeck & Ruprecht, 2000), 141–42, 148–49.

15. Achim von Arnim and Jacob and Wilhelm Grimm, *Briefwechsel*, ed. Reinhold Steig (Stuttgart: Cotta, 1904), 364, cited in Reif, "Von der Stände- zur Klassengesellschaft," 79.

16. Weber, *Economy and Society*, 2:932.

17. Cited from Mordechai Breuer, "Frühe Neuzeit und Beginn der Moderne," in *Deutsch-jüdische Geschichte in der Neuzeit*, by Mordechai Breuer and Michael Graetz, ed. Michael A. Meyer, vol. 1, *Tradition und Aufklärung* (Munich: C. H. Beck, 1996), 83–247, here 233 and 235. In 1932, Jakob Lestschinsky even estimated that at the end of the eighteenth century 80% of all Jews belonged to the lower classes and lived from hand to mouth; see Jakob Lestschinsky, *Das wirtschaftliche Schicksal des deutschen Judentums* (Berlin: Energiadruck, 1932), 21,

cited in Monika Richarz, "Jewish Social Mobility in Germany during the Time of Emancipation (1790–1871)," *Year Book of the Leo Baeck Institute* 20 (1975): 69–77, here 70. A regional differentiation of the social situation may be found, e.g., in Cilli Kasper-Holtkotte, *Juden im Aufbruch: Zur Sozialgeschichte einer Minderheit im Saar-Mosel-Raum um 1800* (Hanover: Hahn, 1996), 15–34; according to her, the Jewish population in the area she investigated was even "poorer . . . than the non-Jewish" population, since, unlike Christians, Jews did not even possess land (33).

18. "Bericht des Obervorsteherkollegiums an den Breslauer-Polizeipräsidenten vom 21. August 1829, betr. die Synagogalverhältnisse in der Stadt," Żydowski Instytut Historyczny w Polsce, Gmina żydówska we Wrocławiu, no.14, fols. 12–15, cited in Andreas Reinke, *Judentum und Wohlfahrtspflege in Deutschland: Das jüdische Krankenhaus in Breslau, 1744–1944* (Hanover: Hahnsche Buchhandlung, 1999), 30–31.

19. Yuri Slezkine, *The Jewish Century* (Princeton, N.J.: Princeton University Press, 2004), 1.

20. See, e.g., Hartmut Kaelble, "Eras of Social Mobility in 19th and 20th Century Europe," *Journal of Social History* 17 (1984): 489–504, here 494: "All in all the Industrial Revolution was not an era of a dramatic rise in social mobility and of exceptional opportunities for newcomers from social classes, as is often assumed. . . . However, it seems more appropriate to regard it as a period of crisis for important strata of society rather than as a golden age of high social mobility with opportunities open to all talents." That is also confirmed by local studies, such as Sylvia Schraut, *Sozialer Wandel im Industrialisierungsprozeß: Esslingen, 1800–1870* (Sigmaringen: Thorbecke, 1989); a critique of the "common idea of a golden age of social mobility under the conditions of the Industrial Revolution" may also be found in Peter Lundgreen, Margret Kraul, and Karl Ditt, *Bildungschancen und soziale Mobilität in der städtischen Gesellschaft des 19. Jahrhunderts* (Göttingen: Vandenhoeck & Ruprecht, 1988), 13, and Hans-Ulrich Wehler, *Deutsche Gesellschaftsgeschichte*, 2nd ed., vol. 2, *1815–1845/49: Von der Reformära bis zur industriellen und politischen "Deutschen Doppelrevolution"* (Munich: C. H. Beck, 1989), 184–85, and *Deutsche Gesellschaftsgeschichte*, vol. 3, *1849–1914: Von der "Deutschen Doppelrevolution" bis zum Beginn des Ersten Weltkrieges* (Munich: C. H. Beck, 1995), 716.

21. On the total population, see Jürgen Kocka, "Zur Schichtung der preußischen Bevölkerung während der industriellen Revolution," in *Geschichte als Aufgabe: Festschrift für Otto Büsch*, ed. Wilhelm Treue (Berlin: Colloquium Verlag, 1988), 357–90, here 388–89.

22. See *Allgemeine Zeitung des Judenthums* 25 (1861): 29, cited in Toury, *Soziale und politische Geschichte*, 110. Toury does not specify whether it is the city council or the Landtag elections and states, incorrectly, that the Jewish proportion of the population was 1.2% (the correct figure comes from *Breslauer Statistik*, vol. 9 [Breslau: Morgenstern, 1885], 138).

23. "Volkszählung und Volksbeschreibung," *Preußische Statistik* 5–6 (1864): 152–53.

24. Toury, *Soziale und politische Geschichte*, 114. Toury's figures are usually adopted uncritically, such as in Marion Kaplan, "Freizeit—Arbeit: Geschlechterräume im deutsch-jüdischen Bürgertum, 1870–1914," in *Bürgerinnen und Bürger: Geschlechterverhältnisse im 19. Jahrhundert,* ed. Ute Frevert (Göttingen: Vandenhoeck & Ruprecht, 1988), 157–74, here 10, or in David Sorkin, *The Transformation of German Jewry, 1780–1840* (New York: Oxford University Press, 1987), 110. By contrast, Stefanie Schüler-Springorum is more careful in her judgment; see her *Die jüdische Minderheit in Königsberg/Preußen, 1871–1945* (Göttingen: Vandenhoeck & Ruprecht, 1996), 30–33: the "broad majority of Königsberg Jews were able to secure their economic survival in the mid-nineteenth century, but they were not prosperous or even rich" (32); even after the turn of the century, "the majority of the Jewish minority belonged to the moderately earning lower or middle bourgeoisie" (57); these passages make it all the more incomprehensible how Schüler-Springorum could nevertheless adopt Toury's thesis (42). Even Claudia Prestel, who has published one of the few analyses of Jewish poverty and also covers the 1850s and 1860s, argues that around 1870 "only 5–25%" could "be designated as marginal [or] poor"; see Claudia Prestel, "Zwischen Tradition und Moderne: Die Armenpolitik der Gemeinde zu Fürth (1826–1870)," *Tel Aviver Jahrbuch für deutsche Geschichte* 20 (1991): 135–62, here 141.

25. Monika Richarz, "Die Entwicklung der jüdischen Bevölkerung," in *Deutsch-jüdische Geschichte in der Neuzeit,* by Steven M. Lowenstein, Paul Mendes-Flohr, Peter Pulzer, and Monika Richarz, ed. Michael A. Meyer, vol. 3, *Umstrittene Integration, 1871–1918* (Munich: C. H. Beck, 1997), 13–38, here 13 and 16 ("most Jews belonged to the bourgeoisie"); see also her conclusion to the same volume, p. 382.

26. Shulamit Volkov, "Die Verbürgerlichung der Juden in Deutschland: Eigenart und Paradigma," in *Bürgertum im 19. Jahrhundert: Deutschland im europäischen Vergleich,* ed. Jürgen Kocka, vol. 2 (Munich: Deutscher Taschenbuch Verlag, 1988), 343–71, here 344; Volkov, *Die Juden in Deutschland, 1780–1914* (Munich: Oldenbourg, 1994), 53, and "Jüdische Assimilation und Eigenart im Kaiserreich," in her *Jüdisches Leben und Antisemitismus im 19. und 20. Jahrhundert* (Munich: C. H. Beck, 1990), 131–45, here 136–37, esp. 136: "a broad prosperous middle class with a small, very rich stratum . . . and a small, poor lower class." The thesis that the Jews belonged the German bourgeoisie occurs without qualification, however, in Moshe Zimmermann, *Die deutschen Juden, 1914–1945* (Munich: Oldenbourg, 1997), 14: the "control group" with which one should compare the German Jews is not the total population but rather the "German bourgeoisie."

27. Andrea Hopp, *Jüdisches Bürgertum in Frankfurt am Main im 19. Jahrhundert* (Stuttgart: Franz Steiner, 1997), 37.

28. Nipperdey, *Deutsche Geschichte, 1866–1918,* 1:398; Volker R. Berghahn, *Imperial Germany, 1871–1914* (Providence, R.I.: Berghahn Books, 1994), 104–5, here 105.

29. Nipperdey, *Deutsche Geschichte, 1866–1918*, 1:378; Peter Gay, *Schnitzler's Century: The Making of Middle-Class Culture, 1815–1914* (New York: W. W. Norton, 2002), 6. According to Heinz-Gerhard Haupt, among the majority of the "petit bourgeoisie . . . bourgeois norms hardly gained currency"; Heinz-Gerhard Haupt, "Kleine und große Bürger in Deutschland und Frankreich am Ende des 19. Jahrhunderts," in *Bürgertum im 19. Jahrhundert*, ed. Jürgen Kocka, vol. 2, *Verbürgerlichung, Recht und Politik* (Munich: Deutscher Taschenbuch Verlag, 1988), 252–75, here 274.

30. Eugen Altmann, "Mein Leben in Deutschland vor und nach dem 30. Januar 1933," 21–22, manuscript collection "My Life in Germany Before and After January 30, 1933," Houghton Library, Harvard University, Cambridge, Mass. Altmann was referring to the well-known anti-Semitic politician of the 1890s Hermann Ahlwardt (1846–1914), and the Socialist journalist, politician, and prominent member of the Berlin free church Adolph Hoffmann (1858–1930), whose *Die zehn Gebote und die besitzende Klasse* (Berlin: Hoffmann, [ca. 1890]) had gone through eighteens edition by the early 1920s.

31. Adolf Riesenfeld, Tagebücher und Erinnerungen, 2 vols., A 16/3, vol. 1, entry for January 14, 1941, Archives of the LBI, New York. Riesenfield is, of course, atypical. Since he had fallen out with his father after a bitter fight, and his father had not supported him financially as was the norm (entry from January 17, 1917, and in vol. 2, entry for January 15, 1942). Despite the fight, it was nevertheless assumed that the son would take over his father's shipping business. Because of his good economic prospects, the young shop assistant, who earned only about 1,000 marks per year, was regarded, he said, as "a young man from a passably well-off and well respected bourgeois family" (entry for February 17, 1941).

32. Ibid., vol. 1, entry for February 7, 1917.

33. Ibid., vol. 1, from entries in the following: March 7, 1917, January 14, 1917, April 3, 1917, April 22, 1917, and November 1, 1917.

34. Ibid., vol. 1, entries for November 3, 1917, November 11, 1917, and October 25, 1917.

35. Ibid., vol. 1, entries for May 3 and 13, 1917.

36. Uziel Schmelz's thorough and comprehensive study on Hessen does not contain any data on income; see Uziel O. Schmelz, *Die jüdische Bevölkerung in Hessen: Von der Mitte des 19. Jahrhunderts bis 1933* (Tübingen: Mohr Siebeck, 1996), esp. 189–310.

37. Recent investigations of Jewish income structure are provided in Shulamit Volkov, "Die Jüdische Gemeinde in Altona 1877–1890: Ein demographisches Profil," in *Von der Arbeiterbewegung zum modernen Sozialstaat: Festschrift für Gerhard A. Ritter*, ed. Jürgen Kocka, Hans-Jürgen Puhle, and Klaus Tenfelde (Munich: Saur, 1994), 601–18; and Avraham Barkai, *Jüdische Minderheit und Industrialisierung: Demographie, Berufe und Einkommen der Juden in Westdeutschland, 1850–1914* (Tübingen: Mohr Siebeck, 1988).

38. Werner Sombart, *Die Juden und das Wirtschaftsleben* (Leipzig: Duncker & Humblot, 1912), 217–20, quotation from 217. Sombart's figures for Berlin, e.g., are based on data from an "official at the Protestant city synod." A critique of Sombart's methods may be found in Jakob Segall, *Die beruflichen und sozialen Verhältnisse der Juden in Deutschland* (Berlin: Schildberger, 1912), 72–74; Barkai, *Jüdische Minderheit und Industrialisierung*; Berghahn, *Imperial Germany*, 104–5: "[W]hen assessing tax liabilities, an adequate yardstick can be gained only if we compare Jewish-middle-class taxpayers with their non-Jewish counterparts, rather than with the total population. Unfortunately, such data are as yet unavailable."

39. Arthur Ruppin, "Die sozialen Verhältnisse der Juden in Preussen und Deutschland," *Jahrbücher für Nationalökonomie und Statistik* 78 (1902): 374–87 and 760–85, here 776, and *Die Juden der Gegenwart: Eine sozialwissenschaftliche Studie*, 3rd ed. (Berlin: Jüdischer Verlag, 1918), 338.

40. *Zeitschrift für Demographie und Statistik der Juden* 1, no. 4 (1905): 12–13. Yet average figures can be, as Avraham Barkai stressed repeatedly, "deceptive"; see his "Die Juden als sozioökonomische Minderheitsgruppe in der Weimarer Republik," in *Juden in der Weimarer Republik: Skizzen und Porträts*, ed. Walter Grab and Julius H. Schoeps (Stuttgart: Burg-Verlag, 1986), 330–46, here 338.

41. *Zeitschrift für Demographie und Statistik der Juden* 1, no. 4 (1905): 12–13; on Hamburg, see Helga Krohn, *Die Juden in Hamburg: Die politische, soziale und kulturelle Entwicklung einer jüdischen Großstadtgemeinde nach der Emanzipation, 1848–1918* (Hamburg: Christians, 1974), 78.

42. Schüler-Springorum, *Die jüdische Minderheit*, 57; in general, see also Barkai, *Jüdische Minderheit und Industrialisierung*, 61–62; the lower incomes are also missing in Helga Krohn's analysis of the incomes of Hamburg Jews for 1887; even if one neglected, as Krohn does, all incomes under 800 marks, around the turn of the century two-thirds of Jewish taxpayers in Hamburg would not have had a "bourgeois" income; see Krohn, *Die Juden in Hamburg*, 68–70. How many Hamburg Jews earned less than 800 marks per year cannot be learned either from Krohn or from Hamburg's statistics; in nearby Altona, half of all taxpayers (thus Jewish and non-Jewish) earned between 420 and 800 marks; see "Die Einkommensteuer im Hamburgischen Staate in den Jahren 1883 bis 1892," *Statistik des Hamburgischen Staates* 17 (1895): 22–23.

43. Toury, *Soziale und politische Geschichte*, 114.

44. Frank W. Taussig, *Principles of Economics* (New York: Macmillan, 1924), 254; Arthur Friedmann estimates that from 1891 to 1911 the income earners with an annual income of over 3,000 marks hid on average 10% of their income, and annual incomes of less than 3,000 marks were estimated too low even more frequently; Arthur Friedmann, "Die Wohlstandsentwicklung in Preußen von 1891–1911," *Jahrbücher für Nationalökonomie und Statistik* 103 (1914): 1–51, here 13–14. An employee of the Breslau Statistics Bureau judged in retrospect in 1920 "that over time tax estimates became increasingly better."

Thus "the increase in income was in reality a bit more moderate than it would seem from the tables"; see Ernst Kieseritzky, "Löhne, Einkommen und Haushaltskosten in Breslaus während der letzten Jahrzehnte," in *Breslauer Statistik*, vol. 36, pt. 2 (Breslau: Morgenstern, 1920), 52–99, here 65. According to Adolf Riesenfeld, his father, the owner of Spedition Arnold Freund, had "intentionally left the accounting in very bad shape." Although his father estimated the annual revenues at 15–20,000 marks, they actually were, as Adolf Riesenfeld discovered after he become a partner in the shipping firm, easily 30,000 marks. See Riesenfeld, Tagebücher und Erinnerungen, vol. 2, entry for January 16, 1942, pp. 99–100.

45. Barkai, *Jüdische Minderheit und Industrialisierung*, 58.

46. The following section owes much to the thorough and stimulating sociostructural analysis by Manfred Hettling, whom I would also like to thank for placing the data sets on the total population of Breslau at my disposal. Isolated divergences from Hettling's results arose because I am not investigating the Jewish population on the basis of the data sets on the total population of Breslau but rather on the basis of all Jewish taxpayers in 1876 and my sample of every tenth Jewish taxpayer in 1906. Since the number of Jewish taxpayers in the data sets on the total population is lower, these are hardly suitable for an analysis of the professional and income structure of Breslau Jews. Hettling sets the proportion of the Jewish lower classes, for example, in 1876 at 5% and in 1906 at 11% and concludes from these figures that the Jewish lower classes grew in the course of the German Empire (Hettling, *Politische Bürgerlichkeit*, 53). By contrast, the figures I have obtained from my far larger data sets give a different picture. Even if one limits oneself, like Hettling, to economically active males alone (and nothing speaks for doing so in an analysis of the total population), the proportion of the Jewish lower classes was a good 15% in 1876 but nearly 9% in 1906. The proportion of economically active Jewish men in the lower classes therefore decreased rather than increased.

47. "Die Ergebnisse der Berufs- und Gewerbezählung vom 14. Juni 1895," in *Breslauer Statistik*, vol. 18 (Breslau: Morgenstern, 1900), 26.

48. See the table on the denominational structure of the Breslau population in 1875 in *Breslauer Statistik*, vol. 9 (Breslau: Morgenstern, 1885), 10, 129, 138, as well as *Breslauer Statistik*, vol. 27 (Breslau: Morgenstern, 1909), 151, for 1905.

49. I diverge here from Hettling, who estimates the proportion of the bourgeois strata to be 40% since he focuses on only economically active males (Hettling, *Politische Bürgerlichkeit*, 43). Because he wrote a political social history of Breslau, that was legitimate. However, in an analysis of the professional structure of the total population, one cannot exclude the group of economically active females. After all, in 1895 economically active women made up 36.3% of all Breslauers; in 1880, 24.5% of all heads of households in Breslau were unmarried females (without children) or mothers, and in 1905, 28%; see *Breslauer Statistik*, 18:26, and *Breslauer Statistik*, 27:156 (the latter is cited in Hettling, *Politische*

Bürgerlichkeit, 380–81). In the sample data generated from the tax rolls, the proportion of women is even greater. In 1906, 310 (32%) of all Jewish, 522 (46%) of all Protestant, and 310 (46.8%) of all Catholic taxpayers were women. The proportion of economically active women among married women was less than that among single, widowed, or divorced women in Breslau; in 1895, 77% of all single and even 74% of all divorced or widowed women were 18–40 years of age, but only 6% of married women 18–40 years of age were economically active or employed as a maid in a household ("Die Ergebnisse der Berufs- und Gewerbezählung vom 14. Juni 1895," in *Breslauer Statistik*, 18:20); in 1907, 80% of all single and 74% of all divorced or widowed women 18–40 years of age were economically active or employed as a maid in a household, but that held true of only 10% of married women 18–40 years of age ("Die Ergebnisse der Berufs- und Gewerbezählung vom 12. Juni 1907," in *Breslauer Statistik*, vol. 28, pt. 3 [Breslau: Morgenstern, 1909], 1–184, here 13).

50. Wehler, *Deutsche Gesellschaftsgeschichte*, 3:712–13.

51. Peter Pulzer, *Jews and the German State: The Political History of a Minority, 1848–1933* (Oxford: Blackwell 1992); and Barbara Strenge, *Juden im preußischen Justizdienst, 1812–1918: Der Zugang zu den juristischen Berufen als Indikator der gesellschaftlichen Emanzipation* (Munich: Saur, 1995).

52. Incidentally, Reinhard Schüren assigns legal interns to the group of judicial civil servants, a career that was almost completely closed to Jewish legal interns. See Reinhard Schüren, *Soziale Mobilität: Muster, Veränderungen und Bedingungen im 19. und 20. Jahrhundert* (St. Katharinen: Scripta Mercaturae Verlag, 1989). A Jewish legal intern became a lawyer, thus was self-employed, and not a judge or a district attorney. In 1880, 23.7% of all 609 legal interns in the *Oberlandesbezirk* were Jewish, and in 1883, 25.1% of all 561 legal interns were.

53. In Breslau in 1880, only 2% of the childcare and domestic staff in Jewish households were Jewish, while 53% were Protestant and 45% Catholic. All in all, 4,643 people worked as domestic staff in the 7,251 Jewish households in Breslau. Assuming that in every Jewish household with domestic staff there worked an average of one and one-half people, then over 3,000 Breslau Jewish households employed non-Jewish domestic staff. That is another reason why four-fifths of the households with a Jewish head were mixed denominationally; that was the case, however, in only a third of the households with a Protestant head and in only a good 40% of those with a Catholic head; see *Breslauer Statistik*, vol. 15, pt. 4 (Breslau: Morgenstern, 1894), 112–15. At the beginning of the German Empire, the proportion of Jewish households with Christian domestic staff was probably even greater. In any case, the Breslau Statistics Bureau noted that "the proportion of female domestics" had decreased considerably since 1871. "Community facilities, such as the sewage system and running water," the report further noted, "have increasingly rendered an arduous part of housework superfluous; the availability of female domestic staff has decreased due to the competition of industry and the decline of the rural population; the

demands from domestics, perhaps not regarding wages so much as room, board, etc., have increased; and so one prefers to make do with cleaning ladies, washerwomen, who live in their own houses and not in the employer's" ("Die Ergebnisse der Berufs- und Gewerbezählung vom 14. Juni 1895," in *Breslauer Statistik,* 18:18).

54. This thesis is particularly strong in Barkai, *Jüdische Minderheit und Industrialisierung,* 330–46, esp. 333–34, 339–40, and 343. Barkai relies solely on the misleading data from the imperial statistics.

55. Felix A. Theilhaber, *Der Untergang der deutschen Juden: Ein volkswirtschaftliche Studie* (Munich: Reinhardt, 1911), 124.

56. "Ein Briefwechsel: An das Bankhaus Eichborn & Co," *Jüdisches Volksblatt,* May 19, 1922, 3, and "Ein antisemitisches Bankhaus," *CV-Zeitung: Blätter für Deutschtum und Judentum* 1 (1922), 64; see also Altmann, "Mein Leben in Deutschland," 12. Similar complaints about the A. Schaaffhausenschen Bankverein in Cologne are voiced in "Antisemitismus im Bankgewerbe," *Jüdisches Volksblatt* 19 (1913), 209 and 269. The fact that colleagues made up a large proportion of those who intermarried, however, suggests that there also were friendly relations in the workplace; see chap. 3.

57. Manfred Hettling, "Die persönliche Selbständigkeit: Der archimedische Punkt bürgerlicher Lebensführung," in *Der bürgerliche Wertehimmel: Innenansichten des 19. Jahrhunderts,* ed. Manfred Hettling and Stefan-Ludwig Hoffmann (Göttingen: Vandenhoeck & Ruprecht, 2000), 57–78.

58. Dolores L. Augustine, *Patricians and Parvenus: Wealth and High Society in Wilhelmine Germany* (Oxford: Berg, 1994); Werner Mosse, *German-Jewish Economic Élite* (Oxford: Oxford University Press, 1989), and *Jews in the German Economy: The German-Jewish Élite, 1820–1935* (Oxford: Oxford University Press, 1987); Morten Reitmayer, *Bankiers im Kaiserreich: Sozialprofil und Habitus der Deutschen Hochfinanz* (Göttingen: Vandenhoeck & Ruprecht, 2000).

59. The significance of self-employed merchants to the Breslau bourgeoisie cannot be stressed enough. In 1876 almost every other member of the high bourgeois professional group was a merchant, and in 1906 every third still was a merchant (the exact proportion was 48.7% and 31.3%, respectively); calculated on the basis of tax rolls from 1876 (APW, AMW, K 150, vols. 1–18 and 20–36, as well as K 151, vol. 19, and K 146), and the tax rolls from 1906 (APW, AMW, K 156); see also the references in Hettling, *Politische Bürgerlichkeit,* 46–47.

60. Bernhard Breslauer, *Die Zurücksetzung der Juden an den Universitäten Deutschlands* (Berlin: Levy, 1911); Norbert Kampe, "Jüdische Professoren im deutschen Kaiserreich," in *Antisemitismus und jüdische Geschichte,* ed. Rainer Erb and Michael Schmidt (Berlin: Wissenschaftlicher Autorenverlag, 1987), 185–211; Ulrich Sieg, "Im Zeichen der Beharrung: Althoffs Wissenschaftspolitik und die deutsche Universitätsphilosophie," in *Wissenschaftsgeschichte und Wissenschaftspolitik im Industriezeitalter,* ed. Bernhard von Brocke (Hildesheim: August Lax, 1991), 287–306, here 294–97, and "Der Preis des Bildungsstrebens: Jüdische

Geisteswissenschaftler im Kaiserreich," in *Bürger, Juden, Deutsche: Zur Geschichte von Vielfalt und Grenzen, 1800–1933*, ed. Andreas Gotzmann, Rainer Liedtke, and Till van Rahden (Tübingen: Mohr Siebeck, 2001), 67–95.

61. The following figures are based on "Die Ergebnisse der Berufs- und Gewerbezählung vom 14. Juni 1895," in *Breslauer Statistik*, 18:43, and "Die Ergebnisse der Berufs- und Gewerbezählung vom 12. Juni 1907," in *Breslauer Statistik*, vol. 28, pt. 3 (1909), 36 and 85.

62. See the notice in the *Allgemeine Zeitung des Judenthums* 66 (1902): December 12 supplement, 3.

63. Arye Maimon, *Wanderungen und Wandlungen: Die Geschichte meines Lebens* (Trier: Arye Maimon-Institut für Geschichte der Juden, 1998), 29.

64. "Neuregelung der Sonntagsruhe im Handelsgewerbe," *Jüdisches Volksblatt* 18 (1912), 386. "Für die am Sabbat geschlossenen Geschäfte," *Jüdisches Volksblatt* 11 (1905), 301–2; Moritz Neefe, "Ermittelungen über die Lohnverhältnisse in Breslau," in *Breslauer Statistik*, vol. 10 (Breslau: Morgenstern, 1887), 225–73, esp. 240n–o; see also *Jahresbericht der Handelskammer Breslau für das Jahr 1910* (Breslau: Handelskammer, 1911), 81, and "Zur Frage der Sonntagsruhe im Handelsgewerbe," in *Jahresbericht der Handelskammer Breslau für das Jahr 1891* (Breslau: Handelskammer, 1892), 11–18. In general, see Clemens Wischermann, "'Streit um die Sonntagsarbeit': Historische Perspektiven einer aktuellen Kontroverse," *Vierteljahrschrift für Sozial- und Wirtschaftsgeschichte* 78 (1991): 6–38; Wischermann obscures the special status of German Jews because he is interested solely in the "controversy over the priority of social solidarity or individual freedom of choice" (7).

65. In general, see "Weihnachtsbäume und Chanukkageschenke," *Israelitische Wochenschrift* 23 (1892), 417, and Monika Richarz, "Der jüdische Weihnachtsbaum—Familie und Säkularisierung im deutschen Judentum des 19. Jahrhunderts," in *Geschichte und Emanzipation: Festschrift für Reinhard Rürup*, ed. Michael Grüttner, Rüdiger Hachtmann, and Heinz-Gerhard Haupt (Frankfurt a. M.: Campus, 1999), 275–89.

66. On this, see esp. the remarks in Sylvia Schraut, *Sozialer Wandel im Industrialisierungsprozeß: Esslingen, 1800–1870* (Sigmaringen: Thorbecke, 1989), 345–48; she soberly observes that one had "better abstain from studies on social mobility" if one lacks "knowledge of the local practice of classifying professions" (348); in general, see also Michael B. Katz, "Occupational Classification in History," *Journal of Interdisciplinary History* 3 (1972): 63–88, here 71.

67. Marion A. Kaplan, *The Making of the Jewish Middle Class: Women, Family, and Identity in Imperial Germany* (New York: Oxford University Press, 1991); see also Michelle Perrot and Anne Martin-Fugier, "Bourgeois Rituals," in *A History of the Private Life*, ed. Michelle Perrot, vol. 4, *From the Fires of Revolution to the Great War* (Cambridge, Mass.: Belknap Press, 1990), 261–336; Sibylle Meyer, *Das Theater mit der Hausarbeit: Bürgerliche Repräsentation in der Familie der wilhelminischen Zeit* (Frankfurt a. M.: Campus, 1982); on the evening banquets and the high cost of

"station-befitting" living, see Toni Pierenkemper, "Der bürgerliche Haushalt in Deutschland an der Wende zum 20. Jahrhundert—im Spiegel von Haushalts-rechnungen," in *Zur Geschichte der Ökonomik der Privathaushalte*, ed. Dietmar Petzina (Berlin: Duncker & Humblot, 1991), 149–85, here 171–75. There were gray areas, of course, as the example of the employees shows. Around 1890, e.g., a quarter of all employee households employed a maid. Though the proportion sank after 1890, Nipperdey notes that the "subjective will of employees to be 'bour-geois' and to distinguish themselves from the workers" remained intact; Nip-perdey, *Deutsche Geschichte, 1866–1918*, 1:376.

68. Weber, *Economy and Society*, 2:927; see also M. Rainer Lepsius, "Bil-dungsbürgertum als ständische Vergesellschaftung," in *Demokratie in Deutschland* (Göttingen: Vandenhoeck & Ruprecht, 1993), 303–14, here 305 and 313.

69. See also Hettling, *Politische Bürgerlichkeit*, 44–46; Philipp Sarasin, *Stadt der Bürger: Struktureller Wandel und bürgerliche Lebenswelt Basel, 1870–1900* (Basel: Helbing & Lichtenhahn, 1990), 257. On the "central importance of how bourgeois households managed their expenses as a sign of their membership in the bour-geoisie," see Pierenkemper, "Der bürgerliche Haushalt in Deutschland," 151.

70. Nipperdey, *Deutsche Geschichte, 1866–1918*, 1:313; regarding the living conditions of workers, Nipperdey speaks of "the wretched reality and habit of living and consuming" and "the chronic insecurity of existence resulting from inadequate resources to deal with broader threats to survival" (317).

71. On this, see the brief treatment in Wolfgang R. Krabbe, *Die deutsche Stadt im 19. und 20. Jahrhundert* (Göttingen: Vandenhoeck & Ruprecht, 1989), 54–59.

72. Altman, "Mein Leben in Deutschland," 12.

73. The different figures for 1876 and 1906 take into consideration the in-crease in the cost of living between the two sample years. The four-year mean of the index of the cost of living, as calculated by Ashok Desai, increased dur-ing the period under investigation here by 9.4% from 106 (1875–1878) to 116 (1905–1908); Ashok V. Desai, *Real Wages in Germany, 1871–1913* (Oxford: Claren-don Press, 1968), 117; on Breslau, see Else Neißer, "Preisbewegung und Haus-haltungskosten in Breslau, 1893–1912," in *Untersuchungen über Preisbildung*, sec. C, *Die Kosten der Lebenshaltung in deutschen Großstädten*, pt. 1, *Ost- und Norddeutschland*, ed. Franz Eulenberg, Schriften des Vereins für Sozialpolitik 145 (Leipzig: Duncker & Humblot, 1915), 441–80, and "Wachstum der Einkommen in Bres-lau," in *Breslauer Statistik*, vol. 29 (Breslau: Morgenstern, 1911), 270–72.

74. Unlike Sarasin, who regards his posited income threshold as decisionis-tic, I am claiming plausibility here. Instead of setting the limits at 2,750 and 3,000 marks, respectively, they could have been set at 5,000 or 10,000 marks, but then the limit would have been less plausible; see Sarasin, *Stadt der Bürger*, 257–60, esp. 258.

75. See the overview in the *Breslauer Zeitung*, October 20, 1895, and January 14, 1896, cited in Hettling, *Politische Bürgerlichkeit*, 411. Even though they earned considerably more than 3,000 marks per year, many Breslau bourgeois voted in

the same electoral class as workers, craftsmen, and employees from about 1890 on; in general, see Krabbe, *Die deutsche Stadt im 19. und 20. Jahrhundert*, 58.

76. As an example of *Gymnasium* teachers' salaries, see APW, AMW, K 156, district 16, nos. 5 and 21, as well as district 41, no. 3; Heinrich Dittenberger, "Die Einkommensenquete," *Juristische Wochenschrift* 43 (1914): 745–48, here 747, cited in Hannes Siegrist, *Advokat, Bürger und Staat: Eine vergleichende Geschichte der Rechtsanwälte in Deutschland, Italien und der Schweiz (18.–20. Jahrhundert)* (Frankfurt a. M.: Klostermann, 1996), 619. On ministers' wages, see Oliver Janz, *Bürger besonderer Art: Evangelische Pfarrer in Preußen, 1850–1914* (Berlin: de Gruyter, 1994), 336–83 and 517–19; also around 1900 "a minister's income marked," according to Janz, "the lowest limit of the high bourgeoisie," although since 1875 even poorly paid ministers after twenty years of service had an income of 3,000 marks (381 and 366). On the salaries of academic officials in general, see Bernd Wunder, *Geschichte der Bürokratie in Deutschland* (Frankfurt a. M.: Suhrkamp, 1986), 103–4. On the economic situation and on household management of the bourgeoisie in the German Empire, see also William H. Hubbard, *Familiengeschichte: Materialien zur deutschen Familie seit dem Ende des 18. Jahrhunderts* (Munich: C. H. Beck, 1983), 230–39. Further evidence for the plausibility of the limit of 3,000 marks may be found in Hopp, *Jüdisches Bürgertum*, 174, and G. v. Hoeselin, "Aufnahme, Beförderung und Leben in den Logen—eine Geldfrage!" in *Bauhütte* 33 (1890): 2–7, cited in Stefan-Ludwig Hoffmann, *Politik der Geselligkeit*, 144–45.

77. Neefe, "Ermittelungen über die Lohnverhältnisse," 240v.

78. Cited in Wolfgang Mommsen, *Bürgerstolz und Weltmachtsstreben: Deutschland unter Wilhelm II, 1890–1918* (Berlin: Propyläen, 1995), 67–68. Another indication is provided by the average income of the electoral delegates in Prussian Landtag elections, the *Wahlmänner*. The delegates, who would be assigned to the petite bourgeoisie in view of their professions, had an annual income of considerably more than 3,000 marks (1876 = 3,856; 1893 = 3,164; and 1903/1906 = 3,817). This finding is even the more significant when one considers that the average income of all heads of Breslau households with petit-bourgeois professions was lower (in the old middle classes in 1876 = 1,473 marks, and in 1906 = 1,988 marks; in the new middle classes in 1876 = 1,493, and in 1906 = 2,249 marks); see Hettling, *Politische Bürgerlichkeit*, 45–46. This contrast was even more striking in the case of the city councilors; in 1877, the average annual income of the sixteen city councilors who belonged to the old middle classes (ten of them were master craftsmen) was over 8,500 marks and thus was almost six times higher than that of a "normal" member of Breslau's old middle classes (1876 = 1,473 marks); see Hettling, *Politische Bürgerlichkeit*, 103–4; Pierenkemper ("Der bürgerliche Haushalt in Deutschland," 166–69) reports similarly on the difference between petit-bourgeois and bourgeois household incomes, though his results are based largely on the housekeeping-books of high-ranking civil servants and therefore can be applied to the Jewish bourgeoisie only with great caution (see esp. 166–67); see also Hopp, *Jüdisches Bürgertum*, 174.

79. "Die Einkommenssteuer im Hamburgischen Staate," 1–48, here 7.

80. Riesenfeld, Tagebücher und Erinnerungen, vol. 2, entry for January 16, 1942, p. 99.

81. Bertha Badt-Strauss, "My World, and How It Crashed," *Menorah Journal* 39 (Spring 1951): 90–100, here 93. On Badt's income level in 1906, see APW, AMW, K 156, district 34, no. 2039.

82. Georg Simmel, *Soziologie: Untersuchungen über die Formen der Vergesellschaftung* (Frankfurt a. M.: Suhrkamp, 1992), 548.

83. Jürgen Kocka, "Zur Schichtung der preußischen Bevölkerung während der industriellen Revolution," in *Geschichte als Aufgabe: Festschrift für Otto Büsch*, ed. Wilhelm Treue (Berlin: Colloquium Verlag, 1988), 357–90, here 375.

84. See also Shulamit Magnus, *Jewish Emancipation in a German City: Cologne, 1798–1871* (Stanford: Stanford University Press, 1997), 158.

85. Thus, precisely with regard to research on the bourgeoisie, one is justified is doubting the view of Lundgreen, Kraul, and Ditt that "the profession" has "an indicative function for many opportunities in life that are typically connected with it"; *Bildungschancen und soziale Mobilität in der städtischen Gesellschaft des 19. Jahrhunderts* (Göttingen: Vandenhoeck & Ruprecht, 1988), 351.

86. On per capita income, see Heinrich Bleicher, "Einkommens- und Wohlstandsverhältnisse," *Statistisches Jahrbuch deutscher Städte* 6 (1897): 319–36, here 336; see also "Die Einkommenssteuer im Hamburgischen Staate," 22–25 and 29; on day wages, see Kieseritzky, "Löhne, Einkommen und Haushaltskosten," 61–63, quotation from 58; see also Neefe, "Ermittelungen über die Lohnverhältnisse," 240a*–c* and 240e*–f* (the differentiation by individual trades, 240e*, and the overview of salaries of local civil servants in Berlin and Breslau, 240c*). One reason for the lower wages in Breslau may have been the immigration of farm workers from the province of Silesia, especially Upper Silesia.

87. Neefe, "Ermittelungen über die Lohnverhältnisse," 240c*–d* (a comparison of food prices in Berlin and Breslau is also provided there).

88. Hettling, *Politische Bürgerlichkeit*, 56–58. The connection between age and income varied in different class situations; workers earned the highest wages between the ages of twenty-five and forty, whereas the income from bourgeois careers approached its highest point only at the age of forty; see Nipperdey, *Deutsche Geschichte, 1866–1918*, 1:307, and Ritter and Tenfelde, *Arbeiter im Deutschen Kaiserreich*, 529–36.

89. On the poverty of single Jewish women, see also Schüler-Springorum, *Die jüdische Minderheit*, 54.

90. Neefe, "Ermittelungen über die Lohnverhältnisse" (1887), 240z.

91. APW, AMW, K 146, district 17, no. 1995.

92. APW, AMW, K 150, district 55, no. 1171 (Jessy Hirschel) and 1172 (Helene Hirschel); the registration form for Jessy Hirschel: APW, PPB 624, no. 2616. The name of the deceased husband was taken from the marriage certificate of his son Nathan Hirschel, who was born in New York in 1890; see USC, Standesamt

Breslau IV, 1919, no. 63, from February 6, 1919. The family of the forty-four-year-old Sara Neumann, née Fränkel, eked out a similarly impoverished existence. Sara was born in 1862 in Dziergowitz, an Upper Silesian village about fifteen kilometers north of Ratibor. The ex-wife of the agent Max Neumann had an annual income of four hundred marks, from which she had to feed herself and her seven children, the youngest of whom was fourteen years old. The Neumanns lived at Hildebrandstrasse 19, in the Nikolaivorstadt in the western part of Breslau, an area in which primarily members of the lower classes lived; see, APW, AMW, K 150, Steuerbezirk 65, no. 1490. It is unclear whether her ex-husband supported Sara Neumann financially, though it is probable.

93. APW, AMW, K 156, Steuerbezirk 13, no. 2929 (Tax records of Moritz Krebs); "Beschwerde der Bewohner der Otto- und Vincenzstrasse," APW, AMW, III, 8705, fol. 167.

94. See also Wehler, *Deutsche Gesellschaftsgeschichte*, 3:708.

95. Barkai, *Jüdische Minderheit und Industrialisierung*, 75 and 77–78.

96. In view of the "plutocratic" character of the inter-Jewish income distribution, it would seem worthwhile to differentiate the Jewish bourgeoisie according to differences in lifestyle. The question of whether the bourgeoisie was fragmented thus concerns the demarcation both of the Christian from the Jewish bourgeoisie and between the various class situations within the Jewish bourgeoisie. See the references to "intra-Jewish tensions" in Kaplan, *Making of the Jewish Middle Class*, 198, 209, and 286n46.

97. "Ein Kampf um das Wahlrecht," *Jüdisches Volksblatt* 12 (1906), 250–51; "Jüdischer Kommunalfreisinn," *Jüdisches Volksblatt* 12 (1906), 293; see the protocol of the representative council meeting in *Jüdisches Volksblatt* 12 (1906), 344–46, esp. 345; five years later the *Jüdisches Volksblatt* scoffed that in most communities "they [held] on to the old with the tenacity, one can almost say, of the Prussian Junker; they [didn't] want to give up the traditional power of the optimates and the notables"; see "Jüdische Wahlrechtsfragen, *Jüdisches Volksblatt* 17 (1911), 271–72, here 272; on the conflicts over the right to vote and the increasing polarization of the Jewish community elections, see, in general, Steven M. Lowenstein, "Die Gemeinde," in *Deutsch-jüdische Geschichte in der Neuzeit*, by Lowenstein et al., ed. Michael A. Meyer, vol. 3, *Umstrittene Integration, 1871–1918* (Munich: C. H. Beck, 1997), 123–50, here 126–27, and Jack Wertheimer, "The Duisburg Affair: A Test Case in the Struggle for the 'Conquest' of the Communities," *AJS Review* 6 (1981): 185–206.

98. APW, AMW, K 150, district 7, no. 1130 (Gustav Born); ibid., district 25, no. 161 (Fanny Born); ibid., district 19, no. 3275 and state tax roll B 172 (Salomon Kauffmann); Max Born, *Mein Leben* (Munich: Nymphenburger Verlagshandlung, 1975), 11. See also Gustav V. R. Born, "The Wide-Ranging Family History of Max Born," *Notes and Records of the Royal Society of London* 56, no. 2 (2002): 219–62. Salomon Kauffmann's family and his wife, Marie, née Joachimsthal, appear in a somewhat more positive light in the memoirs of Anna

Auerbach, née Silbergleit, whose eldest sister, Elise, married Wilhelm Kauffmann, the youngest brother of Salomon Kauffmann; see Anna Auerbach,
"Die Chronik der Familie Silbergleit" (1905), ME 600, 20–22 and 31, Archives
of the LBI, New York.

99. Born, *Mein Leben*, 28.

100. Ibid., 40.

101. Riesenfeld, Tagebücher und Erinnerungen, vol. 2, entry from February 21, 1941; on Riesenfeld's level of income around 1905, see the entry from
February 17, 1941.

102. "Nieder mit der Reaktion!" *Jüdisches Volksblatt* 11 (1905), 477–78, here
477; see also "Gegen die Feinde des kleinen Mannes," *Jüdisches Volksblatt* 11
(1905), 465–66. The *Jüdisches Volksblatt* repeated the accusations like a prayer
wheel; they were already in one of the paper's first lead articles; see "Kommu-
naler Liberalismus," *Jüdisches Volksblatt*, October 14, 1896, 105–6.

103. "Wahlresultat," *Jüdisches Volksblatt* 11 (1905), 489; APW, AMW, K
156, district 53, no. 1901 (Bloch); ibid., district 52, no. 2833 (Schottländer); ibid.,
district 68, no. 1218 (Schreiber). On the results of the elections, see "Die
Repräsentanten-Wahl," *Jüdisches Volksblatt* 11 (1905), 491; "Das Breslauer Wahlresultat," *Jüdisches Volksblatt* 11 (1905), 504 and 513–14.

104. "Theodor Oschinsky," *Jüdisches Volksblatt* 13 (1907), 273–74; the information on Oschinsky's financial circumstances comes from APW, AMW, K
156, district 47, no. 2510; see also Aron Heppner, *Jüdische Persönlichkeiten in und aus
Breslau* (Breslau: Schatzky, 1931), 35.

105. Because not a single Catholic income earner who made more than
9,200 marks appears in the sample set for 1876, the Catholic proportion can be
only estimated. Of course, there were Breslau Catholics who paid taxes on more
than 9,200 marks per year; e.g., the Molinaris were wealthy Breslau Catholics.

106. Breslau Jews do not seem to have benefited from the age limit in 1876.
Among Jewish men in 1875, over half (54.7%) were under twenty-five years of
age; that corresponded fairly well to the age distribution among Protestants and
Catholics, of whom 51% and 53%, respectively, of the men were too young to
vote. See *Breslauer Statistik*, vol. 1 (Breslau: Morgenstern, 1875), 318.

107. Hettling, *Politische Bürgerlichkeit*, 409 and 411.

108. *Breslauer Statistik*, 1:318, and *Breslauer Statistik*, 27:54–55.

109. "Die Anstellung jüdischer Lehrkräfte an den Breslauer Volksschulen,"
Schlesische Morgen-Zeitung, no. 325, November 27, 1910.

110. "Stadtverordnetenwahlen," *Schlesische Morgen-Zeitung*, no. 320, November 22, 1910.

111. *Allgemeine Zeitung des Judenthums* 51 (1887): 604; Leopold Freund, *Eine Lebensgeschichte*, 2nd ed. (Breslau: Leopold Freund's Verlagshandlung, 1878), 5 and
29 (for additional references to his parents' bitter poverty, see 18–19); on economic advancement, see esp. 33 and 45; on Freund's income level in 1876, see
APW, AMW, K 150, district 4, no. 1610. See also Emanuel Schreiber, *Die sociale*

Stellung der Juden: Offenes Sendschreiben an Herrn Dr. Maass-Breslau (Königsberg: Prange, 1877), 27; "most rich Jews," said Schreiber, who at the time was a rabbi in Elbing, had made their fortunes "though seclusion, extreme frugality, tireless hard work, business sense, a shrewd assessment of the business situation, etc." In general, see Hopp, *Jüdisches Bürgertum*, 29, esp. n.45.

112. "Theodor Oschinsky," *Jüdisches Volksblatt* 13 (1907), 273–74, here 274; APW, AMW, K 150, district 17, no. 1699, and the tax roll APW, AMW, K 146, vol. 21, no. 1302; APW, AMW, K 156, district 47, no. 2510.

113. Emil Ludwig, "Vita und Persönlichkeit," in *Hermann Cohn in Memoriam,* by Ludwig Laqueur, Leonhard Weber, and Emil Ludwig (Breslau: Wohlfarth, 1908), 1–37, here 2. On Ludwig, see Adalbert Wichert, "Emil Ludwig," in *Neue Deutsche Biographie*, vol. 15 (Berlin: Duncker & Humblot, 1987), 426–27.

114. Sorkin, *Transformation of German Jewry;* Robert Liberles, "Dohm's Treatise on the Jews: A Defence of the Enlightenment," *Year Book of the Leo Baeck Institute* 33 (1988): 29–42; see also Shulamit Volkov, "Soziale Ursachen des jüdischen Erfolgs in der Wissenschaft," in her *Jüdisches Leben und Antisemitismus,* 146–65, esp. 146–47.

115. Jacob Toury, "Der Eintritt der Juden ins deutsche Bürgertum," in *Das Judentum in der Deutschen Umwelt, 1800–1850: Studien zur Frühgeschichte der Emanzipation,* ed. Hans Liebeschütz and Arnold Paucker (Tübingen: Mohr, 1977), 139–242.

116. Michaelis Silberstein, *Zeitbilder aus der Geschichte der Juden in Breslau* (Breslau: Jacobsohn, 1890); see the almost identical passage on Königsberg in *Allgemeine Zeitung des Judenthums* 39 (1875), cited in Toury, *Soziale und politische Geschichte,* 124.

117. Theilhaber, *Der Untergang der deutschen Juden,* 75 and 134; see also Arthur Ruppin, *Soziologie der Juden,* vol. 2, *Der Kampf der Juden um ihre Zukunft* (Berlin: Jüdischer Verlag, 1931), 274–75; J. Gottlieb, "Erlösung," *Blau-Weiß-Blätter* 5, no. 5 (1918): 176–77, cited in Jörg Hackeschmidt, *Von Kurt Blumenfeld zu Norbert Elias: Die Erfindung einer jüdischen Nation* (Hamburg: Europäische Verlagsanstalt, 1997), 85. In general see David A. Brenner, *Marketing Identities: The Invention of Jewish Ethnicity in "Ost und West"* (Detroit: Wayne State University Press, 1998), 84–97; Joachim Doron, "Social Concepts Prevalent in German Zionism," *Studies in Zionism* 5 (1982): 1–31, esp. 5–7; Moshe Zimmermann, "Das Gesellschaftsbild der deutschen Zionisten vor dem Ersten Weltkrieg," *Trumah* 1 (1987): 139–58, here 144, 147, and 149; and Derek J. Penslar, *Shylock's Children: Economics and Jewish Identity in Modern Europe* (Berkeley: University of California Press, 1999).

118. Ruppin, *Die Juden der Gegenwart,* 243; Theilhaber, *Der Untergang der deutschen Juden,* 122; see also Hackeschmidt, *Von Kurt Blumenfeld zu Norbert Elias,* 85–86. The "enthusiastic reception" of Werner Sombart's *Die Juden und das Wirtschaftsleben* is also typical; see Friedrich Lenger, *Werner Sombart, 1863–1941: Eine Biographie* (Munich: C. H. Beck, 1994), esp. 211.

119. Norbert Elias, *Über sich selbst* (Frankfurt a. M.: Suhrkamp, 1990), 13 and 20.

Chapter 2. Crossing Boundaries

1. Thomas Nipperdey, "Verein als soziale Struktur in Deutschland im späten 18. und frühen 19. Jh.," in his *Gesellschaft, Kultur, Theorie: Gesammelte Aufsätze zur neueren Geschichte* (Göttingen: Vandenhoeck & Ruprecht, 1976), 174–205, here 181. On Germany, see also Klaus Tenfelde, "Die Entfaltung des Vereinswesens während der industriellen Revolution in Deutschland, 1850–1873," in *Vereinswesen und bürgerliche Gesellschaft in Deutschland,* ed. Otto Dann (Munich: Oldenbourg, 1984), 55–114, and Wolfgang Hardtwig, "Strukturmerkmale und Entwicklungstendenzen des deutschen Vereinswesens in Deutschland 1789–1848," in *Vereinswesen und bürgerliche Gesellschaft,* 11–50. One hears nothing from Nipperdey or from Tenfelde or Hardtwig about the inclusion or exclusion of Jews in associational life. Stimulating treatments of associational life are provided in Leonore Davidoff and Catherine Hall, *Family Fortunes: Men and Women of the English Middle Classes, 1780–1850* (Chicago: University of Chicago Press, 1987), 419–45, and Stuart M. Blumin, *The Emergence of the Middle Class: Social Experience in the American City, 1760–1900* (Cambridge: Cambridge University Press, 1989), 192–229.

2. Otto Dann, "Vorwort," in *Vereinswesen und bürgerliche Gesellschaft,* 5–9, here 5.

3. Nipperdey, "Verein als soziale Struktur," 185 and 189; Hardtwig, "Strukturmerkmale und Entwicklungstendenzen," 39; Alexis de Tocqueville, *Democracy in America,* ed., trans., and with an introduction by Harvey C. Mansfield and Delba Winthrop (Chicago: University of Chicago Press, 2000), 486 and 497–98; similar observations may be found in John Stuart Mill, *On Liberty,* ed. Stefan Collini (Cambridge: Cambridge University Press, 1991), esp. 109–10. Specifically on Breslau, see Manfred Hettling, *Politische Bürgerlichkeit: Der Bürger zwischen Individualität und Vergesellschaftung in Deutschland und der Schweiz von 1860 bis 1918* (Göttingen: Vandenhoeck & Ruprecht, 1999), 212–23.

4. "Die Landtagswahlen," *Breslauer Zeitung,* no. 461, October 3, 1879.

5. This later club euphoria got its running start in the 1850s and 1860s; see Tenfelde, "Die Entfaltung des Vereinswesens."

6. *Adreß- und Geschäfts-Handbuch der Königlichen Haupt- und Residenzstadt Breslau für das Jahr 1876,* ed. Ernst Bruch, pt. 2 (Breslau: Morgenstern, 1876), 362–78; Heinrich Wendt, "Die Anfänge des Breslauer Vereinswesens (bis 1808)," *Zeitschrift des Vereins für Geschichte und Altertum Schlesiens* 36 (1903): 260–85, here 261; Wendt estimates that, in addition to the 650 registered clubs in 1902, there were another 150 unreported clubs; "Die Vereine nach Gruppen geordnet," in *Neues Adreßbuch für Breslau und Umgebung: Unter Benutzung amtl. Quellen,* pt. 4 (Breslau: A. Scherl, 1906), 68–77.

7. Wendt, "Die Anfänge des Breslauer Vereinswesens," 260.

8. David Sorkin, *Transformation of German Jewry, 1780–1840* (New York: Oxford University Press, 1987), 112–13; Andrea Hopp, *Jüdisches Bürgertum in Frankfurt*

am Main im 19. Jahrhundert (Stuttgart: Franz Steiner, 1997), 129–38; Shulamit Volkov, *Die Juden in Deutschland, 1780–1914* (Munich: Oldenbourg, 1994), 14–15.

9. *Freimaurer-Zeitung* 1 (1847), 4–56, here 56, cited in Stefan-Ludwig Hoffmann, "Bürger zweier Welten? Juden und Freimaurer im 19. Jahrhundert," in *Bürger, Juden, Deutsche: Zur Geschichte von Vielfalt und Grenzen, 1800–1933*, ed. Andreas Gotzmann, Rainer Liedtke, and Till van Rahden (Tübingen: Mohr Siebeck, 2001), 97–119; on Rotteck's resistance to the Jewish emancipation, see Reinhard Rürup, *Emanzipation und Antisemitismus: Studien zur "Judenfrage" in der bürgerlichen Gesellschaft* (Frankfurt a. M.: Fischer, 1987), 77; on the topos of Jewish "unsociability" in general, see Hans-Joachim Neubauer, *Judenfiguren: Drama und Theater im frühen 19. Jahrhundert* (Frankfurt a. M.: Campus, 1994), 174–75 and 178. The observation that associational life "aimed at a certain homogeneity of life-style, at a certain 'tone,' which was bound up with social presuppositions," was made already in Nipperdey, "Verein als soziale Struktur," 186.

10. Dietmar Preissler, *Frühantisemitismus in der Freien Stadt Frankfurt und im Groß-herzogtum Hessen (1810–1860)* (Heidelberg: Carl Winter, 1989), 261–87, esp. 263.

11. Julius Hainauer, *Die Gesellschaft der Freunde in Breslau: Erinnerungsblätter für das 50. Stiftungsfest* (Breslau: Hainauer, 1871), 11–12.

12. Jacob Toury, *Soziale und politische Geschichte der Juden in Deutschland, 1847–1871: Zwischen Revolution, Reaktion und Emanzipation* (Düsseldorf: Droste, 1977), 128. Toury relies on the *Allgemeine Zeitung des Judenthums* 15 (1851): 244–45, 278, 291, 520, and 542, as well as the *Allgemeine Zeitung des Judenthums* 16 (1852): 453.

13. Cited in Toury, *Soziale und politische Geschichte*, 128.

14. See Sorkin, *Transformation of German Jewry*, 113–23, "parallel associational life" (113); Henry Wasserman, "Jews, Bürgertum and Bürgerliche Gesellschaft in a Liberal Era in Germany, 1840–1880" (PhD diss., Hebrew University, 1984). Prior to Sorkin and Wasserman, Jacob Katz had already argued that the spread of the Enlightenment among German Jews did not lead to an "inclusion of the enlightened Jews in the society of non-Jews": "Instead, there came into being a particular Jewish variation of enlightened society that had some contact with their non-Jewish counterpart but, on the whole, remained socially aloof"; Katz, *Out of the Ghetto: The Social Background of Jewish Emancipation, 1770–1870* (Cambridge, Mass.: Harvard University Press, 1973; repr., Syracuse, N.Y.: Syracuse University Press, 1998), 54.

15. Sorkin, *Transformation of German Jewry*, 116.

16. Hainauer, *Die Gesellschaft der Freunde in Breslau*, 11–12.

17. Ibid., 74–80.

18. *Statuten der Gesellschaft der Freunde zu Breslau: Festgestellt in der General-Versammlung vom 6. April 1878* (Breslau: Gesellschaft der Freunde, 1878), secs. 4 and 6, BUW, GŚŁ Yz 85. The club motto was Schiller's "Nur aus der Kräfte schön vereintem Streben / Erhebt sich, wirkend, erst das wahre Leben!" (For all the powers, with fair and friendly strife, / Must join to weave the web of manly life!); *Festschrift zur hundertjährigen Stiftungs-Feier der Gesellschaft der Freunde in*

Breslau, im Auftrage der Direktion verfaßt von den Schriftführern (Breslau: Gesellschaft der Freunde, 1921), 20.

19. *Festschrift zur hundertjährigen Stiftungs-Feier,* 6; the *Festschrift* also includes a rough analysis of the professional background of members from 1870 to 1920 (10).

20. Ibid., 38; Heinrich Wendt, *Das erste Jahrhundert der Kaufmännischen Zwinger- und Ressourcen-Gesellschaft zu Breslau, 1805–1905: Festschrift zur Jubelfeier* (Breslau: Kaufmännische Zwinger- und Ressourcen-Gesellschaft, 1905), 29.

21. "Die Gesellschaft der Freunde," *Breslauer Zeitung,* no. 17, January 11, 1871, 116; "Die von der Gesellschaft der Freunde veranstaltete Vorträge 'Ueber die Idee des ewigen Völkerfriedens,'" *Breslauer Zeitung,* no. 68, February 9, 1871, 471.

22. *Festschrift zur hundertjährigen Stiftungs-Feier,* 36; on Poleck, see "Nekrolog Theodor Poleck," *Jahresbericht der Schlesischen Gesellschaft für vaterländische Cultur* 84 (1906): obituary section, 41–44.

23. Hubert Stier, "Gesellschaftshaus für die Gesellschaft der Freunde zu Breslau," *Deutsche Bauzeitung* 11 (1877): 11–12. The banquet hall and the dining hall of the Gesellschaft der Freunde were thus considerably larger than the corresponding halls of both the clubhouse of the Verein christlicher Kaufleute (Christian Merchants Club), which was built at the end of the 1880s, and the Zwingergesellschaft, whose large banquet hall was 300 square meters, its small banquet hall 120 square meters. See "Preisbewerbung für Entwürfe zu einem Gesellschaftshaus des Vereins christlicher Kaufleute in Breslau," *Deutsche Bauzeitung* 22 (1888): 353–54. In general on the significance of the neo-Renaissance style in Breslau, see Agnieszka Zabłocka-Kos, "Die Architektur der Neo-Renaissance in Breslau," in *Renaissance der Renaissance: Ein bürgerlicher Kunststil im 19. Jahrhundert,* ed. G. Ulrich Großmann (Munich: Deutscher Kunstverlag, 1995), 143–60.

24. Ernst Scheyer, "Bildung in Breslau," in *Leben in Schlesien,* ed. Hubert Hupka (Munich: Gräfe & Unzer, 1962), 163–76, here 167.

25. Stefanie Schüler-Springorum, *Die jüdische Minderheit in Königsberg/Preußen, 1871–1945* (Göttingen: Vandenhoeck & Ruprecht, 1996); Hopp, *Jüdisches Bürgertum,* esp. 128; Iris Schröder, "Grenzgängerinnen: Jüdische Sozialreformerinnen in der Frankfurter Frauenbewegung um 1900," in *Bürger, Juden, Deutsche: Zur Geschichte von Vielfalt und Grenzen in Deutschland, 1780–1933,* ed. Andreas Gotzmann, Rainer Liedtke, and Till van Rahden (Tübingen: Mohr Siebeck, 2001), 341–68; Ralf Roth, "Von Wilhelm Meister zu Hans Castorp: Der Bildungsgedanke und das bürgerliche Assoziationswesen im 18. und 19. Jahrhundert," in *Bürgerkultur im 19. Jahrhundert—Bildung, Kunst und Lebenswelt,* ed. Dieter Hein and Andreas Schulz (Munich: C. H. Beck, 1996), 121–39, here 131–32, and "Liberalismus in Frankfurt a. M., 1814–1914: Probleme seiner Strukturgeschichte," in *Liberalismus und Region: Zur Geschichte des deutschen Liberalismus im 19. Jahrhundert,* ed. Dieter Langewiesche and Lothar Gall (Munich: Oldenbourg, 1995), 41–86, here 73–74. (Roth dates the opening to the 1830s, but that seems too early, as can be shown also with regard to Frankfurt am Main. See

Dietmar Preissler, *Frühantisemitismus in der Freien Stadt Frankfurt und im Großherzogtum Hessen (1810–1860)* [Heidelberg: Carl Winter, 1989], and Hopp, *Jüdisches Bürgertum,* 128–31, esp. 131.)

26. On Jewish associational life in the German Empire, see Steven M. Lowenstein, "Die Gemeinde," in *Deutsch-jüdische Geschichte in der Neuzeit,* by Steven M. Lowenstein, Paul Mendes-Flohr, Peter Pulzer, and Monika Richarz, ed. Michael A. Meyer, vol. 3, *Umstrittene Integration, 1871–1918* (Munich: C. H. Beck, 1997), 123–50, here 136–47; Rainer Liedtke, *Jewish Welfare in Hamburg and Manchester, c. 1850–1914* (Oxford: Oxford University Press, 1998); Andreas Reinke, *Judentum und Wohlfahrtspflege in Deutschland: Das jüdische Krankenhaus in Breslau, 1744–1944* (Hanover: Hahnsche Buchhandlung, 1999); Jacob Borut, "A New Spirit among Our Brethren in Ashkenaz" (PhD diss., University of Jerusalem, 1993), English summary; stimulating is David Kaufman, *Shul with a Pool: The "Synagogue-Center" in American Jewish History* (Hanover, N.H. : University Press of New England, 1999).

27. Michael R. Gerber, *Die Schlesische Gesellschaft für Vaterländische Cultur (1803–1945)* (Sigmaringen: Thorbecke, 1988), 7, 21, 25, 84–85; Victor Loewe, "Schlesische Gelehrte Gesellschaften und Vereine," in *Schlesische Landeskunde,* ed. Fritz Frech and Franz Kampers (Leipzig: Veit, 1913), 259–62, here 259.

28. For general background, see Andreas W. Daum, *Wissenspopularisierung im 19. Jahrhundert: Bürgerliche Kultur, naturwissenschaftliche Bildung und die deutsche Öffentlichkeit, 1848–1914* (Munich: Oldenbourg, 1998).

29. Gerber, *Die Schlesische Gesellschaft,* 31 and 92.

30. On Auerbach, see Bruno Kisch, "Forgotten Leaders in Modern Medicine: Valentin, Gruby, Remak, Auerbach," *Transactions of the American Philosophical Society* 44, no. 2 (1954): 139–317; "Nekrolog Leopold Auerbach," *Jahresbericht der Schlesischen Gesellschaft für vaterländische Cultur* 75 (1897): obituary section, 3–9; Paul Grützner, "Leopold Auerbach," in *Allgemeine Deutsche Biographie,* vol. 46 (Leipzig: Duncker & Humblot, 1902), 85–87; APW, AMW, K 151, district 19, no. 115 and the Prussian tax rolls, APW, AMW, K 146, vol. 21, no. 2134. On Oscar Berger, see Jonas Graetzer, *Lebensbilder hervorragender schlesischer Ärzte aus den letzten vier Jahrhunderten* (Breslau: Schottländer, 1889), 166a–d; "Nekrolog Oscar Berger," *Jahresbericht der Schlesischen Gesellschaft für vaterländische Cultur* 63 (1885): 428–29; "Nekrolog Oscar Berger," *Israelitische Wochenschrift* 16 (1885): 252.

31. On Jacobi, see "Nekrolog Joseph Jacobi," *Jahresbericht der Schlesischen Gesellschaft für vaterländische Cultur* 85 (1907): obituaries, 31–32.

32. Gerber, *Die Schlesische Gesellschaft,* 56; on Joseph Jacobi and his wife, Selma, see Max Born, *Mein Leben* (Munich: Nymphenburger Verlagshandlung, 1975), 26–27; "Nekrolog Joseph Jacobi" (see preceding note); and APW, AMW, K 156, district 17, no. 2848.

33. Gerber, *Die Schlesische Gesellschaft,* 70–71; on Hönigswald, see Jörg Hackeschmidt, *Von Kurt Blumenfeld zu Norbert Elias: Die Erfindung einer jüdischen Nation* (Hamburg: Europäische Verlagsanstalt, 1997), 138–48.

34. Gerber, *Die Schlesische Gesellschaft,* 44; see also "Nekrolog Emil Toeplitz," *Jahresbericht der Schlesischen Gesellschaft für vaterländische Cultur* 95 (1917): 42–43.

35. Gerber, *Die Schlesische Gesellschaft,* 71–74 and 95–96.

36. On what follows here, see Stefan-Ludwig Hoffmann, *Die Politik der Geselligkeit: Freimaurerlogen in der deutschen Bürgergesellschaft, 1840–1918* (Göttingen: Vandenhoeck & Ruprecht, 2000), 89–92. Hoffmann bases his account especially on "Acta betr. die Freimaurerloge 'Kosmos' 1849–1851," APW, OPB 345.

37. Bernhard Mann, ed., *Biographisches Handbuch für das Preußische Abgeordnetenhaus, 1867–1918* (Düsseldorf: Droste, 1988), 240; Bernd Haunfelder, ed. *Biographisches Handbuch für das Preußische Abgeordnetenhaus, 1849–1867* (Düsseldorf: Droste, 1994), 159. On Laßwitz and the Johannes-Gymnasium, see chap. 4, sec. 2, of this volume.

38. On the Cologne lodge Minerva, see Stefan-Ludwig Hoffmann, "Bürger zweier Welten?"; see also Jacob Katz, *Jews and Freemasons in Europe, 1723–1939* (Cambridge, Mass.: Harvard University Press, 1970), 129–31; Shulamit Magnus, *Jewish Emancipation in a German City: Cologne, 1798–1871* (Stanford, Calif.: Stanford University Press, 1997), 93 and 101 (the exception was Salomon Oppenheim, who had joined the lodge during the French period and was permitted to remain a member after 1815); Thomas Mergel overlooks the fact that the Cologne lodges were not open to all "heterodox" individuals, namely, that they were closed to Jews; see his *Zwischen Klasse und Konfession: Katholisches Bürgertum im Rheinland im 19. Jahrhundert* (Göttingen: Vandenhoeck & Ruprecht, 1994), 59–62.

39. Stefan-Ludwig Hoffmann, *Die Politik der Geselligkeit,* 121–3.

40. On Hirsch Joachimsohn, see APW, AMW, K 150, vol. 2, no. 48; see the magistracy's tribute to him following his death on March 31, 1883, APW, AMW, III, 2189, fol. 243.

41. Geheimes Staatsarchiv Berlin, Logen 5.2 L 17 Leipzig, Freimaurerloge "Apollo," 1.2.6 Personalakten, no. 185, cited in Stefan-Ludwig Hoffmann, *Die Politik der Geselligkeit,* 176–7.

42. "Eine Zuschrift aus Breslau," *Israelitische Wochenschrift* 5 (1874): 393–94; similar to this is a somewhat earlier piece by the editor of the *Allgemeine Zeitung des Judenthums:* Ludwig Philippson, "Wieder einmal die Freimaurerei," *Allgemeine Zeitung des Judenthums* 35 (1871): 817–21 and 835–38.

43. A parallel development is described in Hopp, *Jüdisches Bürgertum,* 124–26.

44. Ludwig Sittenfeld, "Die Geschichte des Vereins 'Breslauer Dichterschule,'" in *"Der Osten": Ein schlesischer Jubiläumsalmanach herausgegeben anläßlich des 50 jährigen Jubiläums der "Breslauer Dichterschule,"* ed. Carl Biberfeld (Breslau: Koebner, 1909), 4–25, here 14, 17, and 22.

45. Ibid., 6.

46. A good impression of this is provided in the writings in Biberfeld, *"Der Osten,"* 26–72.

47. Sittenfeld, "Die Geschichte des Vereins 'Breslauer Dichterschule,'" 16 and 22; see Ludwig's poems in *Der Osten: Literarische Monatsblätter* 36 (1910): 133–36, 157–61, and 178–81.

48. Sittenfeld, "Die Geschichte des Vereins 'Breslauer Dichterschule,'" 5–6.

49. See Jakob Freund, *Biblische Gedichte* (Breslau: Schletter, 1861); Freund, *Confirmationsreden nebst Anhang: Glaubensbekenntnis und Reden für die Confirmanden* (Breslau: Schletter, 1870; repr., Breslau: J. B. Brandeis, 1908); Freund, *Festkränze: Neue Gelegenheitsgedichte für Kinder* (Breslau: Schletter, 1866); Freund, *Hanna: Gebets- und Andachtsbuch für israelitische Mädchen und Frauen*, 2nd ed. (Breslau: Skutsch, 1874), reprinted as *Hanna: Gebets- und Andachtsbuch für israelitische Frauen und Mädchen; Mit Beiträgen von Abraham Geiger, Moritz Güdemann, Manuel Joel und Moritz Abraham Levy*, 6th ed. (Breslau: Verlag von Wilhelm Koebner, 1890); Freund, *Haman oder die Rechnung ohne Wirth: Posse mit Gesang in fünf Akten* (Breslau: C. H. Storch, 1875); Verein Breslauer Dichterschule, ed., *Album Schlesischer Dichterfreunde*, vol. 7 (Breslau, 1874), 37–55. Many of Freund's writings are now located in the Jewish National and University Library, Jerusalem. See also "Nekrolog," *Allgemeine Zeitung des Judenthums* 41 (1877): 552–53.

50. On Julius Freund, see Marline S. Otte, *Jewish Identities in German Popular Entertainment, 1890–1933* (Cambridge: Cambridge University Press, 2006); Biberfeld, *"Der Osten,"* 74–75.

51. Sittenfeld, "Die Geschichte des Vereins 'Breslauer Dichterschule,'" 10.

52. Bertha Badt, "Hans Sachs auf der Breslauer Festwiese," *Der Osten: Literarische Monatsblätter* 36 (1910): 112–13; Arthur Silbergleit, "Sabbat," *Der Osten: Literarische Monatsblätter* 36 (1910): 132. On Silbergleit, see Dora Segall, "Arthur Segall," *AJR Information* 26, no. 6 (1971): 5, and Paul Mühsam, "In Memoriam Arthur Silbergleit," *Schlesien* 16 (1971): 100–101; see also the "Sammlung Arthur Silbergleit," Deutsches Literaturarchiv Marbach.

53. Gründungsaufruf und Statut des Humboldt-Vereins für Volksbildung, Breslau, July 21, 1869, BUW, GŚL Yv 605; (banker Siegfried Cohn, banker Moritz Gradenwitz, merchant Hermann Haber, book dealer Julius Hainauer, physician Pinoff, merchant Salo Sackur, banker Bernhard Schreyer, and merchant Heinrich Wolfskehl).

54. *Allgemeine Zeitung des Judenthums* 33 (1869): 742, cited in Toury, *Soziale und politische Geschichte*, 129. On the Jewish reverence for Humboldt in general, see Adolph Kohut, *Alexander von Humboldt und das Judenthum* (Leipzig: Pardubitz, 1871), and the book notice in *Breslauer Zeitung*, no. 71, February 11, 1871; "Alexander von Humboldt als Politiker," *Allgemeine Zeitung des Judenthums* 33 (1869): 797–801 and 822–25; "Humboldt und die Juden," *Allgemeine Zeitung des Judenthums* 38 (1874): 594–96.

55. "Humboldtfeier," *Schlesische Zeitung*, no. 347, July 29, 1869, supplement 1.

56. "Was eint uns im Geistes- und Gemütsleben?" in *Festschrift herausgegeben aus Anlass der Feier des 25 jährigen Bestehens des Humboldtvereins für Volksbildung zu*

Breslau am 28. October 1894, ed. Gustav Gärtner (Breslau: Preuss & Jünger, 1894), 71–93, here 81–82.

57. On the limited importance of Humboldt clubs elsewhere, see Daum, *Wissenspopularisierung im 19. Jahrhundert*, 138–67, quotation from 150; for general background on what follows here, see Hettling, *Politische Bürgerlichkeit*, 218 and 220. The importance of the Humboldt-Verein is evident, e.g., in the history of the founding of the Johannes-Gymnasium. Of the four Breslau Jews who vigorously championed a pluralistic school, the dentist Moritz Fränkel and the book dealer Julius Hainauer were members of the Humboldt-Verein. Of the seven non-Jews who were strong advocates of the Johanneum, two were club members, the merchant Carl Wilhelm Laßwitz and the preacher of the Breslau free church, Theodor Hofferichter, as well as another, Moritz Elsner, who was connected to the Humboldt-Verein as a speaker. See *7. Jahresbericht des Humboldt-Vereins für Volksbildung in Breslau für das Vereinsjahr 1875–1876* (Breslau: Breslauer Genossenschafts-Buchdruckerei, 1876), 25–27, as well as the list of talks and lectures held in the Humboldt-Verein during this period in Gärtner, *Festschrift*, 18–20.

58. "Nachrichten," *Schlesisches Protestantenblatt* 2 (1872): 91.

59. *7. Jahresbericht des Humboldt-Vereins für Volksbildung in Breslau für das Vereinsjahr 1875–1876*, 26; *24. Jahresbericht des Humboldt-Vereins für Volksbildung in Breslau für das Vereinsjahr 1892–1893* (Breslau: Breslauer Genossenschafts-Buchdruckerei, 1893), 18; and *37. Jahresbericht des Humboldt-Vereins für Volksbildung für das Vereinsjahr 1905–06* (Breslau: Breslauer Genossenschafts-Buchdruckerei, 1906), 9.

60. Reinke, *Judentum und Wohlfahrtspflege in Deutschland*, 226n141. The Breslau chapter of the Centralverein deutscher Staatsbürger jüdischen Glaubens had a good 700 members in 1905 and a good 800 in 1908; see the *Centralverein deutscher Staatsbürger jüdischen Glaubens. Mitglieder-Verzeichnis, 1905* (Berlin: Hasenstein & Vögler, 1905), 72–80, and *Mitglieder-Verzeichnis, 1908* (Berlin: Hasenstein & Vögler, 1908), 85–94.

61. See the member list in *37. Jahresbericht des Humboldt-Vereins für Volksbildung für das Vereinsjahr 1905–06*.

62. Heinrich Wendt, "Wissenschaftliche Vereine in Breslau," *Zeitschrift des Vereins für Geschichte und Altertum Schlesiens* 38 (1904): 71–109, here 106.

63. Loewe, "Schlesische Gelehrte Gesellschaften und Vereine," 260; see also Wendt, "Wissenschaftliche Vereine in Breslau."

64. Hermann L. Cohn, "Ueber sexuelle Belehrung der Schulkinder," *Allgemeine Medizinische Central-Zeitung* 73 (1904): 931–35, 961–64, 981–84, and 1002–4, here 961.

65. *Gründungsaufruf des Humboldt-Vereins für Volksbildung, Breslau, 21. Juli 1869* (Breslau: Humboldt-Verein für Volksbildung, 1869).

66. *Statut des Humboldt-Vereins für Volksbildung, Breslau, 21. July 1869*, sec. 1, BUW, GŚL Yv 605. From 1888 onward, the Humboldt-Verein refrained from printing the founding statement, which was infused with a naive belief in

progress, as part of its statutes. In the statutes it now says, somewhat more soberly, that the club aims "to work for the continuing intellectual education and moral ennoblement of the people"; *Grundgesetz des Humboldt-Vereins für Volksbildung, Breslau, 16. April 1888*, sec. 2, BUW, GŚL Yv 605. On the Manichean thinking in the liberalism of the 1860s and 1870s, see David Blackbourn, *Volksfrömmigkeit und Fortschrittsglaube im Kulturkampf* (Wiesbaden: Franz Steiner, 1988); Michael B. Gross, "Kulturkampf and Unification: German Liberals and the War against the Jesuits," *Central European History* 30 (1997): 545–66; Róisín Healy, "Religion and Civil Society: Catholics, Jesuits, and Protestants in Imperial Germany," in *Paradoxes of Civil Society: New Perspectives on Modern Britain and Germany*, ed. Frank Trentmann (Oxford: Berghan, 2000), 244–62. In general on the "popular education" movement, see Ludolf Parisius, "Eine Gesellschaft zur Verbreitung von Volksbildung," *Volksfreund* 4 (1871): 131–32, 135–36, 137–39, and 145–46.

67. *7. Jahresbericht des Humboldt-Vereins für Volksbildung in Breslau für das Vereinsjahr 1875–1876*, 22. On Wilhelm Kalisch, see "Nekrolog," in Bericht über das 69. Verwaltungsjahr des Breslauer Handlungsdiener Instituts 1902–03, APW, Regierung Breslau, Justizbüro 7237 Breslauer Handlungsinstitut 1834–1926; Hainauer, *Die Gesellschaft der Freunde in Breslau*, 73. On Wilhelm Koebner, see APW, AMW, K 150, district 18, no. 2292; Koebner published, e.g., Moritz Abraham Levy, *Biblische Geschichte nach dem Worte der heiligen Schrift der israelitischen Jugend erzählt*, ed. Benno Badt, 6th rev. ed. (Breslau: Koebner, 1881), and Benno Badt, *Kinderbibel: Biblische Erzählungen für die israelitische Jugend*, 3rd ed. (Breslau: Koebner, 1905). On David Mugdan, see *Jüdisches Volksblatt* 16 (1910): 248, and state tax roll APW, AMW, K 146, vol. 21, no. 223. On Leopold Piebatsch, see APW, AMW, K 150, district 12, no. 1734; Maciej Łagiewski, *Wrocławscy Żydzi, 1850–1944* (Wrocław: Muzeum Historyczne, 1994), plates 322–24; Hainauer, *Die Gesellschaft der Freunde in Breslau*, 73; and the material in the university archive, BUW, Akc. 1968, 261 and 262. A list of the books contained in the library of the Humboldt-Verein für Volksbildung may be found in *8. Jahresbericht des Humboldt-Vereins für Volksbildung für das Vereinsjahr 1876–1877* (Breslau: Breslauer Genossenschafts-Buchdruckerei, 1877), 4–18, here 6 and 23 (club library at Priebatsch's).

68. *37. Jahresbericht des Humboldt-Vereins für Volksbildung für das Vereinsjahr 1905–06*, 9–10.

69. "Sonntagsvortrag des Humboldtvereins," *Breslauer Zeitung*, no. 100, March 1, 1870, 727; *7. Jahresbericht des Humboldt-Vereins für Volksbildung in Breslau für das Vereinsjahr 1875–1876*, 24–25; on the success of the "Sunday Talks," see Gustav Gärtner, "Auf fünfundzwanzig Jahre," in Gärtner, *Festschrift*, 3–18, here 5; the *Schlesische Nachrichten* and the *Schlesische Presse* published inexpensive offprints of the talks, and the *Breslauer Zeitung*, the *Breslauer Morgen-Zeitung*, and the *Schlesische Zeitung* published extensive summaries of the talks (see Gärtner, *Festschrift*, 6).

70. Adolf Heilberg, "Die Idee des allgemeinen Völkerfriedens," in *24. Jahresbericht des Humboldt-Vereins für Volksbildung in Breslau für das Vereinsjahr 1892–1893* (Breslau: Breslauer Genossenschafts-Buchdruckerei, 1893), 3–16 (reprinted in *Jüdisches Leben in Deutschland*, ed. Monika Richarz, vol. 2, *Selbstzeugnisse zur Sozialgeschichte des Kaiserreichs* [Stuttgart: Deutsche Verlagsanstalt, 1979], 289–96). The other Jewish speakers were the ophthalmologist Hermann Cohn, the lawyer (and husband of Paula Ollendorff, the future women's rights activist) Isidor Ollendorff, the lawyer Julius Mamroth, and Albert Wohlauer, a senior teacher at the Johannes-Gymnasium; see *37. Jahresbericht des Humboldt-Vereins für Volksbildung für das Vereinsjahr 1905–06*, 21–22.

71. *37. Jahresbericht des Humboldt-Vereins für Volksbildung für das Vereinsjahr 1905–06*, 16–17.

72. Ibid., 12–14.

73. "Wir wohnen zwar gar abgelegen / Vom allgemeinen Weltverkehr / Doch was sich zuträgt allerwegen / Kommt schließlich auch bis Breslau her." "Wie Nero Christen einst zur Beute / Den Löwen in den Zwinger gab, / So schließen jene sich noch heute / In Breslaus Zwinger ängstlich ab: / Wie paßt das, aufgeklärte Geister, / Zur freien Schule, die Ihr schafft, / Durch welche unser Bürgermeister / Vermehrt den Ruhm der Bürgerschaft." "Zum 20. Stiftungsfest des hiesigen 'kaufmännischen Vereins,'" *Breslauer Zeitung*, no. 99, March 1, 1870, 713. The "free school" mentioned here is the Johannes-Gymnasium; see chap. 4, sec. 2, of this volume.

74. "Breslau, im Februar," *Allgemeine Zeitung des Judenthums* 40 (1876): 119.

75. On Molinari's relation to Gustav Freytag, see Edward Bialek, Roman Polsakiewicz, and Marek Zybura, eds., *Gustav Freytag an Theodor Molinari und die Seinen: Bislang unbekannte Briefe aus den Beständen der Universitätsbibliothek Wrocław* (Frankfurt a. M.: Peter Lang, 1987).

76. "Der 'Judenfreund' Molinari," *Schlesische Volkszeitung*, no. 168, July 26, 1878. When Molinari stood years later as a candidate of the National Liberals for the Reichstag, the Catholic paper recalled Molinari's role: "Precisely now—when Mr. Molinari is presented to Breslau's Catholic voters ostensibly as a fellow believer—it seems only right to remind all Catholic voters of Molinari's philo-Semitism." One of the first debates on the admittance of Jews had taken place in the late 1830s. It was at that time that the Zwingergesellschaft had specified in its statutes that only Christians could become members. See Wendt, *Das erste Jahrhundert*, 20–21.

77. "Der 'Judenfreund' Molinari," *Schlesische Volkszeitung*, no. 168, July 26, 1878.

78. "Der Zwinger," *Schlesisches Morgenblatt*, no. 279, October 1, 1882, 2; the other installments in the series from October 1882 (listing only day and issue number here) were: 4, no. 281; 6, no. 283; 10, no. 286; 12, no. 289; 12, no. 288, 12; 14, no. 290; 17, no. 292; 19, no. 294; 20, no. 295; 24, no. 298; 26, no. 300.

79. What follows here is based on "Verzeichnis der resp. Mitglieder der kaufmännischen Zwinger- und Ressourcen-Gesellschaft, 1875," BUW, GŚŁ Yz 174. On the history of the club, see Julius Neugebauer, "Der Zwinger und die kaufmännische Zwingerschützenbrüderschaft nebst einer historischen Einleitung über die ehemalige Bürgermiliz und die Bürgerschützen-Brüderschaft," *Zeitschrift des Vereins für Geschichte und Altertum Schlesiens* 13 (1876): supplement, 1–94.

80. Wendt, *Das erste Jahrhundert*, 14; see also the list of club members of "all professions and vocations that [were] assured . . . of a place of honor in the history of [their] hometown" (26). On the balls in the 1860s see p. 28.

81. Ibid., 22.

82. Five of the eight members of the board of directors of the Kaufmännischer Verein in 1882 were Jewish (David Mugdan, Julius Moll, Fedor Koebner, Siegfried Haber, and Betrand Zadig); see *Bericht des kaufmännischen Vereins zu Breslau für das Jahr 1882: Nebst Statut und Mitgliederverzeichnis* (Breslau: n.p., 1883), 9. The club concerned itself above all with concrete matters, such as the railroad tariff, the navigability of the Oder River, the pros and cons of the gold standard, and the experience of members with the legal system in Russia and Poland; see pp. 1–5. On the chamber of commerce, see Hermann Freymark, *Die Handelskammer Breslau, 1849–1924: Festschrift der Industrie- u. Handelskammer Breslau* (Breslau: Schatzky, 1924); *Jahresbericht der Handelskammer Breslau für das Jahr 1891* (Breslau: Handelskammer, 1892); and *Jahresbericht der Handelskammer Breslau für das Jahr 1910* (Breslau: Handelskammer, 1911). On Isidor Friedenthal, see the chamber of commerce's obituary notice and the obituary in the *Schlesische Zeitung*, October 20, 1886; "Nekrolog," *Israelitische Wochenschrift* 17 (1886): 353; and Manuel Joël, "An der Bahre von Isidor Friedenthal," in *Festpredigten*, ed. Adolf Eckstein and Bernhard Ziemlich, vol. 1 (Breslau: Schlesische Buckdruck, Kunst- und Verlags-Anstalt, 1892), 310–14.

83. Wendt, *Das erste Jahrhundert*, 25 and 18.

84. On the social structure of the Zwingergesellschaft, see Hettling, *Politische Bürgerlichkeit*, 220, and "Verzeichnis der resp. Mitglieder."

85. Friedrich Naumann, "Die Leidensgeschichte des deutschen Liberalismus" (1908), in *Werke*, ed. Theodor Schieder, vol. 4 (Cologne: Westdeutscher Verlag, 1964), 291–316, here 292.

86. Schüler-Springorum, *Die jüdische Minderheit*, 79–80; Michael Erbe, "Berlin im Kaiserreich (1871–1918)," in *Geschichte Berlins*, ed. Wolfgang Ribbe, vol. 2, *Von der Märzrevolution bis zur Gegenwart* (Munich: C. H. Beck, 1987), 689–793, here 758–59; Theodor Fontane, "Adel und Judenthum in der Berliner Gesellschaft," *Jahrbuch der deutschen Schillergesellschaft* 30 (1986): 34, 37–39, and 59–66.

87. Shulamit Volkov, "Antisemitism as a Cultural Code: Reflections on the History and Historiography of Antisemitism in Imperial Germany," *Year Book of the Leo Baeck Institute* 23 (1978): 25–46, 34–35. Werner Jochmann has made similar observation in his "Struktur und Funktion des deutschen Antisemitismus,"

in *Juden im Wilhelminischen Deutschland, 1870–1914,* ed. Werner E. Mosse (Tübingen: Mohr Siebeck, 1976), 389–477, here 473–77.

88. Adolf Heilberg, Memoiren, ME257a, 330, Archives of the LBI, New York.

89. *Verzeichnis der Mitglieder der Section Breslau des Deutschen und Österreichischen Alpenvereins, April 1888* (Breslau: Breslauer Genossenschafts-Buchhandlung, 1888). On the history of the club's founding, see *Bericht der Section Breslau des Deutschen und Oesterreichischen Alpenvereins über die ersten fünf Jahre ihres Bestehens (1878–1882)* (Breslau: Stenzel, 1883). Since Breslau was not close to the Alps, the club placed less emphasis on "Alpine excursions" than on "offering to Silesia's educated population, in whom the inclination and opportunity to look around the world more widely [had] instilled an interest in knowing more about the Alps, . . . welcome satisfaction for their hunger for broadening and mutually increasing their knowledge" (4).

90. "Wohin mag man jetzt kommen, / Was hört man? Politik! / Uns thät' dies wenig frommen, / Uns brächte dies kein Glück. / Wir tagen unbekümmert / Um der Parteien Zwist, / Ob Windthorst oder Bennigsen / Jetzt ausschlaggebend ist. / Ob ein Schutzzoll, / Ob ein Trutzzoll / Jetzt dem Volke heilsam sei, / Lasst's den Andern, / Wir, wir wandern / In die Alpen froh und frei. // . . . Nationale-/Liberale, / Neu- und Fortschrittswahlverein, / Alle friedlich /Und gemüthlich / Kommen in den Vorstand 'rein.'" "Stiftungsfest 1882," in *Aus dem Leben der Section Breslau des Deutschen und Österreichischen Alpenvereins den Sectionsgenossen überreicht zum X. Stiftungsfest am 28. Januar 1888* (Breslau: Brehmer & Minuth, 1888), 18–19.

91. "Breslau," *Allgemeine Zeitung des Judenthums* 52 (1888): 825.

92. The *Breslauer Zeitung* reported in early January 1889 that "the position taken against Mr. von Stengel" was "a protest against the unreasonable demand" "to allow this man to be granted an honor, a special salute also from those members against whom Mr. von Stengel had displayed a mentality that could be felt to be nothing but offensive"; cited in "Breslau," *Allgemeine Zeitung des Judenthums* 53 (1889): 25.

93. "Breslau, 21. November," *Allgemeine Zeitung des Judenthums* 52 (1888): 761; for mocking treatments of the events, see "Professor Freiherr von Stengel," *Breslauer Gerichts-Zeitung,* no. 49, December 2, 1888, and "Breslau," *Israelitische Wochenschrift* 19 (1888): 349; the characterization of the speech as a "brutal, anti-Semitic, rabble-rousing speech" (*brutale antisemitische Hetzrede*) is from "Breslau, 2. Januar," *Allgemeine Zeitung des Judenthums* 53 (1889): 25.

94. "Breslauer Zeitung," cited in *Allgemeine Zeitung des Judenthums* 53 (1889): 25.

95. "Breslau," *Allgemeine Zeitung des Judenthums* 53 (1889): 39.

96. *Verzeichnis der Mitglieder der Section Breslau des Deutschen und Österreichischen Alpenvereins, Februar 1889* (Breslau: n.p., 1889).

97. *Verzeichnis der Mitglieder der Section Breslau des Deutschen und Österreichischen Alpenvereins, April 1888;* "Mitgliederverzeichnis," in 9. *Bericht der Section Breslau des Deutschen und Österreichischen Alpenvereins, 29. Vereinsjahr 1906* (Breslau: Stenzel, 1907).

98. Other Breslau Jews who left the club were the banker Gustav Bielschowsky and the merchant Siegfried Bielschowsky, the lawyer Hugo Callomon, the merchant Richard Eppenstein, the merchant Adolf Friedenthal, the lawyer Ernst Friedenthal, and the lawyer Julius Haber; see *Verzeichnis der Mitglieder der Section Breslau des Deutschen und Österreichischen Alpenvereins, April 1888,* and *Verzeichnis der Mitglieder der Section Breslau des Deutschen und Österreichischen Alpenvereins, Februar 1889,* both in BUW, GŚL 26408 II. The only one of these men to rejoin was Adolf Heilberg, and he did so no later than 1898 (see "Verzeichnis der Mitglieder im Februar 1899," in *Bericht der Section Breslau des Deutschen und Oesterreichischen Alpenvereins über das Jahr 1898* [Breslau: Stenzel, 1899], 1–15).

99. *Mitglieder-Verzeichnis der Section Breslau des Riesengebirgs-Vereins am Ende des Jahres 1886,* BUW, GŚL Yz 336; *Festschrift zur Feier des 25 jährigen Bestehens der Ortsgruppe Breslau des Riesengebirgs-Vereins* (Breslau: Woywod, 1906).

100. Oscar Dyhrenfurth, "Geschichte der Sektion," in *Festschrift zur Feier des 25 jährigen Bestehens der Sektion Breslau des Deutschen und Österreichischem Alpenvereins* (Breslau: Sektion Breslau des Deutschen und Österreichischem Alpenvereins, 1902), 3–9, here 5. The festschrift recalls the conflict rather cautiously. "In 1888," wrote Dyhrenfurth, "there was a very undesirable conclusion to the year. The high-rising waves of political excitement due to the Reichstag elections even burst in on our club, which is usually far removed from politics, and gave rise to such a rift that some of the members quit the club" (5).

101. Carl Biberfeld, *Pallas und Germania: Festspiel zum 8. allgemeinen deutschen Turnfest* (Breslau: Festausschreibung des VIII. deutschen Turnfestes, 1894), 85 and 87.

102. *Der Reichsbote,* July 27, 1894, cited in "Das 8. deutsche Turnfest und die Antisemiten," *Mitteilungen aus dem Verein zur Abwehr des Antisemitismus* 4 (1894):, 246; see also 213 and 279; it did not take the anti-Semites long to forget their failure; see, e.g., *Antisemitisches Jahrbuch für 1898* (Berlin: Giese, 1898), 150–51. In general, see Svenja Goltermann, *Körper der Nation: Habitusformierung und die Politik des Turnens, 1860–1890* (Göttingen: Vandenhoeck & Ruprecht, 1998), 285–90.

103. On the following, see Stefan-Ludwig Hoffmann, *Die Politik der Geselligkeit,* 186–92.

104. *Namen-Verzeichnis der Mitglieder der Israelitischen Kranken-Verpflegungs-Anstalt und Beerdigungs-Gesellschaft zu Breslau, 20. April 1906* (Breslau: n.p., 1906); *Riesengebirgs-Verein, Breslau: Mitglieder-Verzeichnis, 1908,* BUW, GŚL Yz 336; 37. *Jahresbericht des Humboldt-Vereins für Volksbildung für das Vereinsjahr 1905–06,* BUW, GŚL Yz 608.

105. His efforts to become naturalized are documented in APW, PPB 75, fols. 55–81. In 1906, Fischhoff earned more that 56,000 marks (APW, AMW, K 156, district 40, no. 695) and was also a member of the Israelitische Kranken- und Verpflegungs-Anstalt und Beerdigungsgesellschaft. On Georg Barasch, see *Breslauer Köpfe: Begegnungen mit prominenten Breslauern* (Breslau: Golland, 1927), 28–29.

106. Pfeffer, who belonged to the circle of the Hermann lodge's sponsors, donated in 1903–4 alone a total of 70,000 marks; see *Rechenschafts-Bericht der Israelitischen Kranken-Verpflegungs-Anstalt und Beerdigungsgesellschaft zu Breslau für die Jahre 1903, 1904 und 1905* (Breslau: n.p., 1906); on Pfeffer's income and financial situation, see APW, AMW, K 156, district 40, no. 2767.

107. On Markt, see "Traueranzeigen," *Breslauer Zeitung*, no. 612, December 1, 1918; "Nekrolog," *Breslauer Zeitung*, no. 611, November 30, 1918; *Namen-Verzeichnis der Mitglieder der Israelitischen Kranken-Verpflegungs-Anstalt und Beerdigungs-Gesellschaft zu Breslau, 5. Mai 1909* (Breslau: n.p., 1909).

108. On his biography, see *Jahresbericht der städtischen höheren Töchterschule am Ritterplatz zu Breslau 1871* (Breslau: n.p., 1871), 37; "Trauerfeier der Johannisloge 'Hermann zur Beständigkeit,'" *Bausteine: Mitteilungen aus der großen Freimaurer-Loge von Preußen, genannt Kaiser Friedrich zur Bundestreue* 6 (1897): 99–101; "Locales and Provinziales," *Schlesisches Morgenblatt*, no. 7, January 9, 1881, supplement.

109. Martin Maass, *Die Soziale Stellung der Juden in Deutschland und das Civil-Ehegesetz* (Löbau: Skrzeczek, 1876), 75–76; see also his *Die Mischehe, das einzig wirksame Mittel einer dauernden Vereinigung zwischen der jüdischen und christlichen Bevölkerung Deutschlands* (Löbau: Skrzeczek, 1881); on the Jewish critique of "melting-pot fantasies," see Emanuel Schreiber, *Die sociale Stellung der Juden: Offenes Sendschreiben an Herrn Dr. Maass-Breslau* (Königsberg: Prange, 1877), esp. 13–14; on Maass, see also Susannah Heschel, *Abraham Geiger and the Jewish Jesus* (Chicago: University of Chicago Press, 1998), 42; Kerstin Meiring, *Die christlich-jüdische Mischehe in Deutschland, 1840–1933* (Hamburg: Dölling & Galitz, 1998), 164; and Alan T. Levenson, "Jewish Reactions to Intermarriage in Nineteenth Century Germany" (PhD diss., Ohio State University, 1990), 130 and 133–34.

110. Alfred Oehlke, "Christenthum, Humanität und Freimaurerei," *Bausteine* 9 (1900): 51–57, here 55, cited in Stefan-Ludwig Hoffmann, *Die Politik der Geselligkeit*, 190.

111. Stefan-Ludwig Hoffmann, *Die Politik der Geselligkeit*, 190–91.

112. Dieter Langewiesche has once again stressed that it is insufficient to consider only formal club membership; see his "Kommentar," in *Stadt und Bürgertum im Übergang von der traditionellen zur modernen Gesellschaft*, ed. Lothar Gall (Munich: Oldenbourg, 1993), 229–36.

113. "Bericht über die Tätigkeit des Schlesischen Geschichtsvereins in den Jahren 1887 und 1888," *Zeitschrift des Vereins für Geschichte und Altertum Schlesiens* 23 (1889): 330–36, esp. 332–33.

114. "Durch der Oder flücht'ge Welle / Dampfbeflügelt eilt der Kahn / Jubelnd schaun wir schon die Stelle / Unsrer Festesfreude nah'n . . . // Hat der

Geist sich mit Behagen / Am Naturgenuss erfrischt, / Wird gewöhnlich auch dem Magen / Seine Mahlzeit aufgetischt . . . // Mädchen, Eurem bangen Warten / Seh' ich endlich Heil erblüh'n, / Schau voll Grazie durch den Garten / Sich die Polonaise ziehn. // Lasst uns fröhlich heut noch schweben / In des Tanzes leichten Flug, / Ernstem Fleiss und rüst'gem Streben, / Beut der Winter Zeit genug." "Dem Humboldtverein für Volksbildung zu seinem Sommerausflug nach Zedlitz, Breslau, den 17. Juni 1882," BUW, GŚL Yv 617. Freyhan was an enthusiastic amateur poet and an active member of the Breslauer Dichterschule.

115. On the climbing tours, see *Aus dem Leben der Section Breslau*, 80–81 and 88–90, esp. 90; on the meetings afterward, see *12. Bericht der Section Breslau des Deutschen und Österreichischen Alpenvereins, 32. Vereinsjahr 1909* (Breslau: Stenzel, 1909), 12.

116. *8. Bericht der Section Breslau des Deutschen und Österreichischen Alpenvereins, 28. Vereinsjahr 1905* (Breslau: Stenzel, 1906), 12–13.

117. Hermann L. Cohn, *Was kann die Schule gegen die Masturbation der Kinder thun? Referat erstattet auf dem 8. internationalen hygienischen Kongress Budapest* (Berlin: R. Schoetz, 1894). At that time, Cohn was the honorary president of the school healthcare division of the conference.

118. For general background on the nineteenth-century discussion of masturbation, see R. P. Neumann, "Masturbation, Madness, and the Modern Concepts of Childhood and Adolescence," *Journal of Social History* 8 (1975): 1–27, and Thomas W. Laqueur, *Solitary Sex: A Cultural History of Masturbation* (New York: Zone Books, 2003). Specifically on the anti-Semitic context, see Klaus Hödl, *Die Pathologisierung des jüdischen Körpers: Antisemitismus, Geschlecht und Medizin im Fin de Siècle* (Vienna: Picus Verlag, 1997), 71–104, quotation from 73; and Sander L. Gilman, *The Jew's Body* (New York: Routledge, 1991), 84, 92, 120, 123, and 222.

119. Cohn, "Ueber sexuelle Belehrung der Schulkinder," 931.

120. Ibid. Cohn expressly meant female pupils as well; he referred to his friend Oscar Berger, who had died in 1885. "Masturbation," Berger argued, "is such a widespread manipulation that of 100 men and girls, 99 do it at some time, and the hundredth person, as I usually say, the pure one, is hiding the truth" (cited in Cohn, "Ueber sexuelle Belehrung der Schulkinder," 931).

121. Ibid., 932.

122. Ibid., 933–34; see also 935.

123. Ibid., 961–62 (Wiedemann), 962–64 (Günther, Hippauf, and Tschirn), and 1002–3 (Michaelis).

124. Ibid., 1003 (Asch), 984 (Fraenkel), 963 (Jacobi), 961 (Chotzen), and 962 (Samosch); Asch, Fraenkel, and Jacobi criticize Hermann Cohn, whereas Chotzen and Samosch support him. Fritz Stern, *Five Germanys I Have Known* (New York: Farrar, Straus & Giroux, 2006), 19; on Ernst Fränkel, see *Deutsche Biographische Enzyklopädie* (Munich: Saur, 1996), 3:383; on Michaelis, see Bert

Becker, *Georg Michaelis: Preußischer Beamter, Reichskanzler, Christlicher Reformer 1857–1936. Eine Biographie* (Paderborn: Schöningh, 2007).

125. Cohn, "Ueber sexuelle Belehrung der Schulkinder," 963 and 1003 (Buchwald), 1003–4 (Neisser), and 962 (Tietze).

126. Ibid., 1002.

127. Kaplan, "Freizeit—Arbeit: Geschlechterräume im deutsch-jüdischen Bürgertum, 1870–1914," in *Bürgerinnen und Bürger: Geschlechterverhältnisse im 19. Jahrhundert*, ed. Ute Frevert (Göttingen: Vandenhoeck & Ruprecht, 1988), 157–74, here 172; Schüler-Springorum, *Die jüdische Minderheit*, 81–86, quotation from 82; Hopp, *Jüdisches Bürgertum*, 150 and 153.

128. Hans Jessen, "Eine schlesische Freundschaft," in *Kritische Solidarität: Festschrift für Max Plaut*, ed. Günter Schulz (Bremen: Röver, 1971), 293–98. The expression "good friends" is from a poem of Holtei's that he dedicated to Kurnik (293); see also Jessen's *Max Kurnik: Ein Breslauer Journalist (1819–1881)* (Breslau: Breslauer Zeitung, 1927).

129. Hans I. Bach, *Jacob Bernays: Ein Beitrag zur Emanzipationsgeschichte der Juden und zur Geschichte des deutschen Geistes im 19. Jahrhundert* (Tübingen: Mohr Siebeck, 1974), 136–37; see also Christhard Hoffmann, *Juden und Judentum im Werk deutscher Althistoriker des 19. und 20. Jahrhunderts* (Leiden: Brill, 1988), 117–33, and Stanley Zucker, "Theodor Mommsen and Antisemitism," *Year Book of the Leo Baeck Institute* 17 (1972): 237–41; on Jacob Bernays, see Anthony Grafton, "Jacob Bernays, Joseph Scaliger, and Others," in *The Jewish Past Revisited: Reflections on Modern Jewish Historians*, ed. David N. Myers and David B. Ruderman (New Haven, Conn.: Yale University Press, 1998), 16–38.

130. Anna Auerbach, Die Chronik der Familie Silbergleit, ME 600, Archives of the LBI, New York.

131. Geheimes Staatsarchiv Dahlem, X. Provinz Brandenburg Rep. 16A, NL Forckenbeck, No. 34: Letters from Marie von Forckenbeck to Max von Forckenbeck, February 24, 1874 (Tümpling), March 5, 1874 (Lewald and Molinari), and February 2, 1876 (Friedenthal).

132. APW, AMW, III, 2462, fol. 3 (municipal council) and fols. 39–42 (syndic); in the course of the city council elections of November 1880, Kirschner vehemently attacked the anti-Semite petition; he, Kirschner, would "make a stand against any and all [anti-Semitic] agitation, against the open and the coarse, as well as against the legitimate, elegantly clad" agitation; see "Bezirks-Verein für den nordwestlichen Theil der inneren Stadt," *Breslauer Communal-Zeitung*, no. 35, November 20, 1880, 7. Later, Kirschner was a cofounder of the Verein zur Abwehr des Antisemitismus (Society for the Defense against Anti-Semitism); see *Allgemeine Zeitung des Judenthums* 55 (1891): 50; on Kirschner's time as the lord mayor of Berlin, see Erbe, "Berlin im Kaiserreich," 762–63.

133. Georg Pick was previously county-court judge in the district town of Oels, approximately 25 kilometers northeast of Breslau; see APW, AMW, III, 2471, fols. 4–8 and 17; Georg Pick was elected for an additional twelve years in

April 1888, but he resigned from his position as municipal councilor in June because the Breslau Discontobank had elected him to its board of directors (fol. 66). On his father, Heinrich Pick, see APW, AMW, K 150, vol. 19, no. 1938.

134. APW, AMW, III, 2462, fol. 52.

135. The second witness to the marriage was the bride's brother, Paul Sachs, a landowner in Mitschau, district of Breslau; see APW, USC, Standesamt Breslau I, March 24, 1881.

136. Born, *Mein Leben*, 98.

137. *Breslauer Köpfe*, 9–10; Trentin signed a petition against the ritual murder legend in March 1912; see "Gegen die Ritualmordlüge," *Jüdisches Volksblatt* 18 (1912), 145–47. On Kerr's time in Breslau, see Alfred Kerr, "Lebenslauf," in *Für Alfred Kerr: Ein Buch der Freundschaft*, ed. Joseph Chapiro (Berlin: Fischer, 1928), 157–82, here 162–78, as well as Deborah Vietor-Engländer, "Die Welt im Drama: Alfred Kerr 1867–1948" (Ms. 1998), chap. 1.

138. Other friendships could easily be adduced, such as that between the young Paul Löbe and bookshop assistant Walter Davidsohn (b. 1887) and his future wife, the teacher Alwine Zell (b. 1890), both Jewish. At their wedding on December 28, 1915, Löbe was one of the two witnesses (USC, Heiratsregister/marriage registry, Standesamt Breslau 3, December 28, 1915). Or there was the friendship between Hans Schäffer, the future under secretary of the Prussian Ministry of Finance, and the Catholic Hans Lukaschek (1885–1960), lord mayor of Hindenburg/Zabrze in 1927–29, Provincial Governor of the Province of Upper Silesia in 1929–33, and member of the Kreisauer Kreis; see Hans Schäffer, "Meine Erinnerungen an Hans Lukaschek," MS 1963, Institut für Zeitgeschichte, Munich, cited in Hans-Ludwig Abmeier, "Hans Lukaschek," in *Schlesische Lebensbilder*, vol. 5 (Breslau: W. G. Korn, 1968), 228–36; see also Ger van Roon, *Neuordnung im Widerstand: Der Kreisauer Kreis innerhalb der deutschen Widerstandsbewegung* (Munich: Oldenbourg, 1967). For literary evidence of friendships between Jews and other Breslauers in the late German Empire and in the Weimar Republic, see Ruth Hoffmann, *Meine Freunde aus Davids Geschlecht* (Berlin: Chronos, 1955), esp. 13–21, 48–51, and 53–59 (according to the catalog of the Jewish National and University Library, Jerusalem, "Ruth Hoffmann" is a pseudonym of Ruth Scheye).

139. Approximately 12% belonged simultaneously to at least two and nearly 6% to at least three general clubs. For each of the two groups, all those members were included whose surnames began with the letter *A* or *B*. The following Jewish clubs were included: Gesellschaft der Freunde (1871), Israelitische Kranken- und Verpflegungs-Anstalt und Beerdigungsgesellschaft (1867), Kranken-Unterstützungs-Verein "Tomche Cholim" (1888), and Verein zur Verbreitung der Wissenschaft des Judenthums (1862), as well as Centralverein deutscher Staatsbürger jüdischen Glaubens (1908), Gesellschaft der Freunde (1904), Israelitische Kranken- und Verpflegungs-Anstalt und Beerdigungsgesellschaft (1906), Verein "Israelitisches Mädchenheim" (1906), the Breslau

chapter of the Jüdischer Frauenbund (1911), Kranken-Unterstützungs-Verein "Tomche Cholim" (1908), Vereinigung jüdischer Frauen (1908), and Verein für jüdische Geschichte und Literatur (1904).

140. This is also emphasized in Jacob Borut, "'Verjudung des Judentums': Was There a Zionist Subculture in Weimar Germany?" in *In Search of Jewish Community: Jewish Identities in Germany and Austria, 1918–1933,* ed. Michael Brenner and Derek J. Penslar (Bloomington: University of Indiana Press, 1998), 92–114, here 95: "What was clearly lacking were Jewish parallels to the German social as well as professional societies. There were no Jewish parallels to the many choral, gymnastic, and local history societies, or to the professional associations of merchants and attorneys. . . . Jews did not want their own subculture, but wanted to be part of the existing bourgeois subculture."

141. On the income structure, see APW, AMW, K 151, district 19, no. 2392, and the national tax roll, APW, AMW, K 146, vol. 21, no. 42; Hainauer, *Die Gesellschaft der Freunde in Breslau,* 73; *Rechenschaftsbericht des Israelitischen Mädchenheims zu Breslau für die Jahre 1905, 1906 und 1907* (Breslau: n.p., 1908); *Rechenschaftsbericht der Gesellschaft der Brüder für das Jahr 1903* (Breslau: n.p., 1904), appendix; *Namen-Verzeichnis der Mitglieder der Israelitischen Kranken- und Verpflegungs-Anstalt und Beerdigungs-Gesellschaft zu Breslau, 20. April 1906; Rechenschafts-Bericht der Israelitischen Kranken- und Verpflegungs-Anstalt und Beerdigungsgesellschaft zu Breslau für die Jahre 1903, 1904 und 1905;* "Mitgliederverzeichnis," in: *7. Jahresbericht des Humboldt-Vereins für Volksbildung in Breslau für das Vereinsjahr 1875–1876; 37. Jahresbericht des Humboldt-Vereins für Volksbildung für das Vereinsjahr 1905–06; Bericht über den Zustand der vereinigten sechs Kleinkinder-Bewahr-Anstalten zu Breslau für 1894–1895* (Breslau: n.p., 1895); *Riesengebirgs-Verein, Breslau: Mitglieder-Verzeichnis 1908.*

142. APW, Regierung Breslau, Justizbüro 7259 Hermann Auerbach'she Stiftung für Waisenkinder ohne Unterschied der Religion, 1919–1924.

143. Burgfeld's annual income of nearly 17,000 marks in 1880 was somewhat less than Auerbach's. APW, AMW, K 151, district 19, no. 3382, and national tax roll APW, AMW, K 146, vol. 21, no. 3106. In 1906, Burgfeld earned a good 50,000 marks per year (and in fact almost exclusively from capital investments); see APW, AMW, K 156, district 52, no. 2877. In general on Burgfeld's activities in Jewish clubs, see Aron Heppner, *Jüdische Persönlichkeiten in und aus Breslau* (Breslau: Schatzky, 1931), 6, and "Nekrolog Louis Burgfeld," *Jüdisches Volksblatt* 18 (1912): 303.

144. *Rechenschaftsbericht der Gesellschaft der Brüder für das Jahr 1903,* appendix; *Statuten, Bericht und Mitgliederverzeichnis des Vereins zur Verbreitung der Wissenschaft des Judenthums, Gestiftet den 9. November 1861* (Breslau: n.p., 1862).

145. *Bericht des kaufmännischen Vereins zu Breslau für das Jahr 1882: Nebst Statut und Mitgliederverzeichnis;* Stefan-Ludwig Hoffmann, *Die Politik der Geselligkeit.*

146. *Bericht über die Thätigkeit des Vereins für Jüdische Geschichte und Litteratur (Breslau) 1903/1904* (Breslau: n.p., 1904), 5ff.; *Centralverein deutscher Staatsbürger jüdischen Glaubens: Mitglieder-Verzeichnis, 1897* (Berlin: Das Vereinsbureau, 1897),

76–77; "Rechenschaftsbericht der Israelitischen Kranken- und Verpflegungs-Anstalt und Beerdigungsgesellschaft für 1915," INV 1435, CAHJP, Jerusalem.

147. *Riesengebirgs-Verein, Breslau: Mitglieder-Verzeichnis, 1908;* see the membership list in Emil Bohn, *Bohn'scher Gesangsverein: Hundert historische Concerte in Breslau, 1881–1905* (Breslau: Hainauer, 1905), 143–44.

148. "Unsere Geselligkeit," *Allgemeine Zeitung des Judenthums* 67 (1903): 145–48 (here referring to Berlin).

149. The idea that the 1860s and 1870s were the "palmy days of integration" may be found in Sorkin, *Transformation of German Jewry,* 113.

150. Shulamit Volkov, "Das geschriebene und das gesprochene Wort: Über Kontinuität und Diskontinuität im deutschen Antisemitismus," in her *Jüdisches Leben und Antisemitismus im 19. und 20. Jahrhundert* (Munich: C. H. Beck, 1990), 54–78, here 58. Along similar lines, see Volkov, *Die Juden in Deutschland,* 45–46; Norbert Kampe, *Studenten und "Judenfrage" im Kaiserreich: Die Entstehung einer akademischen Trägerschicht des Antisemitismus* (Göttingen: Vandenhoeck & Ruprecht, 1988), 211–12; Saul Friedländer, *Nazi Germany and the Jews,* vol. 1, *The Years of Persecution, 1933–1939* (London: Weidenfield, 1997), 86; Helmut Berding, *Moderner Antisemitismus in Deutschland* (Frankfurt a. M.: Suhrkamp, 1988), 110 and 161–62; Jochmann, "Struktur und Funktion," 438 and 444; Ute Frevert, *Frauen-Geschichte: Zwischen bürgerlicher Verbesserung und neuer Weiblichkeit* (Frankfurt a. M.: Suhrkamp, 1986), 109; Toury, *Soziale und politische Geschichte,* 123; Peter Pulzer, "Between Hope and Fear: Jews and the Weimar Republic," in *Jüdisches Leben in der Weimarer Republik—Jews in the Weimar Republic,* ed. Wolfgang Benz, Arnold Paucker, and Peter Pulzer (Tübingen: Mohr Siebeck, 1998), 271–79, here 271–72.

151. Stefan Rohrbacher, "Kaiserreich und Weimarer Republik—Horte innigster deutsch-jüdischer Symbiose?" *Geschichte in Wissenschaft und Unterricht* 43 (1992): 681–87, here 684; Pierre Birnbaum and Ira Katznelson, "Emancipation and the Liberal Offer," in *Paths of Emancipation: Jews, States and Citizenship,* ed. Birnbaum and Katznelson (Princeton, N.J.: Princeton University Press, 1995), 3–36, here 7.

152. Thomas Nipperdey, *Deutsche Geschichte, 1866–1918,* vol. 1, *Arbeitswelt und Bürgergeist* (Munich: C. H. Beck, 1990), 406.

Chapter 3 Jewish-Christian Marriages, the "New Woman," and the Situational Ethnicity of Breslau Jews

1. On the general discussion of mixed marriages, see Elliott R. Barkan, "Race, Religion and Nationality in American Society: A Model of Ethnicity from Contact to Assimilation," *Journal of American Ethnic History* 14 (1995): 38–75, here 52, 54, and 56; David M. Heer, "Intermarriage," in *Harvard Encyclopedia of American Ethnic Groups,* ed. Stephen Thernstrom (Cambridge, Mass.: Harvard University Press, 1980), 513–21; John Hendrickx, Osmund Schreuder, and Wouter Ultee, "Die konfessionelle Mischehe in Deutschland (1901–1986) und

den Niederlanden (1914–1986)," *Kölner Zeitschrift für Soziologie und Sozialpsychologie* 46 (1994): 619–45; Kalmijn Matthijs, "Shifting Boundaries: Trends in Religious and Educational Homogamy," *American Sociological Review* 56 (1991): 768–800.

2. Nathan Stoltzfus, *Resistance of the Heart: Intermarriage and the Rosenstrasse Protest in Nazi Germany* (New York: Norton, 1996); Beate Meyer, *Jüdische Mischlinge: Rassenpolitik und Verfolgungsgefahr, 1933–1945* (Hamburg: Dölling & Galitz, 1999).

3. Todd M. Endelman, *Radical Assimilation in English Jewish History, 1656–1945* (Bloomington: Indiana University Press, 1990).

4. Marion Kaplan, *The Making of the Jewish Middle Class: Women, Family, and Identity in Imperial Germany* (New York: Oxford University Press, 1991); Jacob Toury, *Soziale und politische Geschichte der Juden in Deutschland, 1847–1871: Zwischen Revolution, Reaktion und Emanzipation* (Düsseldorf: Droste, 1977), 123; see also Marsha L. Rozenblit, *The Jews of Vienna, 1867–1914: Assimilation and Identity* (Albany: State University of New York Press, 1984), 127–46; Uriel O. Schmelz, *Die jüdische Bevölkerung in Hessen: Von der Mitte des 19. Jahrhunderts bis 1933* (Tübingen: Mohr Siebeck, 1996), 83–95; Shulamit Volkov, *Die Juden in Deutschland, 1780–1914* (Munich: Oldenbourg, 1994), 56–57; Victor Karady, *Gewalterfahrung und Utopie: Juden in der europäischen Moderne* (Frankfurt a. M.: Fischer, 1999), 48–52. Paula Hyman considers "intermarriage and conversion" to be the "most extreme manifestations of assimilation"; see her *Gender and Assimilation in Modern Jewish History* (Seattle: University of Washington Press, 1995), 19. According to Jacob Katz, intermarriage was "tantamount to defection from the Jewish family and society, for marrying out of faith led . . . to a conversion to Christianity" (Katz, *Out of the Ghetto: The Social Background of Jewish Emancipation, 1770–1870* [Cambridge, Mass.: Harvard University Press, 1973; repr., Syracuse, N.Y.: Syracuse University Press, 1998], 205). For assessments of recent scholarship see Steven M. Lowenstein, "Jewish Intermarriage and Conversion in Germany and Austria," *Modern Judaism* 25, no. 1 (2005): 23–61, and Yfaat Weiss, "Deutsche, Juden und die Weder-Nochs: Neuerscheinungen zum Thema deutsch-jüdische Mischehen," *WerkstattGeschichte* 27 (2000): 73–82.

5. Kerstin Meiring, *Die christlich-jüdische Mischehe in Deutschland, 1840–1933* (Hamburg: Dölling & Galitz, 1998), 10.

6. For surveys of recent research on the history of the family, see Tamara K. Hareven, "The History of the Family and the Complexity of Social Change," *American Historical Review* 96 (1991): 95–124, and her "Formen, Funktionen und Werte," in *Entwicklungstendenzen der Familie*, by Tamara K. Hareven and Michael Mitterauer (Vienna: Picus-Verlag, 1996), 14–38; Karin Hausen, "Familie und Familiengeschichte," in *Sozialgeschichte in Deutschland*, ed. Wolfgang Schieder and Volker Sellin, vol. 2 (Göttingen: Vandenhoeck & Ruprecht, 1986), 64–89; William H. Hubbard, "Die historische Familienforschung," in his *Familiengeschichte: Materialien zur deutschen Familie seit dem Ende des 18. Jahrhunderts* (Munich: C. H. Beck, 1983), 17–35; Hans J. Teuteberg, "Zur Genese und Entwicklung

historisch-sozialwissenschaftlicher Familienforschung in Deutschland," in *Ehe, Liebe, Tod: Zum Wandel der Familie, der Geschlechts- und Generationsbeziehungen in der Neuzeit,* ed. Hans J. Teuteberg and Peter Borscheid (Münster: Coppenrath, 1983), 15–65; Hartmann Tyrell, "Historische Familienforschung und Familiensoziologie," *Kölner Zeitschrift für Soziologie und Sozialpsychologie* 29 (1977): 677–701.

7. Amartya Sen, *Identity and Violence: The Illusion of Destiny* (New York: Norton, 2006), 15.

8. For a general account, see Robert C. Young, *Colonial Desire: Hybridity in Theory, Culture, and Race* (London: Routledge, 1995); regarding the United States, see Peggy Pascoe, "Miscegenation Law, Court Cases, and Ideologies of 'Race' in Twentieth-Century America," *Journal of American History* 83 (1996): 44–69.

9. See the cartoon in Ruth Gay, *Geschichte der Juden in Deutschland* (Munich: C. H. Beck, 1993), 191. "Misalliances" between a woman from a Jewish family and an officer or aristocrat had been a popular subject of serialized novels in Jewish weeklies since 1890; see Meiring, *Die christlich-jüdische Mischehe in Deutschland,* 51 and 53.

10. Emanuel Schreiber, *Die sociale Stellung der Juden: Offenes Sendschreiben an Herrn Dr. Maass-Breslau* (Königsberg: Prange, 1877), 12–13.

11. "Breslau, 18. Februar," *Der Israelit* 33, no. 20 (March 10, 1892): 393–394, here 393. On the connections between gender-specific boundaries of the public sphere and notions of sexuality, see Judith M. Walkowitz, *City of Dreadful Delight: Narratives of Sexual Danger in Late-Victorian London* (Chicago: University of Chicago Press, 1992).

12. Ferdinand Rosenthal, "Die Familie" (1899), in his *Festpredigten* (Berlin: Poppelauer, 1917), 95–101, here 99; Julius Lewkowitz makes similar remarks thirty years later in his article "Familie, Familienleben," in *Jüdisches Lexikon,* ed. Georg Herlitz and Bruno Kirschner (Berlin: Jüdischer Verlag, 1927), 2:585–86. Sharon Gillerman, "The Crisis of the Jewish Family in Weimar Germany: Social Conditions and Cultural Representation," in *In Search of Jewish Community: Jewish Identities in Germany and Austria, 1918–1933,* ed. Michael Brenner and Derek J. Penslar (Bloomington: Indiana University Press, 1998), 176–90, here 178–79.

13. Marcuse, Sombart, Tänzer, and Theilhaber are cited here from Walter Hanauer, "Die Mischehe," *Jüdisches Jahrbuch* 3 (1929): 37–66, here 56–58; in general concerning the connections between "racial hygiene" and the discussion of mixed marriage, see Meiring, *Die christlich-jüdische Mischehe in Deutschland,* 58–65.

14. Felix A. Theilhaber, *Der Untergang der deutschen Juden: Ein volkswirtschaftliche Studie* (Munich: Reinhardt, 1911), 98–117, quotations from 113–15. Theilhaber made an urgent call for an analysis of the "increased hedonism, effemination, nervousness, perversity, and criminality of converts and offspring of mixed marriages" (116).

15. For negative middle-class assessments of working-class sexuality, see Carola Lipp, "Die Innenseite der Arbeiterkultur: Sexualität im Arbeitermilieu

des 19. und frühen 20. Jahrhunderts," in *Arbeit, Frömmigkeit und Eigensinn: Studien zur historischen Kulturforschung*, ed. Richard van Dülmen, vol. 2 (Frankfurt a. M.: Fischer, 1990), 215–20; Cornelia Usborne, "The New Woman and Generational Conflict: Perceptions of Young Women's Sexual Mores in the Weimar Republic," in *Generations in Conflict*, ed. Mark Roseman (Cambridge: Cambridge University Press, 1995), 137–63, here 150–54; Derek S. Linton, "Between School and Marriage: Young Working Women as a Social Problem in Late Imperial Germany," *European History Quarterly* 13 (1988): 387–408.

16. Eugen Altmann, "Mein Leben in Deutschland vor und nach 1933," 14, Houghton Library, Harvard University, Cambridge, Mass.

17. Willy Cohn, *Verwehte Spuren: Erinnerungen an das Breslauer Judentum vor seinem Untergang*, ed. Norbert Conrads (Cologne: Bohlau, 1995), 281. For an assessment similar to Cohn's, see Albert Reibmayr, "Ueber den Einfluß der Inzucht und der Vermischung auf den politischen Standpunkt einer Bevölkerung," *Politisch-Anthropologische Revue* 1, no. 1 (1902), quoted by the Breslau Zionist Aron Sandler in his *Anthropologie und Zionismus: Ein Populärwissenschaftlicher Vortrag* (Brünn: Jüdischer Buch- und Kunstverlag, 1904), 41–42. Incidentally, Altmann's and Cohn's misgivings about Jewish-Christian marriages diminished when they commented on mixed marriages of people close to them. Altmann has nothing but good things to say about his brother's wife, who came from a Protestant minister's family with estate holdings. And Cohn reports favorably on the Königsberg features editor Ludwig Goldstein, the offspring of a Jewish-Christian marriage, and the marriage between Lola Landau, whom he "quite liked," and Armin Wegner, who was "known for his travel books." See Altmann, "Mein Leben in Deutschland vor und nach 1933," 51; Cohn, *Verwehte Spuren*, 325 and 37.

18. Review of Max Schneidewin, *Die jüdische Frage im Deutschen Reich*, in *Hamburger Fremdenblatt*, November 24, 1894, no. 276, quoted in Daniela Kasischke-Wurm, *Antisemitismus im Spiegel der Hamburger Presse während des Kaiserreichs, 1884–1914* (Hamburg: LIT, 1997), 316–17; in general see Meiring, *Die christlich-jüdische Mischehe in Deutschland*, 34–35. The power of this idea of a fusion-based utopia was such that it extended even to the American notion of the "melting pot." Franz Boas, a German-Jewish emigrant, the founder of American cultural anthropology, and a proponent of the "melting pot" idea, argued that intermarriage is the ideal means for solving ethnic and racial conflicts in the United States; see Kamala Visweswaran, "Race and the Culture of Anthropology," *American Anthropologist* 100 (1998): 70–83.

19. Monika Richarz, "Jewish Social Mobility in Germany during the Time of Emancipation (1790–1871)," *Year Book of the Leo Baeck Institute* 20 (1975): 69–77, here 70; see also Lamar Cecil, "Jew and Junker," *Year Book of the Leo Baeck Institute* 20 (1975): 47–58, here 49, who asserts that Berlin Jewish high society entertained Junkers to match their daughters with aristocratic grooms; Dirk Blasius, *Ehescheidung in Deutschland* (Göttingen: Vandenhoeck & Ruprecht, 1992), 159.

20. Todd M. Endelman, "Conversion as a Response to Antisemitism in Modern Jewish History," in *Living with Antisemitism: Modern Jewish Responses*, ed. Jehuda Reinharz (Hanover, N.H.: University of New England Press, 1987), 60–84, here 79; Hannah Arendt, *The Origins of Totalitarianism* (New York: Harcourt, 1951), 64. Although Arendt does not cite the source of her argument, it may have been Arthur Ruppin, *Die Soziologie der Juden*, vol. 1, *Die soziale Struktur der Juden* (Berlin: Jüdischer Verlag, 1930), 219.

21. Alan T. Levenson, "Reform Attitudes, in the Past, toward Intermarriage," *Judaism* 38 (1989): 320–32, here 321 and 330, as well as his "German Zionism and Radical Assimilation before 1914," *Studies in Zionism* 13 (1992): 21–41, here 36.

22. Walter Hanauer, "Die jüdisch-christlichen Mischehen," *Allgemeines Statistisches Archiv* 17 (1928): 513–37, here 517. When compiling statistics on mixed marriages, one must take into account that unions between Jews and non-Jews were not counted as mixed when one member of the couple had converted to the other's religion (see 526–27).

23. See the comparative figures for Königsberg in Stefanie Schüler-Springorum, *Die jüdische Minderheit in Königsberg/Preußen, 1871–1945* (Göttingen: Vandenhoeck & Ruprecht, 1996), 370.

24. By contrast, Robert McCaa attributes the sharp increase in the rate of intermarriage in New York City after 1910 to "heavily skewed sex ratios"; he maintains that the "ethnic marriage squeeze" had forced many immigrants to marry outside their ethnic groups; see his "Ethnic Intermarriage and Gender in New York," *Journal of Interdisciplinary History* 24 (1993): 207–32, here 222 and 231.

25. Herbert Philippsthal, "Die jüdische Bevölkerung Breslaus," *Breslauer Jüdisches Gemeindeblatt* 8 (1931): 52, 67–8, 98–9, here 67.

26. Marriage between Simundt and Margarete Rosalie Sachs, APW, USC, Standesamt Breslau I, March 28, 1882.

27. Marriage between Otto Aron Köppen and Margarete Elisabeth Eliason, APW, USC Standesamt Breslau II, June 7, 1893; concerning the financial circumstances of the father, Löbel Eliason, see APW, AMW K 150, vol. 10, no. 2160.

28. Regarding Catholic-Protestant mixed marriages, so far there has been only one study, which was on the city of Bonn. It demonstrates that the likelihood of intermarriage was far greater in the lower classes than in the upper-middle class. See Gabriele Müller-List, *Die Sozialstruktur der evangelischen Einwohner Bonns im 19. Jahrhundert* (Bonn: Stadtarchiv Bonn, 1980), 152–66 and 219–25. My thanks to Kerstin Meiring for her assistance in analyzing the marriage registers of 1874–94.

29. Unfortunately, it is impossible to analyze the income brackets for the years after 1882, since to do so would require that the evaluation of marriage registers in combination with an analysis of tax rolls, which would make sense only if all Jewish wage earners had been recorded, as occurred in 1876.

30. Marriage of Bernhard Englaender and Rosa Pringsheim, APW, USC, Standesamt Breslau II, September 26, 1876; on Siegmund Pringsheim's income see APW, AMW K 150, vol. 20, no. 259, and APW, AMW K 146, vol. 21.

31. Marriage of Albert Neisser and Antonie Kauffmann, APW, USC, Standesamt Breslau II, March 13, 1883; Marriage of Gustav Neisser and Elsbeth Silberstein, APW, USC, Standesamt Breslau I, June 14, 1891. After the turn of the century, Albert and Antonie "Toni" Neisser would host the best known salon in Breslau; see Josef Jadassohn, "Albert Neisser," in *Schlesische Lebensbilder*, vol. 1 (Breslau: W. G. Korn, 1922), 111–15, and Karl Masner, "Toni Neisser," in *Schlesische Lebensbilder*, 1:115–19.

32. Marriage of Theodor Stahl and Emilie Haertel, APW, USC, Standesamt Breslau II, May 6, 1875; Haertel's conversion and Stahl's financial situation are evident from the tax roll; see APW, AMW K 151, vol. 19, no. 697. The Lutheran shopgirl Anne Ottilie Schüttke, who married the Jewish merchant Moritz August Brandy (annual income: 3,600 marks), in July 1875 also converted to Judaism after the marriage; see APW, USC, Standesamt Breslau I, July 6, 1875, and APW, AMW, K 150, vol. 11, no. 603.

33. Marriage of Otto Rudolf Wagner and Else Rosa Neumann; APW, USC Standesamt I, September 16, 1919.

34. Theodor Fontane, *Frau Jenny Treibel*, in *Werke*, ed. Kurt Schreinert, 3 vols. (Munich: Nymphenburger Verlag, 1968), 1:903.

35. Anna Auerbach, "Die Chronik der Familie Silbergleit, geschrieben aus Anlaß des 70. Geburtstages der Mutter am 21. November 1905," ME 600, 21, LBI, New York. On Wilhelm Silbergleit's financial situation, see APW, AMW, K 151, vol. 19, no. 2577, and tax rolls, APW, AMW, K 146, vol. 21, no. 3071.

36. Peter Gay, *Schnitzler's Century: The Making of Middle-Class Culture, 1815–1914* (New York: W. W. Norton, 2002), 57–58; David Sabean, "Die Ästhetik der Heiratsallianzen: Klassencodes und endogame Eheschließung im Bürgertum des 19. Jahrhunderts," in *Historische Familienforschung*, ed. Josef Ehmer, Tamara K. Hareven, and Richard Wall (Frankfurt a. M.: Campus Verlag, 1997), 157–70; Kaplan, *Making of the Jewish Middle Class*; Andrea Hopp, *Jüdisches Bürgertum in Frankfurt am Main im 19. Jahrhundert* (Stuttgart: Franz Steiner, 1997), 194–95. On the Catholic middle class, see Thomas Mergel, *Zwischen Klasse und Konfession: Katholisches Bürgertum im Rheinland im 19. Jahrhundert* (Göttingen: Vandenhoeck & Ruprecht, 1994), 82–87, esp. 83–84. In general, see Ute Frevert, *Frauen-Geschichte: Zwischen bürgerlicher Verbesserung und neuer Weiblichkeit* (Frankfurt a. M.: Suhrkamp, 1986), 40–41; Peter Borscheid, "Geld und Liebe: Zu den Auswirkungen des Romantischen auf die Partnerwahl im 19. Jahrhundert," in *Ehe, Liebe, Tod: Zum Wandel der Familie, der Geschlechts- und Generationsbeziehungen in der Neuzeit*, ed. Peter Borscheid and Hans J. Teuteberg (Münster: Coppenrath, 1983), 112–34 (Borscheid's argument is primarily based on the marriage patterns in the small Württemberg town of Nürtingen); Gunilla-Friederike Budde, *Auf dem Weg ins Bürgerleben: Kindheit und Erziehung in deutschen und englischen*

Bürgerfamilien (Göttingen: Vandenhoeck & Ruprecht, 1994), 25–43, esp. 31–36; Michelle Perrot, ed., *A History of the Private Life*, vol. 4, *From the Fires of Revolution to the Great War* (Cambridge, Mass.: Belknap Press, 1990), 183–87 and 307–14; Philipp Sarasin, *Stadt der Bürger: Struktureller Wandel und bürgerliche Lebenswelt Basel, 1870–1900* (Basel: Helbing & Lichtenhahn, 1990), 266–92, esp. 279; Heidi Rosenbaum, *Formen der Familie: Untersuchungen zum Zusammenhang von Familienverhältnissen, Sozialstruktur und sozialem Wandel in der deutschen Gesellschaft des 19. Jahrhunderts* (Frankfurt a. M.: Suhrkamp, 1982), 333–34; Oliver Janz, *Bürger besonderer Art: Evangelische Pfarrer in Preußen, 1850–1914* (Berlin: de Gruyter, 1994), 413–18, esp. 413. According to Jürgen Kocka, hardly any young member of the economic middle class still entered into an arranged marriage to accumulate capital but rather did so for love; see his "Familie, Unternehmer und Kapitalismus," *Zeitschrift für Unternehmensgeschichte* 24 (1979): 99–135, here 128. However, the opposition between marriage for money and marriage for love is too simplistic since it fails to take into account class-based aspects. Traditional Jewish forms of matchmaking may have promoted the establishment of bourgeois marriage patterns among German Jews; see: Jacob Katz, *Tradition and Crisis: Jewish Society at the End of the Middle Ages*, newly translated and with an afterword and bibliography by Bernard Dov Cooperman (1958; New York: New York University Press, 1993), 113–24; Jacob Goldberg, "Jewish Marriage in Eighteenth-Century Poland," *POLIN: Studies in Polish Jewry* 10 (1997): 1–37. The main difference lay in the early age at marriage among premodern Jewry. Steven Lowenstein argues, however, that by 1800 Ashkenazic Jews had already tended to marry at a late age, as was typical of the "European marriage pattern"; see his "Ashkenazic Jewry and the European Marriage Pattern," *Jewish History* 8 (1994): 155–75.

37. Anne-Charlott Trepp, *Sanfte Männlichkeit und selbständige Weiblichkeit: Frauen und Männer im Hamburger Bürgertum, 1770–1840* (Göttingen: Vandenhoeck & Ruprecht, 1996), 88–103, quotations from 88 and 103.

38. Auerbach, "Die Chronik der Familie Silbergleit," 66; Arnold Bernstein, Erinnerungen, 1888–1964, ME 55, 31, LBI, New York: "Intermarriage was looked upon with contempt, more so by Jews than by gentiles." Likewise among Königsberg Jews "there was a general disapproval of mixed marriages"; Schüler-Springorum, *Die jüdische Minderheit,* 92.

39. Steffi Granby, letter to the author, London, March 18, 1996; her father, Sigmund Klinenberger, owned a clothing factory in Breslau (letter of September 9, 1995). I would like to thank Steffi Granby for sharing her memories of Jewish-Christian relations in Breslau with me. See also Hopp, *Jüdisches Bürgertum*, 213.

40. Rosenbaum, *Formen der Familie,* 348–50.

41. Ibid.

42. Mary Jo Maynes, *Taking the Hard Road: Life Course and Class Identity in Nineteenth-Century French and German Workers' Autobiographies* (Chapel Hill:

University of North Carolina Press, 1995), 150. Maynes clearly also must acknowledge the limits of her sources (148): "Without necessarily imitating dominant norms, many workers connected sexuality and social identity, and in describing their own sexual experiences they often implicitly contrasted their own behavior with that which they believed to be characteristic of the popular milieux surrounding them. The culture is itself accessible to us, in other words, largely in accounts of workers who separated themselves from and often condemned it."

43. See Maynes, *Taking the Hard Road*, 129–51, esp. 136–39; Rosenbaum, *Formen der Familie*, 425; Ulrich Linse, "'Animierkneipen' um 1900: Arbeitersexualität und Sittenreform," in *Kirmes—Kneipe—Kino: Arbeiterkultur im Ruhrgebiet zwischen Kommerz und Kontrolle, 1850–1914*, ed. Dagmar Kift (Paderborn: Schöningh, 1992), 83–118; Marianne Friese, "Familienbildung und Heiratsstrategien im Bremischen Proletariat des 19. Jahrhunderts," in *Familie und Familienlosigkeit*, ed. Jürgen Schlumbohm (Hanover: Verlag Hahnsche Buchhandlung, 1993), 217–34, here 230–31; to a more limited extent, also Borscheid, "Geld und Liebe," 132. Premarital sex among the lower classes was common practice; roughly half of working-class women in Hanover-Linden were pregnant at the time of marriage; see Heidi Rosenbaum, *Proletarische Familien: Arbeiterfamilien und Arbeiterväter im frühen 20. Jahrhundert zwischen traditioneller, sozialdemokratischer und kleinbürgerlicher Orientierung* (Frankfurt a. M.: Suhrkamp, 1992), 134. Ulrich Linse estimates that two-thirds of working-class women were pregnant at their weddings, and thus that almost all of them would have engaged in premarital sexual relations; see his "Arbeiterschaft und Geburtenentwicklung im Deutschen Kaiserreich von 1871," *Archiv für Sozialgeschichte* 12 (1972): 205–71, here 206.

44. Adolf Riesenfeld, Tagebücher und Erinnerungen, vol. 1, A 16/3, entry for October 25, 1917, Archives of the LBI, New York. On the "hypocritical . . . erotic life" of upper-middle-class Jewish young men in turn-of-the-century Breslau, see Cohn, *Verwehte Spuren*, 86. In general, see Ernst Heilborn, *Zwischen zwei Revolutionen: Der Geist der Bismarckzeit (1848–1918)* (Berlin: Elsner, 1929), 217.

45. For the best analysis of dowries, see Kaplan, *Making of the Jewish Middle Class;* see also Hopp, *Jüdisches Bürgertum*, 195–97 and 202–3; dowries among the Protestant and Catholic upper-middle class is discussed briefly in Budde, *Auf dem Weg ins Bürgerleben*, 28–30.

46. Riesenfeld, Tagebücher und Erinnerungen, vol. 1, entry for January 27, 1917.

47. Ibid., entry for February 26, 1941.

48. Ibid., entries for February 16 and 17, 1941. On the two dance schools, see also Cohn, *Verwehte Spuren*, 84–85: "In those days [1906], there were two dance teachers in Breslau, the baptized Jew Reif and the unbaptized Jew Baer. Reif's dance lessons were considered more refined. They were also attended by my sister. For Jewish reasons, however, I refused and went to Baer, even at the risk of appearing less refined."

49. Riesenfeld, Tagebücher und Erinnerungen, vol. 2, entry for January 16, 1942.

50. Rosenbaum, *Formen der Familie*, 348–50; Perrot, *History of the Private Life*, 4:150–51, and 159: "Virginity remained the most precious form of capital."

51. For a thoughtful exploration of American literary representations of cross-class sexual relations between 1900 and 1930, see Michael Trask, *Cruising Modernism: Class and Sexuality in American Literature and Social Thought* (Ithaca, N.Y.: Cornell University Press, 2003).

52. Riesenfeld, Tagebücher und Erinnerungen, vol. 2, entry for October 16, 1941. Since almost all his friends were Jewish, Riesenfeld's sexual affairs with non-Jewish women were by no means uncommon. Around 1900, the usual duration of an engagement was two years; Budde, *Auf dem Weg ins Bürgerleben*, 37.

53. Riesenfeld, Tagebücher und Erinnerungen, vol. 2, entry for January 1, 1942.

54. Lynn Rapaport makes a similar observation: "The anonymity gained by crossing over to the German world, and the lack of pressure from or surveillance by family, friends, and community," the cultural sociologist has argued, "creates a situation conducive to sexual liaisons"; see her *Jews in Germany after the Holocaust: Memory, Identity, and German-Jewish Relations* (New York: Cambridge University Press, 1997), 232–33.

55. Riesenfeld, Tagebücher und Erinnerungen, vol. 2, entry for January 6–7, 1942, pp. 68–69, 72–73, 74, and 78–79.

56. Budde, *Auf dem Weg ins Bürgerleben*, 39–40; Reinhard Sieder, *Sozialgeschichte der Familie* (Frankfurt a. M.: Suhrkamp, 1987), 204–5; Lipp, "Die Innenseite der Arbeiterkultur," 222–24, 228, 230; Gerhard A. Ritter and Klaus Tenfelde, *Arbeiter im Deutschen Kaiserreich* (Bonn: Dietz, 1992), 619, 623, and 626–27.

57. Lola Landau, *Vor dem Vergessen: Meine drei Leben* (Berlin: Ullstein, 1987), 15; in general, see Birgitta Hamann, *Lola Landau: Leben und Werk. Ein Beispiel deutsch-jüdischer Literatur des 20. Jahrhunderts in Deutschland und in Palästina/Israel* (Berlin: Philo, 2000).

58. Landau, *Vor dem Vergessen*, 64–65.

59. Ibid., 145. Theodor Landau later developed "interest and respect" for Armin Wegner, although he continued to treat him as an "unwelcome son-in-law, a stranger addressed formally and by his last name" (239–40).

60. In general, see Atina Grossmann, "Die 'Neue Frau' und die Rationalisierung der Sexualität in der Weimarer Republik," in *Die Politik des Begehrens: Sexualität, Pornographie und neuer Puritanismus in den USA*, ed. Ann Snitow, Christine Stansell, and Sharon Thompson (Berlin: Rotbuch, 1985), 38–60; Ernst Heilborn, "Die 'neue' Frau," *Die Frau* 7 (1899–1900): 5–11; Frevert, *Frauen-Geschichte*, 171–73. On German-Jewish history in particular, see Eleonore Lappin, "Die jüdische Jugendbewegung als Familienersatz?" in *Die jüdische Familie in Geschichte und Gegenwart*, ed. Sabine Hödl and Martha Keil (Berlin: Philo, 1999), 161–91, and Claudia Prestel, "The 'New Jewish Woman' in Weimar Germany,"

in *Jüdisches Leben in der Weimarer Republik—Jews in the Weimar Republic*, ed. Wolf-gang Benz, Arnold Paucker, and Peter Pulzer (Tübingen: Mohr Siebeck, 1998), 135–56; yet Prestel does not see a connection between the increase in the num-ber of mixed marriages and the rise of the "New Jewish Woman," since she equates the decision to enter into a mixed marriage with a "lack of interest in the Jewish minority"; at the same time, however, Prestel thinks that "the major-ity of those marrying out might have been 'new women'" (148).

61. Between 1905 and 1909, 40% of all Jewish intermarried women had a job, in contrast to only 10% of all women in intra-Jewish marriages (1919–20: 50% to 20%). It was unusual for women to have a job before marrying and re-flected badly on their families. Adolf Asch, a Jewish lawyer from Posen, notes in his memoirs that "it was generally looked down upon for young ladies to have a paid occupation. Even less-wealthy parents and poorer widows kept their daughters at home without a profession in order to avoid a decline in the family's reputation"; quoted in Monika Richarz, ed., *Jüdisches Leben in Deutsch-land*, vol. 2, *Selbstzeugnisse zur Sozialgeschichte des Kaiserreichs* (Stuttgart: Deutsche Verlagsanstalt, 1979), 230.

62. Trepp, *Sanfte Männlichkeit und selbständige Weiblichkeit*, 145.

63. In artistic circles, for which being a member of the middle class was problematic, the number of mixed marriages appears to have been high; prior to 1895, there were five mixed marriages involving actors alone: theatrical agent Ferdinand August Gronwald and actress Selma Herzberg (APW, USC, Standesamt Breslau I, May 20, 1876); actor Ernst Karl Kühne and singer Mal-chen Laufen (APW, USC, Standesamt Breslau I, January 8, 1887); actor Emil Hecht and the unemployed Auguste Josefine Petersen (APW, USC, Standesamt Breslau I, July 6, 1889); actor Aron Oesterreicher and actress Charlotte Marie Bär (APW, USC, Standesamt Breslau II, February 11, 1889); lawyer Salomon Berkowitz and actress Eugenie Bozenhard, née Zucker (APW, USC, Standes-amt Breslau II, June 28, 1891). This is true also of the marriage of the actress Tilla Durieux and the Jewish painter Eugen Spiro, son of the cantor Abraham Baer Spiro, who had died in 1900. Contrary to the wishes of her mother, "who, due to her anti-Semitic outlook, was outraged by this marriage," the actress married Spiro in 1904. Tilla divorced Spiro a few years later, however, and mar-ried Paul Cassirer in 1910; see Tilla Durieux, *Eine Tür steht offen—Erinnerungen* (Berlin: Herbig, 1954), 22–23, 31–33, 40, quotation from 40; the biographical in-formation is from Tilla Durieux, *Meine ersten neunzig Jahre*, 3rd ed. (Munich: Her-big, 1971); on the Spiros, see Wilko von Abercron, *Eugen Spiro: Breslau 1874—New York 1972; Spiegel seines Jahrhunderts* (Alsbach: Drachen, 1990).

64. On women's employment as a flaw in middle-class and lower-middle-class circles, see Hopp, *Jüdisches Bürgertum*, 162; see also Paula E. Hyman, "Jü-dische Familie und kulturelle Kontinuität im Elsaß des 19. Jahrhunderts," in *Jüdisches Leben auf dem Lande*, ed. Monika Richarz and Reinhard Rürup (Tü-bingen: Mohr Siebeck, 1997), 249–69, here 262–63.

65. "Nicht hinunter—sondern hinauf," *Jüdische Volkszeitung,* April 26, 1917, 1.

66. The following figures are based on an analysis of the marriage registers from Breslau's Standesämter I–II, 1874–1894 (APW, USC, Breslau), as well as the marriage registers from Breslau's Standesämter I–IV, 1905–1920 (USC, Breslau). On the taboo of premarital sexuality, see Budde, *Auf dem Weg ins Bürgerleben,* 40; Frevert, *Frauen-Geschichte,* 130–31; Franziska Lamott, "Virginität als Fetisch: Kulturelle Codierung und rechtliche Normierung der Jungfräulichkeit um die Jahrhundertwende," *Tel Aviver Jahrbuch für deutsche Geschichte* 21 (1992): 153–70. On the debate in the 1830s and 1840s about "concubinage" as "one of the chief causes of the ruin . . . of the nation's lower classes," see Ute Gerhard, *Verhältnisse und Verhinderungen: Frauenarbeit, Familie und Rechte der Frauen im 19. Jahrhundert; Mit Dokumenten,* 2nd ed. (Frankfurt a. M.: Suhrkamp, 1981), 351–60; and Lynn Abrams, "Concubinage, Cohabitation, and the Law: Class and Gender Relations in Nineteenth-Century Germany," *Gender and History* 5 (1993): 81–100. In Prussia, "living in sin" (*wilde Ehe*) was still a punishable offense during the Weimar Republic if it caused a public nuisance; see the article "Konkubinat," in *Meyers Lexikon,* 7th ed. (Leipzig: Bibliographisches Institut, 1927), 6:1672–73.

67. On the nexus between marriage age and gender hierarchies, see Budde, *Auf dem Weg,* 40–43; Hopp, *Jüdisches Bürgertum,* 168–69 and 205–8; Leonore Davidoff and Catherine Hall, *Family Fortunes: Men and Women of the English Middle Classes, 1780–1850* (Chicago: University of Chicago Press, 1987), 323.

68. This corresponded to the typical age of middle-class women at marriage; see Karin Hausen, "' . . . eine Ulme für das schwanke Efeu': Ehepaare im deutschen Bildungsbürgertum; Ideale und Wirklichkeit im späten 18. und 19. Jahrhundert," in *Bürgerinnen und Bürger: Geschlechterverhältnisse im 19. Jahrhundert,* ed. Ute Frevert (Göttingen: Vandenhoeck & Ruprecht, 1988), 85–117, here 96.

69. Eva G. Reichmann, "Max Horkheimer the Jew—Critical Theory and Beyond," *Year Book of the Leo Baeck Institute* 19 (1974): 181–96, here 182.

70. Steven Lowenstein has calculated for Berlin Jews around 1800 an average age difference of six years; see his "Ashkenazic Jewry," 166.

71. Thus far, historians have hardly analyzed the role of these witnesses. No reference to them is to be found in Budde, *Auf dem Weg ins Bürgerleben;* Rozenblit, *Jews of Vienna;* or Kaplan, *Making of the Jewish Middle Class.* While reference is made, e.g., in Friese, "Familienbildung und Heiratsstrategien," 223–24, the author analyzes not the social relations between the witnesses and the marriage partners but only the professional background of the witnesses and reaches the hardly surprising conclusion that the witnesses, like the grooms, came at least from the "proletariat."

72. Hartmut Zwahr, *Zur Konstituierung des Proletariats als Klasse: Strukturuntersuchungen über das Leipziger Proletariat während der industriellen Revolution* (Berlin: Akademie-Verlag, 1978), 165.

73. Marriage of Hans Riegner and Elisabeth Bauer, APW, USC, Standesamt Breslau II, October 14, 1889; for the income of their respective parents, see APW, AMW K 151, vol. 19, no. 2017 (the precise amount of Otto Bauer's income is unknown since he paid his Prussian state taxes in Kleinburg); APW, AMW K 150, vol. 19, no. 1878 and the Prussian state tax rolls APW, AMW, K 146, vol. 21, no. 2411, total income in 1876 roughly 8,400 marks (Paul Julius Riegner); on the Bauers, see Dagmar Nick, *Jüdisches Wirken in Breslau: Eingeholte Erinnerung; Der Alte Asch und die Bauers* (Würzburg: Bergstadt, 1998), 72–73. Much the same was true of the witnesses to the aforementioned marriage of Bernhard Englaender and Rosa Pringsheim in 1876; the marriage differed insofar as the man was a Christian with Jewish origins and both witnesses belonged to the woman's family (Marriage of Bernhard Englaender and Rose Pringsheim, APW, USC, Standesamt Breslau II, September 26, 1876). Many parallels are evident as well in the marriage of Albert Neisser and Antonie Kauffmann (APW, USC, Standesamt Breslau II, March 13, 1883) and the marriage of Gustav Neisser and Elsbeth Silberstein (APW, USC, Standesamt Breslau I, June 14, 1891).

74. Lola Landau, "Die Kameradschaftsehe," *Die Tat* 20 (February 11, 1929): 831–35; translated as "The Companionate Marriage," in *The Weimar Republic Sourcebook*, ed. Anton Kaes, Martin Jay, and Edward Dimendberg (Berkeley: University of California Press, 1994), 702–3. Monika Richarz has already proposed that Christian-Jewish marriages were primarily "marriages for love"; see her "Frauen in Familie und Öffentlichkeit," in *Deutsch-jüdische Geschichte in der Neuzeit*, by Steven M. Lowenstein, Paul Mendes-Flohr, Peter Pulzer, and Monika Richarz, ed. Michael A. Meyer, vol. 3, *Umstrittene Integration, 1871–1918* (Munich: C. H. Beck, 1997), 69–100, here 84. In general, see Usborne, "New Woman and Generational Conflict," 137–63, and Frevert, *Frauen-Geschichte*, 146–99.

75. On the following see Andreas Reinke, *Judentum und Wohlfahrtspflege in Deutschland: Das jüdische Krankenhaus in Breslau, 1744–1944* (Hanover: Hahnsche Buchhandlung, 1999), 234–37.

76. On Hirschberg's candidacy in December 1905, see *Jüdisches Volksblatt* 11 (1905): 489. In December 1909, he succeeded in being elected to the *Synagogengemeinde*'s administration; from 1918 on, he belonged to the *Gemeinde*'s board of governors; and in 1921 he became chairman of the regional chapter for Middle and Lower Silesia of the Centralverein deutscher Staatsbürger jüdischen Glaubens (Central Association of German Citizens of Jewish Faith); see Aron Heppner, *Jüdische Persönlichkeiten in und aus Breslau* (Breslau: Schatzky, 1931), 21, and *Im Deutschen Reich* 27 (1921): 300.

77. Cited in Reinke, *Judentum und Wohlfahrtspflege in Deutschland*, 236n174.

78. Blasius, *Ehescheidung in Deutschland*, 159.

79. For the case of Ungerleider and Jakubczik, see APW, USC, Standesamt Breslau, Standesamtsbezirk IV, April 3, 1920. Among couples that intermarried during the First World War, only one out of five such marriages ended in divorce. On divorces in the early Weimar years, see Blasius, *Ehescheidung in*

Deutschland, 157–59; Richard Bessel, *Germany after the First World War* (Oxford: Clarendon Press, 1993), 231–33; Usborne, "New Woman and Generational Conflict," 154.

80. See Stoltzfus, *Resistance of the Heart;* Marion A. Kaplan, *Between Dignity and Despair: Jewish Life in Nazi Germany* (New York: Oxford University Press, 1998); for a critique of Stoltzfus and Kaplan, see Meyer, *Jüdische Mischlinge.* For examples from Breslau, see Altmann, "Mein Leben in Deutschland vor und nach 1933," 51, and Anita Lasker-Wallfisch, *Inherit the Truth, 1939–1945: The Documented Experiences of a Survivor of Auschwitz and Belsen* (London: Giles de la Mare, 1996), 50–51. A fascinating inside view of the difficulties facing these marriages can be gleaned from the diary of Victor Klemperer, *Ich will Zeugnis ablegen bis zum letzten: Tagebücher, 1933–1945,* 2 vols. (Berlin: Aufbau-Verlag, 1995).

81. Marsha Rozenblit has made a similar argument for Vienna; see *Jews of Vienna,* 129.

82. *Statistische Mittheilungen aus den deutschen evangelischen Landeskirchen, 1880–1897* (Stuttgart: Klett, 1883–99); 1900–1909 (Stuttgart: Klett, 1902–27) (for 1880–1925); *Kirchliches Jahrbuch für die evangelischen Landeskirchen Deutschlands* 56 (1929): 90 (for 1926 and 1927).

83. APW, USC, Standesamt Breslau I, February 9, 1922 (no. 137); the marriage license notes the religion of the children and that Gertrud Springer left the Breslau *Synagogengemeinde* in 1941. For further information on the children, see APW, USC, Geburtsregister, Standesamt Breslau III, 1926, no. 250, and 1927, no. 1196. See also the examples provided above in note 31.

84. The remarks that follow are based on *Breslauer Statistik,* vol. 15, pt. 4 (Breslau: Morgenstern, 1884): 140; vol. 22 (1903): 89*; vol. 27 (1909): 151; and vol. 33 (1914): 78*.

85. Helmut Krüger, *Der halbe Stern: Leben als deutsch-jüdischer "Mischling" im Dritten Reich* (Berlin: Metropol, 1993), 10–11.

86. On the following, see esp. Meiring, *Die christlich-jüdische Mischehe in Deutschland,* 129–38.

87. Landau, *Vor dem Vergessen,* 274.

88. Hopp also stresses the exceptional character of mixed marriages in the middle class; see her *Jüdisches Bürgertum,* 212–13. However, she does not analyze marriages between Jews and other Frankfurters, which rapidly increased in number, but generalizes based on insights she gained in her study of the middle-class elite.

Chapter 4. Unity, Diversity, and Difference

1. "Hier steht der Liberalismus, er kann nicht anders!" *Breslauer Zeitung,* no. 463, October 4, 1879.

2. See Reinhart Koselleck, "Zur anthropologischen und semantischen Struktur der Bildung," in *Bildungsbürgertum im 19. Jahrhundert,* ed. Reinhart

Koselleck, vol. 2, *Bildungsgüter und Bildungswissen* (Stuttgart: Klett Cotta, 1990), 11–46; Karl-Ernst Jeismann, "Zur Bedeutung der 'Bildung' im 19 Jahrhundert," in *Handbuch der deutschen Bildungsgeschichte*, ed. Karl-Ernst Jeismann and Peter Lundgreen, vol. 3, *1800–1870: Von der Neuordnung Deutschlands bis zur Gründung des Deutschen Reiches* (Munich: C. H. Beck, 1987), 1–21; Ulrich Hermann, "Über 'Bildung' im Gymnasium des wilhelminischen Kaiserreichs," in Koselleck, *Bildungsgüter und Bildungswissen*, 346–68; Margret Kraul, "Bildung und Bürgerlichkeit," in *Bürgertum im 19. Jahrhundert: Deutschland im europäischen Vergleich*, ed. Jürgen Kocka and Ute Frevert (Munich: Deutscher Taschenbuch Verlag, 1988), 3:45–73.

3. See esp. Shulamit Volkov, "The Ambivalence of *Bildung:* Jews and Other Germans," in *The German-Jewish Dialogue Reconsidered: A Symposium in Honor of George L. Mosse*, ed. Klaus L. Berghahn (New York: Peter Lang, 1996), 81–98 and 267–74; George L. Mosse, *German Jews beyond Judaism* (Bloomington: University of Indiana Press; Cincinnati: Hebrew Union College Press, 1985); Stefan-Ludwig Hoffmann, *Die Politik der Geselligkeit: Freimaurerlogen in der deutschen Bürgergesellschaft, 1840–1918* (Göttingen: Vandenhoeck & Ruprecht, 2000); Willi Goetschel, *Spinoza's Modernity: Mendelssohn, Lessing, and Heine* (Madison: University of Wisconsin Press, 2003).

4. See, e.g., Claudia Prestel, *Jüdisches Schul- und Erziehungswesen in Bayern, 1804–1933* (Göttingen: Vandenhoeck & Ruprecht, 1989); Dorothee Schimpf, *Emanzipation und Bildungswesen der Juden im Kurfürstentum Hessen, 1807–1866: Jüdische Identität zwischen Selbstbehauptung und Assimilationsdruck* (Wiesbaden: Staatsarchiv Wiesbaden, 1994). By contrast, several references may be found in Andrea Hopp, *Jüdisches Bürgertum in Frankfurt am Main im 19. Jahrhundert* (Stuttgart: Franz Steiner, 1997), 253–64; Shulamit Volkov, "Jüdische Assimilation und Eigenart im Kaiserreich," in her *Jüdisches Leben und Antisemitismus im 19. und 20. Jahrhundert* (Munich: C. H. Beck, 1990), 131–45, here 142–43. For a summary, see Trude Maurer, *Die Entwicklung der jüdischen Minderheit, 1780–1933: Neuere Forschungen und offene Fragen* (Tübingen: Niemeyer, 1992), 23–35.

5. See James C. Albisetti, "Education," in *Imperial Germany: A Historiographical Companion*, ed. Roger Chickering (Westport, Conn.: Greenwood, 1996), 244–71; James C. Albisetti and Peter Lundgreen, "Höhere Knabenschulen," in *Handbuch der deutschen Bildungsgeschichte*, ed. Christa Berg, vol. 4, *1870–1918: Von der Reichsgründung bis zum Ende des Ersten Weltkriegs* (Munich: C. H. Beck, 1991), 228–78, here 228; Heinz-Elmar Tenorth, "Lob des Handwerks, Kritik der Theorie—Zur Lage der historischen Pädagogik in Deutschland," *Paedagogica Historica* 32 (1996): 343–61, here 349–50.

6. See, e.g., Marjorie Lamberti, *State, Society, and the Elementary School in Imperial Germany* (New York: Oxford University Press, 1989); Thomas Mergel, *Zwischen Klasse und Konfession: Katholisches Bürgertum im Rheinland im 19. Jahrhundert* (Göttingen: Vandenhoeck & Ruprecht, 1994), 157–67 and 235–53; Ludwig Richter, *Kirche und Schule in den Beratungen der Weimarer Nationalversammlung* (Düsseldorf: Droste, 1996).

7. The state of research is now assessed in Berg, *Handbuch der deutschen Bildungsgeschichte*, vol. 4; and Thomas Nipperdey, *Deutsche Geschichte, 1866–1918*, vol. 1, *Arbeitswelt und Bürgergeist* (Munich: C. H. Beck, 1990), 531–67. Specifically concerning Prussia, see Wolfgang Neugebauer, "Das Bildungswesen in Preußen seit der Mitte des 17. Jahrhunderts," in *Handbuch der preußischen Geschichte*, ed. Otto Büsch, vol. 2, *Das 19. Jahrhundert und Große Themen der Geschichte Preußens* (Berlin: de Gruyter, 1992), 605–798; on the other hand, see Paula S. Fass, *Outside In: Minorities and the Transformation of American Education* (New York: Oxford University Press, 1989); and Joel Perlmann, *Ethnic Differences: School and Social Structure among Irish, Italians, Jews and Blacks in an American City, 1880–1935* (Cambridge: Cambridge University Press, 1988).

8. Geoffrey Field, "Religion in the German Volksschule, 1890–1908," *Year Book of the Leo Baeck Institute* 25 (1980): 41–71, here 69; along similar lines, see Norbert Kampe, *Studenten und "Judenfrage" im Kaiserreich: Die Entstehung einer akademischen Trägerschicht des Antisemitismus* (Göttingen: Vandenhoeck & Ruprecht, 1988). On Polish and Danish—though not Jewish—minorities, see Neugebauer, "Das Bildungswesen in Preußen," 742–45; John J. Kulczycki, *School Strikes in Prussian Poland, 1901–1907: The Struggle over Bilingual Education* (New York: Columbia University Press, 1981); Lech Trzeciakowski, *The Kulturkampf in Prussian Poland*, trans. Katarzyna Kretkowska (New York: East European Monographs, 1990).

9. See Sally Tomlinson, "Cultural Diversity and Schooling," *Ethnic and Racial Studies* 18 (1995): 348–54.

10. The tendency can be observed elsewhere, though in a weaker form. See Marjorie Lamberti, *Jewish Activism in Imperial Germany* (New Haven, Conn.: Yale University Press, 1978), 125–26; along the same lines, James C. Albisetti, *Schooling German Girls and Women: Secondary and Higher Education in the Nineteenth Century* (Princeton, N.J.: Princeton University Press, 1988), 56–57 and 216–17; Jacob Toury, *Soziale und politische Geschichte der Juden in Deutschland, 1847–1871: Zwischen Revolution, Reaktion und Emanzipation* (Düsseldorf: Droste, 1977), 163–77; Prestel, *Jüdisches Schul- und Erziehungswesen*, 77–79 and 363. The following quantitative analysis of Breslau secondary schools is based on contemporary school statistics and an analysis of the social background of approximately five thousand Breslau *Gymnasium* graduates (*Abiturienten*) from 1870 to 1910 based on information from annual school reports. The annual reports of secondary schools contain a good deal of information about the graduates for the respective year—specifically, they always include name, father's profession, desired profession, length of attendance, year of birth; almost always: religion, place of birth, release from oral exam; and seldom: final grade and *Wunschstand*, i.e., social class aspiration.

11. Figures are taken from Andreas Reinke, "Zwischen Tradition, Aufklärung und Assimilation: Die Königliche Wilhelmsschule in Breslau 1791–1848," *Zeitschrift für Religions- und Geistesgeschichte* 43 (1991): 193–214, here 209 and 211.

12. See *Breslauer Statistik*, vol. 18, pt. 3 (Breslau: Morgenstern, 1900), 18–19 and 20–21; "Schul- und Bildungswesen," *Verwaltungsberichte des Magistrats der Königlichen Haupt- und Residenzstadt Breslau, 1880/83—1907/10* (Breslau: Grass, Barth & Co., 1897–1911). Concerning the Industrieschule, see chap. 4, sec. 3 of this volume.

13. Quite typical are the accounts given by Julian Kretschmer, "Mein Leben vor und nach 1933," manuscript collection "My Life in Germany Before and After January 30, 1933," 4–5, Houghton Library, Cambridge, Mass.; Arnold Bernstein, Erinnerungen, 1888–1964, ME 55, 2–3, Archives of the LBI, New York, 2–3; Max Born, *Mein Leben* (Munich: Nymphenburger Verlagshandlung, 1975), 48–51; Malwin Warschauer, *Im jüdischen Leben: Erinnerungen des Berliner Rabbiners Malwin Warschauer* (Berlin: Transit, 1995), 40 (in 1890 he graduated from the Realgymnasium am Zwinger).

14. Alfred Kerr, "Lebenslauf," in *Für Alfred Kerr: Ein Buch der Freundschaft*, ed. Joseph Chapiro (Berlin: Fischer, 1928), 157–82.

15. Ludwig Geiger, "Schulfeiern," *Allgemeine Zeitung des Judenthums* 74 (1910): 1–2. In 1907 Adolf Heilberg, a Jewish left-wing liberal from Breslau, argued along the same lines as Geiger; on this, see chap. 4, sec. 3 of this volume. In general, see Kraul, "Bildung und Bürgerlichkeit," 56–73.

16. See the results of the schoolchildren census in Breslau on November 30, 1895, in *Breslauer Statistik* 18, pt. 3, 29–110, here 41; the results were commented upon in "Breslaus confessionelle Schulstatistik," *Jüdisches Volksblatt* 6 (1900): 309–10; in 1880, e.g., only about 20% (550) of all (thus, including those who were no longer obliged to go to school) Jewish schoolchildren attended an elementary school, and in 1892 and 1907 they numbered nearly 17% (449 and 434, respectively); see *Verwaltungsberichte des Magistrats der Königlichen Haupt- und Residenzstadt Breslau, 1892–1895* (Breslau: Grass, Barth & Co., 1897), 189–94; ibid., *1907–1910* (Breslau: Grass, Barth & Co., 1911), 226–28. For more in-depth information on the denominational character of Breslau elementary schools, see chap. 4, sec. 3 of this volume.

17. Viktor Karády has described a parallel development in Hungary, where during the same period Jews avoided the middle schools, which had strong denominational ties. See his "Das Judentum als Bildungsmacht in der Moderne: Forschungsansätze zur relativen Überschulung in Mitteleuropa," *Österreichische Zeitschrift für Geschichtswissenschaften* 8 (1997): 347–61, here 355.

18. For a general account of the socially discriminatory function of school fees, see Achim Leschinsky and Peter Martin Roeder, *Schule im historischen Prozeß: Zum Wechselverhältnis von institutioneller Erziehung und gesellschaftlicher Entwicklung* (Stuttgart: Klett, 1976), 131–37.

19. See the results of the pupil census in Breslau from November 30, 1895, in *Breslauer Statistik* 18, pt. 3, 29–110, here 42. In imperial Germany, the majority of pupils left secondary schools before earning their *Abitur;* see Albisetti and Lundgreen, "Höhere Knabenschulen," 231, as well as Peter Lundgreen, Margret

Kraul, and Karl Ditt, *Bildungschancen und soziale Mobilität in der städtischen Gesell-schaft des 19. Jahrhunderts* (Göttingen: Vandenhoeck & Ruprecht, 1988), 22–23. As an example of a contemporary complaint "that too small a percentage of [secondary school] pupils actually graduate from them," see Heinrich Fiedler, "Beiträge zur Statistik der Breslauer höheren Schulen," in *Programm des Real-gymnasiums am Zwinger zu Breslau 1884* (Breslau: Grass, Barth & Co., 1884), i–x, here ix.

20. See the *Jahresberichte der Augusta- und Viktoriaschule, 1880–1884,* located at the Bibliothek für Bildungsgeschichtliche Forschung, Berlin; on the Ursulinen-schule, which only Catholic girls attended, see *Verwaltungsbericht des Magistrats der Königlichen Haupt- und Residenzstadt Breslau, 1904–1907* (Breslau: Grass, Barth & Co., 1907), 238.

21. *Verwaltungsbericht des Magistrats der Königlichen Haupt- und Residenzstadt Bres-lau, 1877–1880* (Breslau: Grass, Barth & Co., 1881), 77; ibid., *1886–1889* (Breslau: Grass, Barth & Co., 1889), 112; ibid., *1892–1895* (Breslau: Grass, Barth & Co., 1897), 192 and 194; ibid., *1904–1907* (Breslau: Grass, Barth & Co., 1907), 236; ibid., *1907–1910* (Breslau: Grass, Barth & Co., 1911), 231.

22. In the whole of Prussia in 1871, Jews in secondary schools numbered nearly seven times as many as were in the entire population; in 1910, they were still fully five times more common. In 1871, 1.32% of the Prussian population was Jewish, but 8.7% of all *Gymnasium* pupils, 8.0% of all *Realgymnasium* pupils, and 19.1% of all the secondary schools in which Latin was not taught, thus a total of 8.8% of all secondary-school pupils, were Jewish. In 1910, 1.04% of the Prussian population was Jewish, but 6.0% of all *Gymnasium* pupils, 5.8% of all *Realgymnasium* pupils, and 4.9% in all the secondary schools without Latin, thus a total of 5.6% of all secondary-school pupils, were Jewish (calculations based on Hohorst, Kocka, and Ritter, eds., *Sozialgeschichtliches Arbeitsbuch: Materialien zur Statistik des Kaiserreichs, 1870–1918* [Munich: C. H. Beck, 1980], 53 and 55, as well as Detlef K. Müller and Bernd Zymek, eds., *Datenhandbuch zur deutschen Bil-dungsgeschichte,* vol. 2, *Höhere und mittlere Schulen,* pt. 1 [Göttingen: Vandenhoeck & Ruprecht, 1987], 166–67, 200–201, 218–19, and 244–45). In 1906 in Frankfurt, measured against their percentage of the entire population (6.3%), Jews were overrepresented in *Gymnasien* by a factor of 2.5, and in both *Realgymnasien* and girls' secondary schools by a factor of 4.4 (calculation based on Hopp, *Jüdisches Bürgertum,* 261). In Minden, where Jews made up 1.5% of the city's population, Jews were overrepresented during the imperial era in the *Gymnasien* by a factor of 2.7 and in the *Realgymnasien* by a factor of 5.9 (see Lundgreen, Kraul, and Ditt, *Bildungschancen und soziale Mobilität,* 230).

23. The following figures are based on analysis of *Verwaltungsberichte des Magistrats der Königlichen Haupt- und Residenzstadt Breslau, 1880/83 — 1907/10.*

24. For a general account of the "system of qualification," see Albisetti and Lundgreen, "Höhere Knabenschulen," 242–45 and 272–73, as well as Neuge-bauer, "Das Bildungswesen in Preußen," 764–65.

25. Calculations based on Fiedler, "Beiträge zur Statistik," vi–vii.

26. Ibid.

27. Namely, 75% at the Friedrich-Gymnasium, 53% at the Catholic Matthias-Gymnasium, 83% at the Realgymnasium am Zwinger, and 71% at the Realgymnasium zum Heiligen Geist.

28. Between 1900 and 1904, Jews represented 34% of all pupils at the Elisabeth-Gymnasium, 35% of those at the Johannes-Gymnasium, 25% of those at the Maria Magdalena-Gymnasium, and 31% of those at the Wilhelm-Gymnasium. These figures have been calculated based on the "Jahresschulberichte der Breslauer höheren Schulen," i.e., the annual school reports on Breslau's secondary schools; complete runs can be found in the Bibliothek für Bildungsgeschichtliche Forschung des Deutschen Instituts für Internationale Pädagogische Forschung in Berlin.

29. The average age of *Gymnasium* pupils and the percentage of those who were not required to take the oral exam have been calculated based on information about all *Gymnasium* pupils in the "Jahresschulberichte der Breslauer höheren Schulen."

30. Riesenfeld, Tagebücher und Erinnerungen, vol. 1, entries for April 27 and July 6, 1916. In 1988, Arye Maimon recalled his days at the Realgymnasium am Zwinger, whose preparatory school he entered in 1909. His teacher of many years, August Walter, "was a sadist, but an exceptional teacher and educator." The worst aspect of his time there was "the old reactionary spirit that prevailed in the school." The mainstay of the elaborate punitive system was "beatings, and nearly every hour several boys were caned" (Maimon, *Wanderungen und Wandlungen: Die Geschichte meines Lebens* [Trier: Arye Maimon-Institut für Geschichte der Juden, 1998], 6 and 8). Despite all the "mental anguish" he had to endure, however, he "never heard an anti-Semitic remark." The "teachers never discriminated against the Jewish pupils, but judged them by the quality of their work" (9 and 11).

31. Born, *Mein Leben*, 50–51.

32. Ernst Marcus, "Mein Leben in Deutschland vor und nach 1933," 1–2 and 106, Houghton Library, Harvard University, Cambridge, Mass.

33. See the summary of the report from the *Berliner Tageblatt* in *Israelitische Wochenschrift* 17 (1886): 364.

34. Karády, "Das Judentum als Bildungsmacht," 347–61; see also his "Jewish Enrollment Patterns in Classical Secondary Education in Old Regime and Inter-War Hungary," *Studies in Contemporary Jewry* 1 (1984): 225–52.

35. Karády, "Das Judentum als Bildungsmacht," 352–58, quotation from 358. For a similar account, see Marsha L. Rozenblit, *The Jews of Vienna, 1867–1914: Assimilation and Identity* (Albany, N.Y.: State University of New York Press, 1984), 109; and Volkov, "Jüdische Assimilation und Eigenart," 142–43.

36. That is the core of Andrea Hopp's thesis; see Hopp, *Jüdisches Bürgertum*, 254. According to Rozenblit, in the late nineteenth century Jews had "transposed

their famous respect for learning from rabbinic to secular academics"; see Rozenblit, *Jews of Vienna*, 108. Essential in this context is George L. Mosse, *German
Jews beyond Judaism*.

37. Maimon, *Wanderungen und Wandlungen*, 6 (born in Breslau in 1903 as
Herbert Fischer, Maimon was the son of the clothing manufacturer Hermann
Fischer). See also the aforementioned autobiographies by Ernst Marcus and
Max Born.

38. On this, see esp. Sander L. Gilman, *Smart Jews: The Construction of the
Image of Jewish Superiority* (Lincoln: University of Nebraska Press, 1996).

39. The cultural Protestant character of many educational institutions suggests that they were. Yet children of the Catholic middle class also knew the
great significance of educational qualifications; see esp. Mergel, *Zwischen Klasse
und Konfession*, 158–61 and 244–47.

40. Thanks to the contemporary analysis by the principal of the *Oberreal-
schule*, Heinrich Fiedler; see his "Beiträge zur Statistik," vi–vii. However, Fiedler
recorded only the local pupils.

41. Lundgreen, Kraul, and Ditt, *Bildungschancen und soziale Mobilität*, 273.

42. My calculations here are based on Mergel, *Zwischen Klasse und Konfession*,
392–95.

43. The fact that lower-middle-class professional groups were underrepresented among Breslau's graduates throughout the imperial era is astonishing
when one considers that these professional groups were clearly overrepresented
among the *Primaner* (pupils in their final year at the *Gymnasium*) in Minden and
Duisburg during the same period.

44. My calculations here are based on Mergel, *Zwischen Klasse und Konfession*,
392–95. On the increasing social exclusivity of *Gymnasien* in Berlin during the
imperial era, see Detlef K. Müller, *Sozialstruktur und Schulsystem: Aspekte zum Strukturwandel des Schulsystems im 19. Jahrhundert* (Göttingen: Vandenhoeck & Ruprecht,
1977); for a critique of Müller's "segmentation thesis," on which his study is
based, see Lundgreen, Kraul, and Ditt, *Bildungschancen und soziale Mobilität*; and
Fritz K. Ringer, "Bestimmung und Messung von Segmentierung," *Geschichte und
Gegenwart* 8 (1982): 280–85.

45. Neugebauer, "Das Bildungswesen in Preußen," 763.

46. Minden is a prime example of the relative social openness of secondary schools in small cities; see Lundgreen, Kraul, and Ditt, *Bildungschancen und
soziale Mobilität*.

47. On the Catholics' "educational deficit," see Martin Baumeister, *Parität
und katholische Inferiorität: Untersuchungen zur Stellung des Katholizismus im Deutschen
Kaiserreich* (Paderborn: Schöningh 1987); Michael Klöcker, "Das katholische Bildungsdefizit in Deutschland," *Geschichte in Wissenschaft und Unterricht* 32 (1981):
79–98; important objections may be found in Mergel, *Zwischen Klasse und Konfession*, 158–61 and 244–47.

48. On Wilhelm Sohrauer, see APW, AMW K 150, vol. 13, no. 1251.

49. On Pinkus Neustadt, see APW, AMW K 150, vol. 17, no. 1654; on Louis Neustadt, see Leopold Priebatsch, "Louis Neustadt" (obituary), *Jahresbericht der Schlesischen Gesellschaft für vaterländische Cultur* 96 (1918): 67–68.

50. In Vienna, at least, the social profile of Jewish *Gymnasium* pupils was quite distinct. There the percentage of sons from lower-middle-class families at three Viennese *Gymnasien* was roughly equal between Jews (12, 18, and 11%, respectively) and non-Jews (17, 11, and 19%). See Rozenblit, *Jews of Vienna*, 111 and 113.

51. See Shulamit Volkov, "Die Erfindung einer Tradition—Zur Entstehung des modernen Judentums in Deutschland," *Historische Zeitschrift* 253 (1991): 603–28, who follows Eric Hobsbawm and Terence Ranger, eds., *The Invention of Tradition* (Cambridge: Cambridge University Press, 1983); as a typical example of many contemporary reports, see Emanuel Schreiber, *Die soziale Stellung der Juden: Offenes Sendschreiben an Herrn Dr. Maass-Breslau* (Königsberg: Prange, 1877), 23–24. For a thorough study of Jewish upward mobility since the late eighteenth century, see Simone Lässig, *Jüdische Wege ins Bürgertum: Kulturelles Kapital und sozialer Aufstieg im 19. Jahrhundert* (Göttingen: Vandenhoeck & Ruprecht, 2004).

52. Jan Palmowski (*Urban Liberalism in Imperial Germany: Frankfurt am Main, 1866–1914* [Oxford: Oxford University Press, 1999], esp. 163–65 and 189–99) and Ralf Roth ("Liberalismus in Frankfurt a. M., 1814–1914: Probleme seiner Strukturgeschichte," in *Liberalismus und Region: Zur Geschichte des deutschen Liberalismus im 19. Jahrhundert*, ed. Lothar Gall and Dieter Langewiesche [Munich: Oldenbourg, 1995], 87–108, here 76–77) point to parallels with Frankfurt school politics. Likewise, in the city of Schneidemühl there was a bitter struggle between the city and the Prussian educational authorities over the status of Jewish religious instruction; see "Zur Charakteristik des von Mühlerschen Systems," *Breslauer Zeitung*, December 4, 1869; and "Breslau," *Israelitische Wochenschrift* 1 (1870): 4–5.

53. To this day, many interpretations of the Kulturkampf continue to reflect the spirit of the Kulturkampf itself. For studies that suggest more fruitful methods of analysis, see Margaret L. Anderson, *Windthorst: A Political Biography* (Oxford: Clarendon Press, 1981); David Blackbourn, *History of Germany, 1780–1918: The Long Nineteenth Century*, 2nd ed. (Oxford: Blackwell, 2003), 261–63; Mergel, *Zwischen Klasse und Konfession*, 253–307; Lamberti, *State, Society, and the Elementary School*, 40–87; Nipperdey, *Deutsche Geschichte, 1866–1918*, 2:364–81; Christopher Clark and Wolfram Kaiser, eds., *Culture Wars: Secular-Catholic Conflict in Nineteenth-Century Europe* (Cambridge: Cambridge University Press, 2003); on liberal anti-Catholicism, see Michael B. Gross, *The War against Catholicism: Liberalism and the Anti-Catholic Imagination in Nineteenth-Century Germany* (Ann Arbor: University of Michigan Press, 2004); Róisín Healy, *The Jesuit Specter in Imperial Germany* (Leiden: Brill Academic, 2003); and Manuel Borutta, *Liberalismus als Antikatholizismus: Deutschland und Italien im Zeitalter der europäischen Kulturkämpfe* (Göttingen: Vandenhoeck & Ruprecht, 2008).

54. The Johannes-Gymnasium is mentioned in several memoirs and analyses of the history of Breslau Jews. In most cases, however, legends are merely perpetuated; see, e.g., Norbert Conrads, "Einleitung," in *Verwehte Spuren: Erinnerungen an das Breslauer Judentum vor seinem Untergang*, by Willy Cohn, ed. Norbert Conrads (Cologne: Bohlau, 1995), 1–15. The thesis that the special character of the Johannes-Gymnasium was based on "a religious tolerance . . . which had been a tradition in Silesia" (7) seems questionable in view of the fierce resistance to the school from Catholics, anti-Semites, and conservative Protestants.

55. C. F. W. Müller, "Die Eröffnung des Johannesgymnasiums," in *Programm des städtischen Johannes-Gymnasiums zu Breslau für die Zeit von Michaelis 1872 bis Ostern 1874* (Breslau: Graß & Barth, 1874), 1–10, here 1.

56. On Elvenich, see "Elvenich (Peter Josef)," in *Allgemeine Real-Encyclopädie für die gebildeten Stände* (Conversations-Lexikon), 9th ed., vol. 14 (Leipzig: Brockhaus, 1847), 682–83; Heinrich Bacht, SJ, *Die Tragödie einer Freundschaft: Fürstbischof Heinrich Förster und Professor Joseph Hubert Reinkens* (Cologne: Böhlau, 1985), 9n36; and Kurt Engelbert, *Die Geschichte des Breslauer Domkapitels im Rahmen der Diözesangeschichte vom Beginn des 19. Jahrhunderts bis zum Ende des Zweiten Weltkriegs* (Hildesheim: A. Lax, 1964). See Reinkens's letter to his brother Wilhelm from May 11, 1886, in Joseph Hubert Reinkens, *Breife an seinen Bruder Wilhelm (1840–1873)*, ed. Hermann Josef Sieben, 3 vols. (Cologne: Böhlau, 1979), 3:1435.

57. For a summary of the Catholic petition, see "Communales," *Schlesische Volkszeitung*, no. 497, October 24, 1865. The Realgymnasium am Zwinger's principal responded to the Catholic criticism immediately; see "Schlesischer Nouvellen-Courier," *Schlesische Volkszeitung*, no. 501, October 26, 1865. See also "Breslau," *Schlesisches Kirchenblatt* 29 (1863), 285–87, and Ulrich Seng, *Schulpolitik des Bistums Breslau im 19. Jahrhundert* (Wiesbaden: Harrassowitz, 1989), 233–34.

58. "Das höhere städtische Schulwesen in Breslau," *Breslauer Hausblätter*, no. 86, October 28, 1865, 681–83, here 681.

59. "Die Väter der Stadt," *Breslauer Hausblätter*, no. 87, November 1, 1865, 689–91.

60. "Das höhere städtische Schulwesen in Breslau," 681.

61. "Die Väter der Stadt," 691. The anti-Semitism of the *Breslauer Hausblätter* was still uncommon at this time in Breslau's Catholic press. In their analyses of the "Breslau school struggle," the *Schlesisches Kirchenblatt* and the *Katholisches Schulblatt* refrained from anti-Jewish digs, if one disregards the *Kirchenblatt*'s commentary in June 1869 that the magistracy had "really begged" for the "favor" of the "Breslau Jews" ("Die Breslauer Schulfrage und ihr jüngstes Schicksal," *Schlesisches Kirchenblatt* 35 [1869]: 265–67, here 266).

62. In this regard, the terminology was itself a matter of contention. The *Schlesische Zeitung* explicitly emphasized that the planned secondary schools that, "regarding denomination, upheld legal parity" and not — "as some [had] called it with a not very felicitous turn of phrase — 'nondenominational' [*confessionslos*]."

See "Die neueste Eröffnung der Regierung in Sachen der projectirten Lehranstalten," *Schlesische Zeitung*, no. 299, July 1, 1870, supplement, 1. In November
1872, the liberal-Protestant *Schlesisches Morgenblatt* argued that one should call
the Johannes-Gymnasium not nondenominational but rather interdenominational. See "Der evangelische Religionsunterricht an dem confessionslosen
Gymnasium zu Breslau," *Schlesisches Protestantenblatt* 2 (1872): 85–86. In Cologne
in November 1871, liberal city council members protested when the archbishop
called the new school for young ladies "nondenominational"—whereas the liberals regarded it as maintaining "parity"—and warned Catholic parents
against "entrusting their daughters to the nondenominational school for young
ladies"; cited in "Köln, 17. Nov.," *Schlesische Volkszeitung*, no. 278, November 19,
1871. In looking back on the "Breslau school struggle," the *Jüdische Volksblatt*
would use the concept of "interdenominational schools"; see *Jüdische Volksblatt*
11 (1905): 179. See also the remarks by the liberal representative Wehrenpfennig
in the Prussian Landtag in February 1869, in *Stenographische Berichte über die Verhandlungen des preussischen Abgeordnetenhauses, 1868–1869*, vol. 2 (Berlin: n.p., 1869),
esp. 1987–88.

   63. See "Die Väter der Stadt," 690. A brief summary of the diametrically
opposed positions may be found in "Confessionelle oder confessionslose Schulen?" *Allgemeine Zeitung des Judenthums* 33 (1869): 285–89, esp. 287. The same position as the *Breslauer Hausblätter* had been maintained just a few years earlier by
the *Evangelische Kirchen-Zeitung*. Contrary to Wilhelm Freund's claim that the
"majority of the subjects [had] no direct connection to Christianity," the newspaper replied "that Greco-Roman literature, as well as the natural sciences, can
be seen from a Christian and pagan, modern-pagan perspective"; *Evangelische
Kirchen-Zeitung* 68 (1861): 178–79. On the ties between Protestant Conservative
and Center Party members of the Reichstag in early 1872, see Anderson, *Windthorst*, 152–53.

   64. See "Schulbriefe II," *Breslauer Hausblätter*, no. 134, June 1, 1871, 1039–40;
it reads further, citing a Prussian decree concerning public instruction from
1819: "The principal aim of schools is 'to educate the youth such that, with the
knowledge of the relation of man to God, the power and desire will be awakened in them to arrange their lives in accordance with the spirit and the principles of Christianity. What this nation needs is first and foremost Christian discipline.'" The immediate occasion for this article was the book *Freiheit, Autorität
und Kirche* (Mainz: Kirchheim, 1862) by the bishop of Mainz, Wilhelm Emanuel
Freiherr von Ketteler; see "Schulbriefe I," *Breslauer Hausblätter*, no. 98, April 16,
1871, supplement, 1. The *Hausblätter* took the basic ideas in the "Stiehlsche Reg-
ulative" of 1854 concerning elementary schools and applied them to *Gymnasien*.
That decree stated that elementary schools should not be oriented by "general
human education" but by the "foundation of Christianity"; cited after Neugebauer, "Das Bildungswesen in Preußen," 737.

65. "Schulbriefe III," *Breslauer Hausblätter*, no. 135, June 2, 1871, 1046–47.

66. Lamberti, *State, Society, and the Elementary School*, 40–87; Field, "Religion in the German Volksschule," 46, 50–52, and 66; Peter Pulzer, *Jews and the German State: The Political History of a Minority, 1848–1933* (Oxford: Blackwell 1992), 113; Mergel, *Zwischen Klasse und Konfession*, 371–73.

67. *Die Weisheit der Braminen in der konfessionslosen Schule: Ungehaltene Rede eines unabhängigen Freidenkers*, 2nd ed. (Breslau: n.p., 1869), 4–8. The text was first published in early 1869 as an article in the magazine *Rübezahl: Schlesische Provinzial-blätter*, no. 1 (1869); see *Die Weisheit der Braminen*, 8.

68. Ibid. Here also the conflict is reduced to the confrontation between Catholics and Protestants; a late echo of the debate about "denominational subjects" (*Gesinnungsfächer*) may be found in "Jüdische Geschichtslehrer," *Mitteilungen aus dem Verein zur Abwehr des Antisemitismus* 3 (1893): 287–88.

69. "Stadtverordneten Versammlung," *Schlesische Volkszeitung*, no. 503, October 27, 1865. Characteristically, before the meeting the chairman of the city council distributed the pamphlet *Zur Gleichstellung der israelitischen Bürger Preußens*, which the author, Fritz Koch, had sent to the city parliament and which advocated equal status for the Jews; "Stadtverordneten Versammlung," *Breslauer Zeitung*, no. 503, October 27, 1865, 2849.

70. Protokollbücher der Stadtverordnetenversammlung, APW, AMW, H 120, vol. 62, council meeting of October 26, 1865, no. 1133.

71. "Confessioneller Charakter der höheren städtischen Schulen," *Schlesische Zeitung*, no. 503, October 27, 1865. On Elsner, see Albert Teichmann, "Art. Moritz Elsner," in *Allgemeine Deutsche Biographie*, vol. 48 (Leipzig: Duncker & Humblot, 1904), 339–41; Martin Hundt, "Ein schlesischer Junghegelianer," in *Revolution und Reform in Deutschland im 19. und 20. Jahrhundert: Zum 75. Geburtstag von Walter Schmidt*, ed. Helmut Bleiber (Berlin: Trafo-Verlag, 2005), 71–78; and Rolf Hecker, "Die 'Entdeckung' von Marx-Briefen im Nachlass von Moritz Elsner und deren Erstveröffentlichung," *Beiträge zur Marx-Engels-Forschung*, n.s., 2002 (2003): 200–225; Manfred Hettling, *Politische Bürgerlichkeit: Der Bürger zwischen Individualität und Vergesellschaftung in Deutschland und der Schweiz von 1860 bis 1918* (Göttingen: Vandenhoeck & Ruprecht, 1999), 190.

72. Bacht, *Die Tragödie einer Freundschaft*, 124, 157, 203–4, and 206; J. H. Reinkens to W. Reinkens, Breslau, December 5, 1861, in Reinkens, *Briefe an seinen Bruder Wilhelm*, 2:1108.

73. "Confessioneller Charakter der höheren städtischen Schulen."

74. Moreover, Roepell was one of the few university professors who played a leading role in local politics; see Eduard Reimann, "Geheimer Regierungs-rath Roepell: Ein Nekrolog," *Zeitschrift des Vereins für Geschichte und Altertum Schlesiens* 28 (1894): 461–71; as well as Hettling, *Politische Bürgerlichkeit*, 103–4, 161; and Bernd Haunfelder, ed., *Biographisches Handbuch für das Preußische Abgeordnetenhaus, 1849–1867* (Düsseldorf: Droste, 1994), 214.

75. "Confessioneller Charakter der höheren städtischen Schulen"; and "Nochmals Stadtväterliches," *Breslauer Hausblätter,* no. 90, November 11, 1865, 713. Roepell may also have been angry that a few months earlier, on August 1, 1865, he had lost the election for the rectorship of the university to the Catholic Reinkens; J. H. Reinkens to W. Reinkens, Breslau, August 1, 1861, in Reinkens, *Breife an seinen Bruder Wilhelm,* 3:1379.

76. "Confessioneller Charakter der höheren städtischen Schulen"; on Honigmann see "Nekrolog D. Honigmann 1821–1885," *Mittheilungen des Deutsch-Israelitischen Gemeindebundes* 16 (1886): 1–4; the obituary in *Allgemeine Zeitung des Judenthums* 49 (1885): 518; the magistracy's tribute in APW, AMW III, 2189, fol. 265; as well as the appraisal on the centennial of his birthday, "Ein Gedenkblatt," *Allgemeine Zeitung des Judenthums* 85, no. 20 (1921): 229–31.

77. [Wilhelm Freund], *Die Anstellung israelitischer Lehrer an Preußischen Gymnasien und Realschulen: Ein Wort zur Aufhellung der Sachlage von einem praktischen Fachmann* (Berlin: J. Springer, 1860); the authorship is attributed to Freund in the catalog of the Jewish National and University Library, Jerusalem. Freund, born in 1806, had played a leading role in the Reform movement in the 1840s and had asked his friend Abraham Geiger to come to Breslau; see Michael A. Meyer, *Response to Modernity: A History of the Reform Movement in Judaism* (Oxford: Oxford University Press, 1988), 420n36 and 426n113; see also the anti-Semitic repudiation of Freund's text: "Die Juden im Verhältnis zur christlichen Schule und zum christlichen Staate," *Evangelische Kirchen-Zeitung* 68 (1861): 169–73, 177–79, and 203–8; for Freund's biography, see *Allgemeine Zeitung des Judenthums* 50 (1886): 93 and 108; and the article "Wilhelm Freund," in *Große Jüdische National-Biographie,* ed. Salomon Wininger, vol. 2 (Czernowitz: Buchdruckerei "Aria," 1927), 318–19; for general background, see Pulzer, *Jews and the German State,* 113.

78. Protokollbücher der Stadtverordnetenversammlung, APW, AMW, H 120, vol. 62, council meeting of October 26, 1865, no. 1133

79. "Confessionelle oder confessionslose Schulen?" 285–89, esp. 287.

80. "Privatmittheilung, Breslau, 19. August," *Allgemeine Zeitung des Judenthums* 33 (1869): 744.

81. "Stand der Welthändel," *Breslauer Hausblätter,* no. 89, November 8, 1863, 705–6.

82. See Seng, *Schulpolitik des Bistums Breslau,* 233–34.

83. Ludwig Wiese, ed., *Das höhere Schulwesen in Preussen,* 3 vols. (Berlin: Wiegandt & Grieben, 1863–1902); vol. 1 (1863), 165; vol. 2 (1869), 173.

84. Even the name of the department underscored the close connection between church and school. See Franz Schnabel, *Deutsche Geschichte im neunzehnten Jahrhundert,* vol. 2, *Monarchie und Volkssouveränität* (Freiburg i. Br.: Herder, 1933; repr., Munich: Deutscher Taschenbuch Verlag, 1987), 342.

85. Quoted in Wiese, *Das höhere Schulwesen in Preussen,* 2:19–20. Carl Gottfried Scheibert, *Die Confessionalität der höheren Schulen* (Stettin: v. d. Nahmer, 1869), quoted in *Pädagogisches Archiv* 11 (1869): 185–93, quotation from 192; and Hugo

Preuß, *Die Maßregelung jüdischer Lehrerinnen in den Berliner Gemeindeschulen* (Berlin: Cronbach, 1898), 22–23.

86. Müller, "Die Eröffnung des Johannesgymnasiums," 1.

87. "Die neueste Eröffnung der Regierung in Sachen der projectirten Lehranstalten"; see also P. M. [Paul Mazura?], "In welchem Stadium befindet sich gegenwärtig die Breslauer Schulfrage?" *Schlesisches Kirchenblatt* 35 (1869): 541–43, here 543.

88. "Die Errichtung des Johannesgymnasiums," APW, AMW, III, 26365, fols. 23–24; Protokollbücher der Stadtverordnetenversammlung, APW, AMW, H 120, vol. 73, council meeting of July 9, 1868, no. 623.

89. Protokollbücher der Stadtverordnetenversammlung, APW, AMW, H 120, vol. 73, no. 623. Stetter played a prominent role in church life in Breslau; in 1875, e.g., he was a member of the Breslau Comité für den 9. Protestantentag; see *Schlesisches Protestantenblatt* 5 (1875): 149.

90. *Stenographische Berichte*, 2:1983–2009, here 1984–85; on Mallinckrodt, see Anderson, *Windthorst*, 108–10.

91. *Stenographische Berichte*, 2:1994–97 (Laßwitz), 1999–2003 (Lent), and 2008 (text of the motion); on Lent see Bernhard Mann, ed., *Biographisches Handbuch für das Preußische Abgeordnetenhaus, 1867–1918* (Düsseldorf: Droste, 1988), 242; "Zu Ehren der Abgeordneten Lent und Röpell," *Breslauer Zeitung*, no. 91, February 24, 1870, 652–53; on Laßwitz, see Haunfelder, ed., *Biographisches Handbuch*, 159.

92. The year of its founding is taken from the Emil Toeplitz and Paul Malberg, eds., *Kalender für das höhere Schulwesen Preußens*, vol. 5 (Breslau: Trewendt & Granier, 1898), 70.

93. "Stadtverordnetenversammlung," *Schlesische Zeitung*, no. 191, April 27, 1869, supplement 1, 1–2; the proceedings of the city council meeting of April 26, 1869 has been lost, according to the manuscript catalog in the Breslau city archives, since the Second World War.

94. Hermann Markgraf, *Geschichte Breslaus in kurzer Übersicht*, 2nd expanded ed. revised by Otfried Schwarzer (Breslau: Kern, 1913), 99 and 116.

95. "Stadtverordnetenversammlung," 1–2. See also the astute analysis of the intraliberal conflict in "Die Breslauer Schulfrage und ihr jüngstes Schicksal," *Schlesisches Kirchenblatt* 35 (1869): 265–67; while the ultramontane weekly sneered at the magistracy's Christian universalism, the paper granted the left-liberals Bouneß, Hofferichter, and Elsner "the palm of logical consistency" since they "at least said in no uncertain terms what they wanted."

96. "Stadtverordnetenversammlung," 1–2. Under Hobrecht's leadership, the magistracy had recommended to the city council on June 15, 1868, that it "submit to the royal authorities' decree and give the new *Gymnasium* a denominational, and in fact Protestant, character." Although the magistracy had already advertised the post of principal, the city council withheld its consent; see Müller, "Die Eröffnung des Johannesgymnasiums," 2.

97. "Stadtverordnetenversammlung," 1–2.

98. "Etwas vom Judenthum," *Schlesisches Protestantenblatt* 5 (1875): 93; see the rejoinder in "Breslau," *Allgemeine Zeitung des Judenthums* 39 (1879): 429–30.

99. "Breslau," *Katholisches Schulblatt* 15 (1869): 221–22; Seng, *Schulpolitik des Bistums Breslau*, 234 and 250; Paul Mazura, *Die Entwicklung des politischen Katholizismus in Schlesien* (Breslau: Marcus, 1925), 66.

100. *Breslauer Hausblätter*, no. 116 (1869), 286, quoted in Mazura, *Entwicklung des politischen Katholizismus*, 83.

101. F. G. Adolf Weiß, *Chronik der Stadt Breslau von der ältesten bis zur neuesten Zeit* (Breslau: Woywod, 1888), 1160. See also "Die Ueberreicherung der Adresse an Oberbürgermeister Hobrecht," *Schlesische Zeitung*, June 21, 1869, and "Die Ueberreichung der Adresse an den Herrn Oberbürgermeister," *Breslauer Zeitung*, June 20, 1869, 1991. On Moritz Spiegel (ca. 1825–75), see "Nekrolog," *Allgemeine Zeitung des Judenthums* 59 (1895): supplement "Der Gemeindebote," no. 29, and APW, AMW, K 150, district 12, no. 1516, as well as the tax rolls, APW, AMW, K 146, vol. 21, no. 1693. On Moritz Fränkel (ca. 1805 to ?) see APW, AMW, K 150, district 4, no. 2080.

102. "Zur Schulfrage," *Schlesische Zeitung*, no. 371, August 12, 1869, supplement 1.

103. "Stadtverordnetenversammlung [Schulfrage]," *Schlesische Zeitung*, no. 409, September 3, 1869, supplement 1.

104. "Schreiben des Schulprovinzialcollegiums an den Magistrat, 24. Juni 1870," *Schlesische Zeitung*, no. 333, July 21, 1870.

105. In any case, numerous liberal newspapers, including the *Kölnische Zeitung*, the *Magdeburger Zeitung*, the *Weserzeitung*, the *Zeitung für Norddeutschland*, and the *Posener Zeitung*, reprinted the editorial. See "Zur Breslauer Schulfrage," *Schlesische Zeitung*, no. 307, July 6, 1870, 1. The Breslau magistracy exploited the fact that the "school struggle" had received attention far beyond Breslau. In his immediate petition of December 13, 1869, the mayor reminded the Prussian king that, given the stubbornness of the state bureaucracy, there was "no avoiding that our demand and complaint, which had their origin in local circumstances and practical necessity, will be used as a means of political agitation well beyond the borders of our city." Cited from "Stadtverordneten-versammlungs-Sitzung," *Breslauer Hausblätter*, no. 48, March 1, 1870, 331.

106. "Die neueste Eröffnung der Regierung in Sachen der projectirten Lehranstalten." Like the *Schlesische Zeitung*, the Silesian *Provinzial-Korrespondenz* maintained that the magistracy should take von Mühler's offer; see the reference to the *Provinzial-Korrespondenz* in "Die hiesige Schulfrage," *Schlesische Zeitung*, July 8, 1870, supplement 1. On the *Schlesische Zeitung*'s National Liberal orientation before 1876, see Norbert Conrads, "Die *Schlesische Zeitung* (1742–1945)," in *Deutsche Zeitungen des 17.–20. Jahrhunderts*, ed. Heinz-Dietrich Fischer (Pullach bei München: Verlag Dokumentation, 1972), 115–30, here 123–25.

107. "Die neueste Nummer der Israelitischen Wochenschrift," *Breslauer Zeitung*, no. 275, June 17, 1870, 2207.

108. "Der Breslauer Schulstreit," *Israelitische Wochenschrift* 1 (1870): 247–48. The "generally humane character" of the Johanneum, according to the *Wochenschrift*, by no means ruled out that the choice of "the weekly holiday [be made] in accordance with the majority of the teachers and pupils." "Indeed, Sunday and the Christian holidays have assumed more of a social than a religious character anyway, and it is only right that the consideration of the majority is decisive in this case" (ibid.). Later the *Israelitische Wochenschrift* would criticize the diffuse usage of the concept 'Christian,' especially as cultural Protestantism tended to employ it. The Germans regarded every "significant moral force" as "'Christian'!" This "glorification of that which is Christian as the epitome of all virtue" was invented by "Germanic Protestantism." "What, then, is this emphasis on the Christian within the entire spectrum of humanity and morality, this characterization of virtue and charity as a Christian domain," the article concluded, "but a *furor christianissimus* that obscures the truth, that renders impossible the final peace among denominations and the recognition of Judaism." See Peter Buchholz, "Das deutsche Volk und die Juden," *Israelitische Wochenschrift* 2 (1871): 225–27 and 233–34, quotations from 233 and 241.

109. "In Sachen Eröffnung der beiden höheren Lehranstalten," *Schlesische Volkszeitung*, no. 333, July 21, 1870, supplement 1, 1–2. Already in March 1870 the *Allgemeine Zeitung des Judenthums* had interpreted the state bureaucracy's position much as the magistracy would later: if the new "Breslau schools were, by statue, first given 'a Christian character,' this would mean, according to Minister von Mühler's interpretation, nothing other than that only Catholic and Protestant teachers could be hired." See "Breslau," *Allgemeine Zeitung des Judenthums* 36 (1872): 186.

110. "Was erwarten wir von dem neuen preussischen Cultus- und Unterrichtsminister?" *Allgemeine Zeitung des Judenthums* 36 (1872): 97–100, quotation from 98–99.

111. Adolph Wohlauer, Reuschestr. 48 an Herrn Lewald, Stadtverordnetenvorsteher, 25. Feb. 1872, in "Johannes-Gymnasium," APW, AMW, III, 26365, fol. 95a. Concerning Wohlauer, who in 1872 was twenty-nine years old, married, with two (1876: three) children, and a net income (in 1876) of ca. 3,000 marks, see APW, AMW, K 150, district 25, no. 559.

112. Magistrat an Stadtverordnetenversammlung, 11. April 1872 and Stadtverordnetenversammlung an Magistrat, 25. April 1872, in APW, AMW, III, 26365, fols. 99–102; Müller, "Die Eröffnung des Johannesgymnasiums," 3.

113. Magistrat (Hobrecht und Thiel) an Stadtverordnetenversammlung, 3. Mai 1872, APW, AMW, III, 26365, fols. 101–2.

114. Müller, "Die Eröffnung des Johannesgymnasiums," 4–5.

115. "Breslau, im August," *Allgemeine Zeitung des Judenthums* 36 (1872): 690; "Breslau: Anfang August," *Israelitische Wochenschrift* 3 (1872): 268–69.

116. Wiese, *Das höhere Schulwesen in Preussen*, 3:185; *Allgemeine Zeitung des Judenthums* 36 (1872): 690.

117. The principal made his comment in the early days of the Breslau school struggle; quoted in "Schlesischer Nouvellen-Courier," *Schlesische Zeitung*, no. 501, October 26, 1865.

118. "Breslau, im Oktober," *Israelitische Wochenschrift* 5 (1874): 352. For general background, see the following from the same weekly: "Der israelitische Religionsunterricht an den öffentlichen Lehranstalten Preußens," 3 (1872): 27–29, and "Die Einfügung des jüdischen Religionsunterrichts in den Lehrplan der öffentlichen Schulen Preußens," 6 (1875): 233–35; "Moritz Rahmer," 7 (1876): 329–32, 339–40, 349–50; "Der obligatorische Religionsunterricht in der Schule," 23 (1892): 138–40, 145–46, 153–55. The significance of this issue was visible not only in the Jewish weekly press but also in journalism at large; see, e.g., Schreiber, *Die soziale Stellung der Juden*, 5 and 14–15.

119. Around 1900 there were a total of 154 *Gymnasium* professors and senior teachers; 115 (74.7%) were Protestant, 34 (22.1%) Catholic, and 5 (3.2%) Jewish; see Toeplitz and Malberg *Kalender für das höhere Schulwesen Preußens*, 5:70–72; in 1902, there were 5 Jewish teachers and 1 additional teacher charged with religious instruction at the Johanneum; see *Jüdisches Volksblatt* 8 (1902): 213. On Emil Toeplitz's son Otto (1881–1940), who would pass his *Abitur* at the Johanneum in February 1902 and become a well-known mathematician, see Teilnachlass Otto Toeplitz, Universitäts- und Landesbibliothek Bonn. Other Breslau Jews who later taught at the Johanneum include Alfred Cohn (1897–1976) for Latin and Greek, Willy Cohn for history and German, and Hermann Kober (1881–1973) for mathematics; see Maimon, *Wanderungen und Wandlungen*, 27, 30, 34–36, for Alfred Cohn; and W. H. J. Fuchs, "Hermann Kober," *Bulletin of the London Mathematical Society* 7 (1975): 185–90.

120. "Breslau, 14. Oktober," *Israelitische Wochenschrift* 3 (1872): 353–54.

121. Müller, "Die Eröffnung des Johannesgymnasiums," 6–7.

122. "Breslau, 14. Oktober," *Israelitische Wochenschrift* 3 (1872): 353–54.

123. Müller, "Die Eröffnung des Johannesgymnasiums," 7 and 10.

124. *Israelitische Wochenschrift* 3 (1872): 269 and 353–54.

125. Müller, "Die Eröffnung des Johannesgymnasiums," 7 and 10.

126. Ibid., 10.

127. Palmowski, *Urban Liberalism in Imperial Germany*, 257–58. The municipal Humboldt-Gymnasium was founded in Berlin in 1875, the municipal Lessing-Gymnasium in 1882; see Emil Toeplitz and Paul Malberg, eds., *Kalender für das hohere Schulwesen Preußens und einiger anderer deutscher Staaten*, vol. 17 (Breslau: Trewendt & Granier, 1910), 437.

128. See Personalbogen Robert Gregor Depène, Pädagogisches Zentrum, Berlin; and Personalakte Robert Gregor Depène, APW, Oberpräsidium Breslau, 17/II, 3936.

129. Jakob Buchmann, *Popularsymbolik, oder vergleichende Darstellung der Glaubensgegensätze zwischen Katholiken und Protestanten*, 3rd ed., 2 vols. (Mainz: Kirchheim, Schott & Thielmann, 1850).

130. J. H. Reinkens to W. Reinkens, Breslau, June 24, 1864, in Reinkens, *Briefe an seinen Bruder Wilhelm*, 2:1301.

131. Reinkens, *Briefe an seinen Bruder Wilhelm*, 3:1762.

132. J. H. Reinkens to W. Reinkens, Breslau, June 23, 1871, in Reinkens, *Briefe an seinen Bruder Wilhelm*, 3:1770; see also 1762.

133. J. H. Reinkens to W. Reinkens, Breslau, June 23, 1871, in Reinkens, *Briefe an seinen Bruder Wilhelm*, 3:1775, and, Munich, December 30, 1871, ibid., 1785; "Ueber die Amtsentsetzung des Pfarrers Buchmann," *Breslauer Zeitung*, no. 472, October 9, 1871, 3572; Jakob Buchmann, *Über und gegen den Jesuitismus* (Breslau: Gosohorsky, 1872). Moreover, in the autumn of 1872 the archbishop of Breslau slandered Buchmann by telling the magistracy that, during his time as parish priest in Kanth, Buchmann had repeatedly molested minors. After the magistracy had obtained extensive information in Kanth, it sharply rejected the slander. See the correspondence in Johannes-Gymnasium, APW, AMW III 26365.

134. "Die Stadtverordnetenversammlung," *Schlesische Volkszeitung*, no. 269, November 19, 1872; for general background, see Ernst-Rudolf Huber, *Deutsche Verfassungsgeschichte seit 1789*, vol. 4, *Struktur und Krisen des Kaiserreichs* (Stuttgart: Deutsche Verlagsanstalt, 1969), 687–88; the proceedings of the city council meeting of November 15, 1872, have been lost, according to the manuscript catalog in the Breslau city archives, since the Second World War.

135. *Programm des städtischen Johannes-Gymnasiums zu Breslau für die Zeit von Michaelis 1872 bis Ostern 1874*, 11–14 and 17–21.

136. Ibid., 11–14, 17–21, and 28.

137. Ibid., 29.

138. "Verordnungen der Behörden," in *Programm des städtischen Johannes-Gymnasiums zu Breslau für die Zeit von Michaelis 1872 bis Ostern 1874*, 42.

139. For details see "Der jüdische Religionsunterricht an den höheren Schulen," *Allgemeine Zeitung des Judenthums* 40 (1876): 218–19 and 561–65; see also *Allgemeine Zeitung des Judenthums* 41 (1877): 280.

140. "Ein Gutachten über den obligatorischen jüdischen Religionsunterricht," *Israelitische Wochenschrift* 8 (1877): 12–13 and 19–21, here 13 and 19.

141. "Breslau, 24. April," *Israelitische Wochenschrift* 8 (1877): 139.

142. On Julius Hainauer, see Maciej Łagiewski, *Wrocławscy Żydzi, 1850–1944* (Wrocław: Muzeum Historyczne, 1994), plate nos. 334–36; Cohn, *Verwehte Spuren*, 26–29, quotation from 26; Emil Bohn, *Festschrift zur Feier des 25 jährigen Bestehens des Breslauer Orchester-Vereins* (Breslau: Hainauer, 1887), 11; "Rede zum Gedächtnis von Freund Julius Hainauer am 9. Januar 1898," in *Gesellschaft der Freunde: Verwaltungsbericht pro 1897/1898 und 1898/1899* (Breslau: n.p., 1899), 11–13.

143. "Breslau, 24. April," *Israelitische Wochenschrift* 8 (1877): 139.

144. See the reports in *Israelitische Wochenschrift* 8 (1877): 367 and 392.

145. See the report in *Israelitische Wochenschrift* 8 (1877): 392. The Breslau liberals remained proud of their pluralistic school policy. In summer 1879, the *Realschule* principal Franz Meffert appealed to the election meeting of the Breslau

chapter of the Progressive Party (*Fortschrittspartei*): "Seek to preserve a school that strives for the reconciliation of denominational differences and to make the pupils aware that everyone, regardless of creed, indeed belongs to the greater community, whose power and strength is rooted in mutual consideration and toleration and unspoiled harmony! (enthusiastic applause)"; "Allgemeine Wähler-Versammlung der Fortschrittspartei," *Breslauer Zeitung*, no. 454, September 29, 1879, 1–2.

146. *Allgemeine Zeitung des Judenthums* 44 (1880): 795 and 809; *Israelitische Wochenschrift* 11 (1880): 419; Fechner, born in 1834, came from Görlitz and had been a faculty member at the Johanneum since 1872; for biographical information, see Hermann A. Fechner, *Ueber den Gerechtigkeitsbegriff des Aristoteles: Ein Beitrag zur Geschichte der alten Philosophie* (PhD diss., Universität Breslau) (Leipzig: Matthes, 1855), and Personalbogen Hermann Fechner, Pädagogisches Zentrum, Berlin.

147. "Locale und provinzielle Umschau," *Schlesisches Morgenblatt*, no. 267, November 13, 1880; "Locale und provinzielle Umschau," ibid., no. 288, December 8, 1880; "Die Autorität städtischer Behörden und der Fall 'Müller' in Breslau," ibid., no. 290, December 10, 1880; "Die Stadtverordnetenversammlung," *Breslauer Communal-Zeitung*, no. 37, December 4, 1880, 7; see also the summaries in *Allgemeine Zeitung des Judenthums* 45 (1881): 7, and *Israelitische Wochenschrift* 12 (1881): 36–37.

148. "Der Vorstand des neuen Wahlvereins," *Schlesisches Morgenblatt*, no. 29, January 18, 1882.

149. "Der Heimgang Hermann Fechners," *Jüdisches Volksblatt* 16 (1910): 382: "Incidentally," the Jewish weekly added, "Fechner's Jewish pupils have stated . . . back then but also later that toward them he always showed himself to be a just teacher during class."

150. *Die Judenfrage: Verhandlungen des preußischen Abgeordnetenhauses über die Interpellation des Abgeordneten Dr. Hänel am 20. und 22. November 1880* (Berlin: Moeser, 1880), 29 (Reichensperger), 77 (Meyer), and 87 (Bachem). Alexander Meyer (1832–1908) was a "leading member of his faction"; see Mann, *Biographisches Handbuch für das Preußische Abgeordnetenhaus*, 270; see also "Einer von Dreien: Dr. Alexander Meyer," *Breslauer Sonntagsblatt* 2, no. 9 (1882–83): 129–30. Though himself a Protestant, Meyer was guest speaker at one of Breslau's most exclusive Jewish clubs, the Gesellschaft der Freunde; see *Festschrift zur hundertjährigen Stiftungs-Feier der Gesellschaft der Freunde in Breslau* (Breslau: Gesellschaft der Freunde, 1921), 36.

151. "Monstre-Versammlung christlicher Bürger," *Deutscher Volksfreund*, no. 2, January 14, 1881; see also Leonhard Müller, *Der Kampf zwischen politischem Katholizismus und Bismarcks Politik im Spiegel der Schlesischen Volkszeitung: Ein Beitrag zur schlesischen Kirchen-, Parteien- und Zeitungsgeschichte* (Breslau: Müller & Seiffert, 1929), 206–7; "Eine gründliche Lösung der Judenfrage III," *Schlesisches Morgenblatt*, no. 274, November 21, 1880. The series was published shortly thereafter as

Flugblatt Nr. 2 des Schlesischen Morgenblatts under the title *Die gründliche Lösung der Judenfrage: Ein Kampf und Friedenswort von H. Lange* according to an ad in *Schlesisches Morgenblatt*, no. 278, November 26, 1880. On Wick, see "F. X. Seppelt, Josef Wick," in *Schlesische Lebensbilder*, vol. 2 (Breslau: W. G. Korn, 1926), 290–96; see also Josef Wick, *Aus meinem Leben* (Breslau: G. P. Aderholz, 1895).

152. Cohn, *Verwehte Spuren*, 38; see also his "Aus den Erinnerungen eines Johannäers: Zum 50 jährigen Jubiläum des Johannes-Gymnasiums," *Breslauer Neueste Nachrichten*, no. 265, September 27, 1922, supplement 1. Charlotte Schaeffer, "Bilder aus meiner Vergangenheit, 1865–1890," ME 562, LBI, New York, 29; Norbert Elias, *Über sich selbst* (Frankfurt a. M.: Suhrkamp, 1990), 110.

153. Born in 1874 in Breslau, Ernst Cassirer graduated from the Johanneum in spring term 1892; see *Programm des städtischen Johannes-Gymnasiums zu Breslau Ostern 1891 bis 1892* (Breslau: Friedrich, 1892). In Breslau it was common to call the Johanneum the "Judaneum" (Harvey P. Newton [birth name: Hermann Neustadt], letter to the author, Escazu, Costa Rica, September 22, 1994). At the turn of the century, however, there were several anti-Semitic fraternities at the Johannes-Gymnasium, of all places; see *Jüdisches Volksblatt* 8 (1902): 213 and 222–23. The Johanneum's "liberal tradition" (Walter Laqueur) presumably continued beyond January 30, 1933; Laqueur, who attended the school until 1938, recalls a small amount of overt anti-Semitism and individual acts of overt solidarity of non-Jewish with Jewish pupils; see his *Thursday's Child Has Far to Go: A Memoir of the Journeying Years* (New York: Charles Scribner's Sons, 1992), 60–65.

154. See Ferdinand Meister, *Die ersten 25 Jahre des wissenschaftlichen Vereins in Breslau, 1852–1877* (Breslau: n.p., 1877), 6. Hermann Warschauer (b. Krotoschin, October 3, 1840–d. Breslau, July 28, 1880); married (wife born ca. 1841), one son (born ca. 1869); from 1872 on third senior teacher at the Johannes-Gymnasium; see APW, AMW 26365, fol. 146.

155. On Benno Badt, see Bertha Badt-Strauss, "My World, and How It Crashed," *Menorah Journal* 39 (Spring 1951): 90–100; Aron Heppner, *Jüdische Persönlichkeiten in und aus Breslau* (Breslau: Schatzky, 1931), 3; Cohn, *Verwehte Spuren*, 43–46; "Nachruf Benno Badt," *Jahresbericht des städtischen Johannes-Gymnasiums zu Breslau, 1909/1910* (Breslau: Grass, Barth & Co., 1910), 11–12; Maciej Łagiewski, *Macewy mówia* (Breslau: Zaklad Narodowy, 1991), 125; Benno Badt, *Erläuterungen zu den biblischen Geschichten für die israelitische Jugend in Schule und Haus* (Breslau: Wilhelm Koebner, 1890), and *Kinderbibel: Biblische Erzählungen für die israelitische Jugend*, 3rd ed. (Breslau: Wilhelm Koebner, 1905). On Albert Wohlauer, see Heppner, *Jüdische Persönlichkeiten*, 45–46; Cohn, *Verwehte Spuren*, 40.

156. Figures have been calculated based on the annual reports of the schools in question, Breslau city statistics, and Breslau city administrative reports.

157. Georg Bender, cited in "Jüdische Lehrer an städtischen Volksschulen," *Jüdisches Volksblatt* 16 (1910): 482. See also Cohn, *Verwehte Spuren*, 295–96; Wolfgang Pax, "Bist Du auch ein Johanneer? Erinnerungen an die 20er Jahre," *Mitteilungen des Verbandes ehemaliger Breslauer und Schlesier in Israel* 41 (1977): 8–9. On the

liberal spirit prevailing at the Johanneum during the Weimar Republic, see Maimon, *Wanderungen und Wandlungen*, 30–31; and Walter Boehlich, interview in Gerd Mattenklott, *Über Juden in Deutschland* (Frankfurt a. M.: Jüdischer Verlag, 1992), 174–75.

158. The Elisabeth-Gymnasium was founded in 1562, the Maria Magdalena-Gymnasium in 1643 (or possibly 1267), the Friedrich-Gymnasium in 1765; see Toeplitz and Paul Malberg, *Kalender für das höhere Schulwesen Preußens*, 5:70.

159. Fiedler, "Beiträge zur Statistik," vi–vii.

160. This analysis of the social background of *Abiturienten* at the Johanneum thus contradicts Willy Cohn's judgment that the school's "Christian pupils" had belonged "mostly to very diverse social groups"; see Cohn, *Verwehte Spuren*, 38. Cohn's judgment also contradicts his own observation that around 1920 the teachers at the Elisabeth-Gymnasium could "count very little on intellectual cooperation from the families," while "at the Johannes-Gymnasium it was quite common, where even the boys often had access to a family library" (296).

161. *Verwaltungsberichte des Magistrats der Königlichen Haupt- und Residenzstadt Breslau, 1892–1895* (Breslau: Grass, Barth & Co., 1897), 230–31. In 1893 the proportion of pupils on a scholarship at the Elisabeth-Gymnasium was 17%, at the Maria Magdalena-Gymnasium 14%, at the Realgymnasium am Zwinger 12%, and at the Realgymnasium zum Heiligen Geist 16%.

162. It is possible that the price for becoming an elite school was the diminution of the Johanneum's sense of its mission as a model liberal school. When the school celebrated its twenty-five-year anniversary in 1897, there was no reference in the numerous songs to the school's prehistory; see *Jubel-Feier des Johannes-Gymnasiums in Breslau, Lieder zum Festkommers am 16. Oktober 1897* (BUW, GŚL). At the school's fifty-year anniversary, however, the school's parity character did play a role again; see Cohn, "Aus den Erinnerungen eines Johannäers."

163. *Programm des städtischen Johannes-Gymnasiums zu Breslau für das Schuljahr von Ostern 1876 bis Ostern 1877*, 44; *Programm des städtischen Johannes-Gymnasiums zu Breslau für das Schuljahr von Ostern 1877 bis Ostern 1878*, 28. Forckenbeck's successors as Breslau's mayor, Ferdinand Julius Friedensburg (1878–91) and Georg Bender (1892–1912), did not send their sons to the Johanneum. Friedenburg's son, Ferdinand, graduated in 1876—when his father was still a counselor of justice and a city councilor—from the Friedrich-Gymnasium. Georg Bender's son, Carl, graduated in 1892 from the Maria Magdalena-Gymnasium.

164. Nevertheless, several pastors sent their sons to the Johanneum. Ten graduates from the school between 1872 and 1914 were sons of pastors; by contrast, there were twenty-one at the Elisabeth-Gymnasium and eighteen at the Maria Magdalena-Gymnasium.

165. Richard Robert Rive, "Die Entwicklung der preußischen Städte seit dem Erlaß der Städteordnung von 1808," in *Verhandlungen des sechsten allgemeinen preußischen Städtetages am 5. und 6. Oktober 1908 zu Königsberg* 6 (1908): 29–36,

quotation from 34–35. In general, see Wolfgang R. Krabbe, "Kommunale Schul- und Kulturpolitik im 19. Jahrhundert: Münster und Dortmund im Vergleich," in Helmut Lahrkamp, ed., *Quellen und Forschungen zur Geschichte der Stadt Münster* 12 (1987): 139–82, here 139–40; and Palmowski, *Urban Liberalism in Imperial Germany*, 180–83.

166. In general, see Blackbourn, *History of Germany*, 293–94; Nipperdey, *Deutsche Geschichte, 1866–1918*, 2:316 and 322; Gangolf Hübinger, *Kulturprotestantismus und Politik: Zum Verhältnis von Liberalismus und Protestantismus im wilhelminischen Deutschland* (Tubingen: Mohr Siebeck, 1994); Helmut Walser Smith, *German Nationalism and Religious Conflict* (Princeton, N.J.: Princeton University Press, 1995).

167. Abraham Geiger, "Die Schulfrage im preußischen Abgeordnetenhaus," *Jüdische Zeitung für Wissenschaft und Leben* 7 (1869): 216–19. Contrary to Virchow, Geiger asserted that "Christianity" is a "failed attempt to fuse the two great spiritual world powers, Judaism and Hellenism, with each other. But the attempt was completely misguided; Christianity suppressed these two lively, life-giving powers and instead enthroned a grotesque mixture of the two." For general background on Geiger's confrontation with Christianity, see Susannah Heschel, *Abraham Geiger and the Jewish Jesus* (Chicago: University of Chicago Press, 1998).

168. Heinrich von Treitschke, "Unsere Aussichten," quoted in Walter Boehlich, ed., *Der Berliner Antisemitismusstreit* (Frankfurt a. M.: Insel, 1965), 12–13; for a similar argument, see Theodor Mommsen, "Auch ein Wort über unser Judenthum," in *Der Berliner Antisemitismusstreit*, 226.

169. Zygmunt Bauman, *Modernity and Ambivalence* (Cambridge: Polity Press, 1991); Dagmar Herzog, *Intimacy and Exclusion: Religious Politics in Pre-Revolutionary Baden* (Princeton, N.J.: Princeton University Press, 1996), esp. 82–83; Stefan-Ludwig Hoffmann, *Die Politik der Geselligkeit*.

170. Nipperdey, *Deutsche Geschichte, 1866–1918*, 2:369.

171. Carl Schmitt, *Romischer Katholizismus und politische Form* (Munich: Theatiner-Verlag, 1925), 5.

172. With the exception of the 140–150 girls at this school, during the imperial era all Jewish schoolchildren attended public schools in Breslau. See Reinke, "Zwischen Tradition, Aufklärung und Assimilation," 211, and Helga Krohn, *Die Juden in Hamburg: Die politische, soziale und kulturelle Entwicklung einer jüdischen Großstadtgemeinde nach der Emanzipation, 1848–1918* (Hamburg: Christians, 1974), 185–86.

173. On what follows, see Marcus Brann, "Geschichte der Anstalt während des ersten Jahrhunderts ihres Bestehens," in *100. Jahresbericht über die Industrieschule für israelitische Mädchen* (Breslau: n.p., 1901), 3–23; Carl Alexander, *Denkschrift, betreffend die Industrie-Schule für israelitische Mädchen zu Breslau* (Breslau: n.p., 1884); Reinke, "Zwischen Tradition, Aufklärung und Assimilation." For general background on vocational schools (*Industrieschulen*) as "institutions of a pedagogy of poverty," see Leschinsky and Roeder, *Schule im historischen Prozeß*, 283–320.

174. "Die Industrieschule für israelitische Mädchen," *Allgemeine Zeitung des Judenthums* 55 (April 10, 1891): supplement, 2.

175. Brann, "Geschichte der Anstalt," 21; "Breslau," *Jüdisches Volksblatt* 6 (1900): 62; "Die Industrieschule für israelitische Mädchen," *Jüdisches Volksblatt* 13 (1907): 431.

176. "Sogenannter Liberalismus," *Jüdisches Volksblatt* 1 (1896): 105–6.

177. "Die Zurücksetzung jüdischer Lehrer und Lehrerinnen an Breslauer Schulen," *Jüdisches Volksblatt* 10 (1904): 367–68.

178. "Die Industrieschule für israelitische Mädchen," *Jüdisches Volksblatt* 13 (1907): 431; "Die Verhandlungen betreffend die Uebernahme der Industrieschule für israelitische Mädchen durch die Stadtgemeinde: Denkschrift des Magistrats," printed in *Jüdisches Volksblatt* 15 (1909): 250.

179. The following information has been taken from "Isidor Ollendorff," *Jahresbericht der Schlesischen Gesellschaft für vaterländische Cultur* 89 (1911): obituaries, 25–26; "Nekrolog Isidor Ollendorff," *Jüdisches Volksblatt* 17 (1911): 514–15; "Flugblatt: Aufforderung, dem 'Israelitischen Mädchenheim' beizutreten, Juni 1891," BUW, GŚL 29225 III; "Flugblatt zugunsten der galizischen Juden," June 1900, NL Hillel Hugo Schachtel box, A 102, 10, Central Zionist Archives, Jerusalem.

180. "Die Stadtschuldeputation," *Jüdisches Volksblatt* 13 (1907): 163; the *Schlesische Morgen-Zeitung* is cited in that article.

181. "Die Verhandlungen betreffend die Uebernahme der Industrieschule für israelitische Mädchen durch die Stadtgemeinde: Denkschrift des Magistrats," printed in *Jüdisches Volksblatt* 15 (1909): 250.

182. "Die Industrieschule vor dem Verbandstage der jüdischen Gemeinden," *Jüdisches Volksblatt* 15 (1909): 249–50; see also "Der Streit um die Industrieschule," ibid., 259–60.

183. "Protokoll der Repräsentenversammlung vom 28. Juni 1909," *Jüdisches Volksblatt* 15 (1909): 269–70 and 281–82, here 280; see also "Eine Nachtsitzung im Gemeindehause," ibid., 260–61.

184. "Vorlage des Vorstandes, 20. Dez. 1909," printed in *Jüdisches Volksblatt* 16 (1910): 48–49.

185. "Der Kampf um die jüdische Schule in der Repräsentanten-Versammlung," *Jüdisches Volksblatt* 16 (1910): 48.

186. Ibid., 63–65. Many of the representatives who voted against Wohlauer's motion nevertheless shared his position. It was only that they believed it did not lie within the authority of the representative council to close the Industrieschule since a private organization supported it.

187. "Breslau," *Allgemeine Zeitung des Judenthums* 74 (February 4, 1910): supplement, 3.

188. "Der Kampf um die jüdische Schule in der Repräsentanten-Versammlung," *Jüdisches Volksblatt* 16 (1910): 64.

189. Hugo Preuß, *Die Maßregelung jüdischer Lehrerinnen in den Berliner Gemeindeschulen* (Berlin: Cronbach, 1898), 3 and 26.

190. Ibid., 4–18, quotation from 11. See also G. Stein, "Im Verwaltungs-wege," *Im Deutschen Reich* 1 (1895): 246–51, and the report that follows on 255.

191. Preuß, *Die Maßregelung jüdischer Lehrerinnen*, 20, 28, and 36. See also Hugo Preuß, "Die Bekenntnis des Kultusministers und die Konfessionalität der Berliner Schulen," *Die Nation* 16, no. 28 (8 April 1899): 396–98 and "Umschau," *Im Deutschen Reich* 4 (1898): 634–38. And see the minister of education's decree of February 1899, which is reprinted in Gustav Stille, *Die deutsche Schule in Gefahr* (Berlin: W. Giese, 1899), 61–62; Stille's text is representative of the anti-Semitic stance on discussions concerning school policy. Incidentally, the hiring of Jewish teachers in Berlin followed the typical liberal pattern of inclusion; there was no recognition of difference. At any rate, the Berlin municipal school deputation ordered in 1909 that Jewish teachers had to teach and write on Saturdays and Jewish holidays; see "Die Berliner Stadtschuldisputation," *Jüdisches Volksblatt* 15 (1909): 150.

192. "Die Berliner Stadtverordneten und die Anstellung jüdischer Lehrer," *Israelitische Wochenschrift*, no. 44 (1899): 607–700.

193. The statistics on Breslau teachers derive from *Breslauer Statistik*, vol. 24, pt. 1 (Breslau: Morgenstern, 1905), 66–88, esp. 81. It is unclear why the city did not take the offensive and establish interconfessional schools; still, in Frankfurt am Main, where the magistracy had created numerous interconfessional schools, there also was not a single Jewish teacher at a municipal elementary school; see Stein, "Im Verwaltungswege," 247. Jan Palmowski overlooks the exclusion of Jewish teachers from teaching positions at elementary schools; see his *Urban Liberalism in Imperial Germany*.

194. *Allgemeine Zeitung des Judenthums* 68 (1905): 78.

195. APW, AMW, H 120, 292, Protokollbuch der Stadtverordnetenversammlung, March 1–31, 1909, fols. 893–95 (Kurt Nitschke), 899–901 (Hans Trentin), 912–13 (Paul Hein); see also "Stadtverordnetenversammlung," *Schlesische Zeitung*, no. 229, April 1, 1909 (though no mention is made in the latter of the anti-Semitic character of Nitschke's motion). On Paul Hein, see Hettling, *Politische Bürgerlichkeit*, 103; there Hein is mistakenly said to be a Protestant; Hein, however, was on the founding board of directors of the Israelitisches Mädchenheim (see the pamphlet *Aufforderung, dem "Israelitischen Mädchenheim" beizutreten*, June 1891; UBW, GŚL 29225 III) and signed a pamphlet in June 1900 in support of the Galician Jews (NL Hugo Hillel Schachtel, box A 102, 10, Central Zionist Archives, Jerusalem).

196. They could lose their jobs only if they married. See "Betr. Offene Stellen an den Lesehallen und Volksbibliotheken April–Juli 1910," AMW, III, 3105, fols. 333–40. The magistracy had discussed whether it would be possible to dispense with the marriage clause, but ultimately decided against doing so (ibid., fol. 340; "Ein antisemitischer Vorstoß gegen jüdische Damen," *Jüdisches Volksblatt* 15 [1909]: 135).

197. "Die Zurücksetzung der Juden in der Stadtverwaltung: Aus der Breslauer Stadtverordnetenversammlung," *Jüdisches Volksblatt* 13 (1907): 145–46; see also the commentary, "Endlich!" ibid., 140–41. For an unusually biased summary of the debate, which mocked the Jewish city councilors' critique, see "Die Stadtverordnetenversammlung," *Schlesische Zeitung*, no. 235, April 5, 1907. The minutes of the city council meeting of April 4, 1907, have been lost since the Second World War, according to the manuscript catalog.

198. Bender's speech before the upper chamber is cited from "Umschau," *Im Deutschen Reich* 12 (1906): 458–59.

199. "Die Zurücksetzung der Juden in der Stadtverwaltung: Aus der Breslauer Stadtverordnetenversammlung," *Jüdisches Volksblatt* 13 (1907): 145–46.

200. "Die Stadtschuldeputation," ibid., 163.

201. On the aspects of the school law—a law based on a compromise between Conservatives, the Center Party, and National Liberals—that were of interest to German Jews, see Lamberti, *Jewish Activism in Imperial Germany*, 141–75.

202. "Die Verwendung jüdischer Lehrkräfte im städtischen Schuldienste," *Jüdisches Volksblatt* 14 (1908): 319–20.

203. "Lehrer und Schule," *Jüdisches Volksblatt* 16 (1910): 327 and 335.

204. "Antisemitische Kapuzinaden," *Jüdisches Volksblatt* 16 (1910): 354.

205. "Jüdische Lehrer an christlichen Schulen," *Deutsche Tageszeitung*, cited in "Jüdische Lehrer an christlichen Schulen," *Jüdisches Volksblatt* 16 (1910): 327 (issue from August 19, 1910; the reference to the applause of the *Schlesische Volkszeitung* may also be found there). The article from the *Deutsche Tageszeitung* received a good deal of attention; see, e.g., the rejoinder from the *Frankfurter Zeitung* (cited from "Jüdische Lehrer an christlichen Schulen," *Mitteilungen aus dem Verein zur Abwehr des Antisemitismus* 20 [1910]: 267): "The agrarian paper," the rejoinder reads, demands "that constitutional equality simply be abolished. Equal access to [teaching] positions, it says, should not be granted to Jewish teachers, not even when very special reasons, such as in this case the number of Jewish pupils, speak for the employment of Jewish teachers. . . . If German Christian parents want their children to be taught solely by Christian teachers, they have the opportunity [of sending their children to] schools of their own denomination, just as do Jewish parents who want only Jewish teachers for their children. In comprehensive public schools, however, which are supported by public funds, such a demand cannot be made." For references to other anti-Semitic attacks on the magistracy, see "Antisemitische Kapuzinaden," *Jüdisches Volksblatt* 16 (1910): 354.

206. "Der erste Schritt zur religionslosen Schule in Breslau," *Schlesische Volkszeitung*, quoted in "Die Hetze gegen den Breslauer Magistrat wegen der Anstellung jüdischer Lehrer," *Jüdisches Volksblatt* 16 (1910): 335; the reply by the liberal *Breslauer Zeitung* is reprinted in "Die Volksschule ist in Gefahr," *Mitteilungen aus dem Verein zur Abwehr des Antisemitismus* 20 (1910): 289.

207. "Jüdische Lehrer 2. Klasse," *Jüdisches Volksblatt* 16 (1910): 387. Jakob Hacks may have been overly cautious because he had just assumed his position as *Stadtschulrat* and was a member of the Social Democratic Party. Since the 1890s he had taught at the municipal *Gymnasium* in Kattowitz and had served as chairman of the Kattowitz City Council since 1908. During the heady days of the revolution of 1918–19, he published numerous pamphlets advocating educational and cultural reforms such as *Sozialismus und Schule* (Breslau: Volkswacht, 1919), *Die preussischen Bischöfe und die Sozialdemokratie: Erwiderung auf den Hirtenbrief der preussischen Bischöfe über den neuen Kulturkampf* (Breslau: Volkswacht, 1919), and *Der Sozialismus und die katholische Kirche* (Breslau: Volkswacht, 1919).

208. Quoted from "Das antisemitische Geschrei," *Mitteilungen aus dem Verein zur Abwehr des Antisemitismus* 20 (1910): 339.

209. "Anstellung von jüdischen Lehrkräften an Volksschulen," *Jüdisches Volksblatt* 16 (1910): 420–21.

210. "Das Ergebnis der Stadtverordnetenwahlen," *Schlesische Morgen-Zeitung*, no. 315, November 16, 1910. See James J. Sheehan, "Liberalism and the City in Nineteenth Century Germany," *Past and Present* 51 (1971): 116–37, here 132.

211. "Jüdische Lehrer an den städtischen Volksschulen," *Jüdisches Volksblatt* 16 (1910): 481–82 and 485–86. On Hans Herschel, who served as mayor of Breslau from 1924 to 1928, see Gerhard Webersinn, "Dr. Hans Herschel: Bürgermeister von Breslau," *Jahrbuch der Schlesischen Friedrich-Wilhelms-Universität zu Breslau* 12 (1967): 246–306.

212. "Die Anstellung jüdischer Lehrkräfte an den Breslauer Volksschulen," *Schlesische Morgen-Zeitung*, no. 325, November 27, 1910; see also "Stadtverordnetenversammlung," ibid., no. 324, November 26, 1910, supplement. The *Schlesische Zeitung* also condemned the magistracy's policy as an illegal "infringement on the principle of the denominational school"; see "Breslauer Stadtverordnetenversammlung," *Schlesische Zeitung*, no. 826, November 25, 1910.

213. "Jüdische Lehrer an den städtischen Volksschulen: Die Stadtverordnetenversammlung am 24. Nov. 1910," *Jüdisches Volksblatt* 16 (1910): 481–82 and 485–86.

214. Ibid., 481–82 and 485–86. Remarkable also is the contribution of the Social-Democratic city councilor, Paul Löbe, who later would be president of the Reichstag. As long as religious instruction was taught at all in schools, he said, the Jews had just as much right to it as the other denominations. The school was "an institution . . . that grant[ed] every pupil equality." The conservatives and the Catholics, he continued, wanted "to shut up the Jews in a ghetto school, to isolate them, to sharpen differences." He was happy to have the full participation of Jews in political life: "I am happy to see so many Jewish gentlemen on municipal committees who show themselves capable of self-sacrifice in working for the well-being of the municipality, who demonstrate such selflessness— which many a Christian could take as an example. . . . It is time we put an end to medieval anti-Semitism and uphold the great ideal of equality. (Shouts: Bravo!)"

215. Ibid., 481–82 and 485–86.

216. "Die Anstellung jüdischer Lehrkräfte an den städtischen Volksschulen," *Jüdisches Volksblatt* 17 (1911): 33–34 and 45–46, quotation from 33. See also "Stadtverordnetenversammlung," *Schlesische Zeitung*, no. 31, January 13, 1911.

217. "Die Anstellung jüdischer Lehrkräfte an den städtischen Volksschulen," *Jüdisches Volksblatt* 17 (1911): 160–61; *Mitteilungen aus dem Verein zur Abwehr des Antisemitismus* 21 (1911): 55. See also "Die Einrichtung städtischer Religionskurse in Breslau," *Jüdisches Volksblatt* 18 (1912): 158; "Das Rundschreiben in Sachen städtischen Religionsunterrichts," *Jüdisches Volksblatt* 18 (1912): 197.

218. "Der Bericht über die städtischen Religionsschulen," *Jüdisches Volksblatt* 18 (1912): 511–12; see also Louis Neustadt's rather critical article, "Die städtischen Religionsschulen in Breslau," ibid., 563–64.

219. "Die Stadtverordnetenwahlen in Breslau," *Jüdisches Volksblatt* 12 (1906): 491–92 and 543. Perhaps the fact that the proportion of Jewish city councilors had declined also played a role. After the elections in autumn 1904, there were only eighteen Jews among the fifty-one liberal city councilors; after the elections in December 1906, seventeen of the fifty-four liberals were Jewish (ibid.). In general, see Sheehan, "Liberalism and the City," 132, and table 48 in this volume.

220. "Das Ergebnis der Stadtverordnetenwahlen," *Schlesische Morgen-Zeitung*, no. 315, November 16, 1910, supplement; *Jüdisches Volksblatt* 16 (1910): 467. The *Volksblatt* also remarked proudly that the doyen of Breslau liberalism, the Jewish counselor of justice Wilhelm Salomon Freund, was also elected unanimously in his district.

221. See Ilsedore Rarisch, "Arthur Hobrecht," in *Neue Deutsche Biographie*, vol. 9 (Berlin: Duncker & Humblot, 1972), 280; *Jüdisches Volksblatt* 11 (1905): 179.

222. Quoted from "Schulgesetz und Kommune," *Kommunale Praxis* 6, no. 1 (1906): 22.

223. Frank-Michael Kuhlemann, "Niedere Schulen," in *Handbuch der deutschen Bildungsgeschichte*, 4:179–221, here 180–82; Neugebauer, "Das Bildungswesen in Preußen," 751.

224. *Allgemeine Zeitung des Judenthums* 54 (1890): 430.

225. On the following, see Baumeister, *Parität und katholische Inferiorität*, 13–18; Gabriele Haug-Moritz, "Kaisertum und Parität: Reichspolitik und Konfessionen nach dem Westfälischen Frieden," *Zeitschrift für Historische Forschung* 19 (1992): 445–82; Uwe Mazura, *Zentrumspartei und Judenfrage, 1870/71–1933: Verfassungsstaat und Minderheitenschutz* (Mainz: Matthias-Grünewald-Verlag, 1994), 151–65; Kraft Karl Ernst von Moy, "Parität," in *Wetzer und Weltke's Kirchenlexikon oder Encyklopädie der katholischen Theologie und ihrer Hülfswissenschaften*, ed. Joseph Hergenröther and Franz Kaulen, 2nd ed. (Freiburg i. Br.: Herder, 1895), 9:1520–24; Pulzer, *Jews and the German State*, 48–52; in the latter, see also the reference to parallels between the Catholic demands and the prevailing American idea of a "representative bureaucracy, 'responsive to the demands and needs of the community'" (51).

226. See Otto Mejer, "Parität," in *Realencyklopädie für protestantische Theologie und Kirche*, ed. Johann Jakob Herzog, Gustav Leopold Plitt, and Albert Hauck, 2nd ed. (Leipzig: Hinrichs, 1883), 11:223–24, here 223; and Johannes von Pruner, "Bekenntnißfreiheit," in *Staatslexikon*, ed. Adolf Bruder, vol. 1 (Freiburg i. Br.: Herder, 1889), cols. 865–83, here col. 878.

227. Fabius Schach, "Parität," *Im Deutschen Reich* 8 (1902): 1–7.

228. "Preußisches Abgeordnetenhaus," *Jüdisches Volksblatt* 11 (1905): 514. The privileged status of Protestantism and Catholicism conflicted with the general obligation to attend school and with the fact that all taxpayers together financed the schools. Mayor Georg Bender repeatedly drew attention to the latter point.

229. Felix Makower, "Ist Art. 14 der preußischen Verfassung anwendbar auf die im Schulgesetzentwurf geregelten Fragen?" *Deutsche Juristenzeitung* 11 (1906): 195–98; on Makower, see Lamberti, *Jewish Activism in Imperial Germany*, 141–43 and 149–50.

Chapter 5. Liberalism, Anti-Semitism, and Jewish Equality

1. Karl Rohe, *Politik: Begriffe und Wirklichkeiten*, 2nd ed. (Stuttgart: Kohlhammer, 1994), 140.

2. See esp. Joan Wallace Scott, *Gender and the Politics of History* (New York: Columbia University Press, 1988), and Eve Rosenhaft, "Women, Gender, and the Limits of Political History of 'Mass' Politics," in *Elections, Mass Politics, and Social Change in Modern Germany*, ed. Larry E. Jones and James Retallack (Cambridge: Cambridge University Press, 1992), 149–73. In general, see Seyla Benhabib, ed., *Democracy and Difference: Contesting the Boundaries of the Political* (Princeton, N.J.: Princeton University Press, 1996).

3. See, e.g., Peter Pulzer, *Jews and the German State: The Political History of a Minority, 1848–1933* (Oxford: Blackwell 1992); Werner T. Angress, "Prussia's Army and the Jewish Reserve Officer Controversy before World War I," *Year Book of the Leo Baeck Institute* 17 (1972): 19–42; Barbara Strenge, *Juden im preußischen Justizdienst, 1812–1918: Der Zugang zu den juristischen Berufen als Indikator der gesellschaftlichen Emanzipation* (Munich: Saur, 1995); Norbert Kampe, "Jüdische Professoren im deutschen Kaiserreich," in *Antisemitismus und jüdische Geschichte*, ed. Rainer Erb and Michael Schmidt (Berlin: Wissenschaftlicher Autorenverlag, 1987), 185–211.

4. Especially Peter Pulzer and Jack Wertheimer have stressed the significance of national and municipal politics for the social standing of German Jews; see Pulzer, *Jews and the German State*, 129, and Wertheimer, *Unwelcome Strangers: East European Jews in Imperial Germany* (Oxford: Oxford University Press, 1987). See also Inge Schlotzhauer, *Ideologie und Organisation des politischen Antisemitismus in Frankfurt am Main, 1880–1914* (Frankfurt a. M.: Kramer, 1989), 135, 185, 209–20, and 281–84; Ismar Schorsch, "German Antisemitism in the

Light of Post-War Historiography," *Year Book of the Leo Baeck Institute* 19 (1974): 257–71, here 271; and István Deák, "Ethnic Minorities and the Jews in Imperial Germany," *Year Book of the Leo Baeck Institute* 26 (1981): 47–51.

5. Wolfgang R. Krabbe, *Die deutsche Stadt im 19. und 20. Jahrhundert* (Göttingen: Vandenhoeck & Ruprecht, 1989), here 6; Horst Matzerath, *Urbanisierung in Preußen, 1815–1914* (Stuttgart: Kohlhammer, 1985), 347–71, here 371; James Sheehan provides an excellent introduction to this topic in his "Liberalism and the City in Nineteenth Century Germany," *Past and Present* 51 (1971): 116–37; see also: Thomas Nipperdey, *Deutsche Geschichte, 1866–1918*, vol. 2, *Machtstaat vor der Demokratie* (Munich: C. H. Beck, 1995), 154–63; Palmowski, *Urban Liberalism in Imperial Germany: Frankfurt am Main, 1866–1914* (Oxford: Oxford University Press, 1999). By contrast, Wolfgang Mommsen stresses the limits of municipal self-administration that the "old authoritarian state" placed on Prussian cities in his *Das Ringen um den nationalen Staat: Die Gründung und der innere Ausbau des Deutschen Reiches unter Otto von Bismarck, 1850–1890* (Berlin: Propyläen, 1993), 394–405, here 400; Wolfgang Hardtwig argues along similar lines in his "Großstadt und Bürgerlichkeit in der politischen Ordnung des Kaiserreichs," in *Stadt und Bürgertum im 19. Jahrhundert*, ed. Lothar Gall (Munich: C. H. Beck, 1990), 19–64, esp. 57–58. Lothar Gall's "Bürgertumsprojekt" is also based on the premise that the municipal-local sphere is constitutive for the middle class's self-understanding; see Gall, ed., *Stadt und Bürgertum im Übergang von der traditionalen zur modernen Gesellschaft* (Munich: Oldenbourg, 1993).

6. An analysis of anti-Semitism in Dresden is greatly needed; some help in this direction may be found in Gerald Kolditz, "Zur Entwicklung des Antisemitismus in Dresden während des Kaiserreichs," *Dresdner Hefte* 45 (1996): 37–45, and Rudolf Heinze, "Dresden," in *Verfassung und Verwaltungsorganisation der Städte*, by Georg Häpe et al., vol. 4, pt. 1, *Königreich Sachsen*, Schriften des Vereins für Sozialpolitik 120 (Leipzig: Duncker & Humblot, 1905), 85–122, esp. 115–16; on Düsseldorf, Frankfurt, Hamburg, and Nuremberg, see Anthony Kauders, *German Politics and the Jews: Düsseldorf and Nuremberg, 1910–1933* (Oxford: Oxford University Press, 1996); Schlotzhauer, *Ideologie und Organisation;* and Daniela Kasischke-Wurm, *Antisemitismus im Spiegel der Hamburger Presse während des Kaiserreichs, 1884–1914* (Hamburg: LIT, 1997).

7. Dieter Langewiesche, "'Staat' und 'Kommune': Zum Wandel der Staatsaufgaben in Deutschland im 19. Jahrhundert," *Historische Zeitschrift* 248 (1989): 621–35, here 622–23.

8. Manfred Hettling has shown that the Breslau's left-wing liberals' "highest principle" was "the right of free self-determination" in both the political and the commercial spheres; see Hettling, *Politische Bürgerlichkeit: Der Bürger zwischen Individualität und Vergesellschaftung in Deutschland und der Schweiz von 1860 bis 1918* (Göttingen: Vandenhoeck & Ruprecht, 1999), 244–56, here 246.

9. Franz Klühs, "Von Richter zu Luegner," *Kommunale Praxis* 5 (1905): 407–10, here 408; see also in the same issue his "Städtische Arbeiterfürsorge in

Breslau," 626–29; in *Kommunale Praxis* 6 (1906), "Der Breslauer Oberbürger-meister im Umgang mit Arbeitern," 33–34; "Das Koalitionsrecht in freisin-niger Praxis," 53–55; and "Kommunalversammlung und Koalitionsrecht," 169–71; and "Freisinnige Arbeiterfürsorge," *Kommunale Praxis* 8 (1908): 146–47.

10. See Thomas Nipperdey, *Deutsche Geschichte, 1866–1918*, vol. 1, *Arbeitswelt und Bürgergeist* (Munich: C. H. Beck, 1990), 384, and *Deutsche Geschichte, 1866–1918*, 2:312, 316, and 322. See especially Gangolf Hübinger, *Kulturprotestantismus und Politik: Zum Verhältnis von Liberalismus und Protestantismus im wilhelminischen Deutschland* (Tubingen: Mohr Siebeck, 1994). See also Dieter Langewiesche, *Li-beralismus in Deutschland* (Frankfurt a. M.: Suhrkamp, 1988), 114 and 125–26; and Panajotis Kondylis, *Die Aufklärung im Rahmen des neuzeitlichen Rationalismus* (Mu-nich: Deutscher Taschenbuch Verlag, 1986), 540: "[T]he ideological laboratory in eighteenth-century Germany was often not the middle-class house but the parsonage." See Friedrich Naumann, "Liberalismus und Protestantismus: Re-ferat gehalten auf dem 24. Deutschen Protestantentag in Bremen am 22. Sep-tember 1909," in *Werke*, ed. Theodor Schieder, vol. 1 (Opladen: Westdeutscher Verlag, 1960), 773–801.

11. In general, see Peter Pulzer, "Die jüdische Beteiligung an der Politik," in *Juden im Wilhelminischen Deutschland, 1870–1914*, ed. Werner E. Mosse (Tü-bingen: Mohr Siebeck, 1976), 143–240, esp. 186–93.

12. The figures for 1860 and 1874 are from Jacob Toury, *Soziale und poli-tische Geschichte der Juden in Deutschland, 1847–1871: Zwischen Revolution, Reaktion und Emanzipation* (Düsseldorf: Droste, 1977), 110 (though it includes false infor-mation about the Jewish portion of Breslau's population); the figures for 1888 are from the *Schlesische Volkszeitung* (no. 501, October 30, 1888) and the *Breslauer Morgen-Zeitung* (no. 257, October 30, 1888), cited in Hettling, *Politische Bürger-lichkeit*, 69–70.

13. *Neue Preußische Zeitung*, June 8, 1896, cited in Detlef Lehnert, *Kommunale Institutionen zwischen Honoratiorenverwaltung und Massendemokratie: Partizipations-chancen, Autonomieprobleme und Stadtinterventionismus in Berlin, London, Paris und Wien, 1888–1914* (Baden-Baden: Nomos, 1994), 200.

14. John W. Boyer, *Political Radicalism in Late Imperial Vienna: Origins of the Christian Social Movement, 1848–1897* (Chicago: University of Chicago Press, 1981), 85–86; for more information about the differences between Prussian and Viennese municipal electoral law, see pp. 297–300 and 509–10, as well as Leh-nert, *Kommunale Institutionen*, 185–228; on the "predominance of home owners in [Austrian] city councils," see also Detlef Lehnert, "Organisierter Hausbesitz und kommunale Politik in Wien und Berlin, 1890–1933," *Geschichte und Gesell-schaft* 20 (1994): 29–56, here 32 and 54–55.

15. Hettling, *Politische Bürgerlichkeit*, 76–77 and 108–9; on Berlin, see Adolf Wermuth, *Ein Beamtenleben* (Berlin: Scherl, 1922), 333–34.

16. Adolf Heilberg, Memoiren, 1858–1936, ME 257a, 272, Archives of the LBI, New York; partially printed in *Jüdisches Leben in Deutschland*, ed. Monika

Richarz, vol. 2, *Selbstzeugnisse zur Sozialgeschichte des Kaiserreichs* (Stuttgart: Deutsche Verlagsanstalt, 1979), 296.

17. Jan Palmowski, e.g., argues along similar lines regarding Frankfurt school policy; see his *Urban Liberalism in Imperial Germany*, 161–65; see also Pulzer, "Die jüdische Beteiligung an der Politik," 186–93.

18. See *Israelitische Wochenschrift* 3 (1872): 3 and 61. This weekly, which was well informed about the circumstances in Breslau, based its reports on the *Schlesische Volkszeitung* and the *Schlesisches Kirchenblatt;* on early Catholic anti-Semitism in Breslau, see Leonhard Müller, *Der Kampf zwischen politischem Katholizismus und Bismarcks Politik im Spiegel der Schlesischen Volkszeitung: Ein Beitrag zur schlesischen Kirchen-, Parteien- und Zeitungsgeschichte* (Breslau: Müller & Seiffert, 1929), 128–39; see also Rudolf Lill, "Die deutschen Katholiken und die Juden in der Zeit 1850 bis zur Machtübernahme Hitlers," in *Kirche und Synagoge: Handbuch zur Geschichte von Christen und Juden*, ed. Karl Heinrich Rengstorf and Siegfried von Kortzfleisch, vol. 2 (1970; repr., Munich: Deutscher Taschenbuch Verlag, 1988), 358–420, here 381. In general see Olaf Blaschke, *Katholizismus und Antisemitismus im Deutschen Kaiserreich*, 2nd ed. (Göttingen: Vandenhoeck & Ruprecht, 1998); and, specifically concerning Breslau, "'Das Judenthum isolieren!' Antisemitismus und Ausgrenzung in Breslau," in *In Breslau zu Hause? Juden in einer europäischen Metropole der Neuzeit*, ed. Manfred Hettling, Andreas Reinke, and Norbert Conrads (Hamburg: Dölling & Galitz, 2003), 167–84.

19. Cited from "Breslau," *Deutscher Volksfreund*, no. 29, July 13, 1872.

20. Martin Philippson, *Max von Forckenbeck: Ein Lebensbild* (Dresden: Reißner, 1898), 236–37.

21. "Katholish war a, welch a Sturm; / Mer hahn nich lang gefackelt. / Es hat och ünse Rathausthurm / Bis hinte nich gewackelt!" "Wie daß de Breslauer ihren neien Oberbörgermester Herrn Max von Forckenbeck begrißt haben," in X. Provinz Brandenburg Rep. 16A, NL Forckenbeck, no. 28, Geheimes Staatsarchiv Preußischer Kulturbesitz, Berlin-Dahlem. A biographical vignette in the journal *Rübezahl* stressed that the new mayor was "the first Catholic to hold this office since the days of the revolution, a development that [they] gladly welcome[d] as a sign of the coming spring during this extremely turbulent season and fierce fighting"; see "Max von Forckenbeck: Präsident des preußischen Abgeordnetenhauses, Oberbürgermeister von Breslau," *Rübezahl* 12 (1873): 167–69, here 169. Concerning Forckenbeck's Catholicism, see Hermann Oncken, "Max von Forckenbeck," in *Allgemeine Deutsche Biographie*, vol. 48 (Leipzig: Duncker & Humblot, 1904), 630–50, here 640.

22. "Unsere Wahl-Niederlage," *Breslauer Sonntagsblatt*, no. 32, August 11, 1878. The left-wing liberal *Breslauer Zeitung* noted with satisfaction in its commentary on the Landtag elections of 1879 that "by far the largest portion of [their] Catholic population . . . [was] *not* ultramontane"; "roughly 260 delegates were elected, but most of them belong[ed] to the liberal party."

23. Hettling, *Politische Bürgerlichkeit*; Adolf Phillips, ed., *Die Reichstags-Wahlen von 1867 bis 1883* (Berlin: L. Gerschel, 1883), 45–46 (the precise distribution of votes was 54% and 59%).

24. Due to its importance, the *Schlesische Zeitung* incurred the wrath of the Jewish press after it had propagated anti-Semitic positions. In retrospect, the *Israelitische Wochenschrift* wrote in 1882: "[W]e have our most treacherous anti-Semite, the *Schlesische Zeitung* . . . mainly . . . to thank for the fact that anti-Semitism has become respectable here and, in certain circles, almost a sport." *Israelitische Wochenschrift* 13 (1882): 159.

25. See the collection of contemporary articles "Antisemitismus in Breslau 1878/79," BUW, GŚL, Ym 10. The almanac *Der Volksfreund*, which the editor of the *Deutscher Volksfreund*, Franz Goerlich, published, also included popular stories that were widely circulated. See, e.g., "Wie's die Juden manchmal treiben" [How the Jews Often Do It], in *Der Volksfreund: Kalender für 1879* (Breslau, 1878), 73–74; A. Kulik, "Der Schnapsjude" [The Jewish Boozer], in *Der Volksfreund: Kalender für 1881* (Breslau, 1880), 38–46, and "Schimmel und Pony: Eine lustige Pferdejudengeschichte aus Breslau" [The White Horse and the Pony: A Funny Horse-Jew Tale from Breslau], in *Der Volksfreund: Kalender für 1882* (Breslau, 1881), 68–72; "Der König der Juden" [The King of the Jews], in *Der Volksfreund: Kalender für 1882* (Breslau, 1881), 72; "Die Juden im Mittelalter nach Janssen" [The Jews in the Middle Ages according to Janssen], in *Der Volksfreund: Kalender für 1883* (Breslau, 1882), 33–36; "Der angehende Handelsjude" [A Jewish Merchant in the Making], in *Der Volksfreund. Kalender für 1883* (Breslau, 1882), 83.

26. *Breslauer Zeitung*, no. 469, October 8, 1879; "In Betreff der tumultuarischen Vorgaenge bei der Breslauer Abgeordnetenwahl," *Schlesische Zeitung*, no. 472, October 10, 1879; *Deutscher Volksfreund*, no. 42, October 10, 1879; "Locales und Provinzielles," *Deutscher Volksfreund*, no. 43, October 17, 1879; see also Leonhard Müller, *Der Kampf*, 205. The elections were followed closely throughout Germany. Heinrich von Treitschke, e.g., noted in his notorious essay titled "Unsere Aussichten" (Our Prospects): "[T]oday we have already reached the point that the majority of Breslau voters have sworn—clearly not out of great agitation but rather calm deliberation—not to vote for a Jew under any circumstances." Cited in Walter Boehlich, ed., *Der Berliner Antisemitismusstreit* (Frankfurt a. M.: Insel, 1965), 7.

27. Advertisement from the Freie Vereinigung zur Wahl geeigneter Stadtverordneter [Free Union for the Election of Suitable City Councilors], *Schlesisches Morgenblatt*, no. 268, November 14, 1880, 4; on the Freie Vereinigung, see also Leonhard Müller, *Der Kampf*, 206.

28. "Locale und Provinzielle Umschau," *Schlesisches Morgenblatt*, no. 252, October 27, 1880; "Locale und Provinzielle Umschau," *Schlesisches Morgenblatt*, no. 268, November 14, 1880: "And now straight to the ballot box, we have to fight against the hegemony of progress and Semitism in city hall." In

retrospect, the *Israelitische Wochenschrift* characterized the Freie Vereinigung as "a mixture of conservatives, ultramontanes, guildsmen, and anti-Semites"; *Israelitische Wochenschrift* 11 (1881): 37. The Freie Vereinigung even met with the approval of organized political anti-Semites; for instance, in October 1882 Max Liebermann von Sonnenberg wrote: "Incidentally, it is precisely Breslau that now can boast that even liberal elements there have singled themselves out that feel our unbearable dependence upon international capital and are trying to join with other elements to form one great party to which belongs the future." Max Liebermann von Sonnenberg, "Rede gehalten in der Volks-Versammlung des Reform-Vereins am 16. Oktober 1882 im großen Saale des 'Russischen Kaisers' zu Breslau," in *Beiträge zur Geschichte der antisemitischen Bewegung vom Jahre 1880–1885*, ed. Liebermann von Sonnenberg (Berlin: privately published, 1885), 105–22, here 111.

29. The *Deutscher Volksfreund* of November 26, 1880 (no. 40) gives an overview of the election results.

30. *Israelitische Wochenschrift* 10 (1880): 435–36; see also *Israelitische Wochenschrift* 9 (1879): 365 and 435–37, and *Allgemeine Zeitung des Judenthums* 45 (1881): 7 and 90.

31. *Israelitische Wochenschrift* 11 (1881): 36–37.

32. In June 1881, e.g., the *Schlesische Volkszeitung*, which two years earlier was still the principal organ of Silesian anti-Semitism, vehemently attacked the anti-Semitic movement in the person of Ernst Henrici. Anti-Semitism, the paper said, is "a view that arouses the worst emotions and can lead nowhere but to violence and racist outrage against the Jews." This "naked racial hatred," the paper continued, is "the exact opposite of the Christian view of the world and society." *Schlesische Volkszeitung*, June 8, 1881, cited in Margaret L. Anderson, *Windthorst: A Political Biography* (Oxford: Clarendon Press, 1981), 265; see also Müller, *Der Kampf*, 212–16, esp. 213–14 and 219–23. At the end of the 1890s, there was a renewal of the alliance between the Center and Conservative parties (Hettling, *Politische Bürgerlichkeit*, 60). Unlike in the late 1870s, however, after 1900 anti-Semitism does not seem to have formed a key link between the two parties.

33. On Wilhelm Salomon Freund, see Ernest Hamburger, *Juden im öffentlichen Leben Deutschlands: Regierungsmitglieder, Beamte, Parlamentarier in der monarchischen Zeit, 1848–1918* (Tübingen: Mohr Siebeck, 1968), 296–97; K. Schwerin, "Die Juden im wirtschaftlichen Leben Schlesiens," *Jahrbuch der Schlesischen Friedrich-Wilhelms-Universität zu Breslau* 25 (1984): 93–177, here 106; *Allgemeine Zeitung des Judenthums* 79 (September 3, 1915): supplement, 2. Freund's annual income in 1876 was well over 30,000 marks (APW, AMW, K 150, vol. 6, no. 32); on Freund's honorary citizenship, see APW, AMW, III, 3594, fols. 202–7, and "50jaehriges Dienstjubilaeum," *Schlesische Zeitung*, no. 303, May 1, 1901, 2. His political career is very similar to Wolfgang Strassmann's (b. 1821 in Lissa, d. 1885 in Berlin), who was the chairman of the Berlin city council already from 1875 to 1885; however, he never was made an honorary citizen of Berlin. On

Strassmann, see Hamburger, *Juden im öffentlichen Leben Deutschlands*, 329, and "Die Trauerfeier für Strassmann," *Israelitische Wochenschrift* 16 (1885): 387–91.

34. The history of organized political anti-Semitism in Breslau can be written only on the basis of very scant sources. The files of the Silesian capital's political police have been completely destroyed, and even the internal sources from anti-Semitic organizations—even membership registers—are no longer available. The financial difficulties of the Breslau anti-Semites suggest, however, that the business elite did not support them. In contrast to the anti-Semites, other parties had fewer concerns about money. The Conservative-National Liberal Neuer Wahlverein [New Election Association], e.g., at a single election meeting filled the election campaign coffer with the 3,000 marks needed for the 1879 Landtag elections ("Neuer Wahlverein," *Schlesische Zeitung*, no. 385, August 20, 1879). On the costs of election campaigns in general, see Manfred Hettling, *Politische Bürgerlichkeit*, 200, and his "Partei ohne Partei-beamte: Parteisekretäre im Linksliberalismus von 1900 bis 1933," in *Parteien im Wandel: Vom Kaiserreich zur Weimarer Republik*, ed. Dieter Dowe, Jürgen Kocka, and Heinrich August Winkler (Munich: Oldenbourg, 1999), 109–34, here 116–17; and Nipperdey, *Deutsche Geschichte, 1866–1918*, 2:518. The *Deutsche Ostwacht* must serve as the chief source. This "Weekly for the German Middle Class—Organ of the German-Social Provincial-Association for Silesia" (*Wochenschrift für den deutschen Mittelstand—Organ des Deutsch-socialen Provinzial-Verbandes für Schlesien*), as its subtitle read, was published from October 1892 to March 1894 under the editorship of Hugo Kretschmer. Yet precisely because it was a party newspaper, its reports about internal tensions and conflicts are particularly informative. I have also consulted the general daily newspapers and the reports on anti-Semitism in Breslau from the Jewish press. My thanks to Mr. Soboczynsky for his detective skills, which enabled him to retrieve the *Deutsche Ostwacht* from the depths of the Breslau university library. In the meantime, a microfilm of the original may be found at the Zentrum für Antisemitismusforschung, Berlin.

35. "Der Deutsche Reform-Verein," *Deutsche Ostwacht*, January 1, 1893, 9. On the early history of the Deutscher Reform-Verein, see the well-meaning reports of the *Schlesisches Morgenblatt* about the first "genuine meeting of anti-Semites" in Breslau (no. 134, June 14, 1881, 5–6) and the Catholic *Deutscher Volksfreund* ("Bürgerversammlung," no. 24, June 17, 1881), the election announcement "Wahl-Campagne-Lied des Deutschen Reform-Vereins in Breslau: Zur Reichstagswahl am 27. Oktober 1881," BUW, GŚL, Ym 38, as well as the derisive notice in the *Allgemeine Zeitung des Judenthums* 45 (1881): 426.

36. *Deutsche Ostwacht*, November 19, 1892, 5.

37. "Deutsch-nationaler Verein zu Breslau," *Deutsche Ostwacht*, March 4, 1893, 10; see also "Deutsch-nationaler Verein," *Deutsche Ostwacht*, March 18, 1893, 11. Shortly thereafter the *Deutsche Ostwacht* characterized the association as "the right wing of the German-Social movement in Breslau" (ibid., March 25, 1893, 4).

38. Cited from *Deutsche Ostwacht,* March 18, 1893, 9–10.

39. *Deutsche Ostwacht,* March 25, 1893, 4; ibid., April 15, 1893, 5.

40. *Deutsche Ostwacht,* October 14, 1893, 2.

41. *Deutsche Ostwacht,* October 28, 1893, 5. While the *Deutsche Ostwacht* still tried to put a good face on the outcome of the Reichstag elections immediately afterward, Kretschmer admitted in his review of the year's events that neither "of the candidacies" had met with "the desired success"; see his "Die deutsch-sociale Bewegung in Schlesien im Jahre 1893," *Deutsche Ostwacht,* December 30, 1893, 3–4.

42. On Ahlwardt's Breslau speech, see *Deutsche Ostwacht,* March 11, 1893, 5; Hermann Ahlwardt, "Warum muß der Antisemitismus siegen?" *Deutsche Ostwacht,* March 18, 1893, 13–15, and *Deutsche Ostwacht,* March 25, 1893, 10–12; on Böckel's speech, see *Deutsche Ostwacht,* December 8, 1893, 5.

43. H. K. (= Hugo Kretschmer), "Wie können wir die deutsch-sociale Bewegung in Schlesien fördern?" *Deutsche Ostwacht,* February 17, 1894, 4.

44. Hugo Kretschmer, "Unser Bürgerthum," *Deutsche Ostwacht,* March 31, 1894, 2.

45. Ibid. In the preceding September, the lengthy essay "Die Frauenfrage im Lichte der deutsch-socialen Anschauung" had been published (*Deutsche Ostwacht,* September 2, 9, and 16, 1893). According to this essay, the targets of the anti-Semites' misogynistic invectives were "the pretty little things who thoughtlessly shopped in Jewish stores." Anti-Semitic men felt threatened even by the modest power of women as consumers: "The cause of most unhappy marriages is the unhappy upbringing of girls these days." Instead of being instilled with the spirit of "piety, diligence, and fidelity," "young girls learn at home and in society to fritter away their time." Here, too, the primary objective was moral renewal: "If one raises German girls, that is, if one raises them in the German spirit, then there will be German men who court the German virgin as a German woman." The aim of this anti-Semitic gender hierarchy was the "true German housewife" in a familial idyll in which women "show[ed] fidelity not only to their husbands but also to themselves and their people, the German people."

46. Liebermann von Sonnenberg, "Rede," 21. For the general context, see Steven E. Aschheim, "'The Jew Within': The Myth of 'Judaization' in Germany," in *The Jewish Response to German Culture: From the Enlightenment to the Second World War,* ed. Jehuda Reinharz and Walter Schatzberg (Hanover, N.H.: University Press of New England, 1985), 212–41.

47. H. K. (= Hugo Kretschmer), "Klarheit und eigene Prüfung," *Deutsche Ostwacht,* December 23, 1893, 12. In January of that year, Kretschmer had already characterized the *Deutsche Ostwacht* as the "spiritual band that unifies and brings them closer together" (*Deutsche Ostwacht,* January 14, 1893, 4); see also his "Die Zeitung und ihre Leser," *Deutsche Ostwacht,* September 30, 1893, 1–2; the expression "disgraceful hegemony of the Jews" (*unwürdige Judenherrschaft*) occurs, e.g., in *Deutsche Ostwacht,* October 7, 1893, 1–2.

48. See, e.g., *Deutsche Ostwacht*, December 16, 1893, 1–2, and January 13, 1894, 3.

49. *Deutsche Ostwacht,* January 20, 1894, 5.

50. Richard S. Levy, *The Downfall of the Anti-Semitic Political Parties in Imperial Germany* (New Haven, Conn.: Yale University Press, 1975), 116. In all likelihood, the failure of the *Deutsche Ostwacht* was also ultimately an indicator of the disunity among the Silesian anti-Semites. In retrospect, Hugo Kretschmer noted in the final edition of the paper (March 31, 1894, 1) that "during the *Deutsche Ostwacht*'s existence there certainly was no lack of disappointments." "The *Deutsche Ostwacht* even had to endure quite spiteful attacks from some who shared its persuasions, which spoiled many opportunities for political success."

51. Willibald Steinmetz, *Das Sagbare und das Machbare: Zum Wandel politischer Handlungsspielräume; England, 1780–1867* (Stuttgart: Klett-Cotta, 1993), 33. In what follows here on local politics in Breslau, I have derived several ideas from the conceptual framework of Steinmetz's study; like him, my interest is in the "canon of *possible expressions*, the *chances* given therein for *successful argumentation* and the concrete '*actualizations*' of available modes of discourse" (ibid., 44).

52. H. G., "Breslauer Leben," *Deutsche Ostwacht*, March 4, 1893, 10–11, and March 11, 1893, 10–11; there is a similar tone in the lead article, "Kauft nicht bei Juden," *Deutsche Ostwacht*, November 26, 1892, 1–2.

53. "O Breslau du, o Breslau / Du alte Bischofsstadt, / Wo's drinnen so viel Juden / Und Christenfeinde hat. // Wie ist es denn gekommen, / Was hast du denn gemacht, / Daß du es bis zur Herrschaft / Der Juden hast gebracht? // . . . // Sie sitzen schon im Rathe / Fast immer obenan / Und haben Wort und Stimme, / Der Christ—gehorchen kann. // . . . // O wolle doch nicht christlich / Blos nach dem Namen sein, / O richte nach dem Namen / Auch That und Wandel ein. // Verleugne nicht das Zeichen, / Das durch die Wolken bricht, / Denn nur im Kreuz ist Leben, / Im Kreuze Heil und Licht!" H. Hübner, "Mahnung an Breslau," *Breslauer Sonntagsblatt*, no. 40, October 5, 1879.

54. "Zur Judenfrage VI," *Deutscher Volksfreund*, no. 6, February 6, 1880. On the extensive renovation of the Breslau sewage system around 1880, see Architekten- und Ingenieurverein Breslau, ed., *Breslau's Bauten sowie kunstgewerbliche und technische Anstalten* (Breslau: E. Trewendt, [1885]), 17–20. The *Deutscher Volksfreund*'s series on the "Jewish question" ended (no. 7, February 13, 1880) with a mixture of aggressive, threatening gestures and fatalism, in which not only the reference to the "arch-Protestant" Treitschke is remarkable: "Truly, Judaism has sinned often, and if we wanted to exact an eye for an eye, our vengeance would have no end. . . . We are dealing with a powerful enemy, who, led by a secret general staff, threatens the Christian world with religious, moral, and material ruin. It is high time that we join ranks for a decisive spiritual battle, when even a Treitschke exclaims: 'The Jews are our undoing.'"

55. Richard Hofstadter, "The Paranoid Style in American Politics," in *The Paranoid Style in American Politics and Other Essays* (New York: Vintage Books, 1967), 3–40; "Die Stadtverordnetenwahlen," *Breslauer Communal-Zeitung*, no. 23, October 30, 1880; see also "Unscr Programm," *Breslauer Communal-Zeitung*, March 27, 1880: "Independent of and not influenced by any party lines and absolutely free of any discussion of political or religious questions."

56. "Communale Umschau XLVI," *Schlesische Presse*, no. 842, December 1, 1878 6.

57. Wolfgang Hofmann has rightly criticized the idea of an apolitical local politics as a myth; see his *Zwischen Rathaus und Reichskanzlei: Die Oberbürgermeister in der Kommunal- und Stadtpolitik des Deutschen Reiches von 1890–1933* (Stuttgart: Kohlhammer, 1974), 44–45. Yet the specific character of the prevailing understanding of Breslau local politics seems decisive. This is likely what Wolfgang Hardtwig had in mind when he spoke of the "delayed politicization" of municipal government; see his "Großstadt und Bürgerlichkeit in der politischen Ordnung des Kaiserreichs," in *Stadt und Bürgertum im 19. Jahrhundert*, ed. Lothar Gall (Munich: C. H. Beck, 1990), 19–64, here 47. See also James J. Sheehan, "Liberalism and the City in Nineteenth Century Germany," *Past and Present* 51 (1971): 116–37, here 134–35; Thomas Mergel, "Das Rathaus," in *1848: Revolution in Deutschland*, ed. Christof Dipper and Ulrich Speck (Frankfurt a. M.: Insel, 1998), 183–95, esp. 186; and Palmowski, *Urban Liberalism in Imperial Germany*, 14–22, with references to older literature. On Breslau, see Hettling, *Politische Bürgerlichkeit*, 206–7; according to him, "city residents" were concerned "to prevent a disintegration of the municipal administration into political parties."

58. On Julius Friedländer (b. August 28, 1834, in Pleß, d. June 27, 1892, in Breslau), who was of Jewish origin but had converted to Protestantism early, see Hettling, *Politische Bürgerlichkeit*, 101 (there he is mistakenly referred to as "Gustav" Friedländer), as well as the reference to the magistracy's role at his funeral: APW, AMW III, 2190, fols. 37–40b.

59. "Sitzung der Stadtverordnetenversammlung vom 23. März 1880, Neuwahl des Directoriums des Aller-Heiligen-Krankenhauses" (APW, AMW, H 120, vol. 120, fols. 880–82, 902–12, 981–98); Simon (fols. 994–95); Friedländer (fols. 981–82), Seidel (fols. 986–87 and 989), Milch (fols. 987–88).

60. Ibid., Seidel (fols. 986–87 and 989); Milch (fols. 987–88).

61. Ibid., Elsner (fols. 995–97). See also "Stadtverordnetenversammlung vom 23. Maerz 1880," *Schlesische Zeitung*, no. 141, March 1880, supplement 1. On Elsner, see "Der Gymnasiallehrer Dr. Elsner und der Lehrer an der höheren Bürgerschule zu Breslau Dr. Stein, die gegen dieselben eingeleitete Untersuchung wegen Theilnahme an Aufruhr erregenden Bewegungen und staatsgefährlichen Umtrieben überhaupt 1849–1860," I. HA Rep 76 VI, Sektion 8, Geheimes Staatsarchiv Preußischer Kulturbesitz, Berlin-Dahlem; Arno Herzig, "Die unruhige Provinz: Schlesien zwischen 1806 und 1871," in *Schlesien*, ed. Norbert Conrads, Deutsche Geschichte im Osten Europas (Berlin: Siedler,

1994), 466–553, here 539–40; Albert Teichmann, "Moritz Elsner," in *Allgemeine Deutsche Biographie*, vol. 48 (Leipzig: Duncker & Humblot, 1904), 339–41; Leopold Freund, *Eine Lebensgeschichte*, 2nd ed. (Breslau: Leopold Freund's Verlagshandlung, 1878), 42 and 48; as well as chap. 4, n.71 of the present volume. The Aller-Heiligen-Krankenhaus was founded in the fifteenth century and was moved to new facilities in 1830; F. G. Adolf Weiß, *Chronik der Stadt Breslau von der ältesten bis zur neuesten Zeit* (Breslau: Woywod, 1888), 737 and 1128.

62. "Zur Judenfrage IV," *Deutscher Volksfreund*, January 16, 1880, no. 3. In "several timely little rhymes," one could read verses in the Catholic *Schlesische Volkszeitung* already in July 1878 such as the following: "Wenn in der Verwaltung Zweigen / Assessoren führ'n den Reigen, / Die auch Lieferanten sind; / Und bei allen Submissionen / Jacob- und die Isaaksohnen / Stets am Billigsten man findt' / Dann ade ade ade, dann ade Schatz lebe wohl" [When in the administration's branches / Assessors hold the reins / Who also are suppliers; / And when in all the contract bids / The sons of Jacob and Isaac / Are always the lowest bidders / Then adieu adieu adieu, then adieu Dear, farewell] (J. O., "Einige zeitgemässe Reimlein," *Schlesische Volkszeitung*, no. 170, July 28, 1878). The *Schlesisches Morgenblatt* (no. 169, July 23, 1885) regarded an antiliberal reform of the bidding process as "one of the most important means of improving the trades." The magistracy's award policy was said to date back to "an age of economic rationalism" and "in many ways reward[ed] bad work." "The only consideration here is cheapness. . . . But cheapness is in most cases the precondition for bad quality." In general, see Josef Wilden, "Submissionswesen," in *Handwörterbuch der Kommunalwissenschaften*, ed. Josef Brix et al., vol. 4, *Stadt und Stadtverfassung bis Zweckverbände* (Jena: Gustav Fischer, 1924), 154–58.

63. The information on Witkowski is based on "Wahlliste der jüdischen Gemeinde für 1876," no. 2818 (there he is mistakenly listed as "Wittkowsky," though with the same address), Synagogengemeinde Breslau, Żydowski Instytut Historyczny, Warsaw; *Adreß- und Geschäfts-Handbuch der königlichen Haupt- und Residenzstadt Breslau für das Jahr 1877* (Breslau: Morgenstern, 1877), part I/1, 477; *Adreß- und Geschäfts-Handbuch der königlichen Haupt- und Residenzstadt Breslau für das Jahr 1878* (Breslau: Morgenstern, 1878), part I/1, 478 (Witkowski is also listed as "acting district chairman"); the information on the economic situation stems from the tax roll APW, AMW, K 146, vol. 21, no. 4406.

64. "Sitzung der Stadtverordnetenversammlung vom 15. April 1880, Zuschlagserteilung auf Lieferung der Bauhölzer für das Bauholz-Depot auf dem Stadtbauhofe pro 1880–1881 an den Mindestfordernden Isidor Witkowski" (APW, AMW, H 120, vol. 121, fols. 129–30, 161–74); Geier (fols. 164–67), Storch (fols. 169 and 173). Moreover, on Geier's side were Councilor Schaefer (fols. 161–62); the magistracy was also supported by the municipal building surveyor Mende (fols. 162–64) and Councilor Louis Ehrlich (fols. 168–69); the businessman Anton Storch played a prominent role in church life in Breslau; in 1875, e.g., he was a member of Breslau's Comité für den 9. Deutschen Protestantentag

(Committee for the Ninth German Protestant Conference); see *Schlesisches Pro-testantenblatt* 5 (1875): 149.

65. "Die Stadtverordnetenwahlen in Breslau," *Jüdisches Volksblatt* 12 (1906): 491–92 and 543; "Der Rotblock in Aengsten," *Schlesische Morgen-Zeitung*, no. 309, November 12, 1912, 2. On debates on kosher butchering now, see Robin Judd, *Contested Rituals: Circumcision, Kosher Butchering, and German-Jewish Political Life in Germany, 1843–1933* (Ithaca, N.Y.: Cornell University Press, 2007).

66. The phrase "restraining sense of shame" (*Kappzaum der Scham*) stems from Theodor Mommsen's response to Treitschke; cited in Boehlich, *Der Ber-liner Antisemitismusstreit*, 220.

67. "'Ein echt jüdischer Zug,'" *Jüdisches Volksblatt* 11 (1905): 143, 145, 241, and 362.

68. An overview of the "debates on the Jews" in the Reichstag and the Prussian Landtag is provided in Uwe Mazura, *Zentrumspartei und Judenfrage, 1870/71–1933: Verfassungstaat und Minderheitenschutz* (Mainz: Matthias-Grünewald-Verlag, 1994), 73–170; and B. Hentschel, "Juden als Debattenthema im Deut-schen Reichstag, 1871–1914" (master's thesis, Hochschule für Jüdische Studien, Heidelberg, 1989). On the successful anti-Semitic motions in city councils to ban kosher butchering, see, e.g., "Stadtverordnetenversammlung von Post-dam," *Der Israelit* 42 (1901): 837 and 853–54; and "Die Schächtdebatte in der Postdamer Stadtverordnetenversammlung," ibid., 2079–81. Much as in Bres-lau, political anti-Semitism was unsuccessful in Hamburg, where in 1897 the first open anti-Semite was elected to the city parliament. The parliament re-jected all of the anti-Semite's motions without discussion, even when some of his sociopolitical demands were in agreement with the objectives of other oppo-sition groups. No faction, regardless of how critical it was of the liberal major-ity, wanted to be reproached for having worked together with the anti-Semites. See Kasischke-Wurm, *Antisemitismus im Spiegel der Hamburger Presse*, 287–315, esp. 299–300.

69. On Berlin, see Michael Erbe, "Berlin im Kaiserreich (1871–1918)," in *Geschichte Berlins*, ed. Wolfgang Ribbe, vol. 2, *Von der Märzrevolution bis zur Gegen-wart* (Munich: C. H. Beck, 1987), 689–793, here 767–70, esp. 768.

70. See Andreas Fahrmeir, "Nineteenth-Century German Citizenships," *Historical Journal* 40 (1997): 721–52; and Andreas Fahrmeir, *Citizenship: The Rise and Fall of a Modern Concept* (New Haven, Conn.: Yale University Press, 2007).

71. Until the abolition of *Landesangehörigkeit*, that is, provincial citizenship, through the 1934 decree concerning German nationality, however, nationality still followed from one's provincial citizenship. See Rolf Grawert, "Staatsvolk und Staatsangehörigkeit," in *Handbuch des Staatsrechts der Bundesrepublik Deutsch-land*, ed. Josef Isensee and Paul Kirchhoff, vol. 1 (Heidelberg: Müller, 1987), 681.

72. Rogers Brubaker, *Citizenship and Nationhood in France and Germany*, 2nd ed. (Cambridge, Mass.: Harvard University Press, 1994), ix.

73. Etienne Balibar, "Grenzen und Gewalten: Asyl, Einwanderung, Illegalität und Sozialkontrolle des Staates," *Lettre International* 2, no. 37 (Summer 1997): 7–8, here 8.

74. An overview of the differences between the rights of all persons living in the German Empire, on the one hand, and German nationals, on the other, may be found in "Ausländer, ausländische Arbeiter," in *Handwörterbuch der Preußischen Verwaltung*, ed. Rudolf von Bitter, 2nd ed. (Leipzig: Roßberg, 1911), 1: 157–62, esp. 158–59; Klaus Stern, *Das Staatsrecht der Bundesrepublik Deutschland*, vol. 3, pt. 1 (Munich: C. H. Beck, 1988), 410–12, with n.97; and Ernst Fölsche, *Das Ehrenamt in Preußen und im Reiche* (Breslau: Marcus, 1911), 36–38. Yet it could even be risky in some circumstances for foreigners to lay claim to their rights. According to the public assistance domicile law (*Unterstützungswohnsitzgesetz*) of July 6, 1870, for instance, a foreigner living in Germany could, after having lived continuously for two years in the district of a local public assistance organization, request aid in the case of neediness. However, if the foreigner received public assistance, it became considerably more difficult for that person to attain German citizenship. See "Heimatsrecht," in *Brockhaus' Konversations-Lexikon*, 14th ed., vol. 8 (Leipzig: Brockhaus, 1908), 965; and Karl Bachem, "Heimat und Heimatsrecht," in *Staatslexikon*, 3rd ed., vol. 2 (Leipzig: Hirzel, 1909), 1210–18, here 1211–13.

75. A comparative overview of naturalization law may be found in Gerard-René de Groot, *Staatsangehörigkeit im Wandel: Eine rechtsvergleichende Studie über Erwerbs- und Verlustgründe der Staatsangehörigkeit* (Cologne: Carl Heymanns Verlag, 1989), esp. 46–47, 78, 100–101, 114, and 182. From older literature, see esp. Rolf Grawert, *Staat und Staatsangehörigkeit* (Berlin: Duncker & Humblot, 1973). A well-regarded study, from which I have gained many insights, is Rogers Brubaker's *Citizenship and Nationhood;* for an important critique of Brubaker, see Patrick Weil, "Nationalities and Citizenship: The Lessons of the French Experience for Germany and Europe," in *Citizenship, Nationality, and Migration in Europe*, ed. David Cesarani and Mary Fulbrook (London: Routledge, 1996), 74–87; Brubaker also neglects naturalization in practice. Older research on foreign immigration did not address questions of naturalization and expulsion; see, e.g., Christoph Kleßmann, *Polnische Bergarbeiter im Ruhrgebiet, 1870–1945: Soziale Integration und nationale Subkultur einer Minderheit in der deutschen Industriegesellschaft* (Göttingen: Vandenhoeck & Ruprecht, 1978); and Ulrich Herbert, *Geschichte der Ausländerbeschäftigung in Deutschland, 1880–1980: Saisonarbeiter, Zwangsarbeiter, Gastarbeiter* (Berlin: Dietz, 1986). The concrete practice of naturalization is also neglected in Dieter Gosewinkel, *Einbürgern und Ausschließen: Die Nationalisierung der Staatsangehörigkeit vom Deutschen Bund bis zur Bundesrepublik Deutschland* (Göttingen: Vandenhoeck & Ruprecht, 2001). Important information, by contrast, may be found in Fahrmeir, "Nineteenth-Century German Citizenships," and Charles Robert Garris, "Becoming German: Immigration, Conformity, and Identity

Politics in Wilhelminian Berlin, 1880–1914" (PhD diss., University of North
Carolina, Chapel Hill, 1998); see also Eli Nathans, *The Politics of Citizenship in
Germany: Ethnicity, Utility, and Nationalism* (Oxford: Berg, 2004); the older literature is surveyed in Hellmuth Hecker, ed., *Bibliographie zum Staatsangehörigkeitsrecht
in Deutschland in Vergangenheit und Gegenwart* (Frankfurt a. M.: Verlag für Standesamtswesen, 1976).

76. Dieter Gosewinkel, "Die Staatsangehörigkeit als Institution des
Nationalstaats: Zur Entstehung des Reichs- und Staatsangehörigkeitsgesetzes
von 1913," in *Offene Staatlichkeit: Festschrift für Ernst-Wolfgang Böckenförde*, ed. Rolf
Grawert et al. (Berlin: Duncker & Humblot, 1995), 359–78, here 376; see also
his "Staatsangehörigkeit und Einbürgerung in Deutschland während des 19.
und 20. Jahrhunderts," *Geschichte und Gesellschaft* 21 (1995): 533–56.

77. "Die Behandlung der jüdischen Ausländer in Preußen," *Jüdisches Volksblatt* 16 (1910): 109–10; "Naturalisation," *Jüdisches Volksblatt* 15 (1909): 379–80; see
also "Das Rayon-System in Preussen?" *Jüdisches Volksblatt* 17 (1911): 127–28.

78. The most important study is Wertheimer's *Unwelcome Strangers*. Infor-
mation on the late German Empire and the Weimar Republic may also be
found in Ludger Heid, *Maloche—nicht Mildtätigkeit: Ostjüdische Proletarier in
Deutschland, 1914–1923* (Hildesheim: Olms, 1995); Trude Maurer, *Ostjuden in
Deutschland, 1918–1933* (Hamburg: Hans Christian Verlag, 1986); Stefanie
Schüler-Springorum, *Die jüdische Minderheit in Königsberg/Preußen, 1871–1945*
(Göttingen: Vandenhoeck & Ruprecht, 1996), 174–80; and Dirk Walter, "Ungebetene Helfer—Denunziation bei der Münchner Polizei anläßlich der
Ostjuden-Ausweisungen, 1919–1923/24," *Archiv für Polizeigeschichte* 18 (1996): 14–
20. These studies neglect, however, the context of the general policies on mi-
gration and naturalization; information on naturalization and expulsion is even
missing where one would most expect it—e.g., in Peter Pulzer's excellent study
Jews and the German State.

79. *Breslauer Statistik*, vol. 7 (Breslau: Morgenstern, 1881), 124; *Breslauer Statistik*, vol. 9 (Breslau: Morgenstern, 1885), 107*.

80. The figures are from Wertheimer, *Unwelcome Strangers*, 191. The figures
for Berlin also encompass Charlottenburg, Neukölln, Schöneberg, and Wilm-
berdorf. On the Jewish emigration from Eastern Europe in general, see Gerald
Sorin, *A Time for Building: The Third Migration, 1880–1920* (Baltimore: Johns Hopkins University Press, 1992), esp. the overview on p. 58.

81. Gustav von Schmoller, "Über Wesen und Verfassung großer Unternehmungen," in *Zur Social- und Gewerbepolitik der Gegenwart* (Leipzig: Duncker &
Humblot, 1890), 372–440, quotation from 397; in general, see Dieter Langewiesche, "Wanderungsbewegungen in der Hochindustrialisierungsperiode: Regionale, interstädtische und innerstädtische Mobilität in Deutschland, 1880–
1914," *Vierteljahrschrift für Sozial- und Wirtschaftsgeschichte* 64 (1977): 1–40.

82. Julius Neuberger was born on March 29, 1869, in Lipto, Hungary, and
later became an American citizen; he used his "certificate of citizenship" as a

substitute for a passport; "Ausländerliste, ausschließlich Russen und Österreicher," APW, PPB 624, no. 2724. Elia Nissin was born in Sofia on August 1, 1877, and resided at Goldene Radegasse 19 (ibid., no. 2646). Izil Behrmann was born in Bacau on December 25, 1875, and resided at Neudorffstrasse 37a (ibid., no. 2568).

83. Salomon Neumann, *Die Fabel von der jüdischen Masseneinwanderung: Ein Kapitel aus der preußischen Statistik,* 3rd ed. (Berlin: Simion, 1881). According to Helmut Neubach, the East European Jews were a "plague"; see his *Die Ausweisungen von Polen und Juden aus Preussen, 1885/86: Ein Beitrag zu Bismarcks Polenpolitik und zur Geschichte des deutsch-polnischen Verhältnisses* (Wiesbaden: Harrassowitz, 1967), 5 and 12. See also Richard Blanke, "Bismarck and the Prussian Polish Policies of 1886," *Journal of Modern History* 45 (1973): 211–39, here 211–16. On p. 216 it reads: "[W]hat there was in the way of popular pressure upon the government to undertake such a radical solution of the alien problem came from urban, petty-bourgeois interests resentful mainly of alien-Jewish competition."

84. The relative significance of actual persecution, fear of potential persecution, and economic hardship in influencing the decision to emigrate is disputed. On the motivation of Jewish emigrants, see Bernard K. Johnpoll, "Why They Left: Russian-Jewish Mass Migration and Repressive Laws, 1881–1917," *American Jewish Archives* 47 (1995): 17–54.

85. Rainer Fremdling, Ruth Federspiel, and Andreas Kunz, eds., *Statistik der Eisenbahnen in Deutschland, 1835–1989* (St. Katharinen: Scripta Mercaturae Verlag, 1995), 28, and the maps on 59–60 and 63. The volume of people traveling on the Upper Silesian Railroad in the early 1870s was, at roughly two million, greater than that of all other Upper Silesian lines combined and increased by 1880 to almost seven million; see Andreas Kunz and Ruth Federspiel, "Die Verkehrsentwicklung Oberschlesiens im 19. Jahrhundert," in *Industriegeschichte Oberschlesiens im 19. Jahrhundert,* ed. Toni Pierenkemper (Wiesbaden: Franz Steiner, 1992), 217–49, here 232; and in general, Wilhelm Freyhan, *Die Entwicklung Breslaus im Eisenbahnzeitalter* (Breslau: Hochschulverlag, 1922).

86. Zosa Szajkowski, "Sufferings of Jewish Emigrants to America in Transit through Germany," *Jewish Social Studies* 39 (1977): 105–16, here 106; Gerhard Reichberg, "Myslowitz," in *Handbuch der historischen Stätten: Schlesien,* ed. Hugo Weczerka (Stuttgart: Kröner, 1977), 324–25; see also Pamela S. Nadell, "The Journey to America by Steam: The Jews of Eastern Europe in Transition," *American Jewish History* 71 (1982): 269–84.

87. See the reports in the *Israeltische Wochenschrift* (May 23, 1882, 158–59), as well as in the *Allgemeine Zeitung des Judenthums* 46 (1882): 73 and 339. In summer 1869, there had been similar relief efforts elsewhere; see Toury, *Soziale und politische Geschichte,* 136–37.

88. See, e.g., *Israeltische Wochenschrift* 22 (1891): 291; *Jüdisches Volksblatt* 6 (1900): 282–83.

89. "Unterstützung der in Folge der Unruhen in Russland Notleidenden 1906–1907," APW, AMW, III, 3676. In general see also "Polizeipräsidium Breslau an das Polizeipräsidium in Posen über die Behandlung von durchreisenden russischen Staatsangehörigen," January 1913, APW, PPB 634, fols. 78–80.

90. In 1909, e.g., the American immigration authorities denied entry to only 1.03% of all Russian-Jewish immigrants for health reasons (Szajkowski, "Sufferings of Jewish Emigrants," 107); on the cholera epidemics of 1892 and 1905, see APW, AMW, III, 8705 and 8706.

91. The best analysis of the stereotype of the *Ostjude* may be found in Steven E. Aschheim, *Brothers and Strangers: The East European Jew in German and German-Jewish Consciousness, 1800–1923* (Madison: University of Wisconsin Press, 1982). For the period before 1914, I am intentionally avoiding the expression *Ostjude* because it first gained currency in general political language only during the First World War. See the conclusion of this volume.

92. This runs contrary to Helmut Berding's judgment (*Moderner Antisemitismus in Deutschland* [Frankfurt a. M.: Suhrkamp, 1988], 80); the best analysis is still to be found in George L. Mosse, "The Image of the Jew in German Popular Culture: Felix Dahn and Gustav Freytag," *Year Book of the Leo Baeck Institute* 2 (1957): 218–27 (reprinted in his *Germans and Jews: The Right, the Left, and the Search for a Third Force in Pre-Nazi Germany* [New York: Grosset & Dunlap, 1970; repr., Detroit: Wayne State University Press, 1987], 61–76 and 234–36). See also Mark H. Gelber, "Aspects of Literary Anti-Semitism: Charles Dickens' 'Oliver Twist' and Gustav Freytag's 'Soll und Haben'" (PhD diss., Yale University, 1980); Larry L. Ping, *Gustav Freytag and the Prussian Gospel: Novels, Liberalism, and History* (Frankfurt a. M.: Peter Lang, 2006); Hans Otto Horch, "Judenbilder in der realistischen Erzählliteratur: Jüdische Figuren bei Gustav Freytag, Fritz Reuter, Berthold Auerbach und Wilhelm Raabe," in *Juden und Judentum in der Literatur*, ed. Herbert A. Strauss and Christhard Hoffmann (Munich: Deutscher Taschenbuch Verlag, 1985), 140–71; T. E. Carter, "Freytag's *Soll und Haben*: A Liberal Manifesto as Bestseller," *German Life and Letters* 21 (1968): 320–29; Martin Gubser, *Literarischer Antisemitismus: Untersuchungen zu Gustav Freytag und anderen bürgerlichen Schriftstellern* (Göttingen: Wallstein-Verlag, 1998). On the connection between nationalism and anti-Semitism, see the following stimulating studies: Karl-Ernst Jeismann, "Zur Bedeutung der 'Bildung' im 19. Jahrhundert," in *Handbuch der deutschen Bildungsgeschichte*, ed. Karl-Ernst Jeismann and Peter Lundgreen, vol. 3, *1800–1870: Von der Neuordnung Deutschlands bis zur Gründung des Deutschen Reiches* (Munich: C. H. Beck, 1987), 1–21; and Shulamit Volkov, "Nationalismus, Antisemitismus und die deutsche Geschichtsschreibung," in *Nation und Gesellschaft in Deutschland: Festschrift für Hans-Ulrich Wehler*, ed. Manfred Hettling and Paul Nolte (Munich: C. H. Beck, 1996), 208–19.

93. For his biography, see Fritz Martini, "Gustav Freytag," in *Neue Deutsche Biographie*, vol. 5 (Berlin: Duncker & Humblot, 1961), 425–27; the characterization of Freytag as a "poet" also stems from there. The best account of Freytag's

relation to Silesia, while at the same time being a document of the German-Jewish Freytag reception, is R. Koebner, "Gustav Freytag," *Schlesische Lebens-bilder* 1 (1922): 154–64. Yet Freytag is of particular interest not only because of his references to Breslau. Since Freytag is generally regarded as a "consistently liberal thinker," he exemplifies the anti-Semitic dark side of German liberalism; see Walter Bußmann, "Gustav Freytag: Maßstäbe seiner Zeitkritik," *Archiv für Kulturgeschichte* 34 (1952): 261–87, here 261. See also Hans-Ulrich Wehler, *Deutsche Gesellschaftsgeschichte*, vol. 3, *1849–1914: Von der "Deutschen Doppelrevolution" bis zum Beginn des Ersten Weltkrieges* (Munich: C. H. Beck, 1995), 242–43; Thomas Nipperdey, *Deutsche Geschichte, 1800–1866* (1983; 5th ed., Munich: C. H. Beck, 1991), 582; Wolfram Siemann, *Vom Staatenbund zum Nationalstaat: Deutschland, 1806–1871* (Munich: C. H. Beck, 1994), 268; Mommsen, *Das Ringen um den nationalen Staat*, 718–19.

94. Gustav Freytag, "Die Juden Breslaus," *Grenzboten*, no. 30 (1849) (reprinted in his *Vermischte Aufsätze*, vol. 2 [Leipzig: Hirzel, 1903], 339–47). In general here, see Manfred Hettling and Stefan-Ludwig Hoffmann, "Der bürgerliche Wertehimmel: Zum Problem individueller Lebensführung im 19. Jahrhundert," *Geschichte und Gesellschaft* 23 (1997): 333–59.

95. Franz Mehring, *Aufsätze zur deutschen Literaturgeschichte*, ed. Hans Koch, 2nd ed. (Leipzig: Reclam, 1966), 175 and 278. On the editions, see Berding, *Moderner Antisemitismus in Deutschland*, 80; and the catalog of the Stadtbibliothek Mainz (where the 114th edition is located). After Freytag's *Soll und Haben*, the next most successful novels were Felix Dahn's *Ein Kampf um Rom* with 1,688 copies and E. Marlitt's *Goldelse* with 1,285 copies. Far below them lay such "classics" as Gottfried Keller's *Der grüne Heinrich* (630 copies) and Conrad Ferdinand Meyer's *Jürg Jenatsch* (618 copies); see Robin Lenman, John Osborne, and Eda Sagarra, "Imperial Germany: Towards the Commercialization of Culture," in *German Cultural Studies*, ed. Rob Burns (Oxford: Oxford University Press, 1995), 9–52, here 23. According to Alfred Dove, Freytag's biographer for the *Allgemeine Deutsche Biographie*, *Soll und Haben* was "for decades the most frequently read book in the sphere of finer German literature" (Alfred Dove, "Gustav Freytag," in *Ausgewählte Aufsätze und Briefe*, ed. Friedrich Meinecke and Oswald Dammann, 2 vols. [Munich: Bruckmann, 1925], 1:191–222, here 203; first printed in *Allgemeine Deutsche Biographie*, vol. 48 [Leipzig: Duncker & Humblot, 1904], 749–67).

96. "Der Ausgleich von Soll und Haben," *Israelitische Wochenschrift* 1 (1870): 167; "Nachwort der Redaktion," *Allgemeine Zeitung des Judenthums* 50 (1886): 549–50, here 550. As early as 1859, Robert Prutz had characterized *Soll und Haben* as a novel brimming with "hatred for the Jews"; Robert Prutz, *Die deutsche Literatur der Gegenwart 1848 bis 1858* (Leipzig: Voigt & Günther, 1859), 2:110–11, cited in Michael Schmidt, "'Faule Geschichten'? Über den 'Landjuden' und deutsche Literatur," in *Jüdisches Leben auf dem Lande*, ed. Monika Richarz and Reinhardt Rürup (Tübingen: Mohr Siebeck, 1997), 347–71, here 358.

97. "Notizen zum Breslauer Logenleben," *Die Bauhütte* 17 (1874): 58–59; cited in Stefan-Ludwig Hoffmann, *Die Politik der Geselligkeit: Freimaurerlogen in der deutschen Bürgergesellschaft, 1840–1918* (Göttingen: Vandenhoeck & Ruprecht, 2000), 189.

98. Due to poverty or previous convictions, the following applicants were not naturalized: Chaim Hirsch Faust from Czenstochau (APW, AMW, III, 21934, fol. 85), Max Beiner (ibid., fols. 231–33), and Moritz Steigmann/Jacob Neustadt (ibid., fols. 297–99).

99. Naftali Meier Immerglück (APW, AMW, III, 21934, fols. 34–35); Samuel Zarek (ibid., fols. 126–27); David Thumin (ibid., fols. 132–33). The "Petrikau" in the file stands presumably for "Petrikowo," though perhaps for "Petrokow," a city in the western part of Russian Poland.

100. See the naturalization proceedings for Aron Stenger (APW, AMW, III, 21933, fols. 11–19), Moritz Silberstein (ibid., 21934, fols. 234–325), Moritz Töpfer (ibid., fols. 240–41), and Gerson Selkowitz (ibid., fols. 244–45). An overview of the duration of stay normally expected of applicants may be found in Fahrmeir, "Nineteenth-Century German Citizenships," 743; and Wilhelm Cahn, *Reichsgesetz über die Erwerbung und den Verlust der Reichs- und Staatsangehörigkeit*, 3rd ed. (Berlin: Guttentag, 1908), 80.

101. Schüler-Springorum, *Die jüdische Minderheit*, 174.

102. Mommsen, *Das Ringen um den nationalen Staat*, 561; Treitschke, "Unsere Aussichten," cited in Boehlich, *Der Berliner Antisemitismusstreit*, 7–14, quotation from 9.

103. *Schlesische Zeitung*, no. 554, November 27, 1879, 1–2, and no. 598, December 23, 1879; *Schlesische Volkszeitung*, December 23, 1879; "Vermischtes," *Breslauer Sonntagsblatt*, no. 49, December 7, 1879; "Zur Judenfrage VII," *Deutscher Volksfreund*, no. 7, February 13, 1880. Treitschke, "Unsere Aussichten."

104. On the anti-Semite petition, see Peter Pulzer, *The Rise of Political Anti-Semitism in Germany and Austria* (1964; 2nd rev. ed., Cambridge, Mass.: Harvard University Press, 1988), 91 and 247–48; Werner Jochmann, "Akademische Führungsschichten und Judenfeindschaft in Deutschland, 1866–1918," in his *Gesellschaftskrise und Judenfeindschaft in Deutschland, 1870–1945* (Hamburg: Christians, 1988), 13–29, esp. 20; Paul Massing, *Rehearsal for Destruction: A Study of Political Anti-Semitism in Imperial Germany* (New York: Harper & Bros., 1949), 43; Blaschke, *Katholizismus und Antisemitismus*, 123–25; Simon Dubnow, *Weltgeschichte des jüdischen Volkes*, vol. 10 (Berlin: Jüdischer Verlag, 1929), 31–40. According to Richard S. Levy, these four demands remained "the basic program of all future a-S parties for the duration of the German empire" (*The Downfall of the Anti-Semitic Political Parties in Imperial Germany* [New Haven, Conn.: Yale University Press, 1975], 21). The original source on the regional distribution of signatures is possibly Liebermann von Sonnenberg, "Rede," 117–18: "You can see the hegemony of the Jews from the well-known petition against Israel. Silesia has contributed over 50,000 signatures to it and Breslau alone 5,000. . . . Altogether it

has 267,000 signatures. It is an enormous, powerful achievement, for it was done entirely without money. I can testify to that because I worked on it with my friend Förster. The 267,000 signatures represent twice the number of adult Jews and still we have yet to have any tangible success—except for at least one, the occupational statistics."

105. "Eine gründliche Lösung der Judenfrage II," *Schlesisches Morgenblatt*, no. 273, November 20, 1880. The best investigation of government policy on East European Jews is Wertheimer's *Unwelcome Strangers*, esp. 42–74; see also Dieter Gosewinkel, "'Unerwünschte Elemente': Einwanderung und Einbürgerung von Juden in Deutschland, 1848–1933," *Tel Aviver Jahrbuch für deutsche Geschichte* 27 (1998): 71–106, here 91–95. Indispensable regarding the history of mass expulsions is Neubach, *Die Ausweisungen*, even though it remains a captive of the anti-Semitic language of the Prussian administration—e.g., Neubach endorses the judgment of Secretary of the Interior Puttkamer that the immigrating Polish Jews were "a true plague" (5 and 12). Puttkamer was provincial governor of Silesia from 1877 to 1879 and in the early 1880s a patron of Stoecker's "Berlin movement" (Wehler, *Deutsche Gesellschaftsgeschichte*, 3:923). Nevertheless, it is to Neubach's credit to have disclosed the anti-Jewish dimension of the mass expulsions of 1885–86. See also Blanke, "Bismarck and the Prussian Polish Policies," esp. 211–21; and William W. Hagen, *Germans, Poles, and Jews: The Nationality Conflict in the Prussian East, 1772–1914* (Chicago: University of Chicago Press, 1980), 132 and 134. Even "critical" social history has practically ignored the anti-Jewish dimension of the expulsions; see, e.g., Herbert, *Geschichte der Ausländerbeschäftigung in Deutschland*, 18, and Gerhard A. Ritter and Klaus Tenfelde, *Arbeiter im Deutschen Kaiserreich* (Bonn: Dietz, 1992), 181. That holds for the important German migration historian Klaus J. Bade, who focuses almost exclusively on the anti-Polish dimension and tends to play down the expulsion of Jews; see his "'Kulturkampf' auf dem Arbeitsmarkt: Bismarcks 'Polenpolitik,' 1885–1890," in *Innenpolitische Probleme des Bismarckreiches*, ed. Otto Pflanze (Munich: Oldenburg, 1983), 121–42, here 132–33. Bade notes in passing that the Prussian policy—which "tore apart innumerable Prussian-Polish families, some of which had lived for decades in the eastern provinces—also contained allusions to the influx [*sic*] of East European Jews, which was intended to be more than an anti-Polish barrier: It was intended also for those 'Russians of non-Polish tongue . . . who, as experience has shown, exploit the plight of their fellows to their own advantage.'"

106. *Schlesisches Morgenblatt*, no. 239, October 13, 1885. According to the *Israelitische Wochenschrift* 16 (1885): 314, roughly 1,100 Breslau Jews were on the expulsion list in early October 1885. See also *Allgemeine Zeitung des Judenthums* 49 (1885): 577–78, 609, and 761–63; see also *Jahresbericht des Kranken-Unterstützungs-Vereins "Tomche Cholim" pro 1885* (Breslau: n.p., 1885), BUW, GŚL, 28231 III.

107. "Schlesien," *Schlesisches Morgenblatt*, no. 239, October 13, 1885; "Ein Act nationaler Selbsterhaltung," *Schlesische Zeitung*, no. 855, December 6, 1885.

See the critique in the *Allgemeine Zeitung des Judenthums* (49 [1885]: 816–17 and 834) of the *Schlesische Zeitung*'s aiming its anti-Semitism at East European Jews. From the perspective of organized anti-Semitism, the *Schlesische Zeitung* was ever a half-hearted ally. The *Deutsche Ostwacht* mocked it in April 1893, saying the paper was a "posh representative of a faded drawing-room anti-Semitism" (April 29, 1893, 4).

108. Naturalization proceedings, Adolf Wolf Poznanski, APW, PPB 134, fols. 1–18.

109. Ibid. That this was not an isolated case is shown by a list that the Breslau magistracy drew up between 1893 and 1898, presumably in order to be able to demonstrate statistically the anti-Jewish stance of the Prussian government. For thirteen of fourteen Jewish applicants, the city issued a positive report and recommended the rejection of only one application due to poverty. However, the district governor naturalized only two of the fourteen Jewish applicants. By contrast, he naturalized forty-three of a total of sixty-nine applicants. See APW, AMW, III, 4991, fols. 62–68.

110. Application for naturalization, Hermann and Richard Jäger, in Aufenthalt und Naturalisation von Ausländern im preußischen Staate, APW, OPB 342.

111. Naturalisationsverfahren von Martin Leuchtberg, APW, PPB 115. All other references are based on Reichsbund Jüdischer Frontsoldaten, ed., *Die jüdischen Gefallenen des deutschen Heeres, der deutschen Marine und der deutschen Schutztruppen, 1914–1918: Ein Gedenkbuch*, 2nd ed. (Berlin: Der Schild, 1932), 180 (on its publication history, see Ruth Pierson, "Embattled Veterans: Der Reichsbund jüdischer Frontsoldaten," *Year Book of the Leo Baeck Institute* 19 [1974]: 139–54, here 143–44). Martin Leuchtag's father was a prominent member of the Israelitische Kranken- und Verpflegungs-Anstalt und Beerdigungsgesellschaft (Reinke, *Judentum und Wohlfahrtspflege in Deutschland: Das jüdische Krankenhaus in Breslau, 1744–1944* [Hanover: Hahnsche Buchhandlung, 1999], 187–88) and the Jewish Kranken-Unterstützungs-Verein "Tomche Cholim" (*Jahresbericht des Kranken-Unterstützungs-Vereins "Tomche Cholim" pro 1897* [Breslau: n.p., 1897], BUW, GŚŁ, 28231 III); according to section 7 of the statute, only "Israelites born in Austria-Hungary, living in Breslau, with a respectable reputation, and with an independent position, could become members of the society" (Statut des Kranken-Unterstützungs-Vereins "Tomche Cholim" gegründet von und für Oesterreicher-Ungarn, ausgedehnt auf Israeliten jeder Staatsangehörigkeit zu Breslau, 1885, BUW, GŚŁ, 28231 III). Significantly, "tribe" (*Volksstamm*) is in the singular here, a semantic shift that provides evidence for the advance of the ideal of homogeneity.

112. Cahn, *Reichsgesetz*, 80. The introduction of the Nationality Act of July 22, 1913, did not change the role of the local authorities; see Wilhelm Cahn, *Reichs- und Staatsangehörigkeitsgesetz vom 22. Juli 1913, erläutert mit Benutzung amtlicher Quellen und unter vergleichender Berücksichtigung der ausländischen Gesetzgebung* (Berlin: Guttentag, 1914), 69.

113. On Königsberg's inclusive stance, see Schüler-Springorum, *Die jüdische Minderheit,* 174 and 179. The Königsberg city council even protested publicly in 1885 against the mass expulsion of Russian Jews (179).

114. E.g., in the case of Ottilie Benke, née Aust (APW, AMW, III, 7481, fols. 4–5, 9–10, 54–57). The fact that the Prussian government's tendency to deny Jews citizenship was motivated by not economic but "primarily political" (read: anti-Semitic) reasons is also stressed in Gosewinkel, "'Unerwünschte Elemente,'" 105–6. In comparison with the Bavarian government's stance in the early 1920s, the anti-Semitism of the Prussian authorities was still moderate; whereas Prussia did not naturalize wealthy Jews before 1914 *despite* their wealth, the Bavarian government expelled wealthy Jews *because of* their wealth; see Martin H. Geyer, *Verkehrte Welt: Revolution, Inflation und Moderne; München, 1914–1924* (Göttingen: Vandenhoeck & Ruprecht, 1998), 343–44; and Jozef Adelson, "The Expulsion of Jews with Polish Citizenship from Bavaria in 1923," *POLIN: Studies in Polish Jewry* 5 (1990): 57–73.

115. Concerning district prefects, see "Bezirksvorsteher," in Bitter, *Handwörterbuch der Preußischen Verwaltung,* 1:303–4, and Paul Schoen, *Das Recht der Kommunalverbände in Preußen* (Leipzig: Brockhaus, 1897), 142.

116. On Hirsch Chaimoff, see APW, AMW, III, 7480, fols. 47–48; on Josef Chaimoff, see ibid., 7482, fols. 181–82 and 233; on Leo Chaimoff, see ibid., 7482, fols. 195–97 and 286; on Hirsch Chaimoff, see also ibid., 7483, fols. 174–76.

117. APW, AMW, III, 7479, fols. 135–37, rejected January 3, 1910, ibid., fol. 149. Naturalization application of Gertrud Doleschal, widow of a master baker; district prefect advised against naturalization; magistracy did likewise on April 1, 1910 (APW, AMW, III, 7479, fols. 198–99); government president rejected application (fol. 211). Naturalization application of Hedwig Busch, widow of a coachman, née Daumann, Lohestrasse 63a; district prefect advised against naturalization; magistracy did likewise on May 9, 1910 (ibid., fols. 220–21); government president rejected application (fol. 276). Ottilie Benke, née Aust, widow, Schillerstrasse 24; magistracy advised against naturalization: "for quite some time has received welfare assistance" (APW, AMW, III, 7481, fols. 4–5; see also the fundamental position of the public assistance director from February 24, 1912; ibid., fols. 9–10); see also APW, AMW, III, 54–56; government president granted her citizenship on April 4, 1912 (ibid., fol. 57). Nationalization application of journeyman tailor Hugo Horn, Antonienstrasse 18; district prefect advised against his naturalization; magistracy did likewise due to his poverty, 1914 (APW, AMW, III, 7482, fols. 311–12).

118. The magistracy approved the application (APW, AMW, III, 7478, fols. 154–55), but Flor withdrew it (APW, AMW, III, 7479, fol. 7).

119. Application for naturalization, Moritz Weiss (APW, AMW, III, 7481, fols. 272–74). The application presumably was rejected by the district governor. With "Mr. Kober," Jesenich was probably referring to Joseph Kober, a prominent member of the representative council of the Breslau *Synagogengemeinde*

(Aron Heppner, *Jüdische Persönlichkeiten in und aus Breslau* [Breslau: Schatzky, 1931], 25).

120. The judgment of Ernst Bruch, director of the magistracy's statistics office, was similarly positive. Bruch considered the rapid increase in the number of foreigners living in Breslau in the early 1870s to be "very welcome evidence . . . of [the] city's growing importance"; Ernst Bruch, "Zur Bevölkerungs-Statistik der Stadt Breslau," in *Adreß- und Geschäftsbuch der königlichen Haupt und Residenzstadt Breslau für das Jahr 1877* (Breslau: Morgenstern, 1877), 406–11, here 407.

121. Nationalization proceedings of Minna Seelig (APW, AMW, III, 7479, fols. 168–71 and 248). Nationalization proceedings of Bertha Baumann (ibid., 7482, fols. 64–66 and 112).

122. "Arbeitsforderung für Asylisten," *Kommunale Praxis* 5 (1905): 1034.

123. APW, AMW, III, 7479, fols. 111–12. The city showed its negative attitude toward poverty also in the cases of Wenzel Kowarnik (ibid., fols. 309–10); Naturalization application of Hugo Horn in 1914 (APW, AMW, III, 7482, fols. 311–12); Israel Finkenstein (ibid.). Aside from Finkenstein, all the male applicants whose applications the city advised be rejected were presumably not Jewish.

124. APW, AMW, III, 7479, fols. 309–10; district governor rejects application: APW, AMW, III, 7480, fol. 3.

125. Nationalization application of Helene Jankowski, residing at Försterstrasse 5III, July–September 1908, APW, AMW, III, 7478, fols. 144–45.

126. Ibid.

127. On Martha Fischer, née Liebich, who resided in 1911 at Laurentiusstrasse 23, see APW, AMW, III, 7480, fols. 89–92. Similar cases in which the magistracy warned against naturalizing poor women include Gertrud Doleschal (ibid., fols. 198–99); Hedwig Busch, née Daumann (ibid., fols. 220–21); Ottilie Benke, née Aust (ibid., 7481, fols. 4–5); Countess Marina Bianka Finochietti (ibid., 7484, fols. 69–70); Adeline Blümel (ibid., fols. 88–89b).

128. Naturalization application of Rosa Cukiermann, née Walk (APW, AMW, III, 7484, fols. 96–97a) and the naturalization proceedings of Rosa Cukiermann, née Walk (APW, PPB 67, fols. 1–21). On section 10 of the Nationality Act of July 22, 1913, see Cahn, *Reichs- und Staatsangehörigkeitsgesetz*, 74–76.

129. See the district governor's letter to the Lord mayor of Breslau, APW, AMW, III, 7482, fol. 231. The fact that military service did not entitle one to naturalization is stressed in the article "Staatsangehörigkeit," in *Volks-Lexikon*, ed. Emanuel Wurm, vol. 4 (Nuremberg: Wörlein, 1897), 511.

130. See APW, AMW, III, 7482, fol. 138; ibid., 7484, fol. 130. Altogether, in 1914 and 1915 eight times more Jews were naturalized than in the prewar years; see Gosewinkel, "'Unerwünschte Elemente,'" 97.

131. Naturalization of Joseph Chaimoff, APW, AMW, III, 7482, fols. 181–82 and 233. Naturalization of Leo Chaimoff, ibid., fols, 195–97 and 286. The

dates of their deaths are from Reichsbund Jüdischer Frontsoldaten, *Die jüdischen Gefallenen*, 177.

132. Naturalization of Jakob and David Chaimoff, APW, AMW, III, 7484, fols. 58-61a.

133. On the importance of Eastern Europe to Silesian economic activity, see Konrad Fuchs, "Vom deutschen Krieg zur deutschen Katastrophe (1866-1945)," in *Schlesien*, ed. Norbert Conrads, Deutsche Geschichte im Osten Europas (Berlin: Siedler, 1994), 554-692, here 562-64.

134. The proceedings may be found in APW, Oberpräsidium 342; see also *Jahresbericht der Handelskammer Breslau für das Jahr 1894* (Breslau: Handelskammer, 1895), 30-31; the Vorsteheramt der Königsberger Kaufmannschaft painted a similarly positive picture of Russian-Jewish merchants in 1885; see Schüler-Springorum, *Die jüdische Minderheit*, 164 and 179.

135. The chamber of commerce had already made similar requests in 1908 and 1909 (chamber of commerce to government president, May 31, 1911, APW, PPB 634, fol. 37; government president to PPB, June 22, 1911, ibid.): "[A]ccording to the . . . repeated reports from the local chamber of commerce, the expulsion of the Russian-Jewish flax merchants living here would destroy Breslau's important flax trade. For this reason and with the understanding that only such merchants come into consideration here, I want to maintain the mild policy in effect thus far regarding them and ask that you inform N. Aronson that he will be permitted to stay here until May 1, 1913, assuming he does not allow anything negative to happen for which he could be blamed. // However, I do not intend to grant the same privilege to new Russian-Jewish flax merchants who move here" (APW, PPB 634, fols. 38-39). On Russia's significance to the flax trade before 1914, see also the commentary by the flax merchant Eugen Altmann: "Mein Leben in Deutschland vor und nach dem 30. Januar 1933," 15, Houghton Library, Harvard University, Cambridge, Mass.

136. Chamber of commerce, report to Breslau police department, January 21, 1914 (APW, PPB 634, fols. 103-4).

137. Circular from the government president to the Breslau police department and the district administrators, April 14, 1900 (APW, PPB 621, fols. 38-39). That was, of course, nothing specific to the Breslau district governor, but rather part of Prussia's general policy, which aimed to provide German agriculture with as many East European workers as possible from spring to late fall (Herbert, *Geschichte der Ausländerbeschäftigung in Deutschland*, 15-27, esp. 24).

138. Provincial governor to the Breslau police department, January 22, 1912 (APW, PPB 634, fols. 66-67). On the protestations of the Austrian government, see Wertheimer, *Unwelcome Strangers*, 71-72, 218, and 221.

139. Aside from the wave of expulsions in 1885-86, thus far there has been no historical investigation of Prussia's practice of expulsion in the German Empire. Brubaker (*Citizenship and Nationhood*, 69-71), e.g., discusses this aspect only very briefly and traces in broad strokes the formalization of the expulsion

policy. Cursory remarks may also be found in Wertheimer, *Unwelcome Strangers*, 17–18 and 60–62. Nor is Andreas Gestrich, Gerhard Hirschfeld, and Holger Sonnabend, eds., *Ausweisung und Deportation: Formen der Zwangsmigration in der Geschichte* (Stuttgart: Franz Steiner, 1995), very fruitful; the only article therein on the German Empire—Johannes H. Voigt, "Die Deportation—Ein Thema der deutschen Rechtswissenschaft und Politik im 19. und frühen 20. Jahrhundert," 83–102—treats only the legal discussion of whether to introduce in German states deportation as a form of forced relocation of prisoners to distant locations. My analyses here are based especially on contemporary legal literature: Edgar Loening, "Ausweisung," in *Handwörterbuch der Staatswissenschaften*, ed. Johannes Conrad, 3rd ed., vol. 2 (Jena: Fischer, 1909), 314–18 (an overview of the legal situation in other countries is provided on p. 317); Martin Spahn, "Aufenthaltsrecht, Aufenthaltsbeschränkung, Ausweisung," in *Staatslexikon*, 3rd ed., vol. 1 (Leipzig: Hirzel, 1908), 425–35; "Ausweisungen," in Bitter, *Handwörterbuch der Preußischen Verwaltung*, 1:173–75; Hans von Frisch, *Das Fremdenrecht: Die staatsrechtliche Stellung des Fremden* (Berlin: Heymanns, 1910), esp. 137; from a social-democratic perspective: M. Güldenberg, "Die Erwerbung der Staatsangehörigkeit," *Kommunale Praxis* 6 (1906): 1021–24, esp. 1024; a remarkable sketch of a far-reaching legal equality of foreigners as part of a "complete right of hospitality" may be found in Sylvester Jordan, "Gastrecht (Fremdenrecht)," in *Das Staats-Lexikon*, ed. Carl von Rotteck and Carl Welcker, vol. 5 (Altona: Hammerich, 1847), 360–77, esp. 367–77.

140. Heinrich von Treitschke, *Politik: Vorlesungen gehalten an der Universität zu Berlin*, vol. 2 (Leipzig: Hirzel, 1900), 559–60.

141. The analysis is based on all expulsion proceedings with the letters *Ho–Hz;* see the case files concerning the expulsion of foreigners (APW, PPB 643–46).

142. The analysis is based on all expulsion proceedings with the letters *Ha–He;* see the case files concerning the expulsion of foreigners (APW, PPB 639–41).

143. The analysis is based on all expulsion proceedings with the letter *J;* see the case files concerning the expulsion of foreigners (APW, PPB 647–51).

144. On Hennisch, see APW, PPB 641, fols. 27–31; on Cernuch, APW, PPB 636.

145. On Herstein, see APW, PPB 641, fols. 123–51; on Herzfeld, ibid., fols. 114–20.

146. Deák, "Ethnic Minorities and the Jews," 50.

147. The following is based on the expulsion proceedings against Isaak Jackersohn (APW, PPB 647, fols. 25–64, 69–74). See also the innumerable complaints about arbitrary expulsion orders in the Jewish press—for example: "Ausweisungen über Ausweisungen und kein Ende!" *Israelitische Wochenschrift* 16 (1885): 373–74; and "Wo sind wir eigentlich?" *Jüdisches Volksblatt* 13 (1907): 235.

148. APW, PPB 647, fols. 69–74.

149. The foregoing is based on the files of the expulsion proceedings against Isaak Jackersohn (APW, PPB 647, fols. 25–64, 69–74).

150. Ibid., fols. 75–88, 95–112; quotation from fol. 97.

151. APW, PPB 622, fol. 79. The postage stamp on the postcard depicts, oddly enough, the *droits de l'homme*.

152. APW, PPB 622, fols. 84–86. Adolf Lustig was born on September 1, 1872, in Laszk, Galicia; he lived in 1906 with his wife and two children at Feldstrasse 27. His income from the egg shop was roughly 4,700 marks in 1906. Since the tax roll no longer lists him as a foreigner, he was probably naturalized around 1900 (APW, AMW, K 156, vol. 34, no. 414).

153. Letter from Joseph Mandl in Vienna to Breslau police department, dated October 11, 1898 (APW, PPB 622, fols. 8–9).

154. APW, PPB 622, fols. 63–64. See also the case of the Polish-Jewish cigarette maker Markus Klieger from January 1902 (ibid., fols. 89–90).

155. Jordan, "Gastrecht (Fremdenrecht)," 372.

156. People at the time were already familiar with the topos of second-class citizens; see, e.g., Walther Rathenau, "Staat und Judentum: Eine Polemik" (1911), in his *Gesammelte Schriften*, vol. 1, *Zur Kritik der Zeit* (Berlin: Fischer, 1918), 185–207, here 189, cited in Peter Pulzer, "Between Hope and Fear: Jews and the Weimar Republic," in *Jüdisches Leben in der Weimarer Republik—Jews in the Weimar Republic*, ed. Wolfgang Benz, Arnold Paucker, and Peter Pulzer (Tübingen: Mohr Siebeck, 1998), 271–79, here 272.

157. Balibar, "Grenzen und Gewalten," 8.

158. Wolfgang J. Mommsen, "Nationalität im Zeichen offensiver Weltpolitik: Das Reichs- und Staatsangehörigkeitsgesetz des Deutschen Reiches vom 22. Januar 1913," in Hettline and Nolte, *Nation und Gesellschaft in Deutschland*, 128–41. In contrast to Mommsen, see also Gosewinkel, who speaks of the "birth of Prussian naturalization statistics from the spirit of anti-Semitism"; see his "'Unerwünschte Elemente,'" 83.

159. Dubnow, *Weltgeschichte des jüdischen Volkes*, 10:11.

160. Loening, "Ausweisung," 317. Gustav Landauer rightly jested in retrospect in 1916 that the organs of the German state had always expelled every foreigner arbitrarily, even "if it didn't like his nose"; see his "Ostjuden und Deutsches Reich," *Der Jude* 1 (1916/17): 433–39, here 434–35, cited in Ludger Heid, *Maloche—nicht Mildtätigkeit: Ostjüdische Proletarier in Deutschland, 1914–1923* (Hildesheim: Olms, 1995), 194.

161. "Das Rayon-System in Preussen?" 127–28.

162. A similar point is made in Deák, "Ethnic Minorities and the Jews," 51: "Writing in 1980 when the authorities and the public of Munich, Frankfurt and other German cities stubbornly refuse to receive a few hundred Afghan and Ethiopian political refugees, one can only admire the late nineteenth-century German local authorities and public which, in defiance of governmental policy,

ended up accepting a considerable number of East European immigrants." In contrast to that local stance, the Zurich municipal administration pursued an anti-Semitic policy toward Jewish immigrants from Eastern Europe even before 1914; see Karin Huser Bugmann, *Schtetl an der Sihl: Einwanderung, Leben und Alltag der Ostjuden in Zürich, 1880–1939* (Zurich: Chronos, 1998), 95–126, esp. 99–101 and 120–21.

163. A good introduction to the continuously growing literature may be found in Dieter Düding, Peter Friedmann, and Paul Münch, eds., *Öffentliche Festkultur* (Reinbek: Rowohlt, 1988); Manfred Hettling and Paul Nolte, eds., *Bürgerliche Feste: Symbolische Formen des politischen Handelns im 19. Jahrhundert* (Göttingen: Vandenhoeck & Ruprecht, 1993); and Wolfgang Hardtwig, "Bürgertum, Staatssymbolik und Staatsbewußtsein im Deutschen Kaiserreich, 1871–1914," *Geschichte und Gesellschaft* 16 (1990): 269–95.

164. Cited from Christian Engeli and Wolfgang Haus, eds., *Quellen zum modernen Gemeindeverfassungsrecht in Deutschland* (Stuttgart: Kohlhammer, 1975), 377. In general, see Curt Dittrich, "Ehrenbürger," in *Handwörterbuch der Kommunalwissenschaften*, ed. Josef Brix et al. (Jena: Gustav Fischer, 1918), 1:553–54; and "Ehrenbürgerrecht," in Bitter, *Handwörterbuch der Preußischen Verwaltung*, 1:439. On the legal history, see Kurt Adamy, "Ehrenbürger Potsdams in der Kaiserzeit," in *Potsdam: Märkische Kleinstadt—europäische Residenz,* ed. Peter-Michael Hahn, Kristina Hübener, and Julius H. Schoeps (Berlin: Akademie-Verlag, 1995), 237–54, here 238–40; and Karlheinz Spielmann, *Ehrenbürger und Ehrungen in Geschichte und Gegenwart*, 3rd ed. (Dortmund: privately published, 1967), xl–xlvii, though the latter should be used only with caution since the information provided is incomplete and at times false. Almost all of Breslau's honorary citizens are missing, and Julius Schottländer is erroneously named an honorary citizen of Breslau (131–32).

165. Arthur Schopenhauer, "Aphorismen zur Lebensweisheit," in *Sämtliche Werke in fünf Bänden,* ed. Hans Henning, 2nd ed., vol. 4, *Parerga und Paralipomena,* pt. 1 (Leipzig: Insel, 1923), 371–580, here 425.

166. "Jubilaeum Dr. Ferdinand Cohn," *Schlesische Zeitung,* November 13, 1897, no. 799, 4. The Breslau address books contained a list of all of Breslau's living honorary citizens. My list is based on a survey of all address books from 1870 to 1915. During the same period, the municipal authorities in Berlin was even more stringent, naming only sixteen honorary citizens (Otto-Friedrich Gandert et al., *Heimatchronik Berlin* [Cologne: Archiv für deutsche Heimatpflege, 1962], 904–5). In general, see Alastair Thompson, "Honours Uneven: Decorations, the State and Bourgeois Society in Imperial Germany," *Past and Present* 144 (1994): 171–204, here 201; Spielmann, *Ehrenbürger und Ehrungen,* xviii; and Dirk Schumann, *Bayerns Unternehmer in Gesellschaft und Staat, 1834–1914* (Göttingen: Vandenhoeck & Ruprecht, 1992), 250, though the latter concludes from the rarity of the title of honorary citizen that it is not worth considering.

167. In the East Prussian provinces the conferment of honorary citizenship to welfare recipients was even explicitly precluded; see Dittrich, "Ehrenbürger," 553.

168. APW, AMW, III, 3594, fols. 178 and 207.

169. A good introduction to the debate is provided by Thompson, "Honours Uneven"; Hartmut Berghoff, "Aristokratisierung des Bürgertums? Zur Sozialgeschichte der Nobilitierung von Unternehmern in Preußen und Großbritannien," *Vierteljahrschrift für Sozial- und Wirtschaftsgeschichte* 81 (1994): 189–204; David Blackbourn, *History of Germany, 1780–1918: The Long Nineteenth Century*, 2nd ed. (Oxford: Blackwell, 2003), 365–67; Schumann, *Bayerns Unternehmer in Gesellschaft und Staat*, 250–72; Hartmut Kaelble, "Wie feudal waren die deutschen Unternehmer im Kaiserreich?" in *Beiträge zur quantitativen vergleichenden Unternehmensgeschichte*, ed. Richard H. Tilly (Stuttgart: Klett-Cotta, 1985), 148–71; Nipperdey, *Deutsche Geschichte, 1866–1918*, 1:392, 395, and 418–19; Wehler, *Deutsche Gesellschaftsgeschichte*, 3:718–25; for a literary account see, e.g., Theodor Fontane, *Frau Jenny Treibel*, in *Werke*, ed. Kurt Schreinert, vol. 1 of 3 (Munich: Nymphenburger Verlag, 1968), here 841. Interesting information on honors is also provided in Horst Fuhrmann, *Pour le Mérite: Über die Sichtbarmachung von Verdiensten; Eine historische Besinnung* (Sigmaringen: Thorbecke, 1992).

170. Thompson, "Honours Uneven," 171 and 174.

171. Dittrich, "Ehrenbürger," 554.

172. See "Ordensvorschläge 1882," APW, OPB 660; "Ordensvorschläge 1895," APW, OPB 661; "Ordensvorschläge 1896," APW, OPB 662; and "Ordensvorschläge 1898," APW, OPB 664.

173. Thompson, "Honours Uneven," 182 and 199; Thompson speaks of an "ever-increasing spiral of decorations." In Bavaria, the inflationary trends seem to have been less pronounced prior to 1914 (Schumann, *Bayerns Unternehmer in Gesellschaft und Staat*, 250–72). By contrast, during the Weimar Republic Bavaria was inundated with decorations, which led to the protest in December 1928 by the Prussian government and the *Reichskanzler; Das Kabinett Müller II*, ed. Martin Vogt, vol. 1 (Boppard: Boldt, 1970), 337.

174. Thompson, "Honours Uneven," 199.

175. Ludwig Herz, *Spaziergänge im Damals: Aus dem alten Berlin* (Berlin: Freitagstischpresse von Holten, 1933), 44–45, cited in Berghoff, "Aristokratisierung des Bürgertums?" 192–93; see also Nipperdey, *Deutsche Geschichte, 1866–1918*, 1: 419. On the history of Huldschinsky's iron and steel works, see Konrad Fuchs, *Gestalten und Ereignisse aus Schlesiens Wirtschaft, Kultur und Politik* (Dortmund: Universität Dortmund, Forschungsstelle Ostmitteleuropa, 1992), 82–84. Oskar Huldschinsky's father, Salomon, was one of the few Jewish big industrialists who belonged to the conservative party; see Werner E. Mosse, *German-Jewish Economic Élite, 1820–1935: A Socio-Cultural Profile* (Oxford: Oxford University Press, 1989), 228–29.

176. "Ordenvorschläge 1896," APW, OPB 662, fols. 209–18. The refusal of decorations amounted to the refusal of ennoblement, which was common among members of both the Jewish (Carl Fürstenberg, Albert Ballin, and Max Warburg) and the non-Jewish (Emil Kirdorf, Krupp, and Thyssen) upper-middle class; see also Berghoff, "Aristokratisierung des Bürgertums?" 190; Wehler, *Deutsche Gesellschaftsgeschichte*, 3:719.

177. "Ein Erfurter Ehrenbürgerbrief," *Israelitische Wochenschrift* 25 (1894): supplement "Jüdisches Familienblatt" (Jewish Family Page), no. 28, 110–11. Unger had received his doctorate in 1910 from the University of Erfurt, which was closed shortly thereafter. He founded a private mathematical institute around 1820 and ran it until 1844, when the city converted the private institute into a municipal *Realgymnasium* and he had to surrender control because he was Jewish; it was only in 1848 that he received a permanent position as senior teacher. On the honorary citizenship of Lewis Marcus, whom the Schwerin magistracy expressly honored also because of his "many years of work in the highly respected position of chairman of the Israelite community," see Hans-Michael Bernhardt, *Bewegung und Beharrung: Studien zur Emanzipationsgeschichte der Juden im Großherzogtum Mecklenburg Schwerin, 1813–1869* (Hanover: Hahn, 1998), 290–92 (there see n.222, as well as the comment that the small town of Waren in Mecklenburg named a Jew as its first honorary citizen ever in 1871).

178. On Mannheim's first Jewish honorary citizen, Carl Ladenburg, see Lothar Gall, *Bürgertum in Deutschland* (Berlin: Siedler, 1989), 413; and Hermann Schäfer, "Carl Ladenburg," in *Neue Deutsche Biographie*, vol. 13 (Berlin: Duncker & Humblot, 1982), 388–89; on Königsberg, see Schüler-Springorum, *Die jüdische Minderheit*, 65; Herbert M. Mühlpfordt, "Welche Mitbürger hat Königsberg öffentlich geehrt?" *Jahrbuch der Albertus-Universität* 14 (1964): 66–198, here 77–78; Spielmann incorrectly names two additional allegedly Jewish honorary citizens, namely, Walter Simon (1908) and David Hilbert (1930). However, Simon was only of Jewish descent (Schüler-Springorum, *Die jüdische Minderheit*, 61n67), whereas Hilbert was not even that (see the article on him in the *Neue Deutsche Biographie*). Because of such imprecision, Spielmann's statement that in Germany prior to 1933 there was a total of thirty-three honorary citizens is dubious; see Spielmann, *Ehrenbürger und Ehrungen*, xvii. On the honorary citizen of Berlin, Oskar Cassel, see Otto-Friedrich Gandert et al., *Heimatchronik Berlin* (Cologne: Archiv für deutsche Heimatpflege, 1962), 904–5; Ernest Hamburger, *Juden im öffentlichen Leben Deutschlands: Regierungsmitglieder, Beamte, Parlamentarier in der monarchischen Zeit, 1848–1918* (Tübingen: Mohr Siebeck, 1968), 368–69; and Reinhard Rürup, ed., *Jüdische Geschichte in Berlin: Essays und Studien* (Berlin: Edition Hentrich, 1995), 110. By contrast, there were no Jewish honorary citizens of Hamburg (Spielmann, *Ehrenbürger und Ehrungen*, 343–440) or of Potsdam (Adamy, "Ehrenbürger Potsdams in der Kaiserzeit"). Rudolf Mosse was an honorary citizen of his hometown Graetz, Province of Posen, and Albert Mosse became an honorary citizen of Berlin in 1917; see Elisabeth Kraus, *Die*

Familie Mosse: Deutsch-jüdisches Bürgertum im 19. und 20. Jahrhundert (Munich: C. H. Beck, 1999), 187 and 241.

179. On Ferdinand Julius Cohn, see the analysis that follows in the chapter. On the conferment of honorary citizenship to Wilhelm Salomon Freund, see "Verleihung der Ehrenbürgerwürde an den Stadtverordnetenvorsteher Geheimen Justizrath Freund," APW, AMW, III, 3594, fols. 202–7, and "50jaehriges Dienstjubilaeum," *Schlesische Zeitung*, no. 303, May 1, 1901, 2.

180. A list of those who held the positions just named is provided in Hermann Markgraf, *Geschichte Breslaus in kurzer Übersicht*, 2nd expanded ed. revised by Otfried Schwarzer (Breslau: Kern, 1913), 97–111. The absence of clerics among Breslau's honorary citizens is striking; on the other hand, in Potsdam there were only two clerics among the city's thirteen honorary citizens between 1860 and 1910; see Adamy, "Ehrenbürger Potsdams in der Kaiserzeit," 245 and 252–53.

181. A list of the countless awards of honorary citizenship for the old man in Friedrichsruh may be found in Johann Penzler, ed., *Fürst Bismarck nach seiner Entlassung*, vol. 6, *26. Dec. 1894 – Ende 1895* (Leipzig: Fiedler, 1898), 216, 243, 252–53, 284, 286, 307, and 329. On the conflicts preceding the award in Trier, see Emil Zenz, *Die Ehrenbürger der Stadt Trier* (Trier: privately published, 1978), 23–27.

182. "Ehrenbürgerrecht," in Bitter, *Handwörterbuch der Preußischen Verwaltung*, 1:439.

183. The occasion for conferring honorary citizenship on Moltke was his ninetieth birthday on October 26, 1890; Moltke was an honorary citizen of twenty-three cities, including Berlin and Hamburg (both in 1871), Königsberg and Munich (both in 1890). See Heinrich Walle, "Helmuth von Moltke," in *Neue Deutsche Biographie*, vol. 18 (Berlin: Duncker & Humblot, 1997), 13–17, here 16; Spielmann, *Ehrenbürger und Ehrungen*, 343 (Hamburg) and 466 (Cologne). On Tümpling, see Bernhard von Poten, "Wilhelm von Tümpling," in *Allgemeine Deutsche Biographie*, vol. 38 (Leipzig: Duncker & Humblot, 1894), 785–87.

184. Dietz Bering, *Der Name als Stigma: Antisemitismus im Deutschen Alltag, 1812–1933* (Stuttgart: Klett-Cotta, 1987), 206–11, here 206. That a stigma was attached to the name "Cohn" is indirectly indicated by the fact that his two younger brothers changed their names; the writer Oscar Justinus Cohn published as "Oscar Justinus" and his youngest brother, the historian Max Cohn, changed his surname in 1882 to "Conrat"; see *Neue Deutsche Biographie*, vol. 3 (Berlin: Duncker & Humblot, 1957), 314; *Deutsche Biographische Enzyklopädie*, vol. 2 (Munich: Saur, 1995), 352–53 and 365; Hans Kalisch, "Max Conrat (Cohn)," in *Jüdisches Lexikon*, vol. 1 (Berlin: Jüdischer Verlag, 1927), 1437.

185. Friedrich Rosen, "Ferdinand Cohn," in *Schlesische Lebensbilder*, vol. 1 (Breslau: W. G. Korn, 1922), 167–73, here 168; on Jacob Cohn, see also Pauline Cohn, ed., *Ferdinand Cohn: Blätter der Erinnerung* (Breslau: J. U. Kern, 1901), 5 and 8–9 (with the nostalgic depiction of the "poesy of the old Jewish family life");

for background on Hebrew book publishing in Dyhernfurth, see Julian Landsberger, "Zur Geschichte der jüdischen Buchdruckerei in Dyhernfurth und des
jüdischen Buchhandels," *Monatsschrift für Geschichte und Wissenschaft des Judentums*
39 (1895): 120–33, 187–92, and 230–38; on Isaak Cohn, see Pauline Cohn, *Ferdinand Cohn*, 7 (quotation), and "Nekrolog Isaak Cohn," *Allgemeine Zeitung des
Judenthums* 47 (1883): 278; portraits of Ferdinand Julius Cohn may be found in
Maciej Łagiewski, *Wrocławscy Żydzi, 1850–1944* (Wrocław: Muzeum Historyczne,
1994), plates 229 and 240; and Ernst Wunschmann, "Ferdinand Julius Cohn,"
in *Allgemeine Deutsche Biographie*, vol. 47 (Leipzig: Duncker & Humblot, 1903),
503–5.

    186. Pauline Cohn, *Ferdinand Cohn*, 13; p. 173 is also fascinating; there is an
explicit reference to *Soll und Haben* on p. 5. Cohn's wife's characterization of
him is indebted to the bourgeois ethic of achievement: "diligently hardworking, full of fervent enthusiasm for everything beautiful, true, and good, filled
with the highest ideals" (1). The concept of *Bocher* stems from the Hebrew *bachur*
(youth), but the term was often used in a mocking sense in Yiddish (*Jüdisches
Lexikon: Ein enzyklopädisches Handbuch des jüdischen Wissens in vier Bänden*, vol. 1
[Berlin: Jüdischer Verlag, 1927], 672). Ferdinand Julius Cohn's autobiography
first appeared in 1898 in the *Allgemeine Zeitung des Judenthums* (see the reference in
C. Pinn, "Zum Breslauer Universitätjubiläum," *Allgemeine Zeitung des Judenthums*
75 [1911]: 366–67). A similarly self-confident success story may be found in
"Nekrolog Eduard Bielschowsky," *Allgemeine Zeitung des Judenthums* 74 (1910): supplement from April 8, 4–5: the "son of a small landowner succeeded solely by
his own powers, by untiring, iron-willed diligence, combined with a great talent
for business" "to raise up his business step by step and . . . develop it into the
great firm it is today."

    187. The quotation is taken from Rosen, "Ferdinand Cohn," 169; Ferdinand
Julius Cohn, "Curriculum Vitae" (1844), in Pauline Cohn, *Ferdinand Cohn*, 16.

    188. Ferdinand Julius Cohn, "Curriculum Vitae," 20–21.

    189. Pauline Cohn, *Ferdinand Cohn*, 33 and 41–57; Rosen, "Ferdinand
Cohn," 169; "Jubilaeum Dr. Ferdinand Cohn," *Schlesische Zeitung*, no. 799, November 13, 1897, 4.

    190. The original text reads "Vorsichtig, weis', habt ihr dem Wissens-
riesen, / Dem treuen Mann, die letzte Ehre nicht erwiesen, / Dieweil er sprach
und lebte sonder Bangen, / Seid ihr den letzten Weg nicht mitgegangen. / Das
ist nicht neu, ist auch kein Meisterstück, / Ihr bleibt ja immer Nees zurück."

    191. "Ferdinand Julius Cohn," in *Encyclopaedia Britannica*, vol. 5 (1929), 978–
79 (a similar view may be found in Wunschmann, "Ferdinand Julius Cohn,"
503); Rosen, "Ferdinand Cohn," 169–71, quotation from 169; Pauline Cohn,
Ferdinand Cohn, 131; *Komm ich zeige Dir Breslau: Ein zuverlässiger Führer für Breslauer
und Fremde*, pt. 1 (Breslau: Kern, 1926), 34. On Cohn's relationship with Nees
von Esenbeck, see esp. "Nekrolog Ferdinand Cohn," *Mitteilungen aus dem Verein
zur Abwehr des Antisemitismus* 8 (1898): 352 (the mocking poem is also printed

there); in general, see Ernst Wunschmann, "Christian Gottfried Daniel Nees von Esenbeck," in *Allgemeine Deutsche Biographie*, vol. 23 (Leipzig: Duncker & Humblot, 1886), 368–76; and Dietrich v. Engelhardt, ed., *Christian Gottfried Nees von Esenbeck: Politik und Naturwissenschaft in der ersten Hälfte des 19. Jahrhunderts* (Stuttgart: Wissenschaftliche Verlagsgesellschaft, 2004).

192. The conferment of honorary citizenship to exceptional persons, APW, AMW, III, 3594, fols. 170–71.

193. Ibid., 173. Expressly, then, the city did not honor a specialist but rather a generalist who also addressed the broader public. Cohn's pretension to write also for the layman played an important role in many appreciations; he had a "masterful" control of "the form of presentation" (Wunschmann, "Ferdinand Julius Cohn," 503); his "writings are distinguished by an easily understandable, elegant language" ("Jubiläum," *Schlesische Zeitung*, no. 799, November 13, 1897). His greatest success was the book *Die Pflanze: Vorträge aus dem Gebiete der Botanik* (Breslau: J. U. Kern, 1885; 2nd, expanded ed., 1898), according to the *Schlesische Zeitung*, "a work unsurpassed in style and substance."

194. APW, AMW, III, 3594, fols. 177–78.

195. See *Wrocław: Breslau: Fotos aus der Wende vom 19. zum 20. Jahrhundert*, vol. 2, *Breslauer Plätze*, text by Iwona Binkowska (Torun-Wrocław: Via, 1991), plate 9; Maria Zwierz, *Ulica Świdnicka we Wrocławiu*, ed. Zofia Ostrowska-Kębłowska (Wrocław: Via, 1995), plates 61–65 (no. 65 has a view of the facade of Tauenzienstrasse 3a).

196. On the apartment and the view from the loggia, see Pauline Cohn, *Ferdinand Cohn*, 238. A photo of the Eichborn mansion with the New Synagogue in the background may be viewed in Łagiewski, *Wrocławscy Żydzi, 1850–1944*, plate 19; Hubert Stier, "Gesellschaftshaus für die Gesellschaft der Freunde zu Breslau," *Deutsche Bauzeitung* 11 (1877): 11–12. A description of the area may also be found in Anna Auerbach, "Die Chronik der Familie Silbergleit," ME 600, 35–36, Archives of the LBI, New York.

197. The five Jewish dentists in a sample from 1906 earned on average nearly 4,300 marks; the top earner among the five earned nearly 12,000 marks per year.

198. All figures are from the tax rolls from 1897; see APW, AMW, K 154, district 50, nos. 3011–39 (Tauenzienstrasse 3a).

199. Pauline Cohn, *Ferdinand Cohn*, 239.

200. *Rechenschaftsbericht der Gesellschaft der Brüder für das Jahr 1903* (Breslau: n.p., 1904), appendix; *Festschrift zur hundertjährigen Stiftungs-Feier der Gesellschaft der Freunde in Breslau, im Auftrage der Direktion verfaßt von den Schriftführern* (Breslau: n.p., 1921), 36; "Jubiläum," *Schlesische Zeitung*, no. 799, November 13, 1897, 2; "Ferdinand Cohn," *Im Deutschen Reich* 3 (1897): 632–33; the commensurate presence of Jewish and Breslau civic identity is more pronounced at the celebration of the conferment of honorary citizenship on Wilhelm Salomon Freund; see "50jaehriges Dienstjubilaeum," *Schlesische Zeitung*, no. 303, May 1, 1901, 2. Unlike

in the case of Ferdinand Cohn, the two leading rabbis, Jakob Guttmann and Ferdinand Rosenthal, also presented their congratulations to Freund.

201. APW, AMW, III, 3594, fol. 177.

202. The quotation is from Pauline Cohn, *Ferdinand Cohn*, 243–48.

203. "Jubiläum," *Schlesische Zeitung*, no. 800, November 13, 1897, 2; Rosen, "Ferdinand Cohn," 169; the *Schlesische Zeitung* expressly praised "the exceptionally thoughtful speech, in which his great modesty once again found expression" ("Jubiläum," 2).

204. Pauline Cohn, *Ferdinand Cohn*, 243–48; "Jubiläum," *Schlesische Zeitung*, no. 800, November 13, 1897, 2. Dahn's appearance was not an isolated incident. He was also among the prominent well-wishers at the conferment of honorary citizenship on Wilhelm Salomon Freund. Naturally he presented Wilhelm Freund with a copy of *Ein Kampf um Rom* (A Struggle for Rome) and *Die Könige der Germanen* (Germanic Kings); see "50jaehriges Dienstjubilaeum," *Schlesische Zeitung*, no. 303, May 1, 1901, 2. On Dahn's anti-Semitism, see George L. Mosse, "Image of the Jew"; and Florian Krobb, *Die schöne Jüdin: Jüdische Frauengestalten in der deutschsprachigen Erzählliteratur vom 17. Jahrhundert bis zum Ersten Weltkrieg* (Tübingen: Niemeyer, 1993), 132–34; see also "Professor Felix Dahn," *Deutsche Ostwacht*, March 31, 1894, 6.

205. *Im Deutschen Reich* 3 (1897): 565 and 632–33; *Allgemeine Zeitung des Judenthums* 61 (November 26, 1897): supplement, 3; *Mitteilungen des Vereins zur Abwehr des Antisemitismus* 7 (1897): 372; by contrast, no reports on the conferment of honorary citizenship—in fact on either Cohn or on Freund—were published in *Der Israelit: Central-Organ für das orthodoxe Judenthum* (according to an examination of the journal for November 1897 and May 1901).

206. Pauline Cohn, *Ferdinand Cohn*, 237–50, quotation from 250.

207. APW, AMW, III, 3594, fols. 190–93; participation of the magistracy in the funeral, APW, AMW, III, 2190, fol. 134.

208. *Jüdisches Volksblatt* 14 (1908): 222 and 416–17; on the monument, see *Komm ich zeige Dir Breslau*, 70; Łagiewski, *Wrocławscy Żydzi, 1850–1944*, plate 232; "Ilse Conrat, verheiratete von Twardowska," in *Deutsche Biographische Enzyklopädie*, vol. 2 (Munich: Saur, 1995), 365; see also Pinn, "Zum Breslauer Universitätjubiläum."

209. *Jüdisches Volksblatt* 14 (1908): 416–17; "Nachruf Ferdinand Cohn," *Der Israelit* 14, no. 39 (1898): 971–72; Heppner, *Jüdische Persönlichkeiten*, 6–7; a similar development is discernible in the case of Wilhelm Salomon Freund, whose obituary in *Allgemeine Zeitung des Judenthums* 79 (September 3, 1915): supplement, 2–3, began with the formulation "the honorary citizen of our city, Privy Counselor of Justice Dr. Wilhelm Freund [has died]."

Conclusion

1. Peter Gay, "In Deutschland zu Hause . . . : Die Juden in der Weimarer Republik," in *Juden im nationalsozialistischen Deutschland—The Jews in Nazi Germany*

1933–1943, ed. Arnold Paucker, Sylvia Gilchrist, and Barbara Suchy (Tübingen: Mohr Siebeck, 1986), 31–43.

2. Werner T. Angress, "The German Army's 'Judenzählung' of 1916: Genesis—Consequences—Significance," *Year Book of the Leo Baeck Institute* 23 (1978): 117–37; Michael Jeismann, "Der letzte Feind: Nachgeholter Universalismus; Zum Zusammenhang von Nationalismus und Antisemitismus," in *Die Konstruktion der Nation gegen die Juden,* ed. Peter Alter, Claus-Ekkehard Bärsch, and Peter Berghoff (Munich: Fink, 1999), 173–90; Peter Pulzer, "Der Erste Weltkrieg," in *Deutsch-jüdische Geschichte in der Neuzeit,* by Steven M. Lowenstein, Paul Mendes-Flohr, Peter Pulzer, and Monika Richarz, ed. Michael A. Meyer, vol. 3, *Umstrittene Integration, 1871–1918* (Munich: C. H. Beck, 1997), 356–80; Saul Friedländer, "Die politischen Veränderungen der Kriegszeit und ihre Auswirkungen auf die Judenfrage," in *Deutsches Judentum in Krieg und Revolution, 1916–1923,* ed. Werner E. Mosse (Tübingen: Mohr Siebeck, 1971), 27–67; and Helmut Berding, *Moderner Antisemitismus in Deutschland* (Frankfurt a. M.: Suhrkamp, 1988), 165–89.

3. Richard Bessel, *Germany after the First World War* (Oxford: Clarendon Press, 1993), 261–63; Gerald D. Feldman, *The Great Disorder: Politics, Economics, and Society in the German Inflation, 1914–1924* (New York: Oxford University Press, 1993), 702; George L. Mosse, "Der erste Weltkrieg und die Brutalisierung der Politik: Betrachtungen über die politische Rechte, den Rassismus und den deutschen Sonderweg," in *Demokratie und Diktatur: Geist und Gestalt politischer Herrschaft in Deutschland und Europa; Festschrift für Karl Dietrich Bracher,* ed. Manfred Funke et al. (Düsseldorf: Droste, 1987), 127–39; Dirk Schumann, *Politische Gewalt in der Weimarer Republik, 1918–1933: Kampf um die Straße und Furcht vor dem Bürgerkrieg* (Essen: Klartext Verlagsgesellschaft, 2001); Bernd Weisbrod, "Gewalt in der Politik: Zur politischen Kultur in Deutschland zwischen den Weltkriegen," *Geschichte in Wissenschaft und Unterricht* 43 (1992): 391–404.

4. Hannah Arendt was the first to emphasize that the rise of radical, völkish anti-Semitism coincided with the Jews' loss of power; see her *Origins of Totalitarianism* (New York: Harcourt, 1951), 83–87; in general, see David Biale, *Power and Powerlessness in Jewish History* (New York: Schocken, 1986).

5. "Der Oberpräsident der Provinz Schlesien [Wolfgang Jaenicke] an den Reichskanzler, Breslau 10. Mai 1920," in *Das Kabinett Müller I (27. März bis 21. Juni 1920): Akten der Reichskanzlei,* ed. Martin Vogt (Boppard: Boldt, 1971), 213–17, here 216–17. The Jewish press often complained about the radical anti-Semitism of the nationalist organizations and Freikorps in Upper Silesia; see, e.g., "Oberschlesien," *Im Deutschen Reich* 20 (1914): 246–51; "Zeitschau Oberschlesien," *Im Deutschen Reich* 27 (1921): 210–11, 226, and 248; "Die antisemitische Hetze in Oberschlesien," *Jüdische Volkszeitung,* November 28, 1919, 5; "Breslau," *Jüdische Volkszeitung,* November 18, 1921, 4; "Deutsch-völkische Verlogenheit," *Jüdische Volkszeitung,* February 24, 1922, 2–3; "Im deutschen Oberschlesien," *CV-Zeitung: Blätter für Deutschtum und Judentum* 1 (1922): 97–98, and "Aus Oberschlesien," ibid., 189; "Die Nationalsozialisten in Oberschlesien,"

CV-Zeitung 2 (1923): 8, and "Deutschenhaß und Judenhaß in Oberschlesien," ibid., 91 and 102. On the loss of civility and the increasing readiness to engage in violence among the German nationalists in Upper Silesia, see T. Hunt Tooley, *National Identity and Weimar Germany: Upper Silesia and the Eastern Border, 1918–1922* (Lincoln: University of Nebraska Press, 1997), 200–252; on Breslau as a gathering point for volunteers to the "self-defense organizations," see General von Seeckt's communication in "Kabinettssitzung vom 9. Mai 1921," in *Das Kabinett Fehrenbach (25. Juni 1920 bis 4. Mai 1921): Akten der Reichskanzlei*, ed. Peter Wulf (Boppard am Rhein: H. Boldt, 1972), 671.

6. See *Statistik des deutschen Reiches*, vol. 207 (1910), 594–95; and Heinrich Silbergleit, ed., *Die Bevölkerungs- und Berufsverhältnisse der Juden im deutschen Reich* (Berlin: Akademie-Verlag, 1930), 199–200; in general, see Donald L. Niewyk, "The Impact of Inflation and Depression on the German Jews," *Year Book of the Leo Baeck Institute* 28 (1983): 19–36, and *The Jews in Weimar Germany* (Baton Rouge: Louisiana State University Press, 1980), 17–19; Avraham Barkai, "Die Juden als sozioökonomische Minderheitsgruppe in der Weimarer Republik," in *Juden in der Weimarer Republik: Skizzen und Porträts*, ed. Walter Grab and Julius H. Schoeps (Stuttgart: Burg-Verlag, 1986), 330–46, here 338–39; on the downfall of the *rentier*, see Martin H. Geyer, *Verkehrte Welt: Revolution, Inflation und Moderne; München, 1914–1924* (Göttingen: Vandenhoeck & Ruprecht, 1998), 381 and 389.

7. "Die Wandernden nach Herkunft, Ziel und Bekenntnis, 1917–1921," in *Statistisches Jahrbuch der Stadt Breslau für 1922* (Breslau: Morgenstern, 1922), 28–29; "Die Wandernden nach Herkunft, Ziel und Bekenntnis, 1922–1923," in *Statistisches Jahrbuch der Stadt Breslau für 1924* (Breslau: Morgenstern, 1924), 12; Silbergleit, *Die Bevölkerungs- und Berufsverhältnisse*, 201.

8. "Aufruf zur Errichtung einer jüdischen Mittelstandsküche," *Jüdische Volkszeitung*, June 1, 1922, 4; see also "Jüdische Arbeiterfürsorge Breslau," *Jüdische Volkszeitung*, December 9, 1921, 2; "Von jüdischer Not in Breslau," *Jüdische Volkszeitung*, August 25, 1922, 4.

9. Arye Maimon, *Wanderungen und Wandlungen: Die Geschichte meines Lebens* (Trier: Arye Maimon-Institut für Geschichte der Juden, 1998), 5.

10. "Breslauer Brief," *Jüdische Zeitung für Ostdeutschland*, November 18, 1924; and "Die judenfreien Berge," *Jüdische Zeitung für Ostdeutschland*, December 19, 1924.

11. "Streit zwischen jüdischen und christlichen Ärzten in Breslau 1923–1925," Inv. 1434:5, CAHJP, Jerusalem. "Before the war," a leaflet from Jewish doctors reads, "in every collaboration within the Breslau medical profession for economic or professional purposes there was an area from which party-political or religious questions were excluded"; see also "Die jüdischen Ärzte und ihr antisemitischer Geschäftsführer," *Die Freie Meinung*, no. 42, October 11, 1924, supplement, 3.

12. Willy Cohn, *Verwehte Spuren: Erinnerungen an das Breslauer Judentum vor seinem Untergang*, ed. Norbert Conrads (Cologne: Bohlau, 1995), 293–94. During

his time at the Elisabeth-Gymnasium, Cohn grew closer to only the school's principal and his sole Catholic colleague. He said that the Catholic teacher sided with him. "For there they considered being a Catholic," Cohn recalled at the end of the 1930s, "worse than being a Jew" (295).

13. "Judenhetze in der Schule," *Jüdische Volkszeitung,* July 4, 1919, 6; "Antisemitismus und konfessionelle Schule," *Jüdische Volkszeitung,* March 24, 1921, 4; "Alldeutsche Schüler," *Die Freie Meinung,* no. 7, February 14, 1920; "Ein antisemitisches Gymnasium: Das Elisabethaneum," *Die Freie Meinung,* no. 41, October 2, 1920; "Volkserzieher," *Schlesische Arbeiter-Zeitung,* no. 34, April 3, 1920. Similar complaints about anti-Semitism among high school students were also made elsewhere in the early 1920s; see "Antisemitismus in der höheren Schule," *CV-Zeitung* 1 (1922): 273–74; and Anthony Kauders, *German Politics and the Jews: Düsseldorf and Nuremberg, 1910–1933* (Oxford: Oxford University Press, 1996), 85 and 92.

14. Maimon, *Wanderungen und Wandlungen,* 11–12 and 14.

15. Bernd Weisbrod, "The Crisis of Bourgeois Society in Interwar Germany," in *Fascist Italy and Nazi Germany: Comparisons and Contrasts,* ed. Richard Bessel (Cambridge: Cambridge University Press, 1996), 23–39.

16. *Kleines Statistisches Taschenbuch für die Stadt Breslau,* ed. Statistisches Amt Breslau (Breslau: Stadt Breslau, 1928), 51; the Deutschvölkische Freiheitspartei was a successor to the Deutschvölkischer Schutz- und Trutz-Bund (German Völkish Defensive and Offensive Association); see Uwe Lohalm, *Völkischer Radikalismus: Die Geschichte des Deutschvölkischen Schutz- und Trutzbundes, 1919–1923* (Hamburg: Leibnitz-Verlag, 1970), 283 and 316; "Der Antisemitismus der Alldeutschen," *Der Volksstaat,* no. 28, September 19, 1919, 2; "Antisemitische Zuverlässigkeit," *Der Volksstaat,* no. 37, November 23, 1919, 3–4; "Offenes Visier," *Der Volksstaat,* no. 21, May 30, 1920, 1–2. On the erosion of liberal traditions in Silesia generally, see Eric Kurlander, *The Price of Exclusion: Ethnicity, National Identity, and the Decline of German Liberalism, 1898–1933* (New York: Berghahn Books, 2006).

17. "Die Reichspräsidentenwahlen und die Landtags- und Reichstagswahlen im Frühjahr und Sommer 1932 in Breslau," *Monatsberichte des statistischen Amtes der Stadt Breslau* 59 (1932): 47–49, here 48; on cities in general, see Detlef Schmiechen-Ackermann, "Großstädte und Nationalsozialismus, 1930–1945," in *Nationalsozialismus in der Region,* ed. Horst Möller, Andreas Wirsching, and Walter Ziegler (Munich: Oldenbourg, 1996), 253–70, here 253.

18. The minister of the interior is cited in Dieter Gosewinkel, "'Unerwünschte Elemente': Einwanderung und Einbürgerung von Juden in Deutschland, 1848–1933," *Tel Aviver Jahrbuch für deutsche Geschichte* 27 (1998): 71–106, here 100.

19. Ute Gerhard, "Flucht und Wanderung in den Mediendiskursen der Weimarer Republik," in *Die Sprache des Migrationsdiskurses: Das Reden über "Ausländer" in Medien, Politik und Alltag,* ed. Matthias Jung, Martin Wengeler, and Karin Böke (Opladen: Westdeutscher Verlag, 1997), 45–57, here 50; in general, see

Trude Maurer, *Ostjuden in Deutschland, 1918–1933* (Hamburg: Hans Christian Verlag, 1986); and Steven E. Aschheim, *Brothers and Strangers: The East European Jew in German and German-Jewish Consciousness, 1800–1923* (Madison: University of Wisconsin Press, 1982).

20. "Die Ostjudenfrage und die Wohnungsnot" and "Oestliche Einwanderung," both in *Schlesische Zeitung*, no. 6, January 4, 1920; "Antisemitismus und völkischer Gedanke," *Schlesische Tagespost*, no. 165, June 23, 1920; "Völlige Aussaugung des deutschen Volkes durch Juda," *Schlesische Tagespost*, no. 259, November 4, 1923; "Die Stunde drängt," *Schlesische Tagespost*, no. 266, November 13, 1923. From 1922 on, the Breslau Statistics Bureau also used the term *Ostjuden* (Eastern Jews) in its official statistics (*Statistisches Jahrbuch der Stadt Breslau für 1922* [Breslau: Morgenstern, 1922], 28–29).

21. Fritz Becker, "Zur Ostjudenfrage," *Jüdische Volkszeitung*, February 24, 1922. Becker's article did not go without contradiction; see Siegbert Unikover, "Zur Ostjudenfrage," *Jüdische Volkszeitung*, March 17, 1922, 11. See also Dr. W. C. [= Willy Cohn?], "Zur Frage der Einwanderung aus dem Osten," *Die Freie Meinung*, no. 14, April 3, 1920; "Die verdammten Ostjuden!" *Die Freie Meinung*, no. 43, October 16, 1920; "Polizeipräsident und Juden," *Die Freie Meinung*, no. 11, March 12, 1921; "Die Ostjudenfrage," *Jüdisch-liberale Zeitung*, no. 11 (1921).

22. "Einbürgerungsverfahren Selma Farnik, geb. Nothmann," APW, PPB 74. An earlier application for naturalization filed by her daughter, Else Jarnik, was also judged positively because she was "to be ascribed to the German tribe" (ibid.). Typically enough, "tribe" (*Volksstamm*) is used here in the singular; in the nineteenth century it still would have been common to speak of a number of "tribes," which would constitute a unity only in their multiplicity. This semantic shift also confirms the penetration of notions of homogeneity.

23. "Einbürgerungsverfahren Georg Persicaner," APW, PPB 128.

24. "Einbürgerungsverfahren Abraham Pikarsky," APW, PPB 131.

25. Peter Pulzer, "Der Anfang vom Ende," in Paucker, Gilchrist, and Suchy, *Juden im nationalsozialistischen Deutschland*, 3–27, here 9. References to anti-Semitic violence in the Weimar Republic may be found in Martin H. Geyer, "Teuerungsprotest und Teuerungsunruhen, 1914–1923: Selbsthilfegesellschaft und Geldentwertung," in *Der Kampf um das tägliche Brot: Nahrungsmangel, Versorgungspolitik und Protest, 1750–1990*, ed. Manfred Gailus and Heinrich Volkmann (Opladen: Westdeutscher Verlag, 1994), 319–45, here 331, 335, and 343; Maurer, *Ostjuden in Deutschland*, 329–38 and 345–47; Niewyk, *Jews in Weimar Germany*, 51, 79, and 84–85; Stefanie Schüler-Springorum, *Die jüdische Minderheit in Königsberg/Preußen, 1871–1945* (Göttingen: Vandenhoeck & Ruprecht, 1996); and Dirk Walter, *Antisemitische Kriminalität und Gewalt: Judenfeindschaft in der Weimarer Republik* (Bonn: Dietz Verlag, 1999); for the period after 1933, see Michael Wildt, *Volksgemeinschaft als Selbstermächtigung: Gewalt gegen Juden in der deutschen Provinz, 1919–1939* (Hamburg: Hamburger Edition, 2007). Before 1914 there had been only isolated attacks on Jews in Breslau, mostly on Polish-Russian immigrants;

an example from the late 1880s is reported in Malwin Warschauer, *Im jüdischen Leben: Erinnerungen des Berliner Rabbiners Malwin Warschauer* (Berlin: Transit, 1995), 49–50.

26. "Was lehren uns die Ereignisse des 13. März?" *Jüdische Volkszeitung*, March 26, 1920, 1 and 5; "Gedächtnisfeier für Bernhard Schottländer," *Jüdische Volkszeitung*, March 24, 1921.

27. Max Moses Polke, "Mein Leben in Deutschland vor und nach dem 30. Jan. 1933," 27, Manuscript Collection "My Life in Germany Before and After January 30, 1933," Houghton Library, Harvard University, Cambridge, Mass.; similar remarks may be found in Cohn, *Verwehte Spuren*, 394; and Aron Heppner, *Jüdische Persönlichkeiten in und aus Breslau* (Breslau: Schatzky, 1931), 41.

28. "Bernhard Schottlaender zum Gedächtnis" and "Bernhard Schottlaenders Leiche," both in *Schlesische Arbeiter-Zeitung*, no. 70, June 26, 1920; "Schottländers Leiche gefunden," *Breslauer General-Anzeiger*, no. 166, June 24, 1920. On the anti-Semitic context of Landauer's murder, see Werner T. Angress, "Juden im politischen Leben der Revolutionszeit," in *Deutsches Judentum in Krieg und Revolution, 1916–1923*, ed. Werner E. Mosse and Arnold Paucker (Tübingen: Mohr Siebeck, 1971), 137–315, here 264–65; and Norbert Seitz, "Gustav Landauer und die Münchener Räterepublik," in *". . . die beste Sensation ist das Ewige . . ." Gustav Landauer: Leben, Werk und Wirkung*, ed. Michael Matzigkeit (Düsseldorf: Droste, 1995), 267–91, here 272 and 289.

29. *Schlesische Arbeiter-Zeitung*, no. 95, August 28, 1920; *Die Freie Meinung*, no. 35, August 28, 1920; *Schlesische Zeitung*, nos. 432 and 433, August 27, 1920; "Die Drahtzieher der Breslauer Judenhetze," *Jüdische Volkszeitung*, September 3, 1920, 1. Since the demonstrators also attacked the Polish and French consulates, the *New York Times* reported on the anti-Semitic riots (see *New York Times*, August 29, 1920); on the considerable diplomatic embroilments resulting from the attacks on the consulates, see *Das Kabinett Fehrenbach*, 148–52.

30. Stefan Rohrbacher, *Gewalt im Biedermeier: Antijüdische Unruhen im Vormärz und Revolution (1815–1848/49)* (Frankfurt a. M.: Campus, 1993), 229–30.

31. "Zu den Breslauer Unruhen," *Die Freie Meinung*, no. 30, July 28, 1923; see also "Plünderungen in Breslau," *Schlesische Zeitung*, no. 338, July 21, 1923 (the latter contains the remark, "the events . . . suggest an operation that was carried out in accordance with a system that been carefully planned in advance"); *Breslauer Zeitung*, no. 336, July 21, 1923; ibid., no. 338, July 22, 1923; ibid., no. 528, November 10, 1923; "Revolten in Breslau," *Breslauer Neueste Nachrichten*, no. 197, July 21, 1923, 1; "Der blutige Freitag" and "700 Milliarden Tumultschäden," both in *Breslauer Neueste Nachrichten*, no. 199, July 23, 1923, supplement; see also Eugen Altmann, "Mein Leben in Deutschland vor und nach dem 30. Januar 1933," 33, Manuscript Collection "My Life in Germany Before and After January 30, 1933," Houghton Library, Harvard University, Cambridge Mass. I am restricting myself here to collective violence. But the number of individual attacks on Jews also increased in the postwar period; see, e.g., Ludwig Foerder,

"Antisemitismus und Justiz," *Jüdische Volkszeitung,* February 10, 1922, 3; "Hakenkreuz und Davidstern: An die Adresse der *Schlesischen Zeitung,*" *Jüdische Volkszeitung,* June 19, 1922, 1; "Entwischt—durch behördliche Verfügung," *Jüdische Volkszeitung,* July 7, 1922, 4.

32. Willy Cohn, Tagebücher, RP 88, vol. 21, entry for June 27, 1920, CAHJP, Jerusalem.

33. "Schuld und Schuldige," *Schlesische Zeitung,* no. 436, August 29, 1920.

34. "Die Drahtzieher der Breslauer Judenhetze," *Jüdische Volkszeitung,* August 3, 1920, 1.

35. "Unruhen in Schlesien," *Schlesische Zeitung,* July 22, 1923.

36. "Ordnung," *Schlesische Zeitung,* July 21, 1923.

37. Alfred Oehlke, "Das Breslauer Krawall," *Breslauer Zeitung,* no. 337, July 22, 1923, 1–2.

38. It was Horace Kallen, a Jew born in Silesia, who developed the concept of cultural pluralism. He emigrated to the United States and became one of the most prominent social philosophers of American pragmatism. See his *Cultural Pluralism and the American Idea: An Essay in Social Philosophy* (Philadelphia: University of Pennsylvania Press, 1956); see also Higham, "Ethnic Pluralism in Modern American Thought"; and Milton R. Konvitz, "Obituary: Horace Meyer Kallen," *American Jewish Yearbook* 75 (1975): 55–80.

39. Mark Silk, "Notes on the Judeo-Christian Tradition in America," *American Quarterly* 36 (1984): 65–85; the current debate in the United States and Canada about "multiculturalism" is also a confrontation over how far the canon of a Judeo-Christian tradition ought to be opened up; see, e.g., Lawrence W. Levine, *The Opening of the American Mind: Canons, Culture, and History* (Boston: Beacon Press, 1996); and George M. Frederickson, "America's Diversity in Comparative Perspective," *Journal of American History* 85 (1998): 859–75.

BIBLIOGRAPHY

Unpublished Sources

Archiwum Państwowe we Wrocławiu,
Wrocław (State and City Archives of Breslau).

Akta miasta Wrocławia. K 146: Staatssteuerrollen 18 (1876), 20 (1877–78), and 21 (1878–79).

Akta miasta Wrocławia. K 150: Klassensteuerrollen Stadt Breslau 1876 (35 vols.); vol. 19 is missing.

Akta miasta Wrocławia. K 151: Klassensteuerrollen Stadt Breslau 1881, vol. 19.

Akta miasta Wrocławia. K 156: Steuerrollen Stadt Breslau 1906 (160 vols.).

Protokollbücher der Stadtverordnetenversammlung. Akta miasta Wrocławia. H 120.

AMW, III, 2189
AMW, III, 2462
AMW, III, 2471
AMW, III, 3105
AMW, III, 3594
AMW, III, 3676

AMW, III, 4991

AMW III 7363 ("Breslauer Kindergarten-Verein: Rechenschaftsbericht für die Geschäftsjahre 1915/16 und 1916/17")
AMW, III, 7478
AMW, III, 7479
AMW, III, 7480
AMW, III, 7481
AMW, III, 7482

AMW, III, 7483
AMW, III, 7484

AMW, III, 8705
AMW, III, 8706

AMW, III, 21933
AMW, III, 21934
AMW, III, 26365

   Polizei-Präsidium Breslau (PPB)

PPB 67
PPB 75
PPB 115
PPB 134
PPB 621
PPB 622
PPB 634
PPB 636
PPB 639–651

Regierung Breslau, Justizbüro 7237 Breslauer Handlungsdiener Institut 1834–1926.
Regierung Breslau, Justizbüro 7259 Hermann Auerbach'sche Stiftung für Waisenkinder ohne Unterschied der Religion.

Oberpräsidium Breslau, 17/II, 3936, Personalakte Robert Gregor Depène.
Oberpräsidium Breslau, 342.
Oberpräsidum Breslau, 660–664.

APW, Urząd stanu cywilnego, Wrocław. Hauptregister der Breslauer Standesämter I–II, 1874–1894.

Urząd stanu cywilnego, Wrocław

Hauptregister der Breslauer Standesämter I–IV, 1905–1920.
Geburtsregister, Standesamt Breslau III, 1926; 1927.

Biblioteka Uniwersytecka we Wrocławiu, Wrocław

BUW Akc. 1968, 261 and 262.

Żydowski Instytut Historicyczny w Polsce, Warsaw

Bestand 5, Gmina żydowska we Wrocławiu, Wahlliste der jüdischen Gemeinde für 1876.

Central Archives for the History of the Jewish People, Jerusalem

Cohn, Willy. Tagebücher. CAHJP, RP 88.

"Streit zwischen jüdischen und christlichen Ärzten in Breslau, 1923–1925." CAHJP, Inv. 1434, 5.

Central Zionist Archives, Jerusalem

"Flugblatt zugunsten der galizischen Juden, Breslau Juni 1900." NL Schachtel, A 102, 10.

Houghton Library, Harvard University, Cambridge Mass.,
Manuscript Collection "My Life in Germany
Before and After January 30, 1933"

Altmann, Eugen. "Mein Leben in Deutschland vor und nach dem 30. Januar 1933."

Kretschmer, Julian. "Mein Leben in Deutschland vor und nach 1933."

Marcus, Ernst. "Mein Leben in Deutschland vor und nach 1933."

Polke, Max Moses. "Mein Leben in Deutschland vor und nach dem 30. Jan. 1933."

Archives of the Leo Baeck Institute, New York

Auerbach, Anna. "Die Chronik der Familie Silbergleit." ME 600.

Bernstein, Arnold. Erinnerungen, 1888–1964. ME 55.

Heilberg, Adolf. Memoiren, 1858–1936. ME 257a.

Riesenfeld, Adolf. Tagebücher und Erinnerungen. A 16/3.

Schaeffer, Charlotte. "Bilder aus meiner Vergangenheit, 1865–1890." ME 562.

Bibliothek für Bildungsgeschichtliche Forschung des Deutschen Instituts
für Internationale Pädagogische Forschung in Berlin

Jahresschulberichte aller höheren Schulen Breslau, 1870–1910.

Personalbogen Robert Gregor Depène.

Personalbogen Hermann Adolph Fechner.

Geheimes Staatsarchiv, Preußischer Kulturbesitz, Berlin-Dahlem

X. Provinz Brandenburg Rep. 16A, NL Forckenbeck (Akz. 49/1977).

I. HA Rep 76 VI, Sektion 8: "Der Gymnasiallehrer Dr. Elsner und der Lehrer an der höheren Bürgerschule zu Breslau Dr. Stein, die gegen dieselben eingeleitete Untersuchung wegen Theilnahme an Aufruhr erregenden Bewegungen und staatsgefährlichen Umtrieben überhaupt 1849–1860."

Periodicals

Allgemeine Zeitung des Judenthums
Breslauer Communal-Zeitung

Breslauer General-Anzeiger
Breslauer Gerichts-Zeitung
Breslauer Hausblätter
Breslauer Jüdisches Gemeindeblatt
Breslauer Neueste Nachrichten
Breslauer Sonntagsblatt: Beilage der "Schlesischen Volkszeitung"
Breslauer Sonntagsblatt: Illustrierte Schlesische Wochenschrift
Breslauer Zeitung
CV-Zeitung: Blätter für Deutschtum und Judentum
Deutsche Ostwacht
Deutscher Volksfreund
Die Freie Meinung
Im Deutschen Reich
Der Israelit
Israelitische Wochenschrift
Jüdisch-liberale Zeitung
Jüdisches Volksblatt: Unabhängiges Organ für die Interessen von Gemeinde, Schule und Haus
Jüdische Volkszeitung: Unabhängiges Organ für die Interessen von Gemeinde, Schule und Haus
Jüdische Zeitung für Ostdeutschland
Katholisches Schulblatt: Organ der Königlichen katholischen Schullehrerseminare zur Förderung des Elementar-Schulwesens und religiös-sittlicher Erziehung.
Kommunale Praxis
Mitteilungen aus dem Verein zur Abwehr des Antisemitismus
Mittheilungen des Deutsch-Israelitischen Gemeindebundes
Schlesische Arbeiter-Zeitung
Schlesisches Kirchenblatt: Eine Zeitschrift für Katholiken aller Stände
Schlesisches Morgenblatt
Schlesische Morgen-Zeitung
Schlesische Presse
Schlesisches Protestantenblatt
Schlesische Schulzeitung
Schlesische Tagespost
Schlesische Volkszeitung
Schlesische Zeitung
Der Volksstaat: Wochenschrift für die Interessen der "Deutschen Demokratischen Partei" in Schlesien

Primary Sources

7. Jahresbericht des Humboldt-Vereins für Volksbildung in Breslau für das Vereinsjahr 1875–1876. Breslau: n.p., 1876. (BUW, GŚL Yv 608)

8. Bericht der Sektion Breslau des Deutschen und Österreichischen Alpenvereins, 28: Vereinsjahr 1905. Breslau: Stenzel, 1906

8. Jahresbericht des Humboldt-Vereins für Volksbildung für das Vereinsjahr 1876-1877. Breslau: n.p., 1877. (BUW, GŚŁ Yv 608)

9. Bericht der Sektion Breslau des Deutschen und Österreichischen Alpenvereins, 29: Vereinsjahr 1906. Breslau: Stenzel, 1907.

12. Bericht der Sektion Breslau des Deutschen und Österreichischen Alpenvereins, 32: Vereinsjahr 1909. Breslau: Stenzel, 1909.

14. Jahresbericht des evangelischen Local-Vereins zur Fürsorge für entlassene Strafgefangene zu Breslau pro 1895. Breslau: n.p., 1895.

15. Bericht des Vereins für die Besserung der Strafgefangenen in der Provinz Schlesien. Breslau: n.p., 1896. (APW, AMW, III, 7577)

24. Jahresbericht des Humboldt-Vereins für Volksbildung in Breslau für das Vereinsjahr 1892-1893. Breslau: n.p., 1893. (BUW, GŚŁ Yv 608)

37. Jahresbericht des Humboldt-Vereins für Volksbildung für das Vereinsjahr 1905-06. Breslau: n.p., 1906. (BUW, GŚŁ Yv 608)

62. Jahresbericht des Frauen-Vereins zur Speisung und Bekleidung der Armen (Suppen-Anstalten) in Breslau 1893/1894. Breslau: n.p., 1894. (APW, AMW, III, 7434)

70. Jahresbericht des Frauen-Vereins zur Speisung und Bekleidung der Armen (Suppen-Anstalten) in Breslau 1902. Breslau: n.p., 1902. (APW, AMW, III, 7435)

Adreß- und Geschäfts-Handbuch der königlichen Haupt- und Residenzstadt Breslau für das Jahr 1876. Edited by Ernst Bruch. Breslau: Morgenstern, 1876.

Adreß- und Geschäfts-Handbuch der königlichen Haupt- und Residenzstadt Breslau für das Jahr 1877. Breslau: Morgenstern, 1877.

Adreß- und Geschäfts-Handbuch der königlichen Haupt- und Residenzstadt Breslau für das Jahr 1878. Breslau: Morgenstern, 1878.

Alexander, Carl. *Denkschrift, betreffend die Industrie-Schule für israelitische Mädchen zu Breslau.* Breslau: n.p., 1884.

Anonymous. *Die Weisheit der Braminen in der confessionslosen Schule: Ungehaltene Rede eines unabhängigen Freidenkers.* 2nd ed. Breslau: n.p., 1869.

Antisemitisches Jahrbuch für 1898. Berlin: Giese, 1898.

Aus dem Leben der Section Breslau des Deutschen und Österreichischen Alpenvereins den Sectionsgenossen überreicht zum X. Stiftungsfest am 28. Januar 1888. Breslau: Brehmer & Minuth, 1888.

Badt, Benno. *Erläuterungen zu den biblischen Geschichten für die israelitische Jugend in Schule und Haus.* Breslau: Wilhelm Koebner, 1890.

———. *Kinderbibel: Biblische Erzählungen für die israelitische Jugend.* 1890. 3rd ed. Breslau: Wilhelm Koebner, 1905.

Badt-Strauss, Bertha. "My World, and How It Crashed." *Menorah Journal* 39 (Spring 1951): 90-100.

Bericht der Section Breslau des Deutschen und Oesterreichischen Alpenvereins über das Jahr 1898. Breslau: Stenzel, 1899.

Bericht der Section Breslau des Deutschen und Oesterreichischen Alpenvereins über die ersten fünf Jahre ihres Bestehens (1878–1882). Breslau: Stenzel, 1883.

Bericht der Vereinigung Jüdischer Frauen zu Breslau (Kindergarten und Kinderhort) über die Jahre 1906–1908. Breslau: n.p., 1909.

Bericht des kaufmännischen Vereins zu Breslau für das Jahr 1882: Nebst Statut und Mitgliederverzeichnis. Breslau: n.p., 1883. (BUW, GŚL, Yn 234, 235)

Bericht über den Zustand der vereinigten sechs Kleinkinder-Bewahr-Anstalten zu Breslau für 1894/1895. Breslau: n.p., 1895. (BUW, GŚL, 26955 II)

"Bericht über die Thätigkeit des Schlesischen Geschichtsvereins in den Jahren 1887 und 1888." *Zeitschrift des Vereins für Geschichte und Altertum Schlesiens* 23 (1889): 330–36.

Bericht über die Thätigkeit des Vereins für Jüdische Geschichte und Litteratur (Breslau), 1903/1904. Breslau: n.p., 1904. (BUW, GŚL Yv 1516)

Bialek, Edward, Roman Polsakiewicz, and Marek Zybura, eds. *Gustav Freytag an Theodor Molinari und die Seinen: Bislang unbekannte Briefe aus den Beständen der Universitätsbibliothek Wrocław*. Frankfurt a. M.: Peter Lang, 1987.

Biberfeld, Carl, ed. *"Der Osten": Ein schlesischer Jubiläumsalmanach herausgegeben anläßlich des 50 jährigen Jubiläums der "Breslauer Dichterschule."* Breslau: Koebner, 1909.

———. *Pallas und Germania: Festspiel zum 8. allgemeinen deutschen Turnfest*. Breslau: Festausschreibung des VIII. deutschen Turnfestes, 1894.

Boehlich, Walter. Interview. In *Über Juden in Deutschland*, by Gerd Mattenklott, 174–75. Frankfurt a. M.: Jüdischer Verlag, 1992.

Bohn, Emil. *Festschrift zur Feier des 25 jährigen Bestehens des Breslauer Orchester-Vereins*. Breslau: Hainauer, 1887.

———. *Bohn'scher Gesangsverein: Hundert historische Concerte in Breslau, 1881–1905*. Breslau: Hainauer, 1905.

Born, Max. *Mein Leben*. Munich: Nymphenburger Verlagshandlung, 1975.

Brann, Marcus. "Geschichte der Anstalt während des ersten Jahrhunderts ihres Bestehens." In *100. Jahresbericht über die Industrie-Schule für israelitische Mädchen*, 3–23. Breslau: Schueler, 1901.

Breslauer Köpfe: Begegnungen mit prominenten Breslauern. Breslau: Golland, 1927.

Breslauer Radfahrer-Verein "Wratislavia": Mitgliederverzeichnis Mai 1902. Breslau: n.p., 1902. (BUW, GŚL Yz 334)

Breslauer Statistik. Vols. 1–36. Breslau: Morgenstern, 1876–1920.

Breslau's Bauten sowie kunstgewerbliche und technische Anstalten. Edited by Architekten- und Ingenieurverein Breslau. Breslau: E. Trewendt, [1885].

Bruch, Ernst. "Zur Bevölkerungs-Statistik der Stadt Breslau." In *Adreß- und Geschäfts-Handbuch der königlichen Haupt- und Residenzstadt Breslau für das Jahr 1877*, 406–11. Breslau: Morgenstern, 1877.

———. "Zur socialen Statistik der Stadt Breslau." In *Adreß- und Geschäfts-Handbuch der königlichen Haupt- und Residenzstadt Breslau für das Jahr 1876*, 379–82. Breslau: Morgenstern, 1876.

Buchmann, Jakob. *Popularsymbolik, oder vergleichende Darstellung der Glaubensgegen-sätze zwischen Katholiken und Protestanten.* 2 vols. 3rd ed. Mainz: Kirchheim, Schott & Thielmann, 1850.

———. *Über und gegen den Jesuitismus.* Breslau: Gosohorsky, 1872.

Centralverein deutscher Staatsbürger jüdischen Glaubens: Mitglieder-Verzeichnis, 1897. Berlin: n.p., 1897.

Centralverein deutscher Staatsbürger jüdischen Glaubens: Mitglieder-Verzeichnis, 1905. Berlin: Hasenstein & Vögler, 1905.

Centralverein deutscher Staatsbürger jüdischen Glaubens: Mitglieder-Verzeichnis, 1908. Berlin: Hasenstein & Vögler, 1908.

Cohen, Hermann. *Deutschtum und Judentum, mit grundlegenden Betrachtungen über Staat und Internationalismus.* Ergänzt und mit einem kritischen Nachwort als Vorwort. 3rd ed. Gießen: A. Töpelmann, 1916.

Cohn, Hermann L. "Ueber sexuelle Belehrung der Schulkinder." *Allgemeine Medizinische Central-Zeitung* 73 (1904): 931–35, 961–64, 981–84, and 1002–4.

———. *Was kann die Schule gegen die Masturbation der Kinder thun? Referat erstattet auf dem 8. internationalen hygienischen Kongress Budapest.* Berlin: R. Schoetz, 1894.

Cohn, Willy. *Verwehte Spuren: Erinnerungen an das Breslauer Judentum vor seinem Unter-gang.* Edited by Norbert Conrads. Cologne: Bohlau, 1995.

Durieux, Tilla. *Meine ersten neunzig Jahre.* 3rd ed. Munich: Herbig, 1971.

———. *Eine Tür steht offen—Erinnerungen.* Berlin: Herbig, 1954.

"Einkommensstruktur der Frankfurter Juden 1900." *Zeitschrift für Demographie und Statistik der Juden* 1, no. 4 (1905): 12–13.

Elias, Norbert. *Über sich selbst.* Frankfurt a. M.: Suhrkamp, 1990.

Engeli, Christian, and Wolfgang Haus, eds. *Quellen zum modernen Gemeindeverfas-sungsrecht in Deutschland.* Stuttgart: Kohlhammer, 1975.

Fechner, Hermann A. *Ueber den Gerechtigkeitsbegriff des Aristoteles: Ein Beitrag zur Geschichte der alten Philosophie.* PhD diss., Universität Leipzig. Leipzig: Matthes, 1855.

Festschrift für das VIII. deutsche Turnfest zu Breslau 1894. Breslau: Grass, Barth & Co., 1894.

Festschrift zur Feier des 25jährigen Bestehens der Ortsgruppe Breslau des Riesengebirgs-Vereins. Breslau: Woywod, 1906.

Festschrift zur Feier des 25 jährigen Bestehens der Sektion Breslau des Deutschen und Österreichischem Alpenvereins. Breslau: Selbstverlag der Sektion, 1902.

Festschrift zur hundertjährigen Stiftungs-Feier der Gesellschaft der Freunde in Breslau. Im Auftrage der Direktion verfaßt von den Schriftführern. Breslau: n.p., 1921.

Fontane, Theodor. "Adel und Judenthum in der Berliner Gesellschaft." *Jahrbuch der deutschen Schillergesellschaft* 30 (1986): 34, 37 39, and 59–66.

———. *Frau Jenny Treibel.* In *Werke,* edited by Kurt Schreinert, vol. 1. Munich: Nymphenburger Verlag, 1968.

Freund, Jakob. *Biblische Gedichte.* Breslau: Schletter, 1861.

———. *Confirmationsreden nebst Anhang: Glaubensbekenntnis und Reden für die Confirmanden.* Breslau: Schletter, 1870; reprint, Breslau: J. B. Brandeis, 1908.

———. *Festkränze: Neue Gelegenheitsgedichte für Kinder.* Breslau: Schletter, 1866.

———. *Haman oder die Rechnung ohne Wirth: Posse mit Gesang in fünf Akten.* Breslau: C. H. Storch, 1875.

———. *Hanna: Gebets- und Andachtsbuch für israelitische Mädchen und Frauen.* 2nd ed. Breslau: Skutsch, 1874. Reprinted as *Hanna: Gebets- und Andachtsbuch für israelitische Frauen und Mädchen; Mit Beiträgen von Abraham Geiger, Moritz Güdemann, Manuel Joel und Moritz Abraham Levy,* 6th ed (Breslau: Verlag von Wilhelm Koebner, 1890).

Freund, Leopold. *Eine Lebensgeschichte.* 2nd ed. Breslau: Freund's Verlagshandlung, 1878.

[Freund, Wilhelm]. *Die Anstellung israelitischer Lehrer an Preußischen Gymnasien und Realschulen: Ein Wort zur Aufhellung der Sachlage von einem praktischen Fachmann.* Berlin: J. Springer, 1860.

Freymark, Hermann. *Die Handelskammer Breslau, 1849–1924: Festschrift der Industrie- u. Handelskammer Breslau.* Breslau: Schatzky, 1924.

Freytag, Gustav. "Die Juden Breslaus." *Grenzboten* 30 (1849). Reprinted in *Vermischte Aufsätze* 2:339–47 (Leipzig: Hirzel, 1903).

Gärtner, Gustav, ed. *Festschrift herausgegeben aus Anlass der Feier des 25 jährigen Bestehens des Humboldtvereins für Volksbildung zu Breslau am 28. October 1894.* Breslau: Preuss & Jünger, 1894.

Geiger, Abraham. "Die Schulfrage im preußischen Abgeordnetenhaus." *Jüdische Zeitung für Wissenschaft und Leben* 7 (1869): 216–19.

Gesellschaft der Freunde: Einladung zur diesjährigen ordentlichen Generalversammlung am 21. Februar 1904. Breslau: n.p., 1904. (BUW, GŚL Yz 85)

Gesellschaft der Freunde: Verwaltungsbericht pro 1897/1898 und 1898/1899. Breslau: n.p., 1899. (BUW, GŚL Yz 85)

Gesellschaft "Eintracht": Mitgliederverzeichnis, 1880. Breslau: n.p., 1880. (BUW, GŚL Yz 66)

Grimm, Jacob. *Deutsche Grammatik.* Vol. 1. Göttingen: Dieterich, 1819.

Gründungsaufruf des Humboldt-Vereins für Volksbildung, Breslau, 21. Juli 1869. Breslau: Humboldt-Verein für Volksbildung, 1869. (BUW, GŚL Yv 605)

Grundgesetz des Humboldt-Vereins für Volksbildung, Breslau, 16. April 1888. Breslau: Humboldt-Verein für Volksbildung, 1888. (BUW, GŚL Yv 605)

Hainauer, Julius. *Die Gesellschaft der Freunde in Breslau: Erinnerungsblätter für das 50. Stiftungsfest.* Breslau: Hainauer, 1871.

Heilberg, Adolf. "Die Idee des allgemeinen Völkerfriedens." In *24. Jahresbericht des Humboldt-Vereins für Volksbildung in Breslau für das Vereinsjahr 1892–1893,* 3–16. Breslau: n.p., 1893. Reprinted in *Jüdisches Leben in Deutschland,* edited by Monika Richarz, vol. 2, *Selbstzeugnisse zur Sozialgeschichte des Kaiserreichs,* 289–96 (Stuttgart: Deutsche Verlagsanstalt, 1979).

Heilborn, Ernst. "Die 'neue' Frau." *Die Frau* 7 (1899–1900): 5–11.

Heile, Wilhelm. *Stammesfreiheit im Einheitsstaat.* Berlin: Fortschritt, 1919.

Hoffmann, Ruth. *Meine Freunde aus Davids Geschlecht.* Berlin: Chronos, 1955.

Dem Humboldt-Verein für Volksbildung zu seinem Sommerausflug nach Zedlitz, Breslau, den 17. Juni 1882. Breslau: n.p., 1882. (BUW, GŚL Yv 617)

Jadassohn, Josef. "Albert Neisser." In *Schlesische Lebensbilder,* vol. 1 (Breslau: W. G. Korn, 1922), 111–15.

Jahresbericht der Handelskammer Breslau für das Jahr 1891. Breslau: Handelskammer, 1892.

Jahresbericht der Handelskammer Breslau für das Jahr 1894. Breslau: Handelskammer, 1895.

Jahresbericht der Handelskammer Breslau für das Jahr 1910. Breslau: Handelskammer, 1911.

Jahresbericht der Ortsgruppe Breslau des Jüdischen Frauenbundes 1911–12. Breslau: n.p., n.d. (BUW, GŚL Yp 235)

Jahresbericht der städtischen höheren Töchterschule am Ritterplatz zu Breslau 1871. Breslau: n.p., 1871. (BUW, GŚL Yu 1140 u. 1141)

Jahresbericht des Kranken-Unterstützungs-Vereins "Tomche Cholim" pro 1885. Breslau: n.p., 1885. (BUW, GŚL 28231 III)

Jahresbericht des Kranken-Unterstützungs-Vereins "Tomche Cholim" pro 1897. Breslau: n.p., 1897. (BUW, GŚL 28231 III)

Jahresbericht des städtischen Johannes-Gymnasiums für das Schuljahr von Ostern 1883 bis Ostern 1884. Edited by C. F. W. Müller. Breslau: Grass, Barth & Co., 1884.

Jahresbericht des städtischen Johannes-Gymnasiums zu Breslau, 1909/1910. Breslau: Grass, Barth & Co., 1910.

Joël, Manuel. *Festpredigten.* Edited by Adolf Eckstein and Bernhard Ziemlich. Vol. 1. Breslau: Schlesische Buckdruck, Kunst- und Verlags-Anstalt, 1892.

Jordan, Sylvester. "Gastrecht (Fremdenrecht)." In *Das Staats-Lexikon,* edited by Carl von Rotteck and Carl Welcker, 5:360–77. Altona: Hammerich, 1847.

Joseph, Max. "Stammesgemeinschaft." In *Jüdisches Lexikon,* vol. 4, pt. 2, 628–29. Berlin: Jüdischer Verlag, 1930.

"Die Juden im Verhältnis zur christlichen Schule und zum christlichen Staate." *Evangelische Kirchen-Zeitung* 68 (1861): 169–73, 177–79, and 203–8.

Die Judenfrage: Verhandlungen des preußischen Abgeordnetenhauses über die Interpellation des Abgeordneten Dr. Hänel am 20. und 22. November 1880. Berlin: Moeser, 1880.

Die jüdischen Gefallenen des deutschen Heeres, der deutschen Marine und der deutschen Schutztruppen, 1914–1918: Ein Gedenkbuch. Edited by Reichsbund Jüdischer Frontsoldaten. 2nd ed. Berlin: Der Schild, 1932.

Das Kabinett Fehrenbach (25. Juni 1920 bis 4. Mai 1921): Akten der Reichskanzlei. Edited by Peter Wulf. Boppard am Rhein: H. Boldt, 1972.

Das Kabinett Müller I (27. März bis 21. Juni 1920): Akten der Reichskanzlei. Edited by Martin Vogt. Boppard: Boldt, 1971.

Das Kabinett Müller II. Edited by Martin Vogt. Vol. 1. Boppard: Boldt, 1970.

Kerr, Alfred. "Lebenslauf." In *Für Alfred Kerr: Ein Buch der Freundschaft*, edited by Joseph Chapiro, 157–82. Berlin: Fischer, 1928.

Ketteler, Wilhelm Emanuel Freiherr von, Bishop of Mainz. *Freiheit, Autorität und Kirche*. Mainz: Kirchheim, 1862.

Kirchliches Jahrbuch für die evangelischen Landeskirchen Deutschlands 56 (1929): 90.

Kleines Statistisches Taschenbuch für die Stadt Breslau. Edited by Statistisches Amt Breslau. Breslau: Statistisches Amt, 1928.

Kohut, Adolph. *Alexander von Humboldt und das Judenthum*. Leipzig: Pardubitz, 1871.

Komm ich zeige Dir Breslau: Ein zuverlässiger Führer für Breslauer und Fremde. Pt. 1. Breslau: Kern, 1926.

Krojanker, Gustav, ed. *Juden in der deutschen Literatur: Essays über zeitgenössische Schriftsteller*. Berlin: Welt-Verlag, 1922.

Krüger, Helmut. *Der halbe Stern: Leben als deutsch-jüdischer "Mischling" im Dritten Reich*. Berlin: Metropol, 1993.

Landau, Lola. "Die Kameradschaftsehe." *Die Tat* 20 (February 11, 1929): 831–35. Translated as "The Companionate Marriage," in *The Weimar Republic Sourcebook*, edited by Anton Kaes, Martin Jay, and Edward Dimendberg, 702–3 (Berkeley: University of California Press, 1994).

———. *Vor dem Vergessen: Meine drei Leben*. Berlin: Ullstein, 1987.

Landauer, Gustav. "Ostjuden und Deutsches Reich." *Der Jude* 1 (1916/1917): 433–39.

Laqueur, Walter. *Thursday's Child Has Far to Go: A Memoir of the Journeying Years*. New York: Charles Scribner's Sons, 1992.

Lazarus, Moritz. *Was heißt national? Ein Vortrag von Prof. Dr. M. Lazarus*. Forward by Isid. Levy. Berlin: Philo Verlag, 1925.

Levy, Moritz Abraham. *Biblische Geschichte nach dem Worte der heiligen Schrift der israelitischen Jugend erzählt*. Edited by Benno Badt. 6th rev. ed. Breslau: Koebner, 1881.

Lewkowitz, Julius. "Familie, Familienleben." In *Jüdisches Lexikon*, edited by Georg Herlitz and Bruno Kirschner, 2:585–86. Berlin: Jüdischer Verlag, 1927.

Liebermann von Sonnenberg, Max. "Rede gehalten in der Volks-Versammlung des Reform-Vereins am 16. Oktober 1882 im großen Saale des 'Russischen Kaisers' zu Breslau." In *Beiträge zur Geschichte der antisemitischen Bewegung vom Jahre 1880–1885*, edited by Max Liebermann von Sonnenberg, 105–22. Berlin: privately published, 1885.

Ludwig, Emil. "Vita und Persönlichkeit." In *Hermann Cohn in Memoriam*, edited by Ludwig Laqueur, Leonhard Weber, and Emil Ludwig, 1–37. Breslau: Wohlfarth, 1908.

Maass, Martin. *Die Mischehe, das einzig wirksame Mittel einer dauernden Vereinigung zwischen der jüdischen und christlichen Bevölkerung Deutschlands*. Löbau: Skrzeczek, 1881.

————. *Die Soziale Stellung der Juden in Deutschland und das Civil-Ehegesetz.* Löbau: Skrzeczek, 1876.

Maimon, Arye. *Wanderungen und Wandlungen: Die Geschichte meines Lebens.* Trier: Arye Maimon-Institut für Geschichte der Juden, 1998.

Makower, Felix. "Ist Art. 14 der preußischen Verfassung anwendbar auf die im Schulgesetzentwurf geregelten Fragen?" *Deutsche Juristenzeitung* 11 (1906): 195–98.

Masner, Karl. "Toni Neisser." In *Schlesische Lebensbilder,* 1:115–19. Breslau: W. G. Korn, 1922.

"Max von Forckenbeck: Präsident des preußischen Abgeordnetenhauses, Oberbürgermeister von Breslau." *Rübezahl* 12 (1873): 167–69.

Meister, Ferdinand. *Die ersten 25 Jahre des wissenschaftlichen Vereins in Breslau, 1852–1877.* Breslau: n.p., 1877.

Mitgliederlisten der Abtheilung Breslau der Deutschen Kolonial-Gesellschaft, 1896. Breslau: n.p., 1896. (BUW, GŚL Ym 33)

Mitglieder-Verzeichnis der . . . St. Johannisloge "Hermann zur Beständigkeit" im Orient Breslau, 1907. Breslau: n.p., 1907.

Mitglieder-Verzeichnis der Section Breslau des Riesengebirgs-Vereins am Ende des Jahres 1883. Breslau: n.p., 1883. (BUW, GŚL Yz 336)

Mitglieder-Verzeichnis der Section Breslau des Riesengebirgs-Vereins am Ende des Jahres 1886. Breslau: n.p., 1886. (BUW, GŚL Yz 336)

Mitglieder-Verzeichnis der Section Breslau des Riesengebirgs-Vereins am Ende des Jahres 1908. Breslau: n.p., 1908. (BUW, GŚL Yz 336)

Mitglieder-Verzeichnis des Breslauer Bürgerschützen-Corps am 1. Januar 1888. Breslau: n.p., 1888. (BUW, GŚL Yh 523)

Mitglieder-Verzeichniss des Vereins für Velociped-Wettfahren in Breslau, 1894. Breslau: n.p., 1894. (BUW, GŚL 29261 III)

"Mitglieder-Verzeichnis für 1886/87." *Zeitschrift des Vereins für Geschichte und Alter-tum Schlesiens* 21 (1887): 448–63.

"Mitglieder-Verzeichnis für 1901." *Zeitschrift des Vereins für Geschichte und Altertum Schlesiens* 35 (1901): 390–414.

Mitgliederverzeichnis 1905: Johannis-Loge "Settegast zur deutschen Treue"; Or. Breslau, gestiftet am 16. Februar 1901. Breslau: n.p., 1905.

Mommsen, Theodor. "Auch ein Wort über unser Judenthum." In *Der Berliner Antisemitismusstreit,* edited by Walter Boehlich, 212–26. Frankfurt a. M.: Insel, 1965.

Namen-Verzeichnis der Mitglieder der Israelitischen Kranken- und Verpflegungs-Anstalt und Beerdigungs-Gesellschaft zu Breslau, 20. April 1906. Breslau: n.p., 1906.

Namen-Verzeichnis der Mitglieder der Israelitischen Kranken- und Verpflegungs-Anstalt und Beerdigungs-Gesellschaft zu Breslau, 5. Mai 1909. Breslau: n.p., 1909.

Namen-Verzeichniß sämtlicher beitragender Mitglieder der Israelitischen Kranken- und Verpflegungs-Anstalt und Beerdigungsgesellschaft. Breslau: n.p., 1867.

Naumann, Friedrich. "Die Leidensgeschichte des deutschen Liberalismus."

1908. In *Werke*, edited by Theodor Schieder, 4:291 316. Cologne: Westdeutscher Verlag, 1964.

———. "Liberalismus und Protestantismus: Referat gehalten auf dem 24.
Deutschen Protestantentag in Bremen am 22. September 1909." In *Werke*,
edited by Theodor Schieder, 1:773–801. Opladen: Westdeutscher Verlag,
1960.

Neues Adreßbuch für Breslau und Umgebung: Unter Benutzung amtlicher Quellen. Breslau:
A. Scherl, 1906.

Neugebauer, Julius. "Der Zwinger und die kaufmännische Zwingerschützenbrüderschaft nebst einer historischen Einleitung über die ehemalige Bürgermiliz und die Bürgerschützen-Brüderschaft." *Zeitschrift des Vereins für Geschichte und Altertum Schlesiens* 13 (1876): supplement, 1–94.

Pax, Wolfgang. "Bist Du auch ein Johanneer? Erinnerungen an die 20er Jahre."
Mitteilungen des Verbandes ehemaliger Breslauer und Schlesier in Israel 41 (1977): 8–9.

Philippsthal, Herbert. "Die jüdische Bevölkerung Breslaus." *Breslauer Jüdisches
Gemeindeblatt* 8 (1931): 52, 67–68, 98–99.

"Preisbewerbung für Entwürfe zu einem Gesellschaftshaus des Vereins christlicher Kaufleute in Breslau." *Deutsche Bauzeitung* 22 (1888): 353–54.

Preuß, Hugo. "Die Bekenntnis des Kultusministers und die Konfessionalität
der Berliner Schulen." *Die Nation* 16, no. 28 (8 April 1899): 396–398.

———. *Die Maßregelung jüdischer Lehrerinnen in den Berliner Gemeindeschulen*. Berlin:
Cronbach, 1898.

Preußische Statistik. Vols. 5–6. Berlin: Landesamt, 1864.

*Programm des städtischen Johannes-Gymnasiums zu Breslau für das Schuljahr von Ostern
1876 bis Ostern 1877*. Breslau: Grass, Barth & Co., 1877.

*Programm des städtischen Johannes-Gymnasiums zu Breslau für das Schuljahr von Ostern
1877 bis Ostern 1878*. Breslau: Grass, Barth & Co., 1878.

*Programm des städtischen Johannes-Gymnasiums zu Breslau für die Zeit von Michaelis 1872
bis Ostern 1874*. Edited by C. F. W. Müller. Breslau: Grass, Barth & Co., 1874.

Programm des städtischen Johannes-Gymnasiums zu Breslau Ostern 1891 bis 1892. Edited
by C. F. W. Müller. Breslau: Grass, Barth & Co., 1892.

Rathenau, Walther. "Staat und Judentum: Eine Polemik." 1911. In *Gesammelte
Schriften*, Vol. 1, *Zur Kritik der Zeit*, 185–207. Berlin: Fischer, 1918.

*Rechenschafts-Bericht der Israelitischen Kranken- und Verpflegungs-Anstalt und Beerdigungs-
gesellschaft zu Breslau . . . für die Jahre 1903, 1904 und 1905*. Breslau: n.p., 1906.

Rechenschaftsbericht der Gesellschaft der Brüder für das Jahr 1903. Breslau: n.p., 1904,
appendix.

*Rechenschaftsbericht des Israelitischen Mädchenheims zu Breslau für die Jahre 1905, 1906
und 1907*. Breslau: n.p., 1908.

Die Reichstags-Wahlen von 1867 bis 1883. Edited by Adolf Phillips. Berlin: L. Gerschel, 1883.

Reinkens, Joseph Hubert. *Briefe an seinen Bruder Wilhelm (1840–1873)*. Edited by
Hermann Josef Sieben. 3 vols. Cologne: Böhlau, 1979.

Riesengebirgs-Verein, Breslau: Mitglieder-Verzeichnis, 1908. (BUW, GŚL Yz 336)

Rive, Richard Robert. "Die Entwicklung der preußischen Städte seit dem Erlaß der Städteordnung von 1808." *Verhandlungen des sechsten allgemeinen preußischen Städtetages am 5. und 6. Oktober 1908 zu Königsberg* 6 (1908): 29–36.

Rosenthal, Ferdinand Rosenthal. *Festpredigten.* Berlin: Poppelauer, 1917.

Samter, Nathan. *Was thun? Ein Epilog zu den Judentaufen im 19. Jahrhundert.* Edited by Verein für jüdische Geschichte und Literatur. Breslau: Th. Schatzky, 1900.

Sandler, Aron. *Anthropologie und Zionismus: Ein Populärwissenschaftlicher Vortrag.* Brünn: Jüdischer Buch- und Kunstverlag, 1904.

Scheibert, Carl Gottfried. *Die Confessionalität der höheren Schulen.* Stettin: v. d. Nahmer, 1869.

Scheyer, Ernst. "Bildung in Breslau." In *Leben in Schlesien,* edited by Hubert Hupka, 163–76. Munich: Gräfe & Unzer, 1962.

"Schlesischer Verein für Luftschiffahrt: Mitgliederliste." N.d. [ca. 1908]. (BUW, GŚL Yz 315k)

Schopenhauer, Arthur. "Aphorismen zur Lebensweisheit." In *Sämtliche Werke in fünf Bänden,* edited by Hans Henning, vol. 4, *Parerga und Paralipomena: Erster Theil,* 371–580. 2nd ed. Leipzig: Insel, 1923.

Schreiber, Emanuel. *Die sociale Stellung der Juden: Offenes Sendschreiben an Herrn Dr. Maass-Breslau.* Königsberg: Prange, 1877.

Die sechs Vereinigten Kleinkinderbewahr-Anstalten zu Breslau im Jahre 1906/1907. Breslau: n.p., 1907. (BUW, GŚL 26955 II)

Sittenfeld, Ludwig. "Die Geschichte des Vereins 'Breslauer Dichterschule.'" In *"Der Osten": Ein schlesischer Jubiläumsalmanach herausgegeben anläßlich des 50 jährigen Jubiläums der "Breslauer Dichterschule,"* edited by Carl Biberfeld, 4–25. Breslau: Koebner, 1909.

Staatsarchiv Breslau—Wegweiser durch die Bestände bis zum Jahr 1945. Edited by Rościsław Żerelik and Andrzej Dereń. Munich: Oldenbourg, 1996.

Statistik des deutschen Reiches. Vol. 207. Edited by Kaiserlichen Statistischen Amt. Berlin: Puttkammer & Mühlbrecht, 1910.

Statistische Mittheilungen aus den deutschen evangelischen Landeskirchen, 1880–1897. Stuttgart: Klett, 1883–99.

Statistisches Jahrbuch der Stadt Breslau für 1922. Breslau: Morgenstern, 1922.

Statistisches Jahrbuch der Stadt Breslau für 1924. Breslau: Morgenstern, 1924.

Statut des Humboldt-Vereins für Volksbildung, Breslau, 21. Juli 1869. Breslau: n.p., 1869. (BUW, GŚL Yv 605)

Statut des Kranken-Unterstützungs-Vereins "Tomche Cholim" gegründet von und für Oesterreicher-Ungarn, ausgedehnt auf Israeliten jeder Staatsangehörigkeit zu Breslau, 1885. Breslau: n.p., 1885. (BUW, GŚL 28231 III)

Statut und Mitglieder-Verzeichniß der constitutionellen Bürger-Ressource (in Springer's Etablissement) pro 1869/70. Breslau: n.p., 1870.

Statuten, Bericht und Mitgliederverzeichnis des Vereins zur Verbreitung der Wissenschaft des

Judenthums, Gestiftet den 9. November 1861. Breslau: n.p., 1862. (BUW, GŚŁ Yv 1513)

Statuten der Gesellschaft der Freunde zu Breslau: Festgestellt in der General-Versammlung vom 6. April 1878. Breslau: n.p., 1878. (BUW, GŚŁ Yz 85)

Stenographische Berichte über die Verhandlungen des preussischen Abgeordnetenhauses, 1868–1869. Berlin: n.p., 1869.

Stier, Hubert. "Gesellschaftshaus für die Gesellschaft der Freunde zu Breslau." *Deutsche Bauzeitung* 11 (1877): 11–12.

Stille, Gustav. *Die deutsche Schule in Gefahr*. Berlin: Giese, 1899.

Theilhaber, Felix A. *Der Untergang der deutschen Juden: Ein volkswirtschaftliche Studie*. Munich: Reinhardt, 1911.

———. "Zum Preisausschreiben: 'Bringt das materielle und soziale Aufsteigen der Familien Gefahren in rassenhygienischer Beziehung?' Dargelegt an der Entwicklung der Judenheit von Berlin." *Archiv für Rassen- und Gesellschafts-biologie* 10 (1913): 67–92.

Toeplitz, Emil, and Paul Malberg, eds. *Kalender für das höhere Schulwesen Preußens*. Vol. 5. Breslau: Trewendt & Granier, 1898.

———. *Kalender für das höhere Schulwesen Preußens und einiger anderer deutscher Staaten*. Vol. 17. Breslau: Trewendt & Granier, 1910.

Treitschke, Heinrich von. *Politik: Vorlesungen gehalten an der Universität zu Berlin*. Vol. 2. Leipzig: Hirzel, 1900.

Verein "Tomche Cholim" zu Breslau: Einladung zur Generalversammlung am 29. Januar 1889. Breslau: n.p., 1889. (BUW, GŚŁ 28231 III)

Verein "Tomche Cholim" zu Breslau: Einladung zur Generalversammlung am 23. März 1907. Breslau: n.p., 1907. (BUW, GŚŁ 28231 III)

Verwaltungsberichte des Magistrats der königlichen Haupt- und Residenzstadt Breslau, 1880/83—1907/10. Breslau: Grass, Barth & Co., 1881–1911.

Verzeichnis der Mitglieder der Section Breslau des Deutschen und Österreichischen Alpenvereins, April 1888. Breslau: Breslauer Genossenschafts-Buchhandlung, 1888. (BUW, GŚŁ Yz 300, 303)

Verzeichnis der Mitglieder der Section Breslau des Deutschen und Österreichischen Alpenvereins, Februar 1889. Breslau: n.p., 1889. (BUW, GŚŁ Yz 300, 303)

Verzeichnis der resp. Mitglieder der kaufmännischen Zwinger- und Ressourcen-Gesellschaft, 1875. Breslau, n.p., 1875. (BUW, GŚŁ Yz 174)

Der Volksfreund: Kalender für 1879. Breslau: n.p., 1878.

Der Volksfreund: Kalender für 1881. Breslau: n.p., 1880.

Der Volksfreund: Kalender für 1882. Breslau: n.p., 1881.

Der Volksfreund: Kalender für 1882. Breslau: n.p., 1881.

Der Volksfreund: Kalender für 1883. Breslau: n.p., 1882.

Wahl-Campagne-Lied des Deutschen Reform-Vereins in Breslau: Zur Reichstagswahl am 27. Oktober 1881. Breslau: n.p., 1881. (BUW, GŚŁ Ym 38)

Warschauer, Malwin. *Im jüdischen Leben: Erinnerungen des Berliner Rabbiners Malwin Warschauer*. Berlin: Transit, 1995.

Wendt, Heinrich. *Das erste Jahrhundert der Kaufmännischen Zwinger- und Ressourcen-Gesellschaft zu Breslau, 1805–1905: Festschrift zur Jubelfeier.* Breslau: Kaufmännische Zwinger- und Ressourcen-Gesellschaft, 1905.

———. *Katalog der Druckschriften über die Stadt Breslau.* Breslau: Morgenstern, 1903.

———. *Katalog der Druckschriften über die Stadt Breslau: Nachtrag.* Breslau: Morgenstern, 1915.

———."Die Vereine nach Gruppen geordnet." In *Neues Adreßbuch für Breslau und Umgebung: Unter Benutzung amtlicher Quellen,* pt. 4, 68–77. Breslau: A. Scherl, 1906.

———. "Wissenschaftliche Vereine in Breslau." *Zeitschrift des Vereins für Geschichte und Altertum Schlesiens* 38 (1904): 71–109.

Wermuth, Adolf. *Ein Beamtenleben.* Berlin: Scherl, 1922.

Wick, Josef. *Aus meinem Leben.* Breslau: G. P. Aderholz, 1895.

Wininger, Salomon, ed. *Große Jüdische National-Biographie.* Vol. 2. Czernowitz: Buchdruckerei "Aria." 1927.

Secondary Sources

Abercron, Wilko von. *Eugen Spiro: Breslau 1874–New York 1972; Spiegel seines Jahrhunderts.* Alsbach: Drachen, 1990.

Abmeier, Hans-Ludwig. "Hans Lukaschek." In *Schlesische Lebensbilder,* 5:228–36. Breslau: W. G. Korn, 1968.

Abraham, Gary A. *Max Weber and the Jewish Question: A Study of the Social Outlook of His Sociology.* Urbana: University of Illinois Press, 1992.

Abrams, Lynn. "Concubinage, Cohabitation, and the Law: Class and Gender Relations in Nineteenth-Century Germany." *Gender and History* 5 (1993): 81–100.

Adamy, Kurt. "Ehrenbürger Potsdams in der Kaiserzeit." In *Potsdam: Märkische Kleinstadt—europäische Residenz,* edited by Peter-Michael Hahn, Kristina Hübener, and Julius H. Schoeps, 237–54. Berlin: Akademie-Verlag, 1995.

Adelson, Jozef. "The Expulsion of Jews with Polish Citizenship from Bavaria in 1923." *POLIN: Studies in Polish Jewry* 5 (1990): 57–73.

Albisetti, James C. "Education." In *Imperial Germany: A Historiographical Companion,* edited by Roger Chickering, 244–71. Westport, Conn.: Greenwood, 1996.

———. *Schooling German Girls and Women: Secondary and Higher Education in the Nineteenth Century.* Princeton, N.J.: Princeton University Press, 1988.

Albisetti, James C., and Peter Lundgreen. "Höhere Knabenschulen." In *Handbuch der deutschen Bildungsgeschichte,* edited by Christa Berg, vol. 4, *1870–1918: Von der Reichsgründung bis zum Ende des Ersten Weltkriegs,* 228–78. Munich: C. H. Beck, 1991.

Altgeld, Wolfgang. *Katholizismus, Protestantismus, Judentum: Über religiös begründete Gegensätze und nationalreligiöse Ideen in der Geschichte des deutschen Nationalismus.* Mainz: Matthias-Grünewald-Verlag, 1992.

Anderson, Margaret L. *Windthorst: A Political Biography*. Oxford: Clarendon Press, 1981.

Angress, Werner T. "The German Army's 'Judenzählung' of 1916: Genesis—Consequences—Significance." *Year Book of the Leo Baeck Institute* 23 (1978): 117–37.

———. "Juden im politischen Leben der Revolutionszeit." In *Deutsches Judentum in Krieg und Revolution, 1916–1923*, edited by Werner E. Mosse and Arnold Paucker, 137–315. Tübingen: Mohr Siebeck, 1971.

———. "Prussia's Army and the Jewish Reserve Officer Controversy before World War I." *Year Book of the Leo Baeck Institute* 17 (1972): 19–42.

Anschütz, Gerhard. *Die Verfassung des Deutschen Reichs vom 11. August 1919*. 14th ed. Berlin: Hermann Gentner Verlag, 1932.

Apelt, Willibalt. *Geschichte der Weimarer Verfassung*. Munich: Biederstein, 1946.

Arendt, Hannah. *The Origins of Totalitarianism*. New York: Harcourt, 1951.

Aschheim, Steven E. "Between Rationality and Irrationalism: George L. Mosse, the Holocaust, and European Cultural History." *Simon Wiesenthal Center Annual* 5 (1988): 187–202.

———. *Brothers and Strangers: The East European Jew in German and German-Jewish Consciousness, 1800–1923*. Madison: University of Wisconsin Press, 1982.

———. "German History and German Jewry: Boundaries, Junctions, and Interdependence." *Year Book of the Leo Baeck Institute* 43 (1998): 315–22.

———. "'The Jew Within': The Myth of 'Judaization' in Germany." In *The Jewish Response to German Culture: From the Enlightenment to the Second World War*, edited by Jehuda Reinharz and Walter Schatzberg, 212–41. Hanover, N.H.: University Press of New England, 1985.

Augustine, Delores L. *Patricians and Parvenus: Wealth and High Society in Wilhelmine Germany*. Oxford: Berg, 1994.

"Ausländer, ausländische Arbeiter." In *Handwörterbuch der Preußischen Verwaltung*, edited by Rudolf von Bitter, 1:157–62. 2nd ed. Leipzig: Roßberg, 1911.

"Ausweisungen." In *Handwörterbuch der Preußischen Verwaltung*, edited by Rudolf von Bitter, 1:173–75. 2nd ed. Leipzig: Roßberg, 1911.

Bach, Hans I. *Jacob Bernays: Ein Beitrag zur Emanzipationsgeschichte der Juden und zur Geschichte des deutschen Geistes im 19. Jahrhundert*. Tübingen: Mohr Siebeck, 1974.

Bachem, Karl. "Heimat und Heimatsrecht." In *Staatslexikon*, 2:1210–18. 3rd ed. Leipzig: Hirzel, 1909.

Bacht, Heinrich, SJ. *Die Tragödie einer Freundschaft: Fürstbischof Heinrich Förster und Professor Joseph Hubert Reinkens*. Cologne: Böhlau, 1985.

Bade, Klaus J. "'Kulturkampf' auf dem Arbeitsmarkt: Bismarcks 'Polenpolitik,' 1885–1890." In *Innenpolitische Probleme des Bismarckreiches*, edited by Otto Pflanze, 121–42. Munich: Oldenburg, 1983.

Bade, Klaus J., Leonie Herwartz-Emden, and Hans-Joachim Wenzel, eds. *Institut für Migrationsforschung und Interkulturelle Studien (IMIS): Bericht 1991–1997*. Osnabrück: Universitätsverlag Rasch, 1998.

Balibar, Etienne. "Ambiguous Universality." *Differences* 7, no. 1 (1995): 48–74.

———. "Grenzen und Gewalten: Asyl, Einwanderung, Illegalität und Sozialkontrolle des Staates." *Lettre International* 2, no. 37 (Summer 1997): 7–8.

Banks, Marcus. *Ethnicity: Anthropological Constructions*. London: Routledge, 1996.

Barkai, Avraham. "Die Juden als sozioökonomische Minderheitsgruppe in der Weimarer Republik." In *Juden in der Weimarer Republik: Skizzen und Porträts*, edited by Walter Grab and Julius H. Schoeps, 330–46. Stuttgart: Burg-Verlag, 1986.

———. *Jüdische Minderheit und Industrialisierung: Demographie, Berufe und Einkommen der Juden in Westdeutschland, 1850–1914*. Tübingen: Mohr Siebeck, 1988.

Barkan, Elliot R. "Race, Religion, and Nationality in American Society: A Model of Ethnicity from Contact to Assimilation." *Journal of American Ethnic History* 14 (1995): 38–75.

Barth, Fredrick. Introduction to *Ethnic Groups and Boundaries: The Social Organization of Cultural Difference*, edited by Fredrick Barth, 9–38. Bergen: Universitets Forlaget, 1969; reprint, Long Grove, Ill.: Waveland Press, 1998.

Bauman, Zygmunt. *Modernity and Ambivalence*. Cambridge: Polity Press, 1991.

Baumann, Ulrich. *Zerstörte Nachbarschaften: Christen und Juden in badischen Landgemeinden, 1862–1940*. Hamburg: Dölling & Galitz, 2000.

Baumeister, Martin. *Parität und katholische Inferiorität: Untersuchungen zur Stellung des Katholizismus im Deutschen Kaiserreich*. Paderborn: Schöningh, 1987.

Becker, Bert. *Georg Michaelis: Preußischer Beamter, Reichskanzler, Christlicher Reformer 1857–1936. Eine Biographie*. Paderborn: Schöningh, 2007.

Beckstein, Hermann. *Städtische Interessenpolitik: Organisation und Politik der Städtetage in Bayern, Preußen und dem Deutschen Reich, 1896–1923*. Düsseldorf: Droste Verlag, 1991.

Benhabib, Seyla, ed. *Democracy and Difference: Contesting the Boundaries of the Political*. Princeton, N.J.: Princeton University Press, 1996.

Benz, Wolfgang. "The Legend of a German-Jewish Symbiosis." *Year Book of the Leo Baeck Institute* 37 (1992): 95–102.

Berding, Helmut. *Moderner Antisemitismus in Deutschland*. Frankfurt a. M.: Suhrkamp, 1988.

Berghahn, Marion. *German-Jewish Refugees in England: The Ambiguities of Assimilation*. London: Macmillan, 1984.

Berghahn, Volker R. *Imperial Germany, 1871–1914*. Providence, R.I.: Berghahn Books, 1994.

Berghoff, Hartmut. "Aristokratisierung des Bürgertums? Zur Sozialgeschichte der Nobilitierung von Unternehmern in Preußen und Großbritannien." *Vierteljahrschrift für Sozial- und Wirtschaftsgeschichte* 81 (1994): 189–204.

Bering, Dietz. *Der Name als Stigma: Antisemitismus im Deutschen Alltag, 1812–1933*. Stuttgart: Klett-Cotta, 1987.

Bernhardt, Hans-Michael. *Bewegung und Beharrung: Studien zur Emanzipationsgeschichte der Juden im Großherzogtum Mecklenburg Schwerin, 1813–1869*. Hanover: Hahn, 1998.

Bessel, Richard. *Germany after the First World War*. Oxford: Clarendon Press, 1993.

"Bezirksvorsteher." In *Handwörterbuch der Preußischen Verwaltung*, edited by Rudolf von Bitter, 1:303–4. 2nd ed. Leipzig: Roßberg, 1911.

Biale, David. *Power and Powerlessness in Jewish History*. New York: Schocken, 1986.

Bielefeld, Ulrich. "Bürger—Nation—Staat: Probleme einer Dreierbeziehung." In *Staats-Bürger: Deutschland und Frankreich im historischen Vergleich*, edited by Rogers Brubaker, 7–18. Hamburg: Junius, 1994.

Birnbaum, Pierre, and Ira Katznelson. "Emancipation and the Liberal Offer." In *Paths of Emancipation: Jews, States and Citizenship*, edited by Birnbaum and Katznelson, 3–36. Princeton, N.J.: Princeton University Press, 1995.

Blackbourn, David. "The German Bourgeoisie." In *The German Bourgeoisie: Essays on the Social History of the German Middle Class from the Late Eighteenth to the Early Twentieth Century*, edited by David Blackbourn and Richard J. Evans, 1–45. London: Routledge, 1991.

——. *History of Germany, 1780–1918: The Long Nineteenth Century*. 2nd ed. Oxford: Blackwell, 2003.

——. *Marpingen: Apparitions of the Virgin Mary in a Nineteenth-Century German Village*. 2nd ed. New York: Vintage, 1995.

——. *Volksfrömmigkeit und Fortschrittsglaube im Kulturkampf*. Wiesbaden: Franz Steiner, 1988.

Blanke, Richard. "Bismarck and the Prussian Polish Policies of 1886." *Journal of Modern History* 45 (1973): 211–39.

Blaschke, Olaf R. "'Das Judenthum isolieren!' Antisemitismus und Ausgrenzung in Breslau." In *In Breslau zuhause? Juden in einer mitteleuropäischen Metropole der Neuzeit*, edited by Manfred Hettling, Andreas Reinke, and Norbert Conrads, 167–84. Hamburg: Dölling & Galitz, 2003.

——. *Katholizismus und Antisemitismus im Deutschen Kaiserreich*. 2nd ed. Göttingen: Vandenhoeck & Ruprecht, 1998.

Blasius, Dirk. *Ehescheidung in Deutschland*. Göttingen: Vandenhoeck & Ruprecht, 1992.

——. "'Judenfrage' und Gesellschaftsgeschichte." *Neue Politische Literatur* 23 (1978): 17–33.

Bleicher, Heinrich. "Einkommens- und Wohlstandsverhältnisse." *Statistisches Jahrbuch deutscher Städte* 6 (1897): 319–36.

Blumin, Stuart M. *The Emergence of the Middle Class: Social Experience in the American City, 1760–1900*. Cambridge: Cambridge University Press, 1989.

Boehlich, Walter, ed. *Der Berliner Antisemitismusstreit*. Frankfurt a. M.: Insel, 1965.

Boldt, Hans. "Die preußische Verfassung vom 31. Januar 1850: Probleme ihrer Interpretation." In *Preußen im Rückblick*, edited by Hans-Jürgen Puhle and Hans-Ulrich Wehler, Geschichte und Gesellschaft Sonderheft 6, 224–46. Göttingen: Vandenhoeck & Ruprecht, 1980.

Born, Gustav V. R. "The Wide-Ranging Family History of Max Born." *Notes and Records of the Royal Society of London* 56, no. 2 (2002): 219–62.

Borscheid, Peter. "Geld und Liebe: Zu den Auswirkungen des Romantischen auf die Partnerwahl im 19. Jahrhundert." In *Ehe, Liebe, Tod: Zum Wandel der Familie, der Geschlechts- und Generationsbeziehungen in der Neuzeit*, edited by Peter Borscheid and Hans J. Teuteberg, 112–34. Münster: Coppenrath, 1983.

Borut, Jacob. "A New Spirit among Our Brethren in Ashkenaz." PhD diss., Hebrew University, Jerusalem, 1993.

———. "'Verjudung des Judentums': Was There a Zionist Subculture in Weimar Germany?" In *In Search of Jewish Community: Jewish Identities in Germany and Austria, 1918–1933*, edited by Michael Brenner and Derek J. Penslar, 92–114. Bloomington: University of Indiana Press, 1998.

Botstein, Leon. *Judentum und Modernität: Essays zur Rolle der Juden in der deutschen und österreichischen Kultur, 1848 bis 1938*. Vienna: Böhlau Verlag, 1991.

Boyarin, Jonathan, and Daniel Boyarin, eds. *Jews and Other Differences: The New Jewish Cultural Studies*. Minneapolis: University of Minnesota Press, 1997.

Boyer, John W. *Culture and Political Crisis in Vienna: Christian Socialism in Power, 1897–1918*. Chicago: University of Chicago Press, 1995.

———. *Political Radicalism in Late Imperial Vienna: Origins of the Christian Social Movement, 1848–1897*. Chicago: University of Chicago Press, 1981.

Brenner, David A. *Marketing Identities: The Invention of Jewish Ethnicity in "Ost und West."* Detroit: Wayne State University Press, 1998.

Brenner, Michael. "'Gott schütze uns vor unseren Freunden': Zur Ambivalenz des 'Philosemitismus' im Kaiserreich." *Jahrbuch für Antisemitismusforschung* 2 (1993): 174–99.

———. *The Renaissance of Jewish Culture in Weimar Germany*. New Haven, Conn.: Yale University Press, 1996.

Brenner, Michael, Stefi Jersch-Wenzel, and Michael A. Myer. *Deutsch-jüdische Geschichte in der Neuzeit*. Edited by Michael A. Meyer. Vol. 2, *Emanzipation und Akkulturation, 1780–1871*. Munich: C. H. Beck, 1996.

Breslauer, Bernhard. *Die Abwanderung der Juden aus der Provinz Posen*. Berlin: Berthold Levy, 1909.

———. *Die Zurücksetzung der Juden an den Universitäten Deutschlands*. Berlin: Levy, 1911.

Breuer, Mordechai. "Frühe Neuzeit und Beginn der Moderne." In *Deutsch-jüdische Geschichte in der Neuzeit*, edited by Michael A. Meyer, vol. 1, *Tradition und Aufklärung*, by Mordechai Breuer and Michael Graetz, 83–247. Munich: C. H. Beck, 1996.

Bronfen, Elisabeth, and Benjamin Marius. "Hybride Kulturen: Einleitung zur anglo-amerikanischen Multikulturalismusdebatte." In *Hybride Kulturen: Beiträge zur anglo-amerikanischen Multikulturalismusdebatte*, edited by Elisabeth Bronfen, Therese Steffen, and Benjamin Marius, 1–29. Tübingen: Stauffenburg, 1997.

Brubaker, Rogers. *Citizenship and Nationhood in France and Germany*. 2nd ed. Cambridge, Mass.: Harvard University Press, 1994.

Brunner, José, and Yoav Peled. "Das Elend des liberalen Multikulturalismus: Kymlicka und seine Kritiker." *Deutsche Zeitschrift für Philosophie* 46 (1998): 369–91.

Budde, Gunilla-Friederike. *Auf dem Weg ins Bürgerleben: Kindheit und Erziehung in deutschen und englischen Bürgerfamilien.* Göttingen: Vandenhoeck & Ruprecht, 1994.

Buśko, Cezary, et al. *Historia Wrocławia.* Vol. 1, *Od pradziejów do konca czasów habsburskich.* Edited by Adam Galos. Wrocław: Wydaw. Dolnośląskie, 2001.

Bußmann, Walter. "Gustav Freytag: Maßstäbe seiner Zeitkritik." *Archiv für Kulturgeschichte* 34 (1952): 261–87.

Cahn, Wilhelm. *Reichs- und Staatsangehörigkeitsgesetz vom 22. Juli 1913, erläutert mit Benutzung amtlicher Quellen und unter vergleichender Berücksichtigung der ausländischen Gesetzgebung.* Berlin: Guttentag, 1914.

———. *Reichsgesetz über die Erwerbung und den Verlust der Reichs- und Staatsangehörigkeit.* 3rd ed. Berlin: Guttentag, 1908.

Caron, Vicki. *Between France and Germany: The Jews of Alsace-Lorraine, 1871–1918.* Stanford: Stanford University Press, 1988.

Carter, T. E. "Freytag's *Soll und Haben:* A Liberal Manifesto as Bestseller." *German Life and Letters* 21 (1968): 320–29.

Cecil, Lamar. "Jew and Junker." *Year Book of the Leo Baeck Institute* 20 (1975): 47–58.

Chickering, Roger. *Imperial Germany: A Historiographical Companion.* Westport, Conn.: Greenwood Press, 1996.

Cohn, Pauline, ed. *Ferdinand Cohn: Blätter der Erinnerung.* Breslau: J. U. Kern, 1901.

Cohn-Bendit, Daniel, and Thomas Schmid. *Heimat Babylon: Das Wagnis der multikulturellen Demokratie.* Hamburg: Hoffmann & Campe, 1993.

Conrads, Norbert. "Einleitung." In *Verwehte Spuren: Erinnerungen an das Breslauer Judentum vor seinem Untergang,* by Willy Cohn, edited by Norbert Conrads, 1–15. Cologne: Bohlau, 1995.

———. "Die Schlesische Zeitung (1742–1945)." In *Deutsche Zeitungen des 17.–20. Jahrhunderts,* edited by Heinz-Dietrich Fischer, 115–30. Pullach bei München: Verlag Dokumentation, 1972.

Dann, Otto. "Vorwort." In *Vereinswesen und bürgerliche Gesellschaft in Deutschland,* edited by Otto Dann, 5–9. Munich: Oldenbourg, 1984.

Daum, Andreas W. *Wissenspopularisierung im 19. Jahrhundert: Bürgerliche Kultur, naturwissenschaftliche Bildung und die deutsche Öffentlichkeit, 1848–1914.* Munich: Oldenbourg, 1998.

Davidoff, Leonore, and Catherine Hall. *Family Fortunes: Men and Women of the English Middle Classes, 1780–1850.* Chicago: University of Chicago Press, 1987.

Davies, Norman, and Roger Moorhouse. *Microcosm: A Portrait of a Central European City.* London: Jonathan Cape, 2002.

Deák, István. "Ethnic Minorities and the Jews in Imperial Germany." *Year Book of the Leo Baeck Institute* 26 (1981): 47–51.

Desai, Ashok V. *Real Wages in Germany, 1871–1913.* Oxford: Clarendon Press, 1968.

Diner, Dan. "'Rupture in Civilization': On the Genesis and Meaning of a Concept in Understanding." In *On Germans and Jews under the Nazi Regime: Essays by Three Generations of Historians,* ed. Moshe Zimmermann, 33–48. Jerusalem: Magnes Press, 2006.

Dipper, Christof. "Der Freiheitsbegriff im 19. Jahrhundert." In *Geschichtliche Grundbegriffe: Historisches Lexikon zur politisch-sozialen Sprache in Deutschland,* edited by Otto Brunner, Werner Conze, and Reinhart Koselleck, 2:488–538. Stuttgart: Klett-Cotta, 1975.

Dittenberger, Heinrich. "Die Einkommensenquete." *Juristische Wochenschrift* 43 (1914): 745–48.

Dittrich, Curt. "Ehrenbürger." In *Handwörterbuch der Kommunalwissenschaften,* edited by Josef Brix, Hugo Lindemann, Otto Most, Hugo Preuss, and Albert Südekum, 1:553–54. Jena: Gustav Fischer, 1918.

Doron, Joachim. "Social Concepts Prevalent in German Zionism." *Studies in Zionism* 5 (1982): 1–31.

Dove, Alfred. "Gustav Freytag." In *Ausgewählte Aufsätze und Briefe,* edited by Friedrich Meinecke and Oswald Dammann, 191–222. Munich: Bruckmann, 1925. First published in *Allgemeine Deutsche Biographie* (Leipzig: Duncker & Humblot, 1904), 48:749–67.

Duara, Prasenjit. *Rescuing History from the Nation: Questioning Narratives of Modern China.* Chicago: University of Chicago Press, 1995.

Dubnow, Simon. *Weltgeschichte des jüdischen Volkes.* Vol. 10. Berlin: Jüdischer Verlag, 1929.

Düding, Dieter, Peter Friedmann, and Paul Münch, eds. *Öffentliche Festkultur.* Reinbek: Rowohlt, 1988.

Echternkamp, Jörg. *Der Aufstieg des deutschen Nationalismus (1770–1840).* Frankfurt a. M.: Campus, 1998.

Editorial. *Historische Anthropologie* 1 (1993): 1–4.

Ehbrecht, Wilfried, et al. "Neue Veröffentlichungen zur vergleichenden historischen Städteforschung." *Blätter zur deutschen Landesgeschichte* 128 (1992): 387–852.

"Ehrenbürgerrecht." In *Handwörterbuch der Preußischen Verwaltung,* edited by Rudolf von Bitter, 1:439. 2nd ed. Leipzig: Roßberg, 1911.

Eley, Geoff. "Die deutsche Geschichte und die Widersprüche der Moderne: Das Beispiel des Kaiserreichs." In *Zivilisation und Barbare: Gedenkschrift Detlev J. K. Peukert,* edited by Detlef Peukert, Frank Bajohr, Werner Johe, and Uwe Lohalm, 17–65. Hamburg: Christians, 1991.

———. "German History and the Contradictions of Modernity: The Bourgeoisie, the State, and the Mastery of Reform." In *Society, Culture, and the*

State in Germany, 1870–1930, edited by Geoff Eley, 67–103. Ann Arbor: University of Michigan Press, 1996.

———. "Nations, Publics, and Political Cultures: Placing Habermas in the Nineteenth Century." In *Habermas and the Public Sphere,* edited by Craig Calhoun, 289–339. Cambridge, Mass.: MIT Press, 1992.

———, ed. *Society, Culture, and the State in Germany, 1870–1930.* Ann Arbor: University of Michigan Press, 1996.

Eley, Geoff, and David Blackbourn, *The Peculiarities of German History: Bourgeois Society and Politics in 19th Century Germany.* Oxford: Oxford University Press, 1984.

Endelman, Todd M. "Conversion as a Response to Antisemitism in Modern Jewish History." In *Living with Antisemitism: Modern Jewish Responses,* edited by Jehuda Reinharz, 60–84. Hanover, N.H.: University of New England Press, 1987.

———. "The Legitimization of the Diaspora Experience in Recent Jewish Historiography." *Modern Judaism* 11 (1991): 195–209.

———. *Radical Assimilation in English Jewish History, 1656–1945.* Bloomington: Indiana University Press, 1990.

Engelbert, Kurt. *Die Geschichte des Breslauer Domkapitels im Rahmen der Diözesangeschichte vom Beginn des 19. Jahrhunderts bis zum Ende des Zweiten Weltkriegs.* Hildesheim: A. Lax, 1964.

Erbe, Michael. "Berlin im Kaiserreich (1871–1918)." In *Geschichte Berlins,* edited by Wolfgang Ribbe, vol. 2, *Von der Märzrevolution bis zur Gegenwart,* 689–793. Munich: C. H. Beck, 1987.

Eriksen, Thomas Hylland. *Ethnicity and Nationalism: Anthropological Perspectives.* 2nd ed. Ann Arbor: University of Michigan Press, 2002.

Evans, Richard J. *Death in Hamburg: Society and Politics in the Cholera Years, 1830–1910.* Oxford: Clarendon Press, 1987.

———. *Rituals of Retribution: Capital Punishment in Germany, 1600–1987.* 2nd ed. London: Penguin, 1997.

Fahrmeir, Andreas. *Citizens and Aliens: Foreigners and the Law in Britain and the German States, 1789–1870.* New York: Berghahn, 2000.

———. *Citizenship: The Rise and Fall of a Modern Concept.* New Haven, Conn.: Yale University Press, 2007.

———. "Nineteenth-Century German Citizenships." *Historical Journal* 40 (1997): 721–52.

Fass, Paula S. *Outside In: Minorities and the Transformation of American Education.* New York: Oxford University Press, 1989.

Feldman, David. *Englishmen and Jews: Social Relations and Political Culture, 1840–1914.* New Haven, Conn.: Yale University Press, 1994.

———. "Jews and the State in Britain." In *Two Nations: British and German Jews in Comparative Perspective,* edited by Michael Brenner, Rainer Liedtke, and David Rechter, 141–61. Tübingen: Mohr Siebeck, 1999.

Feldman, Gerald D. *The Great Disorder: Politics, Economics, and Society in the German Inflation, 1914–1924.* New York: Oxford University Press, 1993.

Fiedler, Heinrich. "Beiträge zur Statistik der Breslauer höheren Schulen." In *Programm des Realgymnasiums am Zwinger zu Breslau 1884*, i–x. Breslau: Grass & Barth, 1884.

Field, Geoffrey. "Religion in the German Volksschule, 1890–1908." *Year Book of the Leo Baeck Institute* 25 (1980): 41–71.

Fischer, Heinz-Dietrich, ed. *Deutsche Zeitungen des 17.–20. Jahrhunderts.* Pullach bei München: Verlag Dokumentation, 1972.

Fischer, Jens Malte. "Gustav Mahler und das 'Judentum in der Musik.'" *Merkur* 51 (1997): 665–80.

Fölsche, Ernst. *Das Ehrenamt in Preußen und im Reiche.* Breslau: Marcus, 1911.

Frankel, Jonathan. "Assimilation and the Jews in Nineteenth-Century Europe." In *Assimilation and Community: The Jews in Nineteenth-Century Europe*, edited by Jonathan Frankel and Steven J. Zipperstein, 1–37. Cambridge: Cambridge University Press, 1992.

Frederickson, George M. "America's Diversity in Comparative Perspective." *Journal of American History* 85 (1998): 859–75.

Fremdling, Rainer, Ruth Federspiel, and Andreas Kunz, eds. *Statistik der Eisenbahnen in Deutschland, 1835–1989.* St. Katharinen: Scripta Mercaturae Verlag, 1995.

Frevert, Ute. *Frauen-Geschichte: Zwischen bürgerlicher Verbesserung und neuer Weiblichkeit.* Frankfurt a. M.: Suhrkamp, 1986.

Freyhan, Wilhelm. *Die Entwicklung Breslaus im Eisenbahnzeitalter.* Breslau: Hochschulverlag, 1922.

Freytag-Loringhoven, Axel Freiherr von. *Die Weimarer Verfassung in Lehre und Wirklichkeit.* Munich: Lehmann, 1924.

Friedländer, Saul. *Nazi Germany and the Jews.* Vol. 1, *The Years of Persecution, 1933–1939.* London: Weidenfeld, 1997.

Friedmann, Arthur. "Die Wohlstandsentwicklung in Preußen von 1891–1911." *Jahrbücher für Nationalökonomie und Statistik* 103 (1914): 1–51.

Friese, Marianne. "Familienbildung und Heiratsstrategien im Bremischen Proletariat des 19. Jahrhunderts." In *Familie und Familienlosigkeit*, edited by Jürgen Schlumbohm, 217–34. Hanover: Verlag Hahnsche Buchhandlung, 1993.

Friesel, Evyatar. "The German-Jewish Encounter as a Historical Problem: A Reconsideration." *Year Book of the Leo Baeck Institute* 41 (1996): 263–76.

Frisch, Hans von. *Das Fremdenrecht: Die staatsrechtliche Stellung des Fremden.* Berlin: Heymanns, 1910.

Fritzsche, Peter. *Reading Berlin 1900.* 2nd ed. Cambridge, Mass.: Harvard University Press, 1998.

Fuchs, Konrad. *Gestalten und Ereignisse aus Schlesiens Wirtschaft, Kultur und Politik.* Dortmund: Universität Dortmund, Forschungsstelle Ostmitteleuropa, 1992.

———. "Vom deutschen Krieg zur deutschen Katastrophe (1866–1945)." In *Schlesien*, edited by Norbert Conrads, Deutsche Geschichte im Osten Europas, 554–692. Berlin: Siedler, 1994.

Fuhrmann, Horst. *Pour le Mérite: Über die Sichtbarmachung von Verdiensten. Eine historische Besinnung*. Sigmaringen: Thorbecke, 1992.

Gall, Lothar. *Bürgertum in Deutschland*. Berlin: Siedler, 1989.

———, ed. *Stadt und Bürgertum im Übergang von der traditionalen zur modernen Gesellschaft*. Munich: Oldenbourg, 1993.

———. *Von der ständischen zur bürgerlichen Gesellschaft*. Munich: Oldenbourg, 1993.

Galos, Adam, and Kazimierza Popiolka, eds. *Studia e materialy z dziejów slaska*. Vol. 7. Breslau: Zaklad Narodowy im. Ossolinskich, 1966.

Gandert, Otto-Friedrich, et al. *Heimatchronik Berlin*. Cologne: Archiv für deutsche Heimatpflege, 1962.

Garris, Charles Robert. "Becoming German: Immigration, Conformity, and Identity Politics in Wilhelminian Berlin, 1880–1914." PhD diss., University of North Carolina, Chapel Hill, 1998.

Gay, Peter. *Freud, Jews and Other Germans: Masters and Victims in Modernist Culture*. New York: Oxford University Press, 1978.

———. "In Deutschland zu Hause . . . : Die Juden in der Weimarer Republik." In *Juden im nationalsozialistischen Deutschland: The Jews in Nazi Germany, 1933–1943*, edited by Arnold Paucker, Sylvia Gilchrist, and Barbara Suchy, 31–43. Tübingen: Mohr Siebeck, 1986.

———. *Schnitzler's Century: The Making of Middle-Class Culture, 1815–1914*. New York: W. W. Norton, 2002.

Gay, Ruth. *Geschichte der Juden in Deutschland*. Munich: C. H. Beck, 1993.

Gebhardt, Miriam. *Das jüdische Familiengedächtnis: Erinnerung im deutsch-jüdischen Bürgertum, 1890–1932*. Stuttgart: Franz Steiner, 1999.

Gelber, Mark H. "Aspects of Literary Anti-Semitism: Charles Dickens' 'Oliver Twist' and Gustav Freytag's 'Soll und Haben.'" PhD diss., Yale University, 1980.

Gerber, Michael R. *Die Schlesische Gesellschaft für Vaterländische Cultur (1803–1945)*. Sigmaringen: Thorbecke, 1988.

Gerhard, Ute. "Flucht und Wanderung in den Mediendiskursen der Weimarer Republik." In *Die Sprache des Migrationsdiskurses: Das Reden über "Ausländer" in Medien, Politik und Alltag*, edited by Matthias Jung, Martin Wengeler, and Karin Böke, 45–57. Opladen: Westdeutscher Verlag, 1997.

———. *Verhältnisse und Verhinderungen: Frauenarbeit, Familie und Rechte der Frauen im 19. Jahrhundert; Mit Dokumenten*. 2nd ed. Frankfurt a. M.: Suhrkamp, 1981.

Gestrich, Andreas, Gerhard Hirschfeld, and Holger Sonnabend, eds. *Ausweisung und Deportation: Formen der Zwangsmigration in der Geschichte*. Stuttgart: Franz Steiner, 1995.

Geulen, Christian. *Wahlverwandte: Rassendiskurs und Nationalismus im späten 19. Jahrhundert*. Hamburg: Hamburger Edition, 2004.

Geyer, Martin H. "Teuerungsprotest und Teuerungsunruhen 1914–1923: Selbst-hilfegesellschaft und Geldentwertung." In *Der Kampf um das tägliche Brot: Nahrungsmangel, Versorgungspolitik und Protest, 1750–1990*, edited by Manfred Gailus and Heinrich Volkmann, 319–45. Opladen: Westdeutscher Verlag, 1994.

———. *Verkehrte Welt: Revolution, Inflation und Moderne; München, 1914–1924.* Göttingen: Vandenhoeck & Ruprecht, 1998.

Geyer, Michael. "Multiculturalism and the Politics of General Education." *Critical Inquiry* 19 (1993): 499–533.

Geyer, Michael, and Konrad Jarausch. "The Future of the German Past: Transatlantic Reflections for the 1990s." *Central European History* 22 (1989): 229–59.

Gillerman, Sharon. "The Crisis of the Jewish Family in Weimar Germany: Social Conditions and Cultural Representation." In *In Search of Jewish Community: Jewish Identities in Germany and Austria, 1918–1933*, edited by Michael Brenner and Derek J. Penslar, 176–90. Bloomington: Indiana University Press, 1998.

Gillis, John R. "The Future of European History." *Perspectives: American Historical Association Newsletter* 34, no. 4 (1996): 4–6.

Gilman, Sander L. *The Jew's Body.* New York: Routledge, 1991.

———. *Smart Jews: The Construction of the Image of Jewish Superiority.* Lincoln: University of Nebraska Press, 1996.

Gleason, Philip. *Speaking of Diversity: Language and Ethnicity in Twentieth-Century America.* Baltimore: Johns Hopkins University Press, 1992.

Goetschel, Willi. *Spinoza's Modernity: Mendelssohn, Lessing, and Heine.* Madison: University of Wisconsin Press, 2003.

Goldberg, David T., ed. *Multiculturalism: A Critical Reader.* Oxford: Blackwell, 1994.

Goldberg, Jacob. "Jewish Marriage in Eighteenth-Century Poland." *POLIN: Studies in Polish Jewry* 10 (1997): 1–37.

Goldberg, Sylvie Anne. "On the Margins of French Historiography." *Shofar: An Interdisciplinary Journal of Jewish Studies* 14 (1996): 47–62.

Goltermann, Svenja. *Körper der Nation: Habitusformierung und die Politik des Turnens, 1860–1890.* Göttingen: Vandenhoeck & Ruprecht, 1998.

Gordon, Milton Myron. *Assimilation in American Life: The Role of Race, Religion, and National Origins.* New York: Oxford University Press, 1964.

Gosewinkel, Dieter. *Einbürgern und Ausschließen: Die Nationalisierung der Staatsangehörigkeit vom Deutschen Bund bis zur Bundesrepublik Deutschland.* Göttingen: Vandenhoeck & Ruprecht, 2001.

———. "Die Staatsangehörigkeit als Institution des Nationalstaats: Zur Entstehung des Reichs- und Staatsangehörigkeitsgesetzes von 1913." In *Offene Staatlichkeit: Festschrift für Ernst-Wolfgang Böckenförde*, edited by Rolf Grawert, Bernhard Schlink, Rainer Wahl, and Joachim Wieland, 359–78. Berlin: Duncker & Humblot, 1995.

———. "Staatsangehörigkeit und Einbürgerung in Deutschland während des 19. und 20. Jahrhunderts." *Geschichte und Gesellschaft* 21 (1995): 533–56.

———. "'Unerwünschte Elemente': Einwanderung und Einbürgerung von Juden in Deutschland 1848–1933." *Tel Aviver Jahrbuch für deutsche Geschichte* 27 (1998): 71–106.

Graetzer, Jonas. *Lebensbilder hervorragender schlesischer Ärzte aus den letzten vier Jahrhunderten.* Breslau: Schottländer, 1889.

Grafton, Anthony. "Jacob Bernays, Joseph Scaliger, and Others." In *The Jewish Past Revisited: Reflections on Modern Jewish Historians,* edited by David N. Myers and David B. Ruderman, 16–38. New Haven, Conn.: Yale University Press, 1998.

Graml, Hermann. *Reichskristallnacht: Antisemitismus und Judenverfolgung im Dritten Reich.* Munich: Deutscher Taschenbuch Verlag, 1988.

Grawert, Rolf. *Staat und Staatsangehörigkeit.* Berlin: Duncker & Humblot, 1973.

———. "Staatsvolk und Staatsangehörigkeit." In *Handbuch des Staatsrechts der Bundesrepublik Deutschland,* edited by Josef Isensee and Paul Kirchhoff, 1:681. Heidelberg: Müller, 1987.

Grenville, John A. S. "Die Geschichtsschreibung der Bundesrepublik über die deutschen Juden." In *Studien zur jüdischen Geschichte und Soziologie: Festschrift Julius Carlebach,* 195–205. Heidelberg: Carl Winter Universitätsverlag, 1992.

Grimm, Dieter. *Deutsche Verfassungsgeschichte, 1776–1866.* Frankfurt a. M.: Suhrkamp, 1988.

———. "Verfassung." In *Geschichtliche Grundbegriffe,* 6:63–99. Stuttgart: Klett-Cotta, 1990.

Groot, Gerard-René de. *Staatsangehörigkeit im Wandel: Eine rechtsvergleichende Studie über Erwerbs- und Verlustgründe der Staatsangehörigkeit.* Cologne: Carl Heymanns Verlag, 1989.

Gross, Michael B. "Kulturkampf and Unification: German Liberals and the War against the Jesuits." *Central European History* 30 (1997): 545–66.

Grossmann, Atina. "Die 'Neue Frau' und die Rationalisierung der Sexualität in der Weimarer Republik." In *Die Politik des Begehrens: Sexualität, Pornographie und neuer Puritanismus in den USA,* edited by Ann Snitow, Christine Stansell, and Sharon Thompson, 38–60. Berlin: Rotbuch, 1985.

———. "Remarks on Current Trends and Directions in German Women's History." *Women in German Yearbook* 12 (1996): 11–25.

Gubser, Martin. *Literarischer Antisemitismus: Untersuchungen zu Gustav Freytag und anderen bürgerlichen Schriftstellern.* Göttingen: Wallstein-Verlag, 1998.

Guesnet, François. *Lodzer Juden im 19. Jahrhundert: Ihr Ort in einer multikulturellen Stadtgesellschaft.* Leipzig: Simon-Dubnow-Institut für jüdische Geschichte und Kultur, 1997.

Gumpert, Martin, and Alfred Joseph. "Medizin." In *Juden im deutschen Kulturbereich* (1935), edited by Siegmund Kaznelson, 461–526. 2nd ed. Berlin: Jüdischer Verlag, 1959.

Hackeschmidt, Jörg. *Von Kurt Blumenfeld zu Norbert Elias: Die Erfindung einer jüdischen Nation.* Hamburg: Europäische Verlagsanstalt, 1997.

Hacohen, Malachi Haim. "Dilemmas of Cosmopolitanism: Karl Popper, Jewish Identity, and 'Central European Culture.'" *Journal of Modern History* 71 (1999): 105–49.

Hagen, William W. *Germans, Poles, and Jews: The Nationality Conflict in the Prussian East, 1772–1914.* Chicago: University of Chicago Press, 1980.

Hall, Stuart. "Cultural Identity and the Diaspora." In *Identity, Community and Cultural Difference,* edited by Jonathan Rutherford, 222–37. London: Lawrence & Wishart, 1990.

Haltern, Utz. "Die Gesellschaft der Bürger." *Geschichte und Gesellschaft* 19 (1993): 100–134.

Hamann, Birgitta. *Lola Landau: Leben und Werk. Ein Beispiel deutsch-jüdischer Literatur des 20. Jahrhunderts in Deutschland und in Palästina / Israel.* Berlin: Philo, 2000.

Hamburger, Ernest. *Juden im öffentlichen Leben Deutschlands: Regierungsmitglieder, Beamte, Parlamentarier in der monarchischen Zeit, 1848–1918.* Tübingen: Mohr Siebeck, 1968.

Hanauer, Walter. "Die jüdisch-christlichen Mischehen." *Allgemeines Statistisches Archiv* 17 (1928): 513–37.

———. "Die Mischehe." *Jüdisches Jahrbuch* 3 (1929): 37–66.

Hardtwig, Wolfgang. "Alltagsgeschichte heute: Eine kritische Bilanz." In *Sozialgeschichte, Alltagsgeschichte, Mikro-Historie,* edited by Winfried Schulze, 19–32. Göttingen: Vandenhoeck & Ruprecht, 1994.

———. "Bürgertum, Staatssymbolik und Staatsbewußtsein im Deutschen Kaiserreich 1871–1914." *Geschichte und Gesellschaft* 16 (1990): 269–95.

———. "Großstadt und Bürgerlichkeit in der politischen Ordnung des Kaiserreichs." In *Stadt und Bürgertum im 19. Jahrhundert,* edited by Lothar Gall, 19–64. Munich: C. H. Beck, 1990.

———. "Strukturmerkmale und Entwicklungstendenzen des deutschen Vereinswesens in Deutschland, 1789–1848." In *Vereinswesen und bürgerliche Gesellschaft in Deutschland,* edited by Otto Dann, 11–50. Munich: Oldenbourg, 1984.

Hareven, Tamara K. "Formen, Funktionen und Werte." In *Entwicklungstendenzen der Familie,* by Tamara K. Hareven and Michael Mitterauer, 14–38. Vienna: Picus-Verlag, 1996.

———. "The History of the Family and the Complexity of Social Change." *American Historical Review* 96 (1991): 95–124.

Harris, James F. *The People Speak! Anti-Semitism and Emancipation in Nineteenth-Century Bavaria.* Ann Arbor: University of Michigan Press, 1994.

Hartung, Fritz. "Stammesbewußtsein." In *Politisches Handwörterbuch,* edited by Paul Herre, 2:723. Leipzig: Koehler, 1923.

Haug-Moritz, Gabriele. "Kaisertum und Parität: Reichspolitik und Konfessionen nach dem Westfälischen Frieden." *Zeitschrift für Historische Forschung* 19 (1992): 445–82.

Haunfelder, Bernd, ed. *Biographisches Handbuch für das Preußische Abgeordnetenhaus, 1849–1867.* Düsseldorf: Droste, 1994.

Haupt, Heinz-Gerhard. "Kleine und große Bürger in Deutschland und Frankreich am Ende des 19. Jahrhunderts." In *Bürgertum im 19. Jahrhundert: Deutschland im europäischen Vergleich,* edited by Jürgen Kocka, 2:252–75. Munich: Deutscher Taschenbuch Verlag, 1988.

Hausen, Karin. "Familie und Familiengeschichte." In *Sozialgeschichte in Deutschland,* edited by Wolfgang Schieder and Volker Sellin, 2:64–89. Göttingen: Vandenhoeck & Ruprecht, 1986.

———. "'. . . eine Ulme für das schwanke Efeu': Ehepaare im deutschen Bildungsbürgertum. Ideale und Wirklichkeit im späten 18. und 19. Jahrhundert." In *Bürgerinnen und Bürger: Geschlechterverhältnisse im 19. Jahrhundert,* edited by Ute Frevert, 85–117. Göttingen: Vandenhoeck & Ruprecht, 1988.

Healy, Róisín. "Religion and Civil Society: Catholics, Jesuits, and Protestants in Imperial Germany." In *Paradoxes of Civil Society: New Perspectives on Modern Britain and Germany,* edited by Frank Trentmann, 244–62. Oxford: Berghan, 2000.

Hecker, Hellmuth, ed. *Bibliographie zum Staatsangehörigkeitsrecht in Deutschland in Vergangenheit und Gegenwart.* Frankfurt a. M.: Verlag für Standesamtswesen, 1976.

Hecker, Rolf. "Die 'Entdeckung' von Marx-Briefen im Nachlass von Moritz Elsner und deren Erstveröffentlichung." *Beiträge zur Marx-Engels-Forschung,* n.s., 2002 (2003): 200–225.

Heer, David M. "Intermarriage." In *Harvard Encyclopedia of American Ethnic Groups,* edited by Stephen Thernstrom, 513–21. Cambridge, Mass.: Harvard University Press, 1980.

Heffter, Heinrich. *Die deutsche Selbstverwaltung im 19. Jahrhundert: Geschichte der Ideen und Institutionen.* 2nd ed. Stuttgart: Koehler, 1969.

Heid, Ludger. *Maloche—nicht Mildtätigkeit: Ostjüdische Proletarier in Deutschland, 1914–1923.* Hildesheim: Olms, 1995.

Heilborn, Ernst. *Zwischen zwei Revolutionen: Der Geist der Bismarckzeit (1848–1918).* Berlin: Elsner, 1929.

"Heimatsrecht." In *Brockhaus' Konversations-Lexikon,* 8:965. 14th ed. Leipzig: Brockhaus, 1908.

Hein, Dieter. "Soziale Konstituierungsfaktoren des Bürgertums." In *Stadt und Bürgertum im Übergang von der traditionalen zur modernen Gesellschaft,* edited by Lothar Gall, 151–83. Munich: Oldenbourg, 1993.

Hein, Jürgen, and Andreas Schultz, eds. *Bürgerkultur im 19. Jahrhundert: Bildung, Kunst und Lebenswelt.* Munich: C. H. Beck, 1996.

Heinze, Rudolf. "Dresden." In *Verfassung und Verwaltungsorganisation der Städte,* by Georg Häpe et al., vol. 4, pt. 1, *Königreich Sachsen,* Schriften des Vereins für Sozialpolitik 120, 85–122. Leipzig: Duncker & Humblot, 1905.

Heitmann, Margret, and Andreas Reinke, eds. *Bibliographie zur Geschichte der Juden in Schlesien.* Munich: Saur, 1995.

Hendrickx, John, Osmund Schreuder, and Wouter Ultee. "Die konfessionelle Mischehe in Deutschland (1901–1986) und den Niederlanden (1914–1986)." *Kölner Zeitschrift für Soziologie und Sozialpsychologie* 46 (1994): 619–45.

Hentschel, Bernhard. "Juden als Debattenthema im Deutschen Reichstag, 1871–1914." Master's thesis, Hochschule für Jüdische Studien, Heidelberg, 1989.

Heppner, Aron. *Jüdische Persönlichkeiten in und aus Breslau.* Breslau: Schatzky, 1931.

Herbert, Ulrich. *Geschichte der Ausländerbeschäftigung in Deutschland, 1880–1980: Saisonarbeiter, Zwangsarbeiter, Gastarbeiter.* Berlin: Dietz, 1986.

Hermann, Ulrich. "Über 'Bildung' im Gymnasium des wilhelminischen Kaiserreichs." In *Bildungsbürgertum im 19. Jahrhundert,* edited by Reinhart Koselleck, vol. 2, *Bildungsgüter und Bildungswissen,* 346–68. Stuttgart: Klett Cotta, 1990.

Herzig, Arno. "Die unruhige Provinz: Schlesien zwischen 1806 und 1871." In *Schlesien,* edited by Norbert Conrads, Deutsche Geschichte im Osten Europas, 466–553. Berlin: Siedler, 1994.

Herzog, Dagmar. *Intimacy and Exclusion: Religious Politics in Pre-Revolutionary Baden.* Princeton, N.J.: Princeton University Press, 1996.

Heschel, Susannah. *Abraham Geiger and the Jewish Jesus.* Chicago: University of Chicago Press, 1998.

Hettling, Manfred. "Partei ohne Parteibeamte: Parteisekretäre im Linksliberalismus von 1900 bis 1933." In *Parteien im Wande: Vom Kaiserreich zur Weimarer Republik,* edited by Dieter Dowe, Jürgen Kocka, and Heinrich August Winkler, 109–34. Munich: Oldenbourg, 1999.

———. "Die persönliche Selbständigkeit: Der archimedische Punkt bürgerlicher Lebensführung." In *Der bürgerliche Wertehimmel: Innenansichten des 19. Jahrhunderts,* edited by Manfred Hettling and Stefan-Ludwig Hoffmann, 57–78. Göttingen: Vandenhoeck & Ruprecht, 2000.

———. *Politische Bürgerlichkeit: Der Bürger zwischen Individualität und Vergesellschaftung in Deutschland und der Schweiz von 1860 bis 1918.* Göttingen: Vandenhoeck & Ruprecht, 1999.

———. "Von der Hochburg zur Wagenburg: Liberalismus in Breslau von den 1860er Jahren bis 1918." In *Liberalismus und Region: Zur Geschichte des deutschen Liberalismus im 19. Jahrhundert,* edited by Dieter Langewiesche and Lothar Gall, 253–76. Munich: Oldenbourg, 1995.

Hettling, Manfred, and Paul Nolte, eds. *Bürgerliche Feste: Symbolische Formen des politischen Handelns im 19. Jahrhundert.* Göttingen: Vandenhoeck & Ruprecht, 1993.

Hettling, Manfred, and Stefan-Ludwig Hoffmann. "Der bürgerliche Wertehimmel: Zum Problem individueller Lebensführung im 19. Jahrhundert." *Geschichte und Gesellschaft* 23 (1997): 333–59.

Higham, John. "Ethnic Pluralism in Modern American Thought." In his *Send These to Me: Immigrants in Urban America,* 198–232. 2nd ed. Baltimore: Johns Hopkins University Press, 1984.

Hobsbawm, Eric, and Terence Ranger, eds. *The Invention of Tradition.* Cambridge: Cambridge University Press, 1983.

Hödl, Klaus. *Die Pathologisierung des jüdischen Körpers: Antisemitismus, Geschlecht und Medizin im Fin de Siècle.* Vienna: Picus Verlag, 1997.

Hölscher, Lucian. "Die religiöse Entzweiung: Entwurf zu einer Geschichte der Frömmigkeit im 19. Jahrhundert." *Jahrbuch der Gesellschaft für Niedersächsische Kirchengeschichte* 93 (1995): 9–26.

Hoffmann, Christhard. "The German-Jewish Encounter and German Historical Culture." Translated by Louise Willmot. *Year Book of the Leo Baeck Institute* 41 (1996): 277–90.

———. *Juden und Judentum im Werk deutscher Althistoriker des 19. und 20. Jahrhunderts.* Leiden: Brill, 1988.

———. "Politische Kultur und Gewalt gegen Minderheiten: Die antisemitischen Ausschreitungen in Pommern und Westpreußen, 1881." *Jahrbuch für Antisemitismusforschung* 3 (1994): 93–120.

Hoffmann, Stefan-Ludwig. "Bürger zweier Welten? Juden und Freimaurer im 19. Jahrhundert." In *Bürger, Juden, Deutsche: Zur Geschichte von Vielfalt und Grenzen, 1800–1933,* edited by Andreas Gotzmann, Rainer Liedtke, and Till van Rahden, 97–119. Tübingen: Mohr Siebeck, 2001.

———. *Die Politik der Geselligkeit: Freimaurerlogen in der deutschen Bürgergesellschaft, 1840–1918.* Göttingen: Vandenhoeck & Ruprecht, 2000.

Hofmann, Wolfgang. *Zwischen Rathaus und Reichskanzlei: Die Oberbürgermeister in der Kommunal- und Stadtpolitik des Deutschen Reiches von 1890–1933.* Stuttgart: Kohlhammer, 1974.

Hohorst, Gerd, Jürgen Kocka, and Gerhard A. Ritter. *Sozialgeschichtliches Arbeitsbuch: Materialien zur Statistik des Kaiserreichs, 1870–1914.* Munich: C. H. Beck, 1980.

Hollinger, David A. *Science, Jews, and Secular Culture: Studies in Mid-Twentieth-Century American Intellectual History.* Princeton, N.J.: Princeton University Press, 1996.

Holz, Albert. "Kommerzielles Verhalten von Breslau." *Jahresbericht der Schlesischen Gesellschaft für vaterländische Cultur* 69 (1891): 13–23.

Hopp, Andrea. *Jüdisches Bürgertum in Frankfurt am Main im 19. Jahrhundert.* Stuttgart: Franz Steiner, 1997.

Horch, Hans Otto. "Judenbilder in der realistischen Erzählliteratur: Jüdische Figuren bei Gustav Freytag, Fritz Reuter, Berthold Auerbach und Wilhelm Raabe." In *Juden und Judentum in der Literatur,* edited by Herbert A. Strauss and Christhard Hoffmann, 140–71. Munich: Deutscher Taschenbuch Verlag, 1985.

Hubbard, William H. *Familiengeschichte: Materialien zur deutschen Familie seit dem Ende des 18. Jahrhunderts.* Munich: C. H. Beck, 1983.

———. "Die historische Familienforschung." In *Familiengeschichte: Materialien zur deutschen Familie seit dem Ende des 18. Jahrhunderts,* 17–35. Munich: C. H. Beck, 1983.

Huber, Ernst Rudolf, ed. *Deutsche Verfassungsgeschichte seit 1789*. Vol. 3, *Bismarck und das Reich*. 3rd ed. Stuttgart: Kohlhammer, 1963.

———, ed. *Deutsche Verfassungsgeschichte seit 1789*. Vol. 4, *Struktur und Krisen des Kaiserreichs*. Stuttgart: Deutsche Verlagsanstalt, 1969.

———, ed. *Dokumente zur Deutschen Verfassungsgeschichte*. Vol. 1, *Deutsche Verfassungsdokumente, 1803–1850*. 3rd ed. Stuttgart: Kohlhammer, 1978.

———, ed. *Dokumente zur Deutschen Verfassungsgeschichte*. Vol. 2, *Deutsche Verfassungsdokumente, 1851–1900*. 3rd ed. Stuttgart: Kohlhammer, 1986.

Hübinger, Gangolf. *Kulturprotestantismus und Politik: Zum Verhältnis von Liberalismus und Protestantismus im wilhelminischen Deutschland*. Tübingen: Mohr Siebeck, 1994.

Hundert, Gershon David. *The Jews in a Polish Private Town: The Case of Opatów in the Eighteenth Century*. Baltimore: Johns Hopkins University Press, 1992.

Hundt, Martin. "Ein schlesischer Junghegelianer." In *Revolution und Reform in Deutschland im 19. und 20. Jahrhundert: Zum 75. Geburtstag von Walter Schmidt*, edited by Helmut Bleiber, 71–78. Berlin: Trafo-Verlag, 2005.

Huser Bugmann, Karin. *Schtetl an der Sihl: Einwanderung, Leben und Alltag der Ostjuden in Zürich, 1880–1939*. Zurich: Chronos, 1998.

Hyman, Paula E. *Gender and Assimilation in Modern Jewish History*. Seattle: University of Washington Press, 1995.

———. "The Ideological Transformation of Modern Jewish Historiography." In *The State of Jewish Studies*, edited by Shaye J. D. Cohen and Edward L. Greenstein, 143–57. Detroit: Wayne State University Press, 1990.

———. "Jüdische Familie und kulturelle Kontinuität im Elsaß des 19. Jahrhunderts." In *Jüdisches Leben auf dem Lande*, edited by Monika Richarz and Reinhard Rürup, 249–69. Tübingen: Mohr Siebeck, 1997.

———. "Review of Pierre Birnbaum, *The Jews of the Republic: A Political History of State Jews in France from Gambetta to Vichy*." *Journal of Modern History* 70 (1998): 198–99.

Janz, Oliver. *Bürger besonderer Art: Evangelische Pfarrer in Preußen, 1850–1914*. Berlin: de Gruyter, 1994.

Jeismann, Karl-Ernst. *Das preußische Gymnasium in Staat und Gesellschaft*. Vol. 2, *Höhere Bildung zwischen Reform und Reaktion, 1817–1859*. Stuttgart: Klett-Cotta, 1996.

———. "Zur Bedeutung der 'Bildung' im 19. Jahrhundert." In *Handbuch der deutschen Bildungsgeschichte*, edited by Karl-Ernst Jeismann and Peter Lundgreen, vol. 3, *1800–1870: Von der Neuordnung Deutschlands bis zur Gründung des Deutschen Reiches*, 1–21. Munich: C. H. Beck, 1987.

Jeismann, Michael. "Der letzte Feind: Nachgeholter Universalismus; Zum Zusammenhang von Nationalismus und Antisemitismus." In *Die Konstruktion der Nation gegen die Juden*, edited by Peter Alter, Claus-Ekkehard Bärsch, and Peter Berghoff, 173–90. Munich: Fink, 1999.

Jessen, Hans. *Max Kurnik: Ein Breslauer Journalist (1819–1881)*. Breslau: Breslauer Zeitung, 1927.

———. "Eine schlesische Freundschaft." In *Kritische Solidarität: Festschrift für Max Plaut,* edited by Günter Schulz, 293–98. Bremen: Röver, 1971.

Jochmann, Werner. "Akademische Führungsschichten und Judenfeindschaft in Deutschland, 1866–1918." In his *Gesellschaftskrise und Judenfeindschaft in Deutschland, 1870–1945,* 13–29. Hamburg: Christians, 1988.

———. "Struktur und Funktion des deutschen Antisemitismus." In *Juden im Wilhelminischen Deutschland, 1870–1914,* edited by Werner E. Mosse, 389–477. Tübingen: Mohr Siebeck, 1976.

Johnpoll, Bernard K. "Why They Left: Russian-Jewish Mass Migration and Repressive Laws, 1881–1917." *American Jewish Archives* 47 (1995): 17–54.

Judd, Robin. *Contested Rituals: Circumcision, Kosher Butchering, and German-Jewish Political Life in Germany, 1843–1933.* Ithaca, N.Y.: Cornell University Press, 2007.

Kaelble, Hartmut. "Eras of Social Mobility in 19th and 20th Century Europe." *Journal of Social History* 17 (1984): 489–504.

———. "Wie feudal waren die deutschen Unternehmer im Kaiserreich?" In *Beiträge zur quantitativen vergleichenden Unternehmensgeschichte,* edited by Richard H. Tilly, 148–71. Stuttgart: Klett-Cotta, 1985.

Kallen, Horace. *Cultural Pluralism and the American Idea: An Essay in Social Philosophy.* Philadelphia: University of Pennsylvania Press, 1956.

Kalmijn, Matthijs. "Shifting Boundaries: Trends in Religious and Educational Homogamy." *American Sociological Review* 56 (1991): 768–800.

Kampe, Norbert. "Jüdische Professoren im deutschen Kaiserreich." In *Antisemitismus und jüdische Geschichte,* edited by Rainer Erb and Michael Schmidt, 185–211. Berlin: Wissenschaftlicher Autorenverlag, 1987.

———. *Studenten und "Judenfrage" im Kaiserreich: Die Entstehung einer akademischen Trägerschicht des Antisemitismus.* Göttingen: Vandenhoeck & Ruprecht, 1988.

Kaplan, Marion A. *Between Dignity and Despair: Jewish Life in Nazi Germany.* New York: Oxford University Press, 1998.

———. "Freizeit—Arbeit: Geschlechterräume im deutsch-jüdischen Bürgertum, 1870–1914." In *Bürgerinnen und Bürger: Geschlechterverhältnisse im 19. Jahrhundert,* edited by Ute Frevert, 157–74. Göttingen: Vandenhoeck & Ruprecht, 1988.

———. *The Making of the Jewish Middle Class: Women, Family, and Identity in Imperial Germany.* New York: Oxford University Press, 1991.

Karády, Victor. *Gewalterfahrung und Utopie: Juden in der europäischen Moderne.* Frankfurt a. M.: Fischer, 1999.

———. "Jewish Enrollment Patterns in Classical Secondary Education in Old Regime and Inter-War Hungary." *Studies in Contemporary Jewry* 1 (1984): 225–52.

———. "Das Judentum als Bildungsmacht in der Moderne: Forschungsansätze zur relativen Überschulung in Mitteleuropa." *Österreichische Zeitschrift für Geschichtswissenschaften* 8 (1997): 347–61.

Kasischke-Wurm, Daniela. *Antisemitismus im Spiegel der Hamburger Presse während des Kaiserreichs, 1884–1914*. Hamburg: LIT, 1997.

Kasper-Holtkotte, Cilli. *Juden im Aufbruch: Zur Sozialgeschichte einer Minderheit im Saar-Mosel-Raum um 1800*. Hanover: Hahn, 1996.

Katz, David. *The Jews in the History of England, 1485–1850*. Oxford: Clarendon Press, 1994.

Katz, Jacob. *From Prejudice to Destruction: Anti-Semitism, 1700–1933*. Cambridge, Mass.: Harvard University Press, 1980.

———. *Jews and Freemasons in Europe, 1723–1939*. Cambridge, Mass.: Harvard University Press, 1970.

———. "Methodischer Exkurs." In his *Vom Vorurteil bis zur Vernichtung: Der Antisemitismus, 1700–1933*, 236–53. Munich: C. H. Beck, 1989.

———. *Out of the Ghetto: The Social Background of Jewish Emancipation, 1770–1870*. Cambridge, Mass.: Harvard University Press, 1973; reprint, Syracuse, N.Y.: Syracuse University Press, 1998.

———. *Tradition and Crisis: Jewish Society at the End of the Middle Ages*. 1958. Newly translated and with an afterword and bibliography by Bernard Dov Cooperman. New York: New York University Press, 1993.

Katz, Michael B. "Occupational Classification in History." *Journal of Interdisciplinary History* 3 (1972): 63–88.

Kauders, Anthony. *German Politics and the Jews: Düsseldorf and Nuremberg, 1910–1933*. Oxford: Oxford University Press, 1996.

Kaufman, David. *Shul with a Pool: The "Synagogue-Center" in American Jewish History*. Hanover, N.H.: University Press of New England, 1999.

Kaufmann, Robert Uri. "Wie man zum 'Fremden' erklärt wird: Fremd- und Selbstbildnis der Juden in der neueren Schweizer Historiographie." *Traverse* 3 (1996): 120–28.

Kazal, Russell A. "Revisiting Assimilation: The Rise, Fall, and Reappraisal of a Concept in American Ethnic History." *American Historical Review* 100 (1995): 437–71.

Kieseritzky, Ernst. "Löhne, Einkommen und Haushaltskosten in Breslau während der letzten Jahrzehnte." In *Breslauer Statistik*, vol. 36, pt. 2 (1920), 52–99.

Klemperer, Victor. *Ich will Zeugnis ablegen bis zum letzten: Tagebücher, 1933–1945*. 2 vols. Berlin: Aufbau-Verlag, 1995.

Kleßmann, Christoph. *Polnische Bergarbeiter im Ruhrgebiet, 1870–1945: Soziale Integration und nationale Subkultur einer Minderheit in der deutschen Industriegesellschaft*. Göttingen: Vandenhoeck & Ruprecht, 1978.

Klöcker, Michael. "Das katholische Bildungsdefizit in Deutschland." *Geschichte in Wissenschaft und Unterricht* 32 (1981): 79–98.

Kocka, Jürgen. "Das europäische Muster und der deutsche Fall." In *Bürgertum im 19. Jahrhundert*, edited by Jürgen Kocka, 1:9–75. Göttingen: Vandenhoeck & Ruprecht, 1995.

———. "Familie, Unternehmer und Kapitalismus." *Zeitschrift für Unternehmensgeschichte* 24 (1979): 99–135.

———. "Zur Schichtung der preußischen Bevölkerung während der industriellen Revolution." In *Geschichte als Aufgabe: Festschrift für Otto Büsch,* edited by Wilhelm Treue, 357–90. Berlin: Colloquium Verlag, 1988.

Kocka, Jürgen, and Hannes Siegrist, eds. *Die Arbeitsstelle für Vergleichende Gesellschaftsgeschichte, 1992–1997: Ein Bericht.* Berlin: Arbeitsstelle für Vergleichende Gesellschaftsgeschichte, 1997.

Kolditz, Gerald. "Zur Entwicklung des Antisemitismus in Dresden während des Kaiserreichs." *Dresdner Hefte* 45 (1996): 37–45.

Kondylis, Panajotis. *Die Aufklärung im Rahmen des neuzeitlichen Rationalismus.* Munich: Deutscher Taschenbuch Verlag, 1986.

Konvitz, Milton R. "Orbituary: Horace Meyer Kallen." *American Jewish Yearbook* 75 (1975): 55–80.

Kornberg, Jacques. "Vienna, the 1890s: Jews in the Eyes of Their Defenders (The Verein zur Abwehr des Antisemitismus)." *Central European History* 28 (1995): 153–74.

Koselleck, Reinhart. "Volk, Nation, Nationalismus, Masse." In *Geschichtliche Grundbegriffe,* 8:141–431. Stuttgart: Klett-Cotta, 1997.

———. "Zur anthropologischen und semantischen Struktur der Bildung." In *Bildungsbürgertum im 19. Jahrhundert,* edited by Reinhart Koselleck, vol. 2, *Bildungsgüter und Bildungswissen,* 11–46. Stuttgart: Klett Cotta, 1990.

Krabbe, Wolfgang R. *Die deutsche Stadt im 19. und 20. Jahrhundert.* Göttingen: Vandenhoeck & Ruprecht, 1989.

———. "Kommunale Schul- und Kulturpolitik im 19. Jahrhundert: Münster und Dortmund im Vergleich." In Helmut Lahrkamp, ed., *Quellen und Forschungen zur Geschichte der Stadt Münster* 12 (1987): 139–82.

Kraul, Margret. "Bildung und Bürgerlichkeit." In *Bürgertum im 19. Jahrhundert: Deutschland im europäischen Vergleich,* edited by Jürgen Kocka and Ute Frevert, 3:45–73. Munich: Deutscher Taschenbuch Verlag, 1988.

Kraus, Elisabeth. *Die Familie Mosse: Deutsch-jüdisches Bürgertum im 19. und 20. Jahrhundert.* Munich: C. H. Beck, 1999.

Kriedte, Peter. *Eine Stadt am seidenen Faden: Haushalt, Hausindustrie und soziale Bewegung in Krefeld in der Mitte des 19. Jahrhunderts.* Göttingen: Vandenhoeck & Ruprecht, 1991.

Krobb, Florian. *Die schöne Jüdin: Jüdische Frauengestalten in der deutschsprachigen Erzählliteratur vom 17. Jahrhundert bis zum Ersten Weltkrieg.* Tübingen: Niemeyer, 1993.

Krohn, Helga. *Die Juden in Hamburg: Die politische, soziale und kulturelle Entwicklung einer jüdischen Großstadtgemeinde nach der Emanzipation, 1848–1918.* Hamburg: Christians, 1974.

Kuhlemann, Frank-Michael. "Niedere Schulen." In *Handbuch der deutschen Bildungsgeschichte,* edited by Christa Berg, vol. 4, *1870–1918: Von der*

Reichsgründung bis zum Ende des Ersten Weltkriegs, 179–221. Munich: C. H. Beck, 1991.

Kühne, Thomas. *Handbuch der Wahlen zum Preußischen Abgeordnetenhaus 1867–1918.* Düsseldorf: Droste Verlag, 1994.

Kulczycki, John J. *School Strikes in Prussian Poland, 1901–1907: The Struggle over Bilingual Education.* New York: Columbia University Press, 1981.

Kunz, Andreas, and Ruth Federspiel. "Die Verkehrsentwicklung Oberschlesiens im 19. Jahrhundert." In *Industriegeschichte Oberschlesiens im 19. Jahrhundert,* edited by Toni Pierenkemper, 217–49. Wiesbaden: Franz Steiner, 1992.

Kurlander, Eric. *The Price of Exclusion: Ethnicity, National Identity, and the Decline of German Liberalism, 1898–1933.* New York: Berghahn Books, 2006.

Kymlicka, Will. *Multicultural Citizenship: A Liberal Theory of Minority Rights.* 2nd ed. Oxford: Oxford University Press, 1996.

La Vopa, Anthony. "Jews and Germans: Old Quarrels, New Departures." *Journal of the History of Ideas* 54 (1993): 675–95.

Łagiewski, Maciej. *Macewy mówią.* Breslau: Za-klad Narodowy, 1991.

———. *Wrocławscy Żydzi, 1850–1944.* Wrocław: Muzeum Historyczne, 1994.

Laitin, David D. "Liberal Theory and the Nation." *Political Theory* 26 (1998): 221–37.

Lamberti, Marjorie. *Jewish Activism in Imperial Germany.* New Haven, Conn.: Yale University Press, 1978.

———. *State, Society, and the Elementary School in Imperial Germany.* New York: Oxford University Press, 1989.

Lamott, Franziska. "Virginität als Fetisch: Kulturelle Codierung und rechtliche Normierung der Jungfräulichkeit um die Jahrhundertwende." *Tel Aviver Jahrbuch für deutsche Geschichte* 21 (1992): 153–70.

Landsberger, Julian. "Zur Geschichte der jüdischen Buchdruckerei in Dyhernfurth und des jüdischen Buchhandels." *Monatsschrift für Geschichte und Wissenschaft des Judentums* 39 (1895): 120–33, 187–92, and 230–38.

Langewiesche, Dieter. "Kommentar." In *Stadt und Bürgertum im Übergang von der traditionalen zur modernen Gesellschaft,* edited by Lothar Gall, 229–36. Munich: Oldenbourg, 1993.

———. *Liberalismus in Deutschland.* Frankfurt a. M.: Suhrkamp, 1988.

———. "Liberalismus und Region." In *Liberalismus und Region: Zur Geschichte des deutschen Liberalismus im 19. Jahrhundert,* edited by Dieter Langewiesche and Lothar Gall, 1–18. Munich: Oldenbourg, 1995.

———. "'Staat' und 'Kommune': Zum Wandel der Staatsaufgaben in Deutschland im 19. Jahrhundert." *Historische Zeitschrift* 248 (1989): 621–35.

———. "Wanderungsbewegungen in der Hochindustrialisierungsperiode: Regionale, interstädtische und innerstädtische Mobilität in Deutschland, 1880–1914." *Vierteljahrschrift für Sozial- und Wirtschaftsgeschichte* 64 (1977): 1–40.

Laqueur, Thomas W. *Solitary Sex: A Cultural History of Masturbation.* New York: Zone Books, 2003.

Lappin, Eleonore. "Die jüdische Jugendbewegung als Familienersatz?" In *Die jüdische Familie in Geschichte und Gegenwart*, edited by Sabine Hödl and Martha Keil, 161–91. Berlin: Philo, 1999.

Lasker-Wallfisch, Anita. *Inherit the Truth, 1939–1945: The Documented Experiences of a Survivor of Auschwitz and Belsen*. London: Giles de la Mare, 1996.

Laux, Hans-Dieter. "Dimensionen und Determinanten der Bevölkerungsentwicklung preußischer Städte in der Periode der Hochindustrialisierung." In *Die Städte Mitteleuropas im 20. Jahrhundert*, edited by Wilhelm Rausch, 87–112. Linz: Österreichischer Arbeitskreis für Stadtgeschichtsforschung, 1984.

Leggewie, Claus. *Multi Kulti: Spielregeln für die Vielvölkerrepublik*. Berlin: Rotbuchverlag, 1993.

Lehnert, Detlef. *Kommunale Institutionen zwischen Honoratiorenverwaltung und Massendemokratie: Partizipationschancen, Autonomieprobleme und Stadtinterventionismus in Berlin, London, Paris und Wien, 1888–1914*. Baden-Baden: Nomos, 1994.

———. "Organisierter Hausbesitz und kommunale Politik in Wien und Berlin, 1890–1933." *Geschichte und Gesellschaft* 20 (1994): 29–56.

Lenger, Friedrich. "Bürgertum, Stadt und Gemeinde zwischen Frühneuzeit und Moderne." *Neue Politische Literatur* 40 (1995): 14–29.

———. *Werner Sombart, 1863–1941: Eine Biographie*. Munich: C. H. Beck, 1994.

Lenman, Robin, John Osborne, and Eda Sagarra. "Imperial Germany: Towards the Commercialization of Culture." In *German Cultural Studies*, edited by Rob Burns, 9–52. Oxford: Oxford University Press, 1995.

Lepsius, M. Rainer. "Bildungsbürgertum als ständische Vergesellschaftung." In his *Demokratie in Deutschland*, 303–14. Göttingen: Vandenhoeck & Ruprecht, 1993.

———. *Interessen, Ideen und Institutionen*. Opladen: Westdeutscher Verlag, 1990.

Leschinsky, Achim, and Peter Martin Roeder. *Schule im historischen Prozeß: Zum Wechselverhältnis von institutioneller Erziehung und gesellschaftlicher Entwicklung*. Stuttgart: Klett, 1976.

Lestschinsky, Jakob. *Das wirtschaftliche Schicksal des deutschen Judentums: Aufstieg, Wandlung, Krise, Ausblick*. Berlin: Energiadruck, 1932.

Levenson, Alan T. "German Zionism and Radical Assimilation before 1914." *Studies in Zionism* 13 (1992): 21–41.

———. "Jewish Reactions to Intermarriage in Nineteenth Century Germany." PhD diss., Ohio State University, 1990.

———. "Philosemitic Discourse in Imperial Germany." *Jewish Social Studies*, n.s., 2, no. 3 (1996): 25–53.

———. "Reform Attitudes, in the Past, toward Intermarriage." *Judaism* 38 (1989): 320–32.

Levi, Giovanni. "On Microhistory." In *New Perspectives on Historical Writing*, edited by Peter Burke, 93–113. Cambridge: Polity Press, 1992.

Levine, Lawrence W. *The Opening of the American Mind: Canons, Culture, and History*. Boston: Beacon Press, 1996.

Levy, Richard S. *The Downfall of the Anti-Semitic Political Parties in Imperial Germany*. New Haven, Conn.: Yale University Press, 1975.

Liberles, Robert. "Dohm's Treatise on the Jews: A Defence of the Enlightenment." *Year Book of the Leo Baeck Institute* 33 (1988): 29–42.

Lichtblau, Albert. *Antisemitismus und soziale Spannung in Berlin und Wien, 1867–1914*. Berlin: Metropol, 1994.

Liedtke, Rainer. *Jewish Welfare in Hamburg and Manchester, c. 1850–1914*. Oxford: Oxford University Press, 1998.

Lill, Rudolf. "Die deutschen Katholiken und die Juden in der Zeit 1850 bis zur Machtübernahme Hitlers." In *Kirche und Synagoge: Handbuch zur Geschichte von Christen und Juden*, edited by Karl Heinrich Rengstorf and Siegfried von Kortzfleisch, 2:358–420. 1970. Reprint, Munich: Deutscher Taschenbuch Verlag, 1988.

———. "Einleitung: Kulturkämpfe im 19. Jahrhundert." In *Der Kulturkampf*, edited by Rudolf Lill, 9–26. Paderborn: Schöningh, 1997.

Linse, Ulrich. "'Animierkneipen' um 1900: Arbeitersexualität und Sittenreform." In *Kirmes—Kneipe—Kino: Arbeiterkultur im Ruhrgebiet zwischen Kommerz und Kontrolle, 1850–1914*, edited by Dagmar Kift, 83–118. Paderborn: Schöningh, 1992.

———. "Arbeiterschaft und Geburtenentwicklung im Deutschen Kaiserreich von 1871." *Archiv für Sozialgeschichte* 12 (1972): 205–71.

Linton, Derek S. "Between School and Marriage: Young Working Women as a Social Problem in Late Imperial Germany." *European History Quarterly* 13 (1988): 387–408.

Lipp, Carola. "Die Innenseite der Arbeiterkultur: Sexualität im Arbeitermilieu des 19. und frühen 20. Jahrhunderts." In *Arbeit, Frömmigkeit und Eigensinn: Studien zur historischen Kulturforschung*, edited by Richard van Dülmen, 2:215–20. Frankfurt a. M.: Fischer, 1990.

Loening, Edgar. "Ausweisung." In *Handwörterbuch der Staatswissenschaften*, edited by Johannes Conrad, 2:314–18. 3rd ed. Jena: Fischer, 1909.

Loewe, Victor. "Schlesische Gelehrte Gesellschaften und Vereine." In *Schlesische Landeskunde*, edited by Fritz Frech and Franz Kampers, 259–62. Leipzig: Veit, 1913.

Lohalm, Uwe. *Völkischer Radikalismus: Die Geschichte des Deutschvölkischen Schutz- und Trutzbundes, 1919–1923*. Hamburg: Leibnitz-Verlag, 1970.

Lowenstein, Steven M. "Ashkenazic Jewry and the European Marriage Pattern." *Jewish History* 8 (1994): 155–75.

———. *The Berlin Jewish Community: Enlightenment, Family and Crisis, 1770–1830*. Oxford: Oxford University Press, 1994.

———. "Die Gemeinde." In *Deutsch-jüdische Geschichte in der Neuzeit*, by Steven M. Lowenstein, Paul Mendes-Flohr, Peter Pulzer, and Monika Richarz, edited by Michael A. Meyer, vol. 3, *Umstrittene Integration, 1871–1918*, 123–50. Munich: C. H. Beck, 1997.

——. "Jewish Residential Concentration in Post-Emancipation Germany." In his *The Mechanics of Change: Essays in the Social History of German Jewry*, 153–82. Atlanta: Scholars Press, 1992.

Lowenstein, Steven M., Paul Mendes-Flohr, Peter Pulzer, and Monika Richarz. *Deutsch-jüdische Geschichte in der Neuzeit*, edited by Michael A. Meyer, vol. 3, *Umstrittene Integration, 1871–1918*. Munich: C. H. Beck, 1997.

Luhmann, Niklas. *Die Gesellschaft der Gesellschaft*. Frankfurt a. M.: Suhrkamp, 1997.

Lundgreen, Peter. "Die Bildungschancen beim Übergang von der 'Gesamtschule' zum Schulsystem der Klassengesellschaft im 19. Jahrhundert." *Zeitschrift für Pädagogik* 24 (1978): 101–15.

Lundgreen, Peter, Margret Kraul, and Karl Ditt. *Bildungschancen und soziale Mobilität in der städtischen Gesellschaft des 19. Jahrhunderts*. Göttingen: Vandenhoeck & Ruprecht, 1988.

Magnus, Shulamit S. *Jewish Emancipation in a German City: Cologne, 1798–1871*. Stanford, Calif.: Stanford University Press, 1997.

Mann, Bernhard, ed. *Biographisches Handbuch für das Preußische Abgeordnetenhaus, 1867–1918*. Düsseldorf: Droste, 1988.

Mann, Thomas. *Der Zauberberg*. Frankfurt a. M.: Fischer, 1981. Translated by John E. Woods as *The Magic Mountain* (New York: Vintage, 1996).

Markgraf, Hermann. *Geschichte Breslaus in kurzer Übersicht*. 2nd expanded ed. revised by Otfried Schwarzer. Breslau: Kern, 1913.

Massing, Paul. *Rehearsal for Destruction: A Study of Political Anti-Semitism in Imperial Germany*. New York: Harper & Bros., 1949.

Mattenklott, Gerd. "Juden in der deutschsprachigen Zeitschriftenliteratur im ersten Drittel des 20. Jahrhunderts." In *Juden als Träger bürgerlicher Kultur in Deutschland*, edited by Julius H. Schoeps, 149–66. Stuttgart: Burg-Verlag, 1989.

Mattioli, Aram. "Juden und Judenfeindschaft in der schweizerischen Historiographie—Eine Replik auf Robert Uri Kaufmann." *Traverse* 4 (1997): 155–63.

Matzerath, Horst. *Urbanisierung in Preußen, 1815–1914*. Stuttgart: Kohlhammer, 1985.

Maurer, Trude. *Die Entwicklung der jüdischen Minderheit, 1780–1933: Neuere Forschungen und offene Fragen*. Tübingen: Niemeyer, 1992.

——. *Ostjuden in Deutschland, 1918–1933*. Hamburg: Hans Christian Verlag, 1986.

Maynes, Mary Jo. *Taking the Hard Road: Life Course and Class Identity in Nineteenth-Century French and German Workers' Autobiographies*. Chapel Hill: University of North Carolina Press, 1995.

Mazura, Paul. *Die Entwicklung des politischen Katholizismus in Schlesien*. Breslau: Marcus, 1925.

Mazura, Uwe. *Zentrumspartei und Judenfrage, 1870/71–1933: Verfassungstaat und Minderheitenschutz*. Mainz: Matthias-Grünewald-Verlag, 1994.

McCaa, Robert. "Ethnic Intermarriage and Gender in New York." *Journal of Interdisciplinary History* 24 (1993): 207–32.

Medding, Peter Y. "Jewish Identity in Conversionary and Mixed Marriages." *American Jewish Yearbook* 92 (1992): 3–76.

Medick, Hans. "Mikro-Historie." In *Sozialgeschichte, Alltagsgeschichte, Mikro-Historie*, edited by Winfried Schulze, 40–53. Göttingen: Vandenhoeck & Ruprecht, 1994.

Mehring, Franz. *Aufsätze zur deutschen Literaturgeschichte*. Edited by Hans Koch. 2nd ed. Leipzig: Reclam, 1966.

Meiring, Kerstin. *Die christlich-jüdische Mischehe in Deutschland, 1840–1933*. Hamburg: Dölling & Galitz, 1998.

Mejer, Otto. "Parität." In *Realencyklopädie für protestantische Theologie und Kirche*, edited by Johann Jakob Herzog, Gustav Leopold Plitt, and Albert Hauck, 11:223–24. 2nd ed. Leipzig: Hinrichs, 1883.

Mendus, Susan. *Toleration and the Limits of Liberalism*. London: Palgrave Macmillan, 1989.

Mendus, Susan, and David Edwards, eds. *On Toleration*. Oxford: Clarendon Press, 1987.

Mergel, Thomas. "Das Rathaus." In *1848: Revolution in Deutschland*, edited by Christof Dipper and Ulrich Speck, 183–95. Frankfurt a. M.: Insel, 1998.

———. *Zwischen Klasse und Konfession: Katholisches Bürgertum im Rheinland im 19. Jahrhundert*. Göttingen: Vandenhoeck & Ruprecht, 1994.

Mettele, Gisela. *Bürgertum in Köln, 1775–1870: Gemeinsinn und freie Association*. Munich: Oldenbourg, 1998.

Meyer, Beate. *Jüdische Mischlinge: Rassenpolitik und Verfolgungsgefahr, 1933–1945*. Hamburg: Dölling & Galitz, 1999.

Meyer, Michael A. *Response to Modernity: A History of the Reform Movement in Judaism*. Oxford: Oxford University Press, 1988.

Meyer, Sibylle. *Das Theater mit der Hausarbeit: Bürgerliche Repräsentation in der Familie der wilhelminischen Zeit*. Frankfurt a. M.: Campus, 1982.

Mill, John Stuart. *On Liberty: with The Subjection of Women; and Chapters on Socialism*. Edited by Stefan Collini. Cambridge: Cambridge University Press, 1991.

Mommsen, Wolfgang J. *Bürgerstolz und Weltmachtstreben: Deutschland unter Wilhelm II, 1890–1918*. Berlin: Propyläen, 1995.

———. "Nationalität im Zeichen offensiver Weltpolitik: Das Reichs- und Staatsangehörigkeitsgesetz des Deutschen Reiches vom 22. Januar 1913." In *Nation und Gesellschaft in Deutschland: Festschrift für Hans-Ulrich Wehler*, edited by Manfred Hettling and Paul Nolte, 128–41. Munich: C. H. Beck, 1996.

———. *Das Ringen um den nationalen Staat: Die Gründung und der innere Ausbau des Deutschen Reiches unter Otto von Bismarck, 1850–1890*. Berlin: Propyläen, 1993.

Mosse, George L. "Der erste Weltkrieg und die Brutalisierung der Politik: Betrachtungen über die politische Rechte, den Rassissmus und den deutschen Sonderweg." In *Demokratie und Diktatur: Geist und Gestalt politischer Herrschaft in Deutschland und Europa; Festschrift für Karl Dietrich Bracher,* edited by Manfred Funke, Hans-Adolf Jacobsen, Hans-Helmuth Knütter, and Hans-Peter Schwarz, 127–39. Düsseldorf: Droste, 1987.

———. *German Jews beyond Judaism.* Bloomington: University of Indiana Press; Cincinnati: Hebrew Union College Press, 1985.

———. "The Image of the Jew in German Popular Culture: Felix Dahn and Gustav Freytag." *Year Book of the Leo Baeck Institute* 2 (1957): 218–27. Reprinted in his *Germans and Jews: The Right, the Left, and the Search for a Third Force in Pre-Nazi Germany* (New York: Grosset & Dunlap, 1970; reprint, Detroit: Wayne State University Press, 1987), 61–76 and 234–36.

Mosse, Werner E. *German-Jewish Economic Élite, 1820–1935: A Socio-Cultural Profile.* Oxford: Oxford University Press, 1989.

———. *Jews in the German Economy: The German-Jewish Élite, 1820–1935.* Oxford: Oxford University Press, 1987.

Moy, Count Karl Ernst von. "Parität." In *Wetzer und Weltke's Kirchenlexikon oder Encyklopädie der katholischen Theologie und ihrer Hülfswissenschaften,* edited by Joseph Hergenröther and Franz Kaulen, 9:1520–24. 2nd ed. Freiburg i. Br.: Herder, 1895.

Moyn, Samuel. "German Jewry and the Question of Identity: Historiography and Theory." *Year Book of the Leo Baeck Institute* 41 (1996): 291–308.

Mühlmann, Wilhelm E. "Assimilation." In *Wörterbuch der Soziologie,* edited by Wilhelm Bernsdorf, 1:57–58. Frankfurt a. M.: Fischer, 1972.

Mühlpfordt, Herbert M. "Welche Mitbürger hat Königsberg öffentlich geehrt?" *Jahrbuch der Albertus-Universität* 14 (1964): 66–198.

Müller, C. F. W. "Die Eröffnung des Johannesgymnasiums." In *Programm des städtischen Johannes-Gymnasiums zu Breslau für die Zeit von Michaelis 1872 bis Ostern 1874,* edited by C. F. W. Müller, 1–10. Breslau: Grass & Barth, 1874.

Müller, Detlef K. *Sozialstruktur und Schulsystem: Aspekte zum Strukturwandel des Schulsystems im 19. Jahrhundert.* Göttingen: Vandenhoeck & Ruprecht, 1977.

Müller, Detlef K., and Bernd Zymek, eds. *Datenhandbuch zur deutschen Bildungsgeschichte.* Vol. 2, *Höhere und mittlere Schulen,* pt. 1. Göttingen: Vandenhoeck & Ruprecht, 1987.

Müller, Leonhard. *Der Kampf zwischen politischem Katholizismus und Bismarcks Politik im Spiegel der Schlesischen Volkszeitung: Ein Beitrag zur schlesischen Kirchen-, Parteien- und Zeitungsgeschichte.* Breslau: Müller & Seiffert, 1929.

Müller, Theodor. *Die Geschichte der Breslauer Sozialdemokratie.* Vol. 2. Breslau: Sozialdemokratischer Verein, 1925.

Müller-List, Gabriele. *Die Sozialstruktur der evangelischen Einwohner Bonns im 19. Jahrhundert.* Bonn: Stadtsarchiv Bonn, 1980.

Murphy, Raymond. *Social Closure: The Theory of Monopolization and Exclusion.* Oxford: Clarendon Press, 1988.

Nadell, Pamela S. "The Journey to America by Steam: The Jews of Eastern Europe in Transition." *American Jewish History* 71 (1982): 269–84.

Nathans, Eli. *The Politics of Citizenship in Germany: Ethnicity, Utility, and Nationalism.* Oxford: Berg, 2004.

Neißer, Else. "Preisbewegung und Haushaltungskosten in Breslau, 1893–1912." In *Untersuchungen über Preisbildung*, sec. C, *Die Kosten der Lebenshaltung in deutschen Großstädten*, pt. 1, *Ost- und Norddeutschland*, edited by Franz Eulenberg, Schriften des Vereins für Sozialpolitik 145, 441–80. Leipzig: Duncker & Humblot, 1915.

Neubach, Helmut. *Die Ausweisungen von Polen und Juden aus Preussen, 1885/86: Ein Beitrag zu Bismarcks Polenpolitik und zur Geschichte des deutsch-polnischen Verhältnisses.* Wiesbaden: Harrassowitz, 1967.

Neubauer, Hans-Joachim. *Judenfiguren: Drama und Theater im frühen 19. Jahrhundert.* Frankfurt a. M.: Campus, 1994.

Neugebauer, Wolfgang. "Das Bildungswesen in Preußen seit der Mitte des 17. Jahrhunderts." In *Handbuch der preußischen Geschichte*, edited by Otto Büsch, vol. 2, *Das 19. Jahrhundert und Große Themen der Geschichte Preußens*, 605–798. Berlin: de Gruyter, 1992.

Neumann, R. P. "Masturbation, Madness, and the Modern Concepts of Childhood and Adolescence." *Journal of Social History* 8 (1975): 1–27.

Neumann, Salomon. *Die Fabel von der jüdischen Masseneinwanderung: Ein Kapitel aus der preußischen Statistik.* 3rd ed. Berlin: Simion, 1881.

Nick, Dagmar. *Jüdisches Wirken in Breslau: Eingeholte Erinnerung; Der Alte Asch und die Bauers.* Würzburg: Bergstadt, 1998.

Niewyk, Donald L. "The Impact of Inflation and Depression on the German Jews." *Year Book of the Leo Baeck Institute* 28 (1983): 19–36.

——. *The Jews in Weimar Germany.* Baton Rouge: Louisiana State University Press, 1980.

Nipperdey, Thomas. *Deutsche Geschichte, 1800–1866.* 5th ed. Munich: C. H. Beck, 1991.

——. *Deutsche Geschichte, 1866–1918.* Vol. 1, *Arbeitswelt und Bürgergeist.* Munich: C. H. Beck, 1990.

——. *Deutsche Geschichte, 1866–1918.* Vol. 2, *Machtstaat vor der Demokratie.* Munich: C. H. Beck, 1992.

——. "Verein als soziale Struktur in Deutschland im späten 18. und frühen 19. Jh." In his *Gesellschaft, Kultur, Theorie. Gesammelte Aufsätze zur neueren Geschichte*, 174–205. Göttingen: Vandenhoeck & Ruprecht, 1976.

Nipperdey, Thomas, and Reinhard Rürup. "Antisemitismus: Entstehung, Funktion und Geschichte eines Begriffs." In *Emanzipation und Antisemitismus: Studien zur "Judenfrage" in der bürgerlichen Gesellschaft*, by Reinhard Rürup, 120–44. Frankfurt a. M.: Fischer, 1987.

Noiriel, Gérard. *The French Melting Pot: Immigration, Citizenship, and National Identity.* Translated by Geoffroy de Laforcade. Minneapolis: University of Minnesota Press, 1996.

Okamura, Jonathan Y. "Situational Ethnicity." *Ethnic and Racial Studies* 4 (1981): 452–65.

Otte, Marline S. *Jewish Identities in German Popular Entertainment, 1890–1933*. Cambridge: Cambridge University Press, 2006.

——. "Eine Welt für sich? Bürger im Jargontheater, 1890–1920." In *Bürger, Juden, Deutsche: Zur Geschichte von Vielfalt und Grenzen, 1800–1933*, edited by Andreas Gotzmann, Rainer Liedtke, and Till van Rahden, 121–46. Tübingen: Mohr Siebeck, 2001.

Palmowski, Jan. *Urban Liberalism in Imperial Germany: Frankfurt am Main, 1866–1914*. Oxford: Oxford University Press, 1999.

Parkin, Frank. *Marxism and Class Theory: A Bourgeois Critique*. London: Tavistock, 1979.

——. "Strategies of Social Closure in Class Formation." In *The Social Analysis of Class Structure*, edited by Frank Parkin, 1–18. London: Tavistock, 1974.

Pascoe, Peggy. "Miscegenation Law, Court Cases, and Ideologies of 'Race' in Twentieth-Century America." *Journal of American History* 83 (1996): 44–69.

Peal, David. "Anti-Semitism and Rural Transformation in Kurhessen: The Rise and Fall of the Böckel Movement." PhD diss., Columbia University, 1985.

Penslar, Derek J. *Shylock's Children: Economics and Jewish Identity in Modern Europe*. Berkeley: University of California Press, 2001.

Penzler, Johann, ed. *Fürst Bismarck nach seiner Entlassung*. Vol. 6, *26. Dec. 1894–Ende 1895*. Leipzig: Fiedler, 1898.

Perlman, Joel. *Ethnic Differences: School and Social Structure among Irish, Italians, Jews and Blacks in an American City, 1880–1935*. Cambridge: Cambridge University Press, 1988.

Perrot, Michelle, ed. *A History of Private Life*. Vol. 4, *From the Fires of Revolution to the Great War*. Cambridge, Mass.: Belknap Press, 1990.

Perrot, Michelle, and Anne Martin-Fugier. "Bourgeois Rituals." In *A History of Private Life*, edited by Michelle Perrot, vol. 4, *From the Fires of Revolution to the Great War*, 261–336. Cambridge, Mass.: Belknap Press, 1990.

Philippsthal, Herbert. "Die jüdische Bevölkerung Breslaus." *Breslauer Jüdisches Gemeindeblatt* 8 (1931): 52, 67–68, 98–99.

Philippson, Martin. *Max von Forckenbeck: Ein Lebensbild*. Dresden: Reißner, 1898.

Pierenkemper, Toni. "Der bürgerliche Haushalt in Deutschland an der Wende zum 20. Jahrhundert—im Spiegel von Haushaltsrechnungen." In *Zur Geschichte der Ökonomik der Privathaushalte*, edited by Dietmar Petzina, 149–85. Berlin: Duncker & Humblot, 1991.

Pierson, Ruth. "Embattled Veterans: Der Reichsbund jüdischer Frontsoldaten." *Year Book of the Leo Baeck Institute* 19 (1974): 139–54.

Ping, Larry L. *Gustav Freytag and the Prussian Gospel: Novels, Liberalism, and History*. Frankfurt a. M.: Peter Lang, 2006.

Preissler, Dietmar. *Frühantisemitismus in der Freien Stadt Frankfurt und im Großherzogtum Hessen (1810–1860)*. Heidelberg: Carl Winter, 1989.

Prestel, Claudia. *Jüdisches Schul- und Erziehungswesen in Bayern, 1804–1933*. Göttingen: Vandenhoeck & Ruprecht, 1989.

————. "The 'New Jewish Woman' in Weimar Germany." In *Jüdisches Leben in der Weimarer Republik—Jews in the Weimar Republic*, edited by Wolfgang Benz, Arnold Paucker, and Peter Pulzer, 135–56. Tübingen: Mohr Siebeck, 1998.

————. "Zwischen Tradition und Moderne: Die Armenpolitik der Gemeinde zu Fürth (1826–1870)." *Tel Aviver Jahrbuch für deutsche Geschichte* 20 (1991): 135–62.

Priebatsch, Leopold. "Louis Neustadt" (obituary). *Jahresbericht der Schlesischen Gesellschaft für vaterländische Cultur* 96 (1918): 67–68.

Pruner, Johannes von. "Bekenntnißfreiheit." In *Staatslexikon*, edited by Adolf Bruder, vol. 1, cols. 865–83. Freiburg i. Br.: Herder, 1889.

Pulzer, Peter. "Der Anfang vom Ende." In *Die Juden im nationalsozialistischen Deutschland—The Jews in Nazi Germany, 1933–1943*, edited by Arnold Paucker, Sylvia Gilchrist, and Barbara Suchy, 3–27. Tübingen: Mohr Siebeck, 1986.

————. "Between Hope and Fear: Jews and the Weimar Republic." In *Jüdisches Leben in der Weimarer Republik—Jews in the Weimar Republic*, edited by Wolfgang Benz, Arnold Paucker, and Peter Pulzer, 271–79. Tübingen: Mohr Siebeck, 1998.

————. "Der Erste Weltkrieg." In *Deutsch-jüdische Geschichte in der Neuzeit*, by Steven M. Lowenstein, Paul Mendes-Flohr, Peter Pulzer, and Monika Richarz, edited by Michael A. Meyer, vol. 3, *Umstrittene Integration, 1871–1918*, 356–80. Munich: C. H. Beck, 1997.

————. *Jews and the German State: The Political History of a Minority, 1848–1933*. Oxford: Blackwell 1992.

————. "Die jüdische Beteiligung an der Politik." In *Juden im Wilhelminischen Deutschland, 1870–1914*, edited by Werner E. Mosse, 143–240. Tübingen: Mohr Siebeck, 1976.

————. *The Rise of Political Anti-Semitism in Germany and Austria*. 1964. 2nd rev. ed. Cambridge, Mass.: Harvard University Press, 1988.

Rahden, Till van. "'Germans of the Jewish *Stamm*': Visions of Community between Nationalism and Particularism, 1850 to 1933." In *German History from the Margins, 1800 to the Present*, edited by Neil Gregor, Nils Roemer, and Mark Roseman, 27–48. Bloomington: Indiana University Press, 2006.

————. "Ideologie und Gewalt: Neuerscheinungen über den Antisemitismus in der deutschen Geschichte des 19. und frühen 20. Jahrhunderts." *Neue Politische Literatur* 41 (1996): 11–29.

————. "Treason, Fate, or Blessing? Concepts of Assimilation in the Historiography of German-Speaking Jewry since the 1950s." In *Preserving the Legacy of German Jewry: A History of the Leo Baeck Institute, 1955–2005*, edited by Christhard Hoffmann, 349–73. Tübingen: J.C.B. Mohr, 2005.

Rapaport, Lynn. *Jews in Germany after the Holocaust: Memory, Identity, and German-Jewish Relations*. New York: Cambridge University Press, 1997.

Raz, Joseph. "Multiculturalism: A Liberal Perspective." In his *Ethics in the Public Domain: Essays in the Morality of Law and Politics*, 155–76. Oxford: Clarendon Press, 1994.

Reichmann, Eva G. "Max Horkheimer the Jew—Critical Theory and Beyond." *Year Book of the Leo Baeck Institute* 19 (1974): 181–96.

Reif, Heinz. "Von der Stände- zur Klassengesellschaft." In *Scheidewege der deutschen Geschichte*, edited by Hans-Ulrich Wehler, 79–90. Munich: C. H. Beck, 1995.

Reinke, Andreas. *Judentum und Wohlfahrtspflege in Deutschland: Das jüdische Krankenhaus in Breslau, 1744–1944*. Hanover: Hahnsche Buchhandlung, 1999.

———. "Zwischen Tradition, Aufklärung und Assimilation: Die Königliche Wilhelmsschule in Breslau, 1791–1848." *Zeitschrift für Religions- und Geistesgeschichte* 43 (1991): 193–214.

Reitmayer, Morton. *Bankiers im Kaiserreich: Sozialprofil und Habitus der Deutschen Hochfinanz*. Göttingen: Vandenhoeck & Ruprecht, 2000.

Retallack, James. "Conservatives and Antisemites in Baden and Saxony." *German History* 17 (1999): 507–26.

———. *Germany in the Age of Kaiser Wilhelm II*. London: Macmillan, 1996.

Richarz, Monika. "Die Entwicklung der jüdischen Bevölkerung." In *Deutsch-jüdische Geschichte in der Neuzeit*, by Steven M. Lowenstein, Paul Mendes-Flohr, Peter Pulzer, and Monika Richarz, edited by Michael A. Meyer, vol. 3, *Umstrittene Integration, 1871–1918*, 13–38. Munich: C. H. Beck, 1997.

———. "Frauen in Familie und Öffentlichkeit." In *Deutsch-jüdische Geschichte in der Neuzeit*, by Steven M. Lowenstein, Paul Mendes-Flohr, Peter Pulzer, and Monika Richarz, edited by Michael A. Meyer, vol. 3, *Umstrittene Integration, 1871–1918*, 69–100. Munich: C. H. Beck, 1997.

———. "Jewish Social Mobility in Germany during the Time of Emancipation (1790–1871)." *Year Book of the Leo Baeck Institute* 20 (1975): 69–77.

———, ed. *Jüdisches Leben in Deutschland*. Vol. 2, *Selbstzeugnisse zur Sozialgeschichte des Kaiserreichs*. Stuttgart: Deutsche Verlagsanstalt, 1979.

———. "Der jüdische Weihnachtsbaum—Familie und Säkularisierung im deutschen Judentum des 19. Jahrhunderts." In *Geschichte und Emanzipation: Festschrift für Reinhard Rürup*, edited by Michael Grüttner, Rüdiger Hachtmann, and Heinz-Gerhard Haupt, 275–89. Frankfurt a. M.: Campus, 1999.

———. "Luftaufnahme—oder die Schwierigkeiten der Heimatforscher mit der jüdischen Geschichte." *Babylon* 8 (1991): 27–33.

Richter, Ludwig. *Kirche und Schule in den Beratungen der Weimarer Nationalversammlung*. Düsseldorf: Droste, 1996.

Ringer, Fritz K. "Bestimmung und Messung von Segmentierung." *Geschichte und Gegenwart* 8 (1982): 280–85.

Ritter, Gerhard A., and Klaus Tenfelde. *Arbeiter im Deutschen Kaiserreich*. Bonn: Dietz, 1992.

Rohe, Karl. *Politik: Begriffe und Wirklichkeiten*. 2nd ed. Stuttgart: Kohlhammer, 1994.

Rohrbacher, Stefan. *Gewalt im Biedermeier: Antijüdische Unruhen im Vormärz und Revolution (1815–1848/49)*. Frankfurt a. M.: Campus, 1993.

————. "Kaiserreich und Weimarer Republik—Horte innigster deutsch-jüdischer Symbiose?" *Geschichte in Wissenschaft und Unterricht* 43 (1992): 681–87.

Roon, Ger van. *Neuordnung im Widerstand: Der Kreisauer Kreis innerhalb der deutschen Widerstandsbewegung.* Munich: Oldenbourg, 1967.

Rose, Paul Lawrence. *German Question/Jewish Question.* Princeton, N.J.: Princeton University Press, 1992.

Rosen, Friedrich. "Ferdinand Cohn." In *Schlesische Lebensbilder,* 1:167–73. Breslau: W. G. Korn, 1922.

Rosenbaum, Heidi. *Formen der Familie: Untersuchungen zum Zusammenhang von Familienverhältnissen, Sozialstruktur und sozialem Wandel in der deutschen Gesellschaft des 19. Jahrhunderts.* Frankfurt a. M.: Suhrkamp, 1982.

————. *Proletarische Familien: Arbeiterfamilien und Arbeiterväter im frühen 20. Jahrhundert zwischen traditioneller, sozialdemokratischer und kleinbürgerlicher Orientierung.* Frankfurt a. M.: Suhrkamp, 1992.

Rösener, Werner. "Das katholische Bildungsdefizit im Deutschen Kaiserreich—Ein Erbe der Säkularisation von 1803." *Historisches Jahrbuch* 112 (1992): 104–27.

Rosenhaft, Eve. "Women, Gender, and the Limits of Political History of 'Mass' Politics." In *Elections, Mass Politics, and Social Change in Modern Germany,* edited by Larry E. Jones and James Retallack, 149–73. Cambridge: Cambridge University Press, 1992.

Roth, Ralf. "Liberalismus in Frankfurt a. M., 1814–1914: Probleme seiner Strukturgeschichte." In *Liberalismus und Region: Zur Geschichte des deutschen Liberalismus im 19. Jahrhundert,* edited by Dieter Langewiesche and Lothar Gall, 41–86. Munich: Oldenbourg, 1995.

————. *Stadt und Bürgertum in Frankfurt am Main: Ein besonderer Weg von der ständischen zur modernen Bürgergesellschaft 1760–1914.* Munich: Oldenbourg, 1996.

————. "Von Wilhelm Meister zu Hans Castorp: Der Bildungsgedanke und das bürgerliche Assoziationswesen im 18. und 19. Jahrhundert." In *Bürgerkultur im 19. Jahrhundert—Bildung, Kunst und Lebenswelt,* edited by Dieter Hein and Andreas Schulz, 121–39. Munich: C. H. Beck, 1996.

Rozenblit, Marsha L. *The Jews of Vienna, 1867–1914: Assimilation and Identity.* Albany: State University of New York Press, 1984.

Ruppin, Arthur. *Die Juden der Gegenwart: Eine sozialwissenschaftliche Studie.* 3rd ed. Berlin: Jüdischer Verlag, 1918.

————. "Die sozialen Verhältnisse der Juden in Preussen und Deutschland." *Jahrbücher für Nationalökonomie und Statistik* 78 (1902): 374–87 and 760–85.

————. *Soziologie der Juden.* Vol. 1, *Die soziale Struktur der Juden.* Berlin: Jüdischer Verlag, 1930.

————. *Soziologie der Juden.* Vol. 2, *Der Kampf der Juden um ihre Zukunft.* Berlin: Jüdischer Verlag, 1931.

Rürup, Reinhard. "Jüdische Geschichte in Deutschland." In *Zerbrochene Geschichte: Leben und Selbstverständnis der Juden in Deutschland*, edited by Dirk Blasius and Dan Diner, 79–102. Frankfurt a. M.: Fischer, 1991.

———, ed. *Jüdische Geschichte in Berlin: Essays und Studien*. Berlin: Edition Hentrich, 1995.

———. "Zur Entwicklung der modernen Antisemitismusforschung." In his *Emanzipation und Antisemitismus: Studien zur "Judenfrage" in der bürgerlichen Gesellschaft*, 145–58. Frankfurt a. M.: Fischer, 1987.

Rüsen, Jörn. "Identität und Konflikt im Prozeß der Modernisierung: Überlegungen zur kulturhistorischen Dimension von Fremdenfeindschaft heute." In *Universalgeschichte und Nationalgeschichte: Festschrift für Ernst Schulin zum 65. Geburtstag*, edited by Gangolf Hübinger, Jürgen Osterhammel, and Erich Pelzer, 333–43. Freiburg i. Br.: Rombach, 1994.

Sabean, David. "Die Ästhetik der Heiratsallianzen: Klassencodes und endogame Eheschließung im Bürgertum des 19. Jahrhunderts." In *Historische Familienforschung*, edited by Josef Ehmer, Tamara K. Hareven, and Richard Wall, 157–70. Frankfurt a. M.: Campus, 1997.

Sarasin, Philipp. *Stadt der Bürger: Struktureller Wandel und bürgerliche Lebenswelt Basel, 1870–1900*. Basel: Helbing & Lichtenhahn, 1990.

Schieder, Wolfgang. "Sozialgeschichte der Religion im 19. Jahrhundert." In *Religion und Gesellschaft im 19. Jahrhundert*, edited by Wolfgang Schieder, 11–28. Stuttgart: Klett-Cotta, 1993.

Schimpf, Dorothee. *Emanzipation und Bildungswesen der Juden im Kurfürstentum Hessen, 1807–1866: Jüdische Identität zwischen Selbstbehauptung und Assimilationsdruck*. Wiesbaden: Staatsarchiv Wiesbaden, 1994.

Schleunes, Karl A. *The Twisted Road to Auschwitz: Nazi Policy toward German Jews, 1933–1939*. 2nd ed. Urbana: University of Illinois Press, 1990.

Schlotzhauer, Inge. *Ideologie und Organisation des politischen Antisemitismus in Frankfurt am Main, 1880–1914*. Frankfurt a. M.: W. Kramer, 1989.

Schmelz, Uriel O. *Die jüdische Bevölkerung in Hessen: Von der Mitte des 19. Jahrhunderts bis 1933*. Tübingen: Mohr Siebeck, 1996.

Schmidt, Michael. "'Faule Geschichten'? Über den 'Landjuden' und deutsche Literatur." In *Jüdisches Leben auf dem Lande*, edited by Monika Richarz and Reinhard Rürup, 347–71. Tübingen: Mohr Siebeck, 1997.

Schmiechen-Ackermann, Detlef. "Großstädte und Nationalsozialismus, 1930–1945." In *Nationalsozialismus in der Region*, edited by Horst Möller, Andreas Wirsching, and Walter Ziegler, 253–70. Munich: Oldenbourg, 1996.

Schmitt, Carl. *Romischer Katholizismus und politische Form*. Munich: Theatiner-Verlag, 1925.

Schmoller, Gustav von. "Über Wesen und Verfassung großer Unternehmungen." In his *Zur Social- und Gewerbepolitik der Gegenwart: Reden und Afsätze*, 372–440. Leipzig: Duncker & Humblot, 1890.

Schnabel, Franz. *Deutsche Geschichte im neunzehnten Jahrhundert.* Vol. 2, *Monarchie und Volkssouveränität.* Freiburg i. Br.: Herder, 1933. Reprint, Munich: Deutscher Taschenbuch Verlag, 1987.

Schoen, Paul. *Das Recht der Kommunalverbände in Preußen.* Leipzig: Brockhaus, 1897.

Scholem, Gershom. *Judaica.* Vol. 2. Frankfurt a. M.: Suhrkamp, 1970.

Schorsch, Ismar. "German Antisemitism in the Light of Post-War Historiography." *Year Book of the Leo Baeck Institute* 19 (1974): 257–71.

Schraut, Sylvia. *Sozialer Wandel im Industrialisierungsprozeß: Esslingen, 1800–1870.* Sigmaringen: Thorbecke, 1989.

Schröder, Iris. "Grenzgängerinnen: Jüdische Sozialreformerinnen in der Frankfurter Frauenbewegung um 1900." In *Bürger, Juden, Deutsche: Zur Geschichte von Vielfalt und Grenzen in Deutschland, 1780–1933*, edited by Andreas Gotzmann, Rainer Liedtke, and Till van Rahden, 341–68. Tübingen: Mohr Siebeck, 2001.

Schüler-Springorum, Stefanie. "'Denken, Wirken, Schaffen': Das erfolgreiche Leben des Aron Liebeck." In *Bürger, Juden, Deutsche: Zur Geschichte von Vielfalt und Grenzen, 1800–1933*, edited by Andreas Gotzmann, Rainer Liedtke, and Till van Rahden, 369–94. Tübingen: Mohr Siebeck, 2001.

———. *Die jüdische Minderheit in Königsberg/Preußen, 1871–1945.* Göttingen: Vandenhoeck & Ruprecht, 1996.

Schüren, Reinhard. *Soziale Mobilität: Muster, Veränderungen und Bedingungen im 19. und 20. Jahrhundert.* St. Katharinen: Scripta Mercaturae Verlag, 1989.

Schumann, Dirk. *Bayerns Unternehmer in Gesellschaft und Staat, 1834–1914.* Göttingen: Vandenhoeck & Ruprecht, 1992.

———. *Politische Gewalt in der Weimarer Republik, 1918–1933: Kampf um die Straße und Furcht vor dem Bürgerkrieg.* Essen: Klartext Verlagsgesellschaft, 2001.

Schwerin, Kurt. "Die Juden im wirtschaftlichen Leben Schlesiens." *Jahrbuch der Schlesischen Friedrich-Wilhelms-Universität zu Breslau* 25 (1984): 93–177.

Scott, Joan Wallace. *Gender and the Politics of History.* New York: Columbia University Press, 1988.

Segall, Jakob. *Die beruflichen und sozialen Verhältnisse der Juden in Deutschland.* Berlin: Schildberger, 1912.

Seitz, Norbert. "Gustav Landauer und die Münchener Räterepublik." In *". . . die beste Sensation ist das Ewige . . .": Gustav Landauer; Leben, Werk und Wirkung*, edited by Michael Matzigkeit, 267–91. Düsseldorf: Droste, 1995.

Sen, Amartya. *Identity and Violence: The Illusion of Destiny.* New York: Norton, 2006.

Seng, Ulrich. *Schulpolitik des Bistums Breslau im 19. Jahrhundert.* Wiesbaden: Harrassowitz, 1989.

Sheehan, James J. "Different, Ignoble and Alien." *Times Literary Supplement*, July 31, 1992, 8.

———. "Liberalism and the City in Nineteenth Century Germany." *Past and Present* 51 (1971): 116–37.

———. "What Is German History? Reflections on the Role of the 'Nation' in German History and Historiography." *Journal of Modern History* 53 (1981): 1–23.

Sieder, Reinhard. *Sozialgeschichte der Familie.* Frankfurt a. M.: Suhrkamp, 1987.

Sieg, Ulrich. *Aufstieg und Niedergang des Marburger Neukantianismus: Die Geschichte einer philosophischen Schulgemeinschaft.* Würzburg: Königshausen & Neumann, 1994.

———. "Im Zeichen der Beharrung: Althoffs Wissenschaftspolitik und die deutsche Universitätsphilosophie." In *Wissenschaftsgeschichte und Wissenschaftspolitik im Industriezeitalter,* edited by Bernhard von Brocke, 287–306. Hildesheim: August Lax, 1991.

———. "Der Preis des Bildungsstrebens: Jüdische Geisteswissenschaftler im Kaiserreich." In *Bürger, Juden, Deutsche: Zur Geschichte von Vielfalt und Grenzen, 1800–1933,* edited by Andreas Gotzmann, Rainer Liedtke, and Till van Rahden, 67–95. Tübingen: Mohr Siebeck, 2001.

Siegrist, Hannes. *Advokat, Bürger und Staat: Eine vergleichende Geschichte der Rechtsanwälte in Deutschland, Italien und der Schweiz (18.–20. Jahrhundert).* Frankfurt a. M.: Klostermann, 1996.

Siemann, Wolfram. *Vom Staatenbund zum Nationalstaat: Deutschland, 1806–1871.* Munich: C. H. Beck, 1994.

Silbergleit, Heinrich. *Die Bevölkerungs- und Berufsverhältnisse der Juden im deutschen Reich.* Berlin: Akademie-Verlag, 1930.

———, ed. *Preußens Städte.* Berlin: Heymans, 1908.

Silberstein, Michaelis. *Zeitbilder aus der Geschichte der Juden in Breslau.* Breslau: Jacobsohn, 1890.

Silk, Mark. "Notes on the Judeo-Christian Tradition in America." *American Quarterly* 36 (1984): 65–85.

Simmel, Georg. *Die Philosophie des Geldes.* Edited by David Frisby and Klaus Christian Köhnke. Frankfurt a. M.: Suhrkamp, 1989.

———. *Soziologie: Untersuchungen über die Formen der Vergesellschaftung.* Frankfurt a. M.: Suhrkamp, 1992.

Slezkine, Yuri. *The Jewish Century.* Princeton, N.J.: Princeton University Press, 2004.

Smith, Helmut Walser. "Alltag und politischer Antisemitismus in Baden, 1890–1900." *Zeitschrift für die Geschichte des Oberrheins* 141 (1993): 280–303.

———. *German Nationalism and Religious Conflict.* Princeton, N.J.: Princeton University Press, 1995.

———. "Religion and Conflict: Protestants, Catholics, and Anti-Semitism in the State of Baden in the Era of Wilhelm II." *Central European History* 27 (1994): 282–314.

Sollors, Werner. *Beyond Ethnicity: Consent and Descent in American Culture.* New York: Oxford University Press, 1986.

———, ed. *The Invention of Ethnicity.* New York: Oxford University Press, 1989.

———. "Konstruktionsversuche nationaler und ethnischer Identität in der amerikanischen Literatur." In *Nationale und kulturelle Identität: Studien zur Entwicklung des kollektiven Bewußtseins in der Neuzeit,* edited by Bernhard Giesen, 537–69. Frankfurt a. M.: Suhrkamp, 1991.

Sombart, Werner. *Die Juden und das Wirtschaftsleben.* Leipzig: Duncker & Humblot, 1912.

Sorin, Gerald. *A Time for Building: The Third Migration, 1880–1920.* Baltimore: Johns Hopkins University Press, 1992.

Sorkin, David. "Emancipation and Assimilation: Two Concepts and Their Application to German-Jewish History." *Year Book of the Leo Baeck Institute* 35 (1990): 17–34.

———. *The Transformation of German Jewry, 1780–1840.* New York: Oxford University Press, 1987.

Spahn, Martin. "Aufenthaltsrecht, Aufenthaltsbeschränkung, Ausweisung." In *Staatslexikon,* edited by Julius Bachem, 1:425–35. 3rd rev. ed. Freiburg i. Br.: Herder, 1908.

Sperber, Jonathan. "*Bürger, Bürgertum, Bürgerliche Gesellschaft:* Studies of the German (Upper) Middle Class and Its Sociocultural World." *Journal of Modern History* 69 (1997): 271–97.

Spielmann, Karlheinz. *Ehrenbürger und Ehrungen in Geschichte und Gegenwart.* 3rd ed. Dortmund: privately printed, 1967.

"Staatsangehörigkeit." In *Volks-Lexikon,* edited by Emanuel Wurm, 4:511. Nuremberg: Wörlein, 1897.

Staatsarchiv Breslau. *Wegweiser durch die Bestände bis zum Jahr 1945.* Munich: Oldenbourg, 1996.

Steinmetz, Willibald. *Das Sagbare und das Machbare: Zum Wandel politischer Handlungsspielräume; England, 1780–1867.* Stuttgart: Klett-Cotta, 1993.

Stern, Fritz. *Gold and Iron: Bismarck, Bleichröder and the Building of the German Empire.* New York: Knopf, 1977.

———. *Five Germanys I Have Known.* New York: Farrar, Straus & Giroux, 2006.

Stern, Klaus. *Das Staatsrecht der Bundesrepublik Deutschland.* Vol. 3, pt. 1. Munich: C. H. Beck, 1988.

Stichweh, Rudolf. "Inklusion/Exklusion, funktionale Differenzierung und die Theorie der Weltgesellschaft." *Soziale Systeme* 3, no. 1 (1997): 123–36.

———. "Inklusion in Funktionssysteme der modernen Gesellschaft." In *Differenz und Verselbständigung: Zur Entwicklung gesellschaftlicher Teilsysteme,* edited by Renate Mayntz, Bernd Rosewitz, Uwe Schimank, and Rudolf Stichweh, 261–93. Frankfurt a. M.: Campus, 1988.

Stoltzfus, Nathan A. *Resistance of the Heart: Intermarriage and the Rosenstrasse Protest in Nazi Germany.* New York: Norton, 1996.

Strenge, Barbara. *Juden im preußischen Justizdienst, 1812–1918: Der Zugang zu den juristischen Berufen als Indikator der gesellschaftlichen Emanzipation.* Munich: Saur, 1995.

Swartout, Lisa F. "Dueling Identities: Protestant, Catholic, and Jewish Students at German Universities, 1890–1914." PhD diss., University of California at Berkeley, 2002.

———. "Mut, Mensur und Männlichkeit: Die Viadrina, eine jüdische schlagende Verbindung." In *In Breslau zuhause? Juden in einer mitteleuropäischen Metropole der Neuzeit,* edited by Manfred Hettling, Andreas Reinke, and Norbert Conrads, 148–66. Hamburg: Dölling & Galitz, 2003.

Szajkowski, Zosa. "Sufferings of Jewish Emigrants to America in Transit through Germany." *Jewish Social Studies* 39 (1977): 105–16.

Tal, Uriel. *Christians and Jews in Germany: Religion, Politics, and Ideology in the Second Reich, 1870–1914.* Translated by Noah Jonathan Jacobs. 1969. Ithaca, N.Y.: Cornell University Press, 1975.

Taussig, Frank W. *Principles of Economics.* New York: Macmillan, 1924.

Taylor, Charles. *Multiculturalism and the Politics of Recognition.* Edited by Amy Gutmann. Princeton, N.J.: Princeton University Press, 1992.

Tenfelde, Klaus. "Die Entfaltung des Vereinswesens während der industriellen Revolution in Deutschland, 1850–1873." In *Vereinswesen und bürgerliche Gesellschaft in Deutschland,* edited by Otto Dann, 55–114. Munich: Oldenbourg, 1984.

Tenorth, Heinz-Elmar. "Lob des Handwerks, Kritik der Theorie—Zur Lage der historischen Pädagogik in Deutschland." *Paedagogica Historica* 32 (1996): 343–61.

Teuteberg, Hans J. "Zur Genese und Entwicklung historisch-sozialwissenschaftlicher Familienforschung in Deutschland." In *Ehe, Liebe, Tod: Zum Wandel der Familie, der Geschlechts- und Generationsbeziehungen in der Neuzeit,* edited by Hans J. Teuteberg and Peter Borscheid, 15–65. Münster: Coppenrath, 1983.

Thompson, Alastair. "Honours Uneven: Decorations, the State and Bourgeois Society in Imperial Germany." *Past and Present* 144 (1994): 171–204.

Tocqueville, Alexis de. *Democracy in America.* Edited, translated, and with an introduction by Harvey C. Mansfield and Delba Winthrop. Chicago: University of Chicago Press, 2000.

Tomlinson, Sally. "Cultural Diversity and Schooling." *Ethnic and Racial Studies* 18 (1995): 348–54.

Tooley, T. Hunt. *National Identity and Weimar Germany: Upper Silesia and the Eastern Border, 1918–1922.* Lincoln: University of Nebraska Press, 1997.

Toury, Jacob. "Der Eintritt der Juden ins deutsche Bürgertum." In *Das Judentum in der Deutschen Umwelt, 1800–1850: Studien zur Frühgeschichte der Emanzipation,* edited by Hans Liebeschütz and Arnold Paucker, 139–242. Tübingen: Mohr, 1977.

———. *Soziale und politische Geschichte der Juden in Deutschland, 1847–1871: Zwischen Revolution, Reaktion und Emanzipation.* Düsseldorf: Droste, 1977.

Trepp, Anne-Charlott. *Sanfte Männlichkeit und selbständige Weiblichkeit: Frauen und Männer im Hamburger Bürgertum, 1770–1840.* Göttingen: Vandenhoeck & Ruprecht, 1996.

Trzeciakowski, Lech. *The Kulturkampf in Prussian Poland.* Translated by Katarzyna Kretkowska. New York: East European Monographs, 1990.

Tyrell, Hartmann. "Historische Familienforschung und Familiensoziologie." *Kölner Zeitschrift für Soziologie und Sozialpsychologie* 29 (1977): 677–701.

Unckel, Bernhard. "Review of Uriel Tal, *Christians and Jews in Germany: Religion, Politics, and Ideology in the Second Reich, 1970–1914.*" *Historische Zeitschrift* 237 (1983): 738.

Usborne, Cornelia. "The New Woman and Generational Conflict: Perceptions of Young Women's Sexual Mores in the Weimar Republic." In *Generations in Conflict,* edited by Mark Roseman, 137–63. Cambridge: Cambridge University Press, 1995.

Vietor-Engländer, Deborah. "Die Welt im Drama: Alfred Kerr, 1867–1948." Unpublished MS, 1998.

Visweswaran, Kamala. "Race and the Culture of Anthropology." *American Anthropologist* 100 (1998): 70–83.

Voigt, Johannes H. "Die Deportation—Ein Thema der deutschen Rechtswissenschaft und Politik im 19. und frühen 20. Jahrhundert." In *Ausweisung und Deportation: Formen der Zwangsmigration in der Geschichte,* edited by Andreas Gestrich, Gerhard Hirschfeld, and Holger Sonnabend, 83–102. Stuttgart: Franz Steiner, 1995.

Volkov, Shulamit. "The Ambivalence of *Bildung:* Jews and Other Germans." In *The German-Jewish Dialogue Reconsidered: A Symposium in Honor of George L. Mosse,* edited by Klaus L. Berghahn, 81–98 and 267–74. New York: Peter Lang, 1996.

———. "Antisemitismus als kultureller Code." In Volkov, *Jüdisches Leben und Antisemitismus,* 13–36.

———. "Antisemitismus als Problem jüdisch-nationalen Denkens und jüdischer Geschichtsschreibung." In Volkov, *Jüdisches Leben und Antisemitismus,* 88–110.

———. "Die Erfindung einer Tradition—Zur Entstehung des modernen Judentums in Deutschland." *Historische Zeitschrift* 253 (1991): 603–28.

———. "Das geschriebene und das gesprochene Wort: Über Kontinuität und Diskontinuität im deutschen Antisemitismus." In Volkov, *Jüdisches Leben und Antisemitismus,* 54–78.

———. *Die Juden in Deutschland, 1780–1914.* Munich: Oldenbourg, 1994.

———. "Jüdische Assimilation und Eigenart im Kaiserreich." In Volkov, *Jüdisches Leben und Antisemitismus,* 131–45.

———. "Die Jüdische Gemeinde in Altona, 1877–1890: Ein demographisches Profil." In *Von der Arbeiterbewegung zum modernen Sozialstaat: Festschrift für Gerhard A. Ritter*, edited by Jürgen Kocka, Hans-Jürgen Puhle, and Klaus Tennfelde, 601–18. Munich: Saur, 1994.

———. *Jüdisches Leben und Antisemitismus im 19. und 20. Jahrhundert.* Munich: C. H. Beck, 1990.

———. "Minderheiten und der Nationalstaat: Eine postmoderne Perspektive." In *Geschichte und Emanzipation: Festschrift für Reinhard Rürup*, edited by Michael Grüttner, Rüdiger Hachtmann, and Heinz-Gerhard Haupt, 58–74. Frankfurt a. M.: Campus, 1999.

———. "Nationalismus, Antisemitismus und die deutsche Geschichtsschreibung." In *Nation und Gesellschaft in Deutschland: Festschrift für Hans-Ulrich Wehler*, edited by Manfred Hettling and Paul Nolte, 208–19. Munich: C. H. Beck, 1996.

———. "Reflections on German-Jewish History: A Dead End or a New Beginning." *Year Book of the Leo Baeck Institute* 41 (1996): 309–20.

———. "Soziale Ursachen des jüdischen Erfolgs in der Wissenschaft." In Volkov, *Jüdisches Leben und Antisemitismus*, 146–65.

———. "Die Verbürgerlichung der Juden in Deutschland: Eigenart und Paradigma." In *Bürgertum im 19. Jahrhundert: Deutschland im europäischen Vergleich*, edited by Jürgen Kocka, 2:343–71. Munich: Deutscher Taschenbuch Verlag, 1988.

Walkowitz, Judith M. *City of Dreadful Delight: Narratives of Sexual Danger in Late-Victorian London.* Chicago: University of Chicago Press, 1992.

Walter, Dirk. *Antisemitische Kriminalität und Gewalt: Judenfeindschaft in der Weimarer Republik.* Bonn: Dietz Verlag, 1999.

———. "Ungebetene Helfer—Denunziation bei der Münchner Polizei anläßlich der Ostjuden-Ausweisungen, 1919–1923/24." *Archiv für Polizeigeschichte* 18 (1996): 14–20.

Walzer, Michael. "Multiculturalism and Individualism." *Dissent* 41 (1994): 185–91.

Wassermann, Henry. "Jews, Bürgertum and Bürgerliche Gesellschaft in a Liberal Era in Germany, 1840–1880." PhD diss., Hebrew University, 1984.

Weber, Max. *Economy and Society: An Outline of Interpretive Sociology.* Edited by Guenther Roth and Claus Wittich. 2 vols. Berkeley: University of California Press, 1978.

———. *Gesammelte Aufsätze zur Religionssoziologie.* 8th ed. Vol. 1. Tübingen: Mohr Siebeck, 1986.

———. *Gesammelte Aufsätze zur Wissenschaftslehre.* 7th ed. Tübingen: Mohr Siebeck, 1988.

———. *Wirtschaft und Gesellschaft: Grundriß der verstehenden Soziologie.* 1922. 5th ed. Tübingen: Mohr Siebeck, 1980.

Weczerka, Hugo, ed. *Handbuch der historischen Stätten: Schlesien.* Stuttgart: Kröner, 1977.

Wehler, Hans-Ulrich. *Deutsche Gesellschaftsgeschichte*. Vol. 2, *1815–1845/49: Von der Reformära bis zur industriellen und politischen "Deutschen Doppelrevolution."* 2nd ed. Munich: C. H. Beck, 1989.

———. *Deutsche Gesellschaftsgeschichte*. Vol. 3, *1849–1914: Von der "Deutschen Doppelrevolution" bis zum Beginn des Ersten Weltkrieges*. Munich: C. H. Beck, 1995.

———. *Das deutsche Kaiserreich, 1871–1918*. Göttingen: Vandenhoeck & Ruprecht, 1973.

Weil, Patrick. "Nationalities and Citizenship: The Lessons of the French Experience for Germany and Europe." In *Citizenship, Nationality, and Migration in Europe*, edited by David Cesarani and Mary Fulbrook, 74–87. London: Routledge, 1996.

Weingrad, Michael. "Jews (in Theory): Representations of Judaism, Anti-Semitism, and the Holocaust in Postmodern French Writing." *Judaism* 177 (1996): 79–98.

Weisbrod, Bernd. "The Crisis of Bourgeois Society in Interwar Germany." In *Fascist Italy and Nazi Germany: Comparisons and Contrasts*, edited by Richard Bessel, 23–39. Cambridge: Cambridge University Press, 1996.

———. "Gewalt in der Politik: Zur politischen Kultur in Deutschland zwischen den Weltkriegen." *Geschichte in Wissenschaft und Unterricht* 43 (1992): 391–404.

Weiß, F. G. Adolf. *Chronik der Stadt Breslau von der ältesten bis zur neuesten Zeit*. Breslau: Woywod, 1888.

Wendt, Heinrich. "Die Anfänge des Breslauer Vereinswesens (bis 1808)." *Zeitschrift des Vereins für Geschichte und Altertum Schlesiens* 36 (1903): 260–85.

———. "Wissenschaftliche Vereine in Breslau." *Zeitschrift des Vereins für Geschichte und Altertum Schlesiens* 38 (1904): 71–109.

Wertheimer, Jack. "The Duisburg Affair: A Test Case in the Struggle for the 'Conquest' of the Communities." *AJS Review* 6 (1981): 185–206.

———. *Unwelcome Strangers: East European Jews in Imperial Germany*. Oxford: Oxford University Press, 1987.

Wiese, Ludwig, ed. *Das höhere Schulwesen in Preussen*. 3 vols. Berlin: Wiegandt & Grieben, 1863–1902.

Wilden, Josef. "Submissionswesen." In *Handwörterbuch der Kommunalwissenschaften*, edited by Josef Brix, Hugo Lindemann, Otto Most, Hugo Preuss, and Albert Südekum, 4:154–58. Jena: Gustav Fischer, 1924.

Wildt, Michael. *Volksgemeinschaft als Selbstermächtigung: Gewalt gegen Juden in der deutschen Provinz, 1919–1939*. Hamburg: Hamburger Edition, 2007.

Williams, Bill. *The Making of Manchester Jewry, 1740–1875*. Manchester: Manchester University Press, 1976.

Wischermann, Clemens. "'Streit um die Sonntagsarbeit': Historische Perspektiven einer aktuellen Kontroverse." *Vierteljahrschrift für Sozial- und Wirtschaftsgeschichte* 78 (1991): 6–38.

Wodziński, Marcin, ed. *Bibliographie zur Geschichte der Juden in Schlesien II: Bibliography on the History of Silesian Jewry II*. Munich: Saur, 2004.

Wrocław: Breslau; Fotos aus der Wende vom 19. zum 20. Jahrhundert. Vol. 2, *Breslauer Plätze.* Text by Iwona Binkowska. Torun-Wrocław: Via, 1991.

Wunder, Bernd. *Geschichte der Bürokratie in Deutschland.* Frankfurt a. M.: Suhrkamp, 1986.

Young, Robert C. *Colonial Desire: Hybridity in Theory, Culture, and Race.* London: Routledge, 1995.

Zabłocka-Kos, Agnieszka. "Die Architektur der Neo-Renaissance in Breslau." In *Renaissance der Renaissance: Ein bürgerlicher Kunststil im 19. Jahrhundert,* edited by G. Ulrich Großman, 143–60. Munich: Deutscher Kunstverlag, 1995.

Zenz, Emil. *Die Ehrenbürger der Stadt Trier.* Trier: privately printed, 1978.

Ziątkowski, Leszek. *Dzieje Żydów we Wrocławiu.* Wrocław: Wydawnictwo Dolnośląskie, 2000.

———. "Rozwój liczebny Ludnosci żydówskiej we Wrocławiu w latach, 1742–1914." *Sobótka* 46 (1991): 169–89.

Zimmermann, Moshe. *Die deutschen Juden, 1914–1945.* Munich: Oldenbourg, 1997.

———. "Das Gesellschaftsbild der deutschen Zionisten vor dem Ersten Weltkrieg." *Trumah* 1 (1987): 139–58.

———. "Jewish History and Historiography: A Challenge to Contemporary German Historiography." *Year Book of the Leo Baeck Institute* 35 (1990): 35–54.

Zipperstein, Steven J. *The Jews of Odessa: A Cultural History, 1794–1881.* Stanford: Stanford University Press, 1985.

Zucker, Stanley. "Theodor Mommsen and Antisemitism." *Year Book of the Leo Baeck Institute* 17 (1972): 237–41.

Zwahr, Hartmut. *Zur Konstituierung des Proletariats als Klasse: Strukturuntersuchungen über das Leipziger Proletariat während der industriellen Revolution.* Berlin: Akademie-Verlag, 1978.

Zwierz, Maria. *Ulica Świdnicka we Wrocławiu.* Edited by Zofia Ostrowska-Kębłowska. Wrocław: Via, 1995.

INDEX

accounting clerks, 44

Ahlwardt, Hermann, 28, 184, 304n30, 384n42

Alexander, Carl, 153, 159

Allgemeine Zeitung des Judenthums (newspaper), 9, 27, 59, 76, 80, 92, 139, 146–47, 159, 162, 173, 198, 359n109, 389–90n107

Altmann, Eugen, 28, 42, 98–99, 109, 304n30, 336n17, 393n135

Anders, Günther, 76

anti-Catholicism, 149–50, 158, 173

anti-Semitism, 3–4, 9, 12, 65–67, 71, 77–83, 93, 127–28, 171–72, 176, 179–92, 197–201, 210–12, 217–18, 231–42, 353n61, 363n153, 376n32, 382n68, 389–90n107, 391n114, 403n4; anti-Semitic parties, 185, 377n34, 388n104; anti-Semitic petition, 152–53, 200; anti-Semitic violence, 231–32, 236–38; Association for the Defense against Anti-Semitism (Verein zur Abwehr des Antisemitismus), 228, 330n132; Berlin debate on anti-Semitism (*Berliner Antisemitismusstreit*), 9, 199; historiography of, 4–5, 12, 14–16, 177, 290–91n37, 291n40, 377n34; hooligan, 183–84; and racism, 12, 201–2, 376n32

apostasy, 69, 95–96, 102, 115, 117–19, 149, 230

Armer, Hermann, 76, 81

Arnim, Achim von, 25

Asch, Adolf, 342n61

Asch, Robert, 86

Asch, Sigismund, 150

assimilation, 6–7, 10–14, 60, 94–96, 116–20, 154, 204, 222, 230

Association of German Jews (Verband der Deutschen Juden), 174

Association of Jewish Religion Teachers in Silesia and Posen (Verein jüdischer Religionslehrer Schlesiens und Posens), 152

Auerbach, Anna (née Silbergleit), 104–5, 313n98

Auerbach, Berthold, 67

Auerbach, Hermann, 90–92, 241, 332n143

Auerbach, Leopold, 69, 319n30

Bachem, Julius, 153

Badt, Benno, 43, 52, 73, 148, 154

Badt-Strauss, Bertha, 43

Ballin, Albert, 398n176

Bär, Charlotte Marie, 342n63

Barasch, Georg, 82

Bartsch, Carl, 77

Bauch, Hermann, 72

Oesterreicher, Aron, 342n63
Old Catholics, 135, 143, 149–50, 158
Ollendorff, Isidor, 76, 160, 166–67, 170–71, 324n70
Ollendorff, Paula, 324n70
Oppeln (city), 102, 106, 208
Orthodoxy, 54–55, 74, 97–98, 115, 160, 162–63, 169
Oschinsky, Theodor, 54–55, 59
Ost und West (journal), 73

Palakiewicz, Hirsch, 209
parents' councils, 234
parity, 134–35, 137–41, 151–52, 157, 165, 173–74, 292n45, 353–54n62
Persicaner, Georg, 236
Petersen, Auguste Josefine, 342n63
Pfeffer, Simon, 82, 328n106
physicians, 33, 37–39, 44, 61, 85–86, 115–16, 179, 233–34
Pick, Anna (née Sachs), 88
Pick, Georg, 88, 165, 330–31n163
Pick, Heinrich, 88
Pikarsky, Abraham, 236
Poale Zion, 237
Poleck, Theodor, 67, 77
political parties, 79, 83, 164, 176, 181, 194, 376n32, 377n34
Polke, Max Moses, 237
Poor Relief Administration, 203, 205
Poppe, Oskar, 82
Porsch, Felix, 174, 196
Potsdam, 191, 291n38, 398n178, 399n180
poverty, 26, 30–31, 41–57, 103, 133, 205, 211, 216, 233, 303n24, 392n123
Poznanski, Adolf Wolf, 200–201
Preuß, Hugo, 163–64
Preußische Jahrbücher (journal), 199
Priebatsch, Leopold, 75
principle of descent (*ius sanguinis*), 193, 199, 203
principle of territoriality (*ius soli*), 193, 199
Pringsheim, Fedor, 80

Pringsheim, Siegmund, 102
professors, 33, 39, 60, 75, 148, 225, 360n119
Progressive Party (Fortschrittspartei), 82, 99, 156, 361–62n145; *Hamburger Fremdenblatt* (newspaper), 99
prostitution, 106, 210–212
Protestants, 4, 11, 13, 17, 21–22, 24–25, 30, 32–41, 55–56, 62–63, 69, 73, 79, 89, 92, 93, 97, 104–6, 117, 119, 123–27, 129, 131–38, 141–44, 148–49, 156–58, 160, 164, 166–67, 169, 173, 179, 181, 234, 240–41, 306–7n49, 307n53, 314n106, 353n54, 355n68, 359n108, 360n119
provincial governors/government, 201, 208–11, 213, 221, 232
provincial school board, 140, 143–145, 147, 149, 152, 163, 171
Puttkamer, Robert von, 200, 389n105

Realgymnasium am Zwinger, 126, 130, 133, 147, 234, 350n27, 350n30, 353n57, 364n161
Realgymnasium zum Heiligen Geist, 126–27, 350n27, 364n161
refugees, 196, 208, 232, 395–96n162
regional literature, 72
Reich, Carl, 166, 171
Reichenbach, Natalie, 226
Reichensperger, Peter, 153
Reichsbote (newspaper), 81
Reif, Victor, 340n48
Reinkens, Joseph Hubert, 135, 138, 149
religious instruction, 19, 91, 123, 136–39, 149–51, 152, 157, 162–64, 167–68, 171, 240, 352n52, 360n119, 369n214
rentiers, 33, 44, 232–33
representative councils, 52–54, 70–71, 160–63, 182, 227, 366n186, 391n119
Rheinischer Merkur (newspaper), 149
Riegner, Elisabeth Franziska Cäcilie (née Bauer), 114

GEORGE L. MOSSE SERIES
IN MODERN EUROPEAN CULTURAL AND
INTELLECTUAL HISTORY

Series Editors

Stanley G. Payne, David J. Sorkin, and John S. Tortorice